Cyprus in the 19th Century AD

Fact, Fancy and Fiction

Outside the dig house at Enkomi 1960: From right: Olivier Masson, Adonis Orphanou, Vassos Karageorghis, Jacques Raison.

Cyprus in the 19th Century AD

Fact, Fancy and Fiction

*Papers of the 22nd British Museum Classical Colloquium
December 1998*

Edited by

Veronica Tatton-Brown

Oxbow Books

Published by
Oxbow Books, Park End Place, Oxford OX1 1HN

© Veronica Tatton-Brown and the individual authors, 2001

ISBN 1 84217 033 3

A CIP record for this book is available from the British Library

This book is available direct from
Oxbow Books, Park End Place, Oxford OX1 1HN
(Phone: 01865–241249; Fax: 01865–794449)

and

The David Brown Book Company
PO Box 511, Oakville, CT 06779, USA
(Phone: 860–945–9329; Fax: 860–945–9468)

or from our website

www.oxbowbooks.com

Printed in Great Britain at
The Short Run Press
Exeter

Contents

List of Contributors vii
Preface ix

Olivier Masson: 'Luigi Palma di Cesnola – ultimes considérations'
Emilia Masson x

Olivier Masson (1922–1997) – un tribute
Maurice Sznycer xv

Views of Cyprus in the 19th century

1. Cyprus, a new archaeological frontier in the XIXth century: the struggle of European
   Museums for Cypriot antiquities
   Claire Balandier 3
2. Cyprus in the 19th century: perceptions and politics
   Peter W. Edbury 13
3. Imaginary Cyprus. Revisiting the past and redefining the ancient landscape
   Anastasia Serghidou 21
4. Edmond Duthoit: and artist and ethnographer in Cyprus, 1862, 1865
   Rita C. Severis 32

Sites in the 19th century

5. Ormideia: tracing Cesnola's footsteps. Archaeological research and finds
   Maria Hadjicosti 53
6. From Hammer von Purgstall to F.B. Welch. The archaeology of Old Paphos, 1802–1899
   Franz Georg Maier 70
7. A 19th century view of *St George's Hill* in Nicosia: fact or fiction
   Despo Pilides 80
8. An Archaeology of Cult? Cypriot sanctuaries in 19th century archaeology
   Anja Ulbrich 93

Museums and their 19th century Collections

9. 'New' objects from British Museum Tomb 73 at Curium
   Donald M. Bailey and Marilyn Hockey 109
10. Cypriot Antiquities in Italy. Items in the Archaeological Museum of Perugia
    and in the Etruscan-Academy Museum of Cortona
    Marco Bettelli and Silvana Di Paolo 134
11. Les Antiquités de Chypre au Louvre: entre l'Orient et l'Occident
    Annie Caubet 141
12. Excavations in Cyprus and the 'Mycenaean Question'
    J. Lesley Fitton 149

13. Sculptures de la collection Cesnola: le cas du 'prêtre' à la tête de taureau
    Antoine Hermary 153
14. The British Museum and the invention of the Cypriot Late Bronze Age
    Louise Steel 160
15. Excavations in ancient Cyprus: original manuscripts and correspondence in the British Museum
    Veronica Tatton-Brown 168
16. Collecting vases with figurines/protomes in the nineteenth century AD
    Frieda Vandenabeele 184

Early Travellers and excavators

17. Melchior de Vogüé *et alii* and Cyprus
    Lucie Bonato 189
18. The Ohenfalsch-Richter Collection in the Museum für Vor- und Frügeschichte, Berlin
    Melitta Brönner 198
19. Falkland Warren
    H.-G. Buchholz 207
20. Melchior de Vogüé *et alii* and Cyprus: Monsieur Péretié
    Hélène Cassimatis 216
21. T. B. Sandwith and the beginnings of Cypriote archaeology
    R. S. Merrillees 222
22. Lady Brassey, 1870–1886: traveller, writer, collector, educator, woman of means
    and the fate of her Cypriote artefacts
    Lou Taylor 239
23. Max Ohnefalsch-Richter and the Έσπερος
    Ioannis Violaris 248

The Law

24. The fight for the past: Watkins vs. Warren (1885–6) and the control of excavation
    Michael Given 255
25. Archaeology and Islamic Law in Ottoman Cyprus
    G. R. H. Wright 261
26. The Ottoman Law on Antiquities (1874) and the founding of the Cyprus Museum
    Nicholas Stanley-Price 267

27. Cyprus in the 19th century AD: Fact, Fancy and Fiction. A Summing Up
    R. S. Merrillees 276

List of Contributors

DONALD BAILEY
Department of Greek and Roman Antiquities
The British Museum
Great Russell Street
London WC1B 3DG

CLAIRE BALANDIER
14 chemin Gilles Borel
13 100 Aix-en-Provence
France

MARCO BETTELLI
Istituto per gli Studi Micenei
ed Egeo-Anatlicci – CNR
via Giano della Bella
18–0185 Roma
Italy

LUCIE BONATO
153 rue d'Estienne d'Orves
91370 Verrières-le-Buisson
France

MELITTA BRÖNNER
Museum für Vor- und Frühgeschichte
Schloss Charlottenburg
Langshasbau
D-14059 Berlin
Germany

H-G BUCHHOLZ
Espenstrasse 10
D-35428 Langgöns
Germany

HÉLÈNE CASSIMATIS
20 rue La Fontaine
75016 Paris
France

ANNIE CAUBET
Conservateur général du département
des antiquités orientales
Musée du Louvre
34 Quai du Louvre
75058 Paris Cedex 01
France

PETER EDBURY
School of History and Archaeology
Cardiff University
PO Box 909
Cardiff CF1 3XU

J. LESLEY FITTON
Department of Greek and Roman Antiquities
The British Museum
Great Russell Street
London WC1B 3DG

MICHAEL GIVEN
Department of Archaeology
Gregory Building
University of Glasgow
Lilybank Gardens
Glasgow G12 8QQ

MARIA HADJICOSTI
Department of Antiquities
The Cyprus Museum
Nicosia
Cyprus

ANTOINE HERMARY
Centre Camille Jullian
Maison Méditeranéenne des Sciences de l'Homme
5 rue Château de l'Horloge
BP 647
13094 Aix-en-Provence Cedex 2
France

FRANZ GEORG MAIER
Weinmanngasse 60
CH-8700 Küsnacht
Switzerland

EMILIA MASSON
8 rue Leneveux
75014 Paris
France

ROBERT MERRILLEES
CAARI
11 Andreas Demitriou Street
1066 Nicosia
Cyprus

SILVANA DI PAOLO
Istituto per gli Studi Micenei
ed Egeo-Anatlici – CNR
via Giano della Bella
18–0185 Roma
Italy

DESPO PILIDES
Ministry of Communications and Works
1 Museum Street
1516 Nicosia
Cyprus

ANASTASIA SERGHIDOU
Department of History
Hartwick College
Onoenta, New York 13820
USA

RITA C. SEVERIS
15 Them. Dervis Str.
PO Box 1139
1502 Nicosia
Cyprus

NICHOLAS STANLEY-PRICE
ICCROM
Via di San Michele 13
00153 Roma
Italy

LOUISE STEELE
Department of Archaeology
University of Wales
Lampeter
Ceredigion SA48 7ED

MAURICE SZNYCER
2 rue Emile Faguet
75014 Paris
France

VERONICA TATTON-BROWN
Department of Greek and Roman Antiquities
The British Museum
Great Russell Street
London WC1B 3DG

LOU TAYLOR
University of Brighton
School of Historical and Critical Studies
10–11 Pavilion Parade
Brighton BN2 2YB

ANJA ULBRICH
Brennerweg 28
69124 Heidelberg
Germany

FRIEDA VANDENABEELE
Vrije Universiteit Brussel
Faculteit der Letteren en Wijsbegeerte
Vakgroep Kunstwetenshcappen en Archeologie
Pleinlaan 2
1050 Brussel
Belgium

IOANNIS VIOLARIS
23 Ellispontou str.
Dasoupoulis
Nicosia
Cyprus

G.H. WRIGHT
Domaine Bouchony
Ile de la Barthelasse
84 000 Avignon
France

Preface

The 22nd Classical Colloquium, "Cyprus in the nineteenth century AD: Fact, Fancy and Fiction", was held on 2–4 December 1998 in collaboration with the Hellenic Centre, Paddington Street, and with additional generous support from Mr. and Mrs. Constantine Leventis and the international group of supporters of the Department of Greek and Roman Antiquities, the Caryatids.

The colloquium was dedicated to the memory of Professor Olivier Masson, who passed away in 1997, and the theme selected in recognition both of his primary study of the many Cypriot syllabic inscriptions in the British Museum and of his deep interest in the history of the British Museum's outstanding Cypriot collection. We were especially pleased that Madame Emilia Masson was able to attend, as well as Professor Masson's close friend Professor Maurice Sznycer.

The series of papers published here represent most of those that were delivered at the colloquium. To replace those that were not submitted, a few additional papers not given at the colloquium itself have been included as a result of their particular relevance to the theme.

Finally, we are grateful to both the Caryatid Fund and the A.G. Leventis Foundation for generous grants that have made this publication possible. The Caryatids are an international group of supporters of the Greek and Roman Department's work, whose contributions help with displays, research, publications and acquisitions. The A.G. Leventis Foundation's unstinting support for the study and appreciation of Cypriot antiquities throughout the world is, of course, well known and truly remarkable.

Dyfri Williams
Keeper of Greek and Roman Antiquities

Olivier Masson:
'Luigi Palma di Cesnola – ultimes considérations'

Emilia Masson

When he learned, about the middle of November 1996, that the course of his life was about to take its final turn, Olivier had but one concern: to write as much as possible in order to leave behind the judgements, opinions or results that seemed the most important to him. Showing a boundless courage, hurried by time, he worked with determination, constantly going from one article to the other. Although none of these compositions, undertaken during the last three months of his life, reached their final version, each of them, however, was elaborated enough in order to be kept. Guided by the indications he had taken care to leave in the margin of his last writings, his pupil, Laurent Dubois, his colleague, Thomas Drew-Bear and myself[1] have done our best to complete these articles and to improve their presentation.

Olivier's investigations into Cesnola's activities never stopped. Until the end he was looking for more information about this fascinating personality. Cesnola provided Olivier with one of his last triumphs: as if in return for all the detective work, Olivier discovered the existence of Cesnola's granddaughter somewhere in the United States. Suspecting that this ninety-year-old lady could give him some useful information, or might even possess some of Cesnola's objects, he got in touch with Joan Mertens of the Metropolitan Museum of Art, New York and Vassos Karageorghis, suggesting that they pay her a visit.

The text of the main body of this paper was intended for the book that Vassos Karageorghis is preparing at the moment about the Cesnola collection at the Metropolitan Museum. Aware that it was for him the ultimate opportunity to draw up the sum of his considerations about Cesnola, Olivier tried, it seems to me, to present his achievements, as well as his mistakes, and wished to stress what remains to be done. His study was conceived in two periods, the first one was finished or nearly finished, the second just started. As he said himself, this text was 'a version without footnotes'.

Luigi Palma di Cesnola (1832–1904)

Première période – Luigi Palma di Cesnola et le Metropolitan Museum of Art.

En 2004, on pourra songer au centenaire de la disparition de Luigi Palma di Cesnola, ce noble piémontais, devenu par le hasard de l'existence soldat de fortune aux États Unis durant la guerre de Sécession. A ce premier hasard s'en enchaîneront d'autres: entre 1865 et 1876 Cesnola sera Consul des États Unis à Chypre et cette fonction le mènera non moins paradoxalement vers le Metropolitan Museum de New York. Dès le mois de mai 1877, il y occupera le poste de secrétaire général et finira tranquillement ses jours en tant que directeur de ce musée.

Il est inutile de rappeler comment sa personnalité avait été controversée surtout jusque vers 1884. Si ses activités de consul ne semblent pas avoir été critiquées, quelques épisodes, plus ou moins pittoresques, avaient émaillé sa vie. D'une nature, à mon avis, assez honnête, il a néanmoins pêché plusieurs fois par une grande naïveté. A titre d'exemple, on évoquera ici l'épisode de son grade de 'général', qui lui aurait été donné par Lincoln oralement ... la veille de son assassinat: il aurait pu se contenter sans doute de celui de 'brigadier général' qui paraît avoir été plus exact. Quoi qu'il en soit, on l'appellera désormais 'le Général', avec ou sans ironie. Bien plus grave pour la réputation fut l'affaire, assez connue du 'Trésor de Curium', affaire qui a failli compromettre sa carrière aux États Unis.

Au lieu de se contenter d'annoncer, comme il l'avait fait dans ses premières lettres, la découverte de 'riches tombes' dans la nécropole située près de la mer, soit dans la plaine qui s'étend immédiatement à l'est du rocher Kourion, ou Curium sous la forme latine alors plus couramment employée, Cesnola eut la malencontreuse idée d'inventer une version romanesque: les tombes ayant fourni des précieux objets sont déplacées, dans ce scénario, sur l'acropole, et prennent forme d'un souterrain a quatre chambres. J'ai déjà eu l'occasion de raconter en détail cet épisode plutôt comique;[2] ici, ajouterai juste, comme je l'avais indiqué plus récemment,[3] que l'idée de ce 'Trésor' avait été très certainement inspirée par la découverte du 'Trésor de Priam', réalisée par Schliemann, son concurrent inavoué, découverte attribuée à la date du 31 Mai 1873. Bien que les lettres officielles de Cesnola à Schliemann ne tarissent pas d'éloges, sur les travaux du 'grand docteur', d'autres, privées, montrent clairement comment les tombes en question se sont progressivement transformées en 'Trésor'. On y découvre des allusions claires au fouilleur allemand ainsi qu'un désir naïf de l'éclipser.

Cependant, au-delà de sa forte naïveté (avec présomption d'impunité), il convient de rappeler à la décharge de Cesnola, ses grands besoins d'argent: alors que Schliemann était un riche rentier et en conséquence dépourvu de soucis matériels, le Général n'occupait qu'un poste modeste de consul, lequel sera d'ailleurs supprimé par la suite. Outre son épouse et ses deux filles qu'il avait à charge, les voyages entre Larnaca et New York grevaient sensiblement son budget. Aussi, le besoin d'amplifier la valeur des découvertes se faisait-il sentir.

Comme on le sait, le dit Trésor, d'abord très favorablement accueilli, va déchaîner par la suite contre Cesnola la colère exagérée de personnages plus ou moins dangereux. Il s'agit au premier chef de l'irascible mais nullement irréprochable Max Ohnefalsch-Richter. Au nom prédestiné, cet amateur, devenu archéologue, poursuivra Cesnola de ses nombreux libelles, de ses querelles *in situ* et même de ses conférences polémiques jusqu'aux Etats-Unis. L'écho de ces querelles se retrouve encore dans le *Handbook* de John L. Myres,[4] paru en 1914, alors que bien des partis pris anticesnoliens avaient été dépassés depuis longtemps.

La non moins célèbre affaire du procès 'Feuardent versus Cesnola' viendra à la suite de ces remous. Elle se déroule entre 1880 et 1884, alors que le Général était déjà le directeur du Musée de New York. Dans ces nouvelles péripéties, Cesnola est, je crois bien, innocent: les jurés du procès de New York lui donnèrent d'ailleurs raison en 1884. Ayant examiné d'assez près cet épisode, intéressant pour l'époque, j'ai été gagné par l'impression que le mauvais vouloir de l'antiquaire Gaston Louis Feuardent (1841–1893) se trouve à son origine. Fils de Félix Feuardent (1819–1907), célèbre antiquaire et numismate de la place Louvois (firme Rollin et Feuardent), il est d'abord représentant de son père à Londres (vers 1868) et s'établit ensuite (1876) à New York où il se met à persécuter son ancien client. Car Feuardent junior, chargé d'une première exposition chypriote à Londres en hiver 1872, a dû être très déçu par la décision finale de Cesnola (sage décision d'ailleurs!) de vendre en bloc sa première collection à des mécènes américains agissant pour le Metropolitan Museum of Art.[5] Ceci au lieu de faire à Londres des ventes partielles, suivant la mode de l'époque, ventes qui apportaient tout naturellement un profit considérable à l'intermédiaire. Aidé par quelques journalistes que nous dirions aujourd'hui 'à scandale', Feuardent lança toutes sortes d'accusations spectaculaires contre le malheureux Cesnola. Elles allèguent des modifications d'objets, des 'changements' de têtes de statues ou autres méfaits de ce genre. On sait aujourd'hui que tout dans ces accusations n'est pas faux en la matière; cependant, on ne doit pas oublier que vers les années 1880 les critères des érudits et du public étaient bien différents de ceux qui sont en vigueur aujourd'hui, et pas depuis si longtemps d'ailleurs. A défaut de pouvoir montrer des 'Phidias', comme on le disait, les statues endommagées ou acéphales n'étaient pas bien accueillies. Un certain nombre d'ajustements ou de réparations (d'autres restent sans doute encore à faire) sont venues améliorer cet état de choses.

De ce procès, subsistent des libelles et des articles de journaux plus ou moins partiaux, ainsi que des caricatures amusantes comme celle visant à montrer le Directeur en train de fabriquer ses statues... Il y eut en outre un livre venimeux, comportant en réalité un recueil de notes manuscrites et de coupures diverses, assemblées en 1883 par un autre curieux personnage, Henri de Morgan. Spécialiste de préhistoire et collectionneur, Henri de Morgan (1854–1910) est frère du justement célèbre archéologue, Jacques de Morgan (1857–1924). Son livre, resté heureusement à l'état de manuscrit, dort d'un juste sommeil sur un rayon de la Bibliothèque du Musée des Antiquités Nationales à Saint Germain en Laye.[6]

Avant de retracer en détail la carrière de Cesnola au Metropolitan Museum of Art, il me paraît opportun d'évoquer les faits suivants. D'après une certaine légende, des archives concernant Cesnola n'existaient pas à New York, excepté celles relatives au procès. Il en serait de même pour les papiers laissés au Metropolitan Museum of Art par le défunt. Le second point reste à vérifier. Cette tâche reviendra probablement à Joan Mertens, actuel Curator of Greek and Roman Art. Une enquête cherchant à savoir si les papiers en question n'avaient pas été emmenés chez des descendants de Cesnola serait également à faire. Pour ma part, j'avais cru longtemps à cette légende de l'inexistence totale de documents de Cesnola. C'était indéniablement un tort. Comme tous les intellectuels de l'époque, Cesnola avait en effet envoyé et reçu un nombre considérable de lettres. Même si elles n'avaient pas été méticuleusement conservées dans leur totalité, comme ce fut le cas avec celles de personnages beaucoup plus célèbres, Schliemann par exemple, quelques unes doivent en subsister.

Au sujet de la correspondance de Cesnola une mise au point s'impose. Alors que je rédigeais en 1960 mes

Inscriptions chypriotes syllabiques,[7] je n'en connaissais que de très rares pages, notamment celles réunies par Salomon Reinach dans sa notice nécrologique.[8] Péchant par excès de discrétion, Reinach a malheureusement bloqué sa propre correspondance jusqu'en 2000. Elle doit comporter, je suppose, plus d'une lettre de Cesnola, qui lui écrivait souvent.

Je regrette ainsi d'avoir complètement ignoré pendant une longue période l'existence de nombreux dossiers épistolaires de Cesnola. Le premier connu, qui est aussi le plus important par sa richesse, avait été heureusement révélé en 1971 par Elisabeth McFadden, une polygraphe et journaliste, apparentée probablement à G. McFadden, fouilleur de Kourion. Dans sa bibliographie de Cesnola, au titre accrocheur et trop long,[9] l'auteur a en effet réussi à retrouver et à exploiter assez largement un précieux fonds de correspondance cesnolienne, rassemblé par son ami Hiram Hitchcock (1832–1900). Ce dernier préparait une bibliographie du Général mais eut la malchance de disparaître avant lui. Ce lot de lettres, à la fois bien conservées et bien classées, se trouvant actuellement au Dartmouth College (Département des Manuscrits), situé dans la ville de Hanover, New Hampshire, est d'un accès facile.[10] Toutes ces missives renferment plus d'une information précieuse aussi bien sur les trouvailles que sur une chronologie des déplacements de Cesnola, chronologie qui ne ressort pas clairement de son livre trop général *Cyprus*.[11]

Un peu plus tard, un autre fonds est sorti de l'obscurité où il dormait bizarrement depuis tant d'années. Il s'agit du dossier de correspondance conservé au British Museum, non pas au département grec et romain mais au département oriental (actuel Western Asiatic Department). Le regretté Richard Barnett a eu en 1977 l'heureuse inspiration de recopier (non sans quelques erreurs plutôt étranges) des extraits de lettres de Cesnola concernant Amathonte, adressées (avec dessins et photos!) à Samuel Birch (1813–1885), alors conservateur au Département Oriental. On sait que ce spécialiste s'intéressait au déchiffrement du syllabaire chypriote et qu'il avait même collaboré avec l'ingénieux George Smith, le principal décrypteur de ce répertoire. Ces lettres (arrêtées en 1883) sont en conséquence importantes pour l'historique des travaux de Cesnola. Pour ma part, j'ai commencé à en utiliser des éléments (sans oublier le dossier Hitchcock) dans un premier article bref de 1988 et plus largement par la suite.[12]

Les trouvailles appellent parfois d'autres trouvailles. Si la correspondance en français du Général avec notre célèbre compatriote, Georges Perrot, avait été détruite stupidement par sa veuve (vers 1930 seulement, dit-on), d'autres lettres subsistent.[13] Ainsi, des missives très importantes envoyées aux autorités du Musée de l'Ermitage à Saint Pétersbourg datant d'une période où Cesnola s'imaginait pouvoir vendre au Tsar sa première grande collection. Il m'a été également possible de retrouver une série de lettres adressées au célèbre éditeur John Murray (IIIe de cette dynastie, 1808–1892), c'est-à-dire au moment de la publication de *Cyprus* par ses soins.[14] On y trouve entre autres des indications intéressantes sur Schliemann, également 'client' de cet éditeur.

D'autres séries de lettres, plus ou moins inconnues pour nous, ont certainement existé ou existent toujours. Du côté de l'Allemagne je n'ai rien trouvé et on peut envisager que Cesnola, malgré son polyglottisme, n'écrivait pas en allemand. Le hasard a permis de dénicher auprès de la Bibliothèque de l'Institut de France quelques précieuses lettres adressées à Ernest Renan. Cet éminent spécialiste semble voir respecté Cesnola en tant qu'homme. Le courrier que le 'Général' lui avait adressé au sujet de quelques inscriptions phéniciennes témoignent d'une acribie surprenante pour un amateur.[15]

En raison des relations que Cesnola fut obligé d'entretenir comme Consul avec la Sublime Porte jusqu'en 1876, il est à envisager que des lettres de lui se trouvent au Musée archéologique d'Istanbul. Afin d'améliorer ses relations, difficiles, avec l'administration ottomane, il avait fait parvenir des dons importants au Musée de Constantinople: 'J'ai fait cadeau au Musée Impérial Ottoman de plusieurs milliers d'antiquités chypriotes', précise t-il avant 1873.[16] Jusqu'à présent je n'ai pu obtenir aucune information au sujet des rapports directs entre Cesnola et les autorités ottomanes de l'époque, ce que je regrette: une patiente enquête au Musée Archéologique d'Istanbul aboutirait peut-être à des résultats.

Enfin, l'information est malheureusement négative au sujet des relations épistolaires que Cesnola entretenait nécessairement avec son pays d'origine, le Piémont et Turin. Comme on peut le comprendre, Cesnola était en bonnes relations avec le Président de l'Académie des sciences de Turin, le comte Frédéric Sclopis. En janvier 1871, il avait fait lire (*in absentia?*) devant cette Académie une communication sur les fouilles de Golgoi, dédiée à son Président. La correspondance relative à cette communication, assurément accompagnée de photographies (dont Cesnola était prodigue) fut conservée un temps au Secrétariat de l'Académie. Faut-il souligner qu'elle avait été réalisée au cours d'une période remarquable pour les recherches archéologiques à Chypre, soit entre le 8 Mars 1870 (exactement au début des découvertes de Golgoi!) jusqu'en Février 1878.

Selon une indication de M. Gustavo Vagnone, chercheur à Turin, les lettres de Cesnola ont été détruites à une date inconnue, par un personnage dont on maudira l'inadvertance ou l'incompétence. Un album photographique, qui subsiste toujours, apparaît comme une compensation non négligeable à cette perte. Dédié à

Sclopis, il porte cette formule manuscrite de Cesnola: 'A sua Eccellenza il Conte Federigo Sclopis di Salerno, Cipro addi 12 Settembre 1870', L. P. di Cesnola. L'album est pourvu d'un titre spécialement imprimé en français: 'Antiquités de Chypre, photographies des objets trouvés dans le temple de Vénus à Golgoi par le Général L. P. di Cesnola (sic), Consul des États-Unis, 1870'. Cet album ne renferme pas moins de 73 pages non numérotées de photographies d'époque (format environ 13×20) avec également des facsimilés d'inscriptions syllabiques. Même si ces images n'apportent pas de révélations spéciales, elle montrent néanmoins *l'état exact* des objets au cours de l'été 1870. Destinées peut-être à illustrer la communication de Cesnola, elles devaient accompagner les lettres qu'il avaient adressées à Sclopis. Si tel était le cas, ces photographies n'ont pratiquement pas été utilisées étant donné la pauvreté de figures dans cette communication. D'autre part, il est probable que Cesnola ait mêlé aux objets de Golgoi, site auquel était consacré son propos, un petit nombre de pièces trouvées ailleurs. Faut-il rappeler également que les illustrations de l'album en question proviennent du recueil qui fut compilé à Larnaca en 1870, chez Cesnola lui-même, par Johannes Doell, un jeune employé du Musée de l'Ermitage? Ce dernier avait été en effet subventionné par l'Ermitage de Saint Pétersbourg pour établir un catalogue soigneux de la collection, lequel fut très bien publié par l'Académie locale en 1873.[17]

I found these two pages in Olivier's dossier *Cesnola* drafting the beginning of the second period in his own hand. Olivier seemed particularly concerned to put forward his view on the problem of the authorship of the *Descriptive Atlas of the Cesnola Collection of Cypriot Antiquities in the Metropolitan Museum of Art*. This is the reason he raises this question first. This is also the last page of his essay. On the bottom he added the date: 5 février 1997.

Deuxième période – 1884–1904

Les vingt dernières années de l'activité de Luigi Palma di Cesnola peuvent former la seconde période de sa vie. Son début est marqué par un événement, combien important pour notre 'Général': l'achèvement en 1884 du procès Cesnola-Feuardent. La parution en 1885 du premier volume en deux fascicules du grand *Atlas,* préparé depuis des années par Cesnola, en constitue la deuxième date significative ...

Atlas

A propos de l'élaboration de *l'Atlas,* il convient d'évoquer ici avec quelque détail la figure intéressante d'un ami de Cesnola, Isaac Holister Hall (1837–1896). Ceci dans la mesure où J. L. Myres avait cité son nom comme 'auteur' de *l'Atlas* aussi bien dans la bibliographie de son *Handbook,* paru en 1914, que dans un article publié en 1924.[18] Sans le moindre commentaire justificatif, l'éminent spécialiste britannique avait en effet remplacé le nom de Cesnola par celui de Hall. Si ce procédé désinvolte ne permet pas de savoir quelle pouvait être l'intention exacte de Myres, il insinue néanmoins que Hall devait être le véritable auteur de cet imposant ouvrage.

Quoi qu'il en soit, on doit rappeler que Hall était un érudit de New York,[19] sémitisant et enseignant. Il avait consacré ses recherches à la Bible, (Ancien et Nouveau Testament), au syriaque ainsi qu'aux inscriptions et sculptures chypriotes amenées par Cesnola. Au Metropolitan Museum, Hall avait occupé des fonctions comme..............puis comme conservateur des sculptures chypriotes de 1886 jusqu'à sa mort en 1896.[20] Au cours de cette période il a publié plusieurs articles sur les inscriptions syllabiques et les problèmes connexes. Cesnola, ne l'a, lui-même, guère mentionné, sinon pour un voyage à Chypre en 1876, 'When in 1876 I revisited Nea Paphos for the second and last time, I was in compagny with two americans, Prof. Isaac H. Hall,...'[21] Par des allusions de Hall on apprend, en revanche, l'existence de deux voyages (ou d'un seul séjour prolongé?) en octobre 1875 à Kourion et sans doute à Larnaca et en mai 1876, à Larnaca tis Lapithou et à Phasoula.[22] On sait d'autre part que Cesnola lui confia la publication et l'étude de nombreuses inscriptions qu'ils avait découvertes.[23] Tout ceci montre que Cesnola eut souvent recours aux services de Hall: et que, son caractère autoritaire aidant, il l'exploita dans plus d'une circonstance et en particulier pour le long travail sur l'Atlas. Ces faits pourraient expliquer les tentatives maladroites de Myres à réhabiliter un collaborateur dévoué. En tout état de cause, la participation de Hall, si elle fut laissée dans l'ombre, ne put être que bénéfique. Car Hall était assurément un savant consciencieux. Il meurt en 1896, avant la parution du tome trois de l'Atlas qui a lieu seulement en 1904.

Notes

1. 'Nul n'est prophete dans son pays', Olivier used to say. By dedicating this Colloquium to his memory, the organizers proved him right, for the last time. To all participants, they also gave the opportunity to discover on the spot the intense activity of a scholar, who remained involved in his research until the end of his life. My daughters and I are very grateful for this delicate intention. Thank you very much.
2. Cf. *Centre d'Etudes Chypriotes. Cahiers* 1 (1984) 16–25; 2 (1985) 3–14; 25 (1996) 3–39; 'Notes sur le "trésor de Curium", Kypriaka XVI', *BCH* 108 (1984) 77–82.
3. 'L. Palma di Cesnola, H. Schliemann et l'éditeur John

Murray', *Centre d'Etudes Chypriotes. Cahiers* 21 (1994-1) 7–9.

4. *Handbook of the Cesnola Collection of Antiquities from Cyprus* (New York 1914).

5. On trouvera une discussion détaillée sur cette exposition, sur son organisation et sur la vente de la première collection de Cesnola au Musée de New York chez O. Masson, *RDAC* (1990) 290–293.

6. Ce livre-dossier comporte également des lettres de Cesnola, copiées intégralement par H. de Morgan avant 1883, cf. O. Masson, *RDAC* (1990) 288, n. 27 et 291 et n. 54.

7. *ICS* (Paris, Editions de Boccard 1961) et 1983 (seconde édition revue et complétée).

8. *Revue archéologique* Serie iv, tome 5 (1905) 301–4.

9. *The Glitter and the Gold. A spirited account of the Metropolitan Museum of Art's first Director, the audacious and high-handed Luigi Palma di Cesnola* (New York, The Dial Press 1971). De cet ouvrage j'ai eu connaissance seulement quelques années plus tard.

10. On saura gré à la veuve de H. Hitchcock d'avoir fait cet important legs au dit Collège.

11. *Cyprus: its ancient cities, tombs, and temples. A Narrative of Researches and Excavations* (London, John Murray 1877); notons que ce livre est signé 'Général Louis Palma di Cesnola'.

12. 'Les frères Palma di Cesnola et leur correspondance' in Veronica Tatton-Brown ed., *Cyprus and the East Mediterranean in the Iron Age (Proceedings of the VIIth British Museum Classical Colloquium, April 1988*, London 1989) 84–89; 'Correspondances chypriotes: lettres des frères Colonna-Ceccaldi et de L. Palma di Cesnola à J. Froehner' *Centre d'Etudes Chypriotes. Cahier* 14 (1990) 29–44; 'Diplomates et amateurs d'antiquités à Chypre vers 1866–1878' *Journal des savants* (1992) 123–154.

13. Les relations épistolaires entre Cesnola et Georges Perrot sont discutées chez O. Masson, *Journal des savants* (1992) 148–9.

14. Il s'agit d'une trentaine de lettres, échelonnées du 9 Janvier 1877 au 20 Décembre 1878, mais en majorité en 1877, cf. O. Masson, *Centre d'Etudes Chypriotes. Cahier* 21 (1994-1) 9–12.

15. Ecrites directement en français par Cesnola, ces lettres sont *conservées actuellement au Cabinet du Corpus inscriptionum semiticarum*, cf. O. Masson, *Centre d'Etudes Chypriotes. Cahier* 9 (1988) 12-18 et *RDAC* (1990) 294–197.

16. Lettre conservée chez S. Reinach, cf. O. Masson, *Centre d'Etudes Chypriotes. Cahier* 25 (1996) 10–11 et n. 66 avec bibliographie relative à ces objets.

17. Avec le titre *Die Sammlung Cesnola*, cf. O. Masson, 'Diplomates et amateurs d'antiquités à Chypre vers 1866–1878', *Journal des savants* (1992) 141 et n. 82 et 144; également *Centre d'Etudes Chypriotes. Cahier* 25 (1996) 9.

18. *Handbook*, lv, bibliographie, mais rien page XIX, et 'Painted Vases from Cyprus, in the Pitt Rivers Museum at Oxford' in *Essays in Aegean Archaeology presented to Sir Arthur Evans*, (Oxford 1927) 72–89. Cf. discussion à ce sujet chez O. Masson, 'La dispersion des antiquités chypriotes: les deux collections Cesnola' *Centre d'Etudes Chypriotes. Cahier* 25 (1996) 14–15.

19. J'ai déjà évoqué les activité d'Isaac Hall dans *ICS*, 23–24; il n'est, en revanche, jamais mentionné chez McFadden alors que Myres en parle seulement dans les passages cités.

20. O. Masson, *ICS*, 24, n. 1.

21. Cesnola (n.10) 224.

22. *JAOS* 10, 2 (1880) 'Proceedings', cxxxvi sqq.

23. Publiés dans *JAOS* 10,2 (1880) 201–218 et pl. I–VIII et *JAOS* 11, 2 (1885) 209–238, cf. discussion chez O. Masson, *ICS*, 24 et n. 1.

Olivier Masson (1922–1997) – un tribute

Maurice Sznycer

First and foremost I wish to congratulate the organisers of this colloquium for their excellent initiative in dedicating this *22nd British Museum Classical Colloquium* to the memory of Professor Olivier Masson. There can be no doubt that he would willingly have taken part in this session devoted to *Cyprus in the nineteenth century AD: Fact, fancy and fiction*. Amongst other activities, he appreciated research linked to action, intervening on sites, pseudo-scientific activities (with their good and bad sides) of travellers, diplomats, amateurs, collectors, occasionally even adventurers, who followed in the footsteps of archaeologists, and scholars, sometimes even preceding them, in Greece, the Near-East, on the islands and most especially on Cyprus.

And so – a point I should like to insist on – this first scientific colloquium in honour of Olivier Masson's memory, is being organised here, in London, and not in France, his country, our country.

I should also like to thank the organisers of this colloquium, and especially Veronica Tatton-Brown, for inviting me here to speak about my very dear friend and regretted colleague. I must admit that it is much simpler for me to do so in French.

On ne présente pas Olivier Masson devant une telle assistance. Tout le monde ici le connaissait, personnellement ou par sa réputation ou ses oeuvres, certains très bien, d'autres moins bien, mais tous, j'en suis sûr, savent quel savant exceptionnel il était, embrassant de nombreux domaines d'*études grecques*, de préférence ceux qui n'ont pas encore été, à l'époque où il entreprenait ses recherches, suffisamment explorés. D'autre part, tous ici connaissent son apport essentiel, aux *études chypriotes*, dans leurs divers aspects.

Je m'attacherai donc à rappeler, dans leurs grandes lignes, ses travaux de chercheur, de savant, dans les différents domaines qu'il abordait avec une maîtrise incontestée, en insistant plus particulièrement sur les études chypriotes, sans oublier pour autant ses talents de directeur de revue, de rédacteur, et sans négliger son activité, très féconde, d'enseignant, de professeur, d'animateur. On me permettra, enfin, de parler un peu de l'homme que j'ai connu, de l'ami très proche.

Il serait utile, je pense, de rappeler, pour commencer, quelques repères, quelques dates de la carrière universitaire d'Olivier Masson. Né le 23 avril 1922, il a fait de brillantes études secondaires et supérieures à Paris, d'abord au Lycée, puis à la Faculté des Lettres de l'Université de la Sorbonne, où il passe sa Licence d'enseignement et son Diplôme d'Études Supérieures. En 1947, il obtient l'agrégation de grammaire, – celle qui a été et est toujours la plus difficile et la plus convoitée, – et ensuite, il entre comme chercheur au Centre National de la Recherche Scientifique (*C.N.R.S.*), tout en étant pensionnaire à la fondation Thiers de 1948 à 1951. C'est cette année-là, en 1951, qu'il sera nommé à un poste d'enseignement à l'Université de Nancy, d'abord celui d'assistant, puis celui de Maître de Conférences, enfin, celui de professeur; enseignement qu'il exerce jusqu'en 1965, année où il sera élu et nommé Directeur d'Études à la IVe Section de l'*École pratique des Hautes Études* (Sciences historiques et philologiques), l'*É.P.H.É*, qui est, comme on sait, un établissement unique, non seulement en France, mais dans toute l'Europe, puisque sa tâche principale est non pas la transmission du savoir aux étudiants, comme c'est le cas des Universités, mais un enseignement original de recherche et la direction des recherches des auditeurs, et où, pour matérialiser cette différence essentielle, les professeurs portent, depuis sa fondation il y a plus de 130 ans, le titre de *Directeurs d'Études*. La chaire, ou plutôt la direction d'Études, d'Olivier Masson était intitulée *Philologie et Dialectologie Grecques*. En outre, il exerçait parallèlement, de 1972 à 1990, les fonctions de Professeur de Grec ancien à l'Université de Paris – X (Nanterre), où il fut également Directeur de l'Institut d'études grecques.

Parmi ses autres fonctions, on peut mentionner celles de Secrétaire général de l'Association internationale d'Épigraphie grecque et latine (*A.I.É.G.L.*) et rappeler qu'il a été, entre autres, le principal organisateur du Congrès international d'Épigraphie grecque et latine, qui a eu lieu à Nîmes en 1991. Par ailleurs, il était un membre actif de diverses sociétés savantes, françaises et étrangères, qu'il est inutile d'énumérer ici, et était également membre de l'Institut Académique Européen.

Dès le début de sa carrière universitaire, Olivier Masson s'est révélé comme un chercheur aux multiples talents, sérieux et méthodique, s'attaquant de préférence à des sujets réputés difficiles, non encore élucidés, et parfois même considérés comme 'marginaux' par des savants dits 'classiques' ou conformistes (les deux appellations parfois se recoupent). Ainsi, devenu un parfait connaisseur du grec classique, philologue et épigraphiste rigoureux, linguiste passionné, il s'était, dès le début, particulièrement intéressé à la *dialectologie grecque*, aux langues et dialectes encore mal connus, comme le *macédonien*, le *thrace*, ou encore le *carien*, domaines où ses nombreux travaux font autorité. Il est également devenu un maître incontesté de l'*onomastique grecque*, tout en apportant, par ses multiples travaux, toujours pertinents, une contribution essentielle à l'étude des *anthroponymes*, avec leurs particularités régionales si révélatrices. Il a aussi contribué grandement à l'étude rationnelle de l'étymologie du vocabulaire grec ancien. D'autre part, très tôt, il s'était intéressé à la philologie mycénienne, il a été ainsi, dès 1956, Secrétaire du premier Colloque international de Mycénologie, qui s'était tenu à Gif-sur-Yvette, et il a ensuite participé activement aux colloques et congrès de mycénologie, en étant, depuis 1965, Secrétaire du Comité international des Études mycéniennes. Enfin et surtout, de très bonne heure, il commençait à se passionner pour les études chypriotes – ses premiers articles datent de 1951–1952 – qui sont devenues, on peut le dire, l'un de ses domaines de recherche de prédilection. Études chypriotes dans toute leur étendue: écriture et langue du chypro-minoen, documents syllabiques chypriotes, épigraphie grecque alphabétique, dialecte grec chypriote, onomastique de Chypre, numismatique, religions et cultes, géographie et histoire, Phéniciens à Chypre, l'activité des voyageurs, diplomates, collectionneurs à Chypre, particulièrement au XIXe siècle. La seule énumération de ces domaines, si nombreux, d'études chypriotes, auxquelles les travaux d'Olivier Masson ont apporté une contribution souvent essentielle, montre déjà à elle-seule l'étendue des recherches du savant hors pair qu'il était. On y reviendra, bien sûr, tout à l'heure.

La bibliographie d'Olivier Masson est impressionnante: elle compte plus de 400 numéros, dont près de 240 (c'est-à-dire 60%) concerne Chypre, ce qui témoigne éloquemment de la place prépondérante que les études chypriotes ont eu dans son oeuvre. Il n'est pas question ici, bien entendu, de présenter, ni même d'énumérer, ne serait-ce qu'une partie, des publications parues. On se reportera utilement à la 'bibliographie d'Olivier Masson' qui sera publiée dans les *Mélanges de philologie et d'antiquités grecques et proche-orientales en mémoire d'Olivier Masson*, qui sont en préparation, sous la direction d'Emilia Masson et de Laurent Dubois. En ce qui concerne Chypre, on peut d'ores et déjà consulter la 'bibliographie thématique' compilée par Laurent Dubois.[1] Je ne pourrais indiquer ici que quelques rares exemples choisis dans cette masse de publications, avec une attention particulière, évidemment, pour les études chypriotes.

Ainsi, en ce qui concerne, entre autres, l'*onomastique*, sa maîtrise, l'étendue et la variété de ses investigations se manifestent d'emblée dans les nombreux travaux qu'il a consacrés à ce sujet, dont une partie importante a été réunie, dans un vaste recueil, par ses élèves Laurent Dubois et Catherine Dobias.[2] S'il s'est beaucoup occupé de toponymes, domaine où son érudition et son ingéniosité ont fait merveille, ce sont surtout les *anthroponymes* qui ont eu sa faveur, et dans ses recherches, il apportait souvent des solutions définitives. Il s'attachait toujours à situer un anthroponyme donné dans son contexte historique et géographique, et à repérer des noms de personne caractéristiques pour telle ou telle région. On peut citer, entre beaucoup d'autres, comme un exemple typique de ses investigations dans ce domaine, la série intitulée 'Notes d'anthroponymie grecque', qu'il publiait progressivement dans *Revue de Philologie et d'Histoire*, dans *Bulletin de Correspondance Hellénique* ou dans *Zeitschrift für Papyrologie*.[3] Sa maîtrise dans l'utilisation de l'onomastique pour la connaissance tant linguistique qu'historique d'une région éclate déjà, par exemple, dans une contribution passablement ancienne, intitulée 'Les rapports entre les Grecs et les Illyriens d'après l'onomastique d'Apollonia d'Illyrie et de Dyrrachion', publiée en 1968.[4] Dans cet article, après avoir minutieusement examiné toute une série de noms, comme ceux d'*Agrôn*, *Epicados*, *Platôr*, *Grabos*, *Bersantos*, etc., il arrive à des conclusions historiques importantes, qu'il résume ainsi: 'Si l'on étudie la documentation fournie par Apollonia et Dyrrachion du point de vue des rapports entre les Grecs et les Illyriens, on constate, à notre avis, que l'influence illyrienne a dû être assez limitée dans les deux colonies, qui ont conservé pleinement leur caractère hellénique'.

J'ai déjà dit le penchant d'Olivier Masson d'aborder des sujets difficiles et même, à première vue, extérieurs à sa spécialité. Il s'est lancé ainsi, concernant le domaine onomastique, dans les recherches sur les *anthroponymes libyques* en Afrique du Nord. On sait que, si l'écriture libyque est à peu près déchiffrée, la langue libyque ne l'est pas encore, le cas du libyque étant, de ce point de vue, comparable à celui de l'étrusque. Olivier Masson a fait paraître plusieurs articles sur les noms de personne libyques,[5] ainsi qu'une contribution substantielle sur les Grecs et les Libyens.[6] Il a pu dénicher plusieurs noms libyques dans les inscriptions grecques de Cyrénaïque, fait tout à fait nouveau, et il s'est même donné le plaisir de corriger les lectures fautives, présentées par les spécialistes de l'Afrique libyco-punique, dans les transcriptions latines des noms libyques, par exemple, dans la fameuse et longue inscription latine des *Juvenes*, provenant de Maktar, en Tunisie.

Les recherches portant sur les étymologies de noms grecs était une autre de ses passions. Il a consacré à ce sujet plusieurs travaux importants, mais il suffit de mentionner sa collaboration, on peut même dire son apport personnel, au *Dictionnaire étymologique de la langue grecque*, que son maître Pierre Chantraine commençait à publier à partir de 1968,[7] où l'auteur le remercie ainsi: 'M. Olivier Masson a lu le manuscrit et la première épreuve. Son érudition étendue m'a permis d'éviter des fautes et d'apporter d'innombrables améliorations. Je ne saurais dire tout ce que je lui dois'.[8]

Avant de passer aux études chypriotes d'Olivier Masson, je voudrais auparavant mentionner brièvement ses talents d'éditeur, de directeur de revue, de rédacteur. Il a été le fondateur, le directeur et le principal rédacteur des *Cahiers du Centre d'Études Chypriotes*, qu'il avait fondé à l'Université de Nanterre. Ces *Cahiers* paraissaient régulièrement depuis 1984, en deux fascicules par an. Ainsi, 26 *Cahiers* ont été publiés jusqu'en 1997. Le dernier, le *Cahier* 26, a été, comme tous les précédents, conçu, préparé et supervisé par Olivier, déjà bien souffrant, mais il n'a pu paraître que peu de temps après sa disparition. D'autre part, on sait que le *Cahier* 27, paru en 1998, a été consacré aux *Mélanges Olivier Masson*. En outre, Olivier a, entre autres, participé activement à la reprise du flambeau du *Bulletin d'Épigraphie Grecque*, dont il est devenu l'un des principaux collaborateurs, comme il l'était également, celui du *Bulletin de Correspondance Hellénique* (*BCH*), ou celui de l'*Année Épigraphique*. Il était aussi membre actif du Comité de Rédaction de plusieurs revues étrangères, comme *Kadmos*, ou *Minos*.

Concernant les *études chypriotes*, Olivier Masson, comme on l'a déjà dit, a embrassé toute la gamme de ces études. Il a commencé par le *chypro-minoen* et l'*étéochypriote*, mais c'est surtout dans ses recherches et études sur les *inscriptions syllabiques chypriotes* qu'il a eu l'occasion de montrer toute sa maîtrise. Dans ce domaine, ses travaux se sont avérés décisifs: en effet, il a pu, le premier, établir définitivement le syllabaire chypriote, qui, comme on sait, note un dialecte grec, tout en présentant des traductions valables, toujours accompagnées des commentaires détaillés. Ses publications sur ce sujet sont nombreuses, mais il faut souligner, avant tout, l'importance de son ouvrage fondamental, qui est aussi son chef-d'oeuvre, sur les *inscriptions syllabiques chypriotes*, un énorme volume publié il y a près de 40 ans et, chose rare, réimprimé depuis.[9] Après une bien longue et substantielle *Introduction*, présentant, entre autres, les fouilles et les découvertes, les origines du syllabaire chypriote et son évolution suivant les différentes époques, les règles d'emploi et les problèmes historiques et linguistiques, le recueil rassemble toutes les inscriptions syllabiques de quelque importance, celle-ci étant présentées d'après leur provenance géographique, par différents districts et les diverses localités dans chacun de ceux-ci. Chaque inscription est minutieusement décrite, ainsi que chacun des sites, vient ensuite la transcription du texte syllabique, avec souvent sa copie, son équivalent en grec, la traduction accompagnée d'un commentaire aussi détaillé qu'approfondi et, bien entendu, toute la bibliographie correspondante. Qu'en se reporte, par exemple, à l'édition de la grande tablette de bronze provenant du sanctuaire d'Athéna d'Idalion, dont la présentation et l'explication occupent dix grandes pages.[10] On reste confondu devant tant d'érudition, si parfaitement mise en oeuvre.

Olivier Masson, on le sait, a laissé son empreinte dans beaucoup d'autres domaines des études chypriotes: épigraphie grecque alphabétique à Chypre, géographie et histoire de l'île dans l'antiquité, religions et cultes, où il a beaucoup apporté, numismatique chypriote, dont il est devenu un grand connaisseur, comme le montrent ses multiples travaux dans ce domaine.

Travaillant sur Chypre, il ne pouvait pas ne pas y rencontrer les *Phéniciens*, vu le rôle que ceux-ci ont joué dans l'Antiquité et l'influence qu'ils y ont exercé, sur son histoire, ses cultes, sa civilisation, sa culture. Ils l'ont fasciné, je pense, dès le début, et il a été, à l'époque, l'un des rares savants 'classiques' à comprendre et à apprécier d'emblée l'apport, irrécusable, de ces gens venus de l'Est, sur la civilisation de l'île, à partir sans doute du dixième siècle av. J.-C. C'est ainsi, grâce aux Phéniciens, si l'on peut dire, qu'a commencé, il y a une trentaine d'années, notre collaboration, de plus en plus étroite. Nous avons publié ensemble un certain nombre de travaux, que je ne vais pas énumérer ici, en rappelant simplement notre ouvrage intitulé *Recherches sur les Phéniciens à Chypre*,[11] où en regroupant de nombreux témoignages écrits, nous avons pu montrer qu'ils provenaient d'un nombre de localités plus grand qu'on ne le pensait jusque-là, localités situées sur tout le pourtour de l'île, sans parler de celles de l'intérieur, comme Tamasos, Idalion, etc.[12] D'autre part, je peux témoigner qu'Olivier Masson a appris le phénicien, il connaissait bien l'écriture phénicienne, à travers diverses phases de son développement, un peu moins bien, évidemment, la langue. Il pouvait copier parfaitement les inscriptions phéniciennes, et il lui arrivait de consulter avec aisance aussi bien le *Dictionnaire* de Jean et Hoftijzer, le *DISO*,[13] que l'ouvrage de F.L. Benz sur les noms de personne phénico-puniques,[14] de même que les volumes de l'*Ephemeris* de Mark Lidzbarski,[15] ou encore la *Grammaire* de J. Friedrich et W. Röllig.[16]

Je ne vais pas m'étendre ici sur un autre domaine de ses recherches, concernant notamment les activités, souvent controversées, des voyageurs, des diplomates, des collectionneurs ou de simples aventuriers à Chypre, particulièrement au XIXe siècle, ce qui constitue le thème principal du présent Colloque. Je voudrais seulement dire que ces recherches l'attiraient particulièrement, exerçant sur lui un attrait indéniable. Il adorait comme personne fouiller dans les archives de toutes sortes, dans les réserves des bibliothèques ou des musées, dans les collections privées. Il avait le goût et l'âme d'un dépisteur, d'un détective. Je ne l'ai jamais vu aussi content et même joyeux que quand il avait trouvé, concernant tel personnage insoupçonné, quelque chose de nouveau, de préférence troublant et même accablant. Et, comme on sait, il a beaucoup découvert, des intrigues, des fraudes ... Ses articles à ce sujet sont souvent savoureux et non exempts d'humour. Il avait aussi ses personnages de prédilection, dont il ne cessait d'enrichir la connaissance au fil des recherches et des découvertes, comme, par exemple, les frères Colonna-Ceccaldi, ou, plus encore, les frères Cesnola. Il avait amassé, concernant ces derniers, une documentation impressionnante, y compris des photographies et des autographes d'époque. D'ailleurs, l'un des derniers articles qu'il avait rédigé peu avant sa disparition, est consacré précisément, une nouvelle fois, à Luigi Palma de Cesnola.

On me permettra, en conclusion, de dire quelques mots de l'ami que j'ai connu, et qui m'était proche, de nos relations personnelles, qui étaient étroites. Notre collaboration scientifique, centrée essentiellement sur tous les aspects de la présence phénicienne à Chypre, commencée il y a bien longtemps, s'est poursuivie jusqu'à la fin. Nous restions ainsi en contact quasi-permanent, facilité encore par la proximité de nos domiciles réciproques, puisque nous habitions tous les deux le même pâté de maisons, à une cinquantaine de mètres l'un de l'autre. Nous nous voyions donc souvent, et également à la Sorbonne où est logée l'École des Hautes Études, où nos salles étaient voisines et nos cours avaient lieu le même jour (le mardi), ce qui nous a permis, par ailleurs, d'organiser plusieurs séminaires en commun, les deux auditoires réunis, notamment sur les *Phéniciens à Paphos*. Nous avons fait aussi plusieurs missions ensemble à Chypre, et je me rappelle particulièrement notre voyage de 1981, où, en compagnie et dans la voiture de notre collègue Jacques-Claude Courtois, hélas trop tôt disparu, nous avons pu, deux semaines durant, sillonner en long et en large toute l'île, en visitant tous les sites archéologiques, et je garde un souvenir particulier de notre visite de plusieurs jours dans l'ancienne Paphos, où nous fûmes si aimablement accueillis par Franz-Georg Maier, dans son fameux château, logeant la nuit dans le village voisin de Kouklia, chez une vieille paysanne, étant réveillé chaque matin à l'aube par le chant du coq ...

Notre travail en commun avec Olivier Masson m'a donné l'occasion d'apprécier à sa juste mesure ses qualités exceptionnelles de savant, rigoureux dans ses approches et ses méthodes. Sa vaste érudition n'avait d'égale que sa parfaite modestie, toute naturelle. Il fuyait les honneurs et les distinctions, et évitait la langue de bois académique. Il m'était proche. Il était en outre, un homme cultivé, aimant la littérature – chose peu répandue chez nos collègues – et il adorait la musique classique; il travaillait souvent en écoutant, en sourdine, Mozart ou Vivaldi. Homme droit et honnête, il était pour moi un ami cher et proche, notre longue amitié n'ayant jamais connu de nuages. Tel était Olivier Masson. Presque chaque jour, je mesure le vide qu'a laissé sa disparition.

Notes

1. Cf. L. Dubois, 'Bibliographie thématique des travaux d'Olivier Masson concernant Chypre' *Centre d'Etudes Chypriotes. Cahier* 27: *Mélanges Olivier Masson* (1997) 3–13.
2. O. Masson, *Onomastica Graeca Selecta*, introduction et index de Catherine Dobias et Laurent Dubois (Paris-Nanterre 1990) 2 vol., 680 pages.
3. Il a également, dans *Zeitschrift für Papyrologie und Epigraphik*, une série de neuf articles (le premier, en 1974, le dernier, en 1986) sous un titre publié apparemment curieux de 'Pape-Benseleriana', expliqué par l'auteur dès le début: 'J'ai le projet de présenter sous ce titre une série de remarques d'onomastique grecque, sans ordre déterminé, en prenant comme point de départ commode le recueil de Pape et Benseler' (il s'agit du *Wörterbuch der griechischen Eigennamen* de W. Pape et G.E. Benseler).
4. Dans *Actes du Premier Congrès international des études balkaniques et sud-est européennes* (Sofia 1968) 233–239
5. 'Libyca' dans *Semitica* XXV (1975) 75–85 – 'Libyca (suite)', dans *Semitica* XXVII (1977) 41–45, pl. VII et VIII.
6. 'Grecs et Libyens en Cyrénaïque, d'après les témoignages de l'épigraphie', dans *Antiquités Africaines* 10 (1976) 49–62.
7. Pierre Chantraine, *Dictionnaire étymologique de la langue grecque. Histoire des mots*, 4 volumes.
8. Chantraine (n.7) xii (Préface).
9. O. Masson, *Inscriptions Chypriotes Syllabiques. Recueil critique et commenté*, (Paris 1961); 450 pages grand format, 72 planches contenant près de 400 illustrations (Réimprimé avec des suppléments en 1983).
10. Masson (n.9) 235–244.
11. O. Masson et M. Sznycer, *Recherches sur les Phéniciens à Chypre* (Genève – Paris 1972).
12. *Cf.* dans l'ouvrage cité à la note 11, la *carte de Chypre* montrant les principaux sites antiques ou modernes en relation avec la dispersion des documents phéniciens.
13. Ch.-F. Jean et J. Hoftijzer, *Dictionnaire des inscriptions sémitiques de l'Ouest*, (Leiden 1962).
14. F.L. Benz, *Personal Names in the Phoenician and Punic Inscriptions* (Rome 1972).
15. Mark Lidzbarski, *Ephemeris für Semitische Epigraphik*, 3 vol. (Giessen 1902–1915).
16. J. Friedrich – W. Röllig, *Phönizisch-Punische Grammatik* (Rome 1970).

*Views of Cyprus
in the 19th century*

1. Cyprus, a new archaeological frontier in the XIXth century: the struggle of European Museums for Cypriot antiquities

Claire Balandier

'*Mon premier et bref séjour à Chypre, en septembre 1954, consacra un attachement durable à l'île, à ses paysages, à ses antiquités. Un pèlerinage à Amathonte s'imposait (...) Au cours de chaque voyage, je m'arrêtais donc pour grimper sur l'acropole, avec le vague espoir de retourner quelque pierre inscrite, évidemment étéo chypriote, de recueillir quelque tesson remarquable ou quelque monnaie des rois amathousiens, comme il arrivait, dit-on, aux bergers de la région*' (Olivier Masson).[2]

In 1878, in a paper entitled 'Cyprus: its present and future',[3] one reads: 'the mineral wealth of Cyprus may be uncertain, but there can be no doubt of its archaeological riches'. In another report, bearing the eloquent title, *Etude sur l'île de Chypre considérée au point de vue d'une colonisation européenne*, Edmond Paridant-Van der Cammen, a Belgian citizen, talks about the antiquities of Cyprus in the same manner in which he previously described the different mines of the island.[4] Indeed, the antiquities of Cyprus were first regarded as resources which could be of worth to a colonizing nation, just like any other products or resources of a country.

Even if the true worth of Cypriot antiquities was soon appreciated, the spirit of colonization and the continual rivalry between the main European countries, characteristic of the nineteenth century, shifted the focus from the political field to that of the acquisition of Cypriot antiquities for the main European museums.

A number of documents that I consulted in the Gennadios Library in Athens, and more particularly the chronicles of Georges Perrot (Fig. 1.1), the French historian of art, in the *Revue des Deux Mondes*, will help us to follow the evolution of the attitude of the main European museums towards Cypriot antiquities during the nineteenth century. Starting with an initial lack of interest expressed by these museums and the role of the pioneers in the recognition of the value of Cypriot antiquities, we will then turn our attention to the rivalry between these museums in their efforts to form a Cypriot collection. We will consider then how the British Museum established its private archaeological ground on Cyprus and the consequent reaction of the European archaeological community at the dawn of the twentieth century.

Fig. 1.1: Georges Perrot drawn from nature and engraved by Jean Patricot, after G. Perrot and Chipiez, Histoire de l'Art dans l'Antiquité *vol.8, frontispiece (Paris 1903).*

Fig. 1.2: Ktima, the site of Nea Paphos, with the ancient carob storehouse near the harbour, at the beginning of the twentieth century, after Pafos 1924–1984 μεσα απο το φακο του Σπψρου Χηαριτου *(Nicosia 1984) fig. 26.*

Not only the antiquities themselves, but also the scarcity of ancient remains above ground soon disappointed the first hopes of European prospectors, who expected to be rewarded by such sites like those of Egypt, Italy, and Greece. However, in August 1878, in the *Contemporary Review*, one reads that 'the work (in Cyprus) is interesting alone to the serious student of the remote annals of the Mediterranean. To him the antiquities of the island are a precious connecting-link between Egypt, Assyria and Early Greece and the less attractive they are to the artistic eye the more valuable are they to his comparative vision.'[5] So, we can see that Stuart Poole is differentiating between those who search for antiquities and scholars. It is clear that he is not looking for antiquities as a scholar, but that he wants to find remarkable objects, worth sending home.

But, in fact, at the beginning of the nineteenth century, the way scholars thought was not very different and G. Perrot, a very rich source of information on our subject, reported: 'malgré sa réputation, Cypre est une des dernières terres classiques sur lesquelles se soit portée l'attention des érudits. Elle était plus éloignée de l'Italie que la Grèce; elle ne se trouvait point placée, comme les îles de la mer Egée, sur les routes suivies par les voyageurs qui, depuis la fin du siècle dernier (eighteen century), entreprenaient le pèlerinage d'Athènes ou bien allaient visiter Smyrne et l'Ionie, les rivages de Troie et Constantinople.Quelques uns seulement, qui poussaient jusqu'à la Syrie et l'Egypte, avaient été jetés dans l'île de Cypre par les hasards de la voile et du vent; mais de ce détour et de cette relâche, ils n'avaient guère rapporté qu'une déception.Tandis qu'Egine, le Péloponnèse et l'Attique, tandis que toutes les côtes de l'Asie Mineure offraient aux yeux du savant et de l'artiste les murs encore debouts de leurs cités et de leurs acropoles ... Cypre n'avait pour ainsi dire pas gardé de traces apparentes de l'antiquité. Pas un monument de cette époque qui s'élevât au-dessus du sol et qui frappât le regard. A peine ça et là quelques vestiges d'aqueducs et de vieilles murailles ; à peine quelques tombeaux, formés de trois ou quatre grosses pierres rudement assemblées',[6] as it was, for example, in Paphos (Fig. 1.2).

All the same, some antiquities did come to light at Kition, but they still interested nobody. So, Robert Hamilton Lang wrote that in 1849 'one discovered in a garden close to Larnaca, the famous bas-relief that Sargon gave as a present to the Cypriot kings in the 8th century B.C. The British Museum did not want to pay more than 20 pounds ; the Museum of Berlin was cleverer and purchased the monuments for 50 pounds'.[7]

It is certainly thanks to the journey of Ludwig Ross[8] in Cyprus in the spring of 1845 that the Berlin Museum became interested in Cypriot antiquities. G. Perrot reports also that Mas Latrie arrived on the island just before the Sargon stele was bought by the Berlin Museum, but he was not rich enough to buy it. Nevertheless, 'put-il former à Dali et dans d'autres endroits, une petite collection de figurines en calcaire et en terre-cuite. A son retour, ces pièces furent offertes par lui au cabinet des antiques ; mais elles n'y ont jamais été exposées'.[9] He also reports that, in the same way, 'en 1850, c'était M. de Saulci ... qui saisit ... l'importance et l'intérêt des monumens que ses nécropoles commençaient à fournir. Il acquit donc à Larnaca une suite de statuettes que, dès l'année suivante, il cédait au musée du Louvre. En même temps, il y faisait entrer aussi deux objets plus curieux encore peut-être, deux de ces coupes de métal, travaillées au marteau et à la pointe'.[10] G. Perrot notes then that 'les esprits un peu pénétrans pouvaient deviner qu'il y avait là toute une nouvelle province archéologique à conquérir, toute une page de l'histoire de la civilisation à rétablir lettre par lettre et ligne par ligne, à l'aide des monumens figurés'.[11]

Even if the main European museums, apart from the Berlin Museum and to a small degree the Louvre, were not yet aware of the value of the antiquities of Cyprus, individual adventurers and amateurs were active on the island. According to Perrot, 'de 1866 à 1869, tout le monde à Cypre donnait des coups de pioche et remuait la terre avec une activité fiévreuse. On se serait cru en Californie, le lendemain du jour où on y avait signalé la présence de l'or. Chacun avait son filon qu'il suivait avec une ardeur passionnée, ses agens dressés à la recherche des antiquités, ses ouvriers que l'habitude avait rendus singulièrement adroits et expéditifs'.[12]

It appears, however, that the Ottoman rulers tried to stop this flight of antiquities from the island. Indeed, the British consul, Sandwith, tried to obtain a *firman* from the Ottoman Porte that would have given him permission to excavate. The reason given for not granting him this was that the Ottoman government wanted to found a museum, and thus could not let the island be deprived of its treasures. But Sir Sandwith took this to be joke and started to dig anyway.[13]

Anyone who had the energy to dig could make his own fortune, as H. Ridder testified in 1901: 'fourteen years or so ago when I was there, Cyprus was a very happy hunting ground for the lovers of antiquities. Then many desirable things could still be purchased'.[14] He remembered how he had started to pick up ancient objects at the bazaar, but also in the fields. For example at Curium: 'I picked up the lower parts of two of these stone statues and put them into my pocket. As I anticipated, they make excellent letter-weights. What a falling off is here! ... Well perhaps it is more honorable than to be broken up to fill the shovel of a Cyprian roadmaker'.[15] We can see that his conscience was not very clear, but other adventurers were looting the island to a much greater extent and with no bad conscience whatsoever. Indeed, agents of different foreign countries were digging freely in Cyprus, either for their own satisfaction and interest in antiquities or, as we are going to see, for the sake of their nation.

Fig. 1.3: The vase at the moment of its removal, after P. Aupert and M.Ch. Hellmann, Amathonte I Testimonia I *(Ecole Française d'Athènes, Etudes Chypriotes 4, Mémoire 32, Paris 1984) fig. 26.*

Objects found in Cyprus began to be noticed, and the museums of Europe started to desire to have this long forgotten kind of Eastern art represented in their galleries. So, when M. Renan was charged by Napoleon III to explore the coast of ancient Phoenicia, he thought that a necessary complement to his researches on the continent was the careful exploration of Cyprus. For family reasons, he was replaced by M. de Voguë: 'en compagnie de M. Waddington et avec l'aide de M. Duthoit, architecte, il exécuta, dans les premiers mois de 1862, une exploration complète du sol de l'île; il entreprit même sur plusieurs points des fouilles dont le Louvre a largement profité', according to G. Perrot.[16] Amongst the finds were statues and inscriptions found in three deposits in Golgoi. The finds went to the Louvre to join antiquities found on the island by G. Rey and offered by him to the museum in 1860. These two groups formed the core of the new Cypriot gallery at the Louvre.[17] The very distinctive character of these pieces encouraged the administration of the museum to develop this part of the collection.

In 1865, the Louvre arranged through the French ministry of the navy for a warship to go to Cyprus in order to bring the famous Amathousian vase back to France.[18] De Voguë had taken possession of this vase few years before in the name of his nation (Fig. 1.3). This huge vase (1m 85cm high and 3m 20cm in diameter and weighing 14,000 kg) was shipped to Marseille, and from there to Le Havre and, after going up the Seine on a lighter vessel, was exhibited in the Louvre on 13 July 1866.

The local representatives of foreign countries in Cyprus were also in charge of collecting antiquities. The very first

European agent looking for antiquities was the Comte of Maricourt, Vice-Consul of France in Larnaca. According to G. Perrot, 'sa famille et lui avait l'habitude de se promener, les beaux soirs d'été, sur la plage marine ou le long du lac salé... Là, sur la pente d'une petite colline qui domine cette lagune, un jour le consul ... mit au jour une petite statuette de terre-cuite. Cette découverte toute fortuite le mit en goût. On revint le lendemain au même endroit avec quelques pelles et l'on fit de nouvelles trouvailles, distraction précieuse dans la vie monotone d'une petite ville turque. Chaque soir on pouvait voir la bande se diriger vers la colline pour reprendre son travail de la veille; on allait ramasser des statuettes comme en France on va cueillir des fraises ou des champignons. ... En peu de mois, M. de Maricourt eut une collection qui, dit-on, ne manquait pas de valeur'.[19]

Robert Hamilton Lang, bearing the title of Vice-Consul from 1871, was interested in digging and buying antiquities, since European museums, fighting to buy these objects from him, made him rich. Indeed, even if most of his discoveries went to the British Museum, many of the objects he collected can be found in other European museums, above all in Paris and Berlin.

So, it appears that digging did not need much financial support, since the discoveries in themselves largely paid for further work, and absolutely everybody could be involved in the search of antiquities.

Luigi di Cesnola, who arrived on the island on Christmas Day 1865, as Consul of the United States of America in Larnaca, was, of course, largely responsible for these digging activities. Like everybody else he quickly became involved in the hunt for antiquities. The *caïmakan* of Larnaca tried to stop him, but Cesnola managed to obtain a *firman* that allowed him to conduct his researches throughout the island on condition that he first obtained the authorisation of the owner of the land. He was digging at such a rate that 'de temps en temps, les pachas se plaignaient à Constantinople; on l'accusait de miner des mosquées, de profaner les sépultures des vrais croyans; mais le représentant de l'Amérique parlait alors si haut que ces doléances n'étaient pas écoutées. Le ministre lui écrit un jour : "D'après ce que l'on me dit, cher général, des trous que vous percez de tous côtés, je vois que vous avez l'intention de couler l'île un beau matin. Avant qu'elle s'enfonce, mettez en sûreté, je vous prie, les archives du consulat américain"'.[20] This official, who had a sense of humour, did not know how right he was! Indeed, in 1875, at Amathus, a young German scholar, Sigismond, fell and died in a shaft that had been dug by Cesnola in order to reach the entrance of tombs.[21]

The already tough race between different European countries was going to get tougher through the sale of Cesnola's collections.

Cesnola had created his own private museum in Larnaca: there he put together his various finds from Dali, Athienou and Amathus. A lot of people came to visit it and Cesnola often complained about the tourists of the Cook cruises who had the bad habit of helping themselves to a little souvenir from Cyprus: 'lorsque beaucoup de personnes étaient admises à la fois dans les pièces encombrées d'antiquités, il n'était pas toujours facile d'empêcher les visiteurs de manier les petits objets posés sur des tables ..., et plus d'une fois, après le départ de la bande, certains de ces objets ne se retrouvaient point. Des gens qui ont toutes les apparences extérieures de l'honnêteté ne se font aucun scrupule de mettre des antiquités dans leur poche, de casser le nez d'une statue pour le rapporter chez eux, comme un trophée'.[22] But was Cesnola behaving in a very different way?

Not only tourists, but also several experts passing from Cyprus, visited the collection and later spoke about it in Europe. Moreover, Cesnola was taking photographs of the main objects from his museum and sending them to European scholars.

Some public sales of parts of Cesnola's collection took place in some European capitals, like that of the 25 and 26 March 1870 at the Hôtel Drouot in Paris, where the antiquities he found in 1868 were sold.[23] Several museums tried to acquire Cypriot antiquities at this sale, either to form or to increase their Cypriot collections.

The Hermitage itself was interested and, after seeing Cesnola's pictures, 'la Russie envoya à Cypre, dans ce même été 1870, un des conservateurs du musée de l'Ermitage, chargé de négocier un achat. Les négociations n'aboutirent pas; mais l'archéologue auquel avait été confiée cette mission, M. Doell, avait passé près de deux mois à Larnaca, et les avait employés à dresser l'inventaire des richesses, dont le propriétaire lui-même, trop occupé à les augmenter, ne savait pas bien le compte ... L'Académie impériale de Saint-Pétersbourg, en 1873, fit imprimer dans ses *Mémoires* le catalogue qu'avait dressé M. Doell et y joignit dix-sept planches lithographiées'.[24]

According to Perrot, 'ce qui avait peut-être empêché les propositions russes d'être accueillies, c'est que des pourparlers étaient engagés au même moment avec le Louvre ou plutôt avec l'empereur en personne. Celui-ci pouvait se laisser tenter par la pensée de joindre cette galerie, unique dans son genre, à la galerie Campana, qu'il avait achetée dix ans plus tôt; c'était un sûr moyen de relever encore la valeur et le renom de cette partie de nos collections qui avait reçu le titre de *Musée Napoléon III*. La guerre franco-allemande vint interrompre brusquement les négociations. Ce fut alors le Musée britannique qui parla d'acheter; mais on voulait voir les objets à Londres pour pouvoir les étudier et les évaluer à loisir. ... Un mot du gouverneur avertit le général des difficultés qu'il rencontrerait. ... Il lui fit

Fig. 1.4: Picture, undated, of the Metropolitan Museum of New York with a handwritten Greek title: 'Το Μουσειον τώσ Νεασ Ψορκώσ ενδα Κυπριακαι Αρχηιοτώτεσ' (The Museum of New York exhibiting Cypriot Antiquities). This picture belongs to Dr. Demetrios Michaelides, who has generously allowed me to publish it here for the first time, at the time of the conference.

observer que son firman lui permettait bien de fouiller où et quand il lui plairait, mais ne prévoyait ni n'autorisait l'exportation des objets trouvés. M. Lang avait bien une fois fait sortir à la barbe des douaniers, une de ses plus belles statues sur une civière couverte d'un drap. Il était moins facile de dissimuler les trois cent soixante lourdes caisses qui se trouvaient empilées dans les magasins du consulat'.[25] The pasha was asked by the Sublime Porte to prevent the American consul sending his 360 boxes to England. Since the official export ban was addressed to the consul of the United States, Cesnola renewed his request as consul of Russia, a position that was then vacant. Through this stratagem, he sent the collection on a ship to Alexandria from where it was supposed to proceed to London. The Governor General in Nicosia concluded that 'M. de Cesnola aurait mérité de naître Turc; il aurait fait un beau chemin dans la diplomatie orientale'.[26]

Unfortunately, the British Museum had to face an unexpected competitor, the Metropolitan Museum of New York. Private initiative had just given birth to this establishment which, with immense resources at its disposal, had considerable consequences for the art and curiosities market, and for the public galleries of old Europe, even to the richest among them like those of London.

'On insista sur cette idée qu'il siérait de donner la préférence à sa patrie d'adoption et sur le fait qu'à Londres ou Paris, les produits de la plastique et de la céramique chypriotes, plus faits pour intéresser l'archéologue que pour charmer l'artiste, seraient comme écrasés par le voisinage des chefs-d'œuvre de la Grèce et de Rome'.[27]

Fig. 1.5: Engraving showing the 'Main Hall' of the Metropolitan Museum of Art, New York with an exhibition of the Cesnola Collection: statuary from Golgoi can be recognized on the right. After The Art Journal for 1880 *new series, vol. 6 (1880) 181.*

The collection, 10,000 pieces, was bought in 1873 by the Metropolitan Museum for 61,000 dollars. To exhibit the most important pieces, the committee of the Metropolitan Museum rented the Douglas Mansion in 14th street for five years. In 1872, 500,000 dollars were voted by the State of New York to build a museum in Central Park on ground given by the town (Fig. 1.4). Moreover, the trustees, encouraged by the success, sent Cesnola back to Cyprus to lead even larger excavations. These were financed by the Metropolitan Museum to which would belong all that was found. The financial crisis broke this agreement, but Cesnola pursued the search for antiquities on his own. If the excavations at Amathous, Paphos, Soloi and Salamis proved disappointing, the discovery of the so-called Curium Treasure in 1874 was the crowning of Cesnola's career as an archaeologist.[28] This new collection was admired in Paris

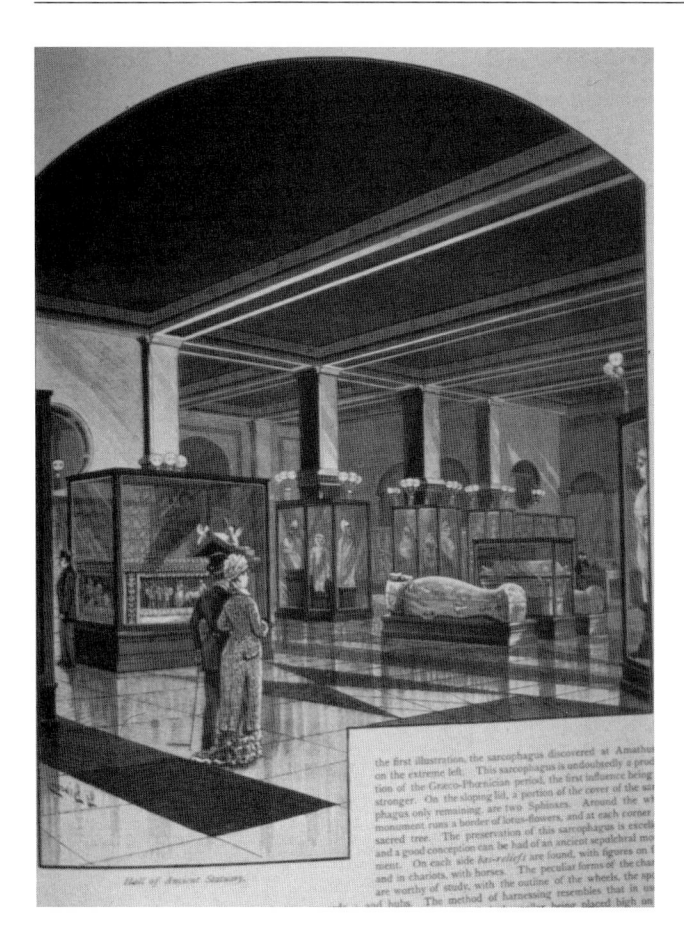

Fig. 1.6: Engraving showing the 'Hall of Ancient Statuary' in the Metropolitan Museum of Art in New York with an exhibition of the Cesnola Collection: the famous sarcophagus discovered at Amathous can be seen on the left, behind a couple of visitors. After The Art Journal for 1880, *new series, vol. 6 (1880) 297.*

and London, but although the main European museums would have liked to buy part of it, Cesnola wanted to keep his entire collection together. It was again the Metropolitan Museum of New York which in 1876 bought it for 45,640 dollars (Fig. 1.5 and 1.6).

By this time Cesnola had left Cyprus for good. Some commented that this was because he did not expect to find more antiquities of the value of the Curium treasure, but we can wonder if it was not the new Ottoman law on antiquities, promulgated in 1874, that dissuaded him from continuing his excavations. Indeed, as it had already been announced in the introduction of the catalogue of the public sale of the Piéridès collection in Paris in February 1873: 'this will not be renewed, since the Ottoman government, touched by the reports of the marvellous discoveries made in the island, had just formerly forbidden any new research of antiquities'.[29] But a few years later, the convention of 4 June 1878 transferred the possession of Cyprus to England.

Opinions were divided about this convention even in England, but this was a great chance for British archaeologists and scholars and above all, of course, for the British Museum. It was said at the time that 'le seul Anglais peut-être dont la satisfaction doive être sans mélange, c'est l'habile et savant conservateur des antiques au Musée britannique, M. Newton. ... Il se voit pénétrant, à la lueur des torches, dans des chambres souterraines comme celle où a été trouvé le fameux trésor de Curium, aujourd'hui la gloire du Musée de New-York. ... Il ira prendre possession du sol, au nom du Musée, comme Sir Garnet Wolseley l'a fait, en juillet dernier [1878], au nom de la couronne d'Angleterre. Avec son expérience et son coup d'œil, il ne lui faudra pas longtemps pour visiter tous les sites antiques, ... et pour établir des chantiers sur les points qui sembleront les plus riches de promesses'.[30]

Even though now a real scholar, the archaeologist was still perceived as an adventurer, no longer working on his own account, but for a great museum: he was the British Museum's ambassador. Indeed, there is no doubt that his real duty was to enrich the Museum's Cypriot collection, something underlined by the clear resentment over the sale of Cesnola's collection to the Metropolitan Museum: 'en ce moment, par suite de l'achat de la collection Cesnola, c'est le Musée métropolitain de New-York qui est le plus riche en objets de provenance cypriote; mais grâce au privilège, on pourrait presque dire au monopole dont va jouir le Musée britannique sur ce sol acquis par l'Angleterre, cette inégalité ne saurait subsister longtemps. ... Si les premiers explorateurs ont eu la main heureuse, ils n'ont pu cependant épuiser, en quelques années, une terre aussi riche, et des efforts bien dirigés, avec des ressources supérieures à celles des simples particuliers, finissent toujours par être couronnés de succès. Avant dix ans, on n'aura plus besoin de passer l'Atlantique pour étudier l'art cypriote; Londres, qui en possède déjà de précieux échantillons, aura complété ses séries au moyen d'objets dont la plupart auront un état civil et une histoire'.[31]

The good will and the scientific guarantee, strongly underlined, could not hide the real aim of the British Museum, to compete with the Metropolitan Museum and to be avenged for Cesnola's affront. To run this competition, huge financial means were provided, 'for the benefit of the Nation'.[32]

Their rule over the island gave Britain the opportunity to constitute a private archaeological land and ensure absolute freedom for excavating where and when required: 'Plus de *firmans* à demander, à attendre pendant de longs mois, comme lors des fouilles de Ninive ou d'Halicarnasse, en Turquie; plus de mauvaises volontés, ouvertes ou cachées, à désarmer ou à déjouer, mais une pleine et entière liberté de creuser partout, aussi profondément que l'on voudra, moyennant une juste indemnité comptée aux propriétaires du terrain'.[33]

We can appreciate that scores had to be settled not only with the former Turkish rulers, but also with other archaeological regulations and restrictions, where the local laws had to be respected: 'Pas de loi jalouse non plus, comme la loi grecque, pour forcer ceux qui retirent du sol les monumens, non sans de grandes fatigues et de grandes dépenses, à les livrer ensuite aux musées d'Athènes; car ce sont là les conditions vraiment trop dures, que les Allemands ont dû accepter avant de fouiller la plaine d'Olympie, et l'Ecole Française l'île de Délos'.[34]

The means provided were great: 'la marine, l'armée, toutes les autorités anglaises prêtent leur concours aux travaux, aideront à enlever les objets découverts et à les faire parvenir, sans qu'ils éprouvent aucun dommage, jusqu'à l'opulent Musée où ils iront prendre leur place dans des séries déjà formées'.[35]

We have already said that the lure of antiquities was camoufflaged under scientific guarantee, but it is true that, at this period, the attitude of European scholars towards excavation methods was changing.

Already in 1879 G. Perrot was criticizing Cesnola and his methods, which previously were considered as the most appropriate ones. From then on, scholars started looking at Cesnola's excavations with new eyes. It seems that this change came about in the year 1879, since the French columnist was speaking with emphasis about Cesnola, compared to Schliemann, Botta or Mariette[36] in his chronicle of January. In that of May of the same year he wrote to the contrary that: 'M. Duthoit nous aurait donné des informations sur la construction et le plan du sanctuaire de Golgos bien plus instructives que celles de M. de Cesnola. Pour ce dernier, les vestiges de ce bâtiment étaient seulement une mine où travailler à la hâte afin de trouver des objets ayant assez de valuer pour être collectionnés ou vendus. La fouille qui est conduite ainsi est rude et destructrice'.[37] The American consul is even described by Haggard as 'the omnivorous Cesnola'.[38] More serious is the report made by W. J. Stillman on the validity of the Cesnola collection, and in particular about the 'Curium treasure'.[39] On 28 March 1885, during a meeting of the American Numismatic and Archaeological Society of New York, he concluded:

> 'while it [the collection] contains many objects of unquestionably great value to the science of archaeology, its utility to students of that science is seriously diminished:
> –First. By a deplorable recklessness of attribution as to the localities of discovery, which makes it quite impossible to determine the place in the general archaeology of Cyprus to which the several pieces can be assigned;
> –Second. By evident repairs and alterations in certain pieces and a thorough system of concealment of the original surfaces of others, and those the most important, which makes it impossible to decide whether they have, or not, undergone similar alterations; ... Any piece of antique sculpture so treated, offered to any of the European museums, or to an intelligent dealer in antiquities, would be rejected, or accepted only as of impaired value, both pecuniarily and archaeologically; and
> –Third. By attributions which assign an important part of the Collection to a single deposit, the principal instance of which ... is the so-called Curium Treasure. ...while some of the objects were certainly of great archaeological value. ...a great part of them were of late Greek work : some were even Byzantine, Barbaric and medieval, with some counterfeits, and one pair of earrings of the nineteenth century, machine-made and of base gold. It is impossible, even for an instant, to grant a collective antique character to this Treasure'.

The British Museum took drastic measures to avoid such a scandal in its own collections and to guarantee the scientific character of archaeological finds.

Consequently, under strict orders from England, the governor of the island, Sir Garnet Wolseley, prohibited all private excavations. 'L'interdiction est générale, elle s'applique aux Européens, aux étrangers, aussi bien qu'aux habitants de l'île'.[40] Indeed, since Cesnola and Lang left Cyprus, their workers, most of them from Dali, now unemployed, had formed cooperatives, under their former foremen and excavated different necropoleis. They now had to lay down their tools, since any excavation had to have the agreement of the British authorities. Only scholars could now lead excavations, of course for the benefit of the British Museum. The British had started to act something like the previous rulers, though not to preserve the antiquities in Cyprus, but, on the contrary, in order to collect, send, and exhibit them only at the British Museum.

Not only archaeologists were unearthing antiquities for the Museum's benefit, but also amateurs: 'veritable antiquities are almost as rare today, owing largely to the prohibition that has been put upon private digging in the interests of the British Museum. ... I procured one or two other objects which I submitted to the British Museum. They said they were worth keeping – and kept them, by way of exchange kindly presenting me with plaster casts edged round with blue paper. Perhaps they are better there. I like to think so'.[41]

This monopolistic approach to antiquities of the British authorities quickly attracted harsh criticism of two kinds. Criticism came from amateur archaeologists. For them, 'the stringent prohibition of the British authorities against a search for antiquities in Cyprus has destroyed the interest which would otherwise have been taken by travellers in such explorations. As ... there are no remains to attract attention upon the surface ... therefore in the absence of permission to excavate, the practical study of the past is impossible, and it is a sealed book'.[42]

Scholars and enlightened people qualified their reaction

Fig. 1.7: The Venetian city-walls of Famagousta in the harbour area in 1903–1904 (Coodes Archives). The original gates have been enlarged to make the passage of trucks easier and to reuse its stones. After Anna G. Marangou, Τα λιμανια τώσ Kυπρου (Nicosia 1997) 40–41, detail.

a little better. They could understand the motives behind the British authorities' decision, but they also toned their criticism down considering the British monopoly on excavations: 'Que certains emplacemens soient ainsi réservés pour de grandes enttreprises archéologiques dignes d'un pays comme l'Angleterre, rien de mieux assurément; mais ne serait-il pas dangereux de donner à cette défense un caractère absolu? L'Angleterre ne saurait se laisser soupçonner de porter ici une autre préoccupation que celle de servir ces intérêts supérieurs qui sont chers à tous les esprits cultivés. Elle devrait donc, sans hésiter, accorder la permission de faire des fouilles à toute personne qui le demanderait afin de résoudre un problème scientifique et non pour faire de l'argent'.[43]

Day by day, the idea of a Cypriot museum, first visualized by the Ottoman rulers, was also growing. Since January 1879, six months after the beginning of British rule in Cyprus, scholars started to discuss it: 'We confess we sympathise with the Turks; it would have been much more fitting for the "Cesnola collection" to have been placed either in the Saint Irene museum, or in one formed on the island, than to have been sold to foreigners'.[44] The same journalist expressed his wish that: 'It is hoped that, under British occupation, what is found will not be suffered to be carried off by private individuals. There should be a Cyprus museum, in which such treasures should be stored'.[45] Another paper in this volume shows that his wish was fulfilled in 1883.[46] In 1900, however, in a touristic guide to the island, it is mentioned that 'formerly permission could be obtained from the Government for exhumation, all objects found being fairly divided between the Government Museum and the exploiters'[47] which is not exactly what was hoped for 25 years earlier.

In the first years of the twentieth century, however surprising it might seem for the period, a French traveller, René Delaporte, wrote that 'le pays attend sa renaissance, et celle-ci-ci se prépare sous la sage administration de l'Angleterre',[48] but he immediately changes his view when it comes to ancient monuments: 'l'autorité anglaise a peu le sens des antiquités et celles-ci disparaîtront, du moins pour les remparts de Nicosie'.[49]

Those who know my passion for city-walls can imagine how hurt I was by this comment and even more so by R. Hamilton Lang's ideas about Famagousta, in 1902 (Fig. 1.7).[50] For him, 'these fortifications are of no value today as such, and for the health of the new town ought to disappear. Archaeologists have already expressed their alarm that such interesting relics of the past as these walls should be demolished. No one who knows the interest I take in the antiquities of Cyprus will suspect me of a spirit of vandalism, and I have no hesitation in saying that these fortifications, *which are only of the 16th century* of our era, are not worth preserving. On the contrary, their demolition and the removal of the stones which encumber the town may yield most interesting archaeological discoveries. All that is desirable is that a small staff of competent archaeologists should assist at the operation, carefully photographing the walls before they disappear, retaining any interesting inscription and statuary, and searching for any concealed objects of interest. The cost of such a mission would be small'. This clearly shows that the preservation of antiquities by the British rulers is understood in a very restrictive sense of the word 'antique'. Despite the fact that Lang is aware of the need for the preservation of memory, that is photographing the Venetian walls before their destruction, the preservation of a monument is subordinate to the interesting finds its demolition could provide.

Fortunately for us, it seems that the cost was higher than Lang expected, or perhaps other archaeologists or historians showed an interest in military and Venetian architecture, because the fortifications are still standing today in the occupied part of the island. Above all, it is certainly the passing of a new Antiquities Law in 1905 which saved them from destruction, since the monuments worthy of protection were now not only those that could be exhibited in museums, and not only those that were ancient, but any building of any period which was bore traces of the history of Cyprus.

Notes

1. I have to express many thanks to Dr. Demetrios Michaelides who read over the first version of this paper. I am also very grateful to him for the picture of the Metropolitan Museum (Fig. 1.4), belonging to his private collection, and for permission to publish it here for the first time at the time of the conference.
2. O. Masson, 'Avant Propos', *Centre d'Etudes Chypriotes. Cahier* 13 (1990) 3.
3. R.S. Poole, 'Cyprus: its present and future', *The Contemporary Review* (August 1878) 150.
4. E. Paridant-Van der Cammen, *Etude sur l'île de Chypre considérée au point de vue d'une colonisation européenne* (Bruxelles 1874) 87.
5. Poole (n.3).
6. G. Perrot, *Revue des Deux Mondes* 31 (Paris 1er janvier 1879) 564–565.
7. R. Hamilton Lang, 'Les tombes et leur contenu', in G. Perrot, *Chypre son passé, son présent et son avenir* (Paris 1879) 222.
8. O. Masson and A. Hermary, 'Le voyage de Ludwig Ross à Chypre en 1845 et les antiquités chypriotes du Musée de Berlin', *Centre d'Etudes Chypriotes. Cahier* 9 (Paris 1988) 3–10.
9. Perrot (n.6) 571.
10. Perrot (n.6) 571.
11. Perrot (n.6) 570.
12. Perrot (n.6) 584.
13. Perrot (n.6) 586–587.
14. H. Rider Haggard, *A Winter Pilgrimage* (London 1901) 115.
15. Haggard (n.14) 119
16. Perrot (n.6) 574.
17. R.C. Severis and L. Bonato (ed.), A. Gautier, 'Antiquities brought to the Louvre Museum by Duthoit', in *Along the most beautiful past in the world. Edmond Duthoit in Cyprus*, Bank of Cyprus Group (Nicosia 1999) 129, 133–137 and pls. 28–30, 146–147.
18. Severis and Bonato (n.17) 131–133.
19. Perrot (n.6) 579. According to G. Perrot, inscriptions had shown that the place was the site of a temple of Demeter Paralia.
20. Perrot (n.6) 579.
21. O. Masson, 'Sur le site d'Amathonte en 1876: J. Siegismund et J.P. Vondiziano', *Centre d'Etudes Chypriotes. Cahier* 7 (Paris 1987) 11–15.
22. Cesnola quoted by Perrot (n.6) 573.
23. W. Froehner, *Antiquités chypriotes des fouilles faites en 1868 par M. de Cesnola*, catalogue de la vente aux enchères publiques à l'hôtel des commissaires-priseurs, 5 rue Drouot à Paris, les vendredi 25 et samedi 26 mars 1870.
24. Perrot (n.6) 594.
25. Perrot (n.6) 594–595.
26. Perrot (n.6) 595.
27. Perrot (n.6) 594.
28. O. Masson, 'Cesnola et le trésor de Curium. Part 1', *Centre d'Etudes Chypriotes. Cahier* 1 (Paris 1984) 16–26 and 'Part 2', *Centre d'Etudes Chypriotes. Cahier* 2 (Paris 1984) 3–16.
29. *Antiquités chypriotes. Collection importante de Verres Antiques, bijoux, terres cuites provenant des fouilles faites dans l'île de Chypre par M. Piéridès*, catalogue of auction sale on Monday 10 February 1873, in Paris, 1.
30. G. Perrot, 'L'île de Cypre, son rôle dans l'histoire. Part 1. Le climat et la nature de l'île. Son agriculture et son industrie', *Revue des Deux Mondes*, tome 30 (Paris 1er décembre 1878) 510–511.
31. Perrot (n.30) 512.
32. *Catalogue of Cypriote Antiquities called the Lawrence-Cesnola collection, the property of Edwin Henry Lawrence, F.S.A.*, collection sold by auction on Friday 1st June 1883.
33. Perrot (n.30) 511.
34. Perrot (n.30) 511.
35. Perrot (n.30) 511.
36. Perrot (n.6) 602 and on the correspondance between L.P. di Cesnola and H. Schliemann, see O. Masson, 'L. Palma di Cesnola, H. Schliemann et l'éditeur John Murray', *Centre d'Etudes Chypriotes. Cahier* 21 (Paris 1994) 7–14.
37. G. Perrot, *Revue des Deux Mondes* 33 (Paris 15 May 1879) 374.
38. Haggard (n.14) 118.
39. This report was privately printed in New York, 28 March 1885 (A copy is now in the Gennadios Library, Athens).
40. Perrot (n.6) 604.
41. Haggard (n.14) 116–117.
42. S.W. Baker, *Cyprus as I saw it in 1879* (London 1879) 145.
43. Perrot (n.6) 604–605.
44. *The London Quarterly Review*, (January 1879) 399.

45. *The London Quarterly Review* (n.44) 393.
46. N.P. Stanley-Price, 'The Ottoman Law on Antiquities (1874) and the founding of the Cyprus Museum', in this volume.
47. Col. Fyler, *The Development of Cyprus*, chapter 5 'Hotels and tours' (London 1900) 92. As an example of the division of antiquities, note those discovered by F. Warren at Frangissa (Tamassos) which were divided between the Museum, the excavator and the owner of the land, see O. Masson, 'Le Colonel Falkland Warren à Chypre, 1878–1890', *Centre d'Etudes Chypriotes. Cahier* 11–12 (Paris 1989) 29–34.
48. R. Delaporte, *L'île de Chypre; séjour de trois ans au pays de Paphie-Vénus* (Paris 1913) 13.
49. Delaporte (n.48) 89.
50. R. Hamilton Lang, 'Cyprus under British rule', *Blackwood's magazine* 1042 (August 1902) 82.

2. Cyprus in the 19th century: perceptions and politics

Peter W. Edbury

There are two dates in the history of Cyprus in the nineteenth century that force themselves on our attention: one is 1821; the other 1878. 1878 was the year of the Congress of Berlin and the British acquisition of Cyprus, and we shall return to that episode presently. March 1821, on the other hand, saw the outbreak of Greek War of Independence. So far as Cyprus is concerned, the story of what happened in that year is perhaps not as well known as it should be, although Professor John Koumoulides and others have studied it in some depth.[1] The Greeks of Cyprus did not follow the example of their compatriots in Greece in taking up arms against their Ottoman masters. They realised that they were too distant from Greece itself and that the Turks could bring troops from Syria or Egypt too readily for an insurrection on the island to get very far. That is not to say that the leading Cypriot Greeks were unsympathetic to the cause of Pan-Hellenic nationalism, and indeed many Cypriots were to fight and die in Greece. What in fact happened was quite appalling. As soon as the rebellion broke out in Greece, the authorities ordered the disarming of all Greeks on the island, even though, as the instructions from Istanbul recognized, in the past when the Turkish community in Cyprus had proved recalcitrant the Greeks had remained passive. But in 1821 the sympathies of the Cypriot Greeks were in little doubt, and the Turkish governor determined on a pre-emptive strike. A list of 486 leading inhabitants was prepared; in June they were rounded up, and in July the executions began. Among the first to be killed was the Greek metropolitan of Cyprus, Archbishop Kyprianos, along with three of his fellow bishops. It is not known exactly how many died at this time, but the total was almost certainly well in excess of the figure of the 486 proscribed individuals. The terror was increased by the fact that troops brought in from Syria mutinied, and their behaviour thoroughly alarmed the European community that was then concentrated at Larnaca. It was commonly believed, at least among the Europeans, that the extent of the slaughter was to be explained by the fact that the Turks could then sequestrate the property of the victims, dispossessing their heirs and families.

Eventually, in 1829, the Ottomans were obliged to recognize the independence of the southern half of what is now Greece. Cyprus, however, remained a part of the Ottoman empire. The atrocities of 1821 and the subsequent repression were never forgotten by the Cypriot Greeks. But – and this is a big 'but' – what happened on the island was hardly known in western Europe at all. Liberal opinion was overwhelmingly philhellene. The romantic idealism of restoring Greek nationhood; the gallant and ultimately tragic involvement of Lord Byron and others; atrocities such as the killing of the ecumenical Patriarch Gregorios V in Istanbul on Easter Sunday 1821 or the massacre on Chios as immortalized by Delacroix – all these things struck a deep chord of sympathy among people educated in the Greek classics, and, though few could manage the grand tour to include Greece itself, there were many who were coming to acquire a greater appreciation of ancient Greek culture thanks to the spate of antiquities that were then finding their way into collections in the West. But Cyprus had never been part of the Grand Tour; apart from merchants and sailors, very few Britons had ever been there. Any news of the events of 1821 that might reach the West was overshadowed in popular perception by what was happening in Greece itself. So far as I have been able to discover, what happened in Cyprus made no impact on opinion in Britain, and the fate of islanders seems to have played no part in the international diplomacy of the time.

All this is by way of introduction. I do not want to tell the story of Cyprus in the nineteenth century, but rather ask what people at the time knew. What would a reasonably well educated and reasonably well informed Englishman, or Englishwoman, think of if someone mentioned 'Cyprus'? What sort of image did people have of Cyprus? How was the island perceived?

Let me try a few suggestions. If in 1800 or 1850 or, for that matter, on the eve of the Congress of Berlin in 1878 you had asked an educated Englishman to say what he knew about Cyprus, maybe the first answer would be that St Paul had visited it with his travelling companion St Barnabas, himself a native of the island, as recorded in the Acts of Apostles chapter 13. Another answer would be that Shakespeare had set his play Othello in the island. Some people might have known that Richard the Lionheart had conquered Cyprus during the Third Crusade – this was in 1191 – although this particular episode seems not to have caught the attention of Sir Walter Scott in his novels, *Ivanhoe* (1819) or *The Talisman* (1825), both of which were set against the background of Richard's exploits in the East. Other people, perhaps more in Continental Europe than in Britain, would have heard of the last queen of Cyprus, the Venetian noblewoman Caterina Cornaro. Caterina had abdicated in 1489 and had then lived in Asolo in northern Italy where she acted as a patron to artists and scholars until her death in 1510. In the course of the nineteenth century her career inspired at least five operas including those by Gaetano Donizetti and Michael William Balfe.

The other thing that people would have known was that Cyprus was a part of the Ottoman empire. In fact the island had been conquered from Venice by the Turks in 1570–71. The siege of Famagusta and the heroic Venetian defence had lasted eleven months and had been a struggle of epic proportions. Christendom's response to the war had culminated the great naval victory over the Turks in the battle of Lepanto in 1571. But it was too late; by then Cyprus had fallen.

Well before 1800, however, western ideas about the Ottomans were changing. No longer was it a matter of the infidels at the gates of Vienna. The peace of Karlowitz of 1699 and then the peace of Passarowitz of 1715 effectively confined the Ottomans to the Balkans. Now that they had ceased to be a threat to Christian Europe, the Turks could be viewed in the West with a benign ambivalence. By turns immoral, raffish, indolent, infuriating, exotic, the Turks were seen as colourful and intriguing. It was the age in which words such as 'sofa', 'divan' and 'ottoman' (in the sense of a padded seat) were added to the language. No matter if reality were something completely different. It was the image that mattered, even if it was sort of construct that Edward Said would castigate as 'Orientalism'. But this indulgent attitude was shattered by the Greek War of Independence, and henceforth the Ottoman empire was to be characterized as the 'Sick Man of Europe'.

Truth to tell, people in Britain did not know very much about the island of Cyprus. So where might our putative 'educated Englishman' have turned for information. One possibility of course would be that great compendium, the *Encyclopaedia Britannica*. By the outbreak of the First World War, the *Encyclopaedia Britannica* had gone through eleven editions, and it might be worth seeing how the entry for Cyprus developed over the course of the nineteenth century and thereby get an impression of what people knew or, rather, what the compilers thought people would need to know about the island.[2]

To begin at the beginning. The first edition of 1773 has only a brief entry giving the approximate, and as it happens inaccurate, latitude and longitude,[3] together with a piece of antiquarian mis-information to the effect that Guy de Lusignan, titular king of Jerusalem at the end of the twelfth century and the first crusader ruler of Cyprus, instituted the 'knights of Cyprus'. This completely groundless assertion was repeated in all subsequent editions down to and including the 8th edition which appeared in the 1850s. Cyprus had in fact fared only slightly better in the famous French *Encyclopédie* of Diderot and d'Alambert. Volume 3 of that work had appeared in 1753, twenty years earlier, and there, in an article on 'Chypre' which fills about 32 column inches, we are told that the fertility of the island had given rise to the alternative name 'Macaria' which means 'fortunate', but that this name is scarcely merited because of the ill-fortune she has suffered in successively passing under foreign domination. Consciously or otherwise, much twentieth-century Cypriot scholarship has echoed this sentiment from the French Enlightenment: despite suffering crusader, Venetian, Turkish and British rule, the Cypriot people have shown tremendous resilience. To return to the *Encyclopaedia Britannica*: the second edition of 1777 has a much larger entry. We are told that, according to Eratosthenes (a late third-century BC polymath), Cyprus 'was first discovered by the Phoenicians two or three generations before the days of Asterius and Minos, kings of Crete: that is, according to Sir Isaac Newton's computation, 2006 years before the Christian era'. The only other ancient authority to be named is Josephus who says that Cyprus was peopled by the descendants of Cittim, a grandson of Japhet (and hence a great grandson of Noah). There then follows a brief and rather garbled outline of Persian, Hellenistic and later rulers down to 1570 when the island was taken by the Turks. We are then informed that the air is 'unwholesome'; that the soil is 'excellent' and 'would produce all the necessaries of life in abundance if properly cultivated'. The entry goes on to say that water is scarce and that, 'by reason of the uncultivated state of the country they are also greatly infested with poisonous reptiles of various kinds. The people are extremely ignorant and lascivious as indeed they are recorded to have been from the remotest antiquity. Anciently the worship of Venus was established in this island, whence her title among the poets of the *Cyprian queen*: and such an inclination had the inhabitants to become the votaries of the goddess, both in theory and practice that the young women used to prostitute themselves in her temple in order to raise themselves portions. Nor are their successors said to be much better at this day'. That was published in 1777, and the entry remained unaltered in the third, fourth, fifth and sixth editions – in other words for almost half a century until 1823. Then in the seventh edition, which appeared in the 1830s, the editors simply cut out the last section – the nonsense about the poisonous reptiles and slur on Cypriot womanhood – and ended with the Turkish acquisition of the island in 1570.

We have to wait until the mid-1850s and the 8th edition for a completely new account. The author clearly preferred classical to modern place-names when describing the geography of the island – I think we can detect here the influence of Strabo – but his account of the history, though brief, seems well researched. He continues: 'Under Turkish rule the material prosperity of Cyprus has greatly declined. In the times of the Venetian supremacy the island maintained a population of 1,000,000: its present population is only about 150,000 of whom the great majority are Greeks. Many parts of the island formerly healthy and fertile are now, from malaria and other causes, barren and uninhabitable. Its trade was at one time valuable and important; now the value of its annual imports does not exceed L26,000; of its exports about L60,000'. For the record, the best modern estimate of the population by the close of the Venetian period is slightly less than 200,000 – far less than the 1,000,000 suggested here – and a census in 1881 produced a figure of 186,183 – in other words, not so very different from the estimate for 1570.[4]

The volume containing the entry for Cyprus in the ninth edition appeared in 1878, on the eve of Britain's acquisition of the island. The writer was Sir Edward Bunbury, the author of *A History of Ancient Geography among the Greeks and Romans* (1879). His entry is substantially longer than the previous one, and his account of the history and geography of the island shows considerably more precision, with appropriate references to Pliny, Strabo and Herodotus. There is no need to summarize the whole entry, but a few points are worth mentioning. Bunbury writes: 'The great central plain ... is in many parts marshy and unhealthy; and indeed the whole interior of the island suffers much from unhealthiness, and is subject to fevers of a peculiarly dangerous description. ... One of the greatest disadvantages of Cyprus is the want of ports, there not being a good natural harbour in the whole island. Larnaca and Limassol, which are the chief places of trade, have nothing but mere roadsteads ...' Bunbury's account of the island's history is, as we might expect from a writer on classical antiquity, stronger on ancient times than on more recent events. He is, however, the first contributor to the *Encyclopaedia Britannica* to mention the atrocities of 1821, although he gets the date wrong, ascribing what he terms the 'frightful massacre of the Greek population' to the year 1823. He is also – and remember he is writing in 1878 – the first to comment on the antiquities: '...within the last few years extensive excavations have been carried on in different parts of the island - especially at Golgos, Idalium, and Curium – by Mr Lang and General de Cesnola, which have brought to light a vast number of statues and other works of the highest interest ... Unfortunately these collections have been removed to New York, while no detailed description of them has yet been published. It is, however, announced that General de Cesnola is engaged in a comprehensive work giving an account of his researches and their results, which will doubtless throw much light on the ancient geography and history of Cyprus'. An extended footnote mentions the deciphering of the Cypriot dialect by George Smith, as well as giving more details of Cesnola's discoveries at Curium.

The tenth edition was conceived as a supplement to the ninth. The entry for Cyprus appeared in 1902, and here of course the British acquisition of the island in 1878 meant that there was much to add. The principal entry was by Claude Cobham, whose collection of travellers' accounts of the island, *Excerpta Cypria* (published in 1908), is still widely used, and this is followed by a full-scale, two page article on 'Cypriote Archaeology' by J.L. Myres, the man who has been described as 'probably the first "modern" archaeologist to work in Cyprus'.[5] Myres listed recent excavations and provided a succinct survey of the island's antiquities and their significance.

There is no doubt in my own mind that these encyclopaedia entries serve as a good indicator of the changing intellectual climate in Britain with regard to British perceptions of Cyprus. The clumsy ignorance of the early editions gave way in the middle of the century to articles that were securely based on the well-known authors of the ancient world – a clear reflection of the prevailing importance of a 'classical education' at that time. Then, from the 1870s, we see an interest in the antiquities, and that fits well with the discoveries and the growing British awareness of the discoveries that began in the 1850s. Where these entries lack strength is in their descriptions of the history of the island from the beginnings of the Christian era onwards. I know from my own work on Cyprus in the later middle ages that what happened in the nineteenth century was that serious study of the crusader period in the later middle ages was almost entirely carried on in France. Indeed, in 1841 the Académie des Inscriptions et Belles-Lettres had announced a competition for the best essay on Lusignan Cyprus, and one of the joint winners, Count Louis de Mas Latrie, went on to make the history of medieval Cyprus his life's work and in so doing lay the foundations of modern scholarship in this field. Apart from a rather disappointing essay by Bishop Stubbs, virtually the only nineteenth-century British contribution to the study of medieval Cyprus of any merit is the catalogue of tombstones from Nicosia published in 1894 by Major Tankerville J. Chamberlayne as *Lacrimae Nicossienses*. In tribute to Gallic pre-eminence in this field, Chamberlayne chose to write in French.

There is much truth in the cliché that in 1878 Cyprus was 'used as a pawn' in great power diplomacy. British politicians, and British opinion generally, were caught between conflicting objectives. On the one hand, there was the anxiety that the Russians would expand into the Balkans and take Istanbul; this must be prevented at all costs, and that in turn meant bolstering the Ottoman sultan. On the other hand, the Turkish atrocities in the Balkans which had precipitated the crisis of 1878 resulted in a considerable body of opinion that looked to free the sultan's Christian subjects from his rule. The pro-Turkish, anti-Russian stance adopted by successive governments had led to frosty relations between Britain and Greece, although in the early 1860s Britain had given Greece the Ionian islands which she had acquired at the end of the Napoleonic Wars. In the background to all this lay fear of Russian advance towards India, and with the opening of the Suez Canal in 1869 and hence the creation of new and quicker route to that 'jewel in the crown', the political and military situation in the eastern waters of the Mediterranean became a matter of concern. What happened in 1878 was that the Ottomans handed over the administration of Cyprus to Britain while retaining nominal sovereignty. The British prime minister, Benjamin Disraeli, had pulled off a remarkable coup. Russia's predatory intent towards the Ottomans had been brought under control; Britain had acquired a site for a naval base in the East Mediterranean to help guard the route to India; a substantial number of Greeks had been freed from the rather less than beneficent attention of Ottoman administrators, soldiers and tax collectors. Disraeli had come close to squaring the circle; he had detached a province of the Ottoman empire in the interests of guaranteeing Ottoman territorial integrity. That at least was how it was portrayed at the time. For many of his contemporaries, the Congress of Berlin was his greatest achievement.

I am not sure when the idea that Britain should want Cyprus first gained currency. Earlier in 1878 and before it was agreed to hold the Congress of Berlin, Lord Derby, the foreign secretary, had resigned rather than agree to a proposal that Britain, using Indian troops, should secretly seize Cyprus or some other place in the Eastern Mediterranean for use as a naval base against the eventuality of the Russians moving on Istanbul.[6] Certainly the British government was advised by its own military representative in Istanbul that, if Britain wanted a base in the eastern Mediterranean, Cyprus was the most practicable of the various possibilities. But we cannot discount the possibility that it was Disraeli himself who cast a covetous eye on the island. While it was generally true that Cyprus was not part of the 'Grand Tour', one young man who had been there as part of his educative travels in the Mediterranean was none other than Benjamin Disraeli. He had made a brief visit to the island at the beginning of 1831.[7] Later, he was to put a strangely prescient remark into the mouth of one of the minor characters in his novel *Tancred*. This was published in 1847. Someone called Barizy says: 'The English want Cyprus ...' and then, about a page later, the same character adds, 'The English will not do the business of the Turks again for nothing' (1877 ed., 237–238).

But if the Conservative prime minister and his foreign secretary, the Marquis of Salisbury, returned from the Congress of Berlin bringing 'Peace with Honour', the Liberal opposition was less enthusiastic. It was not that they wanted to return Cyprus to Ottoman rule, but they certainly took every opportunity to belittle the government's achievements. The British occupation of Cyprus was agreed at Berlin on 4 June. It was not until 11 July that the subject was raised in Parliament. With both the Prime Minister and the Foreign Secretary sitting in the Lords at this period – Disraeli had been ennobled as Lord Beaconsfield a couple of years earlier – it was in the Lords that most of the more interesting altercations took place. These initial exchanges, as reported in Hansard, provide a valuable and at times amusing insight into contemporary attitudes and perceptions.

One of the first to speak was that veteran campaigner, the Earl of Shaftesbury.[8] His question, given his life-long concern, was predictable. What about slavery in Cyprus? Given that by the terms of the treaty sovereignty rested with the Ottomans and that the possibility of Cyprus returning to Ottoman rule remained – there was specific provision for this in the treaty – could the government assure him that slavery would be suppressed? The answer was that it was understood that slavery did not exist in the island, and he would have to wait until the first British High Commissioner, Sir Garnet Wolseley, could report from first hand knowledge. (Wolseley was due to leave for Cyprus the following day – 12 July.) Other questions centred on the numbers of troops that were being sent and the financial aspects of the takeover. For example, one speaker implied that successive crop failures would mean that Britain would have to bear the costs of feeding the population. Two questions are of particular interest in the light of what emerged earlier from the *Encyclopaedia Britannica*. As has been seen, the ninth edition, published that same year, 1878, had noted the absence of port facilities and the unhealthiness of Cyprus. Both issues were raised more than once, and it may be suspected that the Liberals, in looking for ammunition with which to dent the government's pride in its achievements, had found it in the pages of this celebrated work of reference. If there was no good harbour, then surely the value of Cyprus as a naval base was much reduced? If the island was unhealthy, then surely the British garrison would be at risk? Indeed, fears for the health of the garrison was raised repeatedly, fuelled by alarmist press reports.[9]

The problem was that hardly anyone had been to Cyprus. On 15 July there was an exchange in the Lords between Lord Oranmore and the Lord President of the Council, the Duke of Richmond. Oranmore challenged the government on the subject of the health of the island's climate, expressing fears for the British troops, and the duke countered his assertions. It emerged in the course of this exchange that Oranmore was basing his claims on what he had read in the *Pall Mall Gazette*, while the duke was relying on what he in his turn had read in the *Spectator*. The duke of Richmond quoted the *Spectator* as saying '... the island might be a splendid garden; that from the extraordinary variety of its climates it might be a sanatorium for the invalids of Europe; and it would be well if the interesting experiment could be tried of establishing a European colony there'.[10]

A few days later, on 19 July, there was further exchange in the Lords.[11] The foreign secretary, the Marquis of Salisbury, was challenged by Earl Granville, leader of the Liberal Peers. Apparently Salisbury, in a private conversation, had advised Granville to seek the answers to his persistent questions about conditions in Cyprus by referring to various 'geographical authorities'. Now Granville came back at him: 'I can quite understand the government not knowing much about the island of Cyprus. I find on referring to the *Encyclopaedia Britannica* that there are only 15 lines which refer to the state of this island ...' So I was right: educated Englishmen did refer to the article on Cyprus in the *Encyclopaedia Britannica*. But I wonder which edition he was using: perhaps not the new ninth edition of 1878, but more probably the shorter entry to be found in the eighth which by then was over twenty years old. Even so, we could well correct in assuming that it was Sir Edward Bunbury's remarks in the ninth edition on the lack of harbours and the insalubriousness of the island that prompted some of the other questions.

One member of the Upper House, however, had been in Cyprus quite recently. He was Lord Lilford, a Tory peer, who told the Lords that he had been there in April and May 1875, 'his object being principally scientific'.[12] Lilford was in fact a prominent ornithologist who had spent an extended period on a yacht cruising in the Mediterranean, armed no doubt with a rifle as well as his binoculars. He was able to give first-hand reports on the roadstead at Larnaca and the harbour at Famagusta. The harbour at Famagusta was the Venetian port and was 'largely filled up [but] was amply protected from the most troublesome winds. The silting could be removed and the harbour made very practicable'. As for the climate, he quoted Hamilton Lang, the British consul in Cyprus in the early 1870s: 'The island is not unhealthy, but demands simplicity in diet and temperance in habits'. Lilford went on to tell the Lords that he 'had visited almost all the large islands in the Mediterranean – he mentions Corsica, Sardinia and Sicily – and had found none of them more agreeable than Cyprus ... It was only money and enterprise that were required in Cyprus; and in his opinion its acquisition, putting aside political and military considerations altogether, was one of the wisest and best acts done by any Minister in this country for a good while'.

On 23 July there was a major debate in the Lords.[13] It was opened by the Liberal peer, the Earl of Camperdown, and his chief concern was the financial arrangemens agreed with the Ottomans. He made great play of the point which has already emerged from this discussion, that the government knew very little about the island of Cyprus. As reported in Hansard, the Earl of Camperdown said that: 'they [the government] knew that the administration of the island had been distinguished for corruption, rapacity, and ... almost all the faults of which an Administration was capable. They knew that the population had been dwindling. He believed that at one time the population amounted to 1,000,000 souls; but under the benefits of Turkish rule, they had dwindled away to 150,000 or 250,000 persons – he was not sure which.[14] They knew also that the cities were in ruins. They knew that the cultivators of the soil had been harassed by arbitrary exactions. They knew that commerce had been driven away from the island. They knew that the harbour, or whatever used to represent a harbour, had been silted up; and they also knew that even the wells were filled up, and that all sanitary precautions had been neglected. He believed that there were now no roads, or only very bad ones ...' Clearly there was a lot of catching up to do, and the questions was who would pay for it, especially as the government had promised that the surplus revenue would go to the Turkish government. The foreign secretary, Lord Salisbury replied for the government; Earl Granville then came to the support of his Liberal colleague, and then the prime minister himself waded in. This appears to have been the only occasion in which Disraeli (or Beaconsfield as he ought more properly to be called) spoke on Cyprus in the Lords during that year. He ended with a splendid rejoinder: 'With regard to the ports of Cyprus, it is of course easy to pick out musty details from obsolete gazetteers, and to say "there are no ports in Cyprus"; but I venture to say your Lordships will find by this time next year that there are ports sufficient to accommodate British ships'. At the end of the debate Lord Lilford spoke: there were plenty of books about the island, and 'he thought he might fairly say that it was the fault of the noble Lords opposite (i.e. the Liberals) if they were entirely ignorant with regard to Cyprus'. The Liberal accusation against the government of ignorance was thus turned on its head.

Fig. 2.1: Captain Swain's triumphal entry into Lefkoniko. Courtesy of the Bank of Cyprus Cultural Foundation.

Fig. 2.2: Orthodox priests blessing the British flag. Courtesy of the Bank of Cyprus Cultural Foundation.

Fig. 2.3: A court case at Ephtakomi. Courtesy of the Bank of Cyprus Cultural Foundation.

One question that was never raised in either House in 1878 was what the population of Cyprus thought about their change of governors. In his address of welcome the bishop of Kition famously told the High Commissioner, Sir Garnet Wolseley: 'We accept the change of Government inasmuch as we trust that Great Britain will help Cyprus, as it did the Ionian islands, to be united with Mother Greece, with which it is naturally connected'.[15] In 1880 Gladstone, whose Liberals had returned to power earlier that year, privately expressed the idea that Cyprus might indeed be passed on to Greece. But sovereignty remained vested with the Ottomans, and no government would abrogate the terms agreed at Berlin. In any case, when Queen Victoria got to hear rumours to the effect that the government was planning to dispose of the island to Greece, she expressed her opposition in no uncertain terms. That, of course, as is well known, was a issue that would run and run ...

The Parliamentary exchanges in 1878 show that the government had to reassure public opinion in Britain and justify its acquisition of the island. It needed to demonstrate that Cyprus, contrary to the line taken by its critics among the Liberals, was well worth having. Later in 1878 the Illustrated London News carried engravings which were no doubt intended to allay any fears. They have frequently been reproduced, and three of them will suffice to serve as examples:

(i) *Captain Swain's triumphal entry into Lefkoniko.* It is a picture of genuine enthusiasm. The people throng to see this representative of British authority, crowding on the roofs, ringing the bells, running along beside his horse, and Captain Swain, upright in the saddle and raising his helmet to acknowledge the plaudits of the crowd, is clearly the epitome of the English officer and gentleman.

(ii) *Orthodox priests blessing the British flag.* The people have turned out in force. The church is endorsing British rule. The governor looks on gravely, although his aide, slouched against the throne, does rather spoil the solemnity of the occasion – but then it is all decidedly un-English. However, that doesn't matter, because these people in their own peculiar way have accepted us.

(iii) *A court case at Ephtakomi.* British women of course do not wave their arms around when giving evidence, but the British administrators add appropriate *gravitas* to the rustic setting of the tribunal. We, the readers, know that justice will be done. Cyprus may be distant and backward, but we British will not shirk our responsibilities.

That at least is the image projected for the benefit of people back in Britain. How could anyone seeing these pictures in 1878 doubt that acquiring Cyprus was good for Britain and good for the Cypriots? Fortunately, that is a question that does not need to be answered – at least, not here. As is well known, the honeymoon period with the Cypriot Greeks did not last, and anyway, Cyprus never developed into the major military base envisaged in 1878. In this connection it is doubtless significant that in 1880 control in London passed from the Foreign Office to the Colonial Office. The outbreak of the First World War and the destruction of the Ottoman sultanate made the 1878 agreement obsolete, and Cyprus was formally declared a crown colony in 1925.

I want to end with one last point from Hansard for 1878.[16] After the flurry of parliamentary debate in July of that year, interest in Cyprus as expressed in exchanges in either House soon died down. But in December in the Commons Sir Charles Dilke, a prominent Liberal MP whose own career was to collapse in a much publicized scandal a few years later, put a question to the Under Secretary of State for Foreign Affairs. It concerned a certain 'Mr de Cesnola, an American citizen, [who] was tried for an offence against Turkish law in digging up objects of antiquarian interest without a firman, by the district court in Larnaca.' In reply the Under Secretary confirmed that he had indeed been tried and sentenced to a fine and the confiscation of the objects he had found; the fine had subsequently been remitted by the High Commissioner, and Mr de Cesnola had protested about the confiscations. Although overshadowed by his brother, Luigi, who had left Cyprus in 1876 never to return, Alexander Palma de Cesnola has the distinction of being the first named individual resident in Cyprus whose treatment was made the subject of a question in Parliament.

Notes

1. J. Koumoulides, *Cyprus and the Greek War of Independence, 1821–1829* (London 1974).
2. I am much indebted to Dr Veronica Tatton-Brown for obtaining photocopies from the British Library for several of the nineteenth-century editions.
3. 33–36°E and 30–34°N – actually 32–35°E and 34–36°N.
4. B. Arbel, 'Cypriot Population under Venetian rule (1473–1571): A Demographic Study', *Meletai kai Ipomnimata* 1 (1984), 188–90, 211–14; G. Hill, *A History of Cyprus* (Cambridge 1940–52) 4, 34.
5. E. Goring, *A Mischievous Pastime: Digging in Cyprus in the Nineteenth Century* (Edinburgh 1988) 27.
6. R. Blake, *Disraeli* (London 1966) 640.
7. W.F. Moneypenny and G.E. Buckle, *Life of Benjamin Disraeli, Earl of Beaconsfield* (London 1910–20) 1, 171.
8. *Hansard's Parliamentary Debates* (third series, 1830–91) ccxli, 1224–5.
9. *Hansard*, ccxli, 1225–6, 1242–3, 2054–5.
10. *Hansard*, ccxli, 1433–6.
11. *Hansard*, ccxli, 1948–9.
12. *Hansard*, ccxli, 1949–50.
13. *Hansard*, ccxlii, 18–34.
14. *Encyclopaedia Britannica* (8th ed. 1850s) puts the population at 150,000; Bunbury writing in the 9th ed. (1878) has a figure of 135,000. For other estimates, see Hill (n.4) 4, 31–4.
15. Quoted by Hill (n.4) 4, 297.
16. *Hansard*, ccxliii, 636–8.

3. Imaginary Cyprus
Revisiting the past and redefining the ancient landscape

Anastasia Serghidou

Being influenced by the broader 'orientalising' movement of the eighteenth century, the travellers of the nineteenth century often viewed the Island of Cyprus as an unavoidable step towards the Orient.[1] On the way to the 'Biblical Lands', Cyprus marks a frontier, a pause and a link, which allegedly brings together opposed worlds and destinies. It is a threshold which separates and unifies East and West, ancient and modern, exotic and familiar; an apparently attractive locale which persisted throughout history as a scene for cultural interaction, shown by archaeological material and historical testimony. Although, as this paper will reveal, such 'evidence' is rarely straightforward.

Thus, more than a simple geographical region in an exotic environment suggestive of the Orient, Cyprus represented for travellers and antiquarians a particular space imbued with sweet memories of an ancient past – a space which was frequently interpreted by means of its Hellenic affinities and bygone historical realities. What is more, by offering a geographical space which could be visited and described according to the idyllic prototype of Arcadia, the island was also regarded as a depository of an Achaean past, substantiated in the eyes of visitors by the archaeological remains, mostly neglected and yet unexplored at the beginning of the nineteenth century. Emile Deschamps, in his *Au Pays d'Aphrodite,* did not hesitate, for example, to regard the island as the representative landscape of Aphrodite, a place of memories and a reserve of Antiquity. 'Je dois avouer que la pensée de ce sol où la blonde Vénus a laissée des souvenirs jusqu'aujourd'hui, de ce sol choisi par la mythologie pour y établir le délicieux jardin terrestre de la désse, avait un peu influencé mes idées, et je le voyais habité par une population, non point parfaite dans son esthétique, mais encore marquée du secau antique'.[2]

That travellers were primarily interested in the island's archaeological remains is not surprising, and could plausibly be included in the broad antiquarian interest which preceded the emergence of archaeology as a formal discipline. However, this interest acquires deeper significance because it manifestly generates an ideological discourse, which fosters a persistent desire to comprehend current local reality.[3] It is an issue which goes beyond simple antiquarian interest and fascination with the 'unknown', which was prevalent during the Enlightenment. The traveller, who abandons the dreams of the explorer, is invited to be critical; a visitor is not any more an explorer, but an observer.[4] A narrator who implicates himself in the narrative becomes less objective and impersonal. An explorer is expected to advance the infant study of anthropology by gathering political and commercial information along with his increasing interest in ways of life, races and origins. This tendency corroborates the scientific and naturalistic curiosities of the epoch promoting the idea of voyage, not as an adventure, but as a study.[5]

In 1903 H.V. Hilprecht, referring to previous explorers of Asia, wrote that: 'Other travellers, like Marco Polo, visited the same regions without even referring to the large artificial mounds which they must frequently have noticed on their journeys. Travelling to the valleys of the Euphrates and Tigris, in those days, was more for adventure or commercial and religious purposes than for the scientific exploration of the remains of a bygone race, about which even the most learned knew but little'.[6] Reflecting the ideas of the nineteenth century and what was to become modern field archaeology, Hilprecht underlines the necessity of observing and recording material culture – activities which had obviously been neglected by his predecessors. While he was not the only one to underline the necessity of such an approach to the neglected material culture of the Orient, his discourse is relevant to our understanding of the way in which travellers and antiquarians were expected to observe and describe the relatively familiar, although archaeologically unexplored, landscape of the East. To what extent did contemporary ideological tendencies influence the exploration of Cypriot land? This is the question which I will pose and explore in this paper.

When the Revd. Edward Daniel Clarke arrived in Cyprus in the warm summer of 1801, he did not omit to insist on the regrettable view of a broadly abandoned landscape, ostensibly neglected by the inhabitants of the island, whose primary concern was how to survive, rather than how to lead a pleasant existence in an Arcadian frame. However, besides testifying to a damaged landscape, Clarke's observations point to his significant preoccupation with antiquities: 'This island, that had so highly, excited, amply gratified our curiosity by, its most interesting antiquities. Although there is nothing in its present state pleasing to the eye, instead of a beautiful and fertile land, covered with groves of fruit and fine woods, once rendering it the paradise of Levant, there is hardly, upon earth a more wretched spot than it now exhibits. Few words may forcibly describe it: Agriculture neglected-inhabitants oppressed-population destroyed- pestiferous air-contagion-poverty-indolence- desolation'.[7]

So writes Clarke, who considers Cyprus as a soil, a surface layer of earth, exposed to harm and pain, as well as a depository of memory, an enclave of reminiscence, which alludes to history, through ruins and damaged stones of the past, while also exhibiting the mishaps of a decadent present. This antiquarian approach effects a significant transition from a historical opulence to a current social crisis, a crisis which apparently disturbs the viewer's eye and troubles the mental vision of the observer. However, this decadence, which relies on visual effects, contradicts the concealed reserve of memory and material abundance, which is carefully buried in the ground: 'Its antiquities alone', he writes, 'render it worthy of resort; and these, if any person had leisure and opportunity to search for them, would amply repay the trouble'.[8]

Hence digging up the soil appears to be an activity which can plausibly provide an answer to questions of cultural and natural interest, a procedure which takes its roots in the enquiring minds of renaissance antiquaries.[9] In this respect, the landscape of the country appears to be inscribed on a vertical axis combining the top, that is the visible part of the cultivated soil, with its dispersed and often mute ruins, and the potentially eloquent subterranean space which is reserved for archaeological testimony. 'The inhabitants of Larnaca rarely dig near their town without discovering either the traces of ancient buildings, subterranean chambers, or sepulchres', Clarke notices. Numerous examples testify to such an experience. 'Not long before our arrival', he reports, 'the English Consul, Signor Peristiani, a Venetian, dug up, in one place, above thirty idols belonging to the most ancient mythology of the heathen world'.

Indeed, turning back to the past and trying to understand the adventures of time gone by, implies a digging activity. This is an experience which, following the intellectual trends of the epoch, permits the exposure of a pagan world, whose affinities with mythology, for example, enhance the intellectual environment within which observers are invited to contemplate and decipher. This environment is not only one of culture and history, but is also one of topography, in that the world is no longer seen as invisible and subterranean. However, the world had not yet been discovered in the archaeological sense. Instead, this particular archaeological concern corroborates the scientific interests of Professor Clarke and hardly reflects a broader antiquarian curiosity or real archaeological interest. Being neither a collector nor an antiquarian, but an eminent mineralogist, it follows naturally that Clarke should focus his investigation on the exploration of the soil. This process implies for him, at any rate, a travel in time, a voyage in history, which encourages a fruitful investigation of the cultural past; an attitude which, manifestly, brings about an obsolete reception of the archaeological remains. It should be remembered, for example, that in medieval times archaeological remains were viewed as miraculously rising from the earth.[10]

However, this connection between archaeological remains, whether concealed in the ground or not, and the idea of cultural heritage as hypothetical mining, is not new. Fauvel,[11] for example, referring to travellers who arrived in large numbers in Greece in order to admire Greek antiquities, confirmed that they regarded Greece as an unexplored and inexhaustible 'mine'. This metaphor shows the impact of geology, which was evidently considered at the time to be an authentic historical science that aimed to explain the present state of the planet.[12]

The association of abundance of soil and cultural heritage, as it is attested through archaeological remains, is eminently relevant and one need simply consider the notorious treasure hunting for Greek antiquities in the nineteenth century.[13] It is probably within this context of the search for underground treasures that Ali Bey, namely Don Dorningo Badia-y-Leublich, who visited Cyprus in 1806, chose to focus his interest on the mining treasures of the island of Cyprus. These treasures confer their names on toponyms whose uncertain origin might be discovered within the antique framework. 'This was the village of which I spoke above', he writes. 'If fortuitous, this identity of the vulgar and mineralogical name is certainly remarkable: or, if otherwise, what mineralogist founded or named the village of Corno could learn nothing on the origin of the village, so it must be ancient'.[14]

This parallelism between the surface layer of earth and

antiquity, alluding to the cultural origins of the country, is not surprising. It manifestly brings about the particular ethnographic interest of nineteenth-century scholars. This was the age, for example, of the foundation of several archaeological associations which, as has been attested, were directly influenced in their constitutions by the contemporary development of geology and the emergence of romanticism, as well by the appearance of the new disciplines of anthropology and ethnography.[15] It was also the time when man was in search of his origins, and the period during which the ideal model of the traveller-philosopher, which emerged during the Enlightenment, gave way to the 'observer'. A model, which in France, for example, was to be represented by such associations as the *Société des Obsevateurs de l'homme*. At the end of the eighteenth century, this society gave birth to a club of 'ideologists':[16] an association of scholars, which included several physicians, philosophers, moralists and naturalists. They aspired to a new domain of knowledge in which man was expected to be comprehended with reference to his physical, psychic, social and cultural environment.[17] In a different, less idealistic context the main interest in human beings and their origins was to be expressed, some decades later, by evolutionist ideas. In turn, both in France and England, evolutionist theories fostered the idea of European superiority during the period of imperialist expansion.[18]

It is within this evolutionist context that Hepworth W. Dixon[19] was to try to define the ethnic, rather than the social, profile of the camel drivers in Cyprus. Thus in his ethnological descriptions, in which he tries to define the origins of the newly-acquired colony of Cyprus, he instigates a dialogue which is pertinent to our enquiry. Being impressed by some exotic names, such as Mousa or Jousouf, supposedly connected with the group of *linobambakoi*,[20] he is also surprised by the colour of their skin, which prompts him to inquire, about their ethnic origins and their birth place. 'Who, then, are these Cypriots?' He asks. 'Do they stand apart – one of those underived and primitive stocks which "spring from the soil", and have no history elsewhere'.[21] '..."Men of the soil" is an expression in every zone, and in every form of human speech. In the most ancient record of Cyprus the peasants and shepherds are described as "children of the black earth". Mousa is a child of this black earth....'[22] The interpretation he provides is not impressive because it simply recalls some of the same beliefs held by American tribes that the author had the opportunity to meet. But he goes further in his interpretations and, being faithful to the naturalistic and anthropological tendencies of his epoch, plainly relates this group to the world of plants and animals. 'Like cats and lizards', he says, 'they can lie in the glare all day, basking in the fire from pure delight in warmth'.

His ethnological interests are also supplemented by his linguistic interests, which lead him to give several racial interpretations and to formulate various associations with ancient toponyms. This approach most likely corresponded with the linguistic and anthropological concerns of the century that closely connected ethnic and ethno genetic problems with the origins of Indo-European languages.[23]

'A second remnant of an ancient stock bears the nickname of "horn-faced". They live in the mountains, and in the mountains only... These horn-faced people are a primitive type. What type? Mongolian, perhaps. It is a curious fact that one of the oldest names of Cyprus is Kerastis, – the Horned; a name more likely to have sprung from the inhabitants than from their island; which, in truth, has no resemblance to a horn. These horn-faced Cypriots are few in number fewer than the children of black earth, and have no greater weight in Cyprus than the "Wild Cornish" have in Great Britain'.

Although his association with the ancient name of *kerastis* demonstrates the author's familiarity with ancient texts,[24] his conclusions reveal an anthropological thesis which manipulates historical references in the interests of formulating a racial physiognomy. The analogy with the spurious case of the so-called 'Wild Cornish' in England shows how for him both 'mythologised' peoples provide a tangible link with the past and define the present within a national scope.[25] This issue very likely structures the anthropological thesis of the author by classifying the inhabitants of the island according to social criteria which are racially interpreted. We are thus confronted with a use and an abuse of history which supposedly permitted the author to make a link between the past and the present.

These pseudo-historical references in effect lead to an ancient discourse on names and origins enhanced by other discriminating elements. Clothing, for example, becomes a criterion of race and social significance. More than a simple ethnographic curiosity, costume and appearance offer discriminating material which fosters a model of classification and interpretation of origins and local mentalities. This is what induced Pococke, almost a century before, to write that: 'The common people here, dress much in the same manner as they do in the other islands of the Levant; but those who value themselves on being somewhat above the vulgar, dress like the Turks, but wear a red cap turned up with fur, which is the proper Greek dress, and used by those of the islands in whatever parts of Levant they live'.[26]

Certainly the contiguous line between ancient and modern subsidised by elements of clothing or external appearance in general, is not a specificity of Pococke or even Dixon on his own. One could refer to the standard archaeological investigations of the nineteenth century, according to which primary archaeological interests consisted of comparing the archaeological testimony, most often uncertain, with objects belonging to the so-called

Fig. 3.1: Modern priest and stone head from Golgoi.

savage people of the colonised countries. However if, for Dixon, this comparison between the ancient and the modern helps him to define a logical criterion for race investigation, it allows others not to determine the present, but the past.[27] A case in point is the fanciful history offered by Cesnola: 'At Ormidia, I first remarked that the Greek priests in interior, who work in the fields like the peasants, wear a conical hat, not unlike those represented in the statues discovered at Golgoi, and it appears to me not improbable that this fashion of hat has been handed down from the times of the Cypriot priests of Venus' (Fig. 3.1).[28]

For Cesnola, this bonnet is a trade mark of a very eloquent past, which speaks through statues and archaeological finds of any kind – this continuity is marked by artefacts and attested by the current life of human beings, who plausibly have the right to claim their ancestry within the context of tombs and ruins. An equivalence is thus established between life and death, between ancient testimony and present-day remains. Hence the priest's bonnet is an archaeological memory which is reflected in the current life of the inhabitants. Continuity is tangibly inscribed on the priest's face: 'Not only this', he writes, 'but there seemed to me also to be a resemblance between the features of priest who here attracted my attention and his sculptured predecessors'.[29]

Confronted by the mobility of the present, the archaeological discourse of the author seems indeed to be determined by the frozen image of the past, plainly reflected in the immobility of sculptured stones. Stones become in this case the outspoken landmarks of a deadlocked ancestry and the tangible keys to decipherment of a present reality. In the same way, Clarke, referring to Cypriot female garments, writes that: 'The interesting costume presented in the dress of the Cyprian ladies ought not to pass without notice. Their head apparel was precisely, modelled after the kind of *Calathus* represented upon the Phoenician idols of the country, and upon Egyptian statues'.[30]

It is worth noting that this model of continuity, between past and present, which is basically fostered by the expressive world of artefacts, is not only an element of discourse. It is also attested within the context of visual representations, namely drawings, supposedly well-suited to represent a visual combination between artefacts and human figures, as in the case of the priest's bonnet. This procedure, nonetheless, reflects the general tendency of the first archaeologists to juxtapose images of archaeological research with modern natives.[31] One can observe, for example, how Ohnefalsch-Richter integrates ancient jewellery into modern reality when he associates in his drawings ancient ornaments with contemporary pieces and human figures.[32] This particular instance takes the divergent ethnic communities into consideration, given that the author neglects in his drawings neither the Turkish element present in the island and symbolically represented by Ottoman splendour, nor the Greek element represented by a meticulous woman's portrait. The latter association is of interest because it actually becomes a point of reference in the travellers' discourse which constantly evokes the beauty of local women by recalling the divine splendour of Aphrodite.[33] '...nous partons...pour Chypre, île aux belles femmes...', wrote V. Hugo.[34]

In his search for beauty and Hellenic elegance, Clarke insists on the relevant continuity between the contours of a sculptured beauty and the humanized appearance of the female posture.

'Notwithstanding the extraordinary pains they (Grecian women) use to disfigure their natural beauty by all sorts of ill-selected ornaments, the women of Cyprus are handsomer than those of any other Grecian island. They have a taller and more stately figure; and the features, particularly of the women of Nicosia, are regular and dignified, exhibiting that elevated cast of countenance so universally admired in the works of Grecian artists. At present, this kind of beauty seems peculiar to the women of Cyprus; the sort of expression exhibited by one set of features may be traced, with different gradations, in them all. Hence were possibly derived those celebrated models of female beauty conspicuous upon the statues, vases, medals, and gems of Greece, models selected from the throng of Cyprian virgins, who, as priestesses of Venus, officiated at the Paphian shrine. Indefinite as our notions of beauty are said to be, we seldom differ in assigning the place of its abode. That assemblage of graces, which in former ages gave celebrity to the women of Circassia, still characterises their descendants upon Mount Caucasus; and with the same precision that enables us to circumscribe the limits of its residence, we may refer to countries where it never was indigenous'.[35]

Indeed, the divine figure of Aphrodite as well as her ancient followers becomes a determinant element in the definition and description of the Cypriot cultural environment and geographical landscape. For Captain Charles Colville Frankland, the deity becomes a parameter of ethnic identity and even of discrimination, since she embodies an ideal model of grace and attractiveness with which her descendants must be identified. Any distance or deviation from this model stresses abnormality, deformity and disgrace: elements that deny continuity between past and present, and dismantle a cultural and ethnic uniformity. '...on our way out saw a few Cyprians. God only knows how this island ever attained its celebrity for beauty, for to judge of it from the specimens we saw one would have said it was the last place which Venus would have chosen in which to fix her favourable residence. I am told, however that in the neighbourhood of Paphos (whose temple still exists) <il y a le plus beau sang possible>. The male part of the population is handsome and robust: and, perhaps their laughing and wanton goddess had an eye to these circumstances'.[36]

The connection between the origins of Cypriot settlers and Aphrodite is not surprising, given that the goddess Aphrodite functions as a relevant figure of the past, who combines within the literary discourse a nostalgic ancient memory and current cultural reality. Thus for the anonymous Gentleman – author of 'a journal kept on a journey from Bestiary to Baghdad', who visited the island at the end of the eighteenth century, Cyprus is not deprived of the ancient tradition which manifestly thought that the whole island was consecrated to Venus. As he attests: 'Ancient tradition, says the whole island was consecrated to Venus, and she is represented by the poets as taking a particular pleasure in visiting this country and to have holden her court there'.

Nevertheless, continuity between past and present may be neglected and dismantled through the vicissitudes of history and cultural evolution. Thus in his eyes rises a rather unpleasant view of the present, which manifestly ignores the effects of the grace and charm of Aphrodite: 'Be this as it may; very few of her representatives are there to be found at present' he says.[37] However, even if continuity between past and present seems to be irrelevant in the matter of habits, morals and external human appearance, it is crucial in the case of archaeological landscape, where ancient vestiges become the hallmarks of the local history and the cultural identity of the Cypriots.

Thus the first contact with cities shows the meeting of new culture with ancient vestiges. So J. Macdonald Kinneir writes in 1814: 'I had scarcely put my, foot upon the shore, before I was beset by a tribe of Custom house officers and other vagabonds, imperiously demanding baksheesh; but, without attending to their clamours, I entered the sea-gate, and walked about a quarter of a mile through deserted streets and decayed churches, to a small coffee-house an inhibited part of the town. Famagusta, which is said to have derived its name from Cape Ammochostos, is situated above five miles to the S. of the ancient Salamis, now called Eski of Lusignan, and is said to have been founded by a colony from Consantia, fortified by Guy of Lusignan, afterwards embellished by Venetians.'[38]

Indeed, following ancient prototypes, Salamis functions for the moderns as a status symbol; an element of duplicity which unifies Greece and Cyprus. Furthermore, it is a meeting point which links the ancient and the modern and minimises the idea of the exotic.[39] Pococke,[40] who preceded Kinneir and influenced certain later travellers, wrote in his meticulous description that: 'Ancient geographers, mention two islands of Salamis which are not now seen.[41] On examining the ground I imagine the sea might have left these islands, and I saw near the port some rising grounds with channels near them, which might formerly have been filled by sea. There appears to have been a more modern city here than that ancient one built by Teuker, and there are great remains of the foundations of the wall of the new town, which was about half as big as the old cities. The inner walls are supposed to be those of the new town, and the outer ones those of the old city'.[42]

This geographical co-existence is, of course, enhanced by mythical figures of the past, which function as markers of place and time. In this sense, the figure of Teukros is a relevant example. 'Having travelled about four hours', Pococke wrote, 'we went to the left of the ancient convent of Jalousa, there is also a bay here of the same name, and as there is a place so called near Scanderoon, which is the bay that had the ancient name of Sinus Issicus in Cilicia; this, without doubt, must be Sinus Issicus of Cyprus, which was in this part of the island. This is probably the shore of the Acheans where Teuker first landed'.

Constantius, Archbishop of Sinai, trying to define the origins of the Cypriots in his *Cypriad* wrote that 'The Greeks who inhabit the island, the much-suffering, and long-suffering descendants of that wonderful Teucer, brother of Ajax the son of Telamon, are well proportioned and good looking: the more refined classes especially and dwellers in Leucosia, Larnaca, Scala, and some few in Lemesos, are sociable, affable, sumptuous and hospitable, ready, quick-witted, fond of amusement, a little given to ostentation, fond of work, thrifty and apt at business, to which the great spur is gain, that inevitable ill, whether to a commonwealth of men, or to each individual member thereof'.[43]

Similarly, Alexander Drummond,[44] who visited Cyprus in approximately the same era, focussed his interest on some other symbolic ancient figures who could be considered as the Greek predecessors of the Cypriot inhabitants. 'When Solon', he writes, 'the famous Athenian law-giver, came to Cyprus, he lived sometime with Philokyprus, one of the Kings, whose capital, Apeia, was built, in the mountains, by Demophoon, son of Theseus; it was strong, because almost inaccessible, but the adjacent lands were barren and bare, though near the river Clarius; the sage advised him to remove from these naked rocks into the fertile plains, where he might build a larger and fairer city'.[45]

In this way, places, names and heroic figures, contribute to local definitions and profiles. Geography, history and mythology appear to form a significant junction which fosters the comprehension and interpretation of cultural specificity and ethnic identities – this way of approaching the history of the past in many cases contributed to the formation and establishment of national identities in Europe.[46] Observation often falls short of the explanations proposed and questions remain unanswered, since the evidence provided is not necessarily accessible to the eyes of the traveller. 'This place', Drummond writes 'I take to be the Treta of the ancients, because a river runs between it and Piscopi, and Treta was situated east of a fine river. But I find it impossible to reconcile the ancient geography with what I saw, and what I may reasonably suppose from appearances and the traditions of the country'.[47]

Clarke was to be confronted by a similar dilemma a century later. 'The ancient geography of Cyprus is involved in greater uncertainty than seems consistent with its former celebrity among enlightened nations. Neither Greeks nor Romans have afforded any clue by which we can fix the locality of its Eastern cities. Certain of them, it is true, had disappeared in a very early period. Long prior to the time of Pliny, the towns of Cinyria, Malium and Idalium, so necessary in ascertaining the relative position of other places, no longer existed. Both the nature and situation of important land-marks, alluded to by the ancient geographers, are also uncertain'.[48]

As examples of this incompatibility, Clarke refers to several ancient writers: 'According to Strabo', he writes, 'the Cleides were two islands upon the north-east coast; Pliny makes their number four; and Herodotus mentions a promontory that had the name given to these islands. If we consult the text of Strabo, his description of Cyprus appears to be expressed with more than usual precision and perspicacity. Yet of two renowned cities, Salamis and Citium, the first distinguished for the birth of the historian Aristus, and the last conspicuous by the death of Cimon, neither the situation of the one nor of the other has been satisfactorily determined'. However Clarke goes further in his thoughts by recognizing the precious character of the archaeological perspective. With reference to Drummond's and even Pococke's ocular testimony he finally attests that 'Perhaps, the antiquities now described may hereafter serve to confirm an opinion of Drummond's, founded upon very diligen inquiry, and repeated examination of the country'.[49]

To this extent the archaeological remains functioned more than anything else as elements of reality, or visual markers, which could convincingly reveal or conceal the past. This perception was seemingly influenced by an antiquarian trend, which tended to take into consideration both material culture and literary evidence. Within this range of evidence, artefacts were regarded as supporting evidence for knowledge gained from the study of classical authors.[50] This approach preceded, and consequently paved the way for the accumulation of artefacts in private collections and, later, in public museums. What is more, this tendency also affected the selection of monuments for investigation. Keeping with this antiquarian orientation, the investigators sought to attribute to the sites aspects of cult or funerary-ritual significance. Recalling the necessity of discovering an 'underground' civilisation, travellers, collectors and antiquarians focused their interests on the concealed treasures of the cavity of tornbs, which had hitherto become a depository of knowledge and a key to the decipherment of the past.[51]

Thus, it follows naturally that Clarke, by mentioning the Phoenician city of 'Larneca' insists on the relevant 'sepulchral remains'. 'The sepulchral remains' he writes, 'occupying so considerable a portion of the territory where the modern town is situated, appear to have been those of the Necropolis of Citium; and this city probably extended from the port all the way to Larneca, called also Lame, and Larnic (Larnaca is the name in most common acceptation among foreign nations; but the inhabitants call it Lamec, and the Abbé Mariti writes it Larnic. The Bay of Salines is also sometimes called Larneca Bay); implying, in its etymology, independently of its tombs, "*a place of burial*".[52] Though the connection between the name of the city and its archaeological site remains logical, this paragraph goes further than that because it simply stresses a recurrent antiquarian motive.

It is worth noting that one of the primary concerns of collectors and archaeologists, such as Cesnola or Ohenfalsch-Richter, was the search for tombs. Luigi Palma di Cesnola was to focus an extensive part of his archaeological activities on tombs and his writings are remarkably orientated towards the determinant role of tombs in his excavation programme.[53] This interest is even expressed by the drawings in his published work. Tombs are dispersed throughout the deserted Cypriot landscape, which becomes

Fig. 3.2: How tombs were excavated and with what tools.

increasingly eloquent with the help of the perceiving eye of the archaeologist and the revealing effect of the 'spade'. This issue is illustrated in a scene juxtaposing the precious tools of the excavator with the subterranean space of the tomb (Fig. 3.2).

But tombs are not isolated from the surrounding social environment. Interpolated human figures (Fig. 3.3), reproductions of the architectural original layout (Fig. 3.4), significant continuity between nature and archaeology through often humanised space (Fig. 3.5) attest a prolific archaeological curiosity, which in this case combines the visible world of an ongoing reality and the invisible subterranean, material of the tombs (Fig. 3.6).

Thus one can assert that the persistent inventory of funeral items enhanced the vivid interest of travellers, who were the first to emphasise the necessity of digging the soil to discover the past and therefore determine the present. This vision, that could merely be considered as an illuminating procedure, even though politically, embarrassing in the long term, as was suggested by the American Minister at Consantinople (modem Istanbul). A close friend of Cesnola, he casually alerted him to the dangerous aspect of his proliferate 'digging' activities . 'I see, dear General', he says 'that you intend sinking the island one of these days, with all the holes you are boring everywhere; pray, before doing so, save, at least, the archives of the American Consulate'.[54]

It is most likely within this archaeological aspiration of funerary rituals, cult places and their significance that Aphrodite's sanctuaries often persist in the visitor's discourse. This is an issue which entangles modern history with ancient sacred geography. If the memory of Aphrodite's functions as a beauty, which, as we have already seen, is an anthropological criterion, her places are landmarks of time and space. They are pinpoints of the past which define the landscape of the present, thus offering a geography of mind, which structures the Cypriot landscape.[55]

Travellers focus their descriptions on the imposing presence of the goddess on the island. Ruins and monuments enhance, in this case, a spacio-temporal perception which explores the meaning of the visible material culture. Dr J. Sibthorp's arrival on the island, for example, is marked by significant curiosity focused on ruins which defuses a melancholic image of a neglected past and becomes a scenery which precondition one's view and mental perception.[56] 'We anchored', he says, 'about eight in the morning about five miles to east of Bafo. The town now presents a melancholy ruin; few of the houses being inhabited.... At the distance of about forty yards were two smaller pillar; one of them was fluted. This was probably the site of an ancient temple of Venus: near it stood a beautiful village called Iftinia...'.[57]

However, the ruins of temples and monuments are often supplemented by an Arcadian landscape which entails Aphrodite's world. With reference to Carpasia and some other places in the eastern part of Cyprus, R. Pococke[58] juxtaposes Aphrodite's world with surrounding nature. 'These mountains (the high hills near to cape *Chaulbernou*) take up all that narrow tract, which seems to have been called the *Olympian promentory*, and probably *Venus Urania* or the chaste *Venus* for there was a city in this part called *Urania*, which was destroyed by *Diogenes Poliorcetes* and it was not lawful for any woman to enter this temple, or so much as look on it'.[59] By compiling various ancient sources, the author seems to combine beliefs concerning Aphrodite with ancient incidents related to the conquest of the island by Demetrius Poliorectes. The latter, for example is attested by Diodorus Siculus[60] who, by contrast with Herodotus,[61] does not allude to a specific temple of Aphrodite Ourania. Pococke seems to refer in this case both to the Orphic[62] and Platonic[63] Aphrodite Ourania. She is a chaste figure, who is manifestly opposed to the exuberant Aphrodite Pandemos; the daughter, as Plato asserts, of Zeus and Deone.[64] The Aphrodite *Ourania* seems indeed to dominate Pococke's description, which

Fig. 3.3: The two hills called Ambelliri.

Fig. 3.4: Sketch of family sepulchre.

Fig. 3.5: Interior of the sepulchre in Fig. 3.4 showing the skeleton plant on the walls.

Fig. 3.6: Section of a tomb at Dali.

generally emphasises feminine chastity and decent behaviour. 'The women' he says 'are little superior to their ancestors with regard to their virtue; and as they, go unveiled, so they, expose themselves in a manner that in these parts is looked on as very indecent. They go every Whit Sunday in procession to the sea in remembrance of Venus' coming out of it, which was anciently attended with some other circumstances'.[65]

Nevertheless, the prevalent figure of Aphrodite, which becomes a veritable mark of Cypriot cultural identity, is less the Ourania of Pococke than the Paphian initiator of love, whose figure overwhelms the traveller's discourse a century later. J. M. Kinneir, for example, combines the idyllic landscape of Cyprus with the place where the Paphian Aphrodite was born. 'The most fertile as well as the most agreeable parts of the island are in the vicinities of Cerina and Baffo, the ancient Paphos, where, according to Tacitus, Venus rising from the waves was wafted to the shore. Here we find forests of oak, beech and pines, groves of olives and plantations of mulberries'.[66]

Thus the enchantment of nature, connected with the presence of Aphrodite on the island, is expressed by the Sacred Gardens of the goddess: this idyllic area of contemplation and visual pleasure evokes both the ritual aspect of the divinity and the magnificence of the natural scenery. A.-F. Didot confirms that he would like to see 'Idalion, Paphos, Amathonte and the Gardens of Venus, famous in old times'[67] and Ali Bey does not deny that these gardens were magnificent: 'At last at a quarter to seven we reached Yeroschippos, a Greek word meaning "sacred garden" the name which the place has borne from the most remote ages. It is pointed out as the site of sacred garden of Venus, when the goddess dwelt at Paphos'.[68]

Hence, *Yeroshippos* became a point of reference, a toponym which denotes both the past and the present in an island rich in archaeology and geography. 'The whole neighbourhood of Baffo', says Turner, 'and the metropolis and Ieros Kipos ... this village is built on a rocky hill. In the valley below it, to the south, are gardens watered by a stream gushing from the rock, and this stream is said to have been the baths of Venus'.[69]

The sacred landscape is thus incorporated into a naturalistic discourse, most likely inspired by the intellectual approaches of the nineteenth century. Closely related to the visual understanding of an unknown geographical space, nature becomes, in this case, a significant interlocutor, which permits the understanding of a broader cultural space filled with ruins of the past and monuments of history.

Furthermore, Ali Bey, relates the broader Hellenic world of Aphrodite to the Cypriot landscape. Kytheran Aphrodite can thereby be equated with the Cypriot local divinity, an equivalence which stresses the specificity of certain places and a charming environment.[71] 'The great plain of Nicosia stretches to the outskirts of Kythera which is surrounded by mounds of clayey soil. How a poetic imagination would warm up at the sight of these spots consecrated of old to the mother of Love! I had met at Limassol an English traveller, Mr Rooke, who had visited Kythera, and told me that his fancy had filled up the blanks of the real scene, so that he had pictured to himself as present with the goddess surrounded by her court. My brain, little given to illusions, failed here to supply me visions in contrast with what offered itself to my senses; the Graces, Nymphs and Loves would not lend their charm to the view of poor Kythera, which I can only, compare to the most wretched hamlet of the Comté Venaissin, or the Limagne of Auvergne. It is just a slip of country, of irregular shape, with orchards and mulberry trees, about a league from N. to S. but quite narrow'.[71]

Certainly, Ali Bey is aware of the differences in the matter of cults and locations. He does not omit to underline the specificity of the Cypriot Aphrodite in comparison with other expressions and cults of the divinity in the region: 'I do not remember ever having read a description of Cyprus'. He says. 'I do not know even what other travellers have thought about it. But whatever may be their opinion, mine is that the Venus of Paphos is not the same as the Venus of Kythera and Idalium'.[72]

So Venus, her cult and gardens haunt the minds of travellers. By constructing their discourses and stimulating their imagination, she fosters a logic of interpretation which bridges the gap that originally separated the invisible world of the ancients and the visible ruins of the present. She gives reason to their travel and provides answers to their intellectual preoccupation, perhaps recalling that the path of the Orient is always strewn with the misadventures of the mind and the vicissitudes of history; a state of affairs which originates from the personal intellectual itinerary of these writers or antiquarians, who obviously prepared the ground for the development of Cypriot field archaeology within an intellectual and political environment crucially influenced by anthropological investigations, colonialism and national concern.

Notes

1. See for example F.R. de Chateaubriand, *Itinéraire de Paris à Jérusalem* (Paris 1811) 102–103; A. de Lamartine, *Souvenirs, impressions, pensées et paysages pendant un voyage en Orient, 1832–1833* (Paris 1835) 137–138.
2. Emile Deschamps, *Au Pays d'Aphrodite* (Paris 1898) 7.
3. On the archaeological discourse and the construction of national identities, see P.L. Kohl and C. Fawcett, *Nationalism, Politics and the practice of archaeology* (Cambridge 1995). See also, S. Jones, *The Archaeology of Ethnicity* (London, New York 1997). On archaeological narratives in general and the way archaeologists design and produce the past see M. Shanks and I. Hodder, 'Processual, post processual and interpretive archaeologies', in I. Hodder *et al.*(ed.), *Interpreting Archaeology* (London 1995) 2–29.
4. On the difference between the *bourgeois* voyage of modern times and the preceeding humanistic travel see F. Wolfzettel, *Le discours du voyageur* (Paris 1996).
5. On travel and narration in the nineteenth century as well the idea of revisiting a place which denied the spirit of adventure proper to the first explorers see I. Daunais, *L'Art de la mesure ou l'invention de l'espace dans les récits d'Orient, XIX siècle* (Paris 1996). On the change of travel literature in the nineteenth century see R.A. Orman, *The Explorers, 19th Century Expeditions in Africa and the American West* (New Mexico 1983) 61–71.
6. Cf. H.V. Hilprecht, *Explorations in the Bible Lands during the 19th Century* (Philadelphia 1903) 13.
7. E.D. Clarke, *Greece, Egypt and the Holy Land. Travels in Various Countries of Europe, Asia and Africa* (edited 1812) 308–356, cited in *Excerpta Cypria (translated for a history of Cyprus)* [hereafter *EC*] (Cambridge 1908).
8. Clarke (n.7) [*EC 378*].
9. On these matters see A. Schnapp, *The Discovery of the Past* (English translation, London 1996) 139–177.
10. It was the time when the discovery of ancient vases in the ground was the object of numerous irrational interpretations and representations, see Schnapp (n.9) 143–148.
11. Cf. *Dècade Philosophique* 30 (1795) 531–537.
12. Cf. J. Malina and Z. Vasicek, *Archaeology Yesterday and Today* (Cambridge 1990).
13. Cf. G. Tolias, 'Introduction' in *Ο πυρετός των μαρμάρων* (Athens 1996) 7–39.
14. Ali Bey el Abbassi, *Voyages en Afrique et en Asie 1803–1806* (Paris 1814) [*EC* 393].
15. S. Piggot, 'The Origins of the English County archaeological societies', *Transactions of the Birmingham and Warwickshire Society* 86 (1974) 1–16.
16. See, for example, the work of De Gérando, *Considerations sur les diverses methodes à suivre dans l'observation des peuples savages* (Paris 1800) (inaccessible).
17. Cf. F. Laplantine, *L'Anthropologie* (Paris 1987) 57.
18. On the biological evolutionism which served in the nineteenth century as a model of history see Malina and Vasicek (n.12) 41–47.
19. W. Hepworth Dixon, *British Cyprus* (London 1879).
20. Moslemized Cypriots.
21. Hepworth Dixon (n.19) 20.
22. Hepworth Dixon (n.19) 22.
23. On these problems see Malina & Vasicek n.12, 23.
24. See for example, Hesychius, s.v Κεραστιάς ή Κύπρος ποτέ and *Scholia Dionysius Periegeta*, 509.
25. This parallelism enters into a nationalistic discourse that is closely bound up with the divided national identity of Great Britain which led to the idea of a unique nation with its own peculiarities bred through the separate countries of England, Wales and Scotland. The people of Cornwall were marginalised within this range, segregated and identified as the wildest and most undeveloped local elements. On these particular problems see T. Champion, 'Three nations or one? Britain and the national use of the past', in M. Diaz-Andreu and T. Champion (eds.), *Nationalism and Archaeology in Europe* (1996) 119–145.
26. R. Pococke, *A description of the East and some other countries* (London 1743–1745) [*EC* 268].
27. On these problems see A.B. Kehoe, 'Contextualizing Archaeology' in A.L. Christenson (ed.), *Tracing Archaeology's past* (Carbondale/Edwardsville 1989) 102.
28. Cf. L. Palma di Cesnola, *Cyprus. Its Ancient Cities, Tombs and Temples* (1st edition, London 1877; reprinted with additional material, Nicosia 1991) 180.
29. Cesnola (n.28) 180.
30. Clarke (n.7).
31. This tendency, which was to be continued within the context of early modern archaeology, has been considered to be a significant procedure which led to the humanisation and also homogenisation of the past. On these matters and the way they have been expressed in several ethnographic and archaeological contexts, see P. Gathercole and D. Lowenthal, *Politics of the Past* (London 1990).
32. M. Ohnefalsch-Richter, *Kypros. Die Bibel und Homer* (Berlin 1893) Pl.125.
33. This tendency had been characterised as 'biblical'. It meant that certain stock characters, often removed from the flow of history, were inserted into illustrations of excavated sites. Cf. C.M. Hinsley, 'Revising and Revisioning the History of Archaeology: Reflections on Region and Context', in Christenson (n.27) 94.
34. V. Hugo, *La Legende des Siècles* (Paris 1883).
35. Clarke (n.7).
36. Capt. C.C. Frankland [*EC* 456].
37. 'Journal kept on a journey from Bassora to Bagdad, over

the little desert to Aleppo, Cyprus, Rhodes, Zante, Corfu, and Otranto....' [*EC* 324].
38. J. Macdonald Kinneir, *Journey through Asia Minor, Armenia and Koordistan* (London 1818) [*EC* 412].
39. A. Serghidou, 'L'altérité du Chypriote dans le discours grec antique. *Kyprios charactère, quelle identité Cypriote*, in *Sources, Travaux Historiques* 43–44 (1995) 36–38.
40. See, for example, L. De Mas Latrie, *Chypre, sa situation présente et ses souvenirs du moyen âge* (Paris 1879) 119. The author refers to a number of sage travellers such as Pococke, Drummond or Tournefort whose work preceeded his own investigation. He is not the only one to appropriate the Classical background of his predecessors. R. Walpole, *Travels in Various Countries of the East* (London 1820) 26 was to compare, for example, his own observation of nature with that of Tournefort: 'Among the stones of a ruined village we observed the Lacerta Stellio, the same which Tournefort had found among the ruins of Delos'.
41. This confirmation is confused. The author probably alludes to the 'Islands' (Νησιά) mentioned in *Acta Barnabae*, 22–26.
42. Pococke (n.26) 256.
43. Constantius, Archbishop of Sinai, Κυπριὰς χαρίεσσα καὶ ἐπίτομος (Venice 1819) [*EC* 312]
44. A. Drummond, *Travels through different cities of Germany, Italy, Greece and several parts of Asia* (London 1794) [*EC* 296].
45. Drummond (n.44).
46. On the appropriation of Hellenic heroes in medieval Europe see G. Huppert, *The Idea of Perfect History* (Urbana/Chicago/London 1970) 72 ss. For similar arguments, see R. Starn, 'Reinventing heroes in Renaissance Italy', in R.I. Rotberg and T.K. Rabb (eds.), *Art and History, Images and their Meaning* (Cambridge 1986) 67–84. See also H.A. MacDougall, *Racial myth in English History: Trojans, Teutons, and Anglo-Saxons* (Hanover and London 1982).
47. Drummond (n.44).
48. Clarke (n.7).
49. Clarke (n.7). On the intellectual affinities of travellers of the nineteenth century with their predecessors see n.40 above.
50. Cf. Malina and Vasicek (n.12).
51. For tombs, their symbolic power and the way they were read see Schnapp (n.9) 19, 27, 28.
52. Clarke (n.7).
53. Cesnola (n.28).
54. Cesnola (n.28). The prolific excavations of Cesnola could indeed be considered excessive in the eyes of the Turkish authorities.
55. For different ways of reading and structuring landscapes within an ideological, political and, nonetheless, intellectual context see J. Douglas Porteous, *Landscapes of the Mind. Worlds of Sense and Metaphor* (Toronto 1990).
56. See S. Piggot, *Ruins in a landscape: essays in antiquarianism* (Edinburgh 1976).
57. Editor of the *Flora Graeca* and founder of a chair of rural economy at Oxford, died 1796 [*EC* 331].
58. Cf. Pococke (n.26).
59. *EC* 257
60. Diodorus Siculus 20.47,1–2.
61. Herodotus 1.105,2–3.
62. *Orphic Hymns* 55.1–28
63. Plato, *Symposium* 180d.
64. Plato, *Symposium* 180d and see also Pausanias 9.16,3–4
65. Pococke (n.26).
66. Kinneir (n.38).
67. A.F. Didot, *Notes d'un voyage fait dans le levant, en 1816–1817* (Paris 1826) 324.
68. Ali Bey [*EC* 405].
69. W. Turner, *Journal of a Tour in the Levant* (London 1820) [*EC* 443].
70. For the digression into natural science and the consideration of nature as the cradle of all things see Malina and Vasicek (n.12) 91–92.
71. Ali Bey [*EC* 398].
72. Ali Bey [*EC* 410].

4. Edmond Duthoit: an artist and ethnographer in Cyprus, 1862, 1865

Rita C. Severis

It was Olivier Masson who put me on the trail of Edmond Duthoit late one evening in 1996 when I called him from Cyprus to ask if he had seen any of Duthoit's artwork. He had seen only some sketches but encouraged me to pursue the matter and write an article for the *Cahier du Centre d' Etudes Chypriotes*. My research led me to the Musée de Picardie in Amiens where a series of over one hundred drawings and watercolours by Edmond Duthoit unfolded in front of my eyes giving a unique picture of the island as it was seen and perceived by the artist during his visit in 1862. The majority of these works have never been published or exhibited, and do not only present Cyprus as it was in the nineteenth century; examined in conjunction with the artist's letters and notes they reveal precious ethnographic evidence and information on the island, meticulously collected and presented by Edmond Duthoit.

Born in Amiens in 1837 in a family which enjoyed great reputation in the art circles – his father and uncle were accomplished sculptors and decorators – he studied at the Jesuit college of Brugelette in Belgium, in Saint Clement in Metz and in Amiens as a designer of religious buildings. In 1857 he joined the studio of Viollet-le-Duc, and became one of his most promising students of architecture. It was in fact Viollet-le-Duc that proposed Duthoit to Melchior de Vogüé as a capable and reliable draughtsman. The latter was searching for an architect and artist to accompany him to the Orient where he had accepted to undertake the continuation of the French Phoenician Mission in 1862, originally headed by Ernest Renan.

Edmond Duthoit was just 24 years old when he embarked with Melchior de Vogüé for the Orient. They arrived in Beirut in January 1862 where they joined up with the third party of their group, Henry William Waddington, and by February they were on their way to Cyprus aboard the *Stella*. They reached the port of Larnaca on the 28th of the same month. This was to be the first visit to the island within the framework of the mission whose aim was to collect information and antiquities for the French Government, and which lasted from February to end of May 1862. Duthoit re-visited Cyprus from May to August 1865, this time on his own, in order to complete the work of the mission and its main objective, which was now to make arrangements for the transportation of the great vase of Amathus to France.

By the middle of the nineteenth century Cyprus had started to come out of the desolate state it was in as a small province of the Ottoman Empire. Although under Ottoman administration the island continued to show characteristics of material decay and negligent rule, the reforms introduced by Sultan Mahmut II in 1830–39 and the increasing influence of the major powers, particularly that of Britain and France in the Eastern Mediterranean, had some beneficial effects.

It was, therefore, no surprise that Cyprus was included in the French Phoenician Mission at a time when antiquarian and scientific interests constituted a forum for the competitive spirit amongst European powers. The island had been famous since ancient times, primarily in relation to Aphrodite and its wines. Travellers visited Cyprus and wrote about the island. Their number, though, cannot be compared to that of visitors to Italy or Greece, as Cyprus was never part of the Grand Tour. Some travellers included illustrations in their texts, although these were but a few: the Russian monk, Basil Gregorevich Barsky, visited Cyprus several times between 1726 and 1736, producing some naïve drawings of monasteries (Fig. 4.1) and churches as well as some town views (Fig. 4.2). In 1750, the British consul in Aleppo, Alexander Drummond (Fig. 4.3), made some austere and formal illustrations of edifices, while Louis François Cassas (Fig. 4.4) in 1785 presented romanticised views of the island. Seven years later Luigi Mayer (Fig. 4.5) painted ancient sites, including the vase of Amathus; during the eighteenth century illustrations of Cyprus were topographical, containing monuments of historical reference. In the early nineteenth century a number of visitors came to Cyprus and made a few drawings (Fig. 4.6) and watercolours, mostly of Larnaca and the sea front (Fig. 4.7); most of them did not penetrate into the island's hinterland. However, during the middle of the nineteenth century there was an apparent increase in travelling and the island was included in the itineraries of tours to the Orient. It was then that the first ethnographic illustrations of Cyprus appeared, mainly by French artists or scholars, amongst whom the most prolific was perhaps Edmond Duthoit.

It would only be fair to mention that the French Phoenician Mission's interest was first drawn to Cyprus by a native Frenchman, Sosténe Grasset d'Orcet, who was recommended to Melchior de Vogüé and his company by Ernest Renan himself. Grasset knew the island well and had written articles about it in French magazines accompanied by his own illustrations. But Grasset was a voice from within. He illustrated (Fig. 4.8) Cyprus in a manner that he felt would be attractive to the French salons, beautifying the people and the landscape, and making use of artistic license (Fig. 4.9). He was placed at the disposal of the researchers to help and guide them in Cyprus, although he had aspired to conduct the mission himself. Unfortunately, Duthoit never liked Grasset, 'le plus parfait ennuyeux du monde', as he wrote to his mother.[1] This kind of comment was often expressed by the 24-year old Duthoit. In his letters to his mother, he often comes through as a self-assured, self-possessed and arrogant character who had a rather contemptuous attitude towards most people, including his own countrymen: Count de Maricourt, the French consul in Cyprus, was making 'boulette sur boulette,'[2] while the French consular agent in Limassol was regarded by Duthoit as a comic affair. The Greek Cypriots were 'une bien horrible race'.[3] However, there was another side to his character, which exhibited a very sensitive and disciplined nature, enthusiasm and hard work, but above all, the ability to appreciate beauty. He never stopped drawing: 'croquis faits à la hâte, le plus souvent sans même descendre du cheval', he wrote to his mother, 'malgré cela tous les albums que j'ai apportés de France sont sur le point de se finir. J'en ai commandé 6 à Paris'...[4].

He mainly used small sketchbooks of beige, light blue or grey paper, measuring approximately 15×7 cm or 11×15 cm, the largest being 40×30 cm. His drawings are linear, quick, and sketchy; but often, the artist would outline a monument (Fig. 4.10) in a hurry and concentrate on a small aspect of it, which he would work in detail and bring to perfection. Sometimes he would use watercolours, pencil, crayons and gouache achieving a most atmospheric effect. In fact, he intended to work his drawings into a series of paintings when back in France. 'Je dessine beaucoup, mais à la hâte... J'ai l'intention de publier mon voyage à Chypre car je suis le seul voyager qui connaît bien cette île'.[5] A large part of these sketches and the diary have not yet been located.

Duthoit had a special relation with nature and the landscape; it inspired him, especially in Cyprus where it underlined the setting of most of his drawings (Fig. 4.11). Particularly impressive are Duthoit's drawings of Buffavento and Kantara castles which appear as eagles' nests perched on the mountain cliffs (Figs. 4.12, 4.13). The precipice of the position is accentuated, the ruins are drawn in detail, and the fairy-tale quality of the sites dominates the pictures. Some of these drawings were later borrowed by the French scholar Camille Enlart to illustrate his famous book *L'Art Gothique et la Renaissance en Chypre*.[6] A most lyrical description is found in Duthoit's letter to his mother of 24 February:[7] 'De Nicosie nous sommes allés à Kerinia par le plus joli chemin du monde, traversé à mi-côte d'une vallée ou plutôt sur un ravin profond rempli de myrthes et de lauriers roses, la ville elle même située au bord de la mer est d'un effet très pittoresque...Bella est le joyau de l' île nulle part je n'ai vu rien d'aussi joli, ni d'aussi riche pays... De quelque côté qu'on tourne ses yeux le spectacle change mais est toujours ravissant; Rien n'est plus beau que la vue de l'abbaye prise du levant à l'heure où le soleil se puise dans la mer. Les montagnes prennent les couleurs les plus belles et les plus variées, elles poussent successivement du rouge brillant au bleu foncé. La mer prend des teintes analogues, quant au ciel c'est indescriptible, il est d'une pureté surprenante'.

Duthoit stayed in Bellapais three days and drew, as he mentioned in his letter, the bastions, refectory, the church, dormitory and cloisters. As is the case with many of his drawings these are also untraceable.

What seems to have fascinated the artist was the amalgamation of cultures to be found in this small island, which did not permit a straightforward definition of its identity. Its proximity to the East was overwhelmed by the sprinkle of Western edifices that blurred its oriental outlook: 'Famagouste montre d'assez loin les deux tours de sa cathédrale ruinée, des fortifications encore assez bonnes lui donne de loin, l'aspect d'une ville française. Mais les touffes magnifiques de palmiers qui croissent partout détruisent bientôt l'illusion...Famagouste est une ville assez fanatique et il est défendu à tout chrétien d'y loger'.[8]

Yet, 'ce n'est qu' église sur église' (Fig. 4.14), 'chapelle sur chapelle' (Fig. 4.15), 'presque toutes ont été fort belles, enrichies de peintures du haut en bas' (Fig. 4.16).[9] Duthoit studied many Cypriot medieval churches and his meticulous designs of these monuments reflect both Ernest Renan's and Viollet-le-Duc's architectural beliefs. The former was intrigued by the notion that archaeology might reveal a continuous tradition of rationality in architecture.[10] The latter believed that the thirteenth-century Gothic monuments were both the perfect expression of rational construction and the most instructive example for the nineteenth-century architects. Views of the town of Famagusta from the sea (Fig. 4.17) with the Sea Gate bastion in the middle of the picture (Fig. 4.18) reminds one of the island's Venetian period. The Orthodox Christian element is also given its due importance in Duthoit's illustrations. Views of villages dominated by Byzantine churches (Fig. 4.19) and monasteries, sunk in the vegetation of secluded areas in the mountain regions of the island, offer an atmosphere of security and reverence well-captured by the artist, who transmitted historical connotations within the landscape (Fig. 4.20). The mountains had offered refuge to the Orthodox Church since the time of Latin rule in Cyprus. Writing about the monastery of Kykko in the mountainous region of Troodos, Duthoit pays as much attention to the topography as to the architecture: 'Ici point nature terrible, de ces précipices avec pierres déchirées et nues. Il y a, comme partout ailleurs de quoi se casser vingt fois et plus mais partout des fleurs. Les arbres sont vrais bouquets montes; au bord de ruisseaux croissent d'énormes platanes dont la verdure claire et pâle fait un contraste fort agréable avec le feuillage des grands sapins. C'est la première fois que je vois des arbres à Chypre mais ils sont magnifiques…J'ai retrouvé là le type ou, pour mieux dire la représentation idéale que je m'étais faite d'une abbaye au Moyen Age…L'église est une des parties modernes, elle est fort riche en orfèvrerie, bien que les turcs l'aient pillée plusieurs fois…Si le programme est le même que celui des établissements occidentaux, l'architecture est bien différente, il ne faut point chercher de lignes, ici, ou un plan étudié, c'est un amas de bâtiments qui en bois, qui en pierres, qui en terre, agglomérés, suspendus les uns aux autres avec des toits saillants, des galeries couvertes et d'énormes escaliers extérieurs'.[11]

The professionalism of the artist is at its best in his architectural illustrations (Fig. 4.21); particular care is taken over correct dimensions and the inclusion of figures to indicate sizes (Fig. 4.22). Attention is given to the perspective from which an edifice was drawn so as to have it presented to the best advantage for the understanding of its structure, while vegetation and topographical indications are used to determine the location (Fig. 4.23). Often an edifice is drawn from different angles on the same piece of paper (Fig. 4.24). In designing Byzantine churches, the artist tried to understand the local significance of the architectural concept. He later introduced a new style evolved from an understanding of the past which was applied to the needs of the present (Fig. 4.25). Detailed drawings of special antique fragments such as the decor of gables (Fig. 4.26), doorways (Fig. 4.27), windows (Fig. 4.28), columns and capitals (Fig. 4.29), give measurements and some have explanatory notes.

The core of his architectural drawings is constituted by representations of Gothic monuments, either on their own (Fig. 4.30), or in the setting of a street scene (Fig. 4.31). However, in almost all cases, these received alterations or additions to their original appearance by the Ottoman rulers. The minarets, along with the palm trees, the costumes worn by the figures and the humble houses next to the Gothic monuments, add an exotic and oriental touch to many of Duthoit's drawings. Some of these scenes, defined by particular titles, at first glance appear to be purely oriental, such as *Un cimetière turk à Nicosie, '62* (Fig. 4.32) but the Gothic archway on the left of the picture changes the initial impression. The *Sérail à Nicosie 1862* (Fig. 4.33) shows a Turkish figure walking up to the palace of the Turkish Governor which, although shaded by palm trees, being an old Venetian palace bears on top of its doorway the emblem of St. Mark. However, in other street scenes, a purely oriental atmosphere is achieved (Fig. 4.34).

Exotic and oriental elements are abundant in Duthoit's drawings. In fact it may be claimed that it is Duthoit who first introduced these elements into the representations of Cyprus to such a large extent. This becomes even more apparent in his ethnographic drawings which, accompanied with relevant descriptions from his letters, bring alive the Cyprus of the mid-nineteenth century.

The *Paniyiri*, at the church of the Virgin of Chrysoroyiatissa (Fig. 4.35) is one of the main feasts celebrated on the island on 25 March. People gather from everywhere to pay their respects to the Virgin Mary in this mountainous refuge. Duthoit's description of the *Paniyiri* at Kykko compliments the illustration (Fig. 4.36): 'Tous ces pèlerins étaient en fête, les femmes portaient toutes la jasque de velours avec les broderies d'or et, à leur cou, pendait, enfilées comme un collier toutes les pièces de monnaie qui composent leur fortune'.[12] Women in a circle are spinning round to the tunes of music, while others are resting idle on the ground. In the courtyard of the monastery the peddlers have gathered to sell their goods (Fig. 4.37), and the animals, the only means of transport, are lined up to rest after having reached their destination.

Two drawings of the interior of monasteries touch upon another aspect of the social scene on the island: the role of a clergyman as a leading figure in Cypriot life (Fig. 4.38). Thus the Turk, identified by the white, long baggy trousers, is visiting the abbot at the monastery to discuss matters. They are talking intimately and the abbot looks attentively. As late as the end of Ottoman rule, the Church retained its power, which was used for the protection of its people and often for financial gain. Duthoit claims that the Greek clergy is very ignorant and that the people have very little respect for them.[13] Another drawing (Fig. 4.39) presents two novices discussing something between them in the presence of a young woman. The sensitive nature of the artist must have apprehended some kind of mischief in the atmosphere, which he subtly included in his drawing. The two novices are in light-hearted conversation; one has a faint smile on his face, while the other is facing the young woman, who in turn does not seem to portray much reverence in the presence of monks, her posture far from expressing humbleness and respect.

The costumes of the country can be appreciated in most of Duthoit's representations of the population. A young woman carrying a water-pitcher and having under her arm a wide wicker woven basket of Cypriot make (*tsestos*), is dressed in traditional costume (Fig. 4.40). Different parts of the island adhered to variations of Cypriot attire. 'A Acathchi, nous logeâmes chez un papas dont les filles étaient fort belles et portaient les plus jolis costumes que j'ai rencontrés à Chypre'.[14] Tight waistlines accentuated the bosom which was supported by a short kind of jacket (Fig. 4.41). A long apron was often worn over the trousers or the first skirt. A head-dress covered the long plaits while the feet were bare. Another version has the young girl's head tightly covered with a kerchief, an apron over a skirt that covers the long baggy trousers, this time ending at the edge of high boots (Fig. 4.42). A wonderful watercolour with its vivid tones well preserved, portrays two Cypriot girls dancing (Fig. 4.43): 'un petit corsage très ouvert qui se croise au dessous des seins, une mousseline ou des dentelles couvre la poitrine, la gorge reste nue. Une gaze enveloppe la tête et le chignon des personnes qui ne portent pas de magnifiques nattes pendantes sur le dos, des fleurs artificielles ou naturelles sont placées dans les cheveux,' commented Duthoit.[15] Greek men also wore baggy trousers to the knee, known as *vraka*, with wide sashes around their waists and waistcoats over long-sleeved shirts (Fig. 4.44); a man in this attire, portrayed by the artist on one occasion, holds a scythe for reaping wheat. Men wore their moustaches long and well-groomed, regarding them as the proper insignia of manhood and, on festive days they wore the fez, a cap with a thick black silky tassel (Fig. 4.45). The Turks wore long overcoats with wide sleeves and, typically, the turban, a long piece of narrow cloth wrapped capriciously around their head (Fig. 4.46).

Women at work testify to the hard lot of Cypriot female peasantry. At Athienou, a Cypriot mother has gathered her children on a platform, pulled by a pair of skinny oxen, and is threshing the crop (Fig. 4.47).

A number of drawings present local artefacts such as clay pitchers (Fig. 4.48) and water-mills of primitive construction (Fig. 4.49) with the old style wooden wheel. Drawings of interior of houses (Fig. 4.50), devoid of decorative items and restricted to bare essentials, draw the attention to the social conditions within the home. Turkish bathhouses (Fig. 4.51) and khans are examples of public buildings, but also point to the artist's interest in Islamic architecture. 'En Europe on débarque dans une ville, on fait porter ses bagages à l'hôtel, rien n'est plus simple. Ici nous en aurions bien fait autant, mais il ne manquait qu'une seule chose, c'était l'hôtel'.[16] In fact during his second visit to Nicosia, Duthoit discovered and stayed at the *Koumardjilar Khan* or khan of the gamblers (Fig. 4.52).[17] The above, along with copies of Byzantine frescoes (Fig. 4.53), drawings of rusting Venetian cannons (Fig. 4.54) and the famous baroque candelabra found discarded in the castle of Famagusta (Fig. 4.55) testify to the wide diversity of antiquarian material on the island.

A subject that did not escape Duthoit's attention and close examination was the diet of the Cypriots, which in most cases he found boring and repetitive. 'Le poulet est notre nourriture de chaque jour, 2 fois par jour, de la poule avec du riz et du pain d'orge, le vin est assez agréable mais nous en buvons guère qu'au dîner'.[18]

But every now and then he had a stroke of luck. At the village of Cornos, just a few days before his departure, the artist had an unforgettable culinary experience that may sound familiar to those who have visited Cyprus on a Sunday or a feast day: 'A 50 pas de la table on avait tué et dépecé un beau mouton, un grand foyer de braises ardentes renvoyait la fumée de 10 broches longues de 2 m. et que tournaient des gamins. Pour avoir le rôti plus vite on avait imaginé de couper le mouton en tout petit morceaux et de les embrocher sur d'immenses cannes. Le spectacle était fort pittoresque, le dîner succulent, les toasts nombreux et bruyants; nous bûmes si bien à la santé du roi Georges, à l'affranchissement de l'île de Chypre, à la France protectrice, à nos propres santés'.[19] His strong sensitivities took in the atmosphere: 'Dans un beau jardin d'arbres du Levant, orangers, citronniers, mûriers et oliviers, on avait dressé une longue table qui ne brillait pas par l'uniformité du service et la finesse du linge'.[20] One can visualise the oriental feast and imagine the fragrance in the air.

As for various other customs of the island, these never ceased to amaze the French visitor: 'En arrivant chez le pasha on nous fit asseoir ou coucher sur le divan et on apporta des chibouch, longues pipes de 1 m50 a 2 m de long. Ici la pipe, sa dimension, son bouquin d'ambre plus ou moins gros ont leur signification et telle espéce de pipe se donne spécialement à telle espèce d'individu et pas à d'autres. On se dit des compliments et banalités…Ensuite arriva un plateau couvert d'un voile de pourpre constellé d'étoiles d'or ou dorées et porté par quatre officiers. Le café est suivi à quelques distance d'un replateau avec un revoile et les 4 officiers. Ce plateau contient des bols assez grands remplis de limonade ou orangeade, c'est le sorbet. C'est au moment de ces différents services que mon hilarité était fort difficilement contenue. Vois- tu 4 hommes de toutes les couleurs habillés, moitié à l'européene, moitié à la turque, en pantalon et sans bas portant gravement un plateau portant quoi? 4 tasses de café grandes comme des coquetiers'.[21]

While in Paphos: '...j'avais autour de moi une dizaine de grecs et le papas était du nombre, lorsque deux jeunes filles, assez jolies du reste, s'approchèrent de moi. L'une qui paraissait supérieure à la seconde me prit la main, me versa je ne sais quelle eau parfumée et me baisa la main et repartirent toutes deux sans dire un mot'.[22]

At Dali, Duthoit visited the church of St. Mamas, in the outskirts of the village built next to the river. He drew the interior and exterior of the church (Fig. 4.56) and noted that it was wrapped around with cotton string. This is an ancient tradition surviving in Cyprus even today. The island often suffers from drought and special liturgies and litanies accompany the prayers of the faithful for rain. It is the custom, after such ceremonies, to wrap the church with cotton string until the rain comes. In a way, it is an offering to God.

In the early part of June 1865, the artist found himself in Larnaca during the feast of Cataclysmos. Having its roots in the ancient pagan celebrations for Venus, the feast was incorporated in the traditions of the Greek Orthodox Christians. The first Monday after the Pentecost people went, and still go, to the sea to wet themselves in the water. Dancing, singing and merry-making accompanied the ceremony. Crowds gathered and wet each other. Stalls were erected selling sweets, nuts and honey while a colourful array of costumes presented to the artist the wonderful hand made clothes of the island, in danger of soon being replaced by crinolines, chintzes and hats that were making their appearances at the fair, worn by proud females aspiring to the latest European fashions.

Finally, I would like to refer to some examples of Duthoit's antiquarian drawings. While supervising excavations performed by the mission he never stopped sketching, thus accumulating a bulk of representations of tombs (Fig. 4.57), sites and archaeological remnants most of which have long since disappeared. However, he is most appreciated for his thorough study of the colossal vase of Amathus (Fig. 4.58) for the transportation of which to France he procured a *firman* from the Sultan (to the dismay of the British consul who was also eyeing the piece). Duthoit studied and suggested the way by which it should be transported to the beach from the top of the hill and thereon to a French frigate, and went as far as building a wall around it[23] so as to protect it until the time of its transfer. Illustrations of antiquities on the island such as Palaipaphos (Fig. 4.59), otherwise known, according to Duthoit, as the tomb of Venus, or Soli (Fig. 4.60) and his portrayal of scattered Greek columns, refer to and emphasise the Hellenic connections of the country which, although not Duthoit's main preoccupation, nevertheless fascinated him just as much.

It is a pity that the artist spent his last days on the island under distasteful circumstances that left with him a sour taste. 'Mon premier voyage ne fut qu' une longue fête. Que n' en puis-je dire autant du second!'.[24] The outbreak of cholera in Larnaca in August 1865 and the subsequent death of the French consul, Count de Maricourt, from the epidemic, placed Duthoit in the awkward position of having to make arrangements for the funeral and the safekeeping of the Consulate until a new consul was appointed. Of course his contact with a victim of cholera frightened the inhabitants of Larnaca who refused to go anywhere near him or to help him in his duties. This infuriated the tired artist, who could take no more nonsense nor accept or forgive such cowardice: 'Enfin je compte quitter Chypre demain et je veux secouer en partant la poussière de mes souliers, pour ne rien emporter de ce pays où je compte bien ne plus remettre les pieds. J'ai pris Chypre en horreur ou plutôt non, ce n'est pas Chypre que je hais, mais ce sont les Chypriotes'....[25]

However, it is important to realise that these variables in his character, these folds in the artist's personality, which vary from hardness to almost childlike softness, were never allowed to influence his work. What he felt, he kept distant from his representations. The sensitivities present in Duthoits's illustrations are what he perceived from the atmosphere and his subjects and not what came from his heart. This is not to say that his work is devoid of emotions. All of Duthoit's drawings capture faithfully the vibrations of the place, the feeling of the surroundings and the innermost meaning and essence of its subject matter. Thus, Cyprus is presented as a melancholic, decaying land of a multicultural experience which permeates a nostalgic yearning for the past. The feeling of familiarity, to be found in the numerous portrayals of Latin monuments, acquires a special role in this context, as it brings the artist's subject-matter closer to his spectator, forming a personal relationship.

Furthermore the Orientalist[26] representations of Cyprus found in Duthoit's work are carefully treated so as to focus extensively on the exotic aspect of the oriental and avoid any misleading assumptions as to the cultural identity of the island, which is skilfully preserved and persistently presented as an amalgamation of various cultures.

Duthoit's work in Cyprus is multifold: as an academic and draughtsman he fulfilled his task and brought the mission to a successful close. As a discerning traveller he penetrated into the island and by the end of his travels commanded a wide knowledge of the country. As an artist and writer he marvelled at the beauties of the landscape and monuments, representing Cyprus in the most realistic and honest way. Edmond, as a human being, matured in Cyprus and took back with him a wealth of experiences that were to prove invaluable in the success of his future career.[27]

Notes

1. Edmond Duthoit to his mother: letter no. 6, 8 February 1862.
2. Edmond Duthoit to his mother: letter no. 8, 10 July 1865.
3. Duthoit (n.2).
4. E. Duthoit to his mother: letter no. 7, 24 February 1862, Nicosia.
5. E. Duthoit to his mother: letter no. 7, June 1865, Cyprus.
6. Camille Enlart, *L'Art Gothique et la Renaissance en Chypre* (Paris 1899).
7. Duthoit (n.4).
8. Duthoit (n.1).
9. Duthoit (n.1).
10. B. Bergdoll: 'The synthesis of all I have seen: the architecture of Edmond Duthoit 1837–1889)' in Robin Middleton (ed.), *The Beaux-Arts and the nineteenth century* (London 1982) 224.
11. E. Duthoit to his uncle: letter no.11, 5 May 1862, Larnaca-Nicosia.
12. Duthoit (n.11).
13. E. Duthoit to his mother: letter no. 8, Monday, 10 March 1862, Consulate of France, Larnaca.
14. Duthoit (n.11).
15. Duthoit (n.1).
16. Duthoit (n.1).
17. E. Duthoit to his mother: letter 5 bis, Tuesday morning, 30 May, '65, Larnaca.
18. Duthoit (n.4).
19. E. Duthoit to his mother: letter no. 10, 7 August 1865, Larnaca of Cyprus.
20. Duthoit (n.19).
21. Duthoit (n.4).
22. Duthoit (n.13).
23. Jacques Foucart-Bovrille, 'La correspondance chypriote d'Edmond Duthoit', *Centre d'Etudes Chypriotes. Cahier* 4 (1985) 24.
24. Duthoit to Melchior de Vogüé, 7 August 1865, (CHAN 567AP229).
25. Duthoit (n.19).
26. The word *Orientalist* is used here in its sympathetic academic concept that deals with the discovery and study of the Orient.
27. All of Duthoit's drawings and watercolours, except nos. 11–13, are reproduced in this article by kind permission of the Museum of Picardie, Amiens, France.

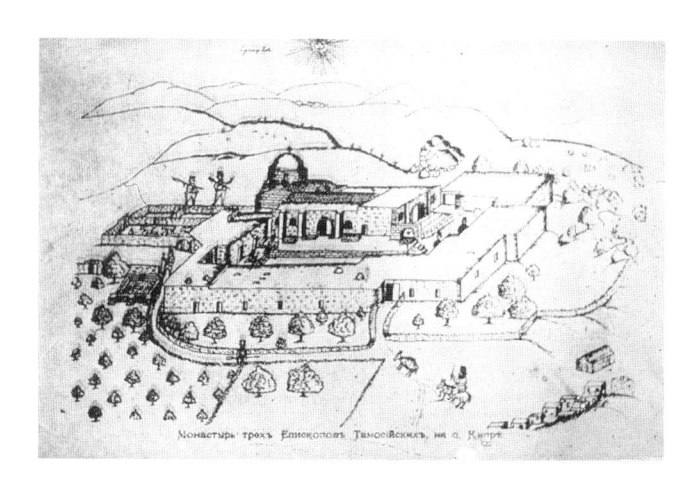

Fig. 4.1: Basil Gregorovich Barsky: Monastery of Saint Herakleidios.

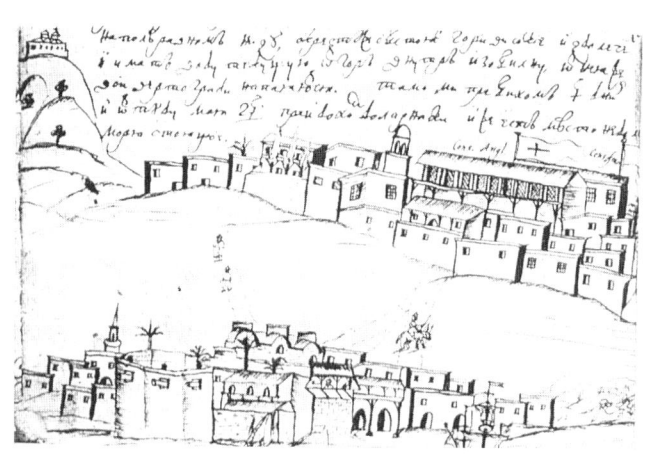

Fig. 4.2: Basil Gregorovich Barsky: Larnaca and Alikas.

Fig. 4.3: Alexander Drummond: The North View of the Grand Commandery Dela Pays.

Fig. 4.4: Louis François Cassas: Vue des Ruines du Monastère de Cazzfone, Chypre.

Fig. 4.5: Luigi Mayer: The Thermae with Piscinae in the neighbourhood of the town of Limassol, the ancient Amathunda in the Island of Cyprus.

Fig. 4.6: Henry Light: Part of Larnica, Cyprus.

Fig. 4.7: W.H. Bartlett: Larneca.

Fig. 4.8: S. Grasset d'Orcet: Les vendanges dans l' isle de Chypre – aspect d'une Phenecha.

Fig. 4.9: S. Grasset d'Orcet: le vin de Chypre – le pressoir.

Fig. 4.10: Edmond Duthoit: Ste. Sophie, Famagusta. (Photo: Marc Jeanneteau)

Fig. 4.11: Edmond Duthoit: Kantara.

Fig. 4.12: Edmond Duthoit: Boufavento.

Fig. 4.13: Edmond Duthoit: Kantara.

Fig. 4.14: Edmond Duthoit: Famagousta, eglise Syrienne. (Photo: Marc Jeanneteau).

Fig. 4.15: Edmond Duthoit: Famagouste. (Photo: Marc Jeanneteau).

Fig. 4.16: Edmond Duthoit: Famagusta. (Photo: Marc Jeanneteau).

Fig. 4.17: Edmond Duthoit: Famagouste. (Photo: Marc Jeanneteau).

Fig. 4.18: Edmond Duthoit: The Sea Gate of Famagusta. (Photo: Marc Jeanneteau).

Fig. 4.19: Edmond Duthoit: Eglise de Dokny. (Photo: Marc Jeanneteau).

Fig. 4.20: Edmond Duthoit: Monastery of Kykko. (Photo: Marc Jeanneteau)

Fig. 4.21: Edmond Duthoit: St. Sophia, Nicosia. (Photo: Marc Jeanneteau).

Fig. 4.22: Edmond Duthoit: The interior of the church of St. Mamas at Dali. (Photo: Marc Jeanneteau).

Fig. 4.23: Edmond Duthoit: Eglise franc dite Djami, Pyrga. (Photo: Marc Jeanneteau).

Fig. 4.24: Edmond Duthoit: Αγιος Γεωργιος, plaine de Messaorie. (Photo: Marc Jeanneteau).

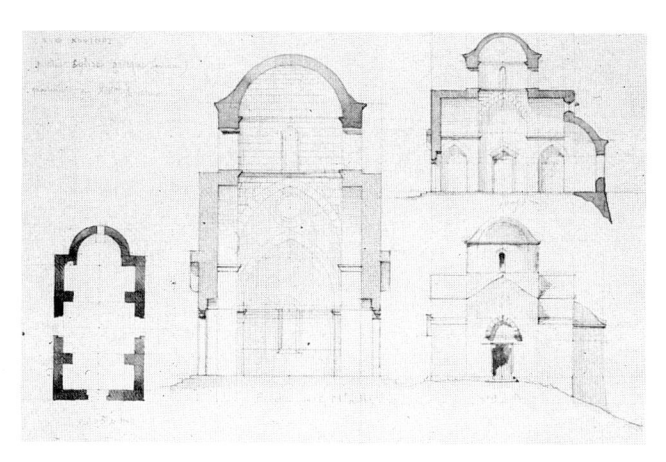

Fig. 4.25: Edmond Duthoit: Κοφινου. (Photo: Marc Jeanneteau).

Fig. 4.26: Edmond Duthoit: Famagouste. (Photo: Marc Jeanneteau).

Fig. 4.27: Edmond Duthoit: Famagouste. (Photo: Marc Jeanneteau).

Fig. 4.28: Edmond Duthoit: Eglise Armenienne de Famagouste. (Photo: Marc Jeanneteau).

Fig. 4.29: Edmond Duthoit: Chap. Georgos, Τρικομο. (Photo: Marc Jeanneteau).

Fig. 4.30: Edmond Duthoit: Ste. Catherine. (Photo: Marc Jeanneteau).

Fig. 4.31: Edmond Duthoit: Nicosia (Omeryie Mosque). (Photo: Marc Jeanneteau).

Fig. 4.32: Edmond Duthoit: Un cimetière turc à Nicosie. (Photo: Marc Jeanneteau).

Fig. 4.33: Edmond Duthoit: Le Sérail à Nicosie. (Photo: Marc Jeanneteau).

Fig. 4.34: Edmond Duthoit: Nicosia. (Photo: Marc Jeaneteau).

Fig. 4.35: Edmond Duthoit: Χρυσοροιατισσα (the church of Chrysoroyiatissa). (Photo: Marc Jeanneteau).

Fig. 4.36: Edmond Duthoit: Παναγια της Χρυσοροιατισσα (the Virgin of Chrysoroiatissa). (Photo: Marc Jeanneteau).

Fig. 4.37: Edmond Duthoit: Interior courtyard of Kykko Monastery. (Photo: Marc Jeanneteau.

Fig. 4.38: Edmond Duthoit: Couvent de Μαχαιρα. (Photo: Marc Jeanneteau).

Fig. 4.39: Edmond Duthoit: Novices in the courtyard. (Photo: Marc Jeanneteau).

Fig. 4.40: Edmond Duthoit: Acathchi. (Photo: Marc Jeanneteau).

Fig. 4.41: Edmond Duthoit: Acathchi. (Photo: Marc Jeanneteau).

Fig. 4.42: Edmond Duthoit: Dali. (Photo: Marc Jeanneteau).

Fig. 4.43: Edmond Duthoit: Girls dancing. (Photo: Marc Jeanneteau).

Fig. 4.44: Edmond Duthoit: Danse de la Paix à Dali. (Photo: Marc Jeanneteau).

Fig. 4.45: Edmond Duthoit: A Greek. (Photo: Marc Jeanneteau).

Fig. 4.46: Edmond Duthoit: A Turk. (Photo: Marc Jeanneteau).

Fig. 4.47: Edmond Duthoit: Αλλωνια Αθιενου (threshing at Athienou). (Photo: Marc Jeanneteau).

Fig. 4.48: Edmond Duthoit: Water pitchers. (Photo: Marc Jeanneteau).

Fig. 4.49: Edmond Duthoit: Dali. (Photo: Marc Jeanneteau).

Fig. 4.50: Edmond Duthoit: Κυτραια (Cythrea). (Photo: Marc Jeanneteau).

Fig. 4.51: Edmond Duthoit: Thermes de bains à Famagouste. (Photo: Marc Jeanneteau).

Fig. 4.52: Edmond Duthoit: The Koumardjilar khan. (Photo: Marc Jeanneteau).

Fig. 4.53: Edmond Duthoit: Copy of a fresco portraying a saint. (Photo: Marc Jeanneteau).

Fig. 4.54: Edmond Duthoit: Canon Venitien et son affut, Famagouste. (Photo: Marc Jeanneteau).

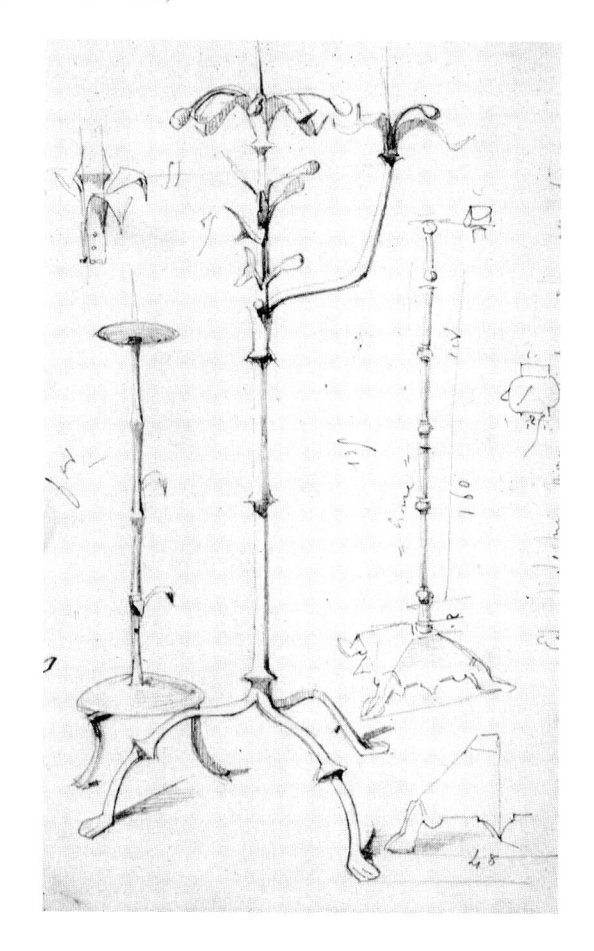

Fig. 4.55: Edmond Duthoit: Candelabra in the Eglise Ste. Sophie, mosquée actuelle de Famagouste. (Photo: Marc Jeanneteau).

Fig. 4.56: Edmond Duthoit: Petite église bâtie dans les derniers...entourée de plusieurs fils de coton en signe de deuil, Αγιος Μαμας, Dali. (Photo: Marc Jeanneteau).

Fig. 4.57: Edmond Duthoit: Bapho. (Photo: Marc Jeanneteau).

Fig. 4.58: Edmond Duthoit: Amathus. (Photo: Marc Jeanneteau).

Fig. 4.59: Edmond Duthoit: Παλαια Papho. (Photo: Marc Jeanneteau).

Fig. 4.60: Edmond Duthoit: Soli. (Photo: Marc Jeanneteau).

Sites in the 19th century

5. Ormideia: tracing Cesnola's footsteps
Archaeological research and finds

Maria Hadjicosti

It was Olivier Masson's suggestion to publish a joint article on the antiquities from Ormideia in *Centre d'Etudes chypriotes. Cahier* 1997/1. In his letter of 8 December 1996 he informed me that he had 'a photocopy of the Cesnola land house at Ormideia (extract from Alexander Cesnola's *Salaminia*, 2nd ed.)' and asked me, as a native of Ormideia, to contribute to this article, and above all to prepare a Cadastral plan showing 'the known or the possible necropoleis'. My answer was that I was delighted with his suggestion, because the study of the material from Ormideia was in my future plans, and that I was ready to contribute, especially under his supervision. In his second letter, dated 7 January 1997, he informed me that he 'began to write something about the site and the 19th century activities, with the two Cesnolas'.[1] He planned for me to study the recent discoveries, to make any other comments about the place, and to find information about the family of the priest illustrated by L.P. di Cesnola (1878, 180). In this paper I will try to examine the nineteenth-century activities and finds and compare them with the recent discoveries, in memory of the great teacher of the younger generation of Cypriot Archaeologists.

Ormideia (Fig. 5.1: 5.2) is, today, a prosperous community of about five thousand inhabitants, situated on the south east coast of Cyprus, about 20 km east of Larnaka and about 30 km south-west of Famagusta, on the boundaries of Larnaka and Famagusta Districts. This village, just like Xylotymbou, is today an island in the middle of the territory of the Sovereign British Base of Dekelia and its village lands come under the jurisdiction of the Bases. The village owes its prosperity to its fertile red soil and to the proximity of the town of Larnaka, the tourist areas of Agia Napa and Paralimni near Famagusta, the British Bases and the sea. Ormeidia is known all over Cyprus as the village of fishermen.

The name of the village (Goodwin 1977, 492–93) most probably derives from the Greek word Ὅρμος, which means bay. Τα Ορμίδεια is the diminutive of the plural of the word Ὅρμος and corresponds with the rocky shore with many small bays, which borders the village on the south (Fig. 5.3). Characteristic is the small harbour for fishing boats, today called Romanzo (Fig. 5.4), which lies not very far from the locality Meridji, where a medieval settlement has been located (CS[2] 1459, Cadastral Plan XLI 22 W2). From the bed of the sea were also collected amphorae of the 'Cannanite' type (M LA[3] 1662–63) and fragments of imported Greek amphorae and other pottery (M LA 1072–73 and M LA 1337). The village appears for the first time in Cypriot Cartography in 1570 (Stylianou 1980, 252), and is also shown on more than thirty old maps until 1911 under the names *Opinidia, Orima, Ormedeia, Ormidia, Ormydia, Ormilia, Ormithia* and *Oromidia*. Leontios Makhairas, in his *Chronicle* dating from the end of the fourteenth or the beginning of the fifteenth century, refers to the village as Ορμετία (Makhairas 1932, 30). The village itself (Fig. 5.1) occupies a narrow valley of about 3km long, between two ranges of small hills and two plateaus, parallel to the sea. An opening to the sea of about 300m long and 500m wide (Fig. 5.5), which has all the characteristics of a marsh, was perhaps a land-locked harbour in antiquity. This area was in the past a source of malaria, which inhibited the growth of the village, and improvement works are still being carried out today. The original village was situated to the north of the marshy corridor on a low hill called *Pithkiavli* (Fig. 5.6), which was, as we will see, the area of an ancient settlement dating from the late Cypro-Geometric to the late Roman period.

Despite the problems created by the marshy area, compared with the surrounding villages of the Famagusta District and the Mesaoria Plain to the north, Ormideia was the only village of this area situated in a picturesque landscape. This is perhaps one of the reasons why it was used in the nineteenth century as the 'summer station' of foreigners, including the diplomatic community living at the time in Larnaka. The second, and most probably the main reason, was that the permanent residence of the Vontizianos family was in this village (Koudounaris 1972, 29), and this was one of the noble families of the time, who were related to the Hadjigeorgakis family of Nicosia and the Pierides family of Larnaka.

Among the diplomats, who used Ormideia as their summer residence, were Luigi and Alexander Palma di Cesnola. Of course, judging from their activities in the area, they did not choose Ormideia only for the reasons mentioned above. It is interesting to read why Luigi Palma di Cesnola chose Idalion to be his first summer residence, soon after his arrival in the island. He writes: 'Another reason, which had great weight in my selection of Dali as a temporary residence, was the fact that an old Greek peasant, called Hadji Jorghi, had brought me from time to time fragments of sculptures from this village, which greatly interested me' (Cesnola 1878, 62). Alexander Palma di Cesnola also writes about Ormideia: 'On arriving in Cyprus at the end of July 1876, I engaged the some house and servants in Larnaka I had before, and also a country house at Ormidia, the later being near the Citium, Idalium, Salamis and other localities which are rich in ancient monuments' (Cesnola 1884, page xii).

Luigi Palma di Cesnola, at the beginning of the passage, referring to his acitivities in Ormideia, says that he arrived in this village early in the spring in 1872 (Cesnola 1878, 177) when, according to his words, he '... resolved to explore as much as possible of the south-east coast of the Island'. After he describes the preparations for his new campaign and his journey along the coast of Pyla (Cesnola 1878, 177–78), he writes: 'Continuing my journey along the coast, I reached a spot where the road takes a northerly direction. Pursuing this, I soon came upon a small village called Ormidia, inhabited exclusively by Greek peasants. It was in a pretty little white cottage on the summit of a low hill near the outskirts of the village that I established in 1873 my summer residence, and this continued to be our summer resort as long as we remained in the island' (Cesnola 1878, 179). By 'we' he means not only his wife and his daughters, but also his brother Alexander Palma di Cesnola (Sternini 1998, 6), who arrived in Cyprus in 1873 (Cesnola 1884, page xi) and, according to his descriptions, in 1876 explored the area of Ormideia and Xylotymbou (Cesnola 1884, page xv) and in 1877 the area of Rizokarpaso, always using the summer house in Ormideia as a base (Cesnola 1884, page xvii). It is interesting to observe that, in the four pages in which Luigi Palma di Cesnola describes his archaeological adventures in the village, while he is precise when speaking about the location of the village, the location of his summer house and the priest, he avoids mentioning the owner of the house and the findspots of his archaeological discoveries. Also the information given in another passage, that he undertook systematic explorations at this area in 1870–71 and 1875 (Cesnola 1878, 181), shows that he visited the village earlier than the year 1872, and that he was familiar with the villagers and the surrounding area.

The position of the village coincides with his description. The few houses of the small community of about 80 inhabitants, were concentrated on the low hill of *Pithkiavli*[4] above two small churches of Agios Damianos and Agios Constantinos Alamanos[5] situated on its southern edge. The two churches of the medieval settlement were replaced in 1901 by the new church of Agios Constantinos Alamanos that we see today (Fig. 5.6). Contrary to the precise location of the village, Cesnola's description of the find spot of archaeological finds is disputable. He writes: 'In the centre of a triangle formed by the villages of Ormidia, Timbo, and Afgoro, I discovered a very extensive burying-ground, which yielded the largest and most highly decorated vases found in Cyprus. The tombs are of a very ancient date. In 1870–71 and 1875 I undertook some systematic explorations at this place, but without finding the slightest traces either of temples or ancient habitations' (Cesnola 1878, 181).

As far as we know, no tomb groups have been recorded in the centre of the triangle between Ormideia, Xylotymbou and Avgorou. Also, on present evidence, all the known burial grounds of Ormideia are located, either in the valley, or on the slopes of the hillocks around the hill of *Pithkiavli*, and closer to the sea. As we will see, there are two main possible areas for Cesnola's cemeteries, not excluding the possibility that he collected his finds from many different areas in the valley and even around his summer house. The localities *Limni* (CS 1464, Cadastral Plan XLI 22 W2) and *Tsifliki* (CS 1465, Cadastral Plan XLI 22 W2) near the house are recorded in the Cyprus Survey Fieldbooks as Geometric necropoleis. Also, at the locality *Ambeli* (MLA 987–91 and MLA 1364, Cadastral Plan XLI 22 W1), the low hill opposite the house to the west (Fig. 5.7),[6] Hellenistic tombs have been excavated (Flourentzos 1990).

Antiquities excavated by Luigi Palma di Cesnola in the area of Ormideia are published and illustrated by himself (Cesnola 1878 and 1894), but also by many others, who were interested in his amazing discoveries (Perrot and Chipiez 1885, 297, fig. 231, 299 fig. 234, 302 fig. 239 and 308, fig. 247; Myres 1914, 76–101).[7] Most of the finest examples date from the Cypro-Geometric III and Cypro-Archaic I periods. Among them there are handmade terracotta figurines representing human figures, such as bearded men holding animals in their arms (Cesnola 1894, pls

VIII:55, 63), tambourine players (Cesnola 1894, pl. VIII:57–8), female figures with uplifted arms (Cesnola 1894, pl. XII:86–91), warriors holding shields (Cesnola 1894, pl. XXXI:257, 259), a man riding a donkey (Cesnola 1894, pl. LXXII:652), as well as horses (Cesnola 1894, pl. LXXI:645–46), double-necked and -headed horses (Cesnola 1894, pl. LXX:643–44), horses-and-riders (Cesnola 1894, pls LXIX:633, LXXI:647–49, LXXII:651, 654), an ape riding a donkey (Cesnola 1894, pl. LXXI:650), a sitting bear (Cesnola 1894, pl. XXVII:219) and a bear holding a vessel (Cesnola 1894, pl. XXVII:221), all recorded as coming from tombs. Very interesting are the two terracottas representing human figures holding or wearing masks (Cesnola 1894, pl. VIII:60 and pl. XXVII:217 respectively). Of great interest is the ceramic material, which, if it is correctly assigned by Cesnola to this area, indicates that in the Cypro-Geometric and Cypro-Archaic periods the land of Ormideia was occupied by thriving communities. The finest examples are a large elaborately decorated amphorae with geometric motifs on neck (Cesnola 1894, pls CX:873–74; CXI:878–881) and floral motifs on the neck and the shoulder (Cesnola 1878, 181 and 1894, pl. CXII:882–85; Perrot and Chipiez 1885, 287, fig. 231; Myres 1914, 86–7), a stemmed bowls with floral motifs and pictorial representations (Cesnola 1894, pl. CXV:896–97, 899–900; Karageorghis and de Gagniers 1974, 280 XXV.a.11), an oinochoe with geometric decoration (Cesnola 1894, pl. CXXII:927–30), pictorial representations of birds (Cesnola 1894, pls CXXVI:948, CXXVIII:956–60, CXXX:966–70), human figures, fish, animals and a boat (Cesnola 1894, pl. CXXIX:961–65; Karageorghis and de Gagniers 1974, 66, VII.5), as well as amphoriskoi with rich floral motifs and pictorial representations of birds (Cesnola 1894, pls CXV:898, CXVIII:910, 912–13, CXXI:922–25, CXXIII:931–35, CXXXI:971–75) and other vases with rich geometric and floral decoration (Cesnola 1878, 181 and 1894, pl. CXVIII:909). Among the most interesting pieces is the famous Ormideia amphora in the Metropolitan Museum of Art with a pictorial representation of two enthroned female deities (Perrot and Chipiez 1885, 308, fig. 247; Karageorghis and de Gagniers 1974, 10–11), which can be compared with the Hubbard amphora (Karageorghis and de Gagniers 1974, 6–9); an oinochoe depicting horse-and-rider (Karageorghis and de Gagniers 1974, 16–17, 1.2), which has a close parallel of unknown provenance (Myres 1914, 99, fig. 768), although there are also representations of horses-and-riders from Dekelia (Karageorghis and de Gagniers 1974, 20, I.5) and Aradippou (Karageorghis and de Gagniers 1974, 18–19, I.3); an amphora with a bird eating a fish depicts a typical design of the eastern part of the island (Karageorghis and de Gagniers 1974, 269, XXIV.b.46). It is obvious that most of the vases, assigned by Cesnola to Ormideia, represent the best examples of the production characteristic of the eastern part of the island, which has a long tradition and appears in the areas of Karpasia, but also in the surroundings of Kition and the areas along the south-west coast, not very far from Kition. Some examples from the last area, apart from the vases from Ormideia, are an oinochoe from Dekelia (Karageorghis and de Gagniers 1989, 41, SXVI.3), an amphora from Pyla (Karageorghis and de Gagniers 1974, 48–49, VI.2) and the famous bowl from Achna (Karageorghis and de Gagniers 1974, 91–92, VIII.16). Thus the area of Ormideia, as the centre of a wider area, where pictorial representations on vases were for a long time the preference of the local people, must have played an important role in the production and distribution of this luxurious class of pottery.

Nevertheless, despite the above picture, a question arises as to whether all the material assigned by Cesnola to Ormideia was really found in the area of this village. These doubts concern mainly the amphoriskoi, which have their parallels in amphoriskoi from Idalion, some illustrated by Cesnola on the same plates (Cesnola 1885, pl. CXXI: 926 from Idalion). Similar amphoriskoi from Idalion, excavated by the Swedish Cyprus Expedition, in a stratified settlement context at the top of the hill of Ampileri (Gjerstad *et al.* 1935, pls CLXII, CLXIII), indicate that this material was most probably produced in local workshops at Idalion and, apart from the finds from Ormideia, there is no other evidence for its distribution in other areas of the island. These observations lead us to assume that, most probably, the Ormideia finds in the Cesnola collection were mixed up with material from Idalion.

However, although the area of Ormideia is not one of the most important archaeological sites of the island, and relatively few antiquities from this area have been recorded in recent years, a considerable amount of pottery, comparable to Cesnola's finds, has been discovered. This material was found at a number of localities in the narrow valley and the surrounding hills, and indicate that the area was continuously inhabited from the Cypro-Geometric II period.

The localities *Limni, Tsifliki, Ambeli* and *Meridji*, mentioned above, produced Cypro-Geometric, Hellenistic and medieval material. At the locality *Konizero* (Cadastral Plan XLI 22 W1) on the slope of the hill west of *Ambeli* (Fig. 5.8) a tomb of the Cypro-Archaic I period has been excavated (M LA 1182, Tomb 1). The most interesting finds are a large amphora with elaborate geometric motifs on the neck and shoulder, a stemmed bowl with floral motifs, and a Phoenician bowl illustrated by Karageorghis (1985, 922, figs. 66–68). To the same tomb also belongs an amphora of Black-on-Red II (IV) ware (Fig. 5.9). A barrel-shaped jug with concentric circles, now in the Cyprus Museum (CM 1961/V-5/1), comes from the same locality.

From the locality *Chalitiki Gi* (Cadastral Plan XLI 22 E1), on the slopes of the north hills east of the village (Fig. 5.10), two accidental discoveries, a cooking pot and a large amphora of Bichrome IV ware, are recorded in the Larnaca District Museum (M LA 1702, Fig. 5.11). At the locality *Koutsopetri* (Cadastral Plan XLI 14 W1), on the slopes of the north hills west of the village (Fig. 5.12), a tomb of the Cypro-Archaic I-II period has been excavated (M LA 1534, Tomb 3/1–11). The earliest material in the whole area of Ormideia comes from a cemetery at the locality *Louri* (Cadastral Plan XLI 14 W2), which is also situated on the north slopes, west of the locality *Koutsopetri* (Fig. 5.13). Ceramic material collected from two looted tombs (M LA 1539 (CS 2110) Tomb 1/1–6 and M LA 1540 (CS 2137), Tomb 2/1–7) dates the cemetery to the Cypro-Geometric II–III and Cypro-Archaic I periods. Typical of the finds is a large amphora of White Painted II ware (Fig. 5.14) and a stemmed bowl of Bichrome III ware (Fig. 5.15). Rich material dating from the Late Roman and Early Christian periods has been also found at the locality *Agios Georgios Angonas*, near the medieval church, north of the village, between Ormideia and Avgorou (M LA 1396, Tomb 1/1–218). Around the church, the remains of a settlement and of the installation of an olive-oil press are still visible. A plot of land with medieval silos, and looted tombs of the Cypro-Archaic period, have also been located by the writer at the locality *Vattena*. The first lies in a field north of the refugees' camp, and the second is situated further west, next to the bend of the asphalt road leading to Xylotymbou, on the boundaries of the two villages.

The investigation of recent discoveries from Ormideia shows that none of the above-mentioned localities corresponds to Cesnola's description of the findspot of his discoveries. The only area which more or less coincides with Cesnola's 'burying-ground' is the locality *Lacsha tou Solomou* (Cadastral Plan XLI 14 W1), a small valley to the north-west of the centre of the modern village (Fig. 5.16). There are no recorded tombs from this place, but scattered sherds on the surface indicate the existence of a cemetery. Peristianis (1927, 180–81) in 1912 collected two interesting inscriptions in the Cypro-Syllabic script, published by Masson (1961, 307–309), from here. The silver plaque, depicting a stag in relief (Peristianis 1927, 181; Masson 1961, 308, pl. LIII), tells us that Αγαθοκρέων was the artist who produced this piece of art. These objects indicate the existence of a settlement or a sanctuary in this locality. Other evidence for the existence of a sanctuary in the area of Ormideia are the terracotta figurines with uplifted arms found by Cesnola (Cesnola 1894, pl. XII:86–91) and those excavated by Ohnefalsch-Richter (1893, 12, no. 15; Myres and Ohnefalsch-Richter 1899, 10) in 1882.

The main Cypro-Geometric and Cypro-Archaic settlement, as well as the main cemetery of Ormideia, most probably lie in the centre of the village (Fig. 5.6). In 1991 at the locality *Lakkos Glykys* (Fig. 5.17), west of the hill of *Pithkiavli*, architectural remains of a public building were uncovered during a rescue excavation conducted in the yard of a modern house (Fig. 5.18, plot 672) under the supervision of the writer.[8] According to the very few diagnostic sherds (M LA 1572, Figs 5.19–5.20), this structure (Fig. 5.21), which was built of very large hewn limestone blocks (Fig. 5.22–5.23), dates to the Hellenistic and Roman period. The Hellenistic tombs mentioned above, and recently excavated at the locality *Ambeli*, at a distance of about 500 m south of *Lakkos Glykys*, may represent the cemetery of the settlement.

Although the available material dates the settlement to the Hellenistic and Roman periods, the little earlier material indicate that the areas of *Pithkiavli* and *Lakkos Glykys* were inhabited already in the Cypro-Geometric and Cypro-Archaic periods. Information from local builders about walls, terracotta figurines and tombs, found during the construction of the modern houses, helped us to estimate the extent of both the settlement and the cemetery (Fig. 5.18). According to the same information, a tomb containing rich material, including vases with floral motifs and pictorial representations, was recently found during the construction of a house built just below the higher hill, where the elementary school is situated (Fig. 5.18, plot 203). This tomb was looted before the Department of Antiquities realized its existence. A saucer-shaped lamp from this tomb is now recorded in the Larnaka District Museum (M LA 1680, Fig. 5.24). We believe that this area, which at the time of Cesnola was the centre of the village, was also the centre of his interest, and for some reason he avoided mentioning the exact find spots of his discoveries.

Nor do both Cesnolas mention the name of the owner of their summer house, who was a member of a noble family of the time. Also their relations with the owners remain unknown, since they do not explain whether they rented the house or were the owners' guests. This behaviour is understandable from what we know of Luigi Palma Cesnola, who systematically avoids giving the names of his friends and collaborators in Cyprus. More enigmatic remains the attitude of Alexander, who often speaks about his good relations with local personalities, such as Demetrios Pierides and the Bishop and the Archimandrite of Larnaka (Cesnola 1884, page xvi).

An engraving of the house (Fig. 5.25) is included in the second edition of Alexander Cesnola's *Salaminia* (Cesnola 1884, page xi). One can only recognize the house from the word 'Ormidia' at the bottom of the picture. The engraving itself, the information given by local older people and the toponyms *Tsifliki* and *Kousoulato*, the Consulate, used today by the villagers to denote Cesnolas' summer residence, indicate that the house was situated exactly on the area described by Luigi Palma Cesnola. The house is also marked on the Cadastral Plan XLI 22 W2 (Fig. 5.26, Plot 398) surveyed by the Department of Lands and Surveys in 1922 (revised in 1970). Its proximity to the sea-shore, according to Cesnola, gave them the advantage of land and sea breezes and a new pleasure to his wife and little daughters, who used to amuse themselves by collecting tiny sea-shells (Cesnola 1878, 179). It is doubtful whether Cesnola's romantic description of the house mirrors the reality, since it was situated not very far from the marshy area at the locality *Lacsha* (Figs 5.7 and 5.26).

The owner of the house at the time of Cesnola was the merchant Nicolaos Vontizianos (Koudounaris 1972, 29), the nephew of Antonios Vontizianos, who was one of the most powerful men of the island. The estate initially belonged to Antonios Vontizianos, a nobleman of the Ionian island of Cephalonia, who came to Cyprus in 1755 and became Chancellor of the English Consulate in Larnaka (Koudounaris 1972, 13–14). He had very good relations with the Archibishop and the Dragoman (interpreter) Hadjigeorgakis Cornesios, and his daughter Iouliani married the son of the Dragoman Giangos Georgiades (Koudounaris 1972, 14). Antonios Vontizianos adopted his nephew Nicolaos, who came from Kefalonia in 1827, and gave him the estate in Ormideia. At the time of Cesnola, Nicolaos Vontizianos had three sons and one daughter of about 20–30 years old (Koudounaris 1972–29), most probably all living in the house in Ormideia. Two of his sons, Giangos and Pericles Vontizianos, between 1890 and 1906, became members of Parliament (Koudounaris 1972, 29 and 1991, 32). The house was always in the hands of the family. Around 1970 it was demolished and replaced by a modern house for one of the family female descendants.

Another important member of the community of Ormideia, who is mentioned by name and even illustrated by Cesnola (1878, 180), is the Greek priest Papapetros (Fig. 5.27). The reason why he is the only person illustrated in his book is because Cesnola found it remarkable that the Greek priest, who worked in the fields like the peasants, used to wear a conical cap similar to that worn the statues from Golgoi. From this comparison he saw not only a continuation of the tradition from the priests of Aphrodite, but also a resemblance between the features of the priest and those of the statues. Further he mentions that the priest was called Papa Petro, and describes how he managed to photograph him in his working clothes.

Nothing is known about the birthplace of the priest. According to older people from Ormideia, he perhaps came from the village of Derinia near Famagusta in the middle of the nineteenth century and, as a religious young person, he helped with the religious ceremonies in the church. Soon afterwards he became the priest of the community, and he died at the beginning of the twentieth century.[9] Information given by older local people that the priest was one of the persons who distributed goods, such as flour and wheat, by which Cesnola rewarded the poor villagers collecting antiquities, indicates good relations between the two men. Also, according to Cesnola (1878, 182–83), the nephew of the Greek priest was his guide during his visit to the Cape Pyla, the Xylophagou watch-tower and the cave Makaria in the surroundings of Ormideia and Xylophagou.

Thus the examination of both the Cesnolas' relations with nature and the people of Ormideia, a place where they spent much of their time in Cyprus, helps in understanding the policy they used in their effort to collect as much as possible of the antiquities of the island. Undoubtedly the antiquities collected from this village proved to be a real treasure for them. Both Cesnolas' finds and the later discoveries indicate that the area of Ormideia, despite both Cesnolas' and Ohnefalsch-Richter's acitivities, remains a promising unexploited ground for archaeological exploration.

Notes

1. I wish to express my warmest thanks to E. Masson for providing me with Olivier Masson's notes about Ormideia soon after the 22nd British Museum Classical Colloquium. It is a text of three pages with footnotes discussing the position and the name of the village.
2. 'CS' is the abbreviation of the Cyprus Survey and indicates the inventory numbers of the finds recorded in the Cyprus Survey Fieldbooks.
3. 'M LA' is the abbreviation of the Larnaka District Museum and indicates the inventory numbers of antiquities found in the District of Larnaka and stored in the above mentioned museum.
4. Pithkiavli is not marked on the Cadastral Plan, surveyed by the Department of Lands and Surveys in 1922 (Revised 1970). This toponym is used only by the villagers to denote the position of the original village of Ormideia between the church of Agios Constantinos and the elementary school to the north (Fig. 5.6).
5. Agios Constantinos Alamanos is called by Makhairas (1932, 30) στρατιώτης, which means the soldier. A late twelfth-century painting of a local soldier-saint, with the inscription 'the junior from Ormidia' was found between 1975 and 1980 on the south-east pier supporting the dome of the church of St. Anthony in Kellia village, which lies about 8 km north-east of Larnaka and about 20 km west of Ormideia (Stylianou 1985, 437).
6. Cesnola's summer house was situated in the plot where the two modern houses appear in the front of the picture on Fig. 5.7.
7. For further references see Masson 1961, 307, n.2.
8. I express my thanks to the staff of the drawing office, the photographic archive and the photographic studio of the Cyprus Museum for the drawings and the illustrations, as well as to G. Christou of the Cyprus Museum and A. Savva

of the Larnaka District Museum for their help and co-operation. Thanks are also due to Alison Todd and Veronica Tatton-Brown for their revision of the English text.

9. Priest Papapetros married Milia from Xylophagou, who gave him three sons, Antonios, Iakovos and Hadjicostis, and two daughters, Louiza and Eleni. The family today consists of more than two hundred persons, most of them living in Ormideia. His last grandson is Petros Papapetros, the son of Hadjicostis, who is 85 years old. He married Chrysi Theodorou from Pyla, and has seven children. As an active member of the community, he became the first elected president of the community of Ormideia in 1979, which he held until his retirement in 1989.

Bibliography

Cesnola 1884: Alexander Palma di Cesnola, *Salaminia (Cyprus). The History, Treasures and Antiquities* (2nd ed., London).

Cesnola 1878: Luigi Palma di Cesnola, *Cyprus: Its Ancient Cities, Tombs and Temples* (New York, reprinted Limassol 1991).
1894: *A Descriptive Atlas of the Cesnola Collection of Cypriote Antiquities in the Metropolitan Museum of Art, New York* Vol. II (New York).

Flourentzos 1990: P. Flourentzos, 'A Hellenistic tomb from Ormidhia', *RDAC* (1990) 169–172.

Gjerstad, Lindros, Sjöqvist and Westholm 1935: E. Gjerstad, J. Lindros, E. Sjöqvist and A. Westholm, *The Swedish Cyprus Expedition, Vol. 2: Finds and Results in the excavations in Cyprus 1927–1931* (2 vols, Stockholm).

Goodwin 1977: J. Goodwin, *A Toponymy of Cyprus* (2nd ed., Nicosia).

Karageorghis 1985: V. Karageorghis, 'Chronique des fouilles et découvertes archéologiques à Chypre en 1984', *BCH* 109 (1985) 897–967.

Karageorghis and De Gagniers 1974: V. Karageorghis and J. De Gagniers, *La Ceramique chypriote de style figure, Age du fer (1050–500 av. J.-C.)* (Roma).
1979: *Le ceramique chypriote de style figure, Age du fer (1050–500 av. J.-C.). Supplement* (Roma).

Koudounaris 1972: A. Koudounaris, Μερικαί Παλαιαί Οικογένειαι της Κύπρου (Nicosia).
1991: Βιογραφικόν Λεξικόν Κυπρίων *1800–1920* (Nicosia).

Machairas 1932: L. Machairas, 'Recital concerning the Sweet Land of Cyprus entitled "Chronicle"', in R.M. Dawkins (ed.) *Volume* I (Oxford).

Masson 1961: O. Masson, *Les inscriptions chypriotes syllabiques* (Paris).

Myres 1914: J.L. Myres, *Handbook of the Cesnola Collection of Antiquities from Cyprus* (New York).

Myres and Ohnefalsch-Richter 1899: J.L. Myres and M. Ohnefalsch-Richter, *A Catalogue of the Cyprus Museum* (Oxford).

Ohnefalsch-Richter 1893: M.H. Ohnefalsch-Richter, Kypros, the Bible and Homer (trans. from German by W.R. Paton, E. Sellers and others, London).

Peristianis 1927: I.K. Peristianis, 'Η Άρτεμις Ελαφήβολος Κυνηγέτις', Κυπριακά Χρονικά 7, 163–192.

Perrot and Chipiez 1885: G. Perrot and C. Chipiez, *History of Art in Phoenicia and its Dependencies, Vol* II (edited and trans. from French by B.A.W. Armstrong, London).

Sternini 1998: M. Sternini, *La collezione di antichita di Alessandro Palma di Cesnola* (Bari).

Stylianou 1980: A. and J. Stylianou, *The History of the Cartography of Cyprus* (Nicosia).

Stylianou 1985: A. and J. Stylianou, *The Painted Churches of Cyprus. Treasures of Byzantine Art* (London)

Fig. 5.1: The village of Ormideia, facing north.

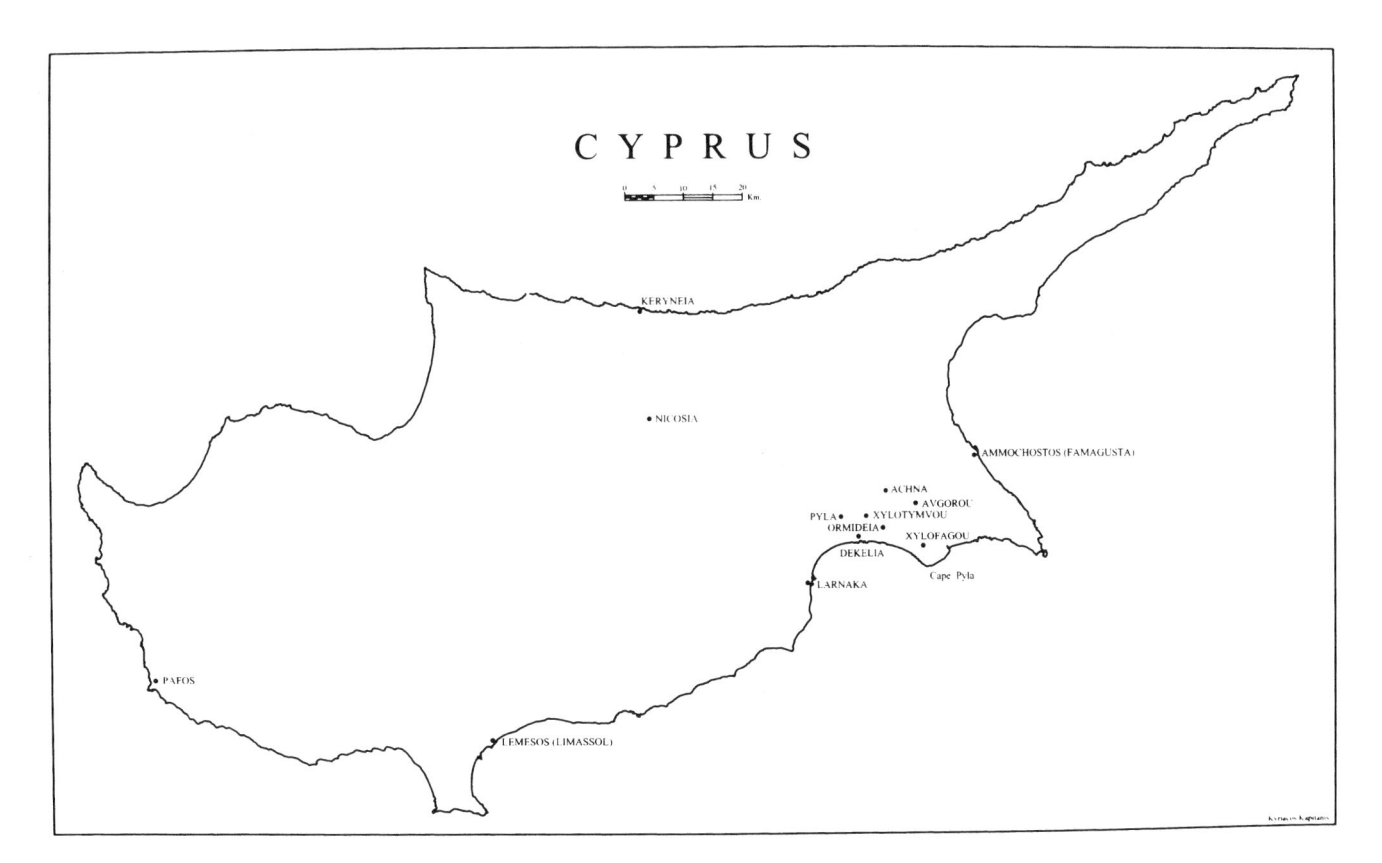

Fig. 5.2: Map of Cyprus showing the area of Ormideia and the surrounding villages mentioned in the text.

Fig. 5.3: The rocky shore of Ormideia, with many small bays, facing east.

Fig. 5.4: The small harbour for fishing boats called Romantzo, facing southeast.

Fig. 5.5: The narrow opening to the sea south of the village, facing south.

Fig. 5.6: The locality Pithkiavli between the church of Agios Constantinos and the elementary school to the north, facing north.

Fig. 5.7: The localities Tsifliki, Limni, Ambeli and Lacsha. Cesnola's summer residence was situated in the plot where are now the two houses in the front of the picture, facing west.

Fig. 5.8: The locality Konizero in the background, facing south.

Fig. 5.9: Jug of Black-on-Red II (IV) ware from the locality Konizero (Tomb 1/9).

Fig. 5.10: The locality Chalitiki Gi, facing east.

Fig. 5.11: Large amphora of Bichrome IV ware from the locality Chalitiki Gi (M LA 1702).

Fig. 5.12: The locality Koutsopetri, facing north.

Fig. 5.13: The locality Louri, facing north.

Fig. 5.15: Stemmed bowl of Bichrome III ware from the locality Louri (Tomb 1/5).

Fig. 5.14: Large amphora of White Painted II ware from the locality Louri (Tomb 2/1).

Fig. 5.16: The locality Lacsha to Solomou in the background, facing north.

Fig. 5.17: The locality Lakkos Glykys below the hill with the elementary school, facing north.

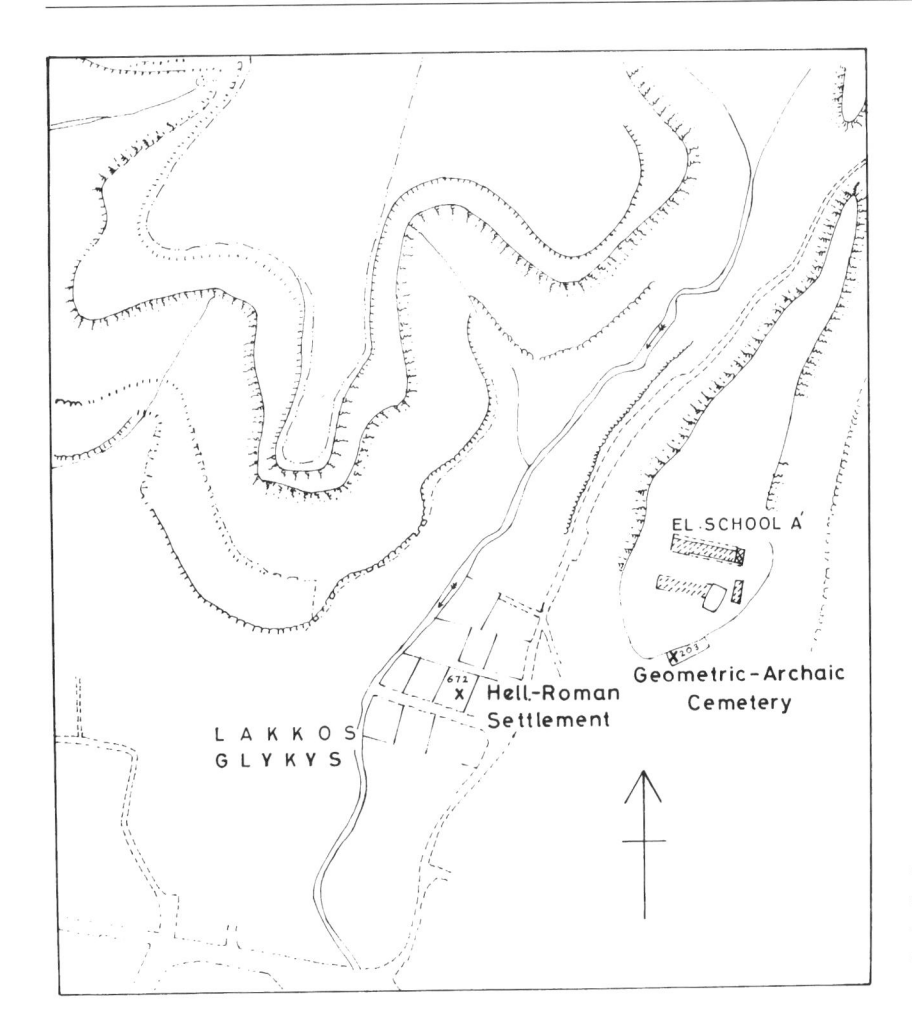

Fig. 5.18: Extract from the Cadastral Plan showing the position of the settlement and the cemetery at the localities Lakkos Glykys and Pithkiavli.

Fig. 5.19: Fragments of pottery of the Hellenistic and Roman periods from the rescue excavation at the locality Lakkos Glykys.

Fig. 5.20: Fragments of large amphoras of the Hellenistic Period from the rescue excavation at Lakkos Glykys.

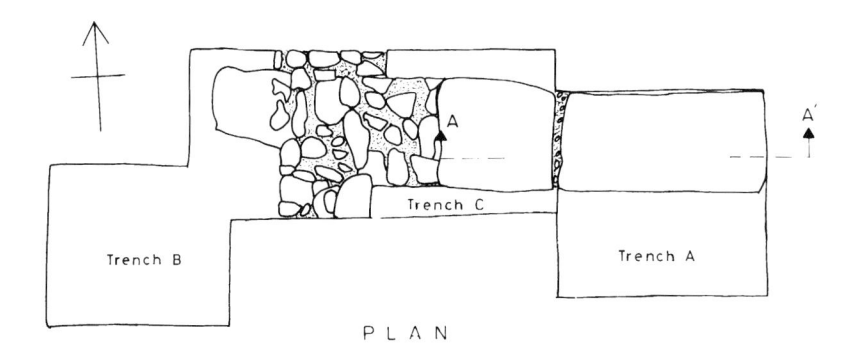

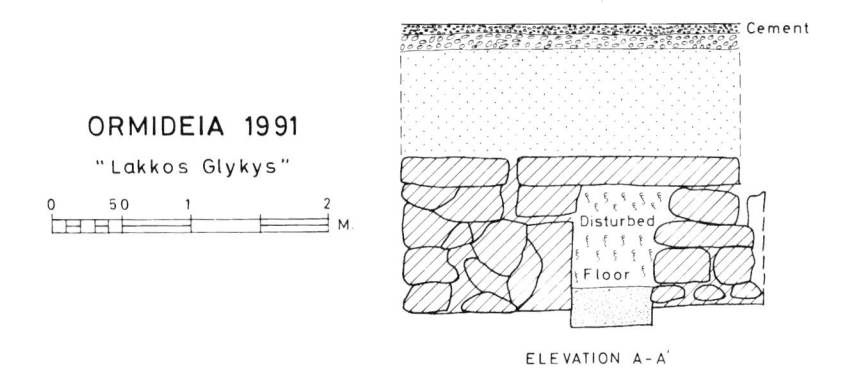

Fig. 5.21: Drawing of the excavated walls at the locality Lakkos Glykys.

Fig. 5.22: The excavated walls at the locality lakkos Glykys, facing west.

Fig. 5.23: Very large hewn blocks with plaster on the wall of a public building excavated at the locality of Lakkos Glykys, facing north.

Fig. 5.24: Saucer-shaped lamp from a looted tomb found on the south slopes of the hill where the elementary school is situated.

Fig. 5.25: Engraving of the Cesnola's summer residence in Ormideia.

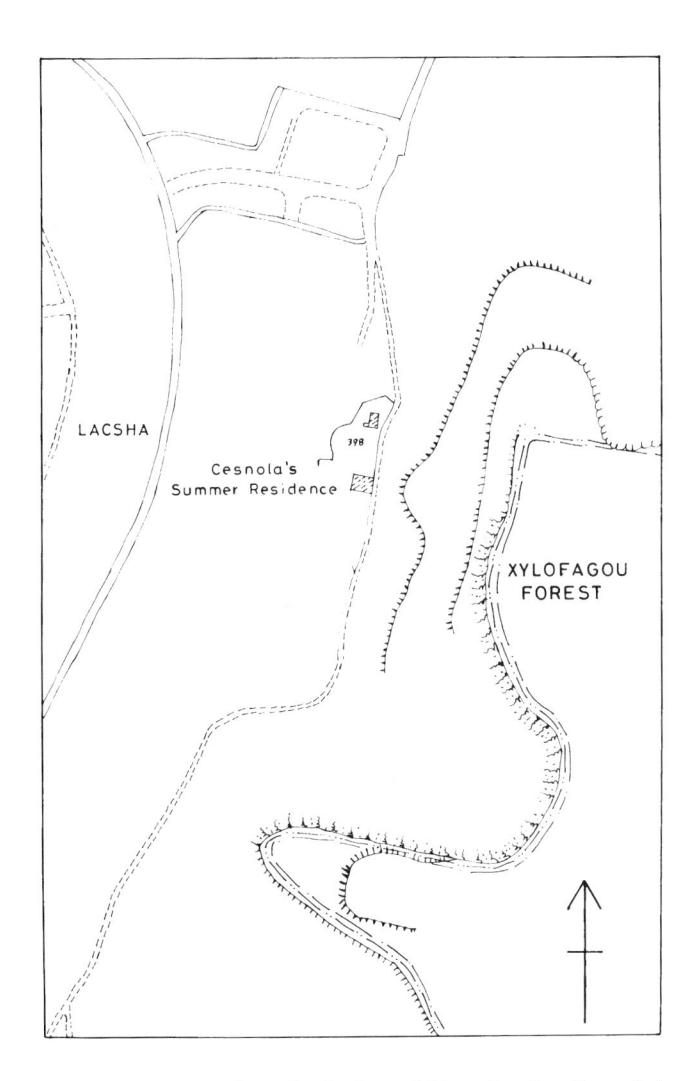

Fig. 5.26: Extract from the Cadastral Plan showing Cesnola's summer residence.

Fig. 5.27: The Greek Priest Papapetros and the head of a statue from Golgoi.

6. From Hammer von Purgstall to F. B. Welch. The archaeology of Old Paphos, 1802–1899

Franz Georg Maier

Fact, fancy and fiction: all that occurs in the archaeology of Old Paphos, as Palaipaphos was called in the nineteenth century. There is plenty of fiction – in Hammer von Purgstall's imaginative description 'der Nachtfeyer der Geburt der Göttinn',[1] or in Cesnola's account of his digging in the temple. There is fancy as well – take Mrs. Lewis' tale of 1893: 'We reached Kouklia, the insignificant clay village which represents old Paphos ...and were conducted to a fine floor of tesselated pavement, designed in stars and wavy lines of beautifully coloured marbles, red, blue, yellow, brown, and white; once the floor of the south stoa of the great temple of Venus. Here luncheon had been laid out for us by the servant of the Commissioner of Papho. That gentleman rode up almost immediately after, and at once administered a most effectual restorative in a draught of foaming light champagne'.[2]

But there are facts also – for instance the interesting fact that we owe our first precise information about the ruins of Palaipaphos to the Royal Navy, at least indirectly. The Navy's contribution to archaeology is often underrated. H.M. ships did not only transport private collections of antiquities (and sometimes lose them at sea). The Navy had captains such as Spratt who assiduously copied inscriptions in the Greek islands (but drove a worried editor of *Inscriptiones Graecae* to the remark 'Sprattius qui quod vidit minime intellexit'). There was also Commodore Sidney Smith – of whom more below.

The archaeology of nineteenth-century Palaipaphos begins with the activities of scholarly travellers. The ruins south of the village of Kouklia had been identified as the Sanctuary of the Paphian Aphrodite by the Swiss Ludwig Tschudi in 1519 and by the Venetian Francesco Attar around 1540.[3] Yet this rediscovery hardly stirred the curiosity of otherwise well-informed travellers. While the inhabitants of Kouklia seem to have been busy to exploit their antiquities,[4] travellers until the end of the eighteenth century tended to dismiss the monuments of Palaipaphos as 'great heaps of ruins' or the like.[5]

Commodore Sir William Sidney Smith changed all that. This colourful character was – to quote Sir George Hill – 'a remarkable, brilliant but sometimes absurd and eccentric Englishman'.[6] Smith became famous in 1799 when he raised the siege of Acre that Napoleon was conducting. This success seems to have gone to his head: under a dubious pretext, and much to the chagrin of his superiors, he embarked upon a policy of his own in the Levant. In the course of these actions his 80-gun ship of the line, the 'Tigre', anchored at Katopaphos on 10 August 1802, to load oxen as provisions.

Sir Sidney's secretary was a young Austrian Oriental scholar, Joseph von Hammer-Purgstall; the stay of the 'Tigre' at Katopaphos gave him an opportunity to visit Palaipaphos.[7] In his book, *Topographische Ansichten gesammelt auf einer Reise in die Levante*, Hammer conveys the impression that he spent considerable time there. Yet, according to his memoirs, published long after his death, he went to Kouklia only on two days. As the ride from Katopaphos took him some three hours, the time left to investigate the ruins must be measured by hours. On a third day the Navy assisted Hammer in rescuing antiquities: 'Auf meine Bitte bewilligte mir Sir Sidney das grosse Schiffsboot und die nötige, mit Hauen und Spitzbeilen versehene Bemannung, um ein von mir entdecktes, wohlerhaltenes Stück Mosaikfussbodens auszugraben und es mit einigen Inschriftsteinen an Bord zu bringen. Keith und Bromley fuhren mit. Bromley wusste alles besser und legte überall mit Hand an. Ich glaube, er hatte an diesem Nachmittag zu viel Port oder Claret im Kopf. Er hieb schonungslos in das Mosaik und hatte es bald ganz zertrümmert. Ich war über diese Barbarei sehr aufgebracht, er lachte mich aber nur

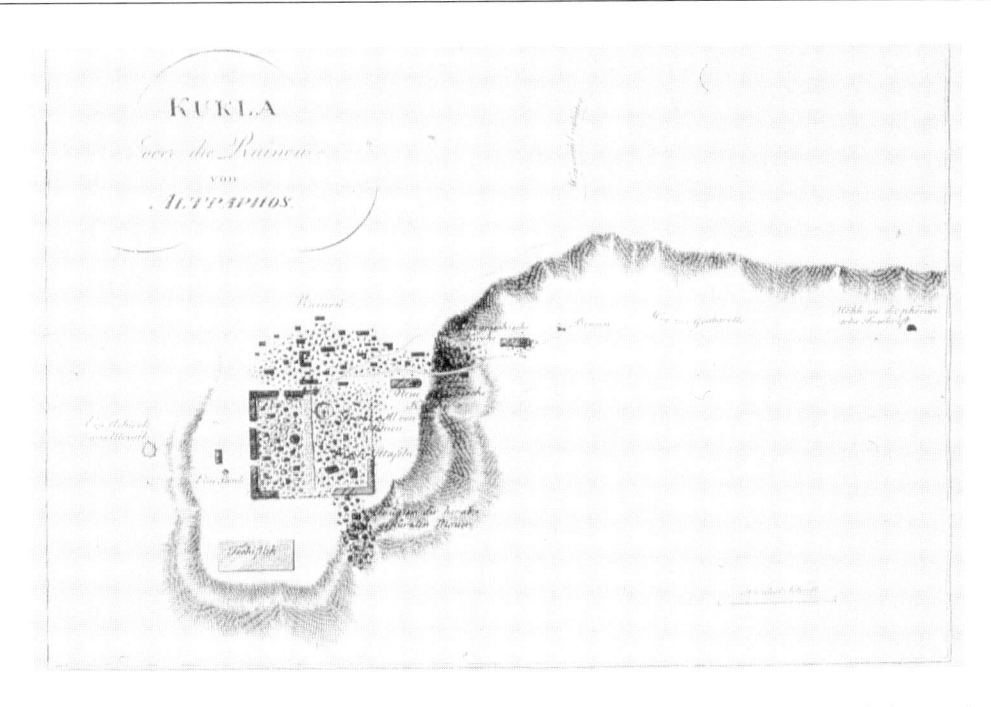

Fig. 6.1: Plan of Old Paphos: J. v. Hammer-Purgstall, Topographische Ansichten gesammelt auf einer Reise in die Levante *(Wien 1811) 150.*

aus. Am folgenden Morgen brachten wir ein Stück Getäfel mit zwei Inschriftsteinen und zwei grosse Stücke des Mosaik an Bord des "Tiger". Der grössere der beiden Steine (Topographische Ansichten Nr.50) wurde von Sir Sidney verschenkt, der kleinere aus rotem Marmor (Nr.49) befindet sich im Kaiserlichen Antikenkabinett in Wien'.[8]

Hammer was the first scholarly traveller to observe and to describe in some detail the ruins at Palaipaphos which Pococke had by-passed 'ohne dieselben zu untersuchen', and to publish a sketch plan of the remains (Fig. 6.1). 'Die Ruinen des alten und berühmten Tempels Aphroditens' he found to be 'ein ununterbrochener Schutthaufen' – 'ungeheuere Steinblöcke zwey bis drey Klaftern lang' of the Temenos wall; damaged statue bases, columns, cornices, and inscriptions; fragments of mosaic floors with geometric patterns of grey, green and red tesserae. Hammer also noted the large holes in the blocks of the Temenos wall and suggested that they served for the transmission of oracles – an improbable interpretation which nonetheless found much favour with later visitors to the site.

Passing over 'andere Ruinen ... hinter denen des Tempels auf der Anhöhe', Hammer devotes some space to two other monuments. Near the mouth of the Diarrhizos he observed in the locality Kouklia-Styllarka, in front of two monoliths, a pit filled with architectural fragments which he thought to represent 'die Reste eines alten und grossen Tempels' near the harbour of Palaipaphos. Incidentally, many travellers were intrigued by the possible religious properties of these monoliths – until S. Hadjisavvas proved them to be an oil mill.[9]

A second point of interest was the large rock-cut Classical chamber tomb in the locality Arkalon east of present-day Kouklia, known as 'Spilaion tis Regainas'. To Hammer we owe the first record of this monument of outstanding interest. He managed to crawl into the tomb through 'eine kleine Oeffnung, durch die man von oben hinab schlieft' at the top of the filled-in dromos and found 'eine Grabstätte derselben Art und Form, wie die bey Neu-Paphos oder Baffa beschriebenen ... Der grosse Marmorblock, der das Todtengemach im Grunde verschloss, ist im Vorgemache an die Wand gelehnt, und eine phönicische Inschrift mit spannlangen Buchstaben darein gehauen ... In den Seitenkammern des Vorgemachs ist nichts als Staub und Würmer übrig'. Hammer copied and published the inscription.[10] His report proves that the Arkalon tomb had been looted fairly thoroughly already by this time.[11]

Only four years later, in 1806, another learned traveller appeared at Kouklia: the slightly mysterious Spaniard Domingo Badia y Leiblich, calling himself Ali Bey al Abbassi (Fig. 6.2).[12] The ruins of the sanctuary, especially the Temenos wall, aroused his curiosity and admiration: 'this colossal work appears to have been raised by gigantic hands. I could hardly believe my eyes'. Ali Bey was the

Fig. 6.2: View of Kouklia (Old Paphos): Travels of Ali Bey in Morocco, Tripoli, Cyprus, Egypt, Arabia, Syria, and Turkey between the years 1803 and 1807 *Vol. I (London 1816) pl. XXXIII.*

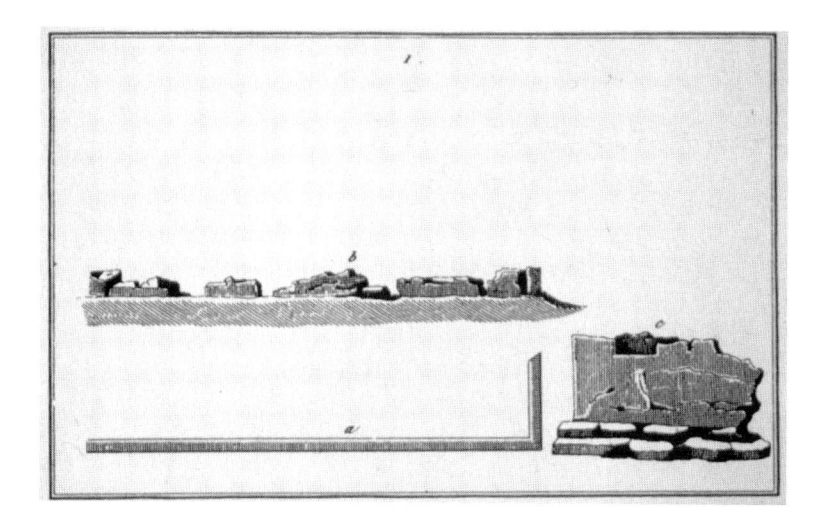

Fig. 6.3: Plan and elevations of the Temenos wall of the Sanctuary of Aphrodite: Travels of Ali Bey *Vol. I, pl. XXXIV 1.*

first traveller who had a plan and two elevations of the Temenos wall drawn (Fig. 6.3): they demonstrate that the wall was practically in the same condition in 1806 as it is today. Ali Bey was also shown 'upon the middle of a hill two spots newly discovered, where were fine mosaic pavements. Each spot was about three feet diameter. I am surprised that some amateur of the fine arts has not discovered the rest, since the coat of earth which covers them is only some inches thick'. As appears from his description, these mosaic fragments – most likely those noted already by Hammer – were situated in the sanctuary itself or in the adjacent Roman peristyle house.

Ali Bey also briefly describes medieval buildings at Kouklia. The ruins near the temple 'which appear to have belonged to the middle age, upon which may be seen inscriptions, bas-reliefs, and some paintings in fresco, of very good colouring' were most likely to have been remains of the cane sugar installations on the sanctuary site. The 'ancient palace, situated upon a high hill..., composed of a large courtyard, surrounded with stables, and storehouses' certainly represents the Royal Manor House. This is the first reference to the Lusignan building after Iodokus von Meggen in 1541.[13]

Subsequent travellers, learned or otherwise, mention the Temple ruins, the 'Spilaion', and the monoliths.[14] They rarely add to our knowledge of Paphian archaeology, but sometimes a piece of relevant information creeps in. Thus Friedrich von Löher records in 1878: 'Auf des höchsten Hügels Spitze fand man ebenfalls Reste von Mauerwerk. Es wurde ringsherum in die Tiefe gegraben, und da ergab sich, dass es blos ein viereckiger Thurm war, der weit in das Erdreich hinein ging. Mit grosser Mühe wurde nun eine Seite des Thurms ganz weggeschafft, doch die gehofften Schätze kamen nicht zum Vorschein'. There can hardly be any doubt that the Koukliotes then quarried the palatial building on Hadji Abdullah (Site KB). Excavations in 1952–53 proved indeed that stone robbers had taken off completely the ashlar blocks of the north wall.[15]

The arrival of the professional archaeologist marks the beginning of a second phase in the archaeology of nineteenth-century Palaipaphos. On 12 March 1845, Ludwig Ross, having recently lost his chair of Archaeology in the University of Athens, rode from Pissouri to Yeroskipos and stopped over for a few hours at Kouklia.[16] The first trained archaeologist to visit Palaipaphos gave a summary account of the temple ruins, concluding with the laconic assessment: 'Die Wichtigkeit der Ruinen des muthmasslichen Heiligthums der phönicischen Aphrodite hat man nach den früheren Reisenden sehr überschätzt; es lässt sich aus ihrem heutigen Zustande nicht viel abnehmen. Alle Versuche, den Plan des Tempels unter Vergleichung der bekannten cyprischen Münzen auf denen das Heiligthum dargestellt ist, danach zu reconstruieren, scheinen mir jedes sicheren Grundes zu entbehren'. Apart from the sanctuary, one monument only seems to have interested Ross: the 'Spilaion tis Regainas'. His account of the royal tomb is brief again, but more accurate than Hammer's description.[17]

Ross created – quite unintentionally – a persistent factoid: the legend of the Panayia Aphroditissa. When the wife of the Papas at Pissouri told him: 'jetzt nennt man sie nicht Aphroditissa, jetzt nennt man sie Chrysopolitissa', Ross did not regard this as reliable information: 'So flossen bei ihr die Vorstellungen in einander, dass sie auch den Namen Aphrodite nur für einen Beinamen der Jungfrau hielt'.[18] Ninety years later, Sir Harry Luke recorded as plain fact: 'barely a hundred years ago the peasants of Paphos were still calling the little Christian church on the outskirts of Kouklia village Panayia Aphroditissa, Our Lady of Aphrodite'.[19]

Ludwig Ross was followed by other, sometimes slightly less professional archaeologists. The French came first. The Duc de Luynes realized that Hammer had discovered a Syllabic inscription and republished it in 1852.[20] Ten years later M. de Vogüé who rated the Kouklia inscription as 'un superbe monument de musée', devoted some of his activities to the 'Spilaion'.[21] This time the French Imperial Navy assisted archaeology. The 'aviso à vapeur' Prométhée was put at the disposal of de Vogüé and 'comme toujours, les officiers de marine se sont montrés les auxiliaires empressés des recherches archéologiques'. In the débris of the first chamber a second Syllabic inscription was found, broken in two pieces. The architect Duthoit observed furthermore 'deux antéfixes et un fragment de corniche d'un style gréco-romaine assez élégant'.[22] The inscriptions were transported with great difficulty to the beach ('ce long et difficile embarquement de Koukla: vous vous ferez une idée des obstacles qu'il a fallu vaincre quand vous saurez que la grotte sépulcrale se trouvait à deux kilomètres du rivage: la pierre principale pesait au moins quatre cents kilogrammes; il a fallu la transporter à force de bras à travers les ravins, les broussailles, les rochers, puis l'embarquer sur une plage ouverte'), and finally reached the Louvre. The texts prove that the 'Spilaion' represents the only true royal tomb in the Paphos area: it served as the burial place of two mid-fourth-century kings of Paphos, Timocharis and Echetimos.[23]

Luigi Palma di Cesnola was next on the scene. He pretends to have excavated at Kouklia in 1869, 1874 and 1875,[24] but as usual exaggerates his activities.[25] *Inter alia*, he claims to have employed, 'with the personal assistance of Dr. Friederichs, of the Berlin Museum', a large number of workmen in 1869.[26] Yet Friederichs stayed one day only at Kouklia; he devotes but one page to the ruins of the sanctuary and the social life of Kouklia, without any reference to digging.[27]

Cesnola's description of the site is partly based on Hammer's book; his plan of the Temple is useless, despite the exact-looking measurements; his reporting is fanciful.[28] It also remains doubtful whether Cesnola actually excavated at the monoliths in the coastal plain; but he confirms Hammer's report of (probably Roman) remains in the vicinity – columns, Doric capitals, and fragments of cornices.

Three years after Cesnola, in 1878, the Sanctuary site was inspected by two French scholars in search for inscriptions, M. Beaudoin and E. Pottier. Their travel journal, surviving in the archives of the Ecole française d'Athènes, contains an interesting sketch plan of the ruins.[29]

The systematic scholarly investigation of the Paphian Sanctuary of Aphrodite began in 1888 with the work of the Cyprus Exploration Fund directed by E.A. Gardner, the then Director of the British School at Athens. Cesnola had summed up in 1869: 'I became convinced that only a government with ample funds at its command could under-

Fig. 6.4: The Sanctuary of Aphrodite in 1888, after the excavations of the Cyprus Exploration Fund, photographed by J.P. Foscolo: A. Malecos (ed.), J.P. Foscolo (Nicosia 1992) 87 (Courtesy of the Cultural Centre of the Cyprus Popular Bank).

take to remove the many feet of rubbish accumulated there by the successive rebuildings of the temple. Without accomplishing this preliminary work, which would be expensive and unremunerative, no hope can be entertained of unearthing any objects of art belonging to the earliest Phoenician sanctuary'.[30] The British team executed part of this 'unremunerative' work (Fig. 6.4).[31]

Having recently published a paper dealing with various aspects of the 1888 excavations,[32] I may be permitted to be brief here. For the first time a large part of the surviving sanctuary buildings were laid bare, conveying a general idea of its plan and architecture. It has to be admitted that the full extent of the sanctuary area was not recognized; that digging methods left something to be desired; that the chronology was rather tentative (the earliest buildings being considered Phoenician). But if we judge by the standards of the time, no criticism can detract from the fact that the British dig at Kouklia represents the only project in the nineteenth-century archaeology of Cyprus that was carefully planned, systematically conducted, and adequately published (and this only a year after the work had ended).

Two years after the British excavations, Wilhelm Dörpfeld visited Kouklia. Although he did not dig there, he left an important legacy: a series of photographs which supplement the records of the 1888 excavation.[33] According to M. Ohnefalsch-Richter, who seems to have acted as his guide (and sometimes as his photographer), Dörpfeld believed 'that the ancient shrine of the Paphian goddess had not been discovered there in the village of Kouklia, and that it must be sought elsewhere in the neighbourhood'.[34] Ohnefalsch-Richter himself, unreliable and vainglorious, contributed nothing to the archaeology of Palaipaphos but a few inscriptions.[35]

Work of high scholarly quality was done in 1890 by the French art historian C. Enlart, who published the first substantial account of the Royal Manor House with a detailed plan and a view of the Gothic Hall.[36] The end of the century is marked by the somewhat enigmatic and lonely figure of F.B. Welch who appeared at Palaipaphos in 1899.

Welch had taken his degree at Magdalen College Oxford and was Craven University Fellow at the British School at Athens 1898–1900.[37] In 1920–1922 he catalogued the Finlay Papers at the School, being then 'Vice Consul attached to the Passport Control Office'[38] – a post which lends plausibility to what A.W. Lawrence once told me: 'I knew this man, I met him at Athens – he was in Intelligence'.

The only record of Welch's single-minded and single-handed archaeological activities consists of a letter to the Keeper of Greek and Roman Antiquities at the British Museum, A.S. Murray, in which he briefly relates his doings at Kouklia.[39] This document merits quotation at some length, as it illustrates certain aspects of nineteenth-century field archaeology: 'On March 3rd I arrived at Limassol and went the next day to Kouklia, where we began work on Monday 6th. We first tried the fields on either side of the path leading Southeast from the village to Orites and the

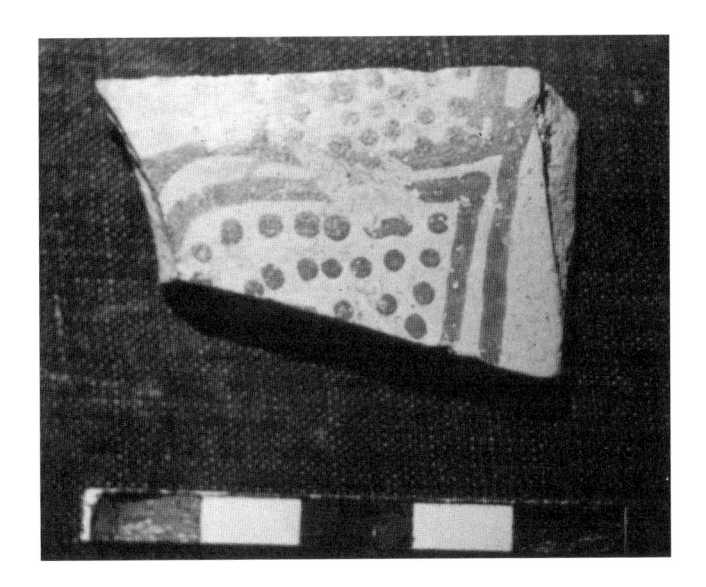

Fig. 6.5: LH IIIA2 krater fragment 'Kouklia, Alonia 1899'.

Kha River. Here we picked up a few fragments of the white slip bowls with dark brown decorations but could only find early Cypriote tombs, dating just after the time of Mycenaean importations, as we found many copper bowls and 4 Bügelkanne in Cypriote ware as well as a cup with a bird in a metope in an imitation of Mycenaean ware. Along with these were the usual Cypriote red ware, bronze weapons, spirals, fibulae. In a later tomb we found broken some hollow clay Phoenician images of Egyptian ... statues; also scarabs, and in the loose earth of a tomb a Phoenician glass bottle. On March 15th we left this site and tried the ravine just North of the threshing floor by the Chiftlik, where we picked up pieces of a Mycenaean vase with men in chariots – but could only find Roman tombs with glass. On the 18th we sent a few men to a mound just South of the Chiftlik, but only found late foundations, so on the 19th moved all to the S.end of the plateau, running S. from Kouklia. This was known to contain large Roman and Greco-Phoenician tombs on the slopes – but on the surface on top were pieces of early ware. However, all we found was a small earth tomb with a Bügelkanne of Cypriote ware. On the 21st we moved all across the stream to the promontory formed by the meeting of the Kouklia South ravine, and the ravine South, coming from Orites. Here after much work we finally found in the middle of our previous diggings, a solitary tomb, containing the black ware with white lines, some dark grey bowls with twisted handles, and two Mycenaean vases, a broken stamnos and a small coup. Besides this we only found Roman and Greco-Phoenician tombs, so on the 25th we gave up Kouklia'.

Part of the material obtained during this fortnight of tomb hunting found its way into the British Museum and the Ashmolean Museum; one single sherd of the 'Mycenaean vase with men in chariots' survives in the sherd collection of the British School at Athens (Fig. 6.5).[40] The archaeological topography of Palaipaphos allows us to locate the areas where Welch dug his tombs. But it is impossible to determine from which particular tomb the surviving finds come – with the possible exception of a Proto White-Painted stirrup jar from 'the small earth tomb with a Bügelkanne of Cypriote ware' at Kato Alonia.[41]

To sum up. From 1802 to 1899, the archaeology of Palaipaphos is fairly well documented. In methods and results it reflects the varying standards of contemporary Mediterranean field archaeology. The range of monuments investigated up the end of the century is fairly restricted: the Sanctuary; a large but indeterminate number of tombs, ranging in date from Late Bronze Age to Roman (including the royal tomb at Arkalon); the monoliths in the coastal plain; and the Manor House. This comparatively narrow panorama is due to two factors: on the one hand the prominence of the Temple in the literary tradition, on the other hand the obsession of many ninteenth-century archaeologists with tombs – tombs not as testimonia for the life of a society, but as repositories of objects of ancient art. One general conclusion can be drawn with regard to the monuments of Palaipaphos: nearly no important ruins above ground seem to have disappeared during the nineteenth century. The remains of the Sanctuary seem to have presented more or less the same aspect to Hammer, Cesnola, and the British excavators of 1888 (Figs 6.3, 6.6, 6.7).[42]

The knowledge of the history and monuments of Palaipaphos attained by 1900 was fairly circumscribed. It was to remain so for another half-century, because the 1888 campaign was followed by a long period of archaeological neglect – illustrated, inter alia, by a number of photographs taken by the Paphos Boy Scouts between 1915 and 1918 (Figs 6.8, 6.9).[43] It was a hiatus that unfortunately prompted further damage to ancient monuments.[44] Only in 1950 did the activities of T.B. Mitford and J.H. Iliffe mark the renewal of archaeological fieldwork at Palaipaphos – but that would be another story.

Fig. 6.6: The Temenos wall of the Sanctuary of Aphrodite in 1869: L. Palma di Cesnola, Cypern, seine alten Städte, Gräber und Tempel *(Jena 1879) 174.*

Fig. 6.7: The Temenos wall of the Sanctuary of Aphrodite in 1890 (Courtesy Deutsches Archäologisches Institut Athen, Neg. CYP 7).

Fig. 6.8: The Sanctuary of Aphrodite in 1915/18: A.K. Phylaktou (ed.), Ημερολογιον Προσκοπον Παπηου (1915–1918) (Nicosia 1992) 109 (Courtesy of the Cultural Centre of the Cyprus Popular Bank).

Fig. 6.9: The Royal Manor House at Kouklia in 1915/18: A.K. Phylaktou (ed.), Ημερολογιον Προσκοπον Παπηου (1915–1918) (Nicosia 1992) 66 (Courtesy of the Cultural Centre of the Cyprus Popular Bank).

Notes

1. J. v. Hammer-Purgstall, *Topographische Ansichten gesammelt auf einer Reise in die Levante* (Wien 1811) 148–49.
2. Mrs. Lewis, *A Lady's Impressions of Cyprus in 1893* (London 1894) 109–110.
3. L. Tschudi, *Reiss und Bilgerfahrt zum Heyligen Grab* (Rorschach 1606) 91–92; F. Attar, *Relatione del regno di Cipro*, ed. by L. de Mas Latrie, *Histoire de l'île de Chypre sous le règne des princes de la maison de Lusignan III* (Paris 1855) 528; see F.G. Maier and M.-L. von Wartburg, 'Strangers at Palaepaphos', *RDAC* (1988) 275–6.
4. G. Mariti, Viaggi per l'isola di Cipro (Lucca 1769), transl. by C.D. Cobham, *Travels in the Island of Cyprus* (Cambridge 1909) 85: 'Many curious antiquities used to be found here [Kouklia], especially in tombs. Now the Turks view all excavations with jealousy, and everyone fears in attempting such to expose himself to fresh extortions'.
5. R. Pococke, *A Description of the East* vol. II. 2 (London 1745) 227; see further, Maier and von Wartburg (n.3) 276.
6. G. Hill, *A History of Cyprus* vol. IV (Cambridge 1952) 101.
7. J. v. Hammer-Purgstall (n.1) 134–5, 142, 147–156.
8. J. v. Hammer-Purgstall, *Erinnerungen aus meinem Leben, 1774–1852*, ed. by R. Bachofen v. Echt (Wien und Leipzig 1940) 74–75. Hammer's estimate of the riding time is corroborated by Ludwig Ross who gives 3–4 hours: L. Ross, *Reisen nach Kos, Halikarnassos, Rhodos und der Insel Cypern* (Halle 1852) = *Reisen auf den griechischen Inseln* IV (1852) 183. For the inscriptions mentioned by Hammer see Maier and von Wartburg (n.3) 277 n.21.
9. S. Hadjisavvas, *Olive Oil Processing in Cyprus from the Bronze Age to the Byzantine Period* (Nicosia 1992) 93–97.
10. J. v. Hammer-Purgstall (n.1) 190 no.69.
11. The tomb was re-investigated in 1990–91: F.G. Maier and M.-L. von Wartburg, 'Excavations at Kouklia (Palaepaphos). 16th Preliminary Report: seasons 1989 and 1990', *RDAC* (1991) 255–6 and 'Excavations at Kouklia (Palaipaphos). Seventeenth Preliminary Report: seasons 1991 and 1992', *RDAC* (1994) 115–8 and 'Ausgrabungen in Alt-Paphos. 16. Vorläufiger Bericht: Grabungskampagne 1989 und 1990', *AA* (1992) 585–6 and 'Ausgrabungen in Alt-Paphos. 17. Vorläufiger Bericht: Grabungskampagnen 1991–1995', *AA* (1998) 105–110; F.G. Maier, 'A Tomb of Paphian Kings: the Spilaion tis Regainas at Kouklia-Arkalon', *Centre d'Etudes Chypriotes. Cahier* 18 (1992) 10–11. A more detailed report will appear in the forthcoming volume 5 of *Ausgrabungen in Alt-Paphos*.
12. *Travels of Ali Bey in Morocco, Tripoli, Cyprus, Egypt, Arabia, Syria, and Turkey betweeen the years 1803 and 1807*. Written by himself. Vol. I (London 1816) 290–1, 299–300, with pls. XXXIII. XXXIV 1. XXXV 1. (a photostatic edition of the original text, with an introduction by R. Bidwell, has been published by Garnet Publishing Ltd., Reading 1993). D.G. Hogarth, *The Penetration of Arabia* (London 1904) 79–83 gives an interesting appreciation of Ali Bey's work.
13. Iodoci a Meggen Patricii Lucerini, *Peregrinatio Hierosolymitana* (Dillingen 1580) 153–4.
14. See Maier and von Wartburg (n.3) 277–8.
15. F. v. Löher, *Cypern. Reiseberichte über Natur und Landschaft, Volk und Geschichte* (3rd ed., Stuttgart 1879) 228–9. Only one brief report of the 1952–53 excavations has been published: J. Schäfer, *OpAth* 3 (1960) 155–175; see further F.G. Maier and M.-L. von Wartburg, *RDAC* 1994, 118; *AA* 1998, 110.115.
16. Ross (n.8), 180–182 (Ross was at that time not 'in the service of the new kingdom of Greece', as stated erroneously by F.G. Maier, 'A hundred years after Hogarth: digging at Aphrodite's sanctuary at Palaipaphos', *Centre d'Etudes Chypriotes. Cahier* 27 (1997) 128). For Ross' biography see C. Schwingenstein in: R. Lullies und W. Schiering (eds.), *Archäologenbildnisse* (Mainz 1988) 29–30.
17. Ross (n.8) 181–2: 'Der Eingang war aus Quadern gebaut und einst mit grossen Steinbalken bedeckt, ist aber jetzt fast ganz verschüttet; man kommt dann in eine 4 Meter breite und 6 1/2 Meter lange Kammer, an welche an jeder Seite zwei kleine Grabkammern anstossen; auf derselben Achse liegt ein zweites ähnliches Gemach, und an dieses schliesst sich hinten ein dritter kleinerer Raum von 3 Meter Länge und Breite. Einer der Durchgänge war vor Alters durch eine grosse Platte oder Thür aus Sandstein verschlossen, die jetz an der Wand lehnt. Auf ihr findet sich in grossen mehrzölligen und sehr deutlichen Buchstaben eine Inschrift, die auch schon Hammer gesehen und abgeschrieben hat....Die Inschrift weicht von der gewöhnlichen phönicischen Schrift ganz ab, und erinnert sehr an die lycischen Buchstaben'. Identical description in *Archäologische Zeitung* 9 (1851) 323–4, with an incomplete and schematic plan, pl. XXVIII 1.
18. Ross (n.8) 178.
19. H. Luke, *More Moves on an Eastern Chequerboard* (London 1935) 151 and *Cyprus. A Portrait and an Appreciation* (London 1957) 26.
20. H. de Luynes, *Numismatique et inscriptions cypriotes* (Paris 1852) 50–51. He translated part of Ross' description and reproduced, on pl.XI, his plan; Ross' copy he considered 'la plus fidèle'.
21. Extrait d'une lettre de M. Melchior de Vogüé à M. Renan', *RA* n.s. 5 (1862) 346; 'Lettre de M. Melchior de Vogüé à M. Renan écrite de Chypre', *RA* n.s. 6 (1863) 246–7; *Mélanges d'archéologie orientale* (Paris 1868) 96–7 and pl. III 2. F. Unger und Th. Kotschy, *Die Insel Cypern* (Wien 1865) 559–60 (who visited the site a few weeks before de Vogüé); J. Seiff, *Skizze von einer Reise durch die Insel Cypern* (Dresden 1874) 95; *Reisen in der asiatischen Türkei* (Leipzig 1875) 117; and Löher (n.14) 228 briefly describe the tomb, but add no new information. The Cyprus Excavation Fund cleared only the dromos of the tomb in 1888: D.G. Hogarth and M.R. James, *JHS* 9 (1888) 159–160, 264, 267. Their sketch plan (266 fig.1) is only partially correct, although slightly more realistic than Ross' schematic drawing (above n.17).
22. Letter to Viollet-le-Duc, 30 July 1862: see J. Foucart-Borville, 'La correspondance chypriote d'Edmond Duthoit (1862 et 1865)', *Centre d'Etudes Chypriotes. Cahier* 4 (1985) 37. Duthoit also states: 'une petite partie seulement

de la grotte était déblayée lors de mon depart'. The re-investigation of the tomb showed that the débris had indeed been removed only partially.

23. O. Masson, *Les inscriptions chypriotes syllabiques* (Paris 1961) 112–115, nos. 16 and 17.
24. L. Palma di Cesnola, *Cyprus. Its ancient cities, tombs, and temples* (3rd ed., New York 1878) 204–216.
25. See the critical remarks of D.G. Hogarth, *Devia Cypria* (London 1889) 18 n.1 (who states that Cesnola stopped 'one day only at Old Paphos') and L. Dyer, 'The Temple of Aphrodite – I', *The Nation* 47 (1888) 191–2; now also O. Masson, 'Quelques épisodes de la vie des frères Palma di Cesnola', *RDAC* (1990) 285–289.
26. Cesnola (n.24) 206.
27. C. Friederichs, *Kunst und Leben. Reisebriefe aus Griechenland, dem Orient und Italien* (Düsseldorf 1872) 47. At Larnaca Friederichs inspected Cesnola's collection and selected a number of votive terracottas from the temple site for the Berlin Museum: 32,50; see further Maier (n.16) 129.
28. Thus Cesnola asserts that he sank a shaft 52 feet deep in the southeastern corner of the Manor House. Excavation in 1985 showed that almost everywhere in the building bedrock occurs only a few cms below the present surface. Deeper foundations exist in the southeastern corner, yet even there bedrock is reached at a depth of 2.10 m; see F.G. Maier and M.-L. von Wartburg, 'Excavations at Kouklia (Palaepaphos). Fourteenth Preliminary Report: season 1985', *RDAC* (1986) 55–58.
29. A. Hermary kindly procured a copy of this plan. See further O. Masson, 'Deux "Athéniens" à Chypre en 1878, M. Beaudoin et E. Pottier', *BCH* 119 (1995) 405–413.
30. Cesnola (n.24) 207–8.
31. Report by E.A. Gardiner, D.G. Hogarth, M.R. James and R.E. Smith, 'Excavations in Cyprus, 1887–88', *JHS* 9 (1888) 149–271.
32. Maier (n.16) 127–136.
33. The glass negatives of these photographs are still kept in the German Archaeological Institute at Athens. They include a view of Dörpfeld on the roof of a Kouklia house; see Maier (n.16) pl. XXXIII:1.
34. M. Ohnefalsch-Richter, *The Times*, 27 July 1910, col. 4.
35. M. Ohnefalsch-Richter, 'Entdeckung des bei Homer erwähnten Räucheraltarplatzes der Aphrodite in Paphos auf Cypern', *Globus* 98 (1910) 296–7; his remark 'auchau dieser Stelle [Kouklia] hat Dr. Zahn versuchsweise graben lassen und einige Bildwerke gefunden' is – as often with him – pure fancy. See also O. Masson, 'Les visites de Max Ohnefalsch-Richter à Kouklia (Ancienne-Paphos),1890 et 1910', *Centre d'Etudes Chypriotes. Cahier* 3 (1985) 19–28. Ohnefalsch-Richter's cavalier way of treating the archaeological evidence is illustrated by the terracotta group which he published 1911 as a new find from Rantidi, although it appeared already in *A Catalogue of the Cyprus Museum* by J.L. Myres and M. Ohnefalsch-Richter (Oxford 1899) 113 nr.3303; see V. Tatton-Brown, 'Two finds allegedly from Rantidi', *RDAC* (1982) 174–182.
36. C. Enlart, *L'art gothique et la Renaissance en Chypre* vol. 2 (Paris 1899) 697–699; English translation by D. Hunt (1987) 503–505. For the present state of the Royal Manor House: Maier and von Wartburg (n.27) 55–58; F.G. Maier, 'The archaeology of the Royal Manor House at Kouklia', *Epeteris* 19 (1992) 251–55.
37. *ABSA* 6 (1899–1900) 152.
38. H. Waterhouse, *The British School at Athens. The first hundred years* (London 1986) 26.72.135; according to the letters of Winifred Lamb he was greatly liked by the students. A photograph of Welch in R. Hood, *Faces of Archaeology in Greece* (Camberley 1998) 74. I am greatly indebted to Mrs. Hood for information about F.B. Welch.
39. Letter written 16.6.1899, in the archives of the Greek and Roman Department of the British Museum; rediscovered by H.W. Catling, 'Kouklia: Evreti Tomb 8', *BCH* 92 (1968) 162 n.4.
40. Fragment of a LH IIIA2 chariot krater, marked on the back: 'Kouklia, Alonia 1899'.
41. H.B. Walters, *Catalogue of the Greek and Etruscan Vases in the British Museum* I. 2 (London 1912) 132; either C 695 or C 696 must come from this tomb. Welch's use of the German term 'Bügelkanne' raises an interesting question: who was responsible for the English translation 'stirrup jar'? The translator obviously knew only this particular meaning of the fairly comprehensive term 'Bügel' – he may well have belonged to the riding fraternity.
42. In this context it is interesting that Hammer observed in the Sanctuary a large column drum sticking out of a cistern. There it still rested in 1972, showing that the excavators of 1888 had not investigated this particular pit.
43. The Cultural Centre of the Cyprus Popular Bank published recently an interesting and amusing book: A.K. Phylaktou (ed.), Ημερολογιον Προσκοπον Παπηου (1915–1918) (Nicosia 1992) which reproduces these photographs.
44. Since 1888 some parts of the Sanctuary buildings have been destroyed – above all the fairly well-preserved western end of the South Stoa: compare F.G. Maier, 'The Temple of Aphrodite at Old Paphos', *RDAC* (1975) pl. XI:5 (one of the precious photographs taken by Dörpfeld) with F.G. Maier and V.Karageorghis, *Paphos* (Nicosia 1984) 89 fig.72. E. Pfuhl, *Ostgriechische Reisen* (Basel 1945) 54, still refers to such dilapidations in 1938.

7. A 19th century view of *St. George's Hill* in Nicosia: fact or fiction

Despo Pilides

This paper's aim is to corroborate observations or comments made in the nineteenth century concerning antiquities found on a little hill in the very heart of Nicosia, known as *St. George's Hill*, with the preliminary results of recent rescue excavations undertaken on the site. In addition an attempt will be made, on the strength of the evidence found in the State Archives[1] to reconstruct, as far as possible, occupation or use of the site in the nineteenth century, during the period of British rule in Cyprus.

There is an indirect connection between the late Olivier Masson, who studied epigraphic material considered to refer to the ancient kingdom of Ledroi or Ledra, and this site, which is amongst the candidates for the location of this elusive kingdom (Masson 1980, 232–235; Masson 1983, 229; Mitford 1961, 136–138).

The summit of this little hill is now occupied by the Meteorological Station, a proto-industrial installation still in use, which was put into operation for the first time in 1899, according to the records of the Meteorological Service.

At the western part of the hill, directly across the Government Secretariat, there is a stone-built shelter with a heavy iron door, possibly constructed for defensive purposes, which is probably why information about its construction and use is not readily available. The eastern part of the lower slope of the hill is now the parking place for the offices of the Ministry of Communications and Works. Part of the northern slope of the hill was cut off to create a parking space for the old premises of the Trade Union of Civil Servants, constructed in the 1950s. Very close to this, now disused, building there is a small chapel dedicated to St. George the Healer.

At the south-eastern extremity of the hill an olive-press was excavated in 1985 (Karageorghis 1986, 874; Hadjisavvas 1992, 27–33) prior to construction of the government offices in the area. The excavator refers to an olive-press associated with a sanctuary on the evidence of the presence of *bothroi* of various sizes, the earliest use of which was assigned to the Cypro-Archaic II; it continued in use until the Hellenistic period. Of particular interest is a bronze figurine, now on exhibition in the Cyprus Museum, retrieved from a *bothros* in the same area in 1982 (Karageorghis 1983, 952, fig. 78). At the top of the adjacent hillock, directly above the olive-press and very close to the new building of the Trade Union of Civil Servants, a huge cistern was found, 5m in diameter, lined with several layers of lime plaster, which, although not fully excavated, is considered to have provided the olive-press with water via a stone channel (Hadjisavvas 1992, fig. 47).

This is the area selected for the erection of a new building for the House of Representatives, an area covering 15,745sq. m. which had to be investigated before the commencement of construction. The first season of excavations was carried out in the summer of 1996, a second season followed in 1997 and a third and fourth season in the spring and autumn of 1998.[2]

Nicosia in itself seemed to have been of little interest to Cesnola as he declares in a statement in his book *Cyprus, its Cities, Tombs and Temples* in the following words: 'with the exception of the church of Sta. Sophia, now converted into a mosque, half a dozen palaces and a few churches in a delapidated condition, there is nothing in Nicosia which would attract the attention of an archaeologist' (Cesnola 1877, reprinted in 1991, 247).

Max Ohnefalsch-Richter, on the other hand, mentions in his book in 1893 'a temenos, of which little now remains, on an eminence between Nicosia and the nearest village to the south, Agios Omologitades . The site', he continues, 'is now occupied by the English church. A Greek church, dedicated to I know not whom of their saints, is said to have

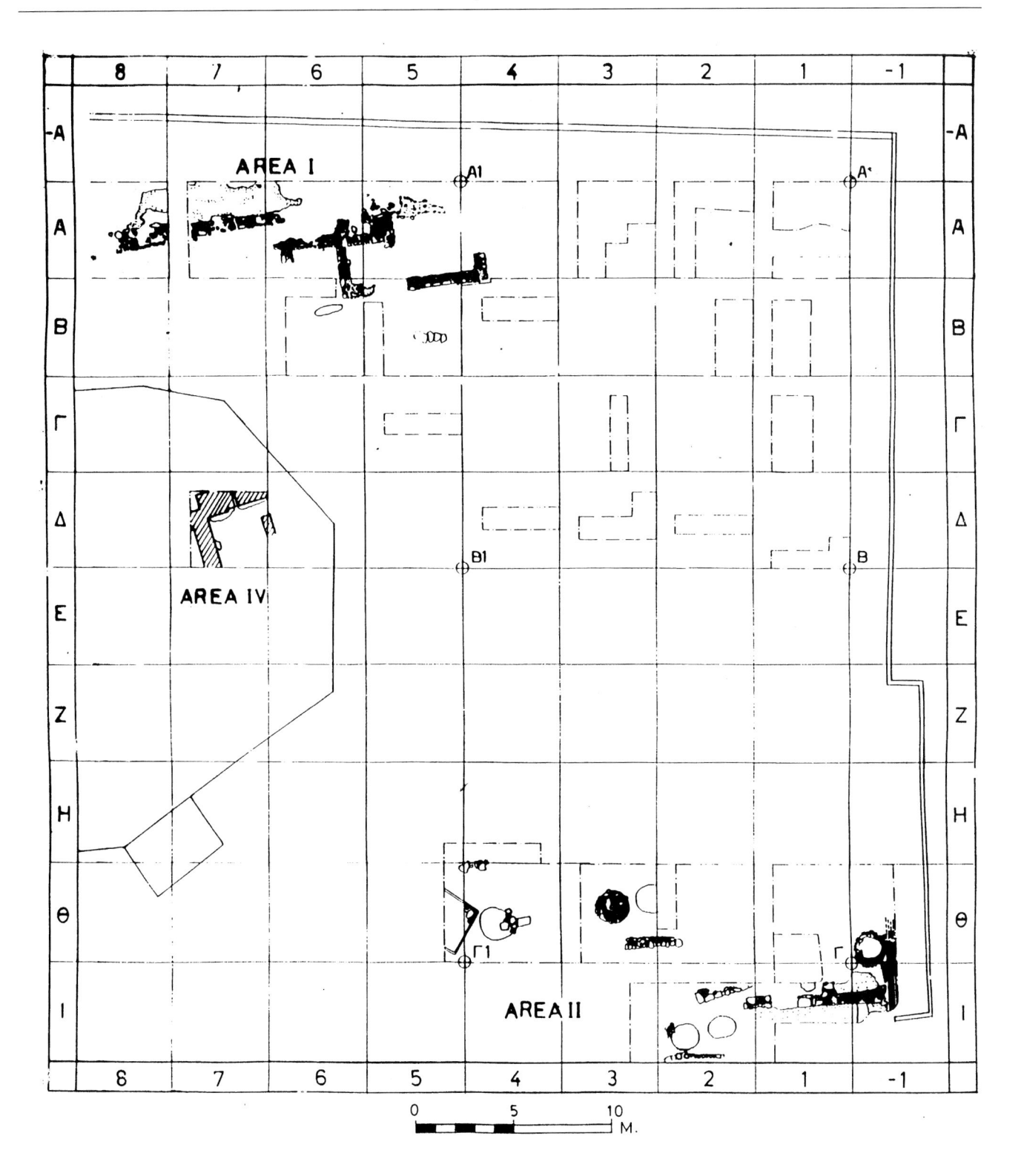

Fig. 7.1: Areas I, II and IV.

formerly stood on the spot, and until a few years ago, the ground was still looked upon as consecrated and, on certain occasions, candles were lit, and service performed. In digging the foundations for the Protestant church, the workers came upon stone statues and ancient votive offerings, as well as fine large Hellenistic draped statues of good treatment, portions of an older chariot combat executed in stone and fragments of columns' (Ohnefalsch-Richter 1893, 13). In an earlier report in 1886, he refers to the Anglican church, 'built in old English style, during the construction of which remains of columns and fragments from an important Phoenician terracotta chariot model were found as well as large stone statues. These findings were not publicised', he goes on, 'so that the construction of this little church, indispensable to the British community, would not be discontinued. Therefore, the church-bell of the Anglican church tolls calling the small English community to prayers precisely over the remains of an ancient sanctuary or necropolis' (Ohnefalsch-Richter 1886, 206).

Small-scale research was carried out at the top of the hill within the Meteorological station in 1997 with the kind permission of the Meteorological Service,[3] which, however, had to be limited to a single test trench of 5×5 m. to avoid disturbing the underground apparatus of the Meteorological station. The trench was sunk at the point where stones from a sandstone wall were protruding through the surface. A thick wall, turning at a 90° angle was located, resting on a thick cement plaque (Fig. 7.1, Area IV). Surprisingly, this building was constructed on thick deposits of pure sand and gravel. A recent geological study of the area concluded that these layers were the result of the erosion of the calcarenite bedrock by an old river, which gradually caused the formation of a river bed with layers of sand and gravel. The same stratigraphy was observed in the eastern and south-eastern part of the hill, where a coin from the siege of Famagusta, dated to 1570 AD, was found in these layers in association with ceramics of the same period. Ancient remains in these areas lay beneath the levels of sand and gravel.

Investigations proved that the short stretch of wall uncovered must have belonged to St. Paul's Anglican church, which was originally built on this hill in 1885, on a plan drafted by William Williams of the Public Works Department. For a few years after the arrival of the British in Cyprus, Anglican services were held in the house of the chaplain. In 1882, a committee was set up to raise subscriptions to build a church, and in 1885 Williams was assigned to design the church building after a long search for an appropriate site, according to the archive records, an article in the *Cyprus Herald* (8 December 1884) and as implied by Ohnefalsch-Richter. The foundation stone was laid on *St. George's Hill* opposite the Government Secretariat. The first service was held on Christmas Day 1885.

At the beginning of 1888, cracks began to appear in the church because the soil of the little hill, on which it was built, was shifting. At the end of 1889 the building was declared dangerous and was dismantled, its material carefully put into storage. In March of the following year a new church, St. Paul's, the cathedral of the Anglican Diocese of Cyprus and the Gulf (Shaar, Given, Theocharous 1995, 28) was built at a short distance to the north, of the old materials and to the same design.[4] The large quantities of rubble uncovered down the east slope of the hill, next to the offices of the Ministry, were thus explained. It may be possible that, as in the eastern and south-eastern part of the hill, the ancient remains from which Ohnefalsch-Richter's finds derived are lying at some depth below the walls of the church, which we were not able to reach due to the restrictions mentioned above. Future investigation after the transfer of the Meteorological Station will put Ohnefalsch-Richter's statements to test. On the north side, where the hill was actually cut off for the construction of the parking space of the old premises of the Trade Union of Civil Servants, *in situ* layers were found going down to a depth of at least 1.3m. before the natural clay bedrock was reached. Hellenistic remains began to appear just before the end of this excavation season. Large quantities of ochre and two fragments of figurines were retrieved from this area (Fig. 7.5, Area VII).

It is recorded in the Department of Public Works' Archives that plans were made in 1880 by Williams for an office building and a hospital that were originally to be part of the Pioneer Barracks' complex. The intended site for the hospital was *St. George's Hill*, east of the barracks' block, where the elevated building would catch the prevailing westerly wind (Schaar, Given, Theocharous 1995, 19; PWD Archives C42, SA/1/940/1885). The Pioneers were disbanded before the hospital and office could be built.

References to houses built in the area in the State Archive records are accompanied by rough sketches which cannot be identified with certainty with the excavated remains of ninteenth- or early twentieth- century residences. One of the earliest houses in the area appeared for sale in the *Cyprus Herald* on 12 July 1884. It belonged to Colonel H.A. Gordon and was built in 1881 in 'Swiss style, comprising 11 rooms and situated on a fine salubrious eminence above and near the Government offices, commanding an unobstructed view of the city and surrounding country with the Kyrenia hills to the north . The whole estate, an area of 8 acres, consisted apart from the house, of gardens and vineyards, two wells, a water tank, stables and a coach house'.

Part of another, possibly earlier house was excavated on the eastern part of the slope built directly over ancient remains of the Classical and Archaic periods, in the walls of which a piastre with a Turkish inscription dating to the

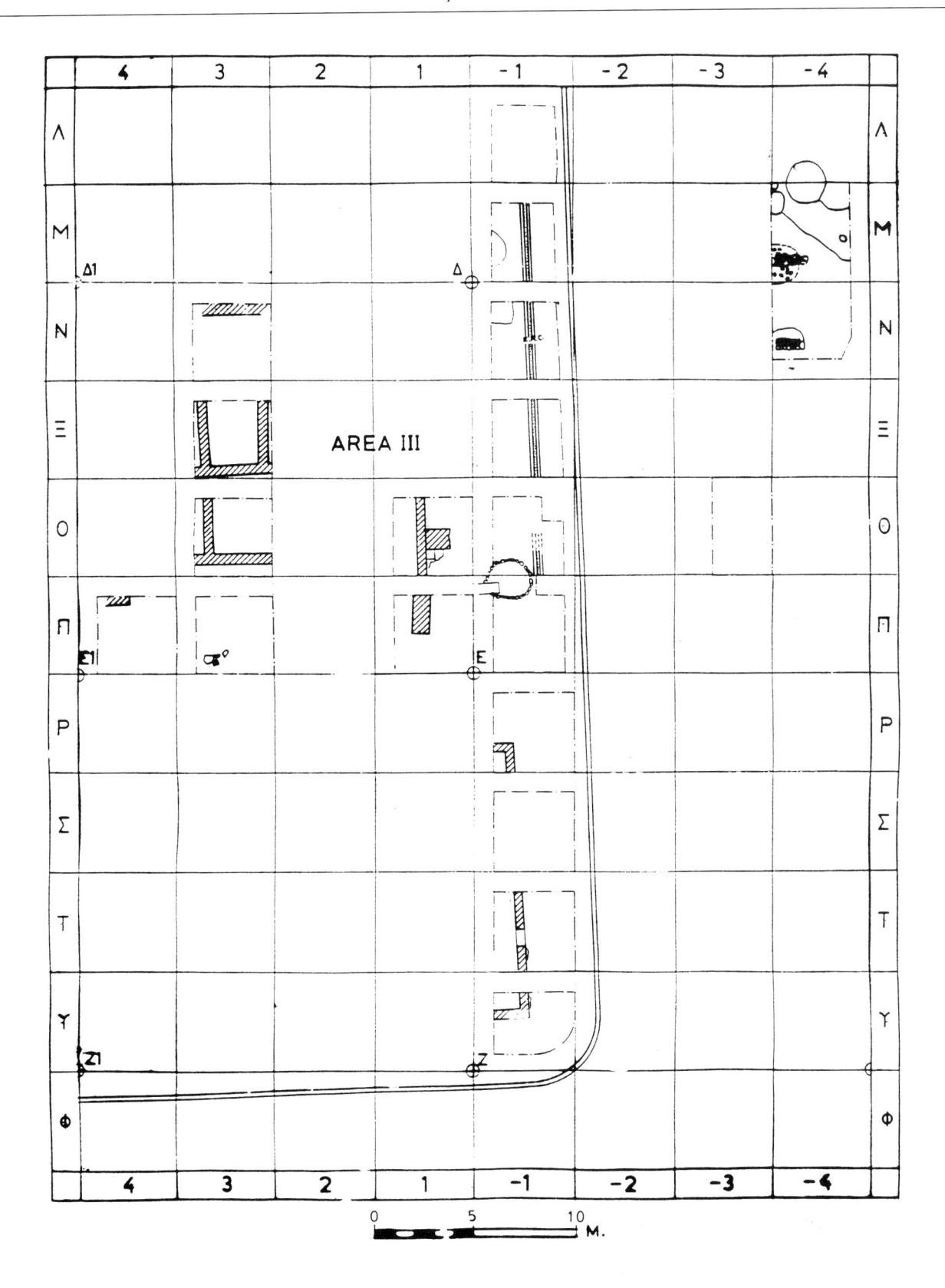

Fig. 7.2: Area III.

Fig. 7.3a-b: Silver denier of undetermined Lusignan king. Diam. about 14mm.

Fig. 7.4a-b: Copper coin of anonymous follis, Rex Regnantium *coinage. Diam. about 26mm.*

regnal year 14 of Mahmud, 1821 AD,[5] was found (Fig. 7.2, Area III).

One more residence of the early twentieth century was excavated on the south-western part of the plot, also overlying remains of the early Classical, Archaic and even earlier periods. According to the archive records the site was a candidate for the first housing scheme proposed by the government for ex-patriate officers in 1920. In spite of the letter from the office of the Divisional Engineer who had undertaken the geophysical study of the site, to the Director of the Public Works' Department in which he states that the whole of this area is 'made ground and should be condemned as a building site', the project went ahead with the result that the tenants were constantly demanding the repair of cracks in the walls of their houses. To the second building scheme, planned and implemented in 1947 belong the house presently occupied by the Office of the Minister of Communications and Works and the house occupied until recently by the Office of the Director of the Department of Public Works.

Ohnefalsch-Richter's references to a church in the area are based on a common belief that St. George's chapel was built on the ruins of an earlier church. Ruins of a church are marked on a map of the early twentieth century (Sheet no. XXI/54W) south of Andreas Demetriou Street, then Queen Mary Street, possibly at the spot of the little chapel. Medieval accounts refer to a church, the location of which is not specified, that was demolished at the time when the

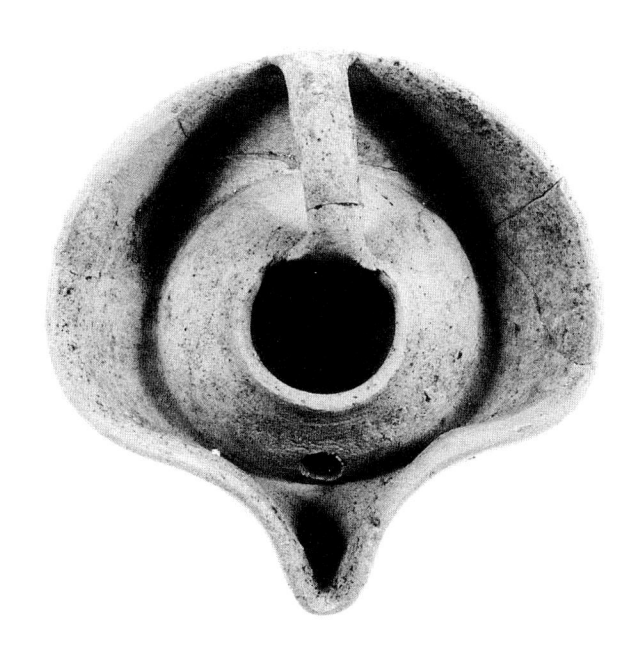

Fig. 7.5: Clay lamp from section on A. Demetriou Street, Nicosia. Diam. about 38mm.

Venetians decided to rebuild the walls of Nicosia with a much shorter circumference than their Lusignan counterparts. Fr. Etienne de Lusignan mentions that amongst the churches demolished in the above process was a monastery of monks called Manchana built by Queen Helena Palaeologina, wife of John II, 1432–1458 (Cobham 1908, reprinted in 1986, 120). Gio. Sozomeno who served as an engineer during the siege of Nicosia in 1570, says that the Turks began constructing forts in preparation for the attack. The first was built on the hill of Santa Marina, at a distance of 270 paces from the Podecattero bastion while the second was built on the hill of S. Giorgio di Magniana, from where they battered the houses of the inhabitants (Cobham 1908, reprinted in 1986, 82). Gio. Pietro Contarini also reports that the infantry of the Turks camped before Nicosia on the hill of Mandia where wells were dug and plenty of water was found (Contarini 1572, 10). This hill is not, however, described or otherwise specified in any of the above accounts. As far as the church is concerned, its location and date of construction are conjectural. According to Hackett's view it was built by Queen Helena Palaeologina, around the year 1453 as a refuge for the monks that fled to Cyprus after the fall of Constantinople (Hackett 1901, 361) and was demolished by the Venetians in 1567 at the time of the construction of the Venetian walls of Nicosia. Recent discussions, however, refute Hackett's argument and place its construction at the period of the Comnenian emperors of Constantinople between the years 1054 and 1191; on the evidence of 14th century records which refer to its location as 'near Nicosia', it is thought to have been located outside the contemporary (Lusignan) walls of Nicosia, (Richard 1986, 67–68, Koureas 1994, 276).

Our evidence for occupation of the hill during these periods consists of remains of the Medieval period which have only begun to be revealed towards the end of the last excavation season.

Excavation in the area north of the chapel began only a short time before the end of this season but revealed wide, well-constructed walls (Fig. 7.6, Area VIII) associated with Medieval pottery, including some pottery wasters and fragments of clay lining, indicating the presence of kilns somewhere in close proximity. Amongst the coins recovered from the area is a denier of an undetermined Lusignan king, probably of the fourteenth to fifteenth century A.D. from a stratified deposit (Fig. 7.3a,b). It is expected that further investigation in the following season will clarify their extent and function as well as their connection with remains and burials on the north slope of the hill (Fig. 7.1, Area I), which have survived the construction of the parking space for the old premises of the Trade Union of Civil Servants. A small section under these remains revealed a stretch of a destroyed earlier wall of which little else could have been said had it not been for the recovery of a copper coin of the *Rex Regnantium* in the wall itself which provides dating evidence for its construction (976–1034 A.D.), (Fig. 7.4a-b, cf. Grierson 1973, pl. LV). Clearly visible in the section of the hill in Andreas Demetriou Str. are large rectangular stones in two or three courses bound together by mortar. Three lamps were found protruding from the section dating to the eleventh or twelfth century AD (Fig. 7.5, cf. Oziol 1977, pl. 48 nos. 889–890 and p. 288).

Underlying the house of the period of British rule on the south-west part of the hill, mentioned above, superimposed remains of various periods were excavated.

A circular stone structure was found directly over bedrock, below a building of several reconstruction phases initially constructed in the Cypro-Archaic period. The foundations of the later structures were built within the interior of the circular construction while its northern part was used as a direct support for the later walls, thus almost totally obliterating the chronological evidence and other material remains belonging to the earlier structure (Fig. 7.7). The building technique, however, and the small sherds found in the foundation trenches indicate that it may belong to the Late Chalcolithic period and could be associated to the site of *Agios Prodromos*, located in 1935, at a short distance to the south-west by P. Dikaios and described as situated on the left bank of the river Pedieos, opposite the Nicosia Government offices (Dikaios 1935, 12, 1938, 77).

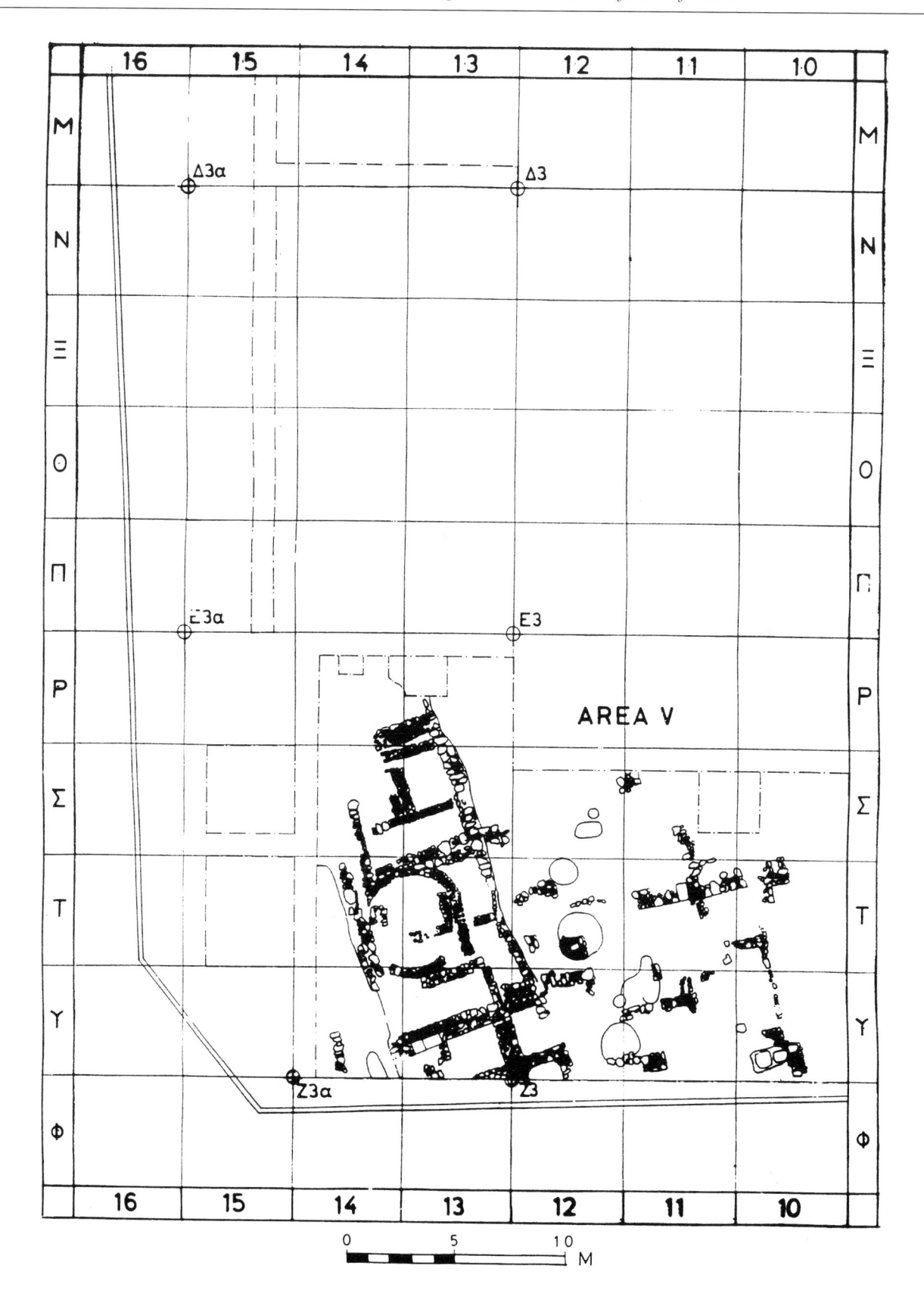

Fig. 7.6: Area V.

Fig. 7.7: Fragmentary walls of stone circular structure underlying later remains.

No evidence of habitation on the hill was found to date that could be assigned to the long intervening period between the Late Chalcolithic and the later parts of the Iron Age. Walls of small riverstones, surviving to a height of only one course of stones belonged to a building that may have extended to the south under the modern road (Skyros Street). It seems to be rectangular in plan and oriented in a north-west to south-east direction. At its south-eastern part large flagstones were used to pave at least part of the two adjoining areas divided by an east-west wall. Finds in these layers were extremely scarce and consisted mainly of small quantities of plain ware sherds. The overlying building seems to have retained the orientation and general plan of the earlier structure, indicating some form of continuity.

Three phases of reconstruction were identified. A long buffer wall on the eastern side was probably constructed to retain the soft crumbling clay bedrock (Fig. 7.6, Area V). Only a short part of what may have been a parallel wall has been preserved on the west side. The interior was subdivided into smaller areas by transverse walls. In the floor of the central room a small pit was excavated which contained some Cypro-Archaic painted sherds and parts of a fragmentary clay chariot model. Signs of fire were traced on the floor and walls of the eastern part of the building in this phase. Burnt ceramics of Bichrome V and the only intact figurine from the entire area, a *kourotrophos*, was found lying on the floor. Walls were rebuilt, mainly of material of secondary use and further subdivisions were made to the interior of the building. Finds were in general few, consisting of grinding tools of calcarenite, parts of unbaked vessels, some loomweights and ochre. Chronologically these phases are assigned to the Cypro-Archaic and, possibly, the beginning of the Classical period.

Parts of wide walls belonging to a large Hellenistic building (Fig. 7.6, Area V) extended only partially over these remains but seemed to continue to the south-west, under the modern road (Skyros Street) and may perhaps form part of a large building of the same period said to have been built of worked stone, located in 1955 at the time of the construction of the petrol station across the road. The Hellenistic building was found to continue to the east, when the excavated area was extended in the spring season of 1998. Walls, although of considerable thickness (about 1m.), were too fragmentary to allow a reconstruction of the plan of the building. In the extended area several types of activities were detected. A large variety of stone tools including grinders, pounders, perforated stones, weights and clay loomweights (Fig. 7.10), sometimes inscribed with one or two letters of the Greek alphabet, amphora fragments, plates and bowls in plain or Colour Coated ware were retrieved. In the same layers, scattered throughout the site, small pits with heavy burning were found with small nodules of slag, possibly indicating small scale processing of metal.

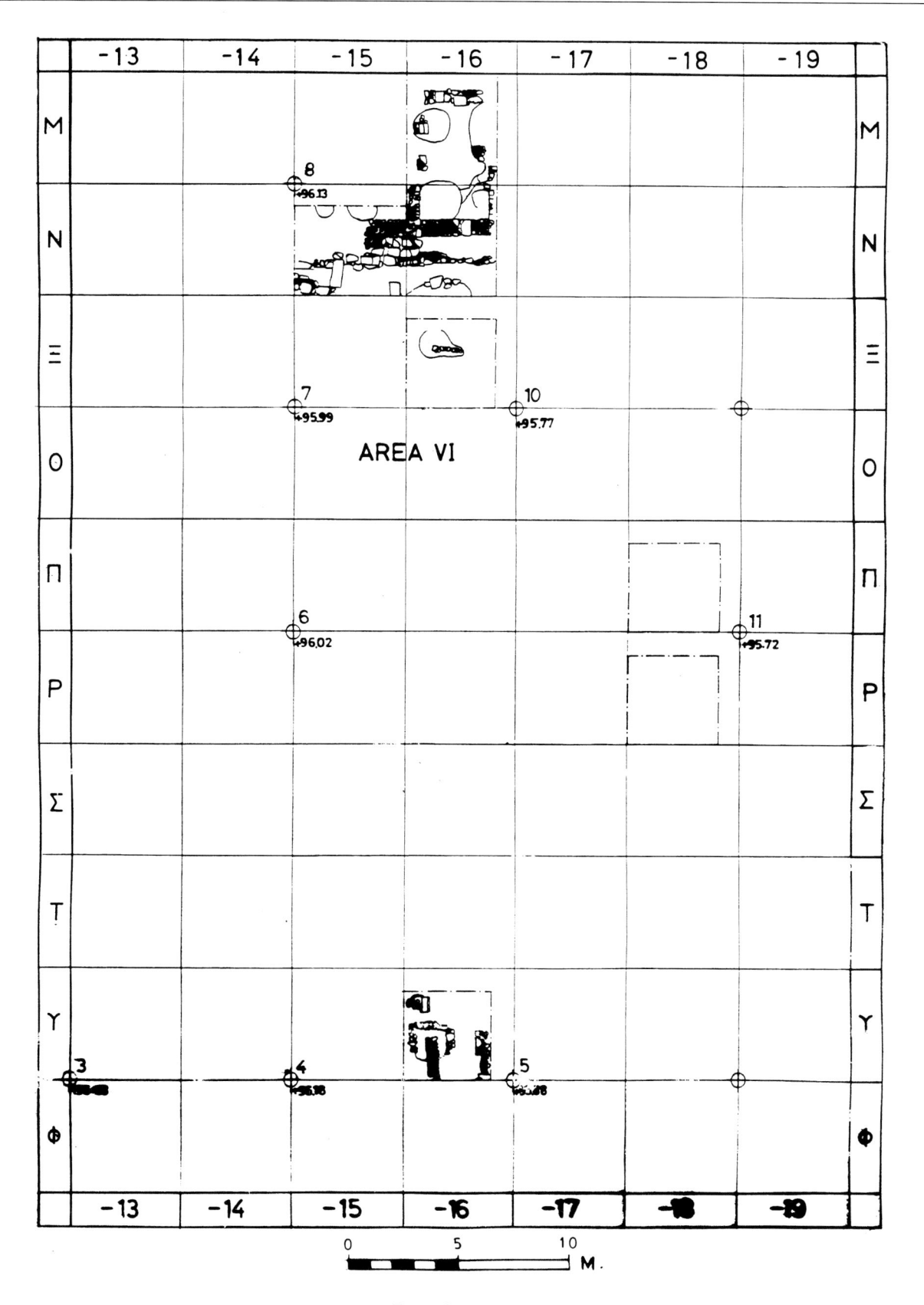

Fig. 7.8: Area VI.

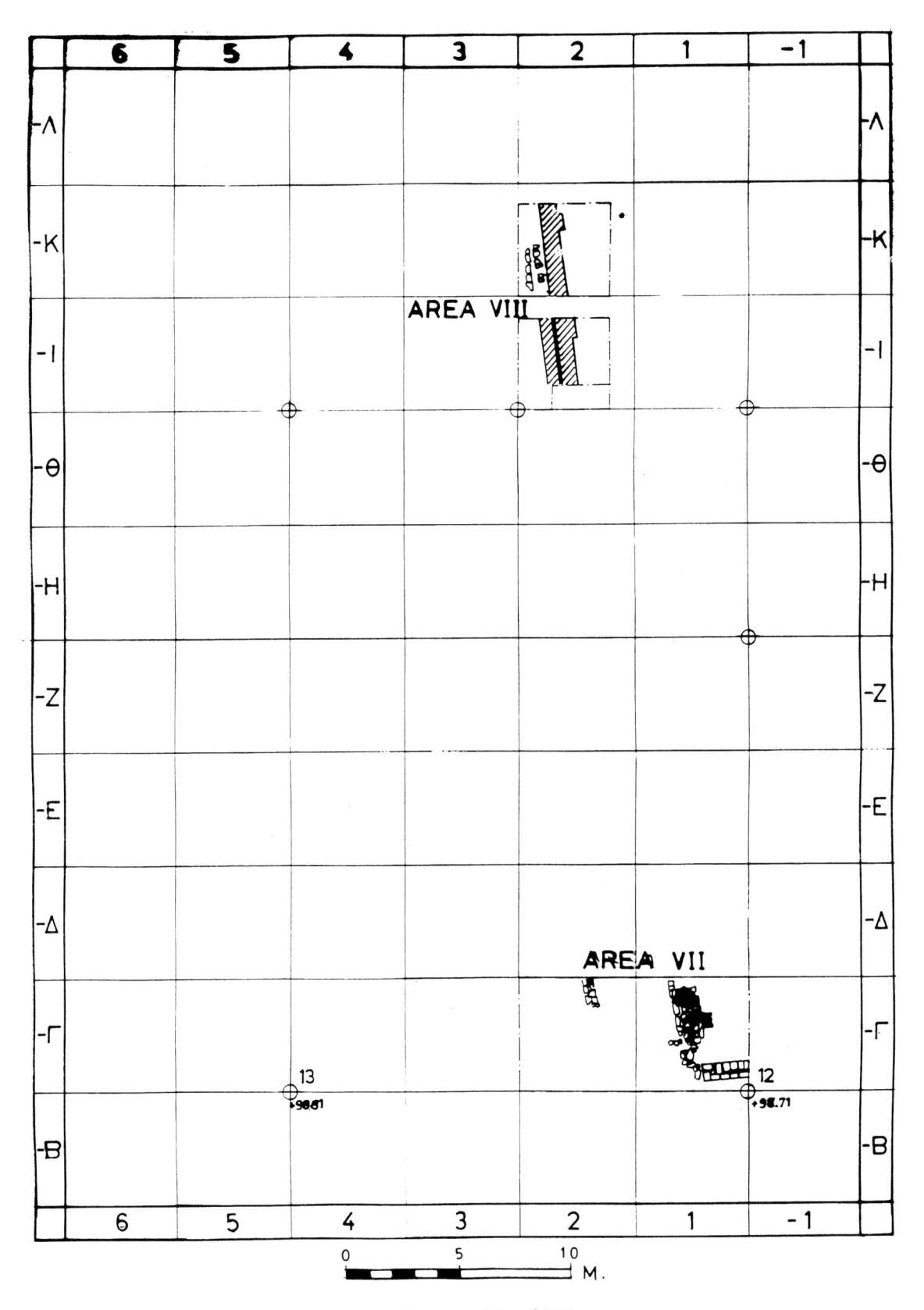

Fig. 7.9: Areas VII and VIII.

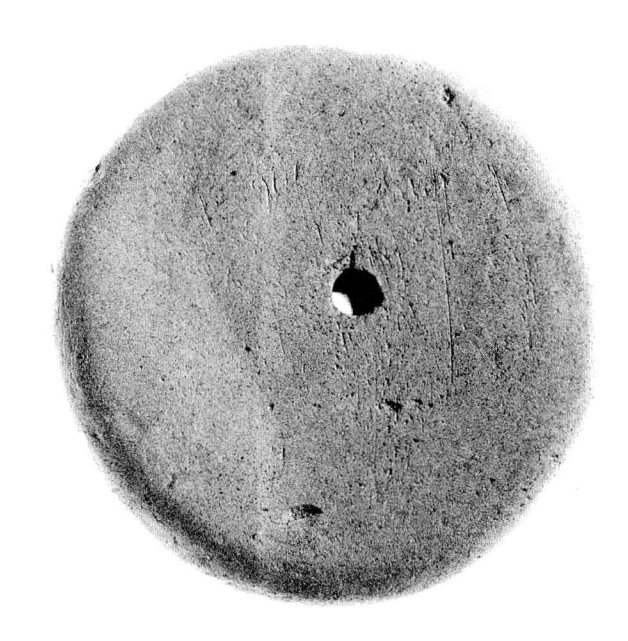

Fig. 7.10: Clay loomweight from Area V. Diam. about 32mm.

To the south-east, a roughly rectangular structure, divided in two compartments, its interior lined with clay and filled with huge quantities of ashes, was excavated. Associated with this area of activity was a small fragmentary limestone figurine. At a small distance a number of intact unguentaria, small bowls, cooking pots, a vessel made of lead, a lead weight and sheets of lead were found. Iron nails, tools and a fragmentary bronze vessel were also amongst the finds. To the west of the kiln, on a sloping area, a pitted stone, the base of a vase with a perforation at its bottom and fragments from another vessel with a double wall were revealed *in situ*, providing perhaps evidence for the small scale processing of some liquid. Deposits of ochre and other copper related substances are common finds. A paved area to the north where a fragmentary sphinx was retrieved, in association with numerous stone tools, probably forms part of the working areas necessary for the above activities. Two coins of Ptolemy II (285–246 B.C.) confirm the chronology already provided by the ceramics for this particular area.

Further to the east, next to the entrance of what is now the parking place of the Ministry of Communications and Works, severely disturbed remains were excavated which yielded large quantities of utilitarian pottery, particularly amphorae of the Hellenistic and possibly the Classical period, overlying pits of various sizes containing material of the Cypro-Archaic II and fragments of human, animal or chariot figurines.

Robust walls belonging to a building of the Hellenistic period were also found at the extreme east of the hill, where more trenches were sunk in the remaining areas not taken up by roads or the prefabricated government offices (Fig. 7.8, Area VI) and close to the olive press installation. The Hellenistic structures were overlying earlier remains but they were considerably more substantial and extensive; at most points they directly overlie Cypro-Archaic remains which mainly consist of habitation material buried in pits. Part of a building was revealed which extends under the modern road to the west and under the various structures on the east and south. Huge quantities of ashes were excavated on either side of an east-west wall. A lamp, a fragment of slag, a loomweight, an incense burner and two small astragali, one of bone and one of lead, were found in the ashy deposits. Large and small grinders, rubbers, pounders and circular loomweights, including a second type in the shape of a truncated pyramid, are once more common finds in these levels. A clay tub with a circular platform and a built-in vessel on the interior, was found close to a hearth (Fig. 7.11, cf. Ginouvès 1962, figs 10–17, Robinson and Graham 1938, pls 53 and 54) while a channel and a circular drain cut in the bedrock, directly to the east, led to an oblong pit. A large, probably imported shell, large blocks of calcarenite and ochre are amongst the raw materials in use. Unbaked loomweights and unbaked fragments of clay indicate that loomweights used for weaving were made on site. Coins belonging to Ptolemy IX, Soter II date these levels to the end of the second century B.C. As already mentioned above, below these remains a large circular pit was excavated containing large quantities of pottery of Cypro-Archaic II date, a variety of stone tools, a fragmentary figurine of a ram, as well as a fragmentary human figurine with a pointed cap and mandibles of sheep, amongst other finds, implying that the use of the site, even though considerably re-arranged, had not essentially changed.

Peristianis (1910, 681), reiterates Ohnefalsch-Richter's report of the presence of a sanctuary on the summit of the hill opposite the barracks of the British army, and extrapolates that it was dedicated to the Paphian Aphrodite and to Apollo as the two gods were traditionally worshipped in the same or neighbouring temples. He in fact assumes the presence of two additional sanctuaries in the area: a sanctuary dedicated to the Paphian Aphrodite at a distance of 800 yards to the south of Richter's findings and very close to the large cistern, where remains of buildings and the base of a stone statue as well as a *kourotrophos* were reported to have been found. Traces of a sanctuary in the area were located in 1985 (Hadjisavvas 1992, 27). The third sanctuary was said to have been located in an obscure plot on the southern boundaries of the city walls.

Although the reports of the nineteenth and early twentieth centuries are inaccurate and appear to be largely

Fig. 7.11: Clay bath from Area VI.

conjectural, it is evident that they are not totally unfounded. There seems to be evidence for the continuous use of the site from the Cypro-Archaic period to the Hellenistic period with small shifts of occupation within the area. Some fragmentary walls and objects such as broken figurines, astragali, incense burners, masks and pottery, buried in pits found all over the site as well as the buildings in the southwest of the site, betray occupation during the Cypro-Archaic period, connected to a sanctuary. Extensive re-use of the site in the Hellenistic period caused disturbance to the earlier structures, although it seems that the more valuable remains of the earlier phases were carefully buried in pits. The evidence for weaving, the manufacture of various types of clay objects in conjunction with the presence of the olive-press and the large cistern in close proximity, which may be viewed as part of this industrial complex, as well as the evidence provided by the extensive cemeteries of the same periods at Ayii Omoloyites (Hadjicosti 1993, Flourentzos 1986), give the impression of a well-organised self-sustaining community, probably also connected with a sanctuary. Similar installations are known in the Near East and in Greece in contemporary contexts (Stager and Wolff 1981, 95–102, Kardara 1961, 261–266). Further excavation in the new year, following the demolition of the abandoned offices and buildings will enhance our understanding of the use of the site and the various phases of habitation, providing new evidence for the little-known but long history of Nicosia.

Notes

1. My thanks are due to the State Archivist for permission to use the records and to the Archives' staff for their assistance. I am also indebted to Michael Given for useful references.
2. During these excavations I was assisted by the technician G. Koumis who acted as foreman and M. Chamberlain who is responsible for the plans and drawings of the site, the staff of the Conservation Laboratories and the Photography department of the Cyprus Museum, Nicosia.
3. I am grateful to the Director and staff of the Meteorological Service for their co-operation and assistance during excavations inside the station.
4. I am grateful to the Venerable M.W. Mansbridge, Provost of St Paul's Cathedral, Nicosia, who allowed me to study the cathedral's archives.
5. My sincere thanks are due to Dr Anne Destrooper-Georgiades for an autopsy and a preliminary identification of the coins from the site.

Bibliography

Cesnola 1877 (reprinted in 1991): L.P. Cesnola, *Cyprus: Its ancient Cities, Tombs and Temples* (Nicosia).

Cobham 1908 (reprinted in 1986): C. D. Cobham, *Excerpta Cypria, Materials for a History of Cyprus* (New York).

Contarini 1572: Gio. Pietro Contarini, *Historia delle cose successe dal principio della guerra mossa da Selim Ottomano à Venetiani* (Venetia).

Dikaios 1935: P. Dikaios, 'Some Neolithic Sites in Cyprus',

Report of the Department of Antiquities of Cyprus, 11–13.
Dikaios 1938: P. Dikaios, 'The Excavations at Erimi, 1933–1935', *Report of the Department of Antiquities of Cyprus*, 1–81.
Flourentzos 1986: P. Flourentzos, 'Tomb groups from the Necropolis in Ay. Omologites, Nicosia', *Report of the Department of Antiquities of Cyprus*, 150–163.
Ginouvès 1962: R. Ginouvés, *Balaneutikè. Recherches sur le Bain dans l'Antiquité Grecque* (Paris).
Grierson 1973: P. Grierson, *Catalogue of the Byzantine Coins in the Dumbarton Oaks Collection and in the Whittemore Collection*, Vol. 3, Part 2 (Washington).
Hackett 1901: J. Hackett, *A History of the Orthodox Church of Cyprus from the Coming of the Apostles Paul and Barnabas to the Commencement of the British Occupation (A.D. 45–A.D. 1878)* (London).
Hadjicosti 1993: M. Hadjicosti, 'The Late Archaic and Classical Cemetery of Agioi Omologites, Nicosia in the Light of New Evidence', *Report of the Department of Antiquities of Cyprus*, 173–193.
Hadjisavvas 1992: S. Hadjisavvas, *Olive Oil Processing in Cyprus From the Bronze Age to the Byzantine Period, Studies in Mediterranean Archaeology* Vol. XCIX, (Nicosia).
Karageorghis 1983: V. Karageorghis, 'Chronique des Fouilles et Découvertes Archéologiques à Chypre en 1982', *Bulletin de Correspondance Hellénique* CVII, 951–952.
Karageorghis 1986: V. Karageorghis, 'Chronique des Fouilles et Découvertes Archéologiques à Chypre en 1985', *Bulletin de Correspondance Hellénique* CX, 874–876.
Kardara 1961: Ch. Kardara, 'Dyeing and Weaving Works at Isthmia', *American Journal of Archaeology* 65, 261–266.
Koureas 1994: N. Koureas, 'Η Μονή Αγίου Γεωργίου των Μαγγάνων επί Φραγκοκρατίας', *Επιστημονική Επετηρίς της Κυπριακής Εταιρείας Ιστορικών Σπουδών*, Τόμος, Β' (Nicosia) 275–286.
Masson 1980: O. Masson, 'Kypriaka XIII–XIV', *Bulletin de Correspondance Hellénique* CIV, 225–235.
Masson 1983: O. Masson, *Les Inscriptions Chypriotes Syllabiques. Recueil Critique et Commenté* (Paris).
Maratheftis 1977: F.S. Maratheftis, *Location and Development of the Town of Levkosia (Nicosia), Cyprus* (thesis submitted to the University of Bristol in 1977, (Nicosia).
Merrillees 1991: R.S. Merrillees, 'Nicosia before Nicosia', *Annual Lectures, The Leventis Municipal Museum of Nicosia* (Nicosia).
Mitford 1961: T.B. Mitford, 'Further Contributions to the Epigraphy of Cyprus', *American Journal of Archaeology* 65, 93–151.
Ohnefalsch-Richter 1886: M.Ohnefalsch-Richter, 'Berichte und Mittheilungen aus Sammlungen und Museen über Staatliche Kunstpflege und Restaurationen, Neue Funde', *Repertorium für Kunstwissenschaft* IX (Berlin und Stuttgart) 205–207.
Ohnefalsch-Richter 1889: M. Ohnefalsch-Richter, 'Ledrai-Lidir and the Copper Bronze Age (Topographical and Ethnographical Studies)', *Journal of Cyprian Studies* (Nicosia) 1–6.
Ohnefalsch-Richter 1893: M. Ohnefalsch-Richter, *Kypros, the Bible and Homer*, Vols I–II (London).
Oziol 1977: Th. Oziol, *Salamine de Chypre VII, Les Lampes du Musée de Chypre* (Paris).
Peristianis 1910 (revised edition 1995): I.K. Peristianis, *Γενική Ιστορία της Νήσου Κύπρου από των Αρχαιοτάτων Χρόνων μέχρι της Αγγλικής Κατοχής* (Nicosia).
Richard 1986: J. Richard, 'Un monastère Grec de Palestine et son domaine chypriote: le monachisme orthodoxe et l'etablissement de la domination franque', *Πρακτικά του Δεύτερου Διεθνούς Κυπριολογικού Συνεδρίου, Λεκωσία 20–25 Απριλίου 1982*, Τόμος Β' (εκδ. Θ. Παπαδόπουλος, Β. Εγγλεζάκης, Λεκωσία) 61–75.
Robinson and Graham 1938: D.M. Robinson and J.W. Graham, *Excavations at Olynthus. Part VIII. The Hellenic House* (London).
Schaar, Given and Theocharous 1995: K.W. Schaar, M. Given and G. Theocharous, *Under the Clock, Colonial Architecture and History in Cyprus, 1878–1960* (Bank of Cyprus, Nicosia).
Stager and Wolff 1981: L.E. Stager and S.R. Wolff, 'Production and Commerce in Temple Courtyards: An Olive Press in the Sacred Precinct at Tel Dan', *Bulletin of the American Schools of Oriental Research* no. 243, 95–102.

8. An Archaeology of Cult?
Cypriot sanctuaries in 19th century archaeology[1]

Anja Ulbrich

In the introduction to his book *Ancient Cyprus*, published in 1937, Stanley Casson gives a short summary and clear evaluation of the development of Cypriot archaeology from its beginnings in the nineteenth century onwards. One of his major complaints concerning this 'strange and sad history'[2] is the preoccupation of Cypriot archaeology with 'tomb-robbing and sanctuary-gutting that had obsessed Cesnola and his followers'.[3] Indeed, records and publications attest that, already by the end of the nineteenth century, at least 77 different sanctuary sites in Cyprus had been discovered, explored and exploited, but rarely scientifically excavated (Fig. 8.1).[4]

This paper investigates the role that Cypriot sanctuaries played during the first wave of large-scale archaeological exploration and exploitation of the island in the second half of the nineteenth century by pursuing the following questions:

- Who explored sanctuary sites and for what reasons?
- Which techniques and principles of excavation were employed?
- Which types of material evidence from sanctuary sites generated the most interest?
- How was the material treated, published and interpreted after the excavations?

In the wake of Napoleon's military expeditions to Egypt, followed by an increasing political and economic involvement of Europe and America in the eastern Mediterranean region, it was primarily French travellers and scholars who made stunning archaeological discoveries in Egypt and the Near East.[5] These finds triggered a surging interest in collecting antiquities from those areas, which became a popular and competitive private, public and even national activity, thereby creating the first large art markets in the eastern Mediterranean, including Cyprus. As tombs and sanctuary sites – first discovered accidentally, but soon purposefully searched for – yielded such desirable antiquities in great numbers, they became the natural targets of the new large-scale archaeological exploration and exploitation on the island in the second half of the nineteenth century.

However, already since the sixteenth century, private and, by the early nineteenth century, public European collections had sporadically received or purchased material from ancient Cypriot sanctuary sites. Such items consisted mainly of terracotta figurines and limestone statuettes which had been accidentally discovered by locals during agricultural activities, dug up and subsequently sold – directly or through the art market in Larnaca – to foreign residents or travellers as a kind of curious souvenir.[6] With the great discoveries in the Near East in the first half of the nineteenth century, such objects became even more popular, thus provoking illicit and unrecorded digging. As foreign and local collectors of antiquities – mostly diplomats and businessmen – lived in Larnaca, and many travellers entered Cyprus through this harbour town, it is not surprising that ancient sites, primarily sanctuaries, in and around Larnaca, as well as in the neighbouring regions, were affected by such 'archaeological' activities conducted by locals and foreigners alike.[7] Two such examples are a sanctuary site near the salt lake of Larnaca and a temenos at Kochi – about 14 km north of Larnaca – both of which were already recorded as 'terribly ransacked' in the late 1870s and 1880s by Ohnefalsch-Richter. Concerning Kochi he wrote: 'In the days of Turkish rule valuable finds were made here and sold to the Consuls in Larnaka...The work of destruction and depredation that has gone on here is indescribable...'.[8] Whereas Ohnefalsch-Richter recognised such sites as cult places, the first scholars, who directly or indirectly exploited them, did not identify and study them as such.

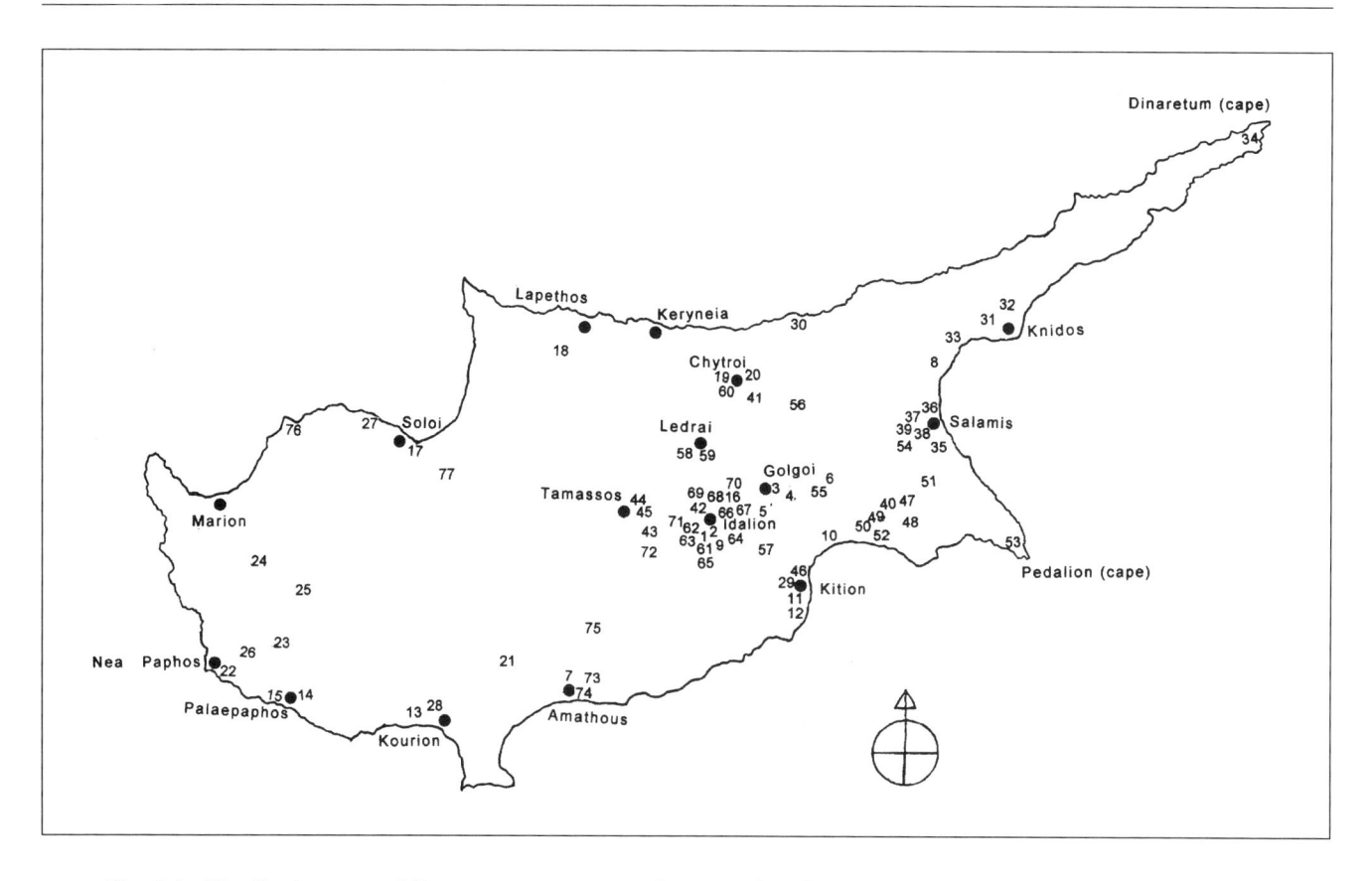

Fig. 8.1: Distribution map of Cypriot sanctuary sites discovered in the nineteenth century. (See Appendix p. 105).

The amateur scholar Duc de Luynes is a fine example. In 1850 he acquired the famous bronze tablet of Idalion and other objects from villagers in Dali, who had found them the previous year on the hill Ambelliri, the western acropolis of ancient Idalion.[9] The discovery of this inscription, its publication by Duc de Luynes himself, and attempts at translation by other scholars, made the eventual decipherment of the Cypro-Syllabic script possible, thus sparking a new interest in Cypriot script and epigraphy. The hitherto unknown historical event of a siege of Idalion by the Kitians, which the text of this inscription attested for the first time, was also a topic of scholarly attention. The actual site of discovery, however, which was very near an ancient Athena sanctuary, is even explicitly mentioned in the text, but did not arouse any immediate scholarly curiosity. Even weapons as well as the bronze and silver objects, which had been discovered in close proximity to the inscription and that in part bore votive inscriptions to Athena, did not evoke any further interest in a more systematic exploration of the area.[10]

Considering the general development of Classical and Near Eastern Archaeology in the nineteenth century, it is not surprising that French scholars conducted the first real archaeological expeditions in Cyprus, which were even financed by the French government. It is revealing that those expeditions, as was the case with every other visit of French scholars to the island, were always connected with a journey to or from the mainland Levant, the focal point of French archaeological activity.[11]

During those campaigns conducted in 1862 and 1865 by the orientalist de Vogue, the epigrapher Waddington and the architect Duthoit, five sanctuary sites, discovered by locals through surface finds, were excavated and exploited to varying degrees.[12] The methods of exploration consisted of collecting pieces of sculpture from the surface, as well as unsystematically digging holes and trenches, all of which yielded limestone sculptures in different quantities. Nothing about these five sites, their topography, the method of exploration, the types of the recovered objects or even particular items was published at the time, and the first impressive collections of Cypriot sculptures simply disappeared into the Louvre. Only some of those sculptures were finally published about 20 years later, in G. Perrot's and Ch. Chipiez, *History of Art in Phoenicia and Cyprus.*

In this monograph the items were treated as isolated objects of art with concern only for their style, chronology and iconography. Almost no references whatsoever to provenience or find context were given, however, let alone to their original contexts, the sanctuaries proper.[13]

The French expeditions of the 1860s are exemplary for what can be called the antiquarian approach and methods, which are characteristic of all early archaeological activities in Cyprus. The primary aim was the acquisition of precious or at least curious antiquities, which brought not only prestige, but also often cash for the discoverer if the objects were sold. Ancient items were retrieved by various methods, often applied simultaneously by the same person, whether scholar or layman.

Objects were either bought directly from villagers, who had accidentally discovered them on their property while engaging in agricultural activities, or they were purchased at the art market in Larnaca. In addition, most foreign professional and amateur scholars also searched for antiquities themselves, often employing local farmers for their knowledge of promising spots. Using an early type of survey technique, they collected objects from the surface or, if they found promising fragments on the surface, searched for more by digging in an unsystematic manner which can hardly be called scientific excavation.[14]

Sanctuary sites exploited in such a way were viewed as a treasure or 'mine of statues' (quotation by Lang, see below), but were often not even identified, let alone perceived or interpreted as sites of ancient worship. Primarily statues, inscriptions and coins from a sanctuary context enjoyed scholarly attention and were studied as isolated objects and as testimonies for Cypriot art, script and the history of these last two.

Until the end of the nineteenth century, antiquarian interests continued to be the major motivation for the excavation of sanctuary sites by unscientific methods employed by locals, professional and amateur scholars alike. Other examples of such activites include the excavations of Tiburce Colonna-Ceccaldi at a temenos on the eastern acropolis of Idalion[15] and of Alexander Palma di Cesnola at several sanctuary sites in the eastern part of the island, that until now remain unidentified.[16]

Sir Robert Hamilton Lang and Luigi Palma di Cesnola, however, although, again, mainly motivated by antiquarian interests, added, albeit inconsistently, new dimensions and approaches to the investigation of sanctuaries: more systematic excavation, recording, documentation, analysis and interpretation of sanctuary sites and related finds. In 1867 Lang was the first of many amateur archaeologists in Cyprus systematically to excavate a Cypriot temenos, at ancient Idalion, and subsequently to publish, though 11 years later, the first excavation report of its kind.[17] Lang's report illustrates a step beyond the antiquarian approach and methods that characterised his earlier investigations of different remains at ancient Idalion, 'the richest antiquarian field yet to be uncovered'.[18]

'In 1868...the Dali men whom I had employed to search for antiquities, came upon (as it were) a mine of statues. Several of these statues were of colossal proportion, a circumstance which convinced me that their position was the site of an ancient temple. Under this conviction I resolved upon entirely uncovering the site... as on no previous occasion had any temple in Cyprus been systematically explored'.[19] Lang's 24-page report provides information on the size of the area under excavation (130 square feet) and the depth which was dug (9 to 11 feet).[20] His method and technique of excavation can be deduced from descriptions in his text which show that, generally, selected and clearly defined areas were dug, but that the workers also excavated along the line of walls discovered in the course of work. The detailed observations and information also suggest some kind of field recording, which is all the more likely as this report was published 11 years after the excavation.

The account informs the reader that the temenos was located at the lower slope of a hill east of a road running south from the village of Dali and passing between two hills on its way to Lymbia.[21] The report also provides observations, descriptions and some illustrations of architecture, single finds and find groups, as well as their relation to each other and their state of preservation. Lang published the first topographical plan of a Cypriot sanctuary site and a small selection of the associated sculptures representing some of the different iconographic types discovered (Figs. 8.2 and 8.3). With regard to the southeastern area of the temenos, he recorded a stratum – and he actually used this word – of ash mixed with animal bones and teeth around a podium, which he tentatively identified as an altar.[22] From his observations on the site and the related finds, Lang deduced the functions of buildings and courts, verbally reconstructed their appearance to the ancient votary and traced the long history of the site.[23] Combining his evidence from dedicatory inscriptions to Apollo Amyklos with Vergil's testimony regarding the Aphrodite cult in Idalion, Lang came to the conclusion that 'It is unlikely that Idalion possessed distinct temples to Aphrodite, Apollo, Ceres, Bacchus, etc., but offerings to each of them at their respective feasts may have been deposited in the chief temple of the city'.[24]

Lang concluded his report by expressing his hope that 'my excavations in Idalion helped to elucidate the question of the early inhabitants of Cyprus, their language, their worship, their customs and their arts'.[25] Such an attitude can be described as a 'kulturhistorischer' (cultural-historical) approach, which is also reflected in the way in which different types of materials were treated,

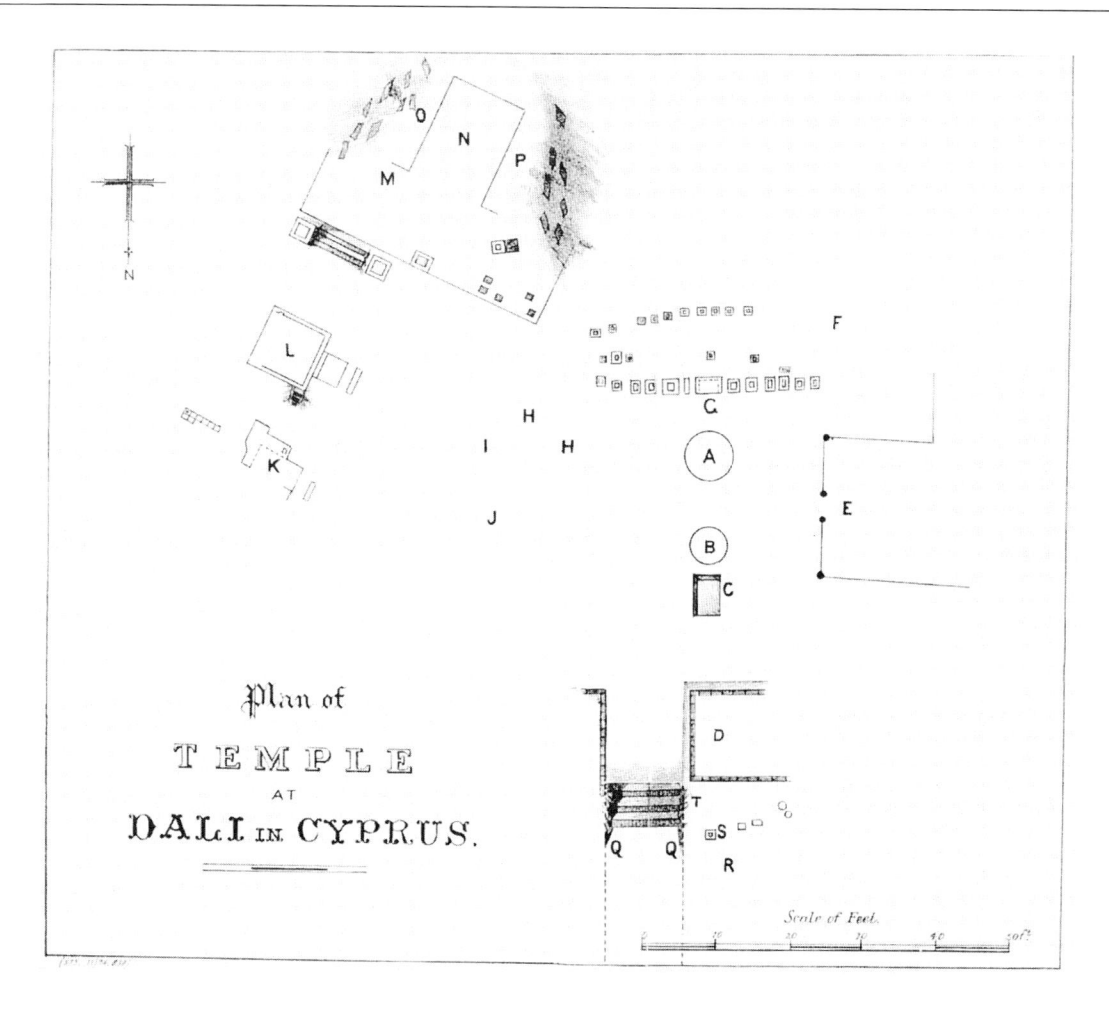

Fig. 8.2: Topographical plan of a sanctuary site at Dali as published by Lang (n.17) 30/31.

documented, discussed and published in Lang's report, as well as in other articles written by him and other British scholars on the material from his excavation at Dali. As Lang was a banker, not a professional archaeologist, he consulted members of the British Museum and the British Antiquarian Society, as well as relevant scholarly literature, in order to analyse and interpret his finds in their cultural and historical context. He explicitly refers to the epigrapher Dr. Birch, a certain Mr. Smith[26] and Dr. Brandis concerning their help with the decipherment and translation of the Cypro-Syllabic and Phoenician inscriptions. Dr. Poole obviously advised him about the coins and also discussed the sculpture of Dali in order to reconstruct its stylistic development and the evolution of Cypriot sculpture in general.[27] In the publications, all the different types of objects from the site – inscriptions, coins and sculpture – were studied to elucidate stylistic developments linking them with the political history of the island and Idalion in particular, both of which were reconstructed from textual and epigraphic evidence. However, the sacred function of the site, though at least recognised, was treated only briefly as another aspect of Cypriot culture and received relatively little attention in comparison with types of objects and particular specimens. The 'cultural-historical' approach became a constant factor and motivation for the investigation of Cypriot sanctuaries, though it never replaced completely the purely antiquarian attitude or financial considerations.

A combination of all three motives was behind Luigi Palma di Cesnola's large-scale archaeological explorations of many different ancient remains in Cyprus between 1866 and 1875. For the 11 sanctuary sites recorded in his book *Cyprus, its Cities, Tombs and Temples* (London 1877), he provided information, although not consistent or complete for every site, on various aspects such as:

1. their specific location,
2. their setting in relation to tombs and settlements,

Fig. 8.3: Stone sculpture from Dali as published by Lang (n.17) 30/31 pl. IV.

3. the nature of the evidence from the respective sites and, sometimes,
4. the identity of the deity, if it could be determined through inscriptions or the iconography of votive sculpture.

Cesnola published illustrations of a small representative selection of sculpture from only three sites at Kourion, Chytroi and Kition.[30] The dedicatory inscriptions, however, are not consistently mentioned and interpreted in their context, but listed by type in an appendix. For all these sites Cesnola did not define his method and scale of investigation, whether involving excavation or merely the collection or extraction of surface finds.

The account and documentation of Cesnola's investigation of the sanctuary site at Ayios Photios near Golgoi, which he explored by intensive excavation in 1870 and 1873, stands in sharp contrast to his superficial remarks on other sites.[31] The type of information and documentation he provided can be compared with, and is strikingly similar to, what is written in Lang's report. Georges Colonna-Ceccaldi recorded that Lang, who had excavated in Dali only three years earlier, was an eye-witness at Cesnola's excavation; there could well have been some kind of information exchange between these two colleagues and rivals.[32] Like Lang's report, Cesnola's account also contains observations concerning the architecture and sculpture as found in different, accurately described contexts. It further describes their state of preservation, their chronological development and includes illustrations of a representative collection of sculpture by type.[33] Cesnola mentioned that he excavated defined areas, as well as along the line of walls, in order to establish the limits of the temenos. He also noticed contexts such as clay layers from decomposed bricks or a layer of ash in the centre of the temple structure in which two horse-and-rider terracotta figurines and an alabaster vase were found.[34] Cesnola also identified iconographic sculptural types including representations of deities and mythological figures such as Hercules, Diana, Venus, and the triple Geryon. Though he quoted the literary evidence for an Aphrodite cult in Golgoi and listed, in an appendix, dedicatory inscriptions for Demeter and Apollo as well as for Zeus from this very site at Ayios Photios,[35] he did not proceed as far as explicitly identifying the deity or deities of the temenos. Similarly to Lang, Cesnola viewed the different types of material as evidence for ancient Cypriot material culture, but did not attempt a more thorough interpretation of the finds in the broader context of Cypriot religion and cults.

Displaying a similar combination of antiquarian and historical approaches and methods, British scholars, whose work had been commissioned and was financed by the Cyprus Exploration Fund as well as the British Museum, recorded at least another 17 sanctuary sites after the establishment of British rule in 1878. The method of exploration followed ranged from surveying the landscape and simply recording diagnostic sculptural finds and inscriptions (partly without context) to full-scale systematic excavations (e.g. at Kouklia, Amargetti and Salamis). All of the sites were recorded in publications, either in general monographs on ancient monuments in Cyprus, such as D. J. Hogarth, *Devia Cypria* (London 1889), or in articles in the *Journal of Hellenic Studies*.[36] The method of publication and documentation shows the same mixture of antiquarian and culture-historical approaches as already detected in Lang's report. However, the presentation is more systematic and the language more scientific. The best and most detailed excavation reports concern the excavations at the sanctuary of Aphrodite at Palaepaphos as well as other ancient cult places at Amargetti, Kition-Kamelarga, and at ancient Salamis. For each site the different types of evidence – architecture, types of finds (sculpture, coins etc.) and inscriptions – are described in some detail and discussed separately, with consideration of stratigraphy and chronology. Though the detailed descriptions of architecture and some iconographic types of sculpture give a good impression of the sites, their chronology and the deity worshipped, actual illustrations of objects by drawings or photographs and topographical plans are largely lacking.

With the exception of the Kouklia sanctuary, the British did not purposefully search for and investigate sanctuaries. When they accidentally discovered and excavated one, the related material was only perceived and interpreted as evidence for ancient Cypriot material culture and history, but not as evidence for cult and religion, an issue which seems not to have enjoyed much interest in British scholarship at the time.

This approach stands in marked contrast to the work of Max Ohnefalsch-Richter. His investigations and excavations between 1879 and 1894 were permitted, actually commissioned and rudimentarily financed by the British authorities in Cyprus, by the newly founded Cyprus Museum, the British Museum, private English residents and, not until later, by the German Archaeological Institute.[37] The German amateur archaeologist discovered, identified and excavated hundreds of tombs and 42 new sanctuary sites: at six of the latter he conducted large-scale excavations and investigated the remaining cult places, either through trial excavations, survey or a combination of both. His monograph *Kypros, the Bible and Homer* (London 1893) contains a catalogue listing 72 different sanctuary sites on the island, which he himself or other scholars had identified and explored by that date. He also provided a topographical map of Cyprus indicating the location of each site in relation to modern villages and towns by a number.[38] Beside this unique catalogue and distribution map of ancient Cypriot cult places, the monograph represents the first comprehensive study of Cypriot sanctuaries and cults. As such a study went beyond the primarily antiquarian interests of Ohnefalsch-Richter's clients, the excavator himself had to provide funding for the documentation, analysis and interpretation of finds.[39]

Ohnefalsch-Richter never actually published systematic, detailed and complete excavation reports, but instead gave comprehensive information as well as many specific details about particular sites including the related finds in his various publications, especially in *Kypros, the Bible and Homer* (subsequently referred to as *KBH*).[40] His explicit ambition to excavate and analyse sites according to the principles and methods of natural science, observing every detail, is reflected in the published information on the site and his manner of documentation of the finds.[41] Going beyond Lang's standard, Ohnefalsch-Richter provided actual stone-by-stone topographical plans, indicating the

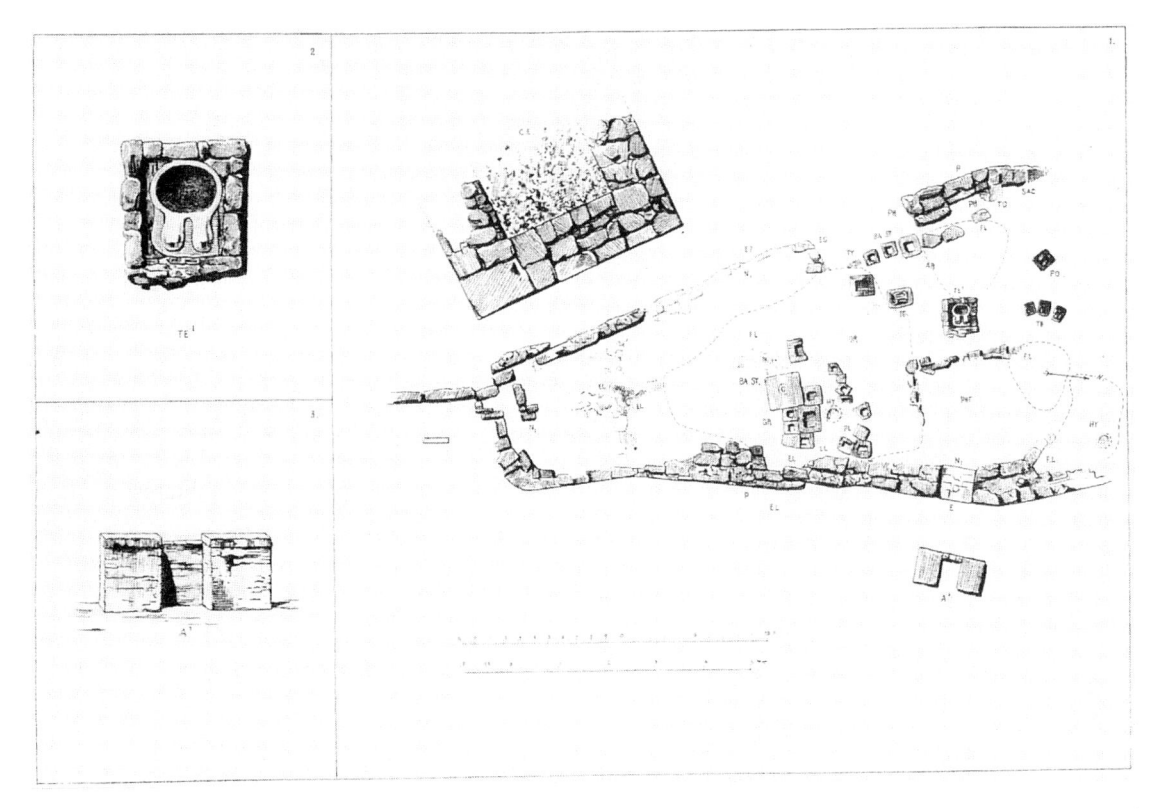

Fig. 8.4: Stone-by-Stone plan of a sanctuary in Achna (KBH No. 1) as published by Ohnefalsch-Richter (n.8) pl. IV.

location of the different structures and sculptures for sites at Achna, Dali, Voni and Tamassos-Frangissa (Fig. 8.4).[42] He also photographed and drew sculpture, sometimes even indicating colours, categorised according to iconographic types and their stylistic development, thus applying an early form of serialisation. Again, the sculpture from Frangissa and Achna (Fig. 8.5) provide good examples.[43] For a site at the Yalias river at Dali, the excavator illustrated the state of preservation, as well as the method and the progress of excavations, in several drawings of the site at different stages of excavation. Moreover, he even depicted a reconstruction of the temenos as it must have looked after its destruction, by putting particular pieces of sculpture in their original place as evident from the context of specific finds (Fig. 8.6).[44]

However, Ohnefalsch-Richter went beyond mere documentation, serialisation and categorisation of the evidence of single sites, and accomplished this in a variety of ways. Comparing the material evidence of 72 sites, he was the first archaeologist who was able to observe patterns concerning architecture, spatial organisation of sanctuaries, votive practice and sacred iconography in their development through the different periods of Cypriot material culture. Close examination of the plates in *KBH* reveals clearly the comparative approach of Ohnefalsch-Richter: Plate X shows a compilation of the topographical plans of seven cult places currently known, which allow a good comparison among themselves and also with depictions on coins and by archaic terracotta models of shrines, which are also assembled on the same plate.

A cornerstone of Ohnefalsch-Richter's work is the study of the historical development of Cypriot iconography as evident from votive sculpture and pictorial representations on pottery and metal objects. He traced the different representations of deities developing from aniconic through vegetal, half anthropomorphic to fully anthropomorphic with different iconographic types between – writing in Ohnefalsch-Richter's terms – the 'prephoenician copper – bronze period'[45] and the Roman period. Chapters 2 and 3 of *KBH*, entitled 'Tree Worship and the Transition to Anthropomorphic Image Worship' and 'Worship of Divinities and Fabulous Beings' both deal extensively with that subject and the iconography of cult and religion in general, comparing the evidence from Cyprus with evidence from other ancient cultures in the eastern Mediterranean. Although Ohnefalsch-Richter often went too far, for example interpreting every depiction of a tree as a religious symbol for a tree deity or even a tree cult[46] and every temple boy as the depiction of Adonis and evidence of his cult at a certain site,[47] his iconological approach to Cypriot cults was a new

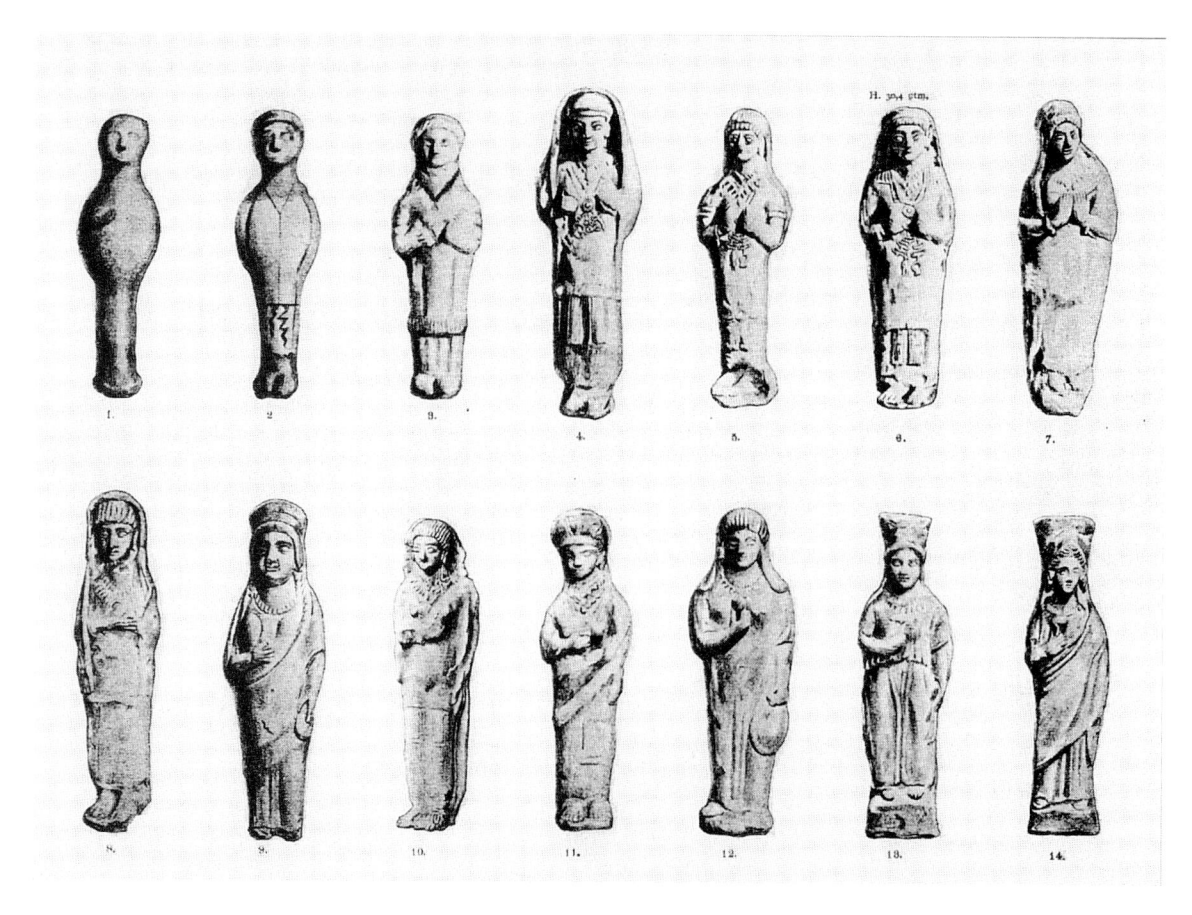

Fig. 8.5: Series of terracottas from Achna (KBH No. 1) as published by Ohnefalsch-Richter (n.8) pl. XI.

and rewarding method of elucidating the nature and history of Cypriot religion.

Applying basic statistics, Ohnefalsch-Richter was also the first scholar to remark on a gender-related votive practice, stating that female deities were usually worshipped by the dedication of female iconographic types, including the representations of goddesses proper, and male deities, accordingly, through male types.[48] This observation provided him with a method of identifying at least the gender of the deity worshipped at a certain site in the absence of dedicatory inscriptions. According to the presence of conclusive representations, he also attempted to name the deities: goddesses identified in such a way were called Astarte, Aphrodite, Artemis, Kybele, Demeter etc., while male deities were Apollo, Heracles, Zeus Ammon, Pan and Dionysos. Thus, Ohnefalsch-Richter actually reconstructed and named the Cypriot pantheon by means of iconography. He also realised that certain iconographic types indicate certain aspects of one deity, and that those types could be abundant in one and completely missing in another sanctuary of the same deity.[49] As a case in point, he observed that terracottas depicting chariots with armed charioteers and armed riders on horseback, which were found in large numbers in Lang's Apollo sanctuary and in Frangissa, were not at all attested for Apollo's temenos at Voni.[50] In Dali, Ohnefalsch-Richter found hundreds of kourotrophos figurines in one of the sanctuaries, while another temenos near the same village predominantly yielded figurines of the naked or dressed Astarte holding her breasts and adorned with rich jewellery. The excavator consequently assigned the first to an Aphrodite-Kourotrophos, whereas the other to Aphrodite-Astarte.[51]

Another major aspect of Ohnefalsch-Richter's research was the location of Cypriot sanctuaries in their natural environment and their relationship to settlements and roads. Applying basic statistics, he observed that 'Of the 72 cultus-sites enumerated in the first chapter, 32 were on mountains (many of them being promontories visible from a long distance) and 36 in valleys and plains, mostly near fountains, brooks or rivers'. He also noted that many sites lay along possibly ancient roads and near the city gates like Lang's sanctuary in Dali.[52] For the city-kingdom of Dali,

Fig. 8.6: Reconstructed view of a temenos at Idalion (KBH No. 3) as published by Ohnefalsch-Richter (n.8) pl. LVI.

the German amateur archaeologist actually reconstructed some sort of sacred landscape indicating the relevant sites in quite accurate maps.[53]

Ohnefalsch-Richter did not study Cypriot sanctuaries and cults in isolation, but interpreted their different aspects in relation to the religion and cults of the other ancient cultures in the eastern Mediterranean. In his book and the explanations of the plates, various passages on Egyptian and Near Eastern cultures, including art, iconography and textual evidence, and their relation to Cypriot culture can be found. His main written sources were the Bible and Homer. For the location of sanctuary sites in Cyprus, he drew heavily on passages in the Bible because Greek sources are silent on this matter. Thus, he saw in every hilltop sanctuary the famous high places of the bible and, overdoing it, reconstructed their design according to biblical descriptions.[54] As two of many iconographic types transmitted from the Near East and Egypt he recognised, for example, depictions of Hathor and Baal Hammon.[55] The title of his monograph, *Kypros, the Bible and Homer*, also reflects his notion of Cyprus as a cross-roads between orient and occident.

In his work Ohnefalsch-Richter referred to evidence discussed in 130 different monographs and articles on Cypriot, Greek, Anatolian, Near Eastern and Egyptian cultures.[56] He also adopted the newly developing systems and methods of categorisation, classification and stylistic serialisation of material, particularly of sculpture. Combining different approaches and methods established by various scholars, Ohnefalsch-Richter found a new way of comparing and interpreting his discoveries with evidence from literary sources about cults and myths. Thus, he introduced an interdisciplinary study of cults and religion into Cypriot archaeology.

Ohnefalsch-Richter's turn to an 'archaeology of cult' was influenced by different factors, such as the state of Cypriot archaeology, developments in German classical archaeology as well as in international scholarship that were affecting all ancient cultures of the eastern Mediterranean. The publications by Lang, Cesnola, Colona-Ceccaldi, Hogarth, Munroe, Tubbs and others providing a comprehensive overview of archaeological remains in Cyprus, were a sound base for further investigation and were amply referred to by Ohnefalsch-Richter. Lang's report, which documented the high value of sanctuary sites as focal points of Cypriot culture, in particular provided a starting point for further investigations concerning cults and religion.

About half of W.H. Engel's, *Kypros* (2 vols., Berlin 1850) had dealt with Cypriot religion as attested by Greek and Latin literary sources, mainly focusing on the Aphrodite cult. Other German scholarly studies had also concentrated on ancient mythology, cults and religion. Ohnefalsch-Richter referred to several important studies: K. Boetticher, *Der Baumkultus der Hellenen* (Berlin 1856), J.A.

Overbeck, 'Das Cultusobjekt bei den Griechen in seinen ältesten Gestaltungen',[57] F.G. Welcker, *Griechische Götterlehre* (3 vols., Göttingen 1857–1863), W.H. Roscher (ed.), *Ausführliches Lexikon der griechischen und römischen Mythologie* (6 vols., Leipzig/Berlin 1884–1937), H.K. Brugsch, *Religion der alten Ägypter* (Leipzig 1888), F.W.A. Baethgen, *Beiträge zur semitischen Religionsgeschichte* (Berlin 1888) and W.W.F. von Baudissin, *Studien zur semitischen Religionsgeschichte* (2 vols., Leipzig 1876–1878).

The German excavations at the Zeus temenos at Olympia, the first publications on the altars by Curtius, and on the bronze votive material published by A. Furtwängler, might also have strengthened Ohnefalsch-Richter's interest in Cypriot religion and its relation to ancient cults on the Greek mainland.

Not only German publications and excavations, but, to a lesser extent, international scholarship reflected a strong interest in the religion and cults of ancient cultures around the eastern Mediterranean. Ohnefalsch-Richter must have been very aware of this trend as he quoted several studies such as A.H. Sayce, *The Religions of Ancient Egypt and Babylon* (the Gifford lectures, Edinburgh 1902) and W.R. Smith, *Lectures on the Religion of the Semites* (rev. ed. London 1894). Even Cypriot cults had been studied in the context of Cypriot culture in A.E. Holwerda, *Die alten Kyprier in Kunst und Kultus* (Leiden 1885).

Thus, we must understand Ohnefalsch-Richter's work as a study in the trend not only of contemporary, mainly German archaeology, but also of international scholarship at the time. Many of his approaches eluded twentieth-century scholarship and some of them, for example the consideration of the topography of sanctuaries, their spatial organisation and the nature of the deities have been rediscovered only fairly recently. In the last three decades of the twentieth century, Cypriot sanctuaries and cults have again become a major focus of excavations and scholarly interest, which is not only reflected by many recent publications, but also by some of the papers given at this very conference.[58] While working on my dissertation on Cypriot sanctuaries from the Archaic to the Hellenistic period, I have collected evidence for almost 300 sanctuary sites in Cyprus for this chronological span alone, which is more than four times as many as Ohnefalsch-Richter knew about. These sites will be studied and interpreted in terms of their location in the natural and human made spatial, social, economic and political landscape of ancient Cyprus. Many of Ohnefalsch-Richter's approaches and observations are still valid and instructive, and his work still constitutes a fundamental base for any modern or contemporary archaeology of Cypriot cults and religion.

Notes

1. The author would like to thank Prof. Dr. Nancy Serwint, Dr. Eric C. Lapp, Dr. John R. Leonard, Dr. Cecilia Beer and Dr. Victor Parker for their kind help and advice in editing this text.
2. S. Casson, *Ancient Cyprus* (London 1937) 8.
3. Casson (n.2) 11–12, 14.
4. For a list of the sanctuaries and their location in Cyprus see appendix and legend for figure 1 (map).
5. See, for example, B.G. Trigger, *A History of Archaeological Thought* (Cambridge 1989) 39–40.
6. For the earliest Cypriot sculptures which came to western Europe already in the seventeenth century see, for example, A. Hermary, 'Histoire des études sur la sculpture chypriote', *Centre d'Études Chypriotes. Cahier* 14 (1990) 2, 7–9.
7. For a contemporary account of how foreign residents and locals were increasingly involved in such activities and on the motivations they had, see R.H. Lang, *Cyprus* (London 1878) 329–340. A summary of the history of archaeological exploration and exploitation of Cyprus before the second half of the nineteenth century is also given in E. Goring, *A Mischievous Pastime* (Edinburgh 1988) 1–5 with further bibliography.
8. M. Ohnefalsch-Richter, *Kypros, the Bible and Homer* (London 1893) 13, no. 20 (Kochi); for the Artemis Paralia sanctuary (Larnaca, Salines) see Ohnefalsch-Richter 11, no. 7 and Lang (n.6) 335–338. See appendix and Fig. 8.1, nos. 57 and 11
9. See O. Masson, *Les inscriptions chypriotes syllabiques* (2nd edition, Paris 1983) 19 for the approximate date of discovery. For all objects discovered at this spot at the time including references, see 233–234 incl. footnotes 1–2. For the circumstances of discovery, acquisition and for the first publications of the bronze tablet proper, 235–236. See appendix and Fig. 8.1, no. 1.
10. The earliest translation of the inscription which mentions the siege of Idalion by the Kitians as well as the Athena sanctuary was given by M. Schmidt, *Sammlung kyprischer Inschriften in epichorischer Schrift* (Jena 1876) 2–3, pl. I; for a dedicatory inscription to Athena on a bronze object (scepter?) see Masson (n.9) 245, no. 218.
11. The fact that Cypriot sculpture was found in the Levant and Phoenician types were found in Cyprus united both cultures in the minds of French scholars as well as art collectors. See, for example, Hermary (n.6) 9–10. Compare the paper of A. Caubet in this volume, and the summary account of the history of the Louvre collection in A. Hermary, *Catalogue des antiquités de Chypre. Sculptures* (Musée du Louvre, Département des Antiquités orientales, Paris 1989) 11–21 passim.
12. Compare with the list of sites (appendix) and Fig. 8.1(map), nos. 3–7. A summary account of those two expeditions is given in Hermary (n.11) 14–19 with further references to unpublished material (mainly letters) in the archives of the Louvre and bibliography. The gigantic stone vase from a sixth located sanctuary on the acropolis of Amathous (see list) had already been known since the Lusignan period (thirteenth-sixteenth century). The French expedition

arranged the transport of this vessel to the Louvre. See P. Aupert et al., *Guide d'Amathonte* (Athens/Nicosia 1996).

13. Compare the list of illustrations in G. Perrot and Ch. Chipiez, *History of Art in Phoenicia and Cyprus* (London 1885) vol. II, IX and X: of 67 pieces of sculpture, only 15 are mentioned with a vague provenience, eight of them from Athienou and two from Dali, but without indication as to the locality (e.g. Ayios Photios, Malloura, Golgoi proper). The remaining five pieces of sculpture with provenience indicated are figurines and come, most likely, from tombs.

14. A good example of employing different methods to acquire objects can be seen in the activities of Lang in Cyprus, summarised by Goring (n.7) 7–10; several objects from Lang's collections were distributed among other museums. Their proveniences indicated as different from Dali or Pyla, where Lang excavated and recorded two sanctuary sites, proves that he kept on buying antiquities found by locals and other amateur archaeologists.

15. Compare with Hermary (n.11) 19, incl. n.46; this is obviously the same temenos which was excavated later by Lang.

16. A. Palma di Cesnola, *Salaminia* (2nd ed., London 1884). The stone objects (85–109; sculptures, altars and thymiateria) and at least some of the terracotta statuettes (177–248; e.g. 204, Fig. 230) illustrated among those pages must have come originally from different sanctuaries sites. The majority of the terracottas, however, originated from tombs or were surface finds according to Cesnola himself. It is not clear from the text which of the objects Cesnola bought and which, if any, he discovered or even personally excavated.

17. H.R. Lang, 'Narrative of Excavations in a Temple at Dali (Idalium) in Cyprus', *Transactions of the Royal Society of Literature* 2nd series XI (1878) 30–79. Compare appendix and Fig. 8.1, no. 9.

18. Lang (n.17) 30.
19. Lang (n.17) 31–32.
20. Lang (n.17) 32.
21. Lang (n.17) 32. From this description Ohnefalsch-Richter (n. 8) pl. III plotted the sanctuary on his map, albeit slightly off site, because every trace of it was annihilated owing to extensive terracing of the slope before Ohnefalsch-Richter visited ancient Idalion. However, the University of Arizona Expedition to Idalion was able to re-identify and uncover part of the site thanks to Lang's plan and his topographical description; compare the paper by Margaret Morden in this volume.

22. Lang (n.17) 37–38.
23. Lang (n.17) 34–42.
24. Lang (n.17) 33–34; 50 (inscriptions).
25. Lang (n.17) 54.
26. This is George Smith, the well-known Assyriologist.
27. Lang (n.17) 50–51 incl. footnotes 10–11 with further references and R.H. Lang, 'On the discovery of some Cypriote inscriptions', *Transactions of the British Academy* 1 (1872) 116–128.

28. Comment by Poole on the sculpture from Dali in Lang (n.17) 54–79. Poole also studied Lang's coin collection, not only from Dali; compare R.H. Lang, 'Treasure-Trove in Cyprus of Gold Staters', *Num.Chron.* 2 (11) (1871) 229–234. Thus, Poole helped Lang to categorise the coins found at the temple in Dali; see R.H. Lang, 'On Coins Discovered During Recent Excavations in the Island of Cyprus', *Num. Chron.* 2 (11) (1871) 1–18.

29. Compare Appendix and Fig. 8.1, nos. 4, 11–21. In the New York edition of Cesnola's book (1878, reprint Nicosia 1991, p. 452) John Taylor lists 15 sanctuary sites. Four of them however are not really sanctuary sites, such as the 'site, where the Curium treasure' was found, which was actually composed from finds from various tombs. The sanctuary at Phasoula is not mentioned in Taylor's list, but in Ohnefalsch-Richter (n.8) no. 46 as discovered by Cesnola. All subsequent citations of this book refer to the pagination of the reprinted text.

30. Cesnola (n.29) 344–347 (Kourion), 50–51 (Kition), 243 (Chytroi).

31. Report on Ayios Photios in Cesnola (n.29) 117–164. The main part of the excavation was conducted in 1873.

32. G. Colonna-Ceccaldi, *Monuments de Chypre, de Syrie et d'Égypte* (Paris 1882) 40 (rivalry), 51–52 (Lang as eye-witness for Cesnola's excavations). After the discovery of the colossal Ayios Photios sculpture, other consuls tried to get to the place before Cesnola, to buy the land and the discoveries made on it, but Cesnola won that race; see Cesnola (n.29) 121.

33. Cesnola (n.29) 139 (plan). Illustrations of sculpture are strewn into the text on the pages 123, 129, 131, 132, 133 (Hercules), 136 (votive relief), 140, 141, 143–145, 149–151, 152 (representation of Venus), 153 (representation of Diana), 156 (Geryon), 157 (Venus), 162.

34. Cesnola (n.29) 150.
35. Cesnola (n.29) 421–422, no. 17 (Demeter and Apollo), no. 20 (Zeus).

36. E.A. Gardner, D.G. Hogarth et al., 'Excavations in Cyprus 1887–8', *JHS* IX (1888) 193–258 (Aphrodite sanctuary in Kouklia); 171–174 (Amargetti); J.A.R. Munroe, H.A. Tubbs, 'Excavations in Cyprus', *JHS* XI (1890), 50–99 (Limniti); 'Excavations at Salamis', *JHS* XII (1891) 59–198 (2 definite and 3 possible sanctuary sites at Salamis); J.L. Myres, 'Excavations in Cyprus in 1894', *JHS* XVII (1897) 164–170 (Larnaca, Kamelarga and Batsalos). Compare appendix and Fig. 8.1, nos. 12, 14, 22–38.

37. For a chronological summary of the archaeological activities of Ohnefalsch-Richter see H-G. Buchholz, 'Max Ohnefalsch-Richter als Archäologe auf Zypern', *Centre d'Etudes Chypriotes. Cahier* 11–12 (1989) 3–27.

38. Ohnefalsch-Richter (n.8) pl. I.
39. M. Ohnefalsch-Richter, *Die antiken Cultusstätten auf Kypros* (Berlin 1891) VI-VII.
40. A list of Ohnefalsch-Richter's publications is given by L. Fivel, 'Ohnefalsch-Richter (1850–1917), essai de bibliographie', *Centre d'Études Chypriotes. Cahier* 11–12 (1989) 35–40.

41. Ohnefalsch-Richter (n.8) V–VI, VIII (scientific approach). Ibid. IX, the author mentions that he documented the progress and results of his work in Polis in fieldnotebooks,

reports, maps, top plans, drawings, photographs and watercolours.
42. M. Ohnefalsch-Richter (n.8) pls. IV (Achna), V (Voni), VI (Tamassos-Frangissa), VII (Idalion).
43. For photographs of the sculptures from Tamassos-Frangissa see H-G. Buchholz, 'Tamassos-Phrangissa (1885)', *Centre d'Etudes Chypriotes. Cahier* 16 (1991) 2, 3–15 pls. 3a-6b; for drawings of the terracotta sculpture from Achna in chronological order (seriation) see Ohnefalsch-Richter (n.8) pls. XI, XII, CCIX–CCXII, colour drawings of terracottas on pl. LXVIII.
44. Ohnefalsch-Richter (n.8) pls. XVI, LVII for the excavation illustration, ibid. pl. LVI for the reconstruction: the statues and statue fragments can clearly be identified with pieces published on pls.XLVIII–LV.
45. Term used by Ohnefalsch-Richter (n.8) 29.
46. Ohnefalsch-Richter (n.8) 36, Fig. 37, 42 Figs. 44–45 and 65, Figs. 76 and 77 are all examples of the depiction of trees and plants as indication of landscape or as decorative patterns. There are no indications that they are meant to be symbols of cult or deities.
47. Ohnefalsch-Richter (n.8) 101–103 (on Cypriot temple boys as images of Adonis); also 202–207. Because of many kourotrophoi as well as temple boys found in sanctuary No. 33 (Idalion; *KBH* 18) he concludes that 'By the side of Astarte-Aphrodite with maternal attributes, Tammuz-Adonis was especially venerated here'.
48. Ohnefalsch-Richter (n.8) 322–323.
49. For the chronology of the different iconographic types of the Cypriote female deities, their different aspects and some of the sites where they were found see Ohnefalsch-Richter (n.8) 269–327; the same for male deities, 327–342.
50. Ohnefalsch-Richter (n.8) 326–327 (warrior aspect); 331 (Voni in comparison to Frangissa).
51. Ohnefalsch-Richter (n.8) 18, no. 33 (Aphrodite Kourotrophos); for many kourotrophoi from this site see 203; for Astarte-Aphrodite sanctuary at Dali see 5–6, no. 3; for the identification of this deity through iconographic types see 267–268. For the identification of such types as Astarte-Aphrodite see 266.
52. Ohnefalsch-Richter (n.8) 229; for the settings of sanctuaries in towns, at city gates and by the waysides see 227; for the different setting of cult places in the natural environment see 227–234; for the setting of Lang's sanctuary at a city gate of Dali see *KBH* 16, no. 30; 231..
53. Ohnefalsch-Richter (n.8) pls. II and III (maps include handwritten legends) and explanation of plates; for the sacred landscape of Idalion compare Margaret Morden's paper in this volume.
54. Ohnefalsch-Richter (n.8) 227–231.
55. Ohnefalsch-Richter (n.8) 186–195 (Hathor capitals and Baal Hammon depictions from Cyprus).
56. I extracted the bibliography used by Ohnefalsch-Richter from the references given in the footnotes of *KBH*. All the publications and authors mentioned in the part of this paper that follows are quoted more or less extensively in *KBH*, often with unsatisfactory bibliographical information by today's standards.
57. *Berichte über die Verhandlungen der Königlich Sächsischen Gesellschaft der Wissenschaften zu Leipzig, Philologisch-historische Klasse* (Leipzig 1864).
58. The most recent overview with bibliography is given in S.M.S. Al-Radi, *Phlamoudhi Vounari: A Sanctuary Site in Cyprus* (Göteborg 1983).

Appendix and legend for the map (Fig. 8.1)

The years given after the excavators indicate the period which they spent in Cyprus; the numbers given before the site name refer to those indicated in the map. The site names (*ancient name*/modern name) correspond to those given in the Administration & Road Map (Scale: 1:250.000), edited by the Department of Lands and Surveys, Cyprus in 1996. The toponyms (names or descriptions) in quotation marks are quoted as in the original publication if no further exploration was made. Each site has only got one number, even if explored several times. The numbers in brackets after the site-names indicate the numbers in the catalogue of cult places published by M. Ohnefalsch-Richter, *Kypros, the Bible and Homer* (London 1893).

The sites *KBH* no. 29 and no. 31 (*Idalion*/Dali, western acropolis) as well as *KBH* no. 48 and no. 49 are different spots of the same site and therefore listed as one site each. The sites *KBH* no. 68 and no. 71 are definitely not sanctuary sites and, consequently, are not included in this list.

List of sanctuary sites, recorded and exploited in the second half of the nineteenth century:

A) French travellers, diplomats and Expeditions (1848–1865)
1. *Idalion*/Dali, Ambelliri (western acropolis)
2. *Idalion*/Dali, Moutti tou Arvili (eastern acropolis) (T. Colonna-Ceccaldi)
3. *Golgoi*/Athienou
4. *Golgoi*/Athienou, Ayios Photios
5. *Golgoi*/ Athienou, Malloura
6. Arsos
7. *Amathous*, acropolis
8. Trikomo (G. Colonna-Ceccaldi)

B) R. H. Hamilton Lang (1861–1872)
9. *Idalion*/Dali, lower Mouti tou Arvili (eastern acropolis)
10. Pyla

C) L. Palma di Cesnola (1865–1873)
11. *Kition*/Larnaka, Salines (Artemis Paralia sanctuary)
12. *Kition*/Larnaka, Batsalos
4. *Golgoi*/Athienou, Ayios Photios
13. *Kourion*, Apollo Hylates sanctuary
14. *Palaepaphos*/Kouklia, Aphrodite temple
15. *Palaepaphos*/Kouklia. Styllarka
16. *Idalion*/ Potamia
17. *Soloi*/ Karavostasi
18. Larnakas Lapithou

19. *Chytroi*/Kythrea (temple 1)
20. *Chytroi*/Kythrea (temple 2)
21. Phasoula (*KBH*, no. 46)

D) British expeditions (1884–1894)
14. *Palaepaphos*/Kouklia, Aphrodite temple
22. *Nea Paphos*/Kato Paphos, east of (Hogarth survey)
23. Amargeti
24. Drymou
25. Ayia Moni
26. Marathounta
27. Limnitis
28. *Kourion*, Demeter and Kore sanctuary
29. *Kition*/Larnaka, Kamelarga
12. *Kition*/Larnaka, Batsalos
30. Kalograia, "Lisies" (Hogarth survey)
31. *Knidos*/Gastria, "Kakoskale" (Hogarth survey)
32. Peristephani (Hogarth survey)
33. Monarga (Hogarth survey)
34. Cap *Dinaretum*/Cape Apostolus Andreas (Hogarth survey)
35. *Salamis*, Toumba
36. *Salamis*, 'Zeus temple'
37. *Salamis*, 'Agora'
38. *Salamis*, "Daemonastasium and Cistern"
39. *Salamis*, "Site A"

E) M. Ohnefalsch-Richter (1878–1889)
40. Achna (*KBH* No. 1)
41. Voni (No.2)
42. *Idalion*/Dali, Yalias River (No. 3)
43. *Tamassos*/Politiko, Frangissa (No. 4)
44. *Tamassos*/Politiko, Chomazoudia (No. 5)
45. *Tamassos*/Politiko, Pedhaios River (No. 6)
46. *Kition*/Larnaka, Bamboula (No. 9)
47. Achna, east of KBH No. 1 (No. 10)
48. Achna, 'in direction of Avgorou' (No. 11)
49. Achna, 'in direction of Xylotymbo' (No. 12)
50. Xylotimbo, 'near threshing floors' (No. 13)
51. Achna, 'in direction to Acheritou' (No. 14)
52. Ormidhia (No. 15)
53. *Pedalion*/Cape Gkreko(No. 16)
54. *Salamis*, 'south of big tumulus' (No. 17)
55. Arsos (No. 18)
56. Marathovounos (No. 19)
57. Kochi (No. 20)
58. *Ledrai*/Nicosia, 'south of Ayios Omoloyitades' (No. 21)
59. *Ledrai*/Nicosia, 'near Ayia Parskevi' (No. 22)
60. *Chytroi*/Kythrea, 'southeast of upper city' (No. 24)
61. *Idalion*/Dali, summit of eastern acropolis (*KBH* No. 29+31)
62. *Idalion*/Dali, slope of western acropolis (No. 32)

63. *Idalion*/Dali, summit of western acropolis (No. 33)
64. *Idalion*/Dali, east of (No. 34)
65. *Idalion*/Dali, south of eastern acropolis (No. 35)
66. *Idalion*/Dali, lower city (No. 36)
67. *Idalion*/Dali, lower city (No. 37)
68. *Idalion*/Dali, east of (No. 38)
69. *Idalion*/Dali, 'one mile north of' (No. 39)
70. Potamia, short distance west from village (No. 40)
71. Nisou (No. 41)
72. Lythrodontas (No. 42)
73. *Amathous*, northeast of (No. 43)
74. *Amathous*, south (No. 44)
75. Kellaki, Moutti Sinoas (No. 47)
76. Pomos Point (No. 51)
77. Katydata, Linou (No. 53)

References to earlier excavations (numbers of this index):

11. *Kition*/Larnaka, Salines (No. 7)
12. *Kition*/Larnaka, Batsalos (No. 8)
 4. *Golgoi*/Athienou, Ayios Photios (No. 25+26)
10. Pyla (No. 27)

 1. *Idalion*/Dali, summit western acropolis (No. 28)
 9. *Idalion*/Dali, lower eastern acroplois (No. 30)
 7. *Amathous*, acropolis (No. 45)
21. Phasoula (No. 46)
13. *Kourion*, Apollo Hylates sanctuary (No. 48–49)
24. Drymou (No. 50)
27. Limnitis (No. 52)
14. *Palaepaphos*/Kouklia (No. 54+55)
15. *Palaepaphos*/Kouklia, Styllarka (No. 57)
22. *Nea Paphos*/Kouklia (No. 56)
23. Amargeti (No. 58)
26. Marathounta (No. 59)
25. Ayia Moni (No. 60)
18. Larnaka Lapithou (No. 61)
33. Monarga (No. 62)
39. *Salamis*, Site A (No. 63)
36. *Salamis*, Temple of Zeus (No. 64)
37. *Salamis*, Agora (No. 65)
38. *Salamis*, Daemonastasium (No. 66)
35. *Salamis*, Toumba (No. 67)
32. Peristephani (No. 69)
34. Cap *Dinaretum*/Cape Andreas (No. 70)

Museums and their 19th century Collections

9. 'New' objects from British Museum Tomb 73 at Curium

Donald M. Bailey and Marilyn Hockey

On receipt of a bequest to the British Museum of £2000 by Miss Emma Turner, for the 'purpose of excavation or survey of sites in Europe, Asia or Africa in furtherance of the study of the antiquities of Greece, Rome or Egypt or of Biblical Antiquities', the money was allocated to the Department of Greek and Roman Antiquities for excavation in Cyprus. In 1893–4, Arthur H. Smith and John L. Myres worked successively in cemeteries at Amathus, Henry B. Walters in 1895 opened tombs at Curium, and in 1896 a Late Bronze Age cemetery and other sites at Enkomi were examined by Alexander S. Murray, Arthur H. Smith and Percy Christian. The three Museum officials eventually, published their work, to some extent, in the comparatively well-illustrated Murray, Smith and Walters 1900. Amathus yielded in the main Archaic and classical-period material, but it becomes clear that both at Curium and Enkomi (and also at some smaller excavations made during the last years of the century) that gathering Mycenaean material became the main aim of the Museum's work in Cyprus. But it is to Curium that we turn in this paper, to one particular tomb there, and one that had no Mycenaean content.

Walters, an Assistant in the Department of Greek and Roman Antiquities of the British Museum, directed excavations at the site of Curium; he was aided by two residents in Cyprus, local agents for the British Museum and both experienced in exploiting the ancient sites of the island, particularly its tombs, John W. Williamson and Percy Christian.[1] Walters, Williamson and Christian excavated 118 tombs between the 24th of January and the 11th of April 1895. They range in date from the Late Bronze Age to Roman times. Working in an ancient cemetery in land belonging to the church of Ayios Ermoyenis, his Site B, Walters opened on the 5th of March Tomb 73 in the British Museum series (Fig. 9.1).[2] His excavation notebook, 'Notes at Curium',[3] which is almost certainly a later transcript compiled from notes made in the field, describes the tomb as 'Full of earth – apparently untouched' and its published description states that it was 'A very large tomb with three chambers, apparently of different dates (500–400 B.C.); full of earth, but apparently intact' (Murray, Smith and Walters 1900, 82). The time-span of the tomb is greater than Walters thought, and like so many chamber-tombs in Cyprus was no doubt constantly opened to receive new burials. A list of 37 numbered items, some of them groups of objects, was included in the published version, but the separate chambers in which they were found were there not defined. 'Notes at Curium', Tomb 73, listing some 44 items, divides the objects into two groups, the second separated from the first by the words 'In other part of tomb'. The published list of 1900 and the excavation notebook list of 1895 can be largely reconciled one with the other, but not wholly so, as will be seen from the lists below. A selective list of the tomb's contents was given by Walters in a letter of 23 March 1895 to the Principal Librarian of the British Museum.[4] A very few sketch plans of tombs taken from the field notes were inserted into 'Notes at Curium', but no plans were made of Tomb 73 and no photographs taken on site seem to exist. The publication of the tomb is inadequate and illustrates only some of the objects found. It is hoped to remedy this situation to a certain degree with the present paper, and to illustrate as many as possible, but with only brief descriptions and few comparanda, although with some emphasis falling on certain silver objects recognised only recently as coming from the tomb. Walters' excavation notebook list, being the primary source, is here transcribed as (**i**), and each item (or group of items) is given a serial number relating to that list and matched as far as possible with the corresponding item, its number in parentheses, in the published list in Murray, Smith and Walters 1900, 82–3: (**ii**); items described in Walters' letter to the Principal

Librarian are quoted in **iii**; the object's Museum Registration Number is given: **(iv)**; and a description follows: **(v)**; and also any published reference is given: **(vi)** (many of these references have full discussions of the type of object, which, to save space, are not necessarily repeated in **(v)**). Numbers **1–29** were apparently found together in one part of the tomb, **30–44** in a different part. It will be noticed that some items are described as 'apparently not kept' or 'not yet identified'. Whether they were discarded in Cyprus or were not registered after reaching the Museum cannot be ascertained. The objects listed under Item 7 below have only recently been identified: hitherto they were lying unregistered in the Department's Research Collections.[5]

Material listed as being from Tomb 73

First Group

1. (i) 'Greek skyphos of black ware – end of 5th cent. B.C.' Fig. 9.2.
   (ii) '(35) Cotylè as last [(34)], of black-glaze ware'.
   (iii) 'Greek cotylè of black glazed ware (red-figure period)'.
   (iv) GR 1896.2–1.396.
   (v) Athenian black-glaze glaux, repaired from fragments, with some loss. Overall black glaze, but reserved within the base-ring; black circle-and-dot at centre of base; reserved area reddened with miltos. H. 6.1, D. of rim 8.1cm. This is Agora skyphos Type B (Sparkes and Talcott 1970, 86, a rare shape): ours probably dates to the early years of the fifth century BC.
   (vi) Murray, Smith and Walters 1900, 77, 83.

2. (i) 'Bronze strigil in fragments'. Apparently not kept.

3 a-c. (i) 'Three fragments of silver bracelet'. Fig. 9.3.
   (iv) (a-b) GR 1896.2–1.353; (c) GR 1896.2–1.354.
   (v) In the Register GR 1896.2–1.353 is described as two fragments of a silver bracelet. One large fragment with its number largely lost may be one of these; the other fragment has not yet been traced. The bracelet appears to be silver with a high bronze content, or with a bronze core. Both terminals are lost. Round in section; one end swells more than the other, but this may be due to corrosion. W. 7.7cm. No intrinsic date, but probably sixth or fifth century BC. The bracelet (c) has lost a terminal. It is more or less evenly round in section, but narrows very slightly to a flattened knobbed terminal, defined by grooves and an elongated chevron design. W. 6.6cm. No intrinsic date, but probably sixth or fifth century BC.
   (vi) Unpublished.

4. (i) 'Bronze mirror'. Apparently not kept.

5a-f. (i) 'Five, six?, spirals (small) of gilt bronze'. Fig. 9.4.
   (ii) '(4) Six gold spirals, plain, of the 5th century B.C.'
   (iii) 'Ring and five spirals of gilt bronze'.
   (iv) (a-f) GR 1896.2–1.143–8.
   (v) Six bronze spirals each overlaid with sheet gold, the tips chased with three lateral grooves from which depend grooves in a horn-shaped pattern: earrings or hair-ornaments. H. 1.6cm. About 450–400 BC?: but compare a closely similar silver example from a tomb at Marion/Arsinoe dated to the first half of the sixth century BC: Ohnefalsch-Richter 1893, pl. LXVII, 5.
   (vi) Murray, Smith and Walters 1900, 82, pl. XIII, 1–6; Marshall 1911, nos 1635–40; Williams and Ogden 1994, no. 163.

6a-b. (i) 'Four large silver bracelets'. Fig. 9.5.
   (ii) '(16) Two pairs of silver bracelets ending in snakes' heads, with hinges and holes for pins to fasten the ends'.
   (iii) 'Four large silver bracelets'.
   (iv) (a) GR 1896.2–1.339–40; (b) GR 1896.2–1.341–2.
   (v) (a) Pair of silver bracelets terminating in stylised snakes' heads and hinged in the middle of the opposite side. The hinge is of the tongue and notch type and was held together by a transverse pin. One has a further pin passing through both elements, behind the heads of the snakes, holding the bracelet closed; the other has holes for such a pin. Scales are indicated on GR 1896.2–1.339 for a short distance behind the head on the back of the snakes; the underside of the heads has less worn detail, with branching patterns, and there are transverse body grooves underneath. Its pair, GR 1896.2–1.340, is much cruder in construction and more corroded, and no decorative detail remains. W. c.8.9cm and c.9.1cm. Fifth century BC or a little

		earlier. (b) Pair of silver bracelets close to (a) but rather smaller in scale. Most details are lost due to corrosion. W. (both) c. 8.1cm. Fifth century BC or a little earlier.			different part of the tomb. W. 3.2cm. About 520–480 BC. (b) Part of a finger-ring of spirally curved silver wire: parts of four turns survive. D. 1.7cm. No intrinsic date, but probably sixth or fifth century BC.
	(vi)	Murray, Smith and Walters 1900, 83.		(vi)	Unpublished.
7.	(i)	'Numerous fragments of silver figures in relief – apparently Egyptian types'. Added later, by Walters: 'BES'. Figs 9.45–9.58	10a-b.	(i)	'Part of silver bar with two gold filagree pendants'. Figs 9.8–9.9.
	(ii)	'(14) A series of silver figures of Bes, in repoussé relief, very much corroded and broken'		(ii)	(a) '(8) Gold vase-shaped pendant decorated with filigree, attached to a thin bar of silver'; (b) '(7) Gold pendant of filigree-work in the form of a ball'.
	(iii)	'Numerous fragments of silver plaques with reliefs of Bes and heads of deities'.		(iii)	'Part of silver necklace with two gold filagree pendants'.
	(iv)	GR 1991.12–11.1–35.		(iv)	(a) GR 1896.2–1.152 and (b) GR 1896.2–1.151.
	(v)	Silver Bes figures and other objects: see below for full descriptions.		(v)	Corroded silver chain with two pendants, one now detached: (a) gold vase-shaped pendant with filigree decoration threaded on a silver loop-in-loop chain, only a part of which survives. H. of pendant 2.0cm; L. of chain 4.2cm; (b) openwork gold-wire pendant with suspension loop. H. 1.6cm. Fifth century BC.
	(vi)	Murray, Smith and Walters 1900, 83.			
8.	(i)	'Fifteen glass beads – several variegated'. Fig. 9.6.			
	(ii)	'(12) Necklace of stone and variegated glass beads, sixteen in number'.			
	(iv)	GR 1896.2–1.156.		(vi)	Murray, Smith and Walters 1900, 82, pl. XIII, 8 and 7; Marshall 1911, nos 1960 and 2030.
	(v)	Series of sixteen oblate spheroid beads that may or may not belong together, collected together by the excavator. Eight of the beads are of an opaque green glass, almost a faience, with a corroded and pitted surface. D. between 1.2 and 1.6cm. Six of the others are matching eye-beads, with blue and white 'eyes' in a green background. D. between 1.2 and 1.3cm. The remaining two are smaller eye-beads (not matching), one with blue, white and black 'eyes' in a blue background, the other with many blue, white and black 'eyes' in a green background. Both 1.0cm in diameter. Eye-beads can be at least as early as the eighth century BC;[6] examples from Etruria are datable to about 550–450 BC,[7] which is probably the date of our Curium examples.	11.	(i)	'Gilt-bronze ring (yellow glass setting fallen out)'. Fig. 9.10.
				(ii)	'(6) Gold-plated bronze ring (broken), with setting for a gem (now lost)'.
				(iv)	GR 1896.2–1.150.
				(v)	Swivel-ring, bronze tapering hoop with thick gold plating and an oval gold mount decorated with two rows of twisted wire; at each end is a socket (with traces of bronze within) surrounded by a beaded collar. The yellow glass setting mentioned in the excavation notebook cannot now be found and was not there when the object was registered in the Museum. D. 2.6cm. Late sixth century BC.
	(vi)	Murray, Smith and Walters 1900, 83.		(vi)	Murray, Smith and Walters 1900, 66, 82, pl. XIII, 10; Marshall 1907, no. 1225.
9a-b.	(i)	'Two small silver rings'. Fig. 9.7.	12.	(i)	'Gold ring with pendant [sic] gem in gold setting'. Fig. 9.11.
	(iii)	A 'Silver ring with rock-crystal setting..'. is probable.		(ii)	'(5) Gold ring with locket attached as pendant in which is a setting of pale yellow paste'.
	(iv)	(a) GR 1896.2–1.357 and (b) probably GR 1896.2–1.358.		(iii)	'Gold ring with pendant gem in gold setting'.
	(v)	(a) Silver swivel-ring hoop, tapering at each end, with most of its mount lost: it perhaps held the gem GR 1896.2–1.157: see **39** below, although the gem is said to be from a		(iv)	GR 1896.2–1.149.
				(v)	Gold ring with a pendent yellow chalcedony scaraboid gem in a gold setting that was once

mounted in a swivel-ring, but now has an applied loop. H. 3.5cm. The swivel-ring setting is of the sixth century BC; the ring and the applied loop are likely to be rather later, probably of the fifth century. Although this is a composite construct, there are examples of purposely made ring-and-pendant jewellery from Cyprus: Ohnefalsch-Richter 1893, pl. XXXIII, 12 (beaded ring with carnelian setting) and pl. XXXIII, 14 (twisted ring with carnelian setting), both from a tomb at Marion/Arsinoe dated to the late fifth, early fourth century; pl. LXVII, 10, also from the same site and of the first half of the sixth century (plain ring with onyx setting).

(vi) Murray, Smith and Walters 1900, 82, pl. XIII, 13; Marshall 1911, no. 2045.

13a-b. (i) 'Two silver rings with flat bezels (one broken)'. Figs 9.12–9.15.

(ii) (a) '(19) Silver ring, with intaglio design on the bezel; Pegasos to right; in the background, palm-trees'; (b) '(20) Similar ring with plain bezel'.

(iii) There is mention of a silver ring: see **14** below.

(iv) (a) GR 1896.2–1.283 and (b) GR 1896.2–1.285.

(v) The broken one mentioned in (i) – probably (13a) – is now repaired; the rings are not similar, as (ii) has it. (a) Electrum or silver ring with a tapering hoop and a flat, rectangularly oval bezel, with an intaglio scene: a winged quadruped, with a branch before it, and possibly a palm tree rising beyond, near the rear. D. 2.2cm. Sixth century BC; (b) silver ring with an oval eroded bezel (of which I can make nothing) and an electrum plug at one end. D. 2.2cm. Fifth century BC.

(vi) Murray, Smith and Walters 1900, 66, 83; Marshall 1907, nos 16 and 1040.

14. (i) 'Three pairs of silver earrings'. Not yet identified.

(iii) 'Three pairs of silver earrings and silver ring'.

15. (i) 'A fine pair of bracelets – gilt bronze – ending in ram's heads'. Fig. 9.16.

(ii) '(1) Pair of gilt-bronze bracelets, ending in rams' heads. Date, about 400 B.C'.

(iii) 'Pair of gilt-bronze bracelets ending in rams' heads – well preserved'.

(iv) GR 1896.2–1.141–2.

(v) Pair of gold penannular bracelets with a bronze core and ram-head terminals; plain tongues on the collar. W. 8.4cm. About 450–400 BC.

(vi) Murray, Smith and Walters 1900, 65, 82, pl. XIII, 11–12; Marshall 1911, nos 1985–6; Higgins 1980, pl. 30A; Deppert-Lippitz 1985, 158, fig. 110; V. Tatton-Brown in Hunt 1990, 89; Pfrommer 1990, 344, TA 143; Williams and Ogden 1994, no. 161.

16. (i) 'Pair of gold earrings – fine filagree work'. Fig. 9.17.

(ii) '(2) Two gold earrings of crescent shape, with honeysuckle patterns in filigree work'.

(iii) 'Pair of gold earrings with good filagree work'.

(iv) GR 1896.2–1.138–9.

(v) Pair of gold crescent-shaped earrings with filigree decoration of spirals and palmettes. H. 2.5cm, W. 2.2cm. About 450–400 BC.

(vi) Murray, Smith and Walters 1900, 65, 82, pl. XIII, 9; Marshall 1911, nos 2451–2; Gjerstad 1948, 163, fig. 34, 7; Williams and Ogden 1994, no. 162.

17. (i) 'Gold ring with filagree on bezel'. Figs 9.18–9.19.

(ii) '(3) Gold ring, with palmettes in filigree on the bezel'.

(iii) 'Gold ring with filagree work on bezel'.

(iv) GR 1896.2–1.140.

(v) Gold finger-ring with a thin gold hoop and a pointed oval bezel decorated with opposed filigree palmettes. W. 1.7cm. About 420–400 BC.

(vi) Murray, Smith and Walters 1900, 66, 82, pl. XIII, 14; Marshall 1907, no. 906; Higgins 1980, 132.

18. (i) 'Gold ring and pendant of turquoise'. Fig. 9.20.

(ii) '(9) Gold and turquoise pendant'.

(iv) GR 1896.2–1.153.

(v) Turquoise pendant modelled as a seated cat, with one ear broken; gold wire is twisted about it, extending to a thicker wire suspension loop. H. 1.5cm. The cat is very probably an import from Egypt and could well be of the sixth or fifth century BC.[8]

(vi) Murray, Smith and Walters 1900, 82, pl. XIII, 20; Marshall 1911, no. 2050.

19a-b. (i) 'Bronze bull and head of another animal in bronze'. Figs 9.21–9.22.
(ii) (a) '(22) Bronze figure of a bull, rather crude, with very short legs, so as to give the proportions of a dog or other small animal'; (b) '(29) Bronze head of some animal, broken from some object'.
(iii) 'Bronze figure of dog or lamb'.
(iv) (a) GR 1896.2–1.162 and (b) GR 1896.2–1.232.
(v) (a) Bronze bull, crudely made, with a slight hump on the neck, and its tail hanging behind the left hind leg; the horns are broken away and the surface corroded. L. 4.7cm, H. 3.3cm. Probably sixth century BC; (b) duck or goose-head cut probably from the handle of a bronze lamp, with a suspension-hole pierced laterally through the nostrils. It might, however, be from the handle of a ladle, but the suspension-hole probably makes against this. L. 2.6cm. If from a lamp, about AD 70–125. If from a ladle, Hellenistic or Roman.
(vi) (a) Murray, Smith and Walters 1900, 67, fig. 86, 83; Walters 1899, no. 235; (b) Murray, Smith and Walters 1900, 83; Bailey 1996, Q 3695 bis.

20. (i) 'R.f cotylè in fragments – owl between laurel-branches'. Figs 9.23–9.24.
(ii) '(34) Red-figured Greek cotylè, on either side an owl between olive branches; one vertical handle'.
(iii) 'Similar [to **1** above] cotylè in fragments – owl and laurel each side'.
(iv) GR 1896.2–1.166.
(v) Athenian red-figured owl-glaux: on both sides, an owl between laurel-sprigs; reserved within base-ring, with circle-and-dot at centre; reserved area reddened with miltos. H. 8.1, D. of rim 10.3cm. Such skyphoi date to the second and third quarters of the fifth century BC: compare Boardman 1989, 39 and fig. 96.
(vi) Murray, Smith and Walters 1900, 76, fig. 139, 77, 83.

21. (i) 'Greek terracotta figure of a Centaur carrying a doe(?) – traces of colouring'. Fig. 9.25.
(ii) '(32) Terracotta figure of a Centaur carrying a doe on his left shoulder, with traces of red, black and white colouring'.
(iii) 'Terracotta figure (Greek) of Centaur carrying doe(?) – traces of colouring'.
(iv) GR 1896.2–1.165.
(v) Cypriote figure of a centaur in terracotta, hand modelled, but the face may be mould made; his hair is long behind. He stands with the upper, human, body half turned to his left and holds a deer on his left shoulder; his tail is extended. He has human genitals, but his front feet are unmodelled and resemble his rear feet: it is uncertain, therefore, whether his forepart is of fully human form, which was, in Donald Strong's immortal phrase,[9] 'propelled, as it were, by the hindquarters of a horse', or had a fully equine body. The human genitalia would point to the former state. Coarse red-brown clay with a buff surface. The whole was once painted white. The beard and hair are black, as is the pubic hair, and the eyes are outlined; there are black stripes over the shoulders and down the human body, and another black stripe extends down his back and along the horse's back. There are narrow black stripes down the deer's back and legs. There is red on the deer's neck and also down the front of the centaur's human torso. L. 15.3cm, H. 14.5cm. Late sixth century BC.
(vi) Murray, Smith and Walters 1900, 70, fig. 110, 83; Walters 1903, A 227.

22. (i) 'Beads of carnelian, stone and silver'. Fig. 9.26.
(ii) '(11) Necklace of carnelian and gold beads, eighteen in number'.
(iv) GR 1896.2–1.155.
(v) Beads from a necklace: ten round and one biconical bead of carnelian; two round gold beads with raised rims round the orifices, and five segmented cylinders of gold. L. as strung 8.0cm. The round carnelian beads could be of any date from the Late Bronze Age on; biconical carnelian beads occur in sixth to fifth-century jewellery from Tharros in Sardinia (Marshall 1911, no. 1546; Barnett and Mendleson 1987, 159, 8/24). The segmented gold beads also occur in the Late Bronze Age in Cyprus, although most are rather larger (compare Marshall 1911, nos 579–80, from Enkomi). The round gold beads are probably of the sixth century or later. If from one necklace, a sixth or fifth-century BC date is likely.
(vi) Murray, Smith and Walters 1900, 83, pl. XIII, 15; Marshall 1911, no. 2017.

23. (i) 'Small Egyptian amulet of porcelain'. Apparently not kept.

24. (i) 'Mask in stone, probably an amulet'. Apparently not kept.

25. (i) 'Small stone object with gold loop for suspension'. Fig. 9.27.
    (ii) '(15) Small fragment of stone fastened to a loop of gold wire'.
    (iv) GR 1896.2–1.167.
    (v) Faience? pendant in the form of a couchant lion on a rectangular base, with gold wire twisted about it and forming a suspension loop. H. 1.2cm. Probably sixth century BC.
    (vi) Murray, Smith and Walters 1900, 83, pl. XIII, 20; Marshall 1911, no. 2051 (where it is described as limestone and as being winged).

26a-e. (i) 'Seven silver spiral rings'. Fig. 9.28.
    (ii) '(18) Five silver spirals, and several fragments of bracelets and spirals'.
    (iii) 'Seven silver spirals'.
    (iv) GR 1896.2–1.345–9.
    (v) Five silver circular loops, round in section, probably small bracelets, tapering at each end, their ends each twisted to one side. No decorative detail is apparent. (a): W. 5.0cm; (b): ends overlapping, W. 4.9cm; (c): one end blunt, perhaps broken, W. 5.0cm; (d): one end blunt, perhaps broken, W. 4.7cm; (e): W. 4.9cm. Not intrinsically datable, but probably of the sixth or fifth century BC. The several fragments mentioned in (ii) were apparently not registered and cannot now be traced with certainty.
    (vi) Murray, Smith and Walters 1900, 83.

27. (i) 'Terracotta objects (pair of paniers?)'. Fig. 9.29.
    (ii) '(33) Terracotta pair of panniers (as from tomb 102)'.
    (iv) GR 1896.2–1.164.
    (v) Hand-modelled terracotta panniers, broken from an object, presumably an animal figurine, a mule or donkey, near Karageorghis 1996, H4. Each pannier has an intentional hole pierced at its lowest point. Buff clay with a reddish core at the scar. L. 8.5cm. Probably sixth century BC.
    (vi) Murray, Smith and Walters 1900, 71, fig. 119, 83; Walters 1903, A 422.

28a-c (i) 'Numerous fragments of uncertain bronze objects'. Figs 9.30–9.32.
    (ii) Most of these were apparently not kept, but they include, (a) '(24) Bronze lid of "seal-box", with design in relief of spread eagle'; (b) '(28) Bronze spoon-shaped object', and item (c), not described in Murray, Smith and Walters 1900, but noted in the Register as being from Tomb 73.
    (iv) GR 1896.2–1.231 = (b); GR 1896.2–1.234 = (c); GR 1896.2–1.286 = (a).
    (v) (a) Lid of a Roman circular bronze seal-box, with a double moulded raised edge and an eagle riveted to its centre. D. 2.0cm. Of the known examples, all, except one from Spain and ours from Cyprus, come from the northern provinces of the Roman Empire and most from the north-west provinces.[10] Second half of the first century AD and the beginning of the second century. (b) Bronze spoon-shaped object of uncertain use, the 'bowl' solid with an attached bronze strip, which fastened the object to a thin sheet of bronze, like the wall of a vessel; the other end is spatulate with a straight edge. Heavily corroded. L. 6.3cm. Not intrinsically datable. (c) Lower part of a vessel handle, crudely made and squarish in section, with an oval handle-plate decorated with random grooves. L. 3.9cm. Not intrinsically datable.
    (vi) (a) Murray, Smith and Walters 1900, 83; Walters 1899, no. 2242; Feugère and Abauzit 1995, 44, fig. 2, 21: (b) Murray, Smith and Walters 1900, 83; Walters 1899, no. 2369.

29a-c. (i) 'Bronze candelabrum of common Cypriote type – in three pieces'. Figs 9.33–9.35.
    (ii) '(31 part) Fragments of bronze candelabra of the common Cypriote type. They consist of three upper parts of stems with tripod-stand above, and inverted flowers, one above the other, below'.
    (iii) 'Bronze candelabrum of common Cypriote type'.
    (iv) GR 1896.2–1.302–4.
    (v) Bronze lampstand tops, socketed for a wooden shaft, each with a lamp-support of three elongated leaves holding a ring, and inverted calices below: (a) and (b) have two calices; (c) has only one calyx, but others may be lost below, together with the socket. (a) has the remains of its yew-wood shaft. (a)

H. 21.0cm, W. 10.6cm; (b) H. 23.2cm, W. 11.8cm; (c) H. 10.2cm, W. 9.1cm. All sixth century BC or perhaps a little earlier.

(vi) (a) Murray, Smith and Walters 1900, 83; Matthäus 1992, 241, fig. 3; Bailey 1996, Q 3853; (b) Murray, Smith and Walters 1900, 67, fig. 88, 83; Jantzen 1972, 45, n. 108; Bailey 1996, Q 3855; (c) Murray, Smith and Walters 1900, 83; Bailey 1996, Q 3859.

Second Group: 'In other part of tomb'

30. (i) 'Bronze archaic Greek female figure – very fine – in Spes attitude – has supported some object'. Fig. 9.36.
    (ii) '(21) Bronze female statuette; archaic Greek work of the 6th century B.C.'; '(31 part) A flat disc which may have fitted on the head of the statuette, No. 21'.
    (iii) 'Archaic bronze statuette (about 500–480 B.C.) – female figure in the "Spes" attitude – in perfect preservation'.
    (iv) GR 1896.2–1.158.
    (v) Bronze lampstand surmounted by a figure of a woman, with a lamp-support upon her head, a tall shaft and a tripod foot terminating in lion's paws: incorporating items **30** here, and **32**, **36**, **41a** below; also GR 1896.2–1.311, the flat disc mentioned in (ii) above. H. 118.0cm. South Italian Greek, about 480 BC.
    (vi) Murray, Smith and Walters 1900, 67, figs 83, 87, 83; Walters 1899, Nos 193 and 247; Pryce 1934–5, pl. XL; Gjerstad 1948, 400; Tatton-Brown 1989, 138, figs 3–4; Williams and Ogden 1994, 228; Bailey 1996, Q 3862.

31. (i) 'Bronze jug with high handle'. Fig. 9.37.
    (ii) '(25) Bronze jug with circular mouth; a good Greek type'.
    (iii) 'Bronze jug'.
    (iv) GR 1896.2–1.161.
    (v) Bronze jug: raised rounded body with offset base, rounded shoulder, and thickened narrow rim, the neck with a concave profile. The heavy cast handle has a subrectangular section and rises high above the rim. It divides at the top into two short straps, each riveted just below the rim, and tapers to an ivy-leaf-shaped escutcheon, also riveted, to the body. Rough corrosion products remaining. A sixth-century date is likely. It is not unlike Cesnola 1903, pl. XLVI, 1, said to be from Curium.

(vi) Murray. Smith and Walters 1900, 83.

32. (i) 'Bronze Ionic column'. Fig. 9.36.
    (ii) '(23) Bronze model of an Ionic column, with capital of archaic type, like those at Bassae'.
    (iii) '[Bronze] model of Ionic column'.
    (iv) GR 1896.2–1.160.
    (v) Part of the lampstand **30** above.
    (vi) Murray, Smith and Walters 1900, 67, fig. 87, 83; plus references in **30** (v).

33. (i) 'Bronze strigil (broken)'. Fig. 9.38.
    (ii) '(26) Bronze strigil, broken; on the back, leaf pattern'.
    (iii) '[Bronze] strigil'.
    (iv) GR 1896.2–1.163.
    (v) Bronze strigil, much damaged, only the lower end of the blade surviving, from which extends a flat waisted handle, once joined to a narrower strip parallel to it, that bends to an elongated palmette-shaped plate fixed to the underside of the blade, which has curved decorative mouldings running along it. L. 16.7cm. Probably fifth century BC.
    (vi) Murray, Smith and Walters 1900, 83; Walters 1899, no. 2427.

34. (i) 'Bronze mirror'. Apparently not kept.

35. (i) 'Bronze phiale'. Apparently not kept.

36. (i) 'Bronze lamp-stand on three feet'. Fig. 9.36.
    (ii) '(31 part) a base of three curved feet ending in claws'.
    (iii) 'Bronze lamp-stand'.
    (iv) GR 1896.2–1.305.
    (v) Part of the lampstand **30** above.
    (vi) Murray, Smith and Walters 1900, 83; plus references in **30** (v).

37. (i) 'Silver bowl – two handles'. Apparently not kept.

38. (i) 'Alabaster vase'. Fig. 9.39.
    (ii) '(36) Alabaster vase, with ears'.
    (iv) GR 1896.2–1.334.
    (v) Alabaster alabastron, probably of Egyptian calcite, with wide flat mouth and two lug-handles. H. 21.1cm. Late sixth or first half of the fifth century BC.
    (vi) Murray, Smith and Walters 1900, 83.

39. (i) 'Silver ring and rock-crystal intaglio with good design of youth holding a hare to which

a dog leaps up – Cypriote syllabary'.
Fig. 9.40.
(ii) '(13) Rock-crystal intaglio scaraboid, with design of a youth holding out a hare in left hand to which a dog leaps up. Inscribed in Cypriote characters la-ma-ti-le-so, Λαμπτίλης'.
(iii) 'Silver ring with rock-crystal setting – intaglio design of youth holding a hare to which a dog leaps up – inscribed with Cypriote syllabry'.
(iv) GR 1896.2–1.157.
(v) Intaglio rock-crystal gem of scaraboid form showing a hunter, nude, wearing petasos and holding a stick; he also holds a hare, in which his hound is most interested; it is inscribed in Eteo-Cypriote *la-va-ti-ri-so*; the silver ring described in the excavation notebook has not been traced, but could be the fragmentary swivel-ring GR 1896.2–1.357 (**9a** above), although that is from another part of the tomb (if its Registration Number has been correctly identified). L. 2.2, W. 1.7cm. About 500–480 BC.
(vi) Murray, Smith and Walters 1900, 63–4, 83, pl. IV, Curium 6; Furtwängler i 1900, pl. IX, 9; Walters 1906, pl. XCI, 23; Walters 1926, no. 502; Masson 1957, 67–8; Mitford 1971, 64–5.

40. (i) 'Gold ring – intaglio of a youth reclining'.
Figs 9.41–9.42.
(ii) '(10) Gold ring engraved with intaglio design of a nude female figure reclining with face to right, resting on right elbow and extending left hand; of late design, probably 4th century'.
(iii) 'Gold ring with intaglio design of youth bending forward'.
(iv) GR 1896.2–1.154.
(v) Gold finger-ring with oval bezel: nude woman wearing a necklace, half-reclining on her right elbow and resting on drapery; she points with her extended left hand. D. 2.0cm. Fourth century BC.
(vi) Murray, Smith and Walters 1900, 66, 82, pl. IV, Curium 7, pl. XIII, 16; Marshall 1907, no. 61; Furtwängler iii 1900, 132.

41a-c. (i) 'Bronze stand and two bronze styli(?)'.
Figs 9.36, 9.43.
(ii) (a) '(31 part) A stand for a lamp'; (b) '(27) Bronze needle or stylus'; (c) '(30) Part of a bronze surgical instrument' (apparently not kept).
(iv) (a) GR 1896.2–1.159; (b) GR 1896.2–1.230.
(v) (a) Bronze stand, the topmost element of the lampstand **30** above. (b) Bronze stirring-rod or kohl-stick, circular in section, and swelling to thickened ends. L. 13.8cm. No intrinsic date.
(vi) (a) Murray, Smith and Walters 1900, 83; plus references in **30** (v); (b) Murray, Smith and Walters 1900, 83; Walters 1899, no. 2690; (c) Murray, Smith and Walters 1900, 83.

42. (i) 'Two silver bracelets ending in snakes' heads'.
Fig. 9.44.
(ii) '(17) A pair of similar [to (16): **6** above] bracelets, small (probably for a child), ending in calves' heads'.
(iii) 'Two silver bracelets ending in snakes' heads'.
(iv) GR 1896.2–1.343–4.
(v) Silver bracelets with calf-head terminals. Very worn plain hoops of circular section, the calves with their ears lying back along the hoop; the heads overlap. Both have traces of gilding between the ears; GR 1896.2–1.343 has V-shaped indications of hatchings behind one of the heads. D. 4.7 and 4.5cm. Probably fifth century BC.
(vi) Murray, Smith and Walters 1900, 65, 83; Marshall 1911, no. 1603.

43. (i) 'Fragments of an iron object'. Apparently not kept, but one of them may be **7f** below.

44. (i) 'Silver coin'.
(ii) '(37) Silver tetradrachm of Alexander the Great (uncertain mint)'. Apparently not kept, nor is it identifiable in the collections of the Department of Coins and Medals.
(vi) Murray, Smith and Walters 1900, 83; Williams and Ogden 1994, p. 228.

This is the full list of objects recorded to have come from Curium British Museum Tomb 73, several of which have not been traced and are known only from the excavation notebook and the published account. Except for two objects, one Roman and one probably so (**28a** and **19b**), the remainder shows that the tomb was used for burials from very late in the seventh to the end of the fourth century BC. It will be seen that no Cypriote pottery of the late Iron Age and Classical periods is mentioned and this seems scarcely credible. To find a tomb intact enough to retain a large quantity of gold, silver and bronze objects, the only fired clay items being two Athenian drinking cups and a couple of terracottas, may suggest that the rest of the pottery was rejected as not worth collecting. If so, this must have been a deliberate policy, it perhaps being thought that the Museum had acquired quite enough Cypriote pottery from the earlier excavations at Amathus, thank you very much. Walters appears to have preserved the bulk of the decorated pottery of the Late Bronze Age found in the tombs of that date, but fewer than a score of vessels from Iron Age or later tombs at Curium were registered in the Museum's collections or were published, even though the excavation report mentions that 'innumerable examples' of such pottery were found, and that 'in some tombs sixty to eighty specimens were found'. (Murray, Smith and Walters 1900, 75–6: this apparently refers to all of the site of Curium). However, Walters in his letter to the Principal Librarian,[4] states that 'There is a remarkable absence of Cypriote pottery'. This probably concerns the whole of Area B, but perhaps only Tomb 83, which he had just been describing.

To return now to item **7** in the list above. While checking through the objects of Tomb 73 because the Cypriote lampstand tops, items **29a-c** above, and the Greek lampstand, item **30**, were to be included in Volume iv of the Catalogue of Lamps in the British Museum (Bailey 1996), the present writer realised that a group of unregistered silver objects from Cyprus must, in part at least but probably wholly, correspond with the Bes figures described in the excavation notebook, 'Notes at Curium', and as no. (14) in the published report of Curium Tomb 73: only Walters' letter to the Principal Librarian mentions 'heads of deities' in addition. These objects, many very fragmentary, and 45 in all, were in such a poor state when excavated that they were not incorporated in the collections when they reached the Museum, but are now registered as GR 1991.12–11.1–35. H.B. Walters, who retired from the Museum thirty years after finding them, was presumably the last person who knew what they were: a further sixty years elapsed before they were recognised again. The objects from Tomb 73 were 'very much corroded and broken' when found (Murray, Smith and Walters 1900, 83 (14)); it is due to the careful, assiduous and extremely skilful work of Marilyn Hockey of the Department of Conservation of the British Museum that they can be presented today in such a splendid state of preservation. Unfortunately, several are still in fragments, with pieces lost, and await conservation, in particular the removal of corrosion products, but they are a remarkably interesting group of objects, with very few parallels, and they deserve to rise from complete obscurity. Whether of Levantine Phoenician origin or made by Cypriote Phoenicians, these silver pendants and plaques add much to the finds already known from Curium Tomb 73, first utilised in the late seventh century BC and continuing in use to late Classical times – the coin of Alexander the Great and the two small Roman objects may point to later use of the tomb

7a *Figures of Bes*

Reg. Nos GR 1991.12–11.1–16.　　　Figs 9.45–9.49.
These quite large Bes figures (they average 6.0cm high) are made with repoussé fronts and flat backs joined, and each had an applied suspension lug. The face and body are full face, but the feet are turned to the left of the figure. There are two short horns on the head, the chest is bare and a double-cable belt holds up a long ?hairy garment reaching almost to the ground; a snake is held in each lowered hand. The front has chased detail: further detail of the construction of all the silver objects are given by Marilyn Hockey below. To add strength and to cause the front and back to adhere they were filled with gypsum in antiquity. Only one of the sixteen figures is so far cleaned and we must wait until the others have been treated before we will know whether a single punch was used for the whole figure. Other than the identity of the god represented there is nothing Egyptian about them, and they are either of Cypriote manufacture or come from a Levantine source. Of the sixteen examples, all of silver, there are eight fairly complete figures, three backplates, and four small fragments, including three faces; four suspension lugs survive on figures and fragments. A seventh to sixth-century date is likely. A Phoenician-style gold repoussé plaque from Cyprus shows a goddess standing to front with her feet turned to the left (Marshall 1911, No. 1488). For Cypriote Bes figures in terracotta holding snakes, see Karageorghis 1996 pl. VII, 7 (discussion on p. 13, D(a)2: this is nearest our silver examples). In Egypt, Bes holding snakes occurs in the Middle Kingdom (cf. Romano 1989, 2,1, 32), but seems to be less common later: a Nineteenth Dynasty example is found on a limestone headrest in the British Museum (Bierbrier 1993, pls 42–3: I am grateful for this reference to John Taylor and Richard Parkinson). Apotropaic figures of Bes with a sword, and a snake gripped in his lowered left hand are known amongst Ptolemaic terracottas, as for example two versions in the Graeco-Roman Museum, Alexandria, Inv. Nos 21123–4, and Bes with a snake is found in the Ptolemaic-period Bes-chambers at Saqqara (Quibell 1907, frontispiece and pls XXVI–VII).

7b *Male figure*

Reg. No. GR 1991.12–11.32, 33, 34c.　　Figs 9.50–9.52.
The greater part of a silver pendent nude standing figure of Bes, 6.0cm high, modelled in the round, but hollow; some gypsum filling survives. The front and the back, and a plinth with beaded decoration curved round the feet, were

separately made in repoussé-work and were soldered together, the seam, although smoothed, showing at the sides. A flat base was applied below the plinth. Much of the head is lost, but is fully bearded, and hair at the rear is indicated by raised points; the right eye survives. The right arm is bent at waist level, the hand fisted; the left fist is adjacent, but its arm is lost. A suspension-loop is soldered on at the rear below the neck; the figure was very likely the main or only pendant of a necklace. Seventh-sixth century BC.

7c Plaques with the busts of two women

Reg. Nos GR 1991.12–11.17–29.　　Figs 9.53–9.54.
Parts of thirteen leaf-gilded silver plaques in very high relief survive; each is about 1.8cm square, made of extremely thin sheet, less than 0.1mm thick in places. They are very weak and fragile and have to be backed with various compounds coated with fibreglass or nylon tissue before the manual removal of corrosion products can commence. The plaques have repoussé fronts but no backs, and show the prominent busts of two women, no doubt goddesses, within a beaded border. Each bust was probably made with a single punch. There is a hole at each corner so that the plaque may be sewn to a garment or a strap. Most of the plaques have minor damage, mainly corners broken away; GR 1991.12–11.23 consists of damaged plaques adhering together by their corrosion products.

The identity of these deities is uncertain: they are naked and each wears a diadem; their hair falls to their shoulders, leaving their ears exposed. One of them is very probably Phoenician Astarte in her Cypriote Aphrodite guise. Antoine Hermary (1982) has suggested that twin goddesses could both be Aphrodite, heavenly and chthonic. Goddesses in pairs in the Cypro-Archaic period are somewhat elusive, but a terracotta in Berlin, has two full-length figures in a shrine (Ohnefalsch-Richter 1893, pls XXXVIII, and CCV, 3). Classical and Hellenistic-period twin deities come in quantity from the same site where this Berlin group was found, the so-called Artemis Paralia shrine on the Salt Lake near Larnaca. Artemis and Cybele or Demeter and Kore have been suggested, but the sanctuary itself may be that of Aphrodite and not Artemis. I must thank Veronica Tatton-Brown for information on twin goddesses.

I am grateful also to Robert Merillees for a reference to a closely similar plaque, probably from the same workshop, published by Ohnefalsch-Richter (1893, pl.XXV, 14). This is one of a series of 18 which, like ours, are from Curium, found in 'an old Graeco-Phoenician grave.....which in 1884 [were] in the possession of Captain Sinclair', no doubt the Lt. Sinclair who, in 1879, filled in the stagnant harbour of Kition with much of the Bamboula site (Bailey 1969, 37–8). Cesnola (1903, pl. XXXIX, 21) published a group of small silver plaques 'from Curium' with heads of a single goddess. Compare perhaps for the type of object, some plaques of the early fifth century BC with the head of Herakles (Karageorghis 1998, p. 89, 47).

7d Figures of lions

Reg. Nos GR 1991.12–11.30–31.　　Figs 9.55–9.57.
Two beads in the form of couchant silver lions, their heads lost or largely so, modelled in the round, but hollow. Both are pierced longitudinally for stringing on a necklace. They are made by the repoussé technique and have flat bases soldered on. The rear of GR 1991.12–11.31 is broken away, but its lower face survives; they are respectively 2.3cm and 1.8cm long. Like much of this group of silver objects, these lion-beads are probably of the seventh or sixth century BC; similar beads, pierced longitudinally, in semi-precious stones, of about the first half of the sixth century are known: cf. Ohnefalsch-Richter 1893, pl. LXVII, 12–14, from Cemetery II, Tomb 131 at Marion/Arsinoe.

7e Unidentified fragments

Reg. Nos. GR 1991.12–11.34a-b, d-j.　　Not illustrated.
Nine small indeterminate silver fragments. Some of these have been and others may eventually be found to join the objects previously described: see Marilyn Hockey's report below.

7f Part of a bracelet?

Reg. No. GR 1991.12–11.35.　　Fig. 9.58.
Small fragment, perhaps of a bracelet or from a piece of furniture, in iron, plated on the outside with silver; it has a floral pattern. There are traces of mineralised wood on the inside. L. 3.7cm. This is perhaps part of **43** above.

CONSERVATION OF THE SILVER PENDANTS AND PLAQUES FROM CYPRUS

by Marilyn Hockey

1. Introduction

A group of thirty-five silver pendants, plaques and fragments (GR 1991.12–11.1 to 35) was sent to the Department of Conservation for investigative cleaning and repair prior to their cataloguing by D.M. Bailey of the Greek and Roman Department.

The group, dating from the seventh century BC, consists of sixteen anthropomorphic pendants, thirteen small plaques decorated with female heads, two small lions, half of a pendant in the form of a male figure, and some associated fragments. The group has been in the collections of the Department of Greek and Roman Antiquities for some years and was excavated in Cyprus. The pieces were uncleaned and very fragile. Surface details were obscured by corrosion. Conservation work included radiography, examination using a binocular microscope (at magnifications up to x 45), manual removal of corrosion, consolidation and repair. X-Ray diffraction analysis of corrosion products and suspected original filling material was carried out by Lorna Lee of the Conservation Research Group (Lee 1997). This report describes observations made during conservation and summarizes the conservation method.

2. Anthropomorphic pendants, GR 1991.12–11.1–16 (Cat. 7a).

Description and condition
These pendants, or fragments of pendant, are each in the form of a bearded figure of Bes. The complete figures are 6cm high. Each was formed from two sheets of silver; a flat back-plate and a front-plate stamped with the Bes figure in relief. The sheets used were extremely thin. Corrosion which occurred during burial has converted the silver to silver sulphide, a compact black corrosion product which now forms a core representing the original sheet, complete with surface detail. This core is about 0.1mm (or less) thick in the back-plate and 0.3mm or less, in the front-plate. The sulphide core is covered with a layer of rough grey silver chloride/silver bromide corrosion, which is in some places a powdery purple or white (Lee 1997). It is not entirely clear how the two plates were joined together, although it appears that the ones which are still joined (GR 1991.12–11.1, 2, 3, 6 & 7) may now be held together only by corrosion. Preliminary cleaning revealed the remains of a plaster-like material on the inside of plates, which appears to be an original adhesive and/or filler and which may have originally both supported and bonded the plates. Analysis identified this material as gypsum (Lee 1997). Four of the figures (GR 1991.12–11.2, 5, 9 and 10) have a suspension loop at the back of the head. There is no apparent evidence of suspension loops on the other figures, either in the corrosion layer or on the original surface where corrosion has been removed. Most of the broken edges are covered by the corrosion layer, indicating that the objects were broken in antiquity.

Conservation
Initial assessment of the pendants indicated that they were extremely fragile and that manual removal of corrosion would be a delicate procedure, since there was no way of applying a backing to support the plates during treatment. For these reasons it was decided initially to remove corrosion from the front surface of GR 1991.12–11.1 and the back of GR 1991.12–11.2, the two most complete pendants.

The silver chloride/bromide layer was removed under a binocular microscope at x 20 magnification, using a fine chisel-tipped needle to carefully lever away the corrosion. This exposed the smooth original surface of the pendants, with details of the figure on the front defined with small linear punch marks, and spots on the snakes made with a round dot punch. On the back of GR 1991.12–11.2 the structure of the suspension loop could be seen to be a short strip of silver, 5mm wide, swaged with three outer longitudinal ridges, bent round in a 'C' shape, the two ends soldered to the back-plate. Some consolidation of friable surfaces was carried out with an acrylic copolymer. Support of vulnerable areas and repairs were made using cellulose nitrate adhesive, where necessary bulked with silica microballoons.

3. Plaques: GR 1991.12–11.17–29 (Cat. 7c)

Description and condition
Objects numbered GR 1991.12–11.17 to 29 in the group form a series of thirteen small gilded silver plaques (each approx. 18 x 18mm). Each of these is decorated with the busts of two female figures in relief, with a beaded edge and a hole in each corner. GR 1991.12–11.23 consisted of one complete plaque and two fragmentary plaques, joined by corrosion. None of the other plaques is entirely complete. Before treatment they were covered in a thick layer of rough, grey silver chloride corrosion, mixed with soil and sand grains.

Investigative cleaning revealed that each plaque was made from extremely thin silver sheet, possibly less than 0.1mm in parts, now completely mineralized, transformed into soft black silver sulphide. This mineralized core, on which the original surface still survives, was covered by the layer of silver chloride. In some places the silver sulphide core was so thin that the chloride corrosion had penetrated through it. This was revealed when the chloride layer was removed from the front during cleaning. Cleaning also revealed the presence of gold leaf on the front of the plaques, on the original surface, between the layers of silver sulphide and silver chloride. This had survived more completely on some plaques than on others. In all cases it was extremely friable and fragmentary and there were no traces at all on plaques GR 1991.12–11.24 and 29.

Conservation
The plaques were extremely weak and fragile. A support had to be applied to the back of each one before the silver chloride corrosion could be removed from the front. The concave areas on the reverse of the plaques were filled with a mixture of cellulose nitrate adhesive and silica micro-

balloons. The whole of the back was then covered with fibre-glass or nylon tissue and cellulose nitrate adhesive. This support has been left in place to provide extra protection for the plaques, but could be easily removed in the future using acetone.

Corrosion was removed from the front of the plaques, under x 20 magnification, using scalpels and fine chisel-tipped needles. The tractability of the chloride layer and its adhesion to the original surface varied from plaque to plaque. In some cases there was a pronounced cleavage plane at the junction of the chloride and the original surface (of silver sulphide or gold leaf), in which case the chloride could be carefully peeled away. In other cases it was necessary to pare the chloride down almost to the surface. Where there was gilding, this was often poorly adhering to the original surface. In these cases it was necessary to consolidate as the work progressed, with a dilute solution (2%-5%) of Paraloid B72 acrylic resin in 50/50 Acetone/Industrial Methylated Spirit.

4. Fragments GR 1991.12–11.30–35
(Cat. 7d, 7b, 7f)

GR 1991–12–11.30 and 31 are two small reclining lions, the more complete one being 23mm long. The heads are missing. The rear half of GR 1991.12–11.31 is also missing. They are hollow, made from silver sheet between 0.1 and 0.3mm thick, now completely mineralized. Surface detail was obscured by a layer of silver chloride corrosion.

Conservation
Both lions were strengthened with a supporting layer of cellulose nitrate adhesive, applied to the interior surface by means of a fine syringe. Chloride corrosion was then removed manually from the outer surface to reveal the punched detail of paws, haunches, manes, faces and open mouths.

GR 1991.12–11.33 is a sheet fragment with a suspension loop. It has a deliberately indented or 'pecked' layer of gypsum on what would have been the inner surface. The broken edges are covered with silver chloride corrosion, indicating that it was broken in antiquity. The sheet appears to be slightly thicker than that of the Bes pendants and is slightly curved. The loop is also heavier than those on the pendent figures GR 1991.12–11.2, 5, 9 and 10, and forms a complete ring. Removal of corrosion revealed a textured surface above the loop which appeared to represent hair, while the surface elsewhere seemed to represent shoulder musculature. Another fragment, formed from three in the box of fragments GR 1991.12–11.34a-j, was found on cleaning to be the front upper part of a figure, the right arm and beard of a Bes. Both fragments were found to join with GR 1991.12–11.32 below to form an almost complete figure. This association had not been identified before cleaning, because each of the fragments was covered with corrosion layers of different colours and textures (some areas were stained with iron salts from adjacent iron in the ground) and the join edges were obscured by corrosion deposits.

GR 1991.12–11.32 is the lower half of a three-imensional standing male figure. The fragment is 4cm high, with an apparent suspension loop on the right thigh. It is formed from sheet silver, hollow, but originally filled with a light-coloured material, possibly gypsum, which can be seen in the broken area. It appeared to have been made from two stamped plates, one forming the front of the figure, one forming the back, which were joined in a seam running around the sides of the body from top to bottom, and joined, probably soldered, to a square plate plinth. The break across the waist is distorted, suggesting that the two halves of the figure were worked back and forth until torn apart. The edges of the break are covered by the corrosion layer, indicating that the figure was broken in antiquity. The whole figure was covered in a thick layer of silver chloride, which was stained green and brown in parts, from nearby copper and iron. This corrosion layer was removed to reveal the original surface, still silvery in parts, the detail of a beaded band around the feet and the crimped seam which joins the front and back plates. It is difficult to determine visually whether or not the seam was also soldered. The supposed suspension loop, which appeared to be attached to the side of the right thigh, was found not to be attached to the figure at all, but merely held in this position by the chloride corrosion. It is a very fine loop of beaded silver wire, which belongs, presumably, to another object. The much more robust suspension loop for this figure, made from ridged silver strip, was attached to fragment GR 1991.12–11.33 above. All the associated fragments were joined with cellulose nitrate adhesive to form a figure 6cm high.

GR 1991.12–11.34a-j were fragments of corroded silver sheet. One of these was found to form part of the back-plate of Bes pendant GR 1991.12–11.6. This, however, means that the feet previously attributed to the latter cannot belong to it. These feet belong with Bes pendant GR 1991.12–11.9. In all, places were found on other objects in the group for six of the fragments GR 1991.12–11.34a-j. Of the remaining four fragments, two are as yet unidentified but may be pieces of pendant for which there are no joins, and two are fragments of decorative stamped plaques. One, with gilding and an attachment hole in the corner, appears to be part of a palmette design. The other appears to be part of a leaf-shaped plaque.

GR 1991.12–11.35 was a fragment of some sort of 'fitting', part of a raised decorative band. It is made from a dark reddish-brown material. A sample was taken for X-ray diffraction analysis and it was confirmed as iron (Lee

1997). It is covered in thin, very degraded, silver sheet, with an openwork running leaf pattern along its outer surface. The other side has a layer of mineralized wood, torn from the object to which it was originally attached.

Conclusion

To date, full cleaning and consolidation has been carried out on the front surfaces of plaques GR 1991.12–11.17–25, revealing full detail of the design and the gilding. Investigative cleaning, repair and consolidation have been carried out on the Bes pendants GR 1991.12–11.1, 2 and 32, and on the lion beads GR 1991.12–11.31 and 32. The objects are physically fragile, but chemically stable. While further repair work will improve their physical stability, no further deterioration from corrosion is to be expected. Although it is probably neither possible nor desirable to carry out full cleaning on all of the objects, some further work is planned to prepare for the probable exhibition of some of the pieces.

Notes

1. For Williamson and the Christian brothers, see E. Goring, *A Mischievous Pastime* (Edinburgh 1988) 27–30.
2. This plan of Site B is taken from a sheet inserted into Walters' excavation notebook, 'Notes at Curium'; see also the published plan in Murray, Smith and Walters 1900, 60.
3. In the library of the Greek and Roman Department.
4. Original Letters and Papers 1895 (in the Museum' Archive Room), P, No. 1, 1341–3: I am grateful to Janet Wallace and Alexander Pullen for locating this letter.
5. It should be said that many objects from the British Museum's excavations in Cyprus which were brought back to the Museum were given to other museums in Britain: these institutions are listed in D.M. Bailey, *A Catalogue of the Lamps in the British Museum* i, *Greek, Hellenistic and Early Roman Pottery Lamps* (London 1975) 206, n. 6, and ii, *Roman Lamps made in Italy* (London 1980) 408. Most of these objects came from Amathus, and John Myres remarks that many intact amphorae from that site were given to the local village women for their modern use.
6. H.C. Beck's 'flush stratified eye beads': *Archaeologia* 77 (1928) 64, fig. 62.
7. Marshall 1911, nos 1450, 1452, both with elements that probably do not belong together.
8. I am grateful to Carol Andrews for help with this amulet.
9. D.E. Strong, 'A lady centaur', *British Museum Quarterly* 30 (1966) 36.
10. For the type cf. Feugère and Abauzit 1995, where the examples known up until 1995 are brought together.

Bibliography

Bailey 1969: D.M. Bailey, 'The Village Priest's Tomb at Aradippou in Cyprus', *British Museum Quarterly* 34 (1969) 36–58.

Bailey 1996: D.M. Bailey, *A Catalogue of the Lamps in the British Museum* iv, *Lamps of Metal and Stone, and Lampstands* (London).

Barnett and Mendleson 1987: R.D. Barnett and C. Mendleson, *Tharros, a Catalogue of Material in the British Museum from Phoenician and other Tombs at Tharros, Sardinia* (London).

Bierbrier 1993: M. Bierbrier, *Hieroglyphic Texts from Egyptian Stelae, etc.* xii (London).

Boardman 1989: J. Boardman, *Athenian Red Figure Vases, the Classical Period* (London).

Cesnola 1903: L.P. di Cesnola, *A Descriptive Atlas of the Cesnola Collection of Cypriote Antiquities in the Metropolitan Museum of Art, New York* iii (New York).

Deppert-Lippitz 1985: B. Deppert-Lippitz, *Griechischer Goldschmuck* (Mainz).

Feugère and Abauzit 1995: M. Feugère and P. Abauzit, 'Les boites à sceau circulaires à décor zoomorphe riveté d'époque romaine', in *Revue archéologique de l'Est et du Centre-Est* 46 (1995) 41–57.

Furtwängler 1900: A. Furtwängler, *Die antiken Gemmen* (Leipzig/Berlin).

Gjerstad 1948: E. Gjerstad, *SCE* iv, 2 (Stockholm).

Hermary 1982: A. Hermary, 'Divinités chypriotes I', *RDAC* (1982) 164–7.

Higgins 1980: R.A. Higgins, *Greek and Roman Jewellery*[2] (London).

Hunt 1990: D. Hunt, (ed.), *Footprints in Cyprus* (2nd edition, London).

Jantzen 1972: U. Jantzen, *Samos* viii, *Ägyptische und orientalische Bronzen aus dem Heraion von Samos* (Bonn).

Karageorghis 1996: V. Karageorghis, *The Coroplastic Art of Ancient Cyprus* vi, *The Cypro-Archaic Period, Monsters, Animals, and Miscellanea* (Nicosia).

Karageorghis 1998: V. Karageorghis, *Greek Gods and Heroes in Ancient Cyprus* (Athens).

Lee 1997: L. Lee, 'Analysis of corrosion products and filler from silver pendants, GR 1991.12–11.1 to 35' in *BM Conservation Research Group Report* CA 1997/71.

Marshall 1907: F.H. Marshall, *Catalogue of the Finger Rings, Greek, Etruscan, and Roman, in the Departments of Antiquities, British Museum* (London; reprint 1968).

Marshall 1911: F.H. Marshall, *Catalogue of the Jewellery, Greek, Etruscan, and Roman, in the Departments of Antiquities, British Museum* (London; reprint 1969).

Masson 1957: O Masson, 'Les inscriptions étéochypriotes III', *Syria* 34 (1957) 64–70.

Matthäus 1992: H. Matthäus, 'Bronzene Kandelaber mit Blattübertall', in P. Åström (ed.), *Acta Cypria* 2 (Jonsered) 214–54.

Mitford 1971: T.B. Mitford, *The Inscriptions of Kourion* (Philadelphia).

Murray, Smith and Walters 1900: A.S. Murray, A.H. Smith and H.B. Walters, *Excavations in Cyprus* (London; reprint 1970).

Ohnefalsch-Richter 1893: M. Ohnefalsch-Richter, *Kypros, the Bible and Homer* (London).

Pfrommer 1990: M. Pfrommer, *Untersuchungen zur Chronologie früh- und hochhellenistischen Goldschmucks* (Tübingen).

Pryce 1934–5: F.N. Pryce, 'A Greek Lampstand' in *British Museum Quarterly* 9 (1934–5) 132–4.

Quibell 1907: J.E. Quibell, *Excavations at Saqqara (1905–1906)* (Cairo).

Romano 1989: J.F. Romano, *The Bes-Image in Pharaonic Egypt* (Ann Arbor).

Sparkes and Talcott 1970: B.A. Sparkes and L. Talcott, *The Athenian Agora* xii, *Black and Plain Pottery of the 6th, 5th and 4th Centuries B.C.* (Princeton).

Tatton-Brown 1989: V.A. Tatton-Brown (ed.), *Cyprus and the East Mediterranean in the Iron Age* (London).

Walters 1899: H.B. Walters, *Catalogue of the Bronzes in the British Museum* (London).

Walters 1903: H.B. Walters, *Catalogue of the Terracottas in the Department of Greek and Roman Antiquities, British Museum* (London).

Walters 1906: H.B. Walters, *The Art of the Greeks* (London).

Walters 1926: H.B. Walters, *Catalogue of the Engraved Gems, Greek, Etruscan and Roman in the British Museum* (London).

Williams and Ogden 1994: D. Williams and J. Ogden, *Greek Gold, Jewellery of the Classical World* (London).

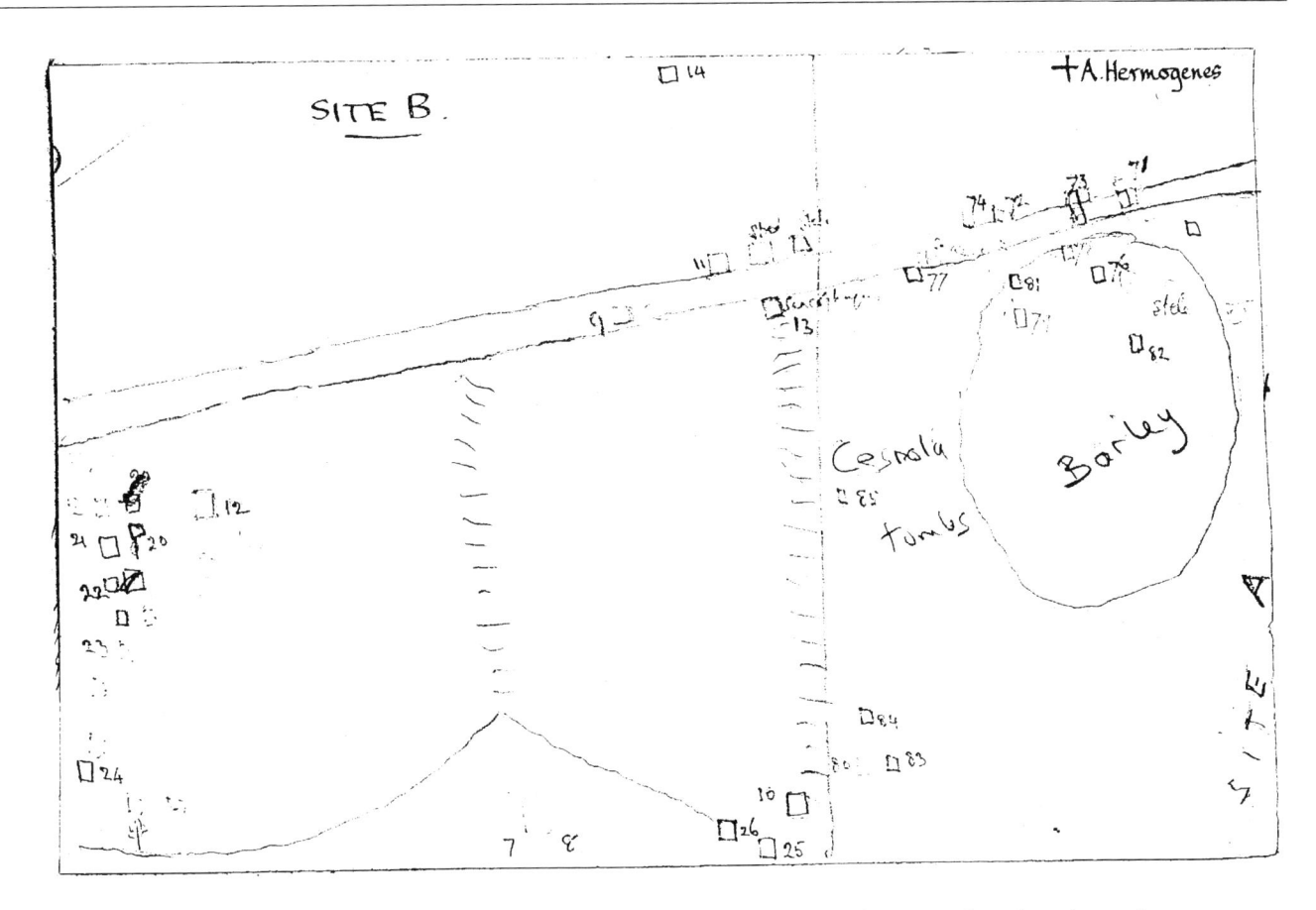

Fig. 9.1: Curium Site B, from Walters' 'Notes at Curium' (some very faint pencil marks enhanced).

Fig. 9.2: 1: Athenian black-glaze glaux.

Fig. 9.3: 3a and 3c: silver bracelets.

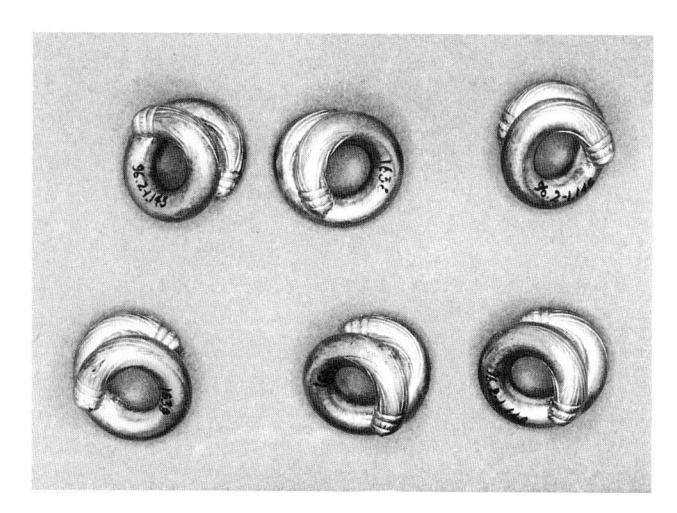

Fig. 9.4: 5: gold-plated bronze spirals.

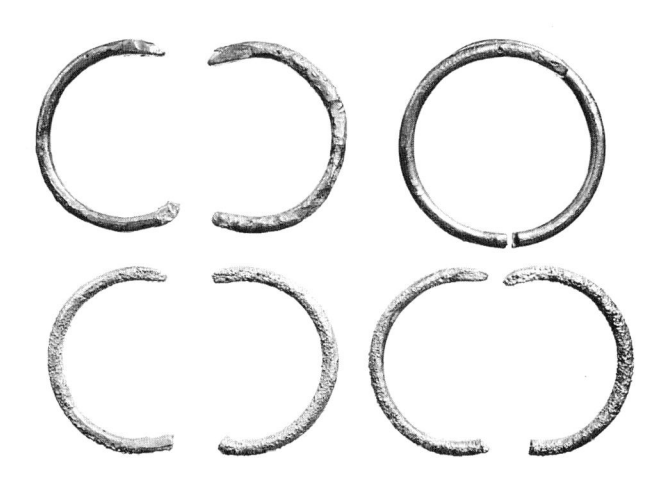

Fig. 9.5: 6: two pairs of silver snake-headed bracelets.

Fig. 9.6: 8: glass beads.

Fig. 9.7: 9: silver swivel-ring and spiral-wire finger-ring.

Fig. 9.8: 10a: silver chain with gold pendant.

Fig. 9.9: 10b: gold pendant

Fig. 9.10: 11: gold plated bronze swivel-ring with empty gold setting.

Fig. 9.11: 12: gold ring with pendent swivel-ring setting.

Fig. 9.12: 13a: silver finger-ring.

Fig. 9.13: 13a: silver finger-ring.

Fig. 9.14: 13b: silver finger-ring.

Fig. 9.15: 13b: silver finger-ring.

Fig. 9.16: 15: pair of gold ram-headed bracelets.

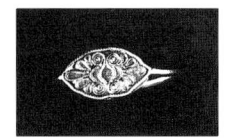

Fig. 9.18: 17: gold finger-ring.

Fig. 9.19: 17: gold finger-ring

Fig. 9.17: 16: pair of gold earrings.

Fig. 9.20: 18: gold pendant holding turquoise cat.

Fig. 9.21: 19a: bronze bull.

Fig. 9.22: 19b: fragment of bronze duck-head handle.

Fig. 9.23: 20: Athenian red-figured owl-glaux.

Fig. 9.24: 20: Athenian red-figured owl-glaux.

Fig. 9.25: 21: terracotta centaur.

Fig. 9.26: 22: carnelian and gold beads.

Fig. 9.27: 25: faience lion with gold-wire suspension loop.

Donald Bailey and Marilyn Hockey

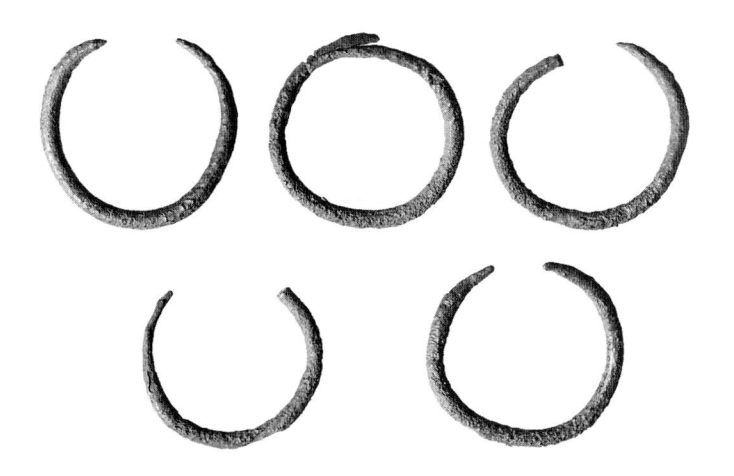

Fig. 9.28: 26: five small silver bracelets.

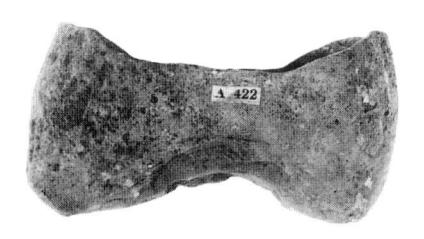

Fig. 9.29: 27: terracotta panniers broken from an equid figure.

Fig. 9.30: 28a: bronze seal-box.

Fig.9.31: 28b: bronze fitting.

Fig. 9.32: 28c: lower part of a bronze handle.

Fig. 9.33: 29a: bronze lampstand top.

Fig. 9.34: 29b: bronze lampstand top.

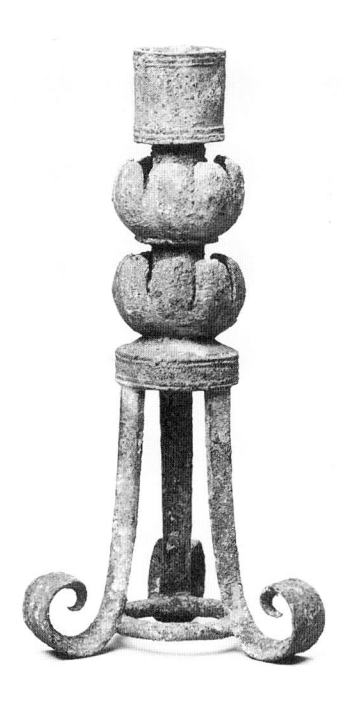

Fig. 9.35: 29c: bronze lampstand top.

Fig. 9.36: 30, 32, 36, 41a: bronze lampstand.

Fig. 9.37: 31: bronze jug.

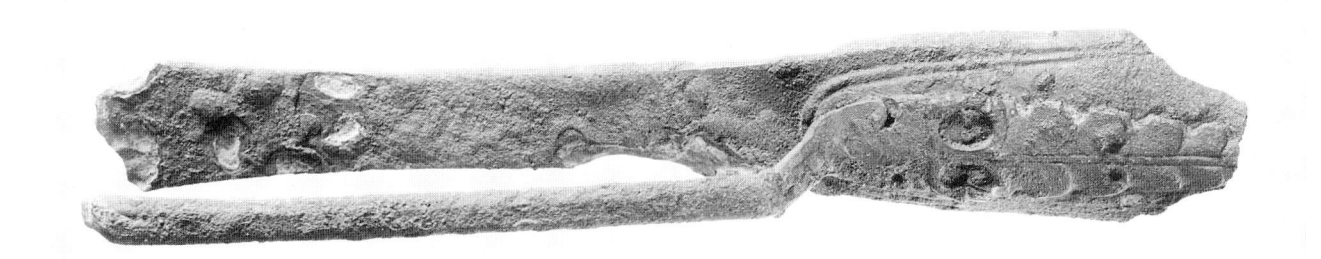

Fig. 9.38: 33: bronze strigil fragment.

Fig. 9.40: 39: rock-crystal scaraboid gem.

Fig. 9.41: 40: gold finger-ring.

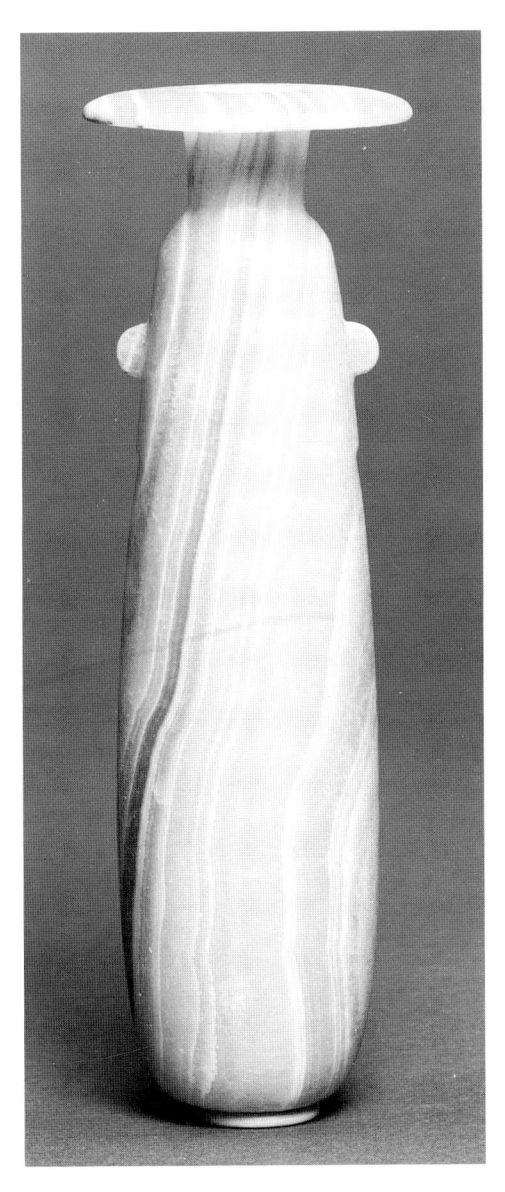

Fig. 9.39: 38: alabaster perfume container.

130 'New' objects from British Museum Tomb 73 at Curium

Fig. 9.42: 40: gold finger-ring.

Fig. 9.43: 41b: bronze stirring-rod.

Fig. 9.44: 42: pair of silver bracelets with calves' heads.

Fig. 9.45: 7a: GR 1991.12–11:1, Bes-pendant (1:1).

Fig. 9.46: 7a: GR 1991.12–11.2, Bes-pendant (1:1).

Fig. 9.47: 7a: GR 1991.12–11.2–10, Bes-pendants (2:3).

Fig. 9.49: 7a: GR 1991.12–11.13–16, Bes-pendants (2:3).

Fig. 9.48: 7a: GR 1991.12–11.5, 11–12, Bes-pendants (2:3).

Fig. 9.50: 7b: Bes-pendant (1:1). *Fig. 9.51: 7b: Bes-pendant (1:1).* *Fig. 9.52: 7b: Bes-pendant (1:1).*

Fig. 9.53: 7c: GR 1991.12–11.19–20, goddess-plaques (2:1).

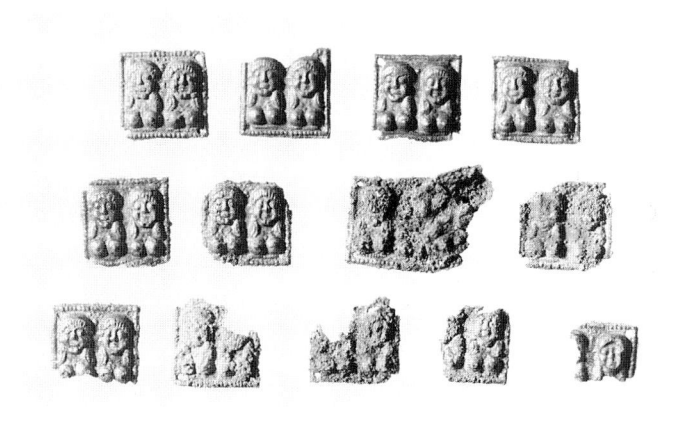

Fig. 9.54: 7c: goddess-plaques (2:3).

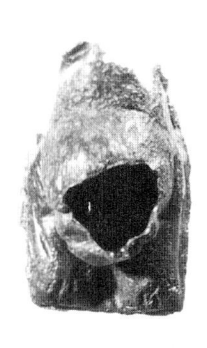

Fig. 9.55: 7d: lion-beads (2:1).

Fig. 9.56: 7d: lion-beads (2:1).

Fig. 9.57: 7d: GR 1991.12–11.31, lion-bead (2:1).

Fig. 9.58: 7f: silver-plated iron fragment (1:1).

10. Cypriot Antiquities in Italy
Items in the Archaeological Museum of Perugia and in the Etruscan-Academy Museum of Cortona

Marco Bettelli and Silvana Di Paolo

Or che di guerra tacion le trombe,
scruta i tesori d'arcane tombe,
scruta di Cipro le prische mura
con dotta cura...
(*G. Regaldi*, Inno a Venere)

The 'Collections Project'

Since 1995, the Institute of Mycenaean and Aegeo-Anatolian Studies (ISMEA) of the CNR in Rome has been working on a research project aimed at identifying, recording and cataloguing the Italian public and private collections, which include Aegean, Cypriot and Near Eastern pieces.[1]

The project, to be carried out in agreement with the hosting Museums concerned, aims to record, study and edit in a systematic and homogenous manner those collections which are as yet unpublished or little known. The purpose is also to examine anew already known material, to re-interpret this in the light of progress made in research, and to contribute to our knowledge of the ways and means by which this particular way of collecting antiquities developed in Italy.

Altogether, to date, thirty-eight groups of material belonging to public and private collections have been recorded. Objects from Cyprus are present in fourteen of these: almost all are pottery vases, although there are also examples of terracotta figurines, stone sculptures and glass vessels. The chronology is quite extensive, extending from the first phases of the Bronze Age to the Roman era.

In this initial phase, the research has concentrated on unpublished material preserved in the Archaeological Museum of Perugia, the Etruscan Academy of Cortona (Arezzo), the Liviano Museum of the University of Padua and the Civic Archaeological Museum of Milan.[2] Here we intend to present a preliminary report on the Perugia and Cortona collections.

Other quite important groups of Cypriot antiquities in Italian Museums are to be found in the Archaeological Museums of Turin[3] and Florence[4] and in the Civic Museum of Trieste.[5] The first consists mainly of a donation made by General Palma di Cesnola.

The Palma di Cesnola collection in Perugia
History of the Collection

The composition of the collection of Cypriot antiquities in the National Archaeological Museum of Perugia recalls, to a great extent, that of the collection owned by the Archaeological Museum of Turin,[6] understandable in the light of events relating to the acquisition of the two groups of objects. Both, in fact, originated in the enormous collection which Luigi Palma di Cesnola assembled during his years in Cyprus as American and Russian Consul. It appears that both consist of duplicates which General Cesnola had chosen as gifts for the museums of the two Italian cities.[7] The selection of the objects was probably made to satisfy a 'didactic' need, and to illustrate the various phases and characteristics of Cypriot civilization in line with the positive ideal '...che i musei fossero all'insegnamento della scienza ciò che i laboratori sono all'insegnamento delle scienze sperimentali..'.[8]

There are discrepancies in the relevant bibliography concerning the date and circumstances of the donation. In fact, some authors date both donations to the great exhibition which Cesnola organized in London in 1872,[9] whilst for others the material went to Turin on an earlier occasion.[10]

The objects preserved in Perugia certainly arrived in the city '...mercé le cure che portava a questo illustre il

Fig. 10.1: Mycenaean piriform jar. Perugia Archaeological Museum (Photo: Soprintendenza Archeologica dell'Umbria).

Fig. 10.2: Base-ring jug. Perugia Archaeological Museum (Photo: Soprintendenza Archeologica dell'Umbria).

benemerito conte Giancarlo Conestabile...'.[11] It is less clear when they were donated. Myres and Roversi,[12] in fact, agree in the event being more or less at the time of the London exhibition, before the entire collection was purchased by the Metropolitan Museum of New York, without, however, providing any further details. Luppatelli, on the other hand, gives far more circumstantial information, saying that the donation was made in the summer of 1875.[13] It is very likely that this latter version is the more probable. When writing of the donations made to the Museum of Perugia in 1871 and 1872 – roughly at the same time, therefore, as the London exhibition – Conestabile makes no mention of the acquisition of Cypriot pieces which would, indeed, have been remarked upon as one of the most important events.[14] It would thus seem reasonable to assume that the only group of Cypriot objects was that recorded, with due attention to detail, by Luppatelli.

The vases and sculptures were soon put on display and remained so until very recently.[15]

The objects

The collection consists of 88 pieces. There are both pottery vases – with a few examples of glass – and small figurines in clay and stone. The chronology varies: there are no examples from the earliest phases of the Bronze Age, whilst pottery from the LBA is well represented (six vases of Mycenaean pottery (Fig. 10.1), three pieces of *Base-Ring* (Fig. 10.2), one *White Slip II* bowl). The LBA vases, including the Mycenaean pottery, is partially known in the bibliography, being quoted as comparative material in Åström's classification.[16] Notable among the Mycenaean examples is a quite well-preserved krater decorated on the shoulder with a chariot scene.

Most of the pottery vases date from the Cypro-Geometric and Cypro-Archaic periods, whilst the glass pieces belong to the Roman era. The pottery vases of the Cypro-Geometric, Cypro-Archaic and Cypro-Classical eras include examples of the principal classes of the island's production: *Proto-White Painted Ware, Black Slip Ware I* (Fig. 10.3), *White Painted Ware III – IV* (Fig. 10.4), *Black on Red Ware II – III, Bichrome Red Ware II, III, IV*. There is also a fragment of a jar with a female figure bearing an *oinochoe*.

The terracotta figurines and the stone sculptures belong to the Cypro-Archaic and Cypro-Classical periods. To the

Fig. 10.3: Black Slip jug. Perugia Archaeological Museum (Photo: Soprintendenza Archeologica dell'Umbria).

Fig. 10.4: White Painted juglet. Perugia Archaeological Museum (Photo: Soprintendenza Archeologica dell'Umbria).

Fig. 10.5: Terracotta horseman. Perugia Archaeological Museum (Photo: Soprintendenza Archeologica dell'Umbria).

Fig. 10.6: Stone temple-boy. Perugia Archaeological Museum (Photo: Soprintendenza Archeological dell'Umbria).

first phase we may attribute, almost exclusively, a group of terracotta objects, mainly horsemen (Fig. 10.5), female images and animal figurines. The later phase is represented both by a series of terracotta pieces – amongst these, two miniature temple-boys and a small head of the goddess Athena – and by a group of small stone sculptures including, again, two temple-boys (Fig. 10.6) already partially published,[17] a female figure with an infant, the small head of a *kouros* and one of 'Herakles.'

As may be seen from this brief summary, the selection of objects appears to satisfy quite precise criteria. This is not, in fact, a more or less casual collection of pieces but, as we have suggested, an assortment which was intended to illustrate the various phases of earliest Cypriot history and the different products which characterized them, especially in the field of pottery.

The Corbelli and Pancrazi collections in Cortona

History of the Collection

Two small groups of Cypriot antiquities are preserved in the Museum created inside Palazzo Casati, a Renaissance building, home of the Etruscan Academy of Cortona in the province of Arezzo. The Academy was founded in 1728 by some illustrious members of the Cortona aristocracy, in particular Abbot Onofrio Baldelli and the brothers Marcello, Ridolfino and Filippo Venuti, all antiquarians. Their aim was to promote historical and archaeological studies. This interest was to be linked to so-called 'Etruscheria', a singular and widespread phenomenon of pseudo-scientific dilettantes which started in Tuscany during the eighteenth century and which, by creating the image of an ancient Etrurian hegemony over the entire world, nourished an anti-Roman and anti-Pontifical form of patriotism. This cultural trend benefited from the activities of various universities and academies, such as the Florentine Studio and the Athenaeum of Pisa, as well as the Etruscan Academy of Cortona, which had also amongst its members Montesquieu and Winckelmann.

Over the years, although the political reasons which had, in part, led to its foundation, faded away, the so-called Academy continued to promote archaeological studies also by the acquisition of antiquities of varying origin.[19] Already, at the end of the eighteenth century, we may note the donation of a group of Egyptian pieces by private collectors through the intermediary of the founders of the Academy, the Venuti brothers.[20]

The first group of Cypriot vases, the object of our study, entered the archaeological collection of the Academy towards the end of the last century as part of a larger collection of Egyptian antiquities assembled by Mons. Guido Corbelli (1841–1903). A native of Cortona, he assumed the post of Apostolic Delegate for Arabia and Egypt in 1888 at the request of Pope Leone XIII.[21] Living in Alexandria, he had the opportunity to acquire and, later, to send, in three separate phases from 1891 to 1896, a notable number of pieces from the Nile valley, mainly objects recovered from tombs.[22] The first expedition of 1891, which provided sixty-four pieces, described together with the eighteenth-century nucleus of the collection in a note by E. Schiaparelli,[23] was followed by a second of 26 June 1894.[24] Among the 160 objects loaded on a ship in Alexandria[25] are four of the five vases of the Cypriot group, to which another example was added two years later,[26] although it is difficult to establish exactly when.[27] In 1955 the Egyptian collection was classified by V.G. Botti.[28] Most of the pieces, including those of supposedly Cypriot origin, appear to have come from Alexandria, probably acquired on the antique market.

Information as to the manner in which the Pancrazi Collection was acquired is, on the other hand, extremely fragmentary. This collection is currently housed in the Biscione room together with pieces from the Classical period.[29] The nine vases belonging to this group were donated to the Museum of the Academy in 1931 by Luigi Pancrazi in his role as a member of the Academy elected in 1923.[30] Brother of the more famous expert of literature, Pietro Pancrazi (Cortona 1893-Firenze 1952) he held the position of Librarian in the Academy between 1945 and 1974. These antiquities had originally been the property of his wife, who belonged to the Gozzi family of Turin.[31] The Cypriot part of the Pancrazi collection was donated at the same time as material from the Graeco-Roman period. Apart from a few vases, for which it has not been possible to find the original acquisition number (nos. 2497 = a small jar of uncertain origin, 2200 = a painted vase similar to no. 264 of the Corbelli Collection, 2201–2 = *Base-Ring* jugs), the rest of the collection was erroneously classified as Etruscan (no. 563/2116 = Cypro-Archaic amphora), Greek (no. 583/2100 = Mycenaean jug) or Roman (nos. 577/2102 = *Red Polished* bowl, 579/2115 = Cypro-Archaic amphora, 232/2101 = Cypro-Archaic flask).

The objects

Within the Corbelli collection, the Cypriot group[32] includes, as well as those pieces of certain origin such as no.3289[33] – that is to say, a jug with lenticular body, funnel rim and ribbon handle, derived from the *Base-Ring* class of the advanced phase of the LBA – also pieces of less certain provenance, like the double painted vase of similar date (no. 264) which seems to be a Palestinian product in the Egyptian style.[34] Of dubious Cypriot origin there is a second jug, again from the LBA, which could belong either to the *Black Lustrous Wheel Made Ware* class,[35] or in a group of Palestinian juglets.[36]

Fig. 10.7: Red Polished III bowl. Accademia Etrusca, Cortona (Photo: Soprintendenza Archeologica della Toscana).

Fig. 10.8: Cypro-archaic jug. Accademia Etrusca, Cortona (Photo: Soprintendenza Archeologica della Toscana).

The largest group of Cypriot pottery in the Pancrazi collection consists, as we have indicated, of nine objects. Only a few of these, however, can be easily identified: one *Red Polished III* bowl (Fig. 10.7), two *Base-Ring I* juglets, one Mycenaean stirrup jar, one amphora and one jug of the Cypro-Archaic period (Fig. 10.8).[37]

The three groups of Cypriots objects discussed here, although not very large, are important, not only in terms of their value as documents of Cypriot archaeology, but also, and possibly more so, because they represent different types of collecting. On the one hand, we have the Perugia collection which, as we have attempted to show, based its composition on a pre-eminently didactic objective, seeing as how the pieces, from the very beginning, were most probably acquired with the intention of being displayed in a public museum. On the other hand, the Pancrazi collection in Cortona appears to be linked more to a 'private' form of collecting, apparently lacking a unified aim for the assembly of material. As for the Corbelli group, the obvious concentration on objects dating from the Bronze Age is clearly due to the fact that the pieces come principally from ancient Egyptian tombs. Here, therefore, there is no direct interest in the history of ancient Cyprus and its material culture, but rather a 'derivative product' arising from the collection of Egyptian antiquities.

Notes

1. Participating in the project, coordinated by Lucia Vagnetti, are Anna Lucia D'Agata of ISMEA and the authors of the present paper. Bibliographical and archive data research has been conducted by the authors under a CNR scholarship for 1995. Cf. L. Vagnetti, 'Materiali Egei, Ciprioti e Vicino Orientali in Musei e Collezioni Italiane', *SMEA* XXXVI (1995) 149. We would like to take this opportunity to thank Dr. Lucia Vagnetti who has assisted this project in every way possible, and the Director of ISMEA, Prof. Miroslav Salvini. Our thanks go also to Dr. A.E. Feruglio, Dr. G. Gattobigio of the Archaeological Superintendence of Umbria, to Dr. P. Bruschetti of the Museum of the Etruscan Academy of Cortona and to Dr. M.C. Guidotti of the Archaeological Superintendence of Umbria and of Tuscany.
2. I. Favaretto, *Il Museo del Liviano a Padova* (Padova 1976) 36–38; D. Ciafaloni, 'I vasi ciprioti del Civico Museo Archeologico di Milano', *OA* XXIV (1985) 301–305, pl. 20–21. The Padua and Milan collections are the subject of a seperate study being undertaken by A.L. D'Agata.
3. F.G. Lo Porto, *La Collezione cipriota del Museo di Antichità di Torino* (Roma 1986).
4. D. Levi, *CVA Italia (Firenze) IICa-IIIA*; P.E. Pecorella, *Guida alle antichità mesopotamiche e cipriote* (Firenze 1966) 25–37; Idem, 'Materiali ciprioti, siriani e micenei nelle collezioni egizie del Museo Archeologico di Firenze', in *Studi ciprioti e rapporti di scavo* I (Roma 1971) 193–201. In Florence there is also an important private collection

which dates back to the discoveries made on Cyprus by Alessandro Palma di Cesnola, but only the glass pieces have been published: M. Sternini, *La Collezione di antichità di Alessandro Palma di Cesnola* (Bari 1998).
5. S. Zupancich, *I vasi ciprioti dell'età del bronzo dei Civici Musei di Storia ed Arte di Trieste* (Trieste 1997).
6. Lo Porto (n.3).
7. L. Roversi, *Luigi Palma di Cesnola e il Metropolitan Museum of Art di New York* (New York 1898) 30.
8. A. Luppatelli, *Il Museo etrusco e romano di Perugia* (Perugia 1889) 17.
9. Roversi (n.7) 49. On the temporary exhibition in London, see O. Masson, 'Quelques épisodes de la vie des frères Palma di Cesnola', *RDAC* (1990) 285–297 and 'Diplomates et amateurs d'antiquités à Chypre vers 1866–1878', *Journal des Savants* (1992) 123–154. Photographs of the exhibition, chosen by C.T. Newton, then Keeper of Greek and Roman Antiquities, were published in 1873 by the photographers W.A. Mansell in a volume entitles *Antiquities of Cyprus* with an introduction by Sidney Colvin, see Masson, *RDAC* (1990) 292–3 and n.61b.
10. J.L. Myres, *Handbook of the Cesnola Collection of antiquities from Cyprus* (New York 1914) xvii; Lo Porto (n.3) 25; G. De Agostini, *Delle scoperte archeologiche fatte dal conte Luigi Palma di Cesnola, Generale e Console Americano in Cipro* (Vercelli 1871) 20. On this subject, it is interesting to note that L. Palma di Cesnola stayed in Turin during the first months of 1871, as can been seen from his correspondence: O. Masson, 'Quelques épisodes de la vie des frères Palma di Cesnola', *RDAC* (1990) 290, in particular n.51.
11. The reference is to General L. Palma di Cesnola, A. Luppatelli, *Indicazione degli oggetti più importanti che si trovano nei Musei di Antichità etrusca, romana e medievale esistenti nelle Università di Perugia* (Perugia 1882) 49–51. Giancarlo Conestabile della Staffa was then director of the Museum in Perugia. Bona's hypothesis would seem less reliable. He holds that the archaeological material was donated by Palma di Cesnola because of his friendship with Ariodante Fabretti (1816–1894), the Perugian scholar and Professor of Archaeology at Turin university. It is, however, certain that there existed reciprocal respect on both a scientific and human level among the three characters involved. C.F. Bona, 'Il piemontese Luigi Palma di Cesnola e le antichità cipriote', *Bollettino della Società Piemontese di Archeologica e Belle Arti* 23–24 (1969–70) 16 n.10; A. Fabretti, *Elogio funebre del conte Giancarlo Conestabile dettato da Ariodante Fabretti e pubblicato a cura del patrio Municipio* (Perugia 1878); Masson (n.10).
12. Myres (n.10); Roversi (n.7).
13. '…ma il dono che a tempo del Conestabile ha una importanza tutta speciale, si è la collezione di statuette, di testine in pietra e in terra cotta, di vasi ceramici semplici e dipinti, di vasetti di vetro in varie forme etc., provenienti dagli scavi dell'isola di Cipro, con il più luminoso successo operati dal Console Americano, il generale Luigi Palma di Cesnola, piemontese di nascita e di famiglia. Questo egregio personaggio, legato da lunga amicizia e da altissima stima con il nostro archeologo, interessandosi a quanto esso più volte gli disse del Perugino Museo, nell'estate del 1875 gli faceva giungere improvvisamente franche di porto da Cipro alla sua casa in Perugia, due casse contenenti oltre un centinaio di pezzi che costituivano la collezione di cui sopra si è parlato…', Luppatelli (n.8).
14. G. Conestabile, *Ragguaglio di doni fatti alle diverse collezioni e alla biblioteca archeologica negli anni 1871–1872* (Perugia 1873).
15. Luppatelli (n.11); B. Dozzini, *Museo Archeologico Nazionale dell'Umbria* (Perugia 1983).
16. P. Åström, *The Swedish Cyprus Expedition IV, vol 1C. The Late Cypriote Bronze Age. Architecture and Pottery* (Lund 1972) 157, 293, 300, 313, 343, 345, 361.
17. C. Beer, *Temple-Boys: A Study of Cypriote Votive Sculpture, Part 1; Catalogue (SIMA* 113, Jonsered 1994) 66–7, no. 224, pl. 48:a-c.
18. P. Bruschetti, M. Gori Sassoli, M.C. Guidotti, *Il Museo dell'Accademia Etrusca di Cortona. Catalogo delle Collezioni* (Cortona 1988) 51–65.
19. V.G. Botti, 'La antichità egiziane raccolte nel Museo dell'Accademia Etrusca di Cortona', *Annuario dell'Accademia Etrusca di Cortona*, n.s., 2 (1953) 21–33, figs 1–3 and *Le antichità egiziane del Muso dell'Accademia Etrusca di Cortona ordinate e descritte* (Firenze 1955) 3–4; P. Bocci Pacini, A.M. Maetzke, *Il Museo dell'Accademia Etrusca di Cortona* (Firenze 1992) 11–37.
20. Information about Marcello, a lover of antiquities and the discoverer of the ancient city of Herculaneum, about Ridolfino, the author of a topographical description of the antiquities of Rome and about Filippo Venuti, scientist and botanist, may be found in L. Bert, 'Musei di Provincia. Il Museo dell'Accademia Etrusca', *Antichità Viva* I,2 (1962) 56.
21. Some biographical notes may be found in D.G. Mirri, *I Vescovi di Cortona della istituzione della Diocesi (1325–1971)* (Cortona 1972) 539–560.
22. Information about the creation of the Egyptian collection of Monsignor Corbelli appeared in the appendix to the volume by A. Della Cella, *Cortona antica. Notizie archeologiche, storiche ed artistiche* (Cortona 1900) 299–311.
23. E. Schiaparelli, 'Le antichità egiziane del Museo di Cortona', *Giornale della Società Asiatica Italiana* 7 (1893) 317–338. This initial group of pieces appears to have come from el-Kab and Thebes and is dated to a period between the XVIII and the XX dynasties.
24. Information about the two later expeditions was presented by Della Cella (n.22) 3.
25. The list was drawn up by V.G. Botti, first Conservator of the Museum of Alexandria appointed by J. de Morgan, General Director the Museums of Egypt: C. Guidotti, G. Rosati, 'Il materiale egizio del Museo dell'Accademia Etrusca di Cortona. La ricerca d'archivio', *Annuario dell'Accademia Etrusca di Cortona* 22 (1985–86) 75.
26. In reality, a third expedition was organized in 1895, but part of the material was destined for Cav. A. Brizi and went to Assisi: G. Rosati, 'Antchità egizie ad Assisi I', *OA* 26 (1985) 55–65 and 'Antichità egizie ad Assisi II', *OA* 27 (1986) 59–67.
27. In fact, three groups of antiquities were sent on the 30

January, in the first days of April, and on the 16 of the same month. The epistolary documentation preserved at the Etruscan Academy does not, however, enable us to establish with certainty which of these expeditions included the Cypriot vase: Guidotti, Rosati (n.25) 77–78.
28. This catalogue was written to enable the re-ordering of the various collections owned by the Museum of the Academy, including the Egyptian collection displayed in the room later named after Corbelli: V.G. Botti, *Le antichità egiziane del Museo dell'Accademia Etrusca di Cortona ordinate e descritte* (Firenze 1955) 3–4.
29. Bruschetti, Gori Sassoli, Guidotti (n.18) 33.
30. *Polimnia. Bollettino Ufficiale dell'Accademia Etrusca di Cortona* anno VIII, no. 4 (1931) 1004–1005.
31. Personal communication from Mr. Filippo Pancrazi.
32. Botti (n.28) 104–109, nos. 261, 264, 266, 288, 289.
33. This is the current inventory number used in the RA files of the Suprintendence and derived from the catalogue created by V.G. Botti.
34. At least according to the evaluations made by R. Amiran, *Ancient Pottery of the Holy Land* (Jerusalem 1970) 187, pl. 58:5,6.
35. Åström (n.16) 218.
36. Amiran (n.34) 146.
37. Both the pieces in Perugia and those in Cortona, presented briefly here, are now being studied in depth in preparation for a systematic publication in the near future.

11. Les Antiquités de Chypre au Louvre: entre l'Orient et l'Occident

Annie Caubet

Les antiquités de Chypre du musée du Louvre sont pour l'essentiel conservées dans le département des Antiquités Orientales, contrairement à la situation de ces collections dans d'autres grands musées, comme le British Museum, Berlin ou Vienne... La raison en est évidemment à rechercher dans l'histoire de l'origine de la collection chypriote du Louvre, histoire qu'Olivier Masson, avec ses talents de détective, a contribué plus qu'aucun autre à éclairer : cette communication est un tribut versé au savant et à l'ami.

Créé en 1793 par Dominique Vivant Denon, le musée du Louvre s'est d'abord appelé Museum Central des Arts, établi pour abriter ce qui survivait du patrimoine national après les violences de la révolution. Un département d'antiques est créé en 1800 pour conserver les marbres et les bronzes antiques des collections royales[1] auxquelles s'ajoutent des achats prestigieux comme celui des marbres de la collection Borghese en 1808. En 1826, Jean-François Champollion obtient la création d'une section spéciale pour les antiquités de l'Egypte, où prennent place la fameuse collection Edme-Antoine Durand[2] vendue à Paris en 1825, puis celle de Henry Salt,[3] ancien consul britannique d'Alexandrie, puis les découvertes qu'Auguste Mariette (1821–1881) fait dans le Sérapeum de Memphis.[4]

En 1847 le Louvre ouvre au public le premier musée d'Europe consacré a l'Assyrie:[5] il contient les colosses mis au jour par le consul de France à Mossoul, Paul-Emile Botta, dans les ruines du palais du roi Sargon II à Khorsobad. Pour l'ouverture de la nouvelle galerie, le conservateur des antiques, Adrien de Longpérier (Fig. 11.1) publie une 'Notice'[6] dont le succès justifie deux éditions immédiates en 1849; ce texte est rapidement augmenté avec l'arrivée des nouvelles découvertes de Victor Place à Khorsobad de 1854. La préface de Longpérier à la troisième édition, écrite dès 1852, contient la première référence à un

Fig. 11.1: Adrien de Longpérier, dessin par François Heim 1856. Louvre, Département des Arts Graphiques.

objet chypriote dans les collections du Louvre, il s'agit des deux coupes d'orfèvrerie d'Idalion:[7] 'Depuis l'époque à laquelle a été rédigée la première édition de cette notice, de précieuses découvertes ont été faites en Assyrie par M. Layard...le Musée de Berlin a fait l'acquisition d'une grande stèle représentant ce dernier (Sargon II), monument découvert dans les ruines de l'antique ville de Citium, en

Fig. 11.2: Coupe d'orfèvrerie rapportée par F. de Saulcy, inventaire N 3454.

Fig. 11.3: Coupe d'orfèvrerie acquise en 1853, inventaire N 3455.

Chypre. Plusieurs coupes d'argent doré, de travail assyrien ont été trouvées dans le même lieu et l'une de ces coupes a été donnée au Louvre par M. de Saulcy, tandis qu'une autre, portant des figures en relief, a pu récemment être examinée à Paris par quelques antiquaires'.[8] Longpérier ajoute en note: 'Depuis que ceci a été écrit, cette seconde coupe est entrée dans la collection du Louvre, voir n° 537'.[9]

Longpérier mentionne donc dans la même phrase les deux coupes d'Idalion (Figs. 11.2–11.3) et la stèle de Sargon découverte à Kition en 1844, acquise par le musée de Berlin. Un moulage de la stèle est envoyé au Louvre et Longpérier le fait exposer à côté des reliefs de Khorsabad en l'incluant dans sa Notice sous le n° 617 'L'administration du Musée n'est pas dans l'usage d'exposer dans les mêmes salles les moulages et les monuments originaux... Une exception a été faite pour la stèle de Larnaca, dont le gouvernement prussien a bien voulu accorder un moulage ... ; ce monument pour être étudié convenablement, devant être rapproché des bas-reliefs où paraît le portrait du roi Sargon'.[10]

La stèle suscite un grand intérêt auprès du public, déjà averti par l'ouverture récente du musée assyrien : un dessin un peu maladroit (Fig. 11.4) paraît dès 1847 dans le *Magasin Pittoresque*,[11] bien avant l'étude scientifique proprement dite.[12] La découverte simultanée du palais assyrien de Sargon II à Khorsabad et de la stèle du même roi à Chypre fut déterminante pour l'avenir du département des Antiquités Orientales et la place qu'occupent les

Fig. 11.4: Stèle assyrienne de Kition, d'après le Magasin Pittoresque *(1847).*

Fig. 11.5: F. de Saulcy et son fils, aquarelle d'Eugène Giraud. Cabinet des Estampes, Bibliothèque Nationale de France.

collections de Chypre au Musée du Louvre. Le commentaire de Longpérier sur cette stèle et les coupes d'orfèvrerie est révélateur de l'attitude courante à l'époque à l'égard des antiquités de Chypre, considérée comme un bon terrain d'étude pour les cultures assyrienne et phénicienne; cette attitude sera aussi adoptée par la génération suivante: 'La présence de monuments assyriens dans l'île de Chypre est un fait de la plus haute importance pour l'histoire de l'art. Il nous explique comment, même avant l'avènement des Achéménides et les invasions de ces princes en Asie-Mineure et en Grèce, ces deux contrées avaient pu emprunter à l'Assyrie des notions d'art, des types qui se sont transmis traditionnellement dans toutes les parties de l'Occident où les Grecs s'étaient établis. Dès une époque très reculée, il a dû exister de fréquentes communications entre Chypre, Rhodes, la Crète et la Sicile; et les écoles d'artistes crétois, rhodiens et siciliens auront reçu des leçons et des modèles de ces habiles sculpteurs assyriens, qui, à une époque où Rome existait à peine, étaient si expérimentés dans la pratique de l'art. La découverte, faite à Ceri [Cerveteri], de coupes d'argent de travail asiatique, tellement analogues aux coupes trouvées en Chypre, qu'on peut les croire contemporaines ou du moins sorties des mêmes ateliers, est un fait qui atteste les rapports de l'Assyrie avec la côte orientale de l'Italie'.[13]

Outre la coupe d'orfèvrerie, F. de Saulcy rapporte de Chypre une série d'antiquités. On s'arrêtera un instant sur la carrière scientifique de cet officier artilleur (Fig. 11.5), numismate averti, que ses recherches sur les monnaies conduisent à apprendre les langues orientales: arabe, hébreu, phénicien, punique, puis baylonien...[14] En 1841, il est élu à l'Académie des Inscriptions et Belles Lettres au fauteuil du numismate Théodore Mionnet. En 1850, à la mort de sa femme Pauline de Brye, il invoque son deuil pour obtenir du Ministre de l'Instruction Publique une mission qui lui 'permette de parcourir avec un caractère officiel' la Syrie et l'Asie Mineure. Il demande au Ministre la permission de 'faire scier et rapporter un monument authentique des conquêtes de Sennacherib. Ce serait, sans contredit, enrichir le Musée du Louvre de l'une des reliques les plus précieuses de l'Empire assyrien': ce projet, fort heureusement, n'aboutit pas, il s'agissait tout simplement de découper une des stèles rupestres de la falaise du Nahr el Kelb, au Liban! Mais on voit là que l'intérêt de Saulcy se porte notamment sur les monuments assyriens du Levant.

L'expédition, partie de Marseille en septembre 1849, comprend son fils Félicien Henri,[15] un ami de la famille, Edouard Delessert,[16] un botaniste, l'abbé J.H. Michon,[17] les peintres Léon Belly et Léon Loysel. En décembre, ils sont à Jérusalem où ils sont reçus par le consul de France, qui n'est autre que Paul-Emile Botta, celui-là même qui venait de redécouvrir le palais assyrien de Sargon II à Khorsabad lorsqu'il était en poste à Mossoul: on se doute que la conversation doit rouler sur ces prestigieuses découvertes. En chemin, ils ont fait relâche à Chypre où ils collectent des figurines de terre cuite et une statue de porteuse d'offrande tenant l'image d'un petit taureau (Fig. 11. 6). Ce objet[18] est publié en 1855 par A. de Longpérier comme un exemple d'art phénicien. Il est intéressant de noter que la revue choisie pour cet article, L'Athenaeum français, de tendance maçonnique, a été fondée en 1852 précisément par Félicien de Saulcy, Adrien de Longpérier et Edouard Delessert.

Les enrichissements ultérieurs de la collection chypriote du Louvre se font tous sous le signe de l'orientalisme: ainsi, la deuxième coupe d'orfèvrerie de Chypre mentionnée dans la Notice de Longpérier est acquise grâce à la générosité du duc de Luynes. Ce grand numismate, dont la collection de monnaies et d'antiquités est aujourd'hui conservée au Cabinet des Médailles, se rend à son tour en Orient[19] en 1861 et rapporte de son voyage autour de la Mer Morte la stèle de Schihan repérée par F. de Saulcy. Un autre voyageur orientaliste, Guillaume Alban Rey,[20] contribue à

Fig. 11.6: Porteuse d'offrande rapportée par F. de Saulcy, inventaire MN 1625.

la construction de la collection chypriote par ses dons et ventes, entre 1860 et 1865: au cours de ses premières missions en Syrie et autour de la Mer Morte, il acquiert à Chypre divers petits sujets de terre cuite et une monumentale figure de roi en calcaire (Fig. 11.7) provenant d'Idalion:[21] à cette époque où l'on ignore tout de l'art grec archaïque, une telle figure royale barbue ne peut que frapper par la comparaison avec les reliefs assyriens. Ce sont surtout les découvertes de la mission Vogüé et Duthoit en 1862 et 1865 qui constituent la majeure partie de la collection chypriote. Conçue comme le prolongement naturel de la mission d'Ernest Renan en Phénicie, la mission de Chypre est confiée à Melchior de Vogüé, tout juste de retour d'une expédition dans le désert de Syrie méridionale où il a étudié les monuments du Hauran et collecté des inscriptions du désert du Safa. Sa mission de 1862 est la première tentative d'étude systématique de l'île et la première fouille de grande ampleur, entreprise dans une perspective orientaliste. Ainsi que Duthoit l'écrit à sa mère: 'La mission du gouvernement a pour but de recueillir

Fig. 11.7: Statue royale rapportée par Guillaume Alban-Rey, inventaire N 1085.

les éléments propres à faire connaître les Phéniciens, tout ce qui peut concerner leur histoire, leurs arts, leurs mœurs etc...'[22]

Une seconde expédition dirigée cette fois par le seul Edmond Duthoit suit en 1865. Plus de mille sculptures,[23] des inscriptions, des statuettes de terre cuite, provenant de Golgoi, Malloura (Fig. 11.8), Paphos, Trapeza près de Salamis etc...arrivent au Louvre. L'œuvre la plus spectaculaire est le gigantesque vase d'Amathonte.[24] Cet afflux soudain de milliers d'œuvres au musée, ajoutée aux acquisitions récentes de la mission de Phénicie d'Ernest

Fig. 11.8: Dessin de sculptures fait à Chypre par Edmond Duthoit. Musée d'Amiens.

Renan, semble avoir paralysé le conservateur, Adrien de Longpérier: le fait est qu'il ne procéda pas systématiquement à l'inventaire des pièces au fur et à mesure de leur arrivée. Au cours du temps, leur origine et leur provenance se perdit et il aura fallu attendre les recherches d'Olivier Masson et d'Antoine Hermary pour clarifier les listes[25] et distinguer les apports de la mission Vogüé et Duthoit des activités de leurs successeurs, qu'il s'agisse des frères Colonna Ceccaldi, de Luigi Palma di Cesnola, ou de Max Ohnefalsch-Richter.

Cette première période est marquée par la personnalité du conservateur des antiques, Adrien de Longpérier, en fonction jusqu'en 1870; la période suivante reflète les intérêts très divers de Léon Heuzey.[26] Entré au Louvre cette année là comme adjoint de Félix Ravaisson Mollien, lui-même remplaçant A. de Longpérier, démissionnaire, il a une formation d'archéologue classique (Fig. 11.9). Ancien membre de l'Ecole française d'Athènes, il fouille à Pydna les premières tombes macédoniennes dont une reconstitution est exposée en 1862 au Palais de l'Industrie. Cette exposition présente aussi les découvertes d'Ernest Renan en Phénicie et celles de Georges Perrot en Asie Mineure. Titulaire depuis 1863 de la chaire d'archéologie de l'Ecole des Beaux-Arts, Léon Heuzey y fonde un cours d'expérimentation sur 'modèle vivant' du costume antique de l'Egypte à la Grèce, domaine qui restera un de ses centres d'intérêt tout au long de sa carrière. Une fois au musée du Louvre, Léon Heuzey s'attache d'abord à restaurer les salles

Fig. 11.9: Léon Heuzey. Photo archives département des Antiquités Orientales.

et les œuvres endommagées par les événements de la guerre franco-prussienne, installe en 1875 les découvertes d'Olivier Texier en Asie Mineure à Tralles, Milet, Magnésie du Méandre, Didymes, avant de veiller à une nouvelle présentation des œuvres dans les salles assyriennes, phéniciennes et chypriotes qui s'effectue en 1876–1877.

C'est alors qu'à tous ces envois des missions archéologiques françaises au Levant et en Asie Mineure, s'ajoutent ceux découverts en pays de Sumer par Ernest de Sarzec à partir de 1877. La quantité d'œuvres devient alors telle qu'il faut prendre des mesures pour réorganiser le département des Antiques. Celui-ci est désormais divisé en spécialités et, en 1881, un nouveau département est créé pour abriter les antiquités orientales, avec à sa tête Léon Heuzey. On s'émerveille de l'étendue des aires d'expertise de celui-ci: non content de 'piloter' la publication des fouilles mésopotamiennes exécutées par Ernest de Sarzec puis Gaston Cros,[28] Léon Heuzey joue un rôle déterminant dans la naissance et la défense de l'archéologie ibérique, prenant parti dans les controverses suscitées par les découvertes de Cerro de los Santos en 1888.[29] Entre-temps, il publie l'ouvrage qui lui assure un rang inégalé dans l'histoire de l'archéologie de Chypre, son Catalogue des figurines antiques de terre cuite du Musée du Louvre.[30] La première édition est introduite par une lettre de Heuzey à l'administrateur général du musée, Louis de Ronchaud qui expose bien son propos: 'Le Catalogue dont je vous prie de vouloir bien autoriser l'impression sera, je crois, le premier essai fait par un grand musée pour publier, dans un ordre méthodique, l'ensemble de ses figurines de terre cuite. Chaque classe de monuments réclame une forme de catalogue qui lui soit appropriée. Le nombre presque infini et le caractère souvent indécis des statuettes d'argile m'ont déterminé à multiplier les notices qui expliquent les classifications ou résument les caractères de chaque série. Cette méthode a l'avantage de tracer, pour les visiteurs de nos collections, comme une histoire de la plastique ancienne par les petites images de terre cuite...'

La table des matières est ainsi organisée: une introduction est dédiée aux terre cuites vernissées égyptiennes, car 'L'Egypte précède de si loin ce que nous connaissons de l'antiquité que l'on ne peut étudier aucune industrie ancienne sans rechercher tout d'abord quel degré d'avancement les Egyptiens y étaient parvenus'. Le catalogue proprement dit est divisé en deux parties: les figurines orientales (Assyrie, Babylonie, Chaldée, Susiane, Phénicie) et les figurines des îles asiatiques (Chypre, Rhodes): on voit bien par là que la culture de Chypre reste envisagée sous un angle asiatique! Dans son chapitre sur les figurines chypriotes, qui comprend un résumé historique et une analyse de l'art de l'île, Heuzey rappelle l'importance de l'art assyrien dans la formation de la sculpture de Chypre: 'Les terres cuites de Chypre sont le plus souvent d'un travail si rudimentaire qu'elles ne suffisent pas pour connaître l'art cypriote. Il faut de toute nécessité prendre pour point de départ l'étude de la sculpture, taillée dans la pierre calcaire du pays.....Les statues cypriotes qui paraissent les plus anciennes ont un caractère asiatique prononcé et présentent avec la sculpture assyrienne un air de famille, dont on est frappé tout d'abord. On reconnaît cependant que l'influence de l'Assyrie n'est pas directe et qu'elle a dû s'exercer par l'intermédiaire des ateliers phéniciens... Il faut donc admettre que l'art s'est développé solidairement dans les deux pays et que la sculpture a été introduite dans l'île par les Phéniciens, à l'époque où ceux-ci subissaient eux-mêmes l'influence du style assyrien...'

Dans l'album on reconnaît aujourd'hui quelques rares statuettes remontant à l'âge du Bronze, parmi les œuvres classées dans les 'origines comparées': la planche IV, 6 et 5 présente deux statuettes du Chypriote Récent qui figurent toutes les deux dans le nouveau catalogue de la coroplastique de Chypre publié en 1998;[31] mais dans l'ensemble, Léon Heuzey n'a pas eu connaissance des civilisations de l'âge du Bronze méditerranéen.

Le premier catalogue Heuzey de 1882 connut un grand succès, et fut réimprimé constamment jusqu'à ce qu'en 1923, Edmond Pottier décide d'en produire une seconde édition augmentée[32] incorporant les planches de l'album devenu introuvable. L'adresse de la seconde édition est en forme de lettre d'Edmond Pottier au Directeur J. d'Estournelles de Constant: 'Le succès de vente et les réimpressions nombreuses du Catalogue des Figurines Antiques que M. Heuzey avait rédigé en 1882 montrent qu'au bout de quarante ans ce petit livre répond encore aux désir du public qui vient s'instruire dans nos galeries. Je n'en suis pas surpris, car cette étude, qui en son temps fut la première tentative faite pour expliquer, sous forme de commentaire développé, l'intérêt historique et artistique d'une série spéciale d'antiquités, a gardé toute sa valeur. Des découvertes nouvelles ont eu lieu, nos collections se sont accrues en nombre, mais les principes si heureusement formulés par notre savant maître n'ont pas changé. Mieux encore, ils se sont vérifiés avec le temps écoulé et ils ont acquis la force de lois scientifiques. Les théories de M. Heuzey sur l'action en retour de l'art grec, le rôle exact des Phéniciens, sur le sourire archaïque des figurines grecques, ont passé dans le domaine des idées courantes et beaucoup d'archéologues en font usage, sans même se rappeler que le petit Catalogue du Louvre fut la source de ces pénétrantes remarques. ... Il nous a paru qu'au lieu de procéder, une fois de plus, à une simple réimpression, il serait utile de fournir au public ce même livret sous une forme un peu rajeunie, d'une part en y complétant les références anciennes... d'autre part en y reproduisant les planches qui accompagnaient l'album... aujourd'hui épuisé et introuvable. Dans ces conditions, il n'y aura rien de changé au texte et le lecteur pourra cependant être mis au courant des faits nouveaux...'

A partir de 1884, en effet, Léon Heuzey s'était attaché la personne d'Edmond Pottier (Fig. 11.10) pour le décharger de l'étude de la céramique antique et lui permettre de se consacrer pleinement aux collections chaldéennes. Edmond Pottier raconte ainsi leur première rencontre en

Fig. 11.10: Edmond Pottier. Photo archives département des Antiquités Grecques, Etrusques et Romaines.

1879, lorsqu'il fut 'reçu... pour la première fois au Louvre. Je le trouvai dans le vaste bureau, un peu sombre, tout peuplé d'armoires, de tables et de paperasses entassées, qu'il devait occuper jusqu'à sa retraite et je ne me doutais pas que dans cette chambre d'aspect si sévère, où me parlait à voix presque basse un homme d'allures réservées et discrètes, devaient se dérouler tant d'années heureuses et laborieuses de ma propre existence'.[33] Dans ce cabinet, Pottier prend place en compagnie de son camarade Salomon Reinach pour y rédiger d'abord la publication des figurines de terre cuite provenant de leurs fouilles de Myrina; puis il s'attaque seul à l'étude de la céramique antique et propose un classement du matériel de l'âge du bronze méditerranéen: son volume consacré 'aux origines' paraît en 1896[34] c'est la première tentative de ce genre, peu avant l'établissement de la nomenclature moderne (et en anglais!) de la céramique de Chypre que donnent John Myres et Max Ohnefalsch-Richter dans leur catalogue du musée de Nicosie en 1899.[35] Edmond Pottier répertorie les céramiques de Chypre au musée du Louvre dans ses deux volumes du Corpus Vasorum Antiquorum parus en 1926 et 1928,[36] mais conserve des désignations en français: cela nuisit beaucoup à la postérité de ces précieux volumes!

Les collections chypriotes du musée du Louvre ont donc été abritées dès leur arrivée à Paris parmi les collections assyriennes et asiatiques, elles furent d'abord placées sous la responsabilité de savants de formation diverse, numismates comme Adrien de Longpérier, hellénistes comme Léon Heuzey ou Edmond Pottier. Ces classiques s'étaient 'reconvertis' à des disciplines nouvellement apparues dans le champ de la connaissance, ils se montrèrent capables d'étudier aussi bien les civilisations de Mésopotamie que celles de Carthage ou d'Espagne, ils en encouragèrent la recherche. Chypre, par bien des égards, leur paraissait un jalon indispensable au cœur de la Méditerranée. Ce n'est que lorsque l'afflux des découvertes au cœur du Proche Orient eut entraîné la formation de conservateurs étroitement spécialisés dans ce domaine que les collections de Chypre au musée du Louvre commencèrent à être négligées, perdant même une partie de leur identité: ce désintérêt progressif est marqué par l'éclipse du travail de catalogue après 1928. Dès 1934, le nouveau guide du département des Antiquités Orientales fait une large part aux fouilles récentes des pays du mandat français, mais ne réserve à Chypre qu'un bref paragraphe partagé avec la Troade:'Les antiquités chypriotes sont constituées par les collections de G. Rey (1860) et du marquis de Vogüé (1862), auxquelles il faut joindre les envois de MM Castillon de Saint-Victor et P. Perdrizet. Les importantes découvertes de M. Cl. Schaeffer (1933 et 1934) sur les sites de Vounous et d'Enkomi seront prochainement exposées'.[37]

On ne saurait être trop reconnaissant à Olivier Masson d'avoir donné une nouvelle impulsion aux études chypriotes dans le musée du Louvre.

Notes

1. Voir récemment l'exposition *Les Bronzes de la Couronne*, Paris 1999.
2. M. Bierbrier, *Who Was Who in Egyptology* (3rd. ed., London 1995) 134.
3. Cette collection comprenait notamment le sphinx de Tanis, les Annales de Thumosis III, les statues d'Amenophis et la dame Nat, et le sarcophage en granit de Ramsès III.
4. Voir sur les enrichissments du musée le *Rapport de M. le Comte de Nieuwerkerke.....*(Paris, Didier et Cie 1863).
5. Voir E. Fontan, 'Adrien Longpérier et la création du musée assyrien du Louvre', in E. Fontan et N. Chevalier, *De Khorsobad à Paris. La découverte des Assyriens* (Paris 1994) 226–237.
6. A. de Longpérier, conservateur des Antiques et de la sculpture moderne, *Notice des Monuments d'antiquités assyriennes au Musée du Louvre* (Vinchon imprimeur des Museés Nationaux, Paris 1849) 38 pages; (2ème ed., Paris 1849) 40 pages; A. de Longpérier, *Notice des Antiquités Assyriennes, Babyloniennes, Perses, Hébraïques exposées dans les galeries du Musée du Louvre* (3ème ed., Paris 1854) (écrite en 1852).
7. Inventaire N 3454 (coupe Saulcy) et N 3433: A. Caubet, A. Hermary et V. Karageorghis, *Art Antique de Chypre* (Athènes 1992) no. 82 et no. 83.
8. Longpérier emploie bien sûr le term 'antiquaire' au sens traditionel de connaisseur et amateur d'antiquités.
9. Longpérier (n.6, 3ème ed.) 16.
10. Longpérier (n.6, 3ème ed.) 143.
11. *Le Magasin Pittoresque* (Paris 1847) 328. Nos devons cette information à Marie-Laure Aurenche dont on peut

désormais consulter la thèse: *Edouard Charton et l'invention du Magasin Pittoresque, 1833–1870* (Université Lumière-Lyon II 1999). Un dessin de la stèle, tout aussi approximatif, avait déjà été livré au publique britannique, voir V. Tatton-Brown, 'The British Museum discovers Cyprus', *Centre d'Etudes Chypriotes. Cahier* 28 (1998) 113–5.

12. E. Schrader, *Die Sargonstele des Berliner Museums (Abhandlungen der königlichen Akademie der Wissenchaften zu Berlin,* Berlin 1881); H. Winckler, *Die Keilschrifttexte Sargons* (Leipzig 1889) I, 174–5; II, pls. 46–47. On sait désormais que la stèle provenait du secteur de Kition Bamboula, voir M. Yon, 'La stèle de Sargon II à Chypre. La découverte de la stèle à Larnaca (Chypre)', in A. Caubet (ed.), *Khorsabad, le palais de Sargon II roi d'Assyrie* (Colloque du musée du Louvre, La Documentation Française, Paris 1994) 161–168.
13. Longpérier (n.6, 3ème ed.) préface.
14. Voir P. Amiet, M. de Bry, A. Caubet, S. Dubois, F. Heilbrun et N. Villa, *F. de Saulcy (1807–1880) et la Terre Sainte* (Notes et Documents 5, Paris 1982).
15. Né le 24 décembre 1832 de la première femme de F. de Saulcy, Pauline de Brye, Félicien Henri, mort en 1912, se spécialisa en entomologie.
16. Alexandre Henri Edouard Delessert, fils du banquier Gabriel-Etienne, né à Paris en 1828, mort en 1898, publia ses propres souvenirs de ce voyage, *Vingt et un jours à la Mer Morte* (1851) et *Voyage aux villes maudite* (1853).
17. On lui doit E. Cosson et Kralik (eds.), *Catalogue des plantes observées en Syrie et en Palestine par MM de Saulcy et Michon* (Paris 1854).
18. Inventaire MN 1625: A. de Longpérier, 'Antiquités Orientales', *Bull. arch. de l'Athenaeum français* (mars 1855) 24; Caubet in Amiet et alii (n.14) no. 280; A. Hermary, *Les Antiquités de Chypre. Sculptures* (Paris 1989) 369, no.746.
19. M. le duc de Luynes, *Voyage d'exploration à la Mer Morte, à Petra et sur la rive gauche du Jourdain* (Paris 1871–1865), ouvrage posthume publié sous la direction de M. le comte de Vogüé.
20. A. Caubet, 'Aux origines de la collection chypriote du Louvre: le fonds Guillaume-Rey (1860–1865)', *RDAC* (1984) 221–229. Hermary (n.18) 11.
21. Inventaire N 1085: Hermary (n.18) 126, no.246.
22. J. Foucart-Borville, 'La correspondance chypriote d'Edmond Duthoit (1862 et 1865)', *Centre d'Etudes Chypriotes. Cahier* 4 (1985) 14.
23. Sur ces travaux, nombreuses études d' O. Masson, résumé dans Hermary (n.18) 14–19.
24. Hermary (n.18) 444, no. 918.
25. On se reportera à L. Dubois, 'Bibliographie thématique des travaux d'Olivier Masson concernant Chypre', *Centre d'Etudes Chypriotes. Cahier* 27 (1997) 11–13; Hermary (n.18) 14–15 pour la restitution des listes.
26. M. Peissik et N. Roy, *Léon Heuzey. La recherche des origines 1831–1922* (Monographie de l'Ecole du Louvre, Paris 1991) (manuscrit).
27. Léon Heuzey et Honoré Daumet, *Mission archéologique de Macédoine* (Paris 1876).
28. Ernest de Sarzec et Léon Heuzey, *Découvertes en Chaldée* (Paris 1884); Commandant Gaston Cros, *Nouvelles fouilles de Tello* (publiées avec le concours de Léon Heuzey et de François Thureau-Dangin, Paris 1914).
29. Voir P. Rouillard, *Antiquités de l'Espagne* (Paris 1997) 10.
30. Léon Heuzey, *Catalogue des Figurines antiques de terre cuite du Musée du Louvre* (Paris 1882). Heuzey était conservateur des Antiquités Orientales et Membre de l'Institut.
31. Inventaire MNB 365 et MNB 1304, récemment cataloguées sous la direction d'A. Caubet, Sabine Fourier et Anne Queyrel avec la collaboration de Frieda Vandenabeele, *L'art des modeleurs d'argile. Antiquités de Chypre. Coroplastiques* (Paris 1998) 659, no. 17 (dépôt au musée de La Castre, Cannes) et 51, no. 20.
32. E. Pottier, *Catalogue des Figurines Antiques de terre cuite. Figurines Orientales et Figurines des îles asiatiques* (Paris 1923) in 8E de XXIV–252 pages, 18 planches.
33. E. Pottier, 'Leon Heuzey (souvenirs d'un collaborateur)', *Revue Archéologique* XV (1922) 324–331.
34. E. Pottier, *Etudes sur l'histoire de la peinture et du dessin dans l'Antiquité. Première partie, Les Origines* (Librairies Imprimeries réunies, éditeur des Musées Nationaux, May et Motteroz directeurs, Paris 1896) in 12E, 258 pages, 3 planches, 576 numeros.
35. John Myres & M. Ohnefalsch-Richter, *A Catalogue of the Cyprus Museum* (Oxford 1899).
36. E. Pottier, 'II C Style chypriote: '1, Vases antérieurs à la période hellénique' and '2, Vases appartenant à la période hellénique', *CVA, France* 5, *Louvre* 4 (Paris 1926); 'II C b Style chypriote: 'II, Vases appartenant à la période hellénique (suite)', *CVA France* 8, *Louvre* 5 (Paris 1928).
37. Marguerite Rutten, *Antiquités Orientales, Guide* (*Musées Nationaux, Musée du Louvre,* Paris 1934) 127; 126–130, les collections de figurines et de céramique de Chypre sont cependant décrites dans la salle des origines comparées, héritage d'Edmond Pottier.

12. Excavations in Cyprus and the 'Mycenaean Question'

J. Lesley Fitton

This note briefly discusses the reception of Bronze Age material from Cyprus at the end of the nineteenth century, and how it fitted with the evolving process of characterisation and dating of Mycenaean culture. It is a small contribution to this volume dedicated to the memory of Professor Masson, whose work is a source of inspiration to everyone working on the history of Cypriot scholarship.

It would be tempting to suggest that by AD1900 the battle for understanding of the nature and date of Mycenaean material had largely been won. The publication in 1896 of Tsountas and Manatt's *The Mycenaean Age* can be viewed as an important fixed point, and the work contains in its early pages the confident assertion 'We now know that the Homeric Age was not the childhood of the Greek world. It was rather an age of renaissance from national decline. Back of that decadence we mount up to the meridien of national bloom. This era of Mycenaean culture covers the period approximately from the sixteenth to the twelfth century BC'.[1] The language may be old-fashioned, but the conclusion scarcely needs updating even now.

Tsountas and Manatt acknowledge the fundamental contribution made by Sir Charles Newton, Keeper of Greek and Roman Antiquities in the British Museum from 1861 to 1886, to the understanding of the Greek Bronze Age, saying that in his article of 1878 he 'laid the real foundation of Mycenaean archaeology'.[2] Newton, closely interested in the results of Schliemann's excavations, had been instrumental in linking the Mycenae finds with material from Ialysos already in the British Museum, as well as with Mycenaean material from elsewhere, including Cyprus. He had correctly identified many of the elements typical of Mycenaean culture, and had grappled with the problem of chronology, elaborating a relative scheme in which Mycenaean material was described as 'prae-Daedalian' (i.e. before the type of art works described by Homer, dated by Newton to about 850BC) and certainly before the 'Graeco-Phoenician' period, which according to Newton ended at about 560BC. His absolute date for the Mycenaean period was in about the eleventh century BC.[3]

His chronology was compressed, and Tsountas and Manatt made a better assessment, mainly because they put more trust in connections between the Mycenaean world and Egypt. Nonetheless, Newton had taken the vital step of recognising that Mycenaean culture was early Greek, and the equally vital step of separating it from that of the Phoenicians, with which Mycenaean material was identified by some scholars. He says in so many words that Mycenaean art is the 'product of a race destined ultimately to assimilate and improve the arts and inventions of the Phoenicians and older races, but who had not yet entered into this rich inheritance'.[4]

One might expect that Alexander Murray, Newton's successor as Keeper, would have built confidently on this inheritance, and that it would underpin his publication of the Mycenaean finds made during the important series of excavations conducted by the British Museum in Cyprus between 1894 and 1896. Murray, with his collaborators Smith and Walters, published *Excavations in Cyprus* in 1900, with results from the sites of Enkomi, Amathus and Kourion.[5] Tombs at both Enkomi and Kourion had yielded quantities of material that could instantly be recognised as Mycenaean. On the face of it, there was every possibility that this would be received on the basis of at least a general understanding of where Mycenaean material fitted in the scheme of things, and dated more or less correctly in the period that we now characterise as the Greek Bronze Age. Indeed, one might have expected that the dating of the Mycenaean material would have helped to date the tombs in which it was found, and the Cypriot objects found with it. In fact this was not the case. Murray described the material as 'Mycenaean', but dated it to the seventh century BC.

Why had the picture become unclear? Murray's drastic down-dating of Mycenaean material seems, with hindsight, such a retrograde step. It must, though, be viewed against the climate of thought of the time. The last decade of the nineteenth century was the age of the so-called 'Mycenaean Question' – shorthand for the question of the spatial and temporal limits of the Mycenaean culture, and how it fitted into the sequence of cultures in Greece and the eastern Mediterranean as they were then understood. It is not clear who coined the term, but it was in general use, and indeed Murray refers repeatedly to W. Helbig's article of 1896 which was actually entitled 'La question Mycenniene'.[6] Helbig's own view was a version of the high dating proposed by earlier scholars, in that he placed Mycenaean material in the fourteenth century BC. He felt, though, that this material represented the oldest phase of the Phoenician culture, and that after a period of some seven centuries which saw little artistic development it found its natural successors in the Phoenician bronze and silver bowls found both on Cyprus and elsewhere. Murray saw Mycenaean material as Greek, and moreover wanted to bring it into direct association particularly with east Greek material. For this reason he wanted to lower the dating by about seven centuries. He says 'more and more it is being accepted that the so-called Mycenaean art was the immediate predecessor of the Ionian Greek art of the seventh century BC, as seen in the vase paintings of Cameiros now in the British Museum, and in numerous objects of gold and porcelain from the same site'.[7]

Murray was certainly not alone in feeling that Mycenaean material could be as late as about the eighth century BC. It is interesting to see how Arthur Evans dealt with the problem in the first publication of the Aigina treasure. His article, 'A Mykenaean Treasure from Aigina', appeared in 1893.[8] He recognised the Aigina Treasure as belonging to the same general sphere as the finds from Mycenae, and recognised also 'a prevailing current of influence from the Asiatic side', though noting 'a certain element of originality' in many of the pieces of the treasure which prevented it from seeming to him to be an imported group. He goes on 'Such, nevertheless, is the attitude of a certain school of criticism towards even the masterpieces of Mykenaean art that, in spite of these considerations, it would be too much to expect that no attempt will be made to claim as articles of Phoenician import the most conspicuous of the Aegina relics'.

Evans has a down-to-earth response. 'In spite of every effort to bring it ready-made from Northern Syria or elsewhere, Mykenaean art has an obstinate way of clinging to the mainland and islands of Greece'. In his view the most flourishing period of Mycenaean art could be dated to the fifteenth century BC, on the basis of Petrie's finds of Mycenaean pottery in Egypt and the evidence of scarabs of Amenhotep III and Queen Ti found with Mycenaean material in Greece. Nonetheless, recognising that the Aigina Treasure was not mainstream Mycenaean, and certainly was not identical to the Shaft Grave material, he dated it later – actually to about 800BC. Evans did not want to down-date the whole Mycenaean phenomenon. Instead, he argued that 'pockets' of Mycenaean style could have survived in certain specific places. He felt these might have included the Argolid and some of the Greek islands, where the Mycenaean tradition could have been so strong that it felt, but was not overwhelmed by, otherwise pervasive Oriental influences.

Such an argument might have seemed tenable for the Mycenaean heartland of the Argolid and some of the more remote and small islands. It could hardly be suggested for Cyprus, a large and archaeologically very rich island lying so close to the Syro-Palestinian coast that it clearly was always going to be in the forefront of influences from the east. Murray therefore did have to down-date the whole of the Mycenaean phenomenon if his view was to be consistent. Throughout the pages of *Excavations in Cyprus* he tried to muster all possible arguments in support of this case.

This involved him in repeated and insistent refusal to accept certain sorts of evidence, most notably that of links with Egypt. In particular he dismissed the relevance of scarabs really quite scornfully. For example, the scarab (*Excavations* pl IV no. 608, GR1897.4–1.608) from the very rich tomb 93 at Enkomi bears the name of Queen Ti, wife of Amenhotep III. It might therefore have been felt to reinforce the association of scarabs of Amenhotep III with Mycenaean material at Ialysos and Mycenae that supporters of the high dating, such as Arthur Evans, had already noted and stressed. For Murray, this evidence was negated by the fact that scarabs may be heirlooms, and thus older than their context, or indeed may have been made with names already several centuries old. 'Helbig', he says, 'the latest and most learned champion of the older age of the Mycenaean civilisation, recognises the fact that the Egyptians *sometimes* employed the names of their kings in later ages. It would have been more correct to say *frequently*. At all events, we can no longer lay great stress, as he does, on the argument that only the scarabs of Amenophis and his queen have been found in connection with Mycenaean antiquities'.[9]

Such reservations, while not without foundation, were over-stated. The disappointing fact that scarabs were not always useful for the dating of contexts either in Egypt or abroad seems to have led Murray to caution that almost amounted to disaffection in his treatment of them, and he seriously undervalued their evidence for Aegean dating. Yet in any case the scarabs were only part of the story. Already in 1890 Flinders Petrie had published Aegean pottery from his excavations at Lahun and Gurob which he felt indicated an early date for the Mycenaean world.[10] More specifically related to the Cypriot finds was the fact that glass vases shaped like pomegranates, of which Enkomi Tomb 66 is said to have contained three examples (GR 1897.4–1.1052, 1053 and 1056, though 1897.4–1.1053 has more recently been identified as a lentoid flask),[11] could be compared with similar vessels found at Gurob and dated by Petrie to about 1400BC. Murray notes this in characteristic style. He describes the Enkomi vessels as 'differing but slightly in shape and fabric from the fine series of glass vases obtained from the tombs of Cameiros, and dating from the 7th and 6th centuries, or even later in some cases. It happens, however, that these slight differences of shape and fabric bring our Enkomi glass vases into direct comparison with certain specimens found by Prof. Flinders Petrie at Gurob'.[12] Murray suggests that in both places the pomegranate flasks may be of Phoenician manufacture. But when were they made? 'For the present we must either accept Prof. Petrie's date (about 1400BC), based on scanty observations collected from the poor remains of a foreign settlement in Egypt, or fall back on the ordinary method of comparing the glass vessels of Gurob with those from Greek tombs of the seventh century BC or later...' Again we can see why the material was confusing, but Murray becomes tendentious in his desire to present consistently the case for the down-dating of the Mycenaean material.

Indeed throughout the publication we sense that, having aligned himself firmly on one side of the 'Mycenaean Question', Murray allowed himself to treat all the evidence from a partisan point of view. This is perhaps not a matter for criticism: an adversarial approach to academic argument can be fruitful, and while the modern age has more self-consciously espoused the ideal of impartial assessment of evidence the ideal is not always realisable. Concealed bias is arguably more dangerous than a clearly stated partisan position. We can see now that Murray was on the 'losing' side, but those earlier commentators such as Newton, Tsountas and Mannatt, whose instincts seem to us to have been more sure-footed, were perhaps also lucky. Much early argumentation about chronology can now be shown to have been right for the wrong reasons. Rather as when reading horoscopes, we tend to notice – indeed to hail as prescient – the things that turn out right and ignore the ideas that fell by the wayside. Murray was wrong, but perhaps sometimes he was wrong for the right reasons – like his contemporaries he was trying hard to grope towards the truth on shifting and uncertain ground.

Perhaps the only fair question we can ask is whether there was anything in the finds from the Cyprus excavations that should, even at the time, have made it clear to Murray that his dating was wrong, and here we do come to territory where it is hard to avoid retrospective criticism. Harsh things have rightly been said about the conduct of the British Museum excavations in Cyprus in the last decade of the nineteenth century.[13] Firstly, the motivation would seem, by modern standards, suspect, with the desire for exhibitable and preferably precious objects over-riding any concern for historical understanding. Secondly, the execution suffered from many of the problems of 'absentee supervisors' to which Cypriot archaeology had traditionally been prone. Thirdly, the recording was truly dreadful. This last point is more than apparent from Murray, Smith and Walters' publication, and the surviving excavation notebooks, kept in the British Museum, offer frustratingly little additional information, in spite of the best efforts of generations of twentieth-century scholars who have mined them assiduously.

One might add to this list a very specific weakness relating to the excavation of tombs containing both Cypriot and Mycenaean material, namely the prejudice exhibited by the excavators in favour of the Mycenaean antiquities. It seems there was a consistent tendency to save preferentially the Mycenaean vases and to discard the often plainer local wares, which considerably distorted the picture offered by the tombs. Murray made no real distinction between 'a cemetery of Mycenaean date' and 'a Mycenaean cemetery': he was disposed to view Cyprus as the easternmost extension of the Mycenaean world. He recognised the possibility of local wares, but it would be left to later generations of scholars to pursue the accurate classification of the pottery. Had he taken a less 'Mycenaean' view he might perhaps have recognised the existence of other elements strongly represented in the tombs.

Indeed it was partly the rich mix of influences in the culture of Late Bronze Age Cyprus which was causing the confusion. We now classify the contents of the Enkomi tombs as Cypriot, though recognising both Mycenaean and oriental imports and influences in assemblages of the period from this and other sites. Murray was attempting to interpret some of the finest products of this mixed culture – the ivories from Enkomi are a prime example – in Mycenaean terms. He recognised that they were strongly influenced from the east, but since for him they were Greek he related them to later material belonging to what is now recognised as the 'Orientalising' period in Greek art of the seventh century BC. Helbig, too, was responding to the eastern elements in Cypriot Late Bronze Age art when he elaborated his theory, which, by associating Mycenaean and Phoenician art, was almost the equivalent of stretching the Greek Orientalising period backwards over several centuries.

Murray, then, is perhaps rightly censured as a bad excavator, though he may deserve some sympathy as an unlucky interpreter. Whether a more careful archaeological approach would have helped him to a better chronological understanding must remain debatable. Nonetheless, *Excavations in Cyprus*, published in 1900, looks backwards into the nineteenth century rather than forward into the twentieth, both from the point of view of basic excavation and recording techniques and from the point of view of interpretation – and in fact the nineteenth century had produced better examples of both.

We might, though, conclude with the reflection that, if a truly soundly-based understanding of Greek Bronze Age chronology was a twentieth-century phenomenon, *Excavations in Cyprus* did carry within it some seeds of enlightenment. Arthur Evans' excavations at Knossos, which began in 1900, can be described as one of the pillars supporting this understanding, since once the wealth of material from Minoan Crete was added to the picture the arguments for a high dating for the Greek Bronze Age were massively supported. Already 'Minoika' had begun to emerge in Cyprus, and though, since they predated the discovery and naming of the Minoan culture, they could hardly be expected to be described as such, nonetheless in two instances their Cretan nature was recognised. The first was the octopus stirrup jar, described thus in *Excavations*: 'The large pseudamphora from tomb 50 (fig 128) is made of a peculiar coarse-grained clay, and was probably imported from Crete, where a similar specimen has been found'.[14] The second was 'several small terracotta balls...on which a series of Cypriote letters had been incised previously to the firing. ... On one of these specimens the inscription seems rather to belong to the kind of writing which Mr. Arthur Evans calls pictographs, associating this manner of writing with a very remote period of history'.[15]

Evans' pursuit of early writing in Crete led to his discovery of a whole Bronze Age culture there. As the twentieth century progressed the chronological position of all the Aegean Bronze Age cultures would be more firmly established, and a sophisticated understanding of the complex relations between Crete and Cyprus would be elaborated by both Evans' and Murray's successors in the field. Scholars such as Olivier Masson have consistently reminded us of the debt we owe to predecessors who were often also pioneers. We are perhaps more generous in our retrospective assessment of their contributions when we think how many challenges remain for the twenty-first century.

Notes

1. Tsountas and Mannatt, *The Mycenaean Age: a study of the monuments and culture of pre-Homeric Greece* (London 1896).
2. C.T. Newton, 'Dr Schliemann's Discoveries at Mycenae', *Edinburgh Review* (1878), reprinted in C.T. Newton, *Essays on Art and Archaeology* (London 1880) 246–302.
3. J.L. Fitton, 'Charles Newton and the Discovery of the Greek Bronze Age', in C. Morris (ed.) *Klados: Essays in honour of J.N. Coldstream* (London 1995) 73–8 discusses Newton's reasoning in detail.
4. Newton (n.2) 292.
5. A.S. Murray, A.H. Smith and H.B. Walters, *Excavations in Cyprus* (London 1900) (hereafter *Excavations*).
6. W. Helbig, 'La question Mycenienne', *Memoires de l'Academie des Inscriptions* xxxv pt. 2 (1896).
7. *Excavations*, 23.
8. A.J. Evans, 'A Mykenaean Treasure from Aegina', *JHS* 13 (1892–3) 195–226.
9. *Excavations*, 21.
10. W.F. Petrie, 'The Egyptian Bases of Greek History', *JHS* 11 (1890) 271–7 includes a dating for Mycenaean stirrup-jars between about 1400–1050BC (though Petrie adds 'I will not attempt to limit what their range may be in Cyprus or elsewhere...') This article contains a preliminary discussion of the foreign pottery from Petrie's sites more fully published in W.F. Petrie *Ilahun, Kahun and Gurob* (London 1891).
11. D.B. Harden, *Catalogue of the Greek and Roman Glass in the British Museum* Vol. 1 (London 1981) 34, no. 8.
12. *Excavations*, 23–4.
13. E. Goring, *A Mischievous Pastime: Digging in Cyprus in the Nineteenth Century* (Edinburgh 1988) 29–30 details some of the shortcomings of the Turner Bequest Excavations. Goring convincingly suggests that J.L. Myres deserves credit as the first truly modern, scientific archaeologist to have worked on Cyprus, and it is interesting to sense his underlying reservations about some of the results of the British Museum excavations in his landmark *Catalogue of the Cyprus Museum* (Oxford 1899). Here the Mycenaean period is dated between 1700 and 900 BC, and he says 'The preliminary reports of the British Museum excavations at Kurion, 1895, which assign Mycenaean graves to the seventh century, cannot be allowed to modify this view until they are supported by a full statement of the evidence.'
14. *Excavations*, 73–4 and footnote citing Furtwangler and Loeschcke's publication of Athens Museum no. 58, a similar vase known to be from Crete.
15. *Excavations*, 27.

13. Sculptures de la collection Cesnola: le cas du 'prêtre' à la tête de taureau

Antoine Hermary

Dans l'immense collection d'antiquités constituée par Luigi Palma di Cesnola à Chypre entre 1866 et 1875, les sculptures en calcaire tiennent une place majeure par leur nombre et leur qualité: bien qu'une partie d'entre elles ait été dispersée, les œuvres entrées au Metropolitan Museum of Art de New York forment, aujourd'hui encore, l'ensemble le plus important pour notre connaissance de la statuaire chypriote antique.

À l'occasion de la nouvelle présentation des collections chypriotes du MMA, prévue pour le printemps de l'an 2000, Vassos Karageorghis et les conservateurs du musée ont entrepris la publication d'un nouveau catalogue destiné à remplacer celui de John Myres, qui date de 1914 et dont les illustrations sont très insuffisantes. Ils ont bien voulu me demander de collaborer à cette recherche pour ce qui concerne la sculpture en pierre, et c'est à la suite d'un séjour d'étude effectué à New York en août 1997 que je présente les remarques qui suivent: elles ne reprendront cependant pas l'ensemble du sujet traité dans mon exposé de Londres, car les nouvelles propositions de restitution du sarcophage d'Amathonte (personnage au parasol) et du grand Héraclès de Golgoi demandent encore quelques vérifications.

Très vite après l'arrivée des sculptures à New York et leur première présentation dans le musée, la question de la provenance précise des objets et celle des restaurations effectuées est posée en termes particulièrement violents: dès 1880, en effet, l'antiquaire Gaston Feuardent attaque Cesnola sur ces sujets et deux ans plus tard, dans un ouvrage intitulé *Transformations and Migrations of Certain Statues in the Cesnola Collection*, publié par le même Feuardent, Clarence Cook dénonce 'the frauds which have been committed in the important matter of the ascription of certain object in the Cesnola collection to certain localities', ainsi que 'the impudent restorations that have been made in one out of the many statues in the Museum' (p. 12). L'œuvre dont il est essentiellement question dans ce pamphlet est précisément celle qui sera évoquée ici. John Myres, dans l'introduction de son *Handbook of the Cesnola Collection* (XIX–XXI), rappelle cette controverse qu'il considère alors comme entièrement close, tout en soulignant que le nettoyage des objets effectué en 1909 par Charles Balliard était nécessaire. Il se contente de noter, un peu plus loin, 'certainly a few mistakes were made, as was only to be expected in a very large collection of unfamiliar types and styles, but none of them affect any important specimen' (XXIII–XXIV); pourtant, sa méfiance à l'égard de Cesnola apparaît clairement quand il renonce presque systématiquement à indiquer les provenances données dans *Cyprus*, puis dans l'*Atlas*.

Une nouvelle étude de la collection des sculptures montre que les restaurateurs dont Cesnola disposait à Chypre ont incontestablement effectué quelques faux raccords entre tête et corps, et que la volonté de présenter des documents aussi complets que possible a conduit à altérer le sens primitif de certaines œuvres majeures, comme le sarcophage d'Amathonte et l'Héraclès de Golgoi. Un examen attentif de la collection permet de corriger peu à peu ces interventions abusives et, dans le cas de la statue du 'prêtre' à la tête de taureau, il apporte la preuve que l'on peut encore faire des découvertes sur cette collection plus que centenaire.

Grâce aux recherches d'archives effectuées par Olivier Masson,[1] on sait que la statue enregistrée au Metropolitan Museum of Art sous le numéro d'inventaire 74.51.2463 a été découverte sur le site de Golgoi à la fin de 1868 et qu'elle a été immédiatement rapprochée d'une tête qui ne lui appartenait pas (le no.1291 du catalogue de Myres). Cesnola écrivait en effet à Wilhelm Froehner, le 24 décembre 1868: 'J'ai dernièrement trouvé une statue

Fig. 13.1: Reconstitution fautive de la statue de New York, d'après Clarence Cook.

Fig. 13.2: Statue de la collection Cesnola, Metropolitan Museum of Art, Purchased by Subscription 1874–1875, inv. 74.51.2463. Photo MMA.

colossale en pierre (tête et pieds cassés) qui tient dans une main une tête de bœuf parfaitement conservée. Barbe frisée, lèvres peintes en rouge, de même les narines et les pupilles. Triple couronne (un bras manque). Trouvée à *Golgos*, où M. de Vogüé a fouillé'. Il s'agit donc certainement d'une découverte fortuite effectuée dans le sanctuaire rural de Golgoi-*Ayios Photios*, partiellement fouillé en 1862 par la mission française et où, en 1870, Cesnola mettra au jour l'essentiel de sa collection de sculptures. Dans l'article qu'il publie dans le *Harper's Magazine for July 1872*, l'ami de Cesnola Hiram Hitchcock reprend l'attribution à la statue de la tête couronnée en donnant comme provenance Salamine, contrairement à l'indication précise de Cesnola en 1868. Quand Johannes Doell examine cette œuvre à l'été 1870 pour le compte du musée de l'Ermitage il n'est plus question de la tête, mais les pieds et la plinthe ont été restaurés[2] et il précise que la statue n'appartient pas au

grand ensemble de sculptures mis au jour en 1870 à Golgoi-*Ayios Photios*, sans toutefois indiquer d'autre origine,[3] ni renvoyer à l'article publié par Hitchcock, qu'il mentionne pourtant ailleurs. Le raccord matériel entre la tête et le corps a-t-il réellement été effectué entre la fin de 1868 et l'été 1870, comme le suggère Cook dans son pamphlet (Fig. 13.1)? Il ne fut en tout cas plus question de ce rapprochement après l'article de Hitchcock, et la provenance salaminienne n'a jamais été évoquée par Cesnola lui-même: dans *Cyprus*, en 1877, le personnage est cité dans le chapitre consacré à Golgoi (p. 161 et pl. XIII) et dans le premier volume de l'*Atlas*, en 1885, la légende de l'illustration indique comme provenance 'Golgoi, temple' (no. 914). On peut se demander si le graffito publié ci-dessous, peut-être remarqué après la découverte de l'œuvre et oublié par la suite, n'aurait pas orienté vers cette fausse origine salaminienne.

Ces polémiques et ces contradictions expliquent sans doute l'étonnante absence de la statue dans le catalogue de Myres et, par suite, dans l'ensemble de la bibliographie entre 1885 et l'article du *BCH* dans lequel je la comparai à une statuette d'un personnage à masque de taureau trouvée à Amathonte.[4] Ignorant que cette œuvre était réellement conservée au Metropolitan Museum de New York, j'avais alors reproduit le dessin publié par Doell en 1873. Après avoir été informé de mon erreur par Joan Mertens, je pus examiner directement la statue en 1985, avant d'en donner une photographie dans une étude sur un autre masque de taureau en calcaire de la collection Cesnola.[5] Peu de temps après, elle était de nouveau reproduite par Joan Connelly dans son ouvrage sur la sculpture hellénistique de Chypre.[6] Il ressortait de ces différentes études que cette statue de grande taille (159 cm sans la tête) appartenait presque certainement à la série des personnages portant un masque rituel, même si celui-ci était figuré sous la forme d'une tête de taureau tenue à la main à hauteur de la poitrine. Le style de l'œuvre m'avait paru indiquer une date dans la deuxième moitié du quatrième siècle avant J.-C.

Cependant, je n'avais pas remarqué en 1985 la présence sur le vêtement de quelques graffiti antiques, repérés au moment des prises de vue de l'été 1997 grâce à un éclairage rasant (Fig. 13.2–13.6). De très nombreuses traces sont visibles mais, par prudence, je n'ai pas tenu compte dans le relevé graphique de celles qui n'apparaissent pas avec suffisamment de clarté sur les photographies; d'autres prises de vue, sous un éclairage différent, permettraient peut-être d'aboutir à des lectures complémentaires. On distingue donc principalement, devant le rameau tenu par la main droite, un début d'abécédaire (A, B, Γ, Δ ; hauteur des lettres 25 mm) (Fig. 13.3–13.4) et à hauteur de la cuisse gauche, en plus de quelques lettres isolées (*bèta, kappa, nu, psi*, peut-être un grand *iôta* avec *apex* inférieur), un mot dont il reste suffisamment de lettres (hauteur entre 12.5 et 20 mm) pour que l'on puisse restituer avec une quasi-certitude le nom ΠΝΥΤΑΓΟΡΑΣ, 'Pnytagoras' (Fig. 13.5–13.6). Comme l'a indiqué depuis longtemps Olivier Masson,[7] il s'agit d'un anthroponyme typiquement chypriote et principalement salaminien: en dehors d'une épitaphe syllabique de Marion pour une Pnytila fille de Pnytagoras,[8] il n'est en effet attesté que pour le Salaminien Minokrétès, fils de Pnytagoros, fils de Pnytotimos, sur un graffito syllabique d'Abydos en Égypte,[9] et surtout par deux personnages de la famille royale de Salamine, le fils d'Evagoras Ier et le Pnytagoras qui a régné de 351 à 332.[10] Il est, pour le reste, absent du corpus chypriote à partir de la fin du IVe siècle, si l'on en juge par le recueil d'Ino Nicolaou, *Prosopography of Ptolemaic Cyprus*, et par les autres publications.

On connaît cependant, en dehors de Chypre, quelques autres Pnytagoras: l'un a laissé son nom sur les murs d'une tombe thébaine,[11] un autre est attesté à Érétrie par l'intermédiaire de son fils défunt,[12] et c'est aussi sous la forme d'un patronyme que se présentent les trois exemples connus à Athènes ou en Attique, le père du médecin Aristocratès sur une stèle funéraire,[13] ceux du bouleute Philokratès[14] et d'une défunte anonyme.[15] Dans les textes littéraires, seule une épigramme funéraire de l'*Anthologie Palatine* VII, 374, 5 (Marcus Argentarius, début du premier siècle après J.-C.) mentionne un personnage de ce nom, en dehors bien sûr des témoignages relatifs aux princes salaminiens. Il faut noter que l'emploi du nom est chronologiquement bien défini, puisque l'épitaphe d'Aristocratès est datée de la première moitié du quatrième siècle (l'époque du fils d'Evagoras), tandis que le bouleute athénien apparaît sur une liste de 304/303 et que l'épitaphe d'Érétrie est située au début du troisième siècle, ce qui signifie que les deux pères nommés Pnytagoras sont contemporains du roi de Salamine. La résurgence du nom à l'époque impériale n'est que faiblement attestée par l'épitaphe fragmentaire d'Athènes, la date du graffito de Thèbes restant incertaine. Comment situer, par rapport à ces témoignages, le nom gravé sur la statue de New York ?

Il est évidemment difficile de dater ces graffiti à partir de la forme des lettres, mais le rapprochement avec d'autres ensembles oriente vers l'époque hellénistique plutôt qu'impériale: on pense en premier lieu aux graffiti vasculaires alphabétiques de la grotte de Kaphizin, près de Nicosie, dont les nombreux exemplaires datés se situent entre 225 et 218,[16] mais aussi à ceux de différents sites égyptiens que l'on attribue à l'époque hellénistique.[17] Une date à l'époque hellénistique s'accorderait d'ailleurs avec l'apparente désaffection du sanctuaire de Golgoi-*Ayios Photios* à l'époque impériale. Il convient cependant de rester prudent sur ce point.

La présence de ces modestes textes sur la statue de New York est d'autant plus étonnante que les graffiti sur pierre sont très rares dans le monde chypriote du Ier millénaire, et que les quelques exemples apparemment comparables s'apparentent plutôt à des marques intentionnelles qu'à un libre exercice d'écriture ou de dessin: ainsi, le court texte syllabique 'J'appartiens à la déesse de Paphos' inscrit sur

Fig. 13.3–13.4: Graffiti sur la même statue. Photo MMA et dessin d'après photo.

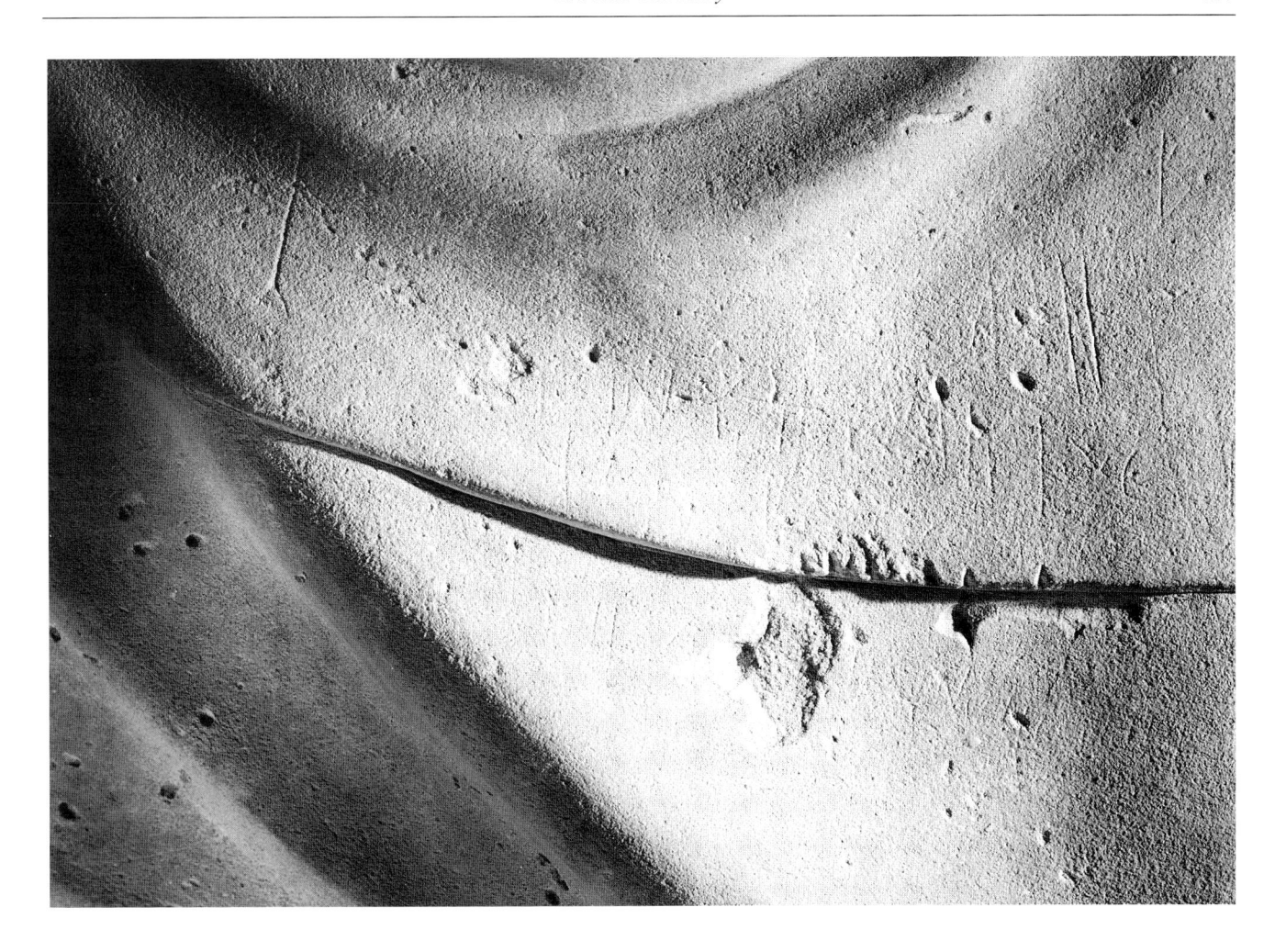

Fig. 13.5–13.6: Autres graffiti sur la statue. Photo MMA et dessin d'après photo.

l'épaule gauche du célèbre 'prêtre à la colombe'[18] et le nom 'Timagoras' gravé, toujours en syllabaire, sur une autre statue de la collection Cesnola[19] paraissent être contemporains de l'érection des statues et correspondre aux nombreuses inscriptions grecques archaïques gravées directement sur les statues. Au contraire, les motifs végétaux récemment repérés par E. Fontan sur un des chapiteaux 'proto-éoliques' du Louvre[20] sont du même ordre que les graffiti de la statue de New York, mais leur date est impossible à déterminer. Cette rareté s'explique sans doute par la disparition à peu près totale, à Chypre, des supports traditionnels des graffiti que sont les murs, les éléments de mobilier (bancs) ou de décor (hermès) des monuments religieux et publics: c'est sur ces surfaces que sont en effet gravés la plupart des graffiti que l'on connaît dans l'Egypte gréco-romaine et à Délos.[21] Un passage des *Ethiopiques* d'Héliodore (V, 5, 1) montre d'autre part que la statuaire faisait partie des supports convenables aux graffiti, puisque Théagène et Chariclée décident, s'ils sont séparés et veulent se retrouver, d'inscrire un message sur les murs des temples, les statues divines les plus en vue, les hermès ou les bornes des carrefours. Qu'une sculpture dressée dans un sanctuaire comme celui de Golgoi porte des graffiti n'a donc, en soi, rien d'étonnant, surtout dans le contexte de la civilisation ptolémaïque. J'ajouterai seulement que la position basse des lettres sur la statue pourrait indiquer que celle-ci était placée sur une base relativement haute, si l'on suppose que l'auteur d'un graffito choisit de préférence, quand la surface est libre, l'endroit où il peut écrire le plus commodément en position debout.

Il reste à évoquer la question de l'interprétation de ces graffiti de Golgoi. Le fait que des lettres et un nom sans rapport entre eux aient été gravés sur une même statue paraît tout à fait normal, suivant la règle qu'un graffito en appelle d'autres. Les lettres isolées peuvent être considérées comme de simples exercices de tracé, et le début d'abécédaire correspond à une pratique courante,[22] qui s'explique d'autant mieux qu'à Chypre l'écriture alphabétique ne s'impose que progressivement au cours de l'époque hellénistique. Reste le nom de Pnytagoras. Comme pour des centaines d'exemples en Egypte, à Délos et ailleurs, il paraît naturel d'y voir celui du personnage qui a rédigé le graffito ou, à la rigueur, celui d'un de ses camarades : ainsi, il est clair que c'est son propre nom qu'a laissé sur le mur d'une tombe de Thèbes le Pnytagoras dont il a été question plus haut.

Toutefois, je ne voudrais pas exclure une autre possibilité, qui est de reconnaître dans ce nom celui du personnage représenté sur la statue. À l'absence tout de même étonnante de cet anthroponyme dans l'onomastique hellénistique de Chypre s'ajoute en effet le sujet très particulier de l'œuvre, qui évoque très probablement des cérémonies masquées du rituel local, comme une tête du même sanctuaire de Golgoi, conservée au Louvre, qui montre de façon plus explicite le personnage relevant sur son crâne le masque de taureau.[23] La découverte à l'intérieur du palais d'Amathonte d'une représentation de ce type (avec le masque sur le visage) confirme le lien qui unissait les rois chypriotes au dieu taureau et à la Grande Déesse de l'île.[24] Il n'y aurait donc rien d'impossible à ce qu'un des membres de la famille royale salaminienne, le fils d'Evagoras Ier ou le roi Pnytagoras lui-même, ait été représenté sous cette forme rituelle dans le sanctuaire de Golgoi-*Ayios Photios*: la date attribuée à cette œuvre parlerait, dans ce cas, en faveur du roi.[25] Cette pratique paraît cependant tout à fait exceptionnelle: je ne peux citer, comme comparaison, qu'une base de Lindos sur laquelle le nom du personnage honoré est répété sous forme de graffito au-dessous de l'inscription officielle.[26] On pourrait aussi supposer, comme variante de cette hypothèse, qu'un personnage portant le même nom que le roi de Salamine a choisi précisément une image de cet homme célèbre pour graver son propre nom.

Quoi qu'il en soit, cette découverte apporte une information supplémentaire sur une sculpture dont l'histoire mouvementée avait intéressé mon ami Olivier Masson: je suis donc particulièrement heureux de dédier ces quelques pages à sa mémoire.

Notes

1. 'Correspondances chypriotes: lettres des frères Colonna-Ceccaldi et de L. Palma di Cesnola à W. Froehner', *Centre d'Etudes chypriotes. Cahier* 14 (1990) 37.
2. J. Doell, *Die Sammlung Cesnola* (Saint-Pétersbourg 1873) 30–31, no. 124, pl. 6:5.
3. 'Nur vereinzelte Sculpturen in Kalkstein, namentlich die unter No. 124 verzeichnete Statue... enstammen nicht dieser Fundstätte [Golgoi-Ayios Photios], sondern theils einigen nahebei gelegenen Gräbern, theils anderen Orten' (Doell (n.2) 7–8).
4. A. Hermary, 'Statuette d'un prêtre masqué', *BCH* 103 (1979) 735–7, fig. 10.
5. A. Hermary, 'Divinités chypriotes, II', *RDAC* (1986) 165, pl. 34:3.
6. B. Connelly, *Votive Sculpture of Hellenistic Cyprus* (Nicosie 1988) 80, pl. 3:115. See now V. Karageorghis, *Ancient Art from Cyprus. The Cesnola Collection in the Metropolitan Museum of Art* (New York 2000) no. 403.
7. 'Notes d'anthroponymie grecque et asianique. I. Les noms grecs en Pnut(o)-, notamment à Chypre', *Beiträge zur Namenforschung* 7 (1956) 1–4 (= *Onomastica Graeca Selecta* I, 238–241); 'Notes d'onomastique chypriote, v-viii', *RDAC* (1974) 157.
8. O. Masson, *Les inscriptions chypriotes syllabiques* (2nd. éd., Paris 1983) no.124.
9. Masson (n.8) no. 403.
10. Les témoignages littéraires et épigraphiques sur ces deux

personnages sont rassemblés par M.-J. Chavane et M. Yon dans *Salamine de Chypre* X (Paris 1978) nos. 242, 266, 279, 290, 294–6, 298–9; voir aussi, sur le roi Pnytagoras, K. Spyridakis, *Kyprioi basileis tou 4 ai. p.Ch.* (Nicosie 1963) 119–124. On ajoutera la liste des théarodoques des concours néméens (323/322) avec, au premier rang des Chypriotes, Nicocréon fils de Pnytagoras: S.G. Miller, 'The theorodokoi of the Nemean games', *Hesperia* 57 (1988) 147–163; *SEG* 36 (1986) 331. Il est probable, mais non certain, que le Pnytagoras père du triérarque Nithaphôn, envoyé en Inde par Alexandre (Arrien VIII, 18,8), est le roi salaminien lui-même.

11. J. Baillet, *Inscriptions grecques et latines des tombeaux des rois ou Syringes* (Le Caire 1926) 66 no. 276.
12. *IG* XII 9, 248B, l. 10.
13. D. Peppas-Delmusu, 'Ein attisches Grabgedicht für einen Artz aus Cypern', *AM* 78 (1963) 154–155, Beil. 74: 1.
14. B.D. Meritt & J.S. Traill, *The Athenian Agora* XV (Princeton 1974) no. 61 l. 317.
15. D.W. Braden, *The Athenian Agora* XVII (Princeton 1974) no. 959.
16. T.B. Mitford, *The Nymphaeum of Kafizin. The Inscribed Pottery* (*Kadmos* Suppl. II, 1980).
17. P. Perdrizet et G. Lefebvre, *Les graffitis grecs du Memnonion d'Abydos* (Nancy/Paris/Strasbourg 1919) passim; A. Bataille, *Les inscriptions grecques du temple de Hatshepsout à Deir El-Bahari* (Le Caire 1951) nos. 22, 43, 48; O. Masson et E. Bernand, 'Les inscriptions grecques d'Abou-Simbel', *REG* 70 (1957) 21–39, en particulier 35 no. 29, graffito d'un certain Boutrys originaire de Kourion.
18. Masson (n.8) no. 262 ('il s'agit d'un prêtre d'Aphrodite').
19. Masson (n.8) no. 263.
20. Il s'agit du chapiteau AM 2754: A. Hermary, *Musée du Louvre. Catalogue des antiquités de Chypre: les sculptures* (Paris 1989) no. 979; L. Bonato, 'Chypre dans les archives de Melchior de Vogüé: à l'origine de la mission de 1862', *Centre d'Etudes chypriotes. Cahier* 28 (1998) 109, pl. I: 3.
21. A. Bernand, 'Graffito II (griechisch)', in *Reallexikon für Antike und Christentum* (Stuttgart 1985) 667–689, avec de nombreuses références, auxquelles on ajoutera M. Th. Couilloud, in J. Audiat, 'Les graffittes du gymnase', *Exploration archéologique de Délos XXVIII. Le gymnase* (Paris 1970) 101–137, et A. Jacquemin, 'Quelques offrandes du gymnase de Délos', *BCH* 105 (1981) 155–169.
22. Voir par exemple M. Lang, *The Athenian Agora* XXI (Princeton 1976) 6–7.
23. Hermary (n.20) no. 588.
24. Hermary (n.4) 734–741.
25. Je pense qu'une date dans la deuxième moitié du quatrième siècle peut être maintenue pour la statue de New York: voir, à propos d'œuvres comparables, Hermary (n. 20) no. 557, et R. Senff, *Das Apollonheiligtum von Idalion* (Jonsered 1993) 40.
26. Ch. Blinkenberg, *Lindos* II (Berlin 1941) 213–4, no.17.

14. The British Museum and the invention of the Cypriot Late Bronze Age

Louise Steel

Investigation into the antiquity of Man developed into the discipline of prehistoric archaeology during the nineteenth century. At its inception archaeology was little more than a glorified treasure hunt, the object of which furnishes many of the large western museums today: the Louvre, the Metropolitan Museum in New York, Berlin, and the British Museum. However, as the nineteenth century progressed this treasure hunt gradually coalesced into a scientific discipline. Darwinism began to affect perceptions of the past and evolutionary principles were applied to the ever-increasing body of material remains from ancient civilisations (Trigger 1989, 114–18).

The classical and biblical heritage of scholars in the nineteenth century informed their interpretation of past civilisations. Montelius's diffusionist cultural typology (1899, 1903) ultimately derived European civilisation from Egypt and the east and so 'appealed to many Christians as a reaffirmation of the biblical view of world history' (Trigger 1989, 161). At the end of the nineteenth century there was an awakening in interest in the pre-Classical remains of Greece, initiated by Schliemann's excavations at the legendary citadel of Troy. Between 1870 and 1873 the German entrepreneur uncovered the remains of a prosperous prehistoric civilisation at the site, which he equated with Priam's city of legend (Schliemann 1880). Subsequently Schliemann turned his attention to Mycenae, Pausanius in hand, and discovered the remains of a magnificent pre-classical, Bronze Age civilisation, giving rise to the discipline of Mycenaean archaeology.

Archaeological investigation began on the island of Cyprus in the nineteenth century, during the final years of Ottoman rule on the island. The emphasis of early archaeological activity on the island, particularly the work of Cesnola (1877), Lang (1878) and Ohnefalsch-Richter (1893), was on its Iron Age heritage, especially the tombs and sanctuaries, and on the island's oriental, mainly Phoenician, connections. This is demonstrated by the precedence of the island's biblical connections before her Homeric past in the title of Ohnefalsch-Richter's 1893 publication *Kypros, the Bible and Homer* (Given 1998, 11). In 1878 Cyprus passed from Ottoman rule into the British Empire and archaeological exploration was placed under control of the British governing authorities (Given 1998, 11). Initially British archaeological discourse remained firmly entrenched within an Orientalist framework, 'reflected in the minarets, palm-trees and camels beloved by travel writers and the artists from the illustrated papers' (Given 1998, 11), but by the turn of the century there was an awakening in interest in the island's Hellenic heritage. While the political background for this shift in interest has been discussed recently (Given 1998), its archaeological dimension remains to be addressed. The turning point in Cypriot archaeology with increasing promotion of the island's classical credentials is marked by the excavations of British Museum in the last decade of the nineteenth century. The British Museum was primarily interested in uncovering material of Mycenaean date and it is no accident today that its Cypriot collection is mainly housed in the Department of Greek and Roman Antiquities, rather than the Western Asiatic Department. These excavations were influenced by the discoveries of Schliemann in Turkey and on the Greek mainland, and the resulting increase in knowledge of the Bronze Age civilisation of the Aegean.

In 1892 the British Museum received a bequest from Miss Emma Turner which it used to finance a series of excavations on the island of Cyprus between 1894 and 1896. These excavations were directed by Arthur Smith, an assistant in the British Museum, John Myres of New College Oxford, and Alexander Murray and Henry Walters, also of the British Museum. Three sites were excavated with the money from the Turner Bequest: Amathus in 1894, Kourion in 1895, and Enkomi in 1896. Walters continued his research on the antiquities of Cyprus excavating the site of Maroni-*Tsaroukkas* in 1897 (Johnson 1980; Steel 1994; Manning and Monks 1998). Also excavated by the British Museum are tombs at the site of Hala Sultan Tekke-*Vyzakia* (Bailey 1972; Manning and Monks 1998, 306). The British Museum excavations concentrated on a series of tomb groups, some of which are published in *Excavations in Cyprus* (1900). The Museum was able to retain the bulk of the finds, which form the core of the magnificent Leventis Gallery. The remainder of the material (one third) – or at least one third of that which was considered of interest and worthy of being kept – was handed over to the Government of Cyprus and is today housed in the Cyprus Museum.

The site of Kourion was chosen partly because of its classical credentials – Kourion occurs occasionally in ancient texts (Herodotus V.113; Strabo XIV.683) and was known to be one of the ten ancient kingdoms of Cyprus – and partly because of the immense riches that had already been found at the site by early explorers such as Cesnola (1877). The British Museum excavated five separate cemeteries at Kourion and their location is roughly indicated on a plan in the final publication (Walters 1900, 56). Of these cemeteries only Site D, some 400m north-east of the village of Episkopi, yielded material of Late Cypriot date and consequently was of most interest to the excavators (Walters 1900, 86). It is also the first site known to have produced Mycenaean pottery in this part of the island (Walters 1900, 61).

The pottery recovered from the tombs was the main focus of interest for the excavators. By the time that the Kourion tombs were published Myres had classified the main Late Bronze Age Cypriot wares in a scheme which remains in use to this day (Myres and Ohnefalsch-Richter 1899). The more familiar (to the excavators) Mycenaean wares were 'invariably associated with two [local] varieties known as the "white slip" -ware and the "base ring" -ware', which Walters notes were commonly found in all [Late] Bronze Age cemeteries (1900, 73). It is noteworthy that Walters correctly identifies a large octopus stirrup jar 'made of peculiar coarse-grained clay' as Cretan (Walters 1900, 74, fig. 128), despite very limited knowledge of Minoan archaeology at the time he was writing. Walters also remarks on the occasional occurrence of a ware that appears to be a local imitation of Mycenaean pottery, which he terms 'sub-mycenaean'. Today such imprecise terminology is the cause of a certain amount of confusion. 'Sub-mycenaean' refers to a specific cultural phase on the Greek mainland at the very end of the LBA and characterised by a particular class of ceramics (Desborough 1972, Mountjoy and Hankey 1988). The term is out of place in a Cypriot context and the so-called 'sub-mycenaean' ware from Kourion should in fact be identified as the White Painted I pottery of Cypro-Geometric date. It is noteworthy, however, that Walter's correctly placed the 'sub-mycenaean' in a crude relative sequence as intermediate between the imported Mycenaean pottery of the Late Bronze Age and 'that of the later or "Graeco-Phoenician" times' (Walters 1900, 74). The actual date of 1050 BC for the transition from Bronze to Iron Age was established as early as 1910 (Myres 1910), and remains the commonly accepted date.

Walters' interpretation of the results of excavations at Kourion marks the beginning of a strongly Hellenic trend in Cypriot archaeology and the development of a certain ambiguity between what is considered indigenous to the island during the Late Cypriot period and what is Mycenaean. Although Site D is identified as Mycenaean (Walters 1900, 72, 86), the Mycenaean pottery from the site is acknowledged to be imported (Walters 1900, 73, 74) and is distinguished from the 'considerable quantity of local ware' (1900, 73) also found in the tombs. At the same time, the discovery of large quantities of Mycenaean vases in the tombs, and the identification of Site D as Mycenaean, is considered sufficient evidence to 'support the statement of Strabo that Curium was an Argive colony' (Walters 1900, 86). This uneasy relationship between the indigenous Late Cypriot remains, intrusive Mycenaean artefacts and the histories of the later Greek and Roman authors was to continue. With Myres' publication of the *Handbook of the Cesnola Collection* in 1914, the equation of Mycenaean pottery with a Mycenaean colonisation of the island became central to twentieth century discourse on the Late Cypriot period, in an archaeological commentary on both the Greek foundation legends of the classical period and the island's linguistic inheritance.

The classical city of Salamis on the east coast of Cyprus was explored by the *Cyprus Exploration Fund* in 1890. According to tradition the city had been founded by Teucros on his return from the Trojan War, and the excavators had hoped to find remains of a Mycenaean city beneath the Greek and Roman remains. In 1896 the British Museum conducted a series of excavations to the south of ancient Salamis, at the site of Enkomi, hoping to confirm the existence of an earlier, pre-Classical city in the region.

The British Museum excavations at Enkomi, which were to have enormous implications for the development of the archaeology of Late Cypriot period, resulted in the discovery of a series of Late Bronze Age tomb groups, although the location of the associated city was not identified. Murray assumed that the cemetery was external to the ancient city, remarking that, although no ancient remains had been found on the nearby high ground, 'It is tempting as one stands on the edge of the long crag which . . . forms one of the boundaries of the burying-ground, to think that the ancient city had in part directly overlooked this wide extent of tombs' (Murray 1900, 3). The tombs were apparently unmarked but, influenced by the *Iliad*, Murray suggested that in antiquity 'the burying-ground of Enkomi had once been covered with low mounds and stelae' (Murray 1900, 4), the due reward of the heroic dead according to Homeric tradition (*Iliad* xvi.675). In fact the perceptions and prejudices of classically-trained archaeologists, who believed that a town's necropolis should be located outside its wall, alongside limited familiarity of the Late Cypriot utilitarian wares – the result of an antiquarian-based interest in the more appealing Late Cypriot fine wares and Mycenaean imports – long impeded the identification of the city of Enkomi. Even Gjerstad, the father of Cypriot archaeology, who excavated a number of tombs at Enkomi in the 1920's, believed that the settlement remains overlying these burials dated to the Byzantine period (Gjerstad 1934). Indeed, the Late Cypriot settlement of Enkomi was only correctly identified in the late 1940's by Schaeffer (1952), simply because the French excavator's experience of intramural burials at the important Late Bronze Age site of Ras Shamra-Ugarit prepared him for a similar situation in Cyprus.[1]

In addition to the Late Cypriot tombs, the British Museum also explored one of a pair of tumuli which dominated the plain of Salamis (Murray 1900, map facing p.1). These tumuli covered large built tombs 'the construction of which leaves no doubt that they belong to the Mycenaean age' (Murray 1900, 1, fig. 1). Ironically, at the time of the British Museum's activities at the site of Enkomi, the local villagers used the tombs as shelters for pigs! The only finds recovered from the tomb, in the *dromos*, were two joining fragments of a pithos with an ink inscription in the Cypro-Syllabic script. Rather than belonging to the Late Cypriot or so-called 'Mycenaean' period, the tumuli should in fact be dated to the Iron Age.

The Enkomi tombs were attributed to the 'Mycenaean age' (Murray 1900, 6), and much of the ensuing discussion of their contents concentrated on the relative chronology of the 'Mycenaean' as opposed to the 'Phoenician' period (e.g. Murray 1900, 27–9). The historical context of the tombs was not broached in the general discussion, although there are fleeting references to subjects which later become embedded in the Late Cypriot discourse. Most notable is the comparison of the feathered head-dress worn by one of the hunters on the famous ivory gaming box to that worn by the enemies of Egypt as depicted on the Ramesside funerary temple of Medinet Habu (Murray 1900, 13, fig. 19). In general, however, Murray's object-oriented publication focused on artistic comparanda from Greece, Egypt and the Near East, with reference to biblical[2] and classical[3] sources.

The tombs excavated by the British Museum remain unique for their immense wealth – in bronze, ivory, gold and silver, glyptic and above all Mycenaean pictorial pottery – despite subsequent excavations of numerous other Late Cypriot tombs both at Enkomi and elsewhere on the island. As a result the site has become central to any discussion of the political and economic organisation of Cyprus during the Late Bronze Age, eclipsing all other Late Cypriot sites. Politically Enkomi has been elevated to the centre of the powerful kingdom of Alashiya known from ancient texts (Dussaud 1952; Knapp 1996; but see Merrillees 1987).

The locality of *Tsaroukkas*, south-east of the modern village of Maroni, was the main focus of excavations in 1897, directed by Walters (Johnson 1980; Cadogan 1992a; Steel 1994). He also made trials at Mari, Kalavasos and Maroni-*Vournes* (Cadogan 1984), but at these locations was less successful in identifying LBA remains of any significance – again reflecting the limited knowledge of the early Cypriot archaeologists of the actual everyday Late Cypriot domestic repertoire. Ironically, Kalavasos-*Ayios Dhimitrios* and Maroni-*Vournes* have been the scene of some of the more spectacular Late Cypriot discoveries of recent years (Cadogan 1984, 1989, 1992; South and Todd 1997 and references), including large ashlar structures with an apparent elite administrative function.

Already by the end of the nineteenth century there was a long history of excavation in the lower Maroni valley (Steel 1994) and the locality of *Tsaroukkas*, near the village of Maroni, was known to be a site with Mycenaean credentials. Cesnola, who identified the site with the ancient city kingdom of Marion, opened numerous tombs in the vicinity. However, it is difficult to reconstruct Cesnola's activities in the area, or indeed the exact focus of his 'excavation'. Even so, he certainly appears to have opened some Late Cypriot tombs and the famous Mycenaean chariot krater, which he ascribes to his excavations at Amathus, appears more plausibly to have come from Maroni (Cesnola 1877, 453; Steel 1994, 89, n.11). Ohnefalsch-Richter also worked in the Maroni valley, concentrating activities on the Early Bronze Age site of Psematismenos. The first archaeologist to report on the rich cemetery of '*Tzarukas*', where Mycenaean sherds were found in copious quantities, was Dümmler (1886, 209) and Ohnefalsch-Richter apparently bought a stone cylinder seal and a Babylonian electron ring from the site (Ohnefalsch-Richter 1893, pls. cli:31 and 35). Myres also visited *Tsaroukkas* in 1894, where he purchased a number of objects of Late Bronze Age date for the Ashmolean Museum, Oxford (Myres 1897, 171). In 1888 Hogarth visited the site of Maroni-*Vournes*, where he describes '. . . a place in the grove where big τετραγωνες πετρες were always to be found when any native of Maroni wished to build himself a house' (Hogarth 1888, 108). These large dressed stones were still visible on the surface of the site at *Vournes* in the 1970's (Johnson 1980, pls. I:IX, V:X, XI).

Between 1897 and 1898 Henry Walters conducted a series of excavations, under the auspices of the British Museum, at the locality of Maroni-*Tsaroukkas*. It was clearly expected that the site would prove to be as rich as that at Enkomi and in many ways the excavations resembled little more than a treasure hunt. Of the tombs opened only twenty-six were listed and others, containing only local Late Cypriot wares or fragmentary remains, were unrecorded (Manning and Monks 1998, 304). The disappointment of the excavators with the limited finds from Maroni might explain its absence from the 1900 publication, *Excavations in Cyprus*.

A study of the finds from Maroni was made by Jane Johnson (1980) and more recently a team from the University of Reading has re-examined the site with the specific aim of identifying the funerary remains excavated by the British Museum (Manning *et al.* 1994; Manning and De Mita 1997; Manning and Monks 1998, 307–08, 347–51). Excavations have uncovered a number of looted tombs, many of which appear to contain debris of the British Museum's activities at the site. The finds recovered from the tombs, including many fragments of Mycenaean pictorial kraters (Manning *et al.* 1994, pl. XII; Manning and Monks 1998, pls. 64d, 65c), mirror the discoveries of the British Museum's excavations. However, it has not been possible to relate the modern excavation results more precisely to those of the British Museum. In particular the Reading team has had little success in relating the remains on the ground to a sketch plan of the site made by Walters (Johnson 1980, pl. III.IV; Manning and Monks 1998, pl. 58a).

The British Museum excavations in Cyprus are very problematic, particularly in terms of modern demands on excavation material, which require more rigorous standards of retrieval, recording and scientific methods of conservation and analysis. Accordingly, there are many lacunae in the data which impede detailed analyses of funerary ritual and social organisation during the Late Cypriote period. While the finds from the tombs are discussed in terms of their artistic affinities, they are not contextualised beyond rudimentary and frequently incomplete tomb lists (Murray 1900, 51–4; Walters 1900, 79–81). The tomb architecture, number of inhumations,[4] disposition of finds within individual tomb groups, associations between particular groups of finds and possibly individual burials and the state of preservation of the funerary material as a whole, were not considered to be of great importance and are only intermittently recorded (Murray 1900, 4–6; Walters 1900, 58–9). The excavators did not explore the context in which the tombs were found, assuming instead that they were elements of an extramural necropolis. The everyday domestic architecture of the ancient Cypriots buried in the tombs did not concern these early archaeologists, who all too often simply resorted to pitting the ancient landscape in search of finds to place in the vaults of the British Museum (Cadogan 1984: Manning and Monks 1998, 306).

Instead, the excavations betray a museum-oriented, nineteenth-century antiquarian's interest in objects. Many of the artifacts recovered from the tombs were not kept, in particular those that were less glamorous, or deemed unsuitable for museum display (Manning and Monks 1998, 304). Consequently, very little interest was shown in the less appealing coarse-wares and fragmentary sherds, which were no doubt discovered in large quantities in the tombs, creating a bias in our understanding of the composition of Late Cypriot burial groups which continues to this day. Thus the interest which has developed in recent years in the utilitarian wares – plain ware, pithos, cooking ware, and monochrome – (Keswani 1991; Pilides 1991, 1996; Russell 1991) cannot always be met by the material from these early excavations. Indeed, other than the Mycenaean pottery, in particular from Kourion, there was greater emphasis on non-ceramic, exotic funerary furniture (Manning and Monks 1998, 349).

Nevertheless, such criticisms take the British Museum excavations out of context. In the late nineteenth century the 'science' of archaeology was still in its infancy. While systematic typologies were being created for the material remains of ancient cultures, their retrieval continued to be somewhat haphazard. The recording and publication of the excavations represent one of the earliest attempts to systematically present archaeological data in a clear and coherent format. The material is attributed to type, and according to tomb group, laying the foundations for the publication of Cypriot tomb groups which continues to the present day. The actual format, still used in the publication of most Cypriot funerary material, is ultimately based on a system devised by Gjerstad to cope with the enormous quantities of Bronze and Iron Age tomb material excavated by the Swedish Cyprus expedition between 1927 and 1931 (Gjerstad 1934, 1935, 1937). However, the basic treatment of material, breaking down a) by tomb group and b) by material – bronzes, ivory, glass, terracotta, pottery etc. – was established in the British Museum publication.

The British Museum excavations were fundamental to the development of the archaeology of the Late Cypriot period during the twentieth century. Not least, these excavations established irrevocably the link between the Mycenaean world and Late Bronze Age Cyprus, a relationship which has continued to dominate the archaeological discourse to this day. However, contacts between the Aegean and Cyprus during the Late Bronze Age are somewhat ambiguous, not least the extent to which the island was hellenized during this period. Much of the confusion results from the British Museum excavators, who too readily ascribed a Mycenaean identity to their Late

Bronze Age finds. Continuing in this vein, in the first real synthesis of Cypriot archaeology, Myres proposed a theory of Mycenaean colonisation of the island (Myres 1914, xxx). However, many of the elements which should accompany a Mycenaean settlement (Niemeier 1998, 26) are simply not present in Cyprus. Instead, this marriage of Mycenaean identity and Late Bronze Age Cyprus should be viewed as one aspect of the philhellenic approach to Cypriot archaeology in the early twentieth century (Given 1998, 11–12). On the other hand, the indigenous development of Late Cypriot culture was not addressed by the British Museum. The over-riding interest in the ceramics was in those of Mycenaean derivation, and the local utilitarian and fine wares received little attention, although by 1899 Myres had established the basic typology for the Late Cypriot fine wares (Myres and Ohnefalsch-Richter 1899).

Classical literature influenced interpretations of the Late Bronze Age tombs and their contents. At both Enkomi and, more categorically, at Kourion (Murray 1900, 1; Walters 1900, 86), the Mycenaean remains were explicitly related to the Greek foundation legends, which identified heroes returning from the Trojan War with the establishment of particular Cypriot city kingdoms. The relationship between the Greek foundation legends and Cypriot archaeology was further refined by Gjerstad (1944), who linked them with changes in the settlement pattern following the destruction of the major Cypriot settlements at the end of the Late Bronze Age. This view-point has become established within the Cypriot archaeological framework. Rather than a Mycenaean colonisation during the Late Bronze Age as proposed by Myres (1914, xxx), it is now more generally accepted that the island was hellenized in the twelfth or eleventh century BC (Fortin 1980; Karageorghis (ed.) 1994; Cadogan 1998, 7).

Perhaps most important of all, the results of the British Museum excavations are the basis for reconstructions of the Late Cypriot landscape, in particular identifying Enkomi as the major Late Bronze Age site on the island. Even in the light of new survey and excavation data, Enkomi remains pre-eminent amongst the Late Cypriot settlements. Together with the other sites explored by the British Museum – Kourion, Maroni and Hala Sultan Tekke – Enkomi continues to dominate Late Cypriot urban topography, although excavations at Kalavasos-*Ayios Dhimitrios* (South and Todd 1997), Kition (Karageorghis and Demas 1985), Alassa (Hadjisavvas 1989, 1994) and Palaepaphos (Maier 1997), and survey work – by the Cyprus Survey in the 1950's (Catling 1963), and more recently in the Vasilikos and Maroni valleys (Todd 1996, 1996a; Manning and de Mita 1997) and lower slopes of the Troodos (Webb and Frankel 1994; Knapp 1997) – are gradually elucidating Late Cypriot urban and rural settlement patterns (Catling 1963; Keswani 1993, 1996; Knapp 1997).

Prior to the British Museum excavations on Cyprus, there was only limited evidence for her prehistoric past. Early exploration had uncovered a wealth of material relating to the Cypriot Iron Age (Cesnola 1877; Ohnefalsch-Richter 1893), but the occupation of Cyprus contemporary with the early Hellenic civilisations being uncovered at Troy, Mycenae and Tiryns was little appreciated, until the excavations of the British Museum.

The major achievements of the work funded by the Turner Bequest and other British Museum activity on the island can be enumerated as follows:

1) They identified a previously little known pre-classical Cypriot culture, contemporary with that of Mycenaean Greece.
2) They laid the foundations for our understanding of Late Cypriot topography of the island, most notably with the discovery of Enkomi.
3) They clearly demonstrated the international connections of Cyprus during the Late Bronze Age.
4) The copious quantities of Mycenaean pottery found in these tombs allowed the excavators to place the tomb groups in their correct chronological contest. While dating techniques are constantly being refined, the correlation of the Late Cypriot sequence with that of Mycenaean Greece remains the basis of the Late Cypriot relative and absolute chronologies.
5) The wealth of the mortuary equipment, found in the tombs at Enkomi in particular, still comprises the cornerstone of our understanding of the prosperity and wide-ranging commercial contacts of Late Bronze Age Cyprus. Indeed, much of the information contained in these early reports concerning Late Cypriot foreign relations is only today being fully assimilated in the archaeological literature, most notably evidence for contacts between Cyprus and Sardinia during the twelfth century BC (Murray 1900, 17; Lo Schiavo *et al.* 1985; Lo Schiavo 1995).

In many ways, the scholars of the nineteenth century had certain advantages over their modern counterparts. While for modern archaeologists a knowledgeable synthesis of widely disparate areas of expertise is all too often impossible, the nineteenth-century scholars were familiar with the work of colleagues in Egypt, the Levant and the Aegean. Standing at the end of a long tradition of classical education, they could draw on a wealth of details from Greek and Roman literature and biblical sources to aid their interpretations of the objects they found. While the dangers of interpreting archaeology strictly in terms of ancient literature have been demonstrated elsewhere, it should not be denied that such texts can throw useful insights on past cultures. And yet, as modern education and research becomes increasingly specialised, with greater emphasis on the scientific core of the curriculum, this knowledge is becoming more esoteric and archaeology is increasingly dependant on scientific data management. Such approaches, however, cannot make any detailed use of the finds from early excavations, as the rigorous techniques which we now demand for systematic retrieval and recording were simply not in place. Yet to dismiss this body of data as irrelevant or simply a source of comparanda for finds from more recent excavations is to diminish our own understanding of the past.

Rather than trying to force the results of the British Museum excavations into a rigid archaeological framework, it is perhaps better to try to understand the aims and perspectives of the early excavators. Their results will never stand up to the quantitative analyses favoured by modern archaeology, and it may not always be possible to answer the same questions that we ask of material from modern, problem-oriented excavations. Instead, it would be more profitable to bear in mind the very different perspectives of the nineteenth century pioneers of Cypriot archaeology, and to allow that old approaches might sometimes be more illuminating of ancient cultures that our own theory-laden perceptions of the past.

Notes

1. When Schaeffer first came upon intramural burials at Minet el-Beida (the port of Ugarit), at about the same time that Gjerstad was excavating Enkomi, he too found it difficult to reconcile the spatial juxtaposition of burial locality and living quarters. His earliest reports of the settlement deposits from the site refer continually to 'dépôts intentionnels' (1932, 2) 'en rapport direct avec des dispositifs rituels assez compliqués' (1932, 3). Today it is clear that these deposits are largely domestic settlement debris. I would like to thank Sophie Marchegay, Maison de l'Orient Méditerranéen, Lyon for her help with the Minet el-Beida material and archives.
2. A wheeled bronze stand, and several bronze wheels (Murray 1900, figs. 24A, 25 no. 1456) are compared to descriptions of metal objects described in I *Kings* vii.27–37 and II *Chronicles* iv.16 (Murray 1900, 15–16).
3. The gold toggle pins from tombs 19 (Murray 1900, pl. VIII), 67 and 92 (Murray 1900, fig. 38), for example, 'illustrate admirably by their stiletto shape the story of Herodotus concerning the pins (peronae) with which the Athenian women had been wont to fasten their dress . . .' (Murray 1900, 20). The Mycenaean chariot kraters are compared to funerary chariots on Late Geometric vases. 'These vases can only indicate a funeral ceremony, and may even have reference to prizes at funeral games, like the series of tripods on a Dipylon vase' (Murray 1900, 9).
4. The skeletal remains were not retrieved, and so anthropological studies of the ancient population and fluctuating demographic patterns of Late Cypriot Enkomi are not possible.

Bibliography

Åström 1972: P. Åström, *The Late Cypriote Bronze Age. Architecture and Pottery. The Swedish Cyprus Expedition* IV.1c. Lund.

Bailey 1972: D.M. Bailey, 'The British Museum Excavations at Hala Sultan Tekke in 1897 and 1898. The Material in the British Museum', in D.M. Bailey and V. Karageorghis *Hala Sultan Tekke* 1. *Excavations 1897–1971* (*SIMA* XLV.1, Göteborg) 1–32.

Cadogan 1984: G. Cadogan, 'Maroni and the Late Bronze Age of Cyprus', in V. Karageorghis and J.D. Muhly (eds), *Cyprus at the End of the Late Bronze Age* (Nicosia) 1–10.

Cadogan 1989: G. Cadogan, 'Maroni and the Monuments', in E.J. Peltenburg (ed.) *Early Society in Cyprus* (Edinburgh) 43–51.

Cadogan 1992: G. Cadogan, 'Maroni VI', *Report of the Department of Antiquities, Cyprus* 51–8.

Cadogan 1992a: G. Cadogan, 'The British Museum's Work at Maroni', in G.C. Ioannides (ed.), *Studies in Honour of Vassos Karageorghis* (Nicosia) 103–08.

Cadogan 1998: G. Cadogan, 'The Thirteenth-Century Changes in Cyprus in their Near Eastern Context', in S. Gitin, A. Mazar, E. Stern (eds), *Mediterranean Peoples in Transition. Thirteenth to Early Tenth Centuries BCE. In Honor of Professor Trude Dothan* (Jerusalem) 6–16.

Catling 1963: H.W. Catling, 'Patterns of Settlement in Bronze Age Cyprus', *Opuscula Atheniensia* 4, 129–69.

Cesnola 1877: L.P. di Cesnola, *Cyprus: its Ancient Cities, Tombs and Temples. A Narrative of Researches and Excavations* (London).

Desborough 1972: V.R. Desborough, *The Greek Dark Ages* (London).

Dümmler 1886: F. Dümmler, 'Mitteilungen von den griechischen Inseln IV. Älteste Nekropolen auf Cypern', *Mitteilungen des Deutschen archäologischen Instituts. Athenische Abteilung* 11, 214, 235–36.

Dussaud 1952: R. Dussaud, 'Note préliminaire. Identification d'Enkomi avec Alasia', in *Enkomi-Alasia* (Paris).

Fortin 1980: M. Fortin, 'La fondation de villes grecques à Chypre: légendes at découvertes archéologiques', in *Mélanges d'Études Anciennes Offerts à Maurice Lebel* (Quebec) 25–44.

Given 1998: M.Given, 'Inventing the Eteocypriots: Imperialist Archaeology and the Manipulation of Ethnic Identity', *Journal of Mediterranean Archaeology* 11, 3–29.

Gjerstad 1934: E. Gjerstad, *The Swedish Cyprus Expedition* I. *Finds and Results of the Excavations in Cyprus 1927–1931* (Stockholm).

Gjerstad 1935: E. Gjerstad, *The Swedish Cyprus Expedition* II. *Finds and Results of the Excavations in Cyprus 1927–1931* (Stockholm).

Gjerstad 1937: E. Gjerstad, *The Swedish Cyprus Expedition* III. *Finds and Results of the Excavations in Cyprus 1927–1931* (Stockholm).

Gjerstad 1944: 'The Initial Date of the Cypriot Iron Age', *Opuscula Archaeologia* 3, 73–106.

Gjerstad 1944a: 'The colonisation of Cyprus in Greek legend', *Opuscula Archaeologia*, 3, 107–23.

Gjerstad 1948: *The Swedish Cyprus Expedition* IV.2. *The Cypro-Geometric, Cypro-Archaic and Cypro-Classical Periods* (Stockholm).

Hadjisavvas 1989: S. Hadjisavvas, 'A Late Cypriot Community at Alassa', in E. Peltenburg (ed.) *Early Society in Cyprus* (Edinburgh) 32–42.

Hadjisavvas 1994: S. Hadjisavvas, 'Alassa: a Regional Centre of Alasia?', *American Journal of Archaeology* 98, 294.

Hogarth 1889: D.G. Hogarth, *Devia Cypria. Notes of an Archaeological Journey in Cyprus in 1888* (London).

Iacovou 1984: M.Iacovou, *The Eleventh Century Pictorial Pottery of Cyprus* (D.Phil thesis, University of Cincinnati).

Iacovou 1988: M. Iacovou, *The Pictorial Pottery of Eleventh Century B.C. Cyprus* (Studies in Mediterranean Archaeology 78, Göteborg).

Iacovou 1991: M.Iacovou, 'Proto-White Painted Pottery: a Classification of the Ware', in J.A. Barlow, D.L. Bolger and B. Kling (eds.), *Cypriot Ceramics: Reading the Prehistoric Record* (University of Pennsylvania, University Monographs 74) 199–205.

Johnson 1980: J. Johnson, *Maroni de Chypre* (Studies in Mediterranean Archaeology 59, Göteborg).

Karageorghis 1994: V. Karageorghis, *Cyprus in the 11th Century B.C.* (Nicosia).

Karageorghis and Demas 1985: V. Karageorghis and M. Demas, *Excavations at Kition V. The Pre-Phoenician Levels* (Nicosia).

Keswani 1991: P.S. Keswani, 'A Preliminary Investigation of Ceramic Production and Distribution in Cyprus during the Late Bronze Age', in J.A. Barlow, D.L. Bolger, and B. Kling (eds), *Cypriot Ceramics: Reading the Prehistoric Record* (Philadelphia, University Monograph 74).

Keswani 1993: P.S. Keswani, 'Models of local exchange in Late Bronze Age Cyprus', *Bulletin of the American Schools of Oriental Research* 292, 73–83.

Keswani 1996: 'Hierarchies, Heterarchies and Urbanization Process: the View from Bronze Age Cyprus', *Journal of Mediterranean Archaeology* 9, 211–50.

Knapp 1996: A.B. Knapp, *Sources for the History of Cyprus* II. *Near Eastern and Aegean Texts from the Third to the First Millennium BC* (Greece and Cyprus Research Centre).

Knapp 1997: A.B. Knapp, *The Archaeology of Late Bronze Age Cypriot Society. The Study of Settlement, Survey and Landscape* (Glasgow).

Lang 1878: R.H. Lang, *Cyprus: its History, its Present Resources, and future prospects.* (London).

Lo Schiavo 1995: F. Lo Schiavo, 'Cyprus and Sardinia in the Mediterranean: trade routes towards the west', in V. Karageorghis and D. Michaelides eds., *Cyprus and the Sea* (Nicosia) 45–59.

Lo Schiavo, Macnamarra and Vagnetti 1985: F. Lo Schiavo, E. Macnamarra and L. Vagnetti, 'Late Cypriot Imports to Italy and their Influence on Local Bronzework', *Proceedings of the British School at Rome* 53, 1–71.

Maier 1997: F.G. Maier, 'The Mycenaean Pottery of Palaipaphos Reconsidered', in *Proceedings of the International Archaeological Conference "Cyprus and the Aegean in Antiquity, from the Prehistoric Period to the 7th Century AD"* (Nicosia) 93–102.

Manning and de Mita 1997: S.W. Manning and F. De Mita Jr., 'Cyprus, the Aegean, and Maroni-*Tsaroukkas*', in *Proceedings of the International Archaeological Conference "Cyprus and the Aegean in Antiquity, from the Prehistoric Period to the 7th Century AD"* (Nicosia) 103–41.

Manning, Steel, Jansen, Conwell, Sewell, Swinton and Collon 1994: S.W. Manning, L. Steel, H.-G. Jansen, D.H. Conwell, D.Sewell, A. Swinton and D.Collon, '*Tsaroukkas*, Mycenaeans and Trade Project: Preliminary Report on the 1993 Season', *Report of the Department of Antiquities of Cyprus* 83–106.

Manning and Monks 1998: S.W. Manning and S.L. Monks, 'Late Cypriot Tombs at Maroni *Tsaroukkas*, Cyprus', *Annual of the British School at Athens* 93, 297–351.

Merrillees 1987: R.S. Merrillees, *Alashiya Revisited* (Cahiers de la Revue Biblique 22, Paris).

Montelius 1899: O. Montelius, *Der Orient und Europa* (Stockholm).

Montelius 1903: O. Montelius, *Die typologische Methode: Die älteren Kulturperioden im Orient und in Europa* I (Stockholm).

Mountjoy and Hankey 1988: 'LHIIIC Late versus Submycenaean: the Kerameikos Pompeion Cemetery reviewed', *Jahrbuch des Deutschen Archäologischen Instituts* 102, 1–37.

Myres 1897: J.L. Myres, 'Excavations in Cyprus in 1894', *Journal of Hellenic Studies* 17, 134–73.

Myres 1910: J.L. Myres, 'A tomb of the early Iron Age from Kition in Cyprus, containing bronze examples of the "sigynna" or Cypriote javelin', *Liverpool Annals of Archaeology and Anthropology* 3, 107–17.

Myres 1914: J.L. Myres, *Handbook of the Cesnola Collection of Antiquities from Cyprus* (New York).

Myres and Ohnefalsch-Richter 1899: J.L. Myres and M. Ohnefalsch-Richter, *A Catalogue of the Cyprus Museum, with a chronicle of excavations undertaken since the British occupation and introductory notes on Cypriot archaeology* (Oxford).

Murray 1900: A.S. Murray, 'Excavations at Enkomi', in A.S. Murray, A.H. Smith and H.B. Walters, *Excavations in Cyprus* (London) 1–54.

Niemeier 1998: W-D Niemeier, 'The Mycenaeans in Western Anatolia and the problem of the origins of the Sea Peoples', in S. Gitin, A. Mazar, E. Stern (eds), *Mediterranean Peoples in Transition. Thirteenth to Early Tenth Centuries BCE. In Honor of Professor Trude Dothan* (Jerusalem) 17–65.

Ohnefalsch-Richter 1893: M. Ohnefalsch-Richter, *Kypros, the Bible and Homer: Oriental Civilization, Art and Religion in Ancient Times* (Berlin).

Pilides 1991: D. Pilides, 'Handmade Burnished Wares of the Late Bronze Age: toward a clearer classification system', in J.A. Barlow, D.L. Bolger, and B. Kling (eds), *Cypriot Ceramics: Reading the Prehistoric Record* (University Monograph 74, Philadelphia) 139–50.

Pilides 1996: D. Pilides, 'Storage Jars as evidence of the economy of Cyprus in the Late Bronze Age', in V. Karageorghis and D. Michaelides (eds), *The Development of the Cypriot Economy from the Prehistoric Period to the Present Day* (Nicosia) 107–24

Russell 1991: P.J. Russell, 'The pot calls the kettle reddish brown (5 YR 3/4): distinguishing among Late Cypriot Monochrome Wares', in J.A. Barlow, D.L. Bolger, and B. Kling (eds), *Cypriot Ceramics: Reading the Prehistoric Record* (Philadelphia, University Monograph 74) 131–7.

Schaeffer 1932: C.F.A. Schaeffer, 'Les Fouilles de Minet-el-Beida et de Ras Shamra. Troisième campagne (printemps 1931). Rapport sommaire', *Syria. Revue d'Art Oriental et d'Archéologie* 13, 1–24.

Schaeffer 1952: C.F.A. Schaeffer, *Enkomi-Alasia (1946–1950)* (Paris).

Schliemann 1880: H. Schliemann, *Ilios: The city and country of the Trojans. The results and discoveries on the site of Troy and throughout the Troad in the years 1871–72–73–78–79* (London).

South and Todd 1997: A. South and I.A. Todd, 'The Vasilikos valley and the Aegean from the Neolithic to the Late Bronze Age', in *Proceedings of the International Archaeological Conference "Cyprus and the Aegean in Antiquity. From the Prehistoric Period to the 7th Century AD"* (Nicosia) 71–6.

Steel 1994: L. Steel, 'History of archaeological research in the Maroni valley before 1990', in Manning *et al.* 1994, 88–91.

Todd 1996: I.A. Todd, 'The Vasilikos Valley: its place in Cypriot and Near Eastern prehistory', in J.E. Coleson and V.H. Matthews (eds), *Go to the Land I Will Show You. Studies in honour of Dwight W. Young*, 317–51.

Todd 1996a: I.A. Todd, 'A Cross-Section through Cypriot history. Surveying the Vasilikos Valley', *Minerva* 7, 19–22.

Trigger 1989: B.G. Trigger, *A History of Archaeological Thought* (Cambridge).

Walters 1900: H.B. Walters, 'Excavations at Curium', in A.S. Murray, A.H. Smith and H.B. Walters, *Excavations in Cyprus* (London) 57–86.

Walters 1912: H.B. Walters, *Catalogue of the Greek and Etruscan Vases in the British Museum I.2. Cypriote, Italian, and Etruscan Pottery* (London).

Webb and Frankel 1994: M. Webb and D. Frankel, 'Making an impression: storage and surplus finance in Late Bronze Age Cyprus', *Journal of Mediterranean Archaeology* 7, 5–26.

15. Excavations in ancient Cyprus: original manuscripts and correspondence in the British Museum

Veronica Tatton-Brown

This paper is dedicated to the memory of Professor Olivier Masson, a dear friend and distinguished colleague, whose work has inspired me to produce this list.[1] Most of the material refers to excavations and collections of the nineteenth century and additions to our holdings of Cypriot antiquities made early in the twentieth century. It seemed best to group the information according to sites as far as possible which means that the site, if identified, takes precedence so that, for example, objects from particular collections or excavations are listed under the site when known. A short list of the major people involved (arranged within groups in alphabetical order) acts as a preface. It includes individuals who, if not mentioned specifically in the second part of this paper, the reader may come across when consulting letters and reports here listed.

Major personae

British Museum[2]

Birch, Samuel:[3] Egyptologist and Orientalist, assistant in the Department of Antiquities under Edward Hawkins (Keeper until 1861), promoted to Assistant Keeper in 1844 and retiring on his death in 1885.
Budge, Ernest Alfred Thompson Wallis (Sir Wallis, 1857–1934): Keeper of Egyptian and Assyrian Antiquities 1894–1924.
Franks, Augustus Wollaston (Sir Augustus, KCB, 1826–1897): first Keeper of British and Medieval Antiquities 1866–1896.
Jones, John Winter: Principal Librarian 1866–1873.
Maunde Thompson, Edward (Sir Edward, GCB, ISO): Principal Librarian 1888–1909, and from 1898 also Director.
Murray, Alexander Stuart: Keeper of Greek and Roman Antiquities 1886–1904.
Newton, Charles (later Sir Charles): first Keeper of Greek and Roman Antiquities 1861–1886.
Payne Knight, Richard (1750–1824): a noted antiquary, MP, trustee and benefactor.
Poole, Reginald Stuart: second Keeper of Coins and Medals 1870–1890.
Read, Charles Hercules (Sir Hercules, 1857–1929): second Keeper of British and Medieval Antiquities 1896–1921.
Ready, W.T.: an antiquities dealer who undertook conservation work for Greek and Roman in the 1880s (and had an office in the Museum).[4]
Smith, Arthur Hamilton (1860–1941):[5] Assistant in the Department of Greek and Roman Antiquities from April 1885 initially under *Sir Charles Newton* and then under *Murray*; promoted to Assistant Keeper in 1904 and Keeper from 1909 until his retirement in 1925.
Walters, Henry Beauchamp: Assistant in the Department of Greek and Roman Antiquities under *Murray*.

Residents and excavators in Cyprus[6]

Antoniou, Gregorios: Resident of Larnaca and superintendent of BM excavations in 1896–7 and of other excavations, notably those of the Cyprus Exploration Fund, as well. He went on to work for D.G. Hogarth at Ephesus in 1904–5.[7]
Bey, Castan: collector, active until 1879.
Cesnola, Major Alexander Palma di (1839–1914): *Luigi*'s brother, in Cyprus (not continuously) until 1879.
Cesnola, General Luigi Palma di (1832–1904): He carried out extensive excavations in Cyprus between 1865 and 1876 while serving as American consul. The bulk of his collection was acquired by the Metropolitan Museum of Art in New York in 1872, and Cesnola himself installed it there during the first half of 1873. A year after his final return to America in 1876, he was appointed to the Board of the Metropolitan

Museum, later becoming Secretary and then its first Director, a post he held until his death in 1904. A number of pieces were obtained by this Museum, some in 1872 when the collection was exhibited in London, and others from individuals who probably acquired them at the same time.[8]

Christian, Charles: Director of the Imperial Ottoman Bank at Larnaca, with *Williamson* acted as agent for the British Museum, arranging for permits etc. from 1893.

Christian, Percy: younger brother of *Charles*.

Colonna-Ceccaldi, T. (1833–1892): French consul in Cyprus 1866–1869.[9]

Crowfoot, J.W.: originally a student at the British School at Athens, arrived in Cyprus in 1898.

Gardner, Ernest A.: Director of the British School at Athens appointed to direct expeditions by the Cyprus Exploration Fund (founded 1887).

Hake, George Gordon: son of Thomas Gordon Hake, a poet in the Rosetta circle; he carried out excavations for *Kitchener* in January 1882; in March 1882 he worked also at Gastria and in the following months at Curium.[10]

Hogarth, David George: Fellow of Magdalen College and Craven Fellow in the University of Oxford; Student at the British School at Athens 1886–7 when he started to co-operate with Gardner in excavations conducted by the Cyprus Exploration Fund (founded 1887). Director of the British School at Athens 1897–1900, during which time he worked in Crete.[11] Excavated on the site of the Artemision at Ephesus for the British Museum 1904–5,[12] and finally became Keeper of the Ashmolean Museum in Oxford.

James, M.R.: as Fellow of King's College, Cambridge, worked with the Cyprus Exploration Fund (founded 1887).

Kitchener, Horatio (later Lord Kitchener of Khartoum): Director of a survey in Cyprus, who also organised excavations in January 1882 that were carried out by *Hake*.

(*Kühn, Dr Julius*: uncle of *Ohnefalsch-Richter* and Professor at Halle University, Germany.)

Lang, Robert Hamilton (later Sir Robert, 1836–1913): a Scotsman and 1863–72 Manager of the Imperial Ottoman Bank's Agency in Cyprus; 1871–2 H.M.'s Consul for Cyprus.

Mavrogordato, A.S.: resident in Cyprus in the 1890s (see miscellaneous letters below).

Munro, J.A.R.: student at the British School at Athens, later Rector of Lincoln College, Oxford, directed excavations for the Cyprus Exploration Fund (founded 1887).

Munro, J.L.: originally a student at the British School at Athens, first arrived in Cyprus in 1893.

Pierides, Dimitrios (1811–1895) of Larnaca:[13] a banker scholar and collector; he held consular posts under the British and was one of the founders of the Cyprus Museum (first established in 1883). He has been described as the first archaeologist and epigraphist of the island of Cyprus.

Pierides, G.D. (Djabra) 1852–1928: son of *Demetrios*; inherited (with his brother *Zeno*) his father's collection to which he made additions and came to hold one of the finest collections of Mycenaean pottery in Cyprus, which is now housed in Nicosia.

Pierides, Kleanthes:[14] businessman of Limassol (related to the Pierides of Larnaca), antiquarian and collector and also purveyor of antiquities in the early years of the last century.

Pierides, Zeno (1839–1911): son of *Demitrios* who, with his brother *Djabra*, inherited his father's collection and, together with his descendants, greatly enriched it. He founded the shipping and banking company, Z.D. Pierides, and acted as Consul for Britain as well as for Sweden and Norway. The present head of the family is his direct descendant.

Smith, R. Elsey: architect, worked with the Cyprus Exploration Fund (founded 1887).

Tubbs, H.A.: of Pembroke College, Oxford, as a student at the British School at Athens directed excavations (with *Munro*) at Salamis (1890) for the Cyprus Exploration Fund.

Welch, F.B.: a student at the British School at Athens in 1898 and in Cyprus in 1899. In the 1920s he was Vice-Consul attached to the Passport Control Office in Greece, and from 1920–22 he was engaged in cataloguing the Finlay papers at the British School at Athens which he saw to completion. He was very popular with the students of the school at this time.[15]

Williamson, J.W.: a prominent British resident in Cyprus, head of the English Club at Limassol and agent for the English-Cyprus Copper Mine Company who, with *Charles Christian*, acted as agent for the British Museum arranging permits etc. from 1893.

British Government officials in Cyprus

Biddulph, Sir Robert: High Commissioner 1879–1886.

Cobham, Claude Delaval: in Cyprus from 1878, became British Commissioner in Larnaca and also held other posts.

Colnaghi, D.E.: British Vice-Consul (later Consul) in Cyprus; presented terracottas and some sculpture to the British Museum in 1866.

(*Colnaghi, K.*: related to *D.E.*)

Haynes-Smith, Sir W.F.: High Commissioner April 1898–October 1904.

Kerr, Niven: British Consul in Cyprus 1833–1846.

Lang, Robert Hamilton (later Sir Robert, 1836–1913): see list above

Luke, Sir Harry K.C.M.G.: b. 1884, Private Secretary to the High Commissioner 1911–12; Commissioner of Famagusta 1918–20.

Michel, Roland District Commissioner of Limassol 1893–4.

Ohnefalsch-Richter, Max:[16] archaeologist (1850–1917);

arrived in Cyprus in 1878 and became Government Inspector.
Sandwith, Thomas Backhouse:[17] British Vice-Consul 1865–1870.
Seager, Major: appointed Assistant Commissioner in 1879 (see *Wolseley* pp. 170–1below); president of the district court in Nicosia in 1891.
Sendall, Sir Walter: High Commissioner 1892–8.
Travers, Mr.: Commissioner of Famagusta in 1896.
Warren, Colonel Falkland (1834–1908):[18] in Cyprus 1878–90, Commissioner at Limassol (1879), Chief Secretary to the Government (appointed 1879) and Honorary Keeper of the Cyprus Museum.
Wolseley, Garnet Joseph (1833–1913):[19] As Lieutenant-General, he became the first High Commissioner of Cyprus in 1878 when the island came under British administration. However, he held this post for less than a year, as he was chosen by the British government to restore the situation in the Zulu war after the disaster at Isandhlwana (27 January 1879). He went on to become the first Viscount Wolseley, a Field-Marshall and Commander in Chief of the British army.

British Military Personnel and others involved in Cypriot affairs

Ashbee, Henry Spencer: eminent bibliophile whose bequest of Cypriot antiquities was received by the Victoria and Albert Museum in 1901 (transferred to the British Museum in 1980).[20]
Chester, Rev. Greville J.(1831–1892): author and traveller, gave and sold antiquities to the British Museum.
Granville, Earl (1815–1891): British Foreign Secretary 1851, 1870–74 and 1880–5, colonial secretary 1868–70, 1886.[21]
Handcock, Captain J.: acted as mediator in the purchase of antiquities in 1890.[22]
Hiristmaitland, Lt. Colonel H. RE: see miscellaneous correspondence below.
Legge, Walter: of the British School at Athens 1889–90
Leighton, Sir Frederic (Lord) (1830–1896): President of the Royal Academy of Arts 1878–1895.
Meister, Richard: philologist of Leipzig in the early twentieth century.
Macmillan, G. A.: Secretary of the Cyprus Exploration Fund 1887–8.
Morel, Léon (1828–1909):[23] resident in France; formed large collection of Gaulish antiquities sold to the British Museum in 1901.
Petrie, Sir William Flinders (1853–1942): English Egyptologist who had no formal education. He first visited Egypt to make a survey of the pyramids 1880–2. He became Hon. Joint Secretary of the Egyptian Exploration Fund in 1883 and dug for the fund 1884–6. After a quarrel, he continued digging with two others from 1887 and in 1894 he set up the Egyptian Research Account, which later expanded to become the British School of Archaeology in Egypt. He rejoined the E.E.F. and worked again for the fund 1896–1906. By the will of Miss Amelia Edwards, who had founded the Department of Egyptology at University College, London, he was appointed to the first chair of Egyptology in England as Edwards Professor, University College, London, a post he held from 1892–1933, becoming Emeritus Professor on his retirement. He received many other academic awards and may be credited with having more major archaeological discoveries than any other archaeologist.
Sayce, Archibald Henry (1845–1933): Distinguished English orientalist and Professor of Assyriology in the University of Oxford 1891–1919. He held a number of lectureships in different years and was awarded a D.Litt., L.L.D and D.D. and became an Hon. F.B.A. He did important work on the Carian script and on the Hittite language and texts, and also travelled extensively in Egypt.[25]
Sinclair, Lt. R.E.: see Larnaca (Bamboola) below.
Torr, Cecil (1857–1928): Aegean specialist who, among other things, challenged conventional ancient chronologies.
White, Lt. Colonel H.G.: see miscellaneous correspondence below.
Wood, J.T.: architect, better known for his excavations at Ephesus for the British Museum (1863–74).

Sponsors etc.

The British Museum: provided some funding for Ohnefalsch-Richters's excavations between 1879 and 1883.[26]
Cyprus Exploration Fund: a learned society formed in London in 1887 to promote interest in the island (for its constitution see *The Athenaeum* 3149, 3 March 1888, p. 282).
Lawrence, Edwin Henry: became father-in-law of Alexander Cesnola, whose excavations at Salamis in the late 1870s he financed.
Turner Bequest: funds for excavations (country not specified in the will) bequeathed to the British Museum by Miss Emma Tourner Turner that were used to finance the BM excavations in Cyprus of 1893–6. A few objects without provenance are also probably part of this bequest as *GR Registers* 1970.6–22.1–10.

The Archives

These comprise departmental registers each recording the antiquities of one department (that in the Greek and Roman department denoted here by *GR Registers*),[27] reports submitted by the Keepers of the different antiquities departments, minutes of Trustee meetings known as *Trustee Minutes*, and letters written to the British Museum and the antiquities departments. Each department houses copies of the Trustee Minutes and also of its own submitted reports (those of the Greek and Roman department are noted here as *GR Reports*), as well as letters written to the department bound in volumes (*Original Letters*)[28] and later kept in files. The later filed letters usually have the replies filed with them; for those in the Greek and Roman *Original Letters* there are also books containing copies of replies, mostly from the Keeper of the department of the time, which are noted below as *Letter Book(s)*.[29] All this information is ordered by year and date and, in the case of letters, according to the name of the sender. In addition the Greek and Roman Department has bound copies of *Parliamentary Reports: Income, expenditure etc.* from 1858–1921.[30]

The Central Archives[31] of the Museum include the minutes of the Museum Trustees, the originals of reports submitted to the Trustees by the Keepers, and letters from within and outside the Museum which were submitted to the Trustees at their meetings. Most of the letters and many of the reports will be found in the series known as the *Original Papers* (1743–1946) [it is to these letters and reports that mentions below under *Trustee Minutes* refer], but reports dating from 1805 to 1869 are in a separate series, the *Officers' Reports*, and reports and correspondence dating from 1897 to 1974 and concerning donations made to the Museum will be found [along with other donations] in the *Book of Presents* (1756–1974). Copies of letters sent out from the Principal Librarian's (later the Director's) Office are contained in *Letter Books* (1829–1946). Correspondence dating from 1946 onwards may be found among the *Registered Files* (1946–present), and more recent reports among the *Board Papers* (1963–date); papers among both these series, which date from before the end of 1966, are open to the public.

Copies of Keepers' reports are also in the relevant departments, and those denoted as *GR Reports* may be consulted in the Greek and Roman department. Some reports and notebooks of excavators, and a bound volume entitled *Correspondence: Excavations in Cyprus*, that contains letters written between 17 October 1892 and 17 January 1900, are also housed in the offices of the Department of Greek and Roman Antiquities, together with one volume of photographs entitled *Miscellaneous Photographs 2* (there is no volume 1); photographs mentioned in letters etc. have rarely survived. I have here summarised the archive material available according to sites and collections as far as possible. The drawings of built tombs mentioned under the sites are the work of A.R. Castioglione undertaken in 1938–9; the Greek and Roman department has recently acquired copies of his drawings and a commentary.[32]

Sites in Cyprus[33]

(included are just brief mentions, particularly from letters in the Correspondence: Excavations in Cyprus volume, and also little-known British publications)

Achna:
Book of Presents, Supplementary Vol. 1: Report of 5 January 1883 from C.T. Newton about Achna referring to female terracotta figurines acquired from Cobham.
Parliamentary Reports 1883, p. 27.
GR Reports 1883–4, pp. 13–17, 5/1/83.
GR Registers 1883.1–6.1–163; 1905.7–12.1,2; 1926.3–24.4; 1969.2–10.1–39; 1969.8–28.1–3.

Alambra:
According to the *Cyprus Museum Catalogue*, published in 1899, objects from Ohnefalsch-Richter's excavations at this site came to the British Museum and mention is made of a Ms. report.[34] Unfortunately no record of their arrival in the Museum is preserved, and Ohnefalsch-Richter's reports have disappeared.[35] It is possible that some of the finds from this site are listed in the series 1884.12–10.1–332, as a note in the register suggests, and these all come from Ohnefalsch-Richter's excavations.

Amargetti:
The Athenaeum 3164, 18 June 1888, p. 442, Hogarth's report.

Amathus:[36]
The Times (newspaper), 29 December 1894.
Myres' excavation notebook entitled *Amathus* (bound).
Transcript from Myres' excavation notebook bound in a volume entitled *Excavations at Amathus* with additional maps and wax impressions of coins.
A.H. Smith's diary bound in a volume entitled A.H. Smith, *Notes at Amathus 1893–4*.
Trustee Minutes 10 June 1893, authorisation of excavations at Amathus.
Original papers 1893, 22 September, Murray's report; 1894, 9 Jan., Murray's report; 5 March, Murray's report; 24 September, Murray's report.
GR Reports 1879–80, pp. 105–7, 20/5/79, pp. 369–73, 8/7/80; 1889–90, p. 77, 7/5/89, p. 245, 9/7/90;[37] 1893–4, p. 101, 22/9/93, pp. 133–4, 9/1/94, pp. 137–8, 12/1/94, p. 161, 5/3/94, pp. 235–6, 24/9/94; 1895–6, p. 9, 4/1/95; 1897–8, p. 101, Feb. 98;[38] 1899–April 1902, p. 40, 3/5/99.
Parliamentary Reports 1880, p. 20; 1894, pp. 60–62; 1896, pp. 67–8; 1899, p. 64.
Correspondence: Excavations in Cyprus: letters of 17 October 1892, 22 November 1892, 9 January 1893, 16 February 1893, 24 April 1893, 8 November 1893, 16 November 1893, 20 November 1893, 3 December 1893, 4 December 1893, 16 December 1893, 28 December 1893, 7

January 1894, 15 January 1894, 3 February 1894 (2 letters), 25 January 1895 (7 letters); 27 January 1895, 31 January 1895, 23 November 1897.
GR Original Letters 1900–1903, no. 198.
GR Registers (see also Limassol below): 1880.7–10.112–126; 1884.10–6.6; 1891.4–18.1–59;[39] 1894.11–1.1–739; 1894.11–2.1; 1899.6–4.2,4; 1900.5–21.4; 1933.4–28.1;[40] 1960.3–2.1;1967.1–2.1; 1969.4–1.1–266; 1973.1–16.1.
ANE Registers 123053 (1933.4–28.1); 135.591 (1971.12–13.1)
Drawing of built tomb.[41]
Aradippou:[42]
GR Reports 1879–80, pp. 117–9, 20/5/79, pp. 365–6, 8/7/80; 1885–6, p. 37, 15/3/85.
Parliamentary Reports 1880, p. 20; 1885, p. 31.
Correspondence: *Excavations in Cyprus*: letters of 23 November 1897, 16 December 1897, 16 June 1899.
GR Registers 1880.7–10.1–22.
Arpera:
Correspondence: *Excavations in Cyprus*: letter of 16 June 1899.
Athienou:
GR Registers 1866.1–1.332, 334.[43]
Ayia Paraskevi:
Correspondence: *Excavations in Cyprus*: letter of 24 February 1895.
GR Registers 1888.9–27.2–35.
Ayios Sozomenos (a tomb between this site and Laksha)
GR Registers 1903.12–15.17; 1913.2–12.1–15.
Curium (Kourion):[44]
Bound volume entitled H.B. Walters, *Notes at Curium*; the inside title page describes it as 'A Record of Excavations at Curium, Cyprus. Second Season Jan-April 1895'.
Papers in paper folder entitled H. B. Walters, *Report on Excavations at Curium. Jan-April 1895*. In this the finds are categorised and the contents of the tombs are described accordingly, thus under the heading 'Inscriptions' are listed the relevant finds in their tombs.
Original Papers 1879, Newton's report of 6 January;[45] 1894, 24 September, Murray's report.
GR Reports 1875–6, pp. 387–8, letter of 11/11/76; 1879–80, p. 27, 11/2/79, pp. 107–111, 121–2, 125–9, 20/5/79; 1885–6, pp. 373–4,18/11/80; 1887–8, p. 218, 10/7/88; 1893–4, p. 235, 24/9//94, p. 259, 6/12/94; 1895–6, pp. 89–91, 6/12/95; p. 207, 10/11/96; 1897–8, p. 24, 3/3/97.
Copy of *Hake's excavation report*.[46]
Parliamentary Reports 1890, p. 61;[47] 1895, pp. 63–5; 1897, p. 51.
Correspondence: *Excavations in Cyprus*: letters of 27 January 1895, 31 January 1895,12 February 1895, 13 February 1895, 24 February 1895, 18 March 1895, 23 March 1895 (and report), 23 April 1895, 2 May 1895, 24 June 1895, 28 June 1895,18 November 1897, 23 November 1897,[48] map of the area at end of the volume.
GR Original Letters 1888, no. 73; 1890, nos 117–9;[49] 1900–1903, no. 215.
GR Registers 1884.12–10.329–332; 1889.11–11.1; 1896.2–1.1–400; 1897.3–16.1; 1909.6–15.1,2; 1917.6–1.244–5, 696, 2073; 1920.12.20.1; 1926.3–24.1; 1991.12–11.1–35; see also **Kitchener-Hake excavations** below.
Miscellaneous Photographs 2, nos 156–8, earrings in Metropolitan Museum of Art, photos presented by Luigi di Cesnola.
Enkomi:[50]
A.H. Smith's notebook bound in volume entitled *Notes at Enkomi 1896*.
Bound volume entitled *Excavations at Enkomi* contains reports by A.H. Smith (tombs 1–37) and by Percy Christian (tombs 38–100), including plans and figures.
Trustee Minutes of 14 March 1896 recording letters from Williamson and Christian and giving authority to excavate; 9 May 1896, recording letter and telegram from Mr Murray on his visit.
GR Reports 1895–6, p. 29, 4/3/96, p. 147, 2/6/96, p. 163, 19/6/96, pp. 169–70, 171, 4/7/96, pp. 223–5, 10/12/96; 1897–8, p. 101, Feb. 98;[51] 1899–April 1902, p. 40, 3/5/99.
Parliamentary Reports 1881, p. 25; 1898, p. 59; 1899, p. 64.
Correspondence: *Excavations in Cyprus*: letters of 17 March 1896, 25 May 1896, 13 July 1896, 16 July 1896, 22 July 1896, 17 August 1896, 22 September 1896, 23 October 1897, 18 November 1897, 23 November 1897, 24 November 1897, 3 December 1897, 16 December 1897, 22 March 1898, 20 March 1899, 18 December 1899, 23 December 1899.
GR Original Letters 1896–7, no. 735.
GR Registers 1881.8–24.1–16, 25,27, 28–30, 38–40;[52] 1897.4–1.1–1572; 1899.2–24.1; 1899.6–4.3; 1900.6–15.1–72; 1921.6–17.1; 1926.3–24.2,6; 1969.5–15.1–14; 1969.7–1.1–57; 1974.11–1.22,39; 1998.3–16.1.
Episkopi:
GR Registers 1906.3–12.2,3; 1924.5–15.6.
Erimi:
GR Registers 1934.11–14.1,2; 1958.12–20.2.
Famagusta (district):
Correspondence: *Excavations in Cyprus*: letter of 12 August 1898.
Gastria (Alaas):
Copy of *Hake's excavation report*.[53]
Letter in the Department of Manuscripts (British Library) of 23rd June 1882 to Gordon Hake from his father Thomas Hake.
GR Registers see **Kitchener-Hake excavations** below.
Golgoi:
GR Reports 1879–80, p. 97, 20/5/79.

Goski:
GR Registers 1884.12–10.268–273,279–291.
Hala Sultan Tekké (Tekké):[54]
Walters' hardback notebook (see also **Maroni**) under heading 'Excavations on Tekké site Dec. 1897'.
GR Reports 1897–8, p. 80, 5/1/98, p. 100, 4/3/98, p. 123–4, 9/5/98.
Parliamentary Reports 1897, pp. 60–2; 1899, p. 67.
Correspondence: Excavations in Cyprus: letters of 24 November 1897, 3 December 1897, 16 December 1897, 25 February 1898, 16 April 1898, 18 April 1898, 22 April 1898, 27 April 1898 (including excavation report), 28 April 1898.
GR Registers 1898.12–1.177–319; 1898.12–31.1–27; 1971.3–25.1,2.
Idalion (Dali) and R.H. Lang's collection:[55]
Blackwood's Magazine May 1905, pp. 622–639, report by Lang entitled 'Reminiscences – archaeological researches in Cyprus'.
Trustees Minutes of 13 Nov. 1869 considering reports by Birch of 11 November, Newton of 10 November; 12 February 1870; 26 February 1870; 12 March 1870, finally considered papers by Poole (with a memorandum by Mr Deutsch of the British Library) of 9 February, Birch and Newton of 11 February (submitted on 12 and 26 Feb.1870); 30 April 1870 considering Lang's letter of 26 March; 11 November 1871 considering Poole's report on coins of 12 Oct., reports from Birch of 13 Oct. and 10 Nov. and from Principal Librarian (John Winter Jones) of 10 November; 13 July 1872 considering Birch report of 5 July and completing purchase of collection; 27 July 1872 considering reports of Poole of 25 and 26 July concerning Lang's coins from Larnaca.
Sub-committee minutes of 25 November 1871.
Poole's manuscript report on Lang's excavations submitted to the Trustees on 12 March 1870 (see above) dated 9 February 1870 bound in volume entitled *Inventory of Mr Lang's Collection*
GR Reports 1867–69, pp. 575–581, 10/11/69, pp. 591–8, 10/11/69; 1870–72, pp. 19–23, 11/2/70, pp. 400–401, 8/11/71; 1873–4, p. 17, 7/1/73; 1879–80, p. 27, 11/2/79, pp. 115–6, 20/5/79.
Parliamentary Reports 1867, p. 22; 1869, p. 15
Correspondence: Excavations in Cyprus: letter of 22 November 1892.
GR Original Letters 1861–68, nos 408–411; 1869–72, nos 358–63.
GR Letter Book 1861–79, pp. 12, 129, 152, 175, 189, 196, 210 (2), 211, 213, 214.
ANE Original Letters (Lang with Birch) 1868–1881, nos 3565–3582 (Sept. 1871– Feb.1876).
GR Registers 1855.11–1.1–29; 1866.1–1.2, 245, 300, 321–4, 328, 337,[56] 353;[57] 1868.8–30.1; 1872.8–16.1–78, 85–98;[58] 1873.3–20.1–347;[59] 1884.12–10.1–332;[60] 1913.2–12.1–34; 1938.11–30.4; 1978.7–17.2.
ANE Registers 117.980 (1872.8–16. 99); 125.315–6 (1872.8–16.80,83); 125.320 (1872.8–16.84); 125.326–8 (1872.8–16.82,81,79);
Miscellaneous Photographs 2, no. 51 and eight loose photographs some of which are reproduced in Senff's study.[61]
Kafizin:
GR Register 1970.9–14.1.
Kalavasos (Kalavassos):
Mentioned in Walters' Maroni/Tekké notebook under entry for Nov.29–Dec.4.
Correspondence: Excavations in Cyprus: letter of 3 December 1897.[62]
Karpas (s)(Carpas) peninsula:
Correspondence: Excavations in Cyprus: letter of 23 October 1897.[63]
GR Original Letters 1896–7, no. 736.
GR Reports 1887–8, pp. 217–8, 10/7/88.
Parliamentary Reports 1896, p. 57.
GR Registers 1888.9–27.1;1896.10.15.1; 1924.5–15.2,5.
Kazaphani:
GR Registers 1932.7–11.1.
Khirokitia:
Final Report on the Khirokitia Excavations, Cyprus 1936–1939 by P. Dikaios, F.S.A., Curator, Cyprus Museum; page of typescript (references on the back) with three plates of photos and a plan, bound together.
Kissonerga:
GR Registers 1980.1–30.1–30.
Kiti:
Correspondence: Excavations in Cyprus: letter of 23 November 1897.
Kition/Citium (Larnaca):[64]
Trustee Minutes of 27 July 1872, Lang's coins from Larnaca.
Book of Presents, Supplementary Vol. 1, no. 2868. Manuscript copy of a *Report on Excavations at the Bamboola-Larnaca* addressed to the Commissioner at Larnaca dated 5.7.1879, by Lieutenant H.M. Sinclair, R.E.
GR Reports 1879–80, 119–121, 20/5/79 (Sinclair's excavations in general), pp. 361–75, 8/7/80; 1895–6, p. 93, 6/12/95, p. 125, 6/2/96, p. 129, 4/3/96, p. 209, 19/11/96;1889–90, p. 123, 18/9/89;1897–8, p. 48, 24/8/97, p. 80, 5/1/98, pp. 123–4, 9/5/ 98.
Parliamentary Reports 1855, p. 12; 1880, p. 20; 1881, p. 25; 1883, p. 27.
Correspondence: Excavations in Cyprus: letters of 31 January 1895, 16 June 1899.
GR Registers 1852.5–17.15; 1852.6–9.1–81;1866.1–1.1, 3–230,231,232–244,246–297,301–312,325–7,329–331,333,336,338–352,354–8;[65] 1868.1–8.1; 1876.11–

14.1,2; 1880.7–10.24–65; 1881.8–24.17–24;[66] 1883.4–29.1–7; 1883.7–25.323,324; 1888–.8–24.1–178; 1883.4–29.1–3; 1899.12–29.1–125 (includes some finds from Kouklia also listed below);1903.12–15.1–66; 1905.10–19.1–16; 1917.1–1.9,11,16–24; 1920.3.17.1–23; 1920.10–12.1,2; 1980.2–3.1
ANE Registers 125080 (1880.7–10.44); 125081 (1880.7–10.43).
Miscellaneous Photographs 2, no. 81 top.[67]
Drawings of two tombs.[68]
Klavdia (Claudia):
GR Reports 1897–8, p. 152, 20/9/98; 1899–April 1902, pp. 81–3, 4/12/99.
Parliamentary Reports 1898, pp. 62, 63; 1899, pp. 67–8.
Correspondence: Excavations in Cyprus: letters of 16 February 1898, 20 March 1899, 16 June 1899.
GR Registers 1899.12–29.27–46, 48–135; 1978.6–17.1.
Koma tou Gialou (Yialou):
Correspondence: Excavations in Cyprus: letter of 16 June 1899.
Kouklia (Old Paphos, Palaipaphos or Palaepaphos):[69]
The Athenaeum 3149, 3 March 1888, p. 282; 3150, 10 March 1888, p. 314; 3154, 7 April 1888, pp. 441–2; 3155, 14 April 1888, pp. 474–5 (monoliths at);[70] 3156, 21April 1888, pp. 506–7; 3158, 5 May 1888, pp. 575–6, Gardner's reports including one in no. 3156 from Elsey Smith.
GR Reports 1867–9, p. 598, 10/11/69; 1887–8, pp. 267–8, 5/11/88; 1893–4, p. 134, 9/1/94; 1899–April 1902, pp. 14–15, 2/2/99, p. 35, 4/3/99, pp. 81–3, 4/12/99.
Parliamentary Reports 1888, p. 36; 1899, pp. 67–9.
Correspondence: Excavations in Cyprus: letters of 18 February 1898, 20 March 1899, 10 April 1899, 28 March 1899, 15 April 1899, 16 June 1899 (and report)
GR Original Letters 1898–9, no. 184, mentions Mr Welch.[71]
GR Registers 1888.11–15.1–20; 1899.12–29.1–26, 47; 1982.2–20.1–55.
Kyrenia (Kerynia):
GR Reports 1879–80, p. 111, 20/5/79.
Parliamentary Reports 1886, p. 44
GR Registers 1980.10–15.1–21.
Drawing of built tomb close to the harbour.[72]
Lapi(e)thos:
GR Original Letters 1900–1903, nos 184–194
GR Registers 1900.7–23.1; 1900.9–3.1–20.
Lefka:
GR Original Letters 1909–10, nos 794–797
GR Registers 1910.10–14.1.
Lefkara:
Correspondence: Excavations in Cyprus: letter of 3 December 1897.
Leonarisa:
Correspondence: Excavations in Cyprus: letter of 22 September 1896.

Leontari Vouno:
Report from M.R.James in *The Athenaeum* 3149, 3 March 1888, p. 282.
Limassol:
GR Reports 1879–80, p. 369, 8/7/80.
Parliamentary Reports 1892, p. 55
GR Registers: 1880.7–10.66–111 (**Amathus** and **Limassol**); 1892.11–28.1,2; 1892. 12–1.1; 1969.10–2.1,2.
Limniti:
Parliamentary Reports 1890, p. 58.
GR Registers 1890.7–31.56, 57.
Miscellaneous Photographs 2, pl.52.
Mari:
Note of 'primitive pottery' in hardback notebook (see **Maroni**) under entry for 11–17 November 1897.
Original Papers 1897, 24 August, Murray's report.
Parliamentary Reports 1889, pp. 40–2.
Correspondence: Excavations in Cyprus: letters of 31 January 1895, 17 March 1896, 23 November 1897, 3 December 1897.[73]
GR Registers 1881.8–24.1–16, 25,27, 28–30, 38–40;[74] 1899.10–15.1–14. See also **Kitchener-Hake excavations** below.
Marion (Polis tis Chysochou):
The Athenaeum 3202, 9 March 1889, p. 320; 3205, 30 March 1889, p. 416; 3210, 4 May, 1889, reports from Gardner (3202) and J.A.R. Munro.
Original Papers 1887, letter of 25 July.
GR Reports 1885–6, pp. 373–4, 18/11/86; 1887–8, pp. 83–4, 25/7/87, p. 133, 4/10/87; 1889–90, pp. 250–1, 10/7/90, pp. 261–3, 30/7/90; 1891–2, p. 99, 29/7/91; 1895–6, p. 185, 3/8/96; 1899–April 1902, p. 15, 2/2/99, p. 287, 27/2/1902.
Parliamentary Reports 1887, pp. 37–8; 1888, p. 37; 1890, pp. 56–58; 1891, p. 57; 1896, p. 55.
Correspondence: Excavations in Cyprus: letters of 17 October 1892; 3 December 1897; 10 April 1899.
GR Original Letters 1888, nos 72,74; 1889, nos 140, 176, 171,178; 1890, nos 190, 191a, 192; 1891, no. 197; 1896–7, no. 733; 1900–1903, no. 200.
GR Registers 1887.8–1. 1,3, 4–20, 22–42,44, 45, 47–61, 64–71; 1890.7–31.1–4, 6,7–14, 18, 22–54, 58, 88–92; 1891.8–6.4, 84,85,93–5; 1896.10–15.2; 1903.10–15.1; 1906.3–12.1; 1919.12–1.1–7; 1926.3–24.3; 1934.3–8.1–4; 1966.2–16.2; 1967.10–22.1,3,8,10; 1967.10–27.1–12; 1967.11–1.1–64; 1967.11–2.1–33; 1969.9–8.1; 1972.2–1.1.
Miscellaneous Photographs 2 nos 33–50 (Ohnefalsch-Richter's excavations).
Maroni:[75]
Tomb lists in hardbound notebook under heading *Maroni excavations 1897.*
Original Papers 1893, 7 November, Murray's request to

purchase items from Charles Christian; 1897, 24 August, Murray's report.
GR Reports 1893–4, p. 117, 7/11/93; 1895–6, p. 125, 6/2/96, p. 129, 4/3/96, p. 209, 19/11/96; 1897–8, p. 48, 24/8/97, p. 80, 5/1/98, pp. 123–4, 9/5/98; 1899–April 1902, p. 40, 3/5/99.
Parliamentary Reports 1893, p. 65; 1897, pp. 60–2; 1898, p. 64; 1899, p. 64.
Correspondence: *Excavations in Cyprus*: letters of 17 October 1892, 24 April 1893, 17 March 1896, 23 October 1897, 18 November 1897 (and report), 23 November 1897, 24 November 1897, 3 December 1897, 16 December 1897, 22 December 1897, 26 February 1898, 17 March 1898, 22 April 1898, 15 April 1899.
GR Original Letters 1900–1903, no. 198.
GR Registers 1893.11–16.1–3; 1898.12–1.1–176; 1899.6–4.4; 1911.4–28.1; 1925.1–1.1–3.
Moni:
Correspondence: *Excavations in Cyprus*: letters of 17 March 1896, 23 October 1897, 23 November 1897, 22 December 1898.
Nicosia:
GR Reports 1879–80, pp. 97–9, 20/5/79 (tombs in the vicinity).
GR Original Letters 1900–1903, no. 198.
GR Registers 1924.10–6.1–6; 1935.8–23.13,14; 1938.11–30.3.
Nicosia, Convent of St. Domenica:
Correspondence: *Excavations in Cyprus*: letters of 22 November 1892, 9 January 1893.
GR Registers 1917.7–1.38.
Nisso (Niso):
GR Letter Book 1880–96, p. 323.
Paphos:
The Athenaeum 3155, 14 April 1888, pp. 474–5 (monoliths at).[76]
GR Original Letters 1896–7, no. 736.
GR Inscription no. cccxc (unregistered).
Drawings of some of 'royal' tombs.[77]
Potamia:
GR Registers 1876.11–14.3 (near).
Pyla:
Parliamentary Reports 1871, p. 16.
GR Registers 1871.5–6.1; 1917.7–1.1–319.
Drawing of built tomb.[78]
Pyrga (Larnaca District):
GR Registers 1866.1–1.298,299,[79] 332,334.[80]
Rizokarpasso:
Correspondence: *Excavations in Cyprus*: letter of 28 April 1898
Salamis:[81]
The Athenaeum 3252, 22 Feb. 1890, p. 250, report from Munro; 3255, 15 March 1890, pp. 346–7, report from Tubbs; 3263, 10 May 1890, pp. 613–4; 3268, 14 June 1890, p. 776, reports from Munro and Tubbs; 3271, 5 July 1890, pp. 39–40, report from Munro.
Trustees Minutes of 14 June 1890 considering letter from the chairman of the Cyprus Exploration Fund concerning transport of the capital; 11 April 1891 considering letters of 30 March and 9 April from the admiralty and a detailed report from the ship's captain giving particulars of transport of the capital - Trustees resolved to grant extra pay to the ship's crew.
Copy of *Hake's excavation report*.[82]
Original Papers 1879, Newton's report of 6 January.[83]
GR Reports 1883–4, p. 13, 3/1/83; 1889–90, pp. 249–50, 10/7/90; 1891–2, pp. 97–9, 29/7/91; 1895–6, p. 125, 5/2/96.
Parliamentary Reports 1885, p. 29; 1891, pp. 55–7.
Correspondence: *Excavations in Cyprus*: letters of 27 January 1895, 24 February 1895, 16 July 1896.
GR Original Letters 1879–82, no. 479; 1889, no. 1555; 1890, nos 190, 191, 191a, 192.
GR Registers 1882.11–10.1;1883.1–6.1, 163; 1884.12–10.239, 246–67; 1885.2–19.2–3; 1891.8–6.1–93; 1909.3–10.1–148; 1914.3–7.1–14; 1928.3–17.5–9; 1949.8–8.1–3;1965. 9–30.707,748–51; 1966.11–1.1; 1967.11–3.21–28; 1967.11–4.1–12; 1967.12–13.1–65; 1968.12–13.1–65; 1969.8–8.1–3; 1972.12–20.1; 1973.5–1.4; 1975.6–20.1–43; 1980.11–27.1–4; 1980.11–27.1–4. See also **Kitchener-Hake excavations** below.
Miscellaneous Photographs 2, no. 101, 6 photos of transport of capital.
Drawings of the Tomb of St Catherine[84] and of a tomb at Ayios Sergios.[85]
Skilloura:
Correspondence: *Excavations in Cyprus*: letter of 16 June 1899.
Soli:
Correspondence: *Excavations in Cyprus*: letters of 17 March 1896, 15 April 1899.
GR Original Letters 1900–1903, no. 191.
Sotira:
PEE Registers 1958.12–20.1.
Tamassos:[86]
GR Registers 1891.6–28.1; 1910.6–20.1–22.
ANE Register 125321–2 (1892.12–13.11, 12).
Miscellaneous Photographs 2, nos 26–32 + loose copies of 26 (2)-28 and one loose of a different view (Warren's excavations).
Drawing of built tomb[87]
Tremithus(a):
GR Reports 1879–80, p. 97, 20/5/79.
GR Registers 1876.11–14.4; 1917.7–1.250.
Correspondence: *Excavations in Cyprus*: letter of 16 June 1899.

Tremithousa, Embelia:
GR Registers 1982.2–25.1–74.
Trikomo (Trichamore):
Correspondence: Excavations in Cyprus: letter of 22 September 1896.
GR Registers 1924.5–15.3,4.
Vounous:
GR Registers 1939.2–17.1–43; 1940.4–24.1–11; 1980.11–26.1–7.
Xylinou:
GR Register (*glass*) 1888.11–12.1.
Xylotymbou:
GR Register 1884.12–10.274–6.
Yeri (Phoenikiais):
GR Registers 1884.12–10.115, 170, 184–202 (and perhaps others in this series, see note in register); 1978.7–17.1.

Collections

Ashbee bequest:
GR Registers 1980.10–7.1–16; 1982.7–21.1–77.
Castan Bey collection:
GR Reports 1879–80, pp. 24–7, 1/2/79; p. 105, 20/5/79.
Cesnola (Luigi Palma di) collection:[88]
Trustee minutes 24 April 1875 considering Birch report of 12 April; 9 October 1875 considering Birch report of 7 October and authorised Smith to visit Cyprus and report on the Cesnola Collection; 8 July 1876 considering Birch report of 7 July; 22 July 1876 considering Birch report of 21 July and resolution not to purchase the collection; 7 August 1880, considering letter from Birch of 6 August and Newton report of the same date, decision not to ask Cesnola to excavate on behalf of the Trustees.
Original Papers 1872 Letter from Cesnola of 14 December; 1879 Newton's report of 6 January.[89]
GR Reports 1875–6, pp. 387–8, letter of 11/11/76, pp. 393–404, 8/12/76; 1879–80, pp. 99–101, 105–7, 111, 121–3, 20/5/79, pp. 389–95, 6/8/80.
Parliamentary Reports 1871, p. 16.
GR Original Letters 1869–72, no. 593 with catalogue of sale of 1869; 1876–8, nos 57–61 (including 60a); 1879–82, nos 90–92; 1900–1903, nos 181–3.
GR Letter Books 1861–79, pp. 320, 451 (2), 453,454,455 (2), 471; 1880–96, p. 31.
ANE Original Letters Cesnola correspondence with Birch:1868–1881, nos 892–908, 910–1044 (December 1870 to July 1881);[90] 1882, nos 46–47 (Sept. 25 and Nov. 30[91]); 1883, no. 76 (11 Jan.).
ANE Original Letters 1868–1881, no. 909 (12 Jan. 1871), Birch to Newton (in Smyrna) enclosing photographs (not preserved) of Cesnola's collection.
GR Registers 1871.1–23.1–13;[92] 1871.2–10.1; 1871.3–11.1,2; 1871.7–8.1–6; 1875.3–10.1; 1876.9–9.1–127;

1876.11–14.1; 1911.11–17.1; 1969.12–31.13–23; 1982.7–26.1–92.
(*ANE Register* 89737 (1825.5.3, R173)).[93]
Colnaghi collection:
Original Papers 1866 Feb.7, Newton's report.
GR Reports 1864–6, pp. 333–4, 7/2/66.
Parliamentary Reports 1866, p. 18.
GR Original Letters 1861–1868, nos 176–195 which includes a report numbered 180; 1873–5, no. 74 (from K. Colnaghi).
GR Letter Books 1861–79, p. 279 (K. Colnaghi); 1880–96, pp. 44, 125 (D.E. Colnaghi)
GR Register 1866.1–1.1–358.[94]
Franks Bequest and other gifts:[95]
GR Registers 1868.8–10.18; 1871.2–10.1; 1871.3–11.1,2; 1876.5–15.1–4; 1879.11–19.2–9; 1885.4–18.1; 1892.5–23.3; 1916.6–1.28;[96] 1917.6–1.135,162–3, 776, 777, 779, 780, 1057,1178, 1182, 1340, 1563, 1564, 1571, 1616,1617; 1969.12–31.11–12, 24–53, 60–63, 135.
Earl Granville's collection:
GR Reports 1879–80, pp. 361–75, 8/7/80.
Greenwell Collection:[97]
GR Registers 1869.12–31.98–131; 1935.8.23.6; 1969.12–31.66.
Lawrence/Cesnola (Alexander) collection:[98]
Ms report in *Original Papers* 1881.
Copies of the catalogues of the 4 portions sold at Sotheby's 1883–1892.
GR Reports 1881–2, pp. 113–116, 22/6/81, pp. 141–2, 7/7/81; 1891–2, p. 201, 13/5/92.
GR Registers 1892.5–19.1–8; 1892.5–23.3; 1895.10–25.2–5; 1928.3–17.5,9; 1980.10–5.1–8; 1975.6–20.1–16; 1980.10–6.2–3; 1980.12–1.5–7, 9, 11–12,14,16, 18–20; 1980.21–2–24; 1981.8–5.2; 1981.8–10.1–11; 1982.3–2.14,16,17,19–28, 32,34.
Morel Collection:
GR Registers 1904.2–4.621; 1969.12–31.67–8.
Payne Knight Coins:
Trustee Minutes of 11 June 1825 records acceptance; 13 May 1826, resolution on publication of catalogue.
F.W. Robins Bequest:[99]
GR Registers 1963.7–15.13,14.
Sandwith Collection:[100]
GR Reports 1875–6, pp. 21–3, 24/2/75; 1897–8, pp. 99–100, Feb.98,[101] p. 133, 1/7/98, p. 152, 20/9/98.
Parliamentary Reports 1870, p. 16.
GR Original Letters 1861–8, nos 681–2; 1869–72, nos 571–5 (and nos 180–1 for mention of Sandwith); 1876–8, nos 305–6.
GR Letter Book 1861–70, pp. 145, 174–5, 243–4, 480–1, 484, 492.
GR Registers 1868.8–10.18; 1869.6–4.1–53; 1870.10–10.1–25; 1875.3–10.1; 1898.2–23.4.

Wellcome Collection:[102]
1975.7–12.83, 87–99, 102.

Miscellaneous Excavations etc.

BM reports, and excavations, purchases and gifts in general:
Original Papers 1846, Niven Kerr's report of 9 April;[103] 1879, Newton's report of 6 January;[104] 1897, Murray's report of 24 August.
Central Archive 'Original Letters' (copies of out-going letters), 4/5/1846 to Niven Kerr.[105]
GR Reports 1877–8, pp. 289–97, 25/7/78, pp. 97–129, 20/5/79 (Newton's Cyprus visit), pp. 389–95, 6/8/80; 1881–2, pp. 162–3, 1/10/81; 1885–6, p. 354, 23/9/86; 1887–8, p. 1, 3/1/87, p. 133, 14/10/87, pp. 217–8, 10/7/88; 1889–90, p. 78, 7/5/89;1891–2, p. 73, 9/6/91; 1891–2, p. 3, 7/1/91 (gift from Warren);1893–4, pp. 51–7, 1/6/93, p. 101, 22/9/93; 1895–6, p. 185, 31/8/96; 1897–8, p. 109, Feb. 98,[106] p. 142, 7/7/98; 1899–April 1902, p. 40, 3/5/99.
Parliamentary Reports 1852, p. 14; 1871, p. 16; 1875, p. 18; 1876, p. 15; 1879, pp. 20–21; 1889, p. 42; 1885, p. 31 (Franks); 1887, p. 37; 1888, p. 36 (Cyprus Exploration Fund); 1891, p. 58; 1892, pp. 58,60; 1894, p. 59 (Cobham gift); 1895, pp. 65, 68;[107] 1896, pp. 55, 57; 1898, p. 64; 1899, p. 64.
GR Original Letters 1879–82, no. 178.
GR Registers 1870.3–15.17,18;[108] 1882.10–12.1–3; 1887.7–12.1; 1900.5–21.1–3, 5–7; 1906.4–11.2; 1914.10–13.1; 1914.10–18.1; 1919.7–12.1; 1922.2–14.1; 1924.5–15.1; 1926.4–7.17; 1926.4–19.4; 1928.5–20.1; 1935.6–11.1–24; 1936.4–14.1; 1938.11–30.5; 1940.3–7.4; 1961.11–21.1; 1962.2–11.1; 1963.10–7.1; 1966.12–13.5, 10,12;[109] 1967.12–31.7–8;[110] 1969.2–25.1; 1971.10–30.1,2; 1973.4–15.1; 1974.11–1.1–21,23–38, 40–64; 1978.7–17.4; 1980.2–1.83; 1982.9–29.1–8;[111] 1985.10–8.1; 1987.11–9.1; 1 1991.7–16.3; 1991.12–18.2,3,15; 1993.4–6.1; 1995.4–3.1; 1998.1–22.1; 1999.8–2.1; 2000.2–14.1; 2001.1–29.1.[112]
ANE Registers 89508–9 (1871.2–9.1,2,4); 89734 and 89734b (1871.2–9.3,5); 1103266 (1871.2–9.6); 103270 (1871.2–9.7); 103273 (1871.2–9.8); 1871.2–9.9–11; 89252 (1871.2–11.1); 103269 (1871.2–11.2); 120283 (1871.2–11.4); 1871.2–11.3; 89122 (1884.6–30.1); 89358 (1884.6–30.2); 89336 (1884.6–30.4); 89338 (1884.6–30.5); 89357 (1884.6–30.6); 89342 (1884.6–30.7); 89360 (1884.10–13.2); 89536 (1888.5–12.778); 134359 (1889.10–15.5); 133026–7 (1962.12–12.1,2).
PEE Register unregistered, flat axe.
Cyprus Exploration Fund:
Correspondence and general finds: *GR Reports* 1887–8, pp. 267–8, 5/1/88.

Parliamentary Reports 1888, p. 36.
GR Original Letters 1898–9, nos 306–7.
GR Registers 1969.12–31.64; 1978.7–20.1.
Kitchener-Hake excavations:
Copy of V&A file detailing Hake's excavations.[113]
GR Reports 1879–80, pp. 297–300, 9/3/80, 361–375, 8/7/80; 1881–2, pp. 162–3, 1/10/81.
GR Registers (from Salamis, Mari, Gastria or Curium) 1980.10–1.1–210 and 1982.7–29.1–596.
Ohnefalsch-Richter's excavations (in general) and finds:
GR Reports 1883–4, pp. 13–17, 3/1/83, p. 335, 6/10/84.
Parliamentary Reports 1882, p. 27; 184, p. 34.
GR Original Letters 1879–82, no. 351; 1886–7 and 1888, miscellaneous now lost;[114] 1890, nos 211–212; 1891, 209–211; 1892–5, no. 844a; 1911–12, nos 504–8 (505 includes copies of earlier letters).[115]
GR Letter Book 1880–96, pp. 120, 144, 201,242, 327.
GR Registers 1868.9–5.1–57; 1881.8–24.1–178; 1884.10.6.1–6; 1884.12–10.1–332; 1895.10–25.1.
Miscellaneous Photographs 2, nos 53–75.
Warren's excavations:
GR Reports 1879–80, p. 3, 20/5/79, 361–375, 8/7/80.
GR Original Letters 1891, 314–8.
GR Letter Book 1880–9; pp. 97, 172, 228.
GR Register 1891.8–1.1.

Correspondence and acquisitions from vendors of Cypriot antiquities:

Castellani, Alessandro: Italian dealer who sold antiquities to the Museum between 1865 and 1882 including occasionally Cypriot pieces.
GR Registers 1873.8–20.747–9.
H. Housepian of Cairo and Limassol:
GR Original Letters 1898–9, nos 236–338; 1900–1903, nos 541–7, 553.
GR Letter Book 1896–1907, pp. 144,162, 213, 218, 225, 229, 144.
GR Register 1900.5–23.1–5.
C. Georgiades & co. of Nicosia:
GR Letter Book 1880–96, p. 323.
Kenon C. Malis of Larnaca:
GR Original Letters 1896–7, nos 372–8.
Karemphylako: mentioned as owner of antiquities in *Correspondence: Excavations in Cyprus* letter of 23 November 1897, but no letters from him survive.
Pilavachi of Limassol:
GR Original Letters 1892–5, nos 937–9.
Rollin and (G.L.) Feuardent of London:
GR Original Letters 1869–72, no. 554.
GR Register 1875.3–13.3,4.

Miscellaneous correspondents[117] and acquisitions without provenance (not listed elsewhere) with which they are associated:

Antoniou, Gregorios:[118]
GR Original Letters 1896–7, no. 192.
Caridi, J.:[119]
GR Original Letters 1889, nos 53–56.
GR Register 1889.11–10.1–3.
Chamberlayne, Tankerville:
GR Original Letters 1900–1903, nos 184–194.
Chester, The Rev. Greville:
GR Registers 1927.1–13.4; 1928.3–17.1,3; 1938.11–30. 6,7; 1969.12–31.11–12,24–53
Christian, Charles:
GR Original Letters 1888, nos 72–4; 1889, no. 70 a-e; 1890 nos 49–54; 1898–9, nos 80–84.
GR Letter Book 1896–1907, p. 54.
Christian, Percy:
GR Original Letters 1896–7, nos 68–72; 1898–9, 85–93; 1900–1903, nos 197–201.
GR Letter Books 1880–96, pp. 108, 118, 122, 179, 181, 184, 205, 258, 259,261, 1896–1907, pp. 43, 112, 118, 125,128, 131,133, 136, 146,151, 155–6, 164,165, 175, 222, 234, 255, 265, 260
GR Registers 1899.6–4.1,5,6; 1901.7–8.1,2; 1902.9–15.1–5; 1902.10.11.1.
Cobham, Claude Delaval:[120]
Correspondence: Excavations in Cyprus: letter of 8 November 1893 (his terracottas).
GR Original Letters 1886–7, nos 144–5; 1896–7, nos 81–2; 1898–9, nos 97–8; 1900–1903, nos 215–216.
ANE Original Letters 1868–1881, nos 1248–9 and 1249a.
GR Letter Books 1880–96, pp. 118–9, 310; 1896–1907, pp. 90–92, 157.
Book of Presents Supplementary vol.1, letter of 11 September 1882.
GR Registers 1894.3–16.1–3; 1894.6–17.1,2.
Colonna-Ceccaldi, T.:
GR Original Letters 1861–8, no. 150.[121]
Colnaghi, D.E.:
GR Original Letters 1861–8, nos 176–7.[122]
Gardner, E.A.:
GR Letter Book 1880–96, pp. 115, 183, 202, 275.
Haynes-Smith, Sir W.:
Correspondence: Excavations in Cyprus: letters of 14 February 1899, 17 February 1900.
Hiristmaitland:
GR Original Letters 1879–82, no. 287.
Legge, Walter:
GR Original Letters 1889, no. 140; 1890, no. 155.
Luke, Sir Harry:
GR Registers 1903.11–17.1.

Macmillan, G.A.:
GR Original Letters 1888, nos 226–8.
Mavrogordato, A.S.:
GR Original Letters 1896–7, nos 390–1.
Munro, J.A.R.:
GR Original Letters 1889, nos 176–8; 1890, nos 190 (and 190a)-193 (with photos); 1891, nos 193–7.
Myres, J.L.:
GR Original Letters 1898–9, nos 347 (refers to Ohnefalsch-Richter), 348.
Pierides, D.:
GR Original Letters 1861–8, nos 582–93; 1869–72, nos 495–7.
GR Registers 1868.9–5.1–57; 1869.6–8.1–48.
Pierides, G.D.:
Correspondence: Excavations in Cyprus: letter of 26 February 1898.
GR Original Letters 1898–9, nos 396–7.
GR Letter Books 1880–96, pp. 353–4, 355; 1896–1907, pp. 140, 264.
GR Registers 1896.10–18.1–5
Pierides, Kleanthes:
GR Original Letters 1906–8, nos 1231–54; 1909–10, nos 603–4; 1911–12, no. 533; 1913–14, nos 469–74.
GR Registers 1909.6–15.1,2.
Pierides, Zeno:
Correspondence: Excavations in Cyprus: letter of 28 April 1898.
Ready, W.T.:
GR Registers 1895.10–25.1.
Seager, Major:
GR Original Letters 1891, nos 270–2 and see under **Wolseley** below.
GR Registers 1891.6–30.1–4.
Sendall, Sir Walter:
Correspondence: Excavations in Cyprus: letters of 14 August 1893, 24 September 1897.
Letter Book 1896–1907, p. 57.
Walters, H.B.:
GR Original Letters 1892–5, no. 1367.
White, Lt. Colonel H.G.:
GR Original Letters 1879–82, nos 543–9.
Williamson, J.W.:
Correspondence: Excavations in Cyprus: letter of 24 June 1895.
GR Original Letters 1892–5, no. 1398; 1896–7, nos 733–741.
GR Letter Book 1896–1907, pp. 108, 166, 172, 244.
GR Registers 1896.10–15.3; 1899.6–3.1, 2.[123]
Wolseley, Garnet Joseph:
MS 41324 in the British Library contains his correspondence relating to Cyprus, the first letter written on 2 August 1876 and the last on 29 June 1879. It includes a letter of

support to Colonel Warren in his dispute with the Bishop of Kition written on 1st May 1879, a letter of 4 May to Major Seager appointing him Assistant Commissioner, and a letter of 5 February about Kitchener's survey. His interest in the British Museum is detailed in the appendix to this article.

Wood, J.T.:
GR Original Letters 1869–72, nos 559–60.

Notes

1. There is only room to briefly list the archives and no attempt is made to evaluate the information. I am most grateful to my colleagues Donald Bailey, who provided me with material and answered my questions, Lesley Fitton who read and commented on an earlier draft of this paper, colleagues from other antiquities departments who helped with their Cypriot archives, and Janet Wallace, Christopher Date, Stephen Corri (since promoted to the Director's Office) and Alexander Pullen of the Central Archive without whom this paper could not have been written.
2. See in general, Edward Miller, *That Noble Cabinet* (London 1973); B.F. Cook in B.F. Cook (ed.), *Cypriote Art in the British Museum* (London 1979) 4–5; V. Tatton-Brown, *Ancient Cyprus* (1st edition, London 1987) 4–6.
3. *Biographical Notices of Dr Samuel Birch* with an introduction by Walter de Gray Birch (London 1886).
4. *GR Reports* 1885–1886, p. 359, 4/10/86. W.T.Ready was probably related to Augustus Ready, conservator working for Birch and others, and perhaps also to W.J.Ready and sons who made electrotypes of some coins for the Museum. My thanks to Christopher Date for this information.
5. F.G. Kenyon, 'Arthur Hamilton Smith', *Proceedings of the British Academy* 37 (1942) 3–14.
6. E. Goring, *A Mischievous Pastime* (Edinburgh 1988) 1–39.
7. D.G. Hogarth, *Excavations at Ephesus. The Archaic Artemisia* (London 1908) 19 writes 'For the supervising of the workmen I used Gregorios Antoniou of Larnaca, who has had a longer experience of excavation work than perhaps any man on the active list in the Levant, having first served as a labourer and then, for over a quarter of a century, as an overseer on all sorts of sites. To his organising capacity, diligence, vigilance, and probity the success of our excavations is largely due.'
8. Cf. a number of papers in this volume, notably that of Emilia Masson; for a spirited account see E. McFadden, *The Glitter and the Gold* (New York 1971) and for a more sober assessment see now *Ancient Art from Cyprus. The Cesnola Collection* (Metropolitan Museum of Art, 2000) 3–15. See also the references in n. 88 below.
9. O. Masson, 'Diplomates et amateurs d'antiquités à Chypre vers 1866–1878', *Journal des Savants* (January-June 1992) 123–138.
10. For these excavations see D.M. Bailey, 'Lamps in the Victoria and Albert Museum', *Op. Ath.* VI (1965) 4–13 and *Catalogue of Lamps in the British Museum* III (1988) 294. Although the material from these excavations was transferred to the British Museum in 1980 (Tatton-Brown n.2), the records remain in the Victoria and Albert Museum. However, a copy of the excavation report is in the Greek and Roman department.
11. H. Waterhouse, *British School at Athens. The First Hundred Years* (London 1986) 10, 15.
12. Hogarth (n.7).
13. For the Pierides family see V. Karageorghis, *Ancient Cypriote Art in the Pierides Foundation Museum* (Larnaca 1985) 13–15 and 10–21 (by Aristides Koudonaris).
14. Cf. O. Masson, 'Nouvelles Variétés Chypriotes', *Centre d'études Chypriotes. Cahier* 24 (1995–2) 8–18 (hereafter, *Cahier*).
15. Waterhouse (n.11) especially 135.
16. See now H-G Buchholz, 'Max Ohnefalsch-Richter als Archäologe auf Zypern', *Cahier* 11–12 (1989) 3–28; Léon Fivel, 'Ohnefalsch-Richter (1850–1917), essai de bibliographie', *Cahier* 11–12 (1989) 35–44 and 'Lettre de M. Ohnefalsch-Richter à A.H. Smith', *Cahier* 21 (1994–1) 23–25 and 'Ohnefalsch-Richter vendeur d'antiquités Chypriotes (1895)', *Cahier* 25 (1996–1) 29–35; Margit Krapita, 'Max Hermann Ohnefalsch-Richter; bibliography and bibliographical remarks', *RDAC* (1992) 337–341; Melitta Brönner, 'Veranstaltungen anlässlich des Nachdrucks der Werke von Max und Magda Ohnefalsch-Richter, Nikosia/Zypern 1994', *Ethnographisch-Archäologisch Zeitschrift* 35 (1994) 320–1.
17. See also R.S.Merrillees, 'Sandwith' in this volume.
18. Olivier Masson, 'Le Colonel Falkland Warren à Chypre', *Cahier* 11–12 (1989) 29–34 and cf. Wolseley, p. 170–1 above.
19. *DNB* 1912–1921, 586–591.
20. See n.10.
21. Sir Robert Ensor, *England 1870–1914* (*the Oxford History of England*, Oxford 1936) 4 note 2.
22. These are the imprecations, see n.47 and n.49 below.
23. I. Stead, *The Gauls, Celtic Antiquities from France* (London 1981) 13.
24. M.L. Bierbrier, *Who was Who in Egyptology* (3rd. revised edition, London 1995) 329–32.
25. Bierbrier (n.24) 375.
26. His reports on these excavations are now lost, see D.M. Bailey, *Catalogue of Lamps in the British Museum* I (London 1975) 205 n.3. The postcard acknowledging receipt of his 'reports etc. of the excavations conducted by me for Sir Charles Newton in the years 1879–1883' is no. 211 in *GR Original Letters* 1891, and the letter of 2 August 1912 is no. 505 in *GR Original Letters* 1911–1912. The latter thanks Murray for returning 'some portion of the correspondence.... with Sir Charles Newton, A.H. Sayce, C.D. Cobham and Lord Leighton' (perhaps the parcel, p. 174 and n. 114 below), and complains that his reports etc. were never returned. This letter contains copies of letters written from Cyprus to Sir Charles Newton on 26 August 1882, and to Lord Leighton on 18 December 1882.
27. Other departments now denoted by PEE (Department Prehistory and Early Europe) and ANE (Department of The Ancient Near East). For coins the reader is referred to G.F. Hill, *Catalogue of The Greek Coins of Cyprus* (London 1904) and I. Carradice, 'The coinage of Roman Cyprus', in

V. Tatton-Brown (ed.), *Cyprus and the East Mediterranean in the Iron Age* (*Proceedings of the Seventh British Museum Classical Colloquium, April 1988*, London 1989) 182–5. Although, generally, archives up to *c.* 1900 have been included, GR registers into the 1990s have been perused in order to include items transferred from other departments in the Museum and from other museums and collections. *GR Register* 1917.7–1.1–303 for the most part re-registers items already included in our registers. Since 1980, the 1917 numbers have been removed, and only those pieces not registered previously are now known by numbers in that series. *GR Registers* 1927.3–18.1–55 and 1928.3–17.1–13 again re-register items that are listed here with their original registration numbers. There is a separate register for glass here denoted as *GR Register* (*glass*).

28. The volumes of *Original Letters*, in which the letters are numbered, are rarely indexed, and it is always necessary to know the name of the sender. All the volumes of GR *Original Letters* for the years 1861–1903 inclusive have been perused and it is hoped that all those relevant to Cyprus have been picked out. Letters from later volumes have come to my attention over the years, often from correspondence with the late Professor Olivier Masson. References here give the number(s) of the letter(s) in the relevant volume, rather than the date.

29. In these the pages (and letters) are numbered and it is to the page numbers that the references in this paper refer.

30. These are bound with several years together in one volume. The dates on the outside of each volume refer to the years in which each report was published, while tickets attached to the relevant places give the year (one year earlier in every case) to which each report refers. It is the latter date that is given in the references below. Not until the report for 1839 (published in 1840) is there any information about the activities of the departments, although three Under Librarians had been appointed to head three departments in 1756, and a Department of Antiquities was established in 1807 (see Miller n.2). The acquisitions listed in these reports have not been matched with the registers and so the objects are not precisely identified

31. Janet Wallace, head of the Central Archive, kindly wrote this section (my annotations in square brackets). For further information see her paper in *Archives* (*Journal of the British Records Association*) XIX, no. 84 (Oct. 1990) 213–222.

32. I would like to thank Mr Roger Castioglione for this gift, a valuable addition to our archives.

33. Cypriot finds from sites in Egypt are recorded in letters from Petrie, *GR Original Letters* 1886–7, nos 219–220; 1889, no. 206 (two letters); 1890, nos 200–1; 1898–9 (M-Z), no. 395

34. J.L. Myres and M. Ohnefalsch-Richter, *Catalogue of the Cyprus Museum* (Nicosia 1899) 2, sv. *Alambra*.

35. See n.26 above.

36. For these excavations see 'Amathonte au xixe siècle', *Cahier* 13 (1990) and *Amathonte I–III, Testimonia 1–3* (Paris 1982–6).

37. This refers to the imprecations (n.47 and n.49) without mention of findspot.

38. The precise date is illegible.

39. These are the imprecations discussed in n.47 and n.49 below.

40. Transferred to the Department of The Ancient Near East (ANE) 5/4/74.

41. E. Gjerstad *et al.*, *Swedish Cyprus Expedition* II (Stockholm 1935) 6–16, fig.6.2–3 and Alfred Westholm, 'Built tombs in Cyprus', *Op. Arch* II (1941) 34, no. 9.

42. D.M. Bailey, 'The village priest's tomb at Aradippou in Cyprus', *British Museum Quarterly* 34 (1969–70) 36–58.

43. These two terracottas may have come from this site see Colnaghi's letter of 28 February 1866 (no. 187 in *GR Original Letters* 1861–68), though 332 is perhaps from Pyrga and listed there also.

44. For the British Museum excavations see now T.B. Mitford, *The Inscriptions of Kourion* (Philadelphia 1971) 1–4. For the 1991 series see the paper by Bailey and Hockey in this volume.

45. GR Reports 1879–80, p. 13 notes that Newton's report of 6 January headed 'Proposed excavations in Cyprus' has been temporarily withdrawn, but a copy, without that specific heading, remains in *Original Papers* for 1879.

46. See n.10 above.

47. These talc imprecations, for which the vendor's letter (below) gives Curium as the provenance, are now believed to be from Amathus. In the register the provenance has been changed to Ayios Tychonas (Amathus) in the same hand as the original entry of Curium, and a letter from David Jordan of the University of California to my colleague Donald Bailey of 20 March 1989 says that 'the smaller collection of selenite [crystallised gypsum] fragments in the Bibliothèque National is part of the same lot from Amathus, for every piece in Paris joins a piece in London.'

48. This letter refers to Kourion as Episkopi inferring that some of the tombs were in fact located at the locality *Phaneromeni*.

49. See n.47 above. The letter in question is no. 119 of 14 January 1890.

50. J-C Courtois in J-C Courtois, J. and E. Lagarce, *Enkomi et le Bronze Récent à Chypre* (Nicosia 1986) 1.

51. See n.38 above.

52. Some of these finds may be from Mari and are listed here under that site also, see J.L. Myres and M. Ohnefalsch-Richter, *Catalogue of the Cyprus Museum* (Oxford 1899) 9.

53. See n.10 above.

54. Paul Åström, D.M. Bailey and Vassos Karageorghis, *Hala Sultan Tekké* I (*Studies in Mediterranean Archaeology* XLV.1, Göteborg 1976) 1–32.

55. See now R. Senff, *Das Apollonheiligtum von Idalion* (*Studies in Mediterranean Archaeology* XCIV, Jonsered 1993) 1–5.

56. Compare sketch in Colnaghi's report *GR Original Letters* 1861–8, no. 180.

57. These are all from Colnaghi's collection, also n.65 below.

58. These objects originally entered into the Department of Egyptian and Assyrian Antiquities. This department was divided into two in 1955 and the original registers of this collection are now housed in the Department of The Ancient

Near East (and not in the Department of Egyptian Antiquities as noted in the Greek and Roman register). The objects were transferred to Greek and Roman in 1917, except for those with Phoenician inscriptions that have the ANE long numbers recorded below. When transferred in 1917 several were re-registered in the series 1917.7–1. In 1980 these 1917 numbers were removed and the objects are now marked only with their original registration numbers (n.27 above).
59. These objects and their records are as for those of the 1872 series, but a copy of the register is now in the Greek and Roman Department.
60. These come from Ohnefalsch-Richter's excavations. A note in the register attributes most of them to 'the neighbourhood of Dali' but certain are known from other sources to come from other sites under which they are listed here.
61. See n.55 above.
62. Cf. G. Cadogan 'The British Museum's work at Maroni', in G.C. Ioaninides (ed.), *Studies in Honour of Vassos Karageorghis* (Nicosia 1992) 126, no. 6.
63. The reference is to Corso-ti-Yialani which is not identified in literature or on recent maps.
64. Bailey (n.42) 36–41.
65. These are from Colnaghi's collection, mentioned again below under collections, most of which probably came from the so-called sanctuary of Artemis Paralia at Larnaca (see D.M. Bailey, *Catalogue of Lamps in the British Museum* III (London 1988) 450, and A. Hermary, 'Divinités Chypriotes I', *RDAC* (1982) 166 note 25, who suggests that this sanctuary may have been dedicated to Aphrodite), though 1866.1–1.231 comes from a different site at Larnaca. Colnaghi's correspondence (also detailed under his name below), notably *GR Original Letters* 1860–1868, no. 187 (28 February 1866) and no. 184 (17 December 1865) provides information about the findspots of some of his finds which are listed here accordingly.
66. For these see *The Graphic* of 25 December 1880, a copy of which is in the *GR Register*.
67. This is Ohnefalsch-Richter's photo see *Kypros The Bible and Homer* (London 1893) 479, fig.263.
68. These are the 'Evangelis' tomb and the 'Cobham' tomb, see now V. Karageorghis, *Kition* (London 1976) 149–152, figs. 26–27.
69. F.G. Maier and V. Karageorghis, *Paphos. History and Archaeology* (Nicosia 1984) 17. The reports etc. usually speak simply of Paphos, but in the records it is often combined with mention of the Temple of Aphrodite, confirming Old Paphos (or Palaipaphos) as the true site.
70. Monoliths at other sites in Cyprus are also mentioned in this article as well as in *The Athenaeum* 3172, 11 August 1888, p. 201; 3174, 25 August 1888, p. 206; 3177; 15 September 1888, pp. 359–60. For those at Palaipaphos see now S. Hadjisavvas, 'The Kouklia monoliths revisited', *RDAC* (1991) 185–90.
71. From R.T. Günther of Magdalen College, Oxford.
72. This does not seem to be mentioned in any literature concerning Cyprus to the end of the Roman period, but Newton mentions tombs here in his report of his visit (20/5/79), *GR Reports* 1879–80 p. 115 (p. 9 of the report).
73. Cadogan (n.62).
74. See n.66 above.
75. J. Johnson, *Maroni de Chypre* (Studies in Mediterranean Archaeology LXIX, Göteborg 1980) 7–8; Cadogan (n.62) 123–6.
76. Cf. n.70 above.
77. See now Maier and Karageorghis (n.69) 267–9.
78. See now Olivier Masson, 'Kypriaka. II, Recherches sur les antiquités de la region de Pyla', *BCH* XC (1966) 9–11, figs. 5–6; also P. Dikaios, 'Built tomb near Pyla', *RDAC* (1934) 9–11, pl. III and plan.
79. See *GR Original Letters* 1861–8 nos 181 (15.4.65), 184 (17.12.65), 187 (28.2.66); first published, Veronica Tatton-Brown, 'A terracotta "Geryon" in the British Museum', *RDAC* (1979) 285–288, pl. xxxii.
80. Colnaghi's collection see n.65 above.
81. Veronica Wilson, 'The Tubbs-Munro excavations at Salamis 1890', in *Salamine de Chypre* (Colloques Internationaux du CNRS no. 578, Paris 1980) 59–70.
82. From 'Lord Kitchener 1882–1910' file at the Victoria and Albert Museum, now housed in the Greek and Roman Department and see n.10 above.
83. See n.45 above.
84. See now, V. Karageorghis, *Excavations in the Necropolis of Salamis* I (Nicosia 1967) 90–116 (Tomb 50).
85. V. Karageorghis, *Excavations in the Necropolis of Salamis* IV (Nicosia 1978) 27–58
86. Hans-Günter Buchholz, 'Tamassos-Phrangissa (1885)', *Cahier* 16 (1991–2) 3–15.
87. See now, H-G Buchholz, 'Tamassos, Zypern 1973. 2. Bericht', *AA* (1974) 554–614 and 'Tamassos, Zypern 1977 bis 1986. Vierter Bericht', *AA* (1987) 165–228.
88. Olivier Masson, 'Quelques épisodes de la vie des frères Palma di Cesnola', *RDAC* (1990) 285–297 and 'La dispersion des antiquités Chypriotes; les deux collections Cesnola', *Cahier* 25 (1996–1) 3–29 and 'Les deux collections Cesnola: quelques complements', *Cahier* 26 (1996–2) 25–28. Note also that texts of four of Cesnola's lectures entitled 'Cyprus: its Ancient Art and History' were published (with illustrations) in a supplement, *Extra No. 47*, to the *New York Tribune* of 27 November 1878.
89. See n.45 above.
90. O. Masson, 'Les frères di Cesnola et leur correspondance', in Tatton-Brown (n.27) 85.
91. This letter (no. 47) enclosed cuttings from American newspapers that are still preserved and pasted in the letter volume.
92. Glass vessels originally in Cesnola's collection bought from a sale at Sotheby and Wilkinson and given by the executors of the late Felix Slade, renowned for his glass collection (see H. Tait, 'Felix Slade. A collector in uncharted waters, 1790–1868', *The Glass Circle Journal* 8 (1996) 70–87).
93. Cesnola claimed that this seal was part of his Kourion treasure, though it has now been shown to have come to the British Museum with the Rich Collection, D. Collon, *Catalogue of the Western Asiatic Seals in the British Museum. Cylinder Seals* III (London 1982) 125, no. 255, pl. xxi. My thanks to Dr Dominique Collon for bringing this to my attention.

94. 1866.1-1.316,318,319 are lamps of the Christian period now housed in the Department of Medieval and Modern Europe (MME), see Bailey (n.10, *Lamps* III) 290-1, 318, Q2352, 2615, 2353.
95. See now M. Caygill and J. Cherry (eds.), *A.W. Franks. Nineteenth century collecting and the British Museum* (London 1997).
96. Given by Lord Avebury.
97. Canon Greenwell's collection was bought and then donated to the Museum by the American millionaire J.Pierpont Morgan in 1909.
98. Cf. Masson (n.88, *RDAC*).
99. D.M. Bailey, 'Some lamps from the F.W. Robins Collection', *BMQ* 37 (1963-4) 88.
100. Only Sandwith's Cyprus connections are listed here. For his activities in Crete see Sinclair Hood, 'An early British interest in Knossos', *ABSA* LXXXII (1987) 85-94.
101. See n.38 above.
102. These form part of the collection of Sir Henry Wellcome (1853-1936), co-founder of the large pharmaceutical firm of Burroughs, Wellcome and co., and an avid collector from 1896. In 1917 the collection was transferred to the Science Museum. When pruning the collection so as to concentrate on medical items, the Wellcome Trustees gave archaeological material to this Museum in 1964, 1975 and 1982.
103. This is an extract as explained in the accompanying letter in *Original Papers* letter of 7 April 1846 and see now, Veronica Tatton-Brown, 'The British Museum discovers Cyprus', *Cahier* 28 (1998) 113-5.
104. See n.45 above.
105. This expresses the trustees' disinclination to excavate in Cyprus, but offers £20.00 for the stele identified as the 'Sargon stele' erected at Kition in about 707BC and now in Berlin, G. Hill, *A History of Cyprus* I (Cambridge 1940) 104 and note 2.
106. See n.100 above.
107. p. 68 records lead weights from Sidon bearing Cypriot and Greek inscriptions which are *GR Register* 1895.10-22.5-7.
108. These came with Biliotti's collection through Rollin and Feuardent. Alfred Biliotti was British Vice-Consul in Rhodes where he excavated. The results of his latest excavations were sold in London in 1885.
109. Given by my colleague Dr Donald Bailey.
110. Also donated by Dr Bailey.
111. Also transferred from the Victoria and Albert Museum.
112. The piece of rope (1991) comes from near Skouriotissa, north of the Troodos mountains, in the copper-yielding area of the island. The statuette (1995) may be from S. Pozzi's collection sold in Paris in 1919. The terracotta figurine (1995) was formerly in the Schmïdt collecion (a Swiss collection of the 1950's).
113. See n.10 above and mention under Wolseley pp. 170-1, above.
114. A note in the relevant place (no. 397) in *GR Original Letters* 1886-7 under the heading 'Max Ohnefalsch-Richter' and dated 26/5/88 reads 'Many letters received between 1886-8 have been withdrawn and placed in a separate parcel pending further orders from Mr Murray', but see n.26 above.
115. Fivel (n.16, *Cahier* 21).
116. Many of these may be from around Idalion, but some may come from Alambra (see p. 163 and n.26 above). Those whose provenances are known from other sources are listed under the appropriate site.
117. Some of the letters given under the sites above are also from these correspondents.
118. He is also mentioned in letters in the volume *Correspondence: Excavations in Cyprus* and see n.7 above.
119. J. Caridi of Caridi, Taylor & Co., general merchants of Gracechurch Street, London. The antiquities belonged to J. Parlides of Cyprus.
120. He is also mentioned several times in Newton's reports as in that of his Cyprus visit and in the presentation of Earl Granville's antiquities, and also as a host in many of the letters in the volume *Correspondence: Excavations in Cyprus*.
121. Bailey (n.10, *Lamps* III) especially 137-8.
122. These letters are not concerned with his collection.
123. See letter from Percy Christian of 29 August 1898, *GR Original Letters* 1898-9, nos 87-88, with wax impression.

APPENDIX

(these minutes were transcribed, and are reproduced here by permission of The British Museum Central Archive).

Transcriptions from the Minutes of the Trustees' Standing Committee (prefixed 'C.')

Cyprus/ Wolseley/ Excavations

(C 14399–400) Meeting of 27.7.1878

The Trustees approved a suggestion made by Mr Newton, in a report dated 25th July, that a representation be made to the Government to the effect that in any contract which the Government may enter into for dredging the harbour of Famagosta [?], or any other ancient harbour in Cyprus, the right to all treasure or antiquities should be reserved; and that in allotting waste land to purchasers, or tenants, it would be well to reserve the right to explore all ancient sites, as was done by the Greek Government after Greece was given up by the Turks.

(C 14419) Meeting of 12.10.1878

A letter dated 6th August, from the Foreign Office, stating that a copy of the Principal Librarian's letter of the 2nd August, representing the wish of the Trustees that the Government should reserve the right to all treasure or antiquities found in Cyprus, will be sent to Sir Garnet Wolseley; and that the suggestions made on the part of the Trustees will be borne in mind (C 14,399–400)

(C 14508–9) Meeting of 14.12.1878

Read a letter, dated 13th of December from the Foreign Office – stating that Sir Garnet Wolseley had expressed a wish that an archaeologist should visit Cyprus and carry on excavation on behalf of the Government:– that Lord Salisbury could not, at present, sanction any expenditure for this purpose out of the revenues of the Island; but that if the Trustees would send out an archaeologist, he would be furnished with letters to Sir Garnet Wolseley, who would give him all assistance in his power:– also a report thereon, dated 14th December, by Mr Newton, recommending Mr R P Pullan as a competent archaeologist to be sent to Cyprus; and stating that the cost of such a mission ought not to exceed one thousand pounds for the first twelve months, and might be much less.
Ordered – That application be made to the Treasury for funds for this purpose.

(C 14532–3) Meeting of 11.1.1879

Read a letter, dated 31st December, from the Treasury, stating that the Lords Commissioners admit to the full the value of the proposed archaeological mission to Cyprus, but regret that they are not prepared [to] sanction the expenditure that would be entailed by it in 1879–80 (C 14508–9); also a report, dated the 6th of January, by Mr Newton, recommending that tentative excavations be commenced; suggesting sites for the earlier researches; proposing that the expenditure be limited in the first instance to such a sum as might be available from unexpended balances of the vote for the current and ensuing financial years; and asking that he might be allowed to visit Cyprus to inspect the sites referred to.
Ordered – That application be made to the Treasury for a grant of £300 to enable Mr Newton to visit Cyprus, and to direct tentative excavations.

(C 14571–2) Meeting of 8.2.1879

The Trustees had before them a letter, dated the 22nd of January, from the treasury, expressing the regret of the Lords Commissioners that they cannot sanction expenditure for the proposed excavations in Cyprus. (C 14,532–3)

The Trustees took into consideration – 1. A report, dated the 1st of February, by Mr Newton, submitting – 2. An extract of a letter, dated the 13th of January, from Colonel Warren, Commissioner at Limasol, respecting the offer for sale of a collection of Cyprian antiquities in Cyprus, belonging to Castan Bey, who had asked £700 for it, but who, it was thought, might possibly take less: 3. A letter, dated the 21st January, from Mr J. Wood, who had recently visited Cyprus, stating that the two most promising sites for excavations are Kurion and Dali.

Mr Newton having stated that he thought it was very desirable that he should have an opportunity of examining and reporting, with as little delay as possible, on the collection belonging to Castan Bey, it was Resolved, That the Trustees agree that Mr Newton's going out for this purpose be sanctioned.

(C 14705–6) Meeting of 24.5.1879

The Trustees had before them a report, dated 20th May, by Mr Newton, giving an account of his mission to Cyprus for the purpose of examining Castan [?] Bey's collection of antiquities (C 14,571–72) and indicating the sites which had come under his notice as suitable for exploration in the case of future excavations in the Island.
Ordered – That the thanks of the Trustees be returned to Sir Garnet Wolseley, the Commissioners of districts, Officers of the Royal Engineers and to others who had assisted Mr Newton in his mission.

16. Collecting vases with figurines/protomes in the nineteenth century AD

Frieda Vandenabeele

I hope that this short detective story about Cypriot jugs with figurines holding an oinochoe, more exceptionally a bull's head, and once a ram's head (leaving aside those with an anthropomorphic face or a zoomorphic protome, which will be treated in detail by Karin Nys in her doctoral thesis to be submitted at the Vrije Universiteit Brussel [Free University Brussels]), will be my last contribution on this subject since my book *Figurines on Cypriote Jugs Holding an Oinochoe* came out as number 120 of the series *Studies in Mediterranean Archaeology* (*SIMA*), Paul Åström's Förlag, Jonsered 1998 (cited hereafter as Vandenabeele 1998a). Nevertheless, I am afraid that some supplements may follow because new items (Athens, National Museum: Vandenabeele 1998a, 111 n. 97; Cyprus, Private Collections; Marion, Neapaphos District Museum: Christou 1997, 900–01, fig. 41–2; and, probably, Manchester, Manchester Museum, University of Manchester, some of which have already been published in an addendum, Vandenabeele 1998a, 223–24, pl. CXXXIII: A-B) have been brought to my attention. I hope others will follow, such as the jugs sold in 1928 by the Trustees of the Metropolitan Museum of Art (cf. *infra*) to J. A. Plimpton and Arnold Genthe. Fortunately, I did not call my study a corpus.

None will contest that these jugs were created by the Cypriots of the western part of the island in the sixth century BC, i.e. in the Cypro-Archaic II period (ca. 600 BC to 475 BC) and that the Cypriots continued to produce this type of vessel until the beginning of the Hellenistic period, i.e. until about 300 BC (Vandenabeele 1998a, chapters I and II).

Forerunners were probably Bichrome IV and Bichrome Red I (IV) jugs of the eighth-seventh centuries BC (i.e. of the Cypro-Archaic I period ca. 750/725 BC to ca. 600 BC) showing a schematic human form with the face rendered on the neck of the jug opposite the handle, the grooved rim suggesting a headdress, two modelled arms on the shoulder of the vessel holding a pierced receptacle and two modelled legs extending underneath onto the belly of the vase (Vandenabeele 1998a, 33–4, pl. I: a-b).

However, it is not until the extensive excavations of Ohnefalsch-Richter at Marion (Hellenistic Arsinoe) in 1886 in necropolis II, to the east of the modern village of Polis Chrysochous, and in necropolis I and III to the west (Vandenabeele 1998a, 103), that for the first time numerous examples were brought to light. A third of the finds and, assumedly, a third of the jugs, remained in Cyprus (Myres & Ohnefalsch-Richter 1899, 78–80); the rest were mostly dispersed by auction in Paris in 1887 (Froehner 1887, passim; Hellmann 1982, passim; Hellmann 1991, passim). According to my initial investigations, published in *Cahier* 22/2 (1994) 19–31 entitled 'Ohnefalsch-Richter – Cesnola: ou la recherche des cruches à terres cuites tenant une oinochoé', cited hereafter as Vandenabeele 1994, the Musée du Louvre, Paris, acquired the largest amount, namely a group of thirty-four jugs or jug fragments (Vandenabeele 1994, 22; Vandenabeele 1998a, 109; Vandenabeele 1998b, 230–31, 397–411). Fourteen more are preserved in other European museums: six in the Staatliche Museen zu Berlin, Preussischer Kulturbesitz, Antikensammlung (Vandenabeele 1994, 23; Vandenabeele 1998a, 109–10), three in the Nationalmuseet, Copenhagen (Vandenabeele 1994, 22; Vandenabeele 1998a, 109), two in the Goluchow collection (Vandenabeele 1994, 22–3; Vandenabeele 1998a, 111), which I traced in the National Museum, Warsaw, two in the British Museum, London (Vandenabeele 1994, 23; Vandenabeele 1998a, 110) and probably one in the Ny Carlsberg Glyptotek, Copenhagen, bought by Løytved in Beirut in 1886 (Vandenabeele 1994, 24; Vandenabeele 1998a, 109 and n. 85). So forty-eight examples from

Ohnefalsch-Richter's excavations are without any doubt in European museums outside Cyprus. In 1994, I could assume that seven more were preserved in the Cyprus Museum, Nicosia (Vandenabeele 1994, 24–6; Vandenabeele 1998a, 108). Meanwhile, further research on the style, and particularly on the workshops, of more than three hundred jugs or jug fragments known to me has enabled me to attribute more jugs to Ohnefalsch-Richter's and Cesnola's excavations.

So, fifteen more jugs, preserved in the Cyprus Museum, Nicosia and catalogued in 1935 as without provenance, come most probably from Ohnefalsch-Richter's excavations. They all belong to a Marion workshop as demonstrated in my book (Vandenabeele 1998a, 82–4). I shall only briefly refer to new and different identifications – no illustrations accompany this paper, but the plate and catalogue number are indicated in bold after Vandenabeele 1998a – scattered throughout the chapters in my book on the history of excavations (Vandenabeele 1998a, 101–6) and the history of collections (Vandenabeele 1998a, 107–13). Seven Bichrome Red II (V) jugs with a figurine holding the oinochoe with both hands, category B of my classification (Vandenabeele 1998a, 57–8), which begins in the Cypro-Archaic II period and continues through Cypro-Classical I and primarily on Bichrome Red vases, could be ascribed to workshops of Marion or of its surroundings and, consequently, most probably come from Ohnefalsch-Richter's explorations. Some of these vessels have a tomb number, but none has a necropolis number. They are inventoried as C 389 (Vandenabeele 1998a, 124 no. 29.B, pl. XVII: 29.B) with further annotation T.33, C 390 (Vandenabeele 1998a, 124 no. 30.B, pl. XVII: 30.B); C 393 (Vandenabeele 1998a, 125–26, pl. XVIII: 32.B) with further annotation T.107.11; C 398 (Vandenabeele 1998a, 127–28 no. 37.B, pl. XX: 37.B), with further annotation T.10.11, C 377 (Vandenabeele 1998a, 129 no. 41.B, pl. XXI: 41.B); C 378 (Vandenabeele 1998a, 137–38 no. 68.B, pl. XXXIII: 68.B) with further annotation T.126/1; and C 381 (Vandenabeele 1998a, 139 no. 71.B, pl. XXXIV: 71.B). To this group we can add one Bichrome Red III (VI) jug, C 388 (Vandenabeele 1998a, 133–34 no. 55.B, pl. XXVII: 55.B) and two figurines C 298 (Vandenabeele 1998a, 134 no. 58.B, pl. XXVIII: 58.B) and C 299 (Vandenabeele 1998a, 130 no. 45.B, pl. XXII: 45.B). Two other jugs with a figurine having the left arm alongside the body, category D of my classification (Vandenabeele 1998a, 58–9), may equally originate from Marion or its surroundings. One (C 310) belongs to the Red Slip IV (VI) class (Vandenabeele 1998a, 149 no. 106.D, pl. XLIX: 106.D), the other (C 376) to the Polychrome (VII) class (Vandenabeele 1998a, 151 no. 116.D, pl. LII: 116.D). A Plain White VII jug (C 408) with two *peplophorai* (Vandenabeele 1998a, 180 no. 196.H, pl. LXXXIV: 196.H) reflecting an Attic style of the second half of the fifth century BC and executed in a Greek technique (that is, hollow, with the front made in different moulds and the back handmade with a rectangular vent) as well as a Cypriot derivative C 294 (Vandenabeele 1998a, 180 no. 197.H, pl. LXXXIV: 197.H) may also be considered as products of Marion together with five similar examples excavated by others. An additional object, which surely can be attributed to Ohnefalsch-Richter's work at Marion, is a fragment with an Eros (C 296: Vandenabeele 1998a, 200 no. 258.L, pl. XC: 258.L), also executed in a Greek technique and closely resembling the Eros of the Aphrodite group found by the Princeton University excavations at ancient Marion (Serwint 1993, 207–21). On the contrary, an attribution to Ohnefalsch-Richter's excavation of a group of three Polychrome (VII) jugs, C 308 (Vandenabeele 1998a, 184–85 no. 208.I, pl. LXXXIX: 208.I), C 316 (Vandenabeele 1998a, 185 no. 209.I, pl. LXXXIX: 209.I) and C 318 (Vandenabeele 1998a, 185 no. 210.I, pl. LXXXIX: 210.I) with a figurine in Boeotian style and most probably belonging to a Marion workshop, is less certain, because one of the jugs, C 308, is marked B.T.8, which possibly stands for British Tomb 8.

The history of Luigi Palma di Cesnola's discoveries and collecting of jugs which have a figurine holding an oinochoe opposite the handle, seems, at first, quite clear, as most of the vessels were acquired by the Metropolitan Museum of Art in New York between 1874 and 1876 (Vandenabeele 1994, 29; Vandenabeele 1998a, 112), except for one which was bought by the British Museum, London in 1876 (Vandenabeele 1994, 29; Vandenabeele 1998a, 110). Problems arose when the Trustees of the Metropolitan Museum of Art made the decision in 1928 to sell part of the Cypriote collection as duplicates (Vandenabeele 1998a, 112 n. 104). Fortunately, the annotated catalogue of the Metropolitan Museum of Art permitted me in 1994 to link one jug with a gift to the Walters Art Gallery, Baltimore after the death of Mrs Samuel C. Lamport in 1955 (Vandenabeele 1994, 29; Vandenabeele 1998a, 170–71 no. 165.G, pl. LXXII: 165.G) and to link another with a jug in the John and Mable Ringling Museum, Sarasota (Vandenabeele 1994, 29, Vandenabeele 1998a, 174–75 no. 177.G, pl. LXXVI: 177.G). A visit to this museum in December 1997 provided new evidence for two seemingly lost Cesnola finds, one illustrated in Palma di Cesnola 1894, pl. CXXXIV: 987 (Vandenabeele 1998a, 163 no. 147.F.bis, pl. LXV: 147.F.bis) and the other probably mentioned in the annotated catalogue *Cypriote & Classical Antiquities. Duplicates of the Cesnola & other Collections. Sold by Order of the Trustees of the Metropolitan Museum of Art, The Anderson Galleries.* (New York 1928) on p. 134 no. 510 without photograph (Vandenabeele 1998a, 208 no. 285.O, pl. CXXII: 285.O). The latter is an unexpected second representation of a Hermes, the first being preserved in the Ny Carlsberg Glyptotek, Copenhagen (Vandenabeele 1998a, 208 no. 284.O, pl. CXXII: 284.O).

Besides the two major collectors, Ohnefalsch-Richter and Cesnola, who were treated in Vandenabeele 1994, some others contributed to the discovery of jugs having a figurine holding an oinochoe opposite the handle, which were discovered at Kourion in the nineteenth century. The Vicomte de Castillon Saint-Victor (see the paper of Dr. Andrew Oliver and Dr. Diana Buitron', 'The Vicomte de Castillon Saint-Victor at Kourion', delivered at the colloquium but to be published elsewhere), consul of France at Larnaca, uncovered two such examples in tomb XV during his 'excavations' of 1886–1887 on the spot of the presumed 'subterranean chambers' of the so-called 'Curium treasure'. The figurine (Vandenabeele 1998a, 117–18 no. 7.A, pl. VIII: 7.A; Vandenabeele 1998b, 396) and the Bichrome Red III (VI) jug (Vandenabeele 1998a, 158–59 no. 134.F, pl. LX: 134.F; Vandenabeele 1998b, 405) are now preserved in the Musée du Louvre, Paris. Another Polychrome (VII) jug was brought to light by the 1882 'excavations' of Lt. Kitchener under the supervision of George Gordon Hake. Until recently, this vessel was preserved in the Victoria and Albert Museum, London, but it was transferred in the 1980's to the British Museum (Vandenabeele 1998a, 188–89 no. 223.I, pl. XCV: 223.I). Finally, once again Ohnefalsch-Richter, who by now was excavating by order of Colonel Falkland George E. Warren in the name of the British Museum, together with Charles Newton of the British Museum, gave us three more jugs: one Plain White VII, preserved in the Ny Carlsberg Glyptotek, Copenhagen (Vandenabeele 1998a, 208 no. 284.O, pl. CXXII: 284.O), one Red Slip V (VII) in the Cyprus Museum (Vandenabeele 1998a, 210 no. 289.Q, pl. CXXIV: 289.Q) and one now lost (Vandenabeele 1998a, 150 no. [112.D], pl. L: [112.D]). The brother of Luigi Palma di Cesnola, Alessandro, provided one more, which cannot now be traced (Vandenabeele 1998a, 215 no. [305.X], pl. CXXIX: [305.X]).

So far the discoveries of the nineteenth century prior to more scientific British excavations by the Cyprus Exploration Fund and by the Trustees of the British Museum in the last quarter of the nineteenth century at Amathus, Enkomi, Kourion, Marion, etc.

In conclusion, I wish to summarize the problems created by predecessors of the late nineteenth-century excavations, primarily Ohnefalsch-Richter and Luigi Palma di Cesnola. Not only has most of the scientific information been lost, with the exception of perhaps the provenance – and therefore one needs a serious sense of detection – but the dispersal throughout so many museums in Europe and the United States made the study of the jugs having a figurine holding an *oinochoe* opposite the handle very difficult. Not only were there considerable travel expenses, but also much time was necessary to visit so many museums and collections, and comparisons had to be made mostly based on a database and photographs. Only in some rare cases could actual jugs be compared side by side.

Bibliography

Christou 1997: D. Christou, 'Chronique des fouilles et découvertes archéologiques à Chypre en 1996', *BCH* 121 (1997), 891–933.

Froehner 1887: W. Froehner, *Antiquités chypriotes. Catalogue des objets trouvé à Arsinoé* (Paris 1887).

Hellmann 1982: M.-Chr. Hellmann, *Wilhelm Froehner (1834–1925)* (Paris 1982).

Hellmann 1991: M.-Chr. Hellmann, 'W. Froehner et Chypre', *Centre des Études Chypriotes. Cahier* 16 (1991), 17–28.

Myres & Ohnefalsch-Richter 1899: J.L. Myres & M. Ohnefalsch-Richter, *A Catalogue of the Cyprus Museum* (Oxford 1899).

Palma di Cesnola 1894: L. Palma di Cesnola, *A Descriptive Atlas of the Cesnola Collection of Cypriote Antiquities in the Metropolitan Museum of Art, New York* II (New York 1894).

Serwint 1993: N. Serwint, 'An Aphrodite and Eros Statuette from Ancient Cyprus', *RDAC* (1993), 207–21.

Vandenabeele 1994: Fr. Vandenabeele, 'Ohnefalsch-Richter – Cesnola: ou la recherche des cruches à terres cuites tenant une oinochoé', *Centre des Études Chypriotes. Cahier* 22/2 (1994), 19–31.

Vandenabeele 1998a: Fr. Vandenabeele, *Figurines on Cypriote Jugs Holding an Oinochoe* (SIMA 120, Jonsered 1998).

Vandenabeele 1998b: Fr. Vandenabeele, 'Les vases à figurines', 'Les figurines vases, les figurines d'applique de vase', in A. Caubet (ed.), S. Fourrier, A. Queyrel, Fr. Vandenabeele, *L'Art des modeleurs d'argile. Antiquitiés de Chypre. Coroplastique. Musée du Louvre, Département des Antiquités Orientales* tomes 1 et 2 (Paris 1998), 230–31, 396–411.

Early travellers and excavators

17. Melchior de Vogüé *et alii* and Cyprus

Lucie Bonato

Study of the archives of Melchior de Vogüé[1] brings about renewed interest in the work of this great scholar. From unpublished information, found essentially in his voluminous correspondence, we can evoke today, with greater accuracy, the relations he had with Cyprus.

Without going into the life and work of Melchior de Vogüé (Fig. 17.1), a multi-talented personality,[2] we can, nevertheless, mention that he was born in Paris on 18 October 1829 and after brilliant studies embarked on a diplomatic career. It was, however, during his first voyage to the Orient from 11 May 1853 to 21 May 1854 that he discovered his orientalist vocation, possibly in Palmyra, where he dreamt of translating the texts he had discovered, or perhaps in Beirut with his friend the antiquarian Aimé Péretié, chancellor of the French consulate, as he wrote in 1854:[3] 'Jamais je n'oublierai les heures passées à admirer les chefs-d'œuvre qu'il a su réunir et à m'instruire à son intéressante conversation'.

In 1861, he decided to revisit the Orient and join his friend Henry William Waddington (1826–1894) who had been in Syria for more than a year. It was during this second voyage, and within the period covering the year 1862, that de Vogüé directed the continuation of Ernest Renan's mission in Phoenicia, one of whose objectives was the exploration of Cyprus. On 17 December 1861 he wrote to Renan:[4] 'C'est à vous, et à vous seul que j'ai affaire. Je vais en Orient, de mon propre mouvement, et une fois là, je me charge, en votre absence, de prendre provisoirement la direction de vos travaux'.

The next day Renan replied with a long letter in which he notes:[5] 'Je ferai le rapport à l'Empereur de toute cette dernière partie de la mission comme je l'ai fait pour la côte de Phénicie'.

These reports, if they ever existed, have disappeared and the results of the mission to Cyprus were never

Fig. 17.1: Melchior de Vogüé (courtesy Marquis Pierre de Vogüé).

published neither by Renan nor by de Vogüé. In the absence of adequate and precise information, no overall synthesis of the progress of the mission has yet been made, but the rediscovery of the circumstances, as well as the results, are well known thanks to the work of Annie Caubet, Antoine

Hermary and the late Olivier Masson. Nevertheless, we now possess new evidence with which to make a case and I propose to concentrate here on certain aspects of the mission.

Melchior de Vogüé, accompanied by Edmond Duthoit, left Marseilles on 22 December 1861 and arrived in Beirut on 2 January 1862 where he re-joined Waddington. On 28 January all three disembarked on the island to which they devoted the first part of their work. The mission lasted four months until 1 June and raises a number of questions.

The first question that we may pose is: what documents and what information had de Vogüé at his disposal before his departure?

We now know that he had in his hands letters of recommendation to the consular agents given by Renan[6] and he possessed information contained in two important letters from which extracts are given below. The first is that mentioned above which was written by Renan and dated 18 December 1861: 'Chacune de nos campagnes en Syrie se composait de deux parties: 1. L'exploration aussi complète que possible du pays, le relevé *absolument complet* des inscriptions du pays, ne laissant aucune indication, quelque vague et peu autorisée qu'elle fût, sans la vérifier; la description et, quand nous le pouvions, le dessin ou la photographie des monuments. 2. Des fouilles sur les points qui nous attiraient et où de pareils travaux n'offraient pas d'insurmontables difficultés. Vous voudrez sans doute faire de même pour Chypre, et nous apporter l'estampage ou la copie de toutes les inscriptions même byzantines'.

The second is a letter from Sosthène Grasset addressed to Renan and dated 10 July 1861.[7] Grasset (1828–1900), a young Frenchman living in the island since 1855, was then hoping to be put in charge of the mission and had contacted Renan to this effect:[8] '...j'ai dit à Madame Cornu que le périple de Chypre est tout maritime et que la meilleure manière de le faire est d'avoir un aviso de l'Etat à sa disposition. On emporte avec soi les bras et les vivres qui manquent partout et on enlève d'emblée et à peu de frais les morceaux qui en valent la peine et qui sont nombreux à la surface du sol, sans compter ce que les fouilles peuvent faire découvrir'. Grasset then gives a detailed list of the sites to visit, namely Salamis, Famagusta, Larnaca, Amathus, Kouklia etc. and mentions Dali as a field of inexhaustible excavations. Attached to this letter was a drawing representing the vase of Amathus and an aeolic capital that he curiously calls 'idalien'. He wrote on the left: 'à Famagouste, côté sud de la cathédrale au pied d'un escalier à environ 50 mètres'. This capital was drawn by Duthoit who also noted on his sketch 'Famagusta'. The Louvre holds a similar aeolic capital, found in Trapeza according to Longpérier.[9] This casts doubt on the origin of this capital.[10]

In addition, while they were already conducting their exploration, probably at the end of February, de Vogüé received from Emmanuel Guillaume-Rey some maps of Cyprus and rough sketches of the fortifications of Famagusta with a letter dated 9 February 1862.[11] In this letter he gave him some advice: 'Vous allez trouver en Chypre Grasset, c'est un garçon intelligent et qui pourra vous être utile. Il est artiste et connaît bien le pays. Dans le cours de vos travaux, je vous signale spécialement la grande vasque d'Amathonte, les églises de Paphos, les ruines de Soli où se trouve une belle inscription[12] que Grasset vous indiquera ainsi que deux stèles qui lui ont été signalées. Dans les ruines de Famagouste, je vous signale un chapiteau de pilastre que je considère comme phénicien ainsi que des débris analogues encastrés dans un mur à Athienou entre Larnaca et Nicosie'. The capital at Famagusta is probably the one mentioned by Grasset. This is not surprising as he guided Guillaume-Rey during his mission in Cyprus in 1857–1858.

The mission, therefore, was not an adventure, but followed a specific plan. The country would first have to be explored to discover inscriptions and then excavations could be undertaken.

Exploration on horseback quite often lasted for seven or eight hours a day[13] and covered almost the entire island. On 11 March de Vogüé and Waddington left for Syria. The same day Duthoit, accompanied by Grasset, settled down to undertake some excavations, first at Athienou and then at Dali. On 12 April they both set out to explore the western part of the island.

We can follow their route on a map made by Louis de Mas Latrie and published in 1862 (Fig. 17.2). They started at Larnaca from where they went to Athienou and Famagusta, and then to Carpasia and Nicosia. After two days in Nicosia, they left for Kyrenia and Bellapais, where Duthoit stayed for three days. During that time, de Vogüé and Waddington went to Soli to find, but without success, the inscription mentioned by Grasset and Guillaume-Rey. They met again in Nicosia and went south to Paphos and back to Larnaca. Duthoit and Grasset's route to Soli, where they finally found the inscription, can also be easily followed.

It is clear that all the sites mentioned by Grasset were visited, even though his idea of a maritime itinerary was not pursued. The information given by Guillaume-Rey was also extremely useful as the Louvre now possesses some of the monuments that he mentions in his letter.

As to the excavations, it is easy to understand why Dali and Athienou were chosen. It was known for a long time that antiquities were to be found there, and it was more or less certain that excavations would produce important discoveries whereas, as de Vogüé explained to Renan,[14]

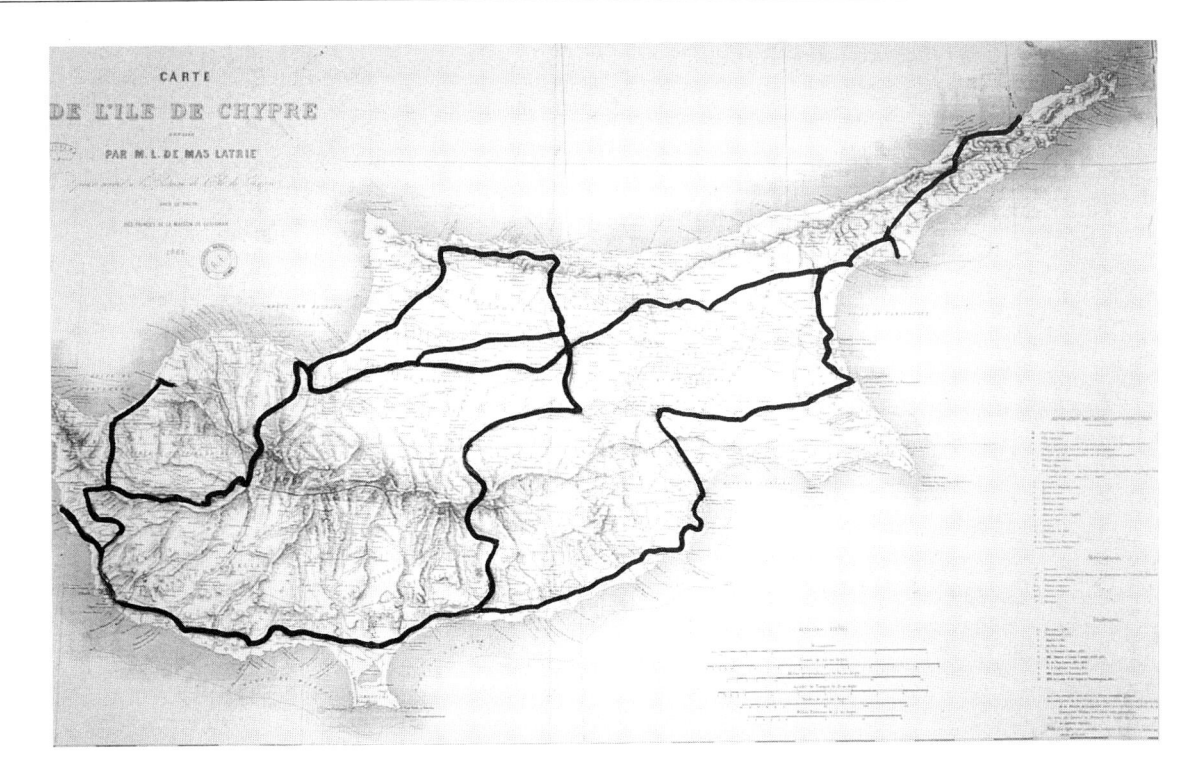

Fig. 17.2: Itinerary of the 'mission de Vogüé' on the map of Louis de Mas Latrie (Bibliothèque Nationale de France, Département des Cartes et Plans, Paris).

with other sites there was a greater risk of finding nothing. Dali and Athienou were not the only sites excavated. Other excavations were carried out at Carpasia and Nea-Paphos, but on a smaller scale.[15]

The work as a whole did not present any difficulties, except perhaps at Dali where they had to use more sophisticated equipment as we can see from a drawing of Duthoit (Fig. 17.3) who wrote to de Vogüé:[16] 'Je fais fouiller des tombeaux que personne ne daigne aller voir et qui m'ont paru infiniment plus intéressants que les bonnes femmes que chacun achète ici. Ils sont, s'il faut en croire leur construction, des temps les plus anciens, en partie creusés dans la roche vive. Ils sont recouverts par des pierres se contrebutant l'une l'autre, d'une dimension qui rappelle Bapho, admirablement jointes entre elles et parfaitement taillées'.

Another point of interest is the assistance they found on the spot. It is worth underlining the role of two people: Sosthène Grasset, mentioned above, and the doctor Charles Gaillardot.

The rather obscure role of Grasset was far from being negligible, and has already been underlined by the late Olivier Masson and Annie Caubet.[17] Although he was not officially part of the mission, he gave all the information he possessed and all his help to Duthoit who barely appreciated

Fig. 17.3: Diggings in Dali, drawing by Edmond Duthoit (Musée de Picardie, Amiens).

him and had even proposed that he should be nominated cook of the mission! Unfortunately he was very little compensated for his zeal, and only de Vogüé appeared to show any understanding and patience towards him.

Doctor Gaillardot, medical director of the Saïda hospital, was an archaeologist and had accompanied Renan in 1860.[18] It was through his intervention that de Vogüé received the firman for Cyprus as well as the tools for the excavations that were transported from Beirut.[19] He also gave some advice at the request of de Vogüé:[20] 'Pour ce qui concerne la manière de fouiller, elle doit être appropriée à la localité qu'on se propose d'étudier et votre architecte en saura plus là-dessus que je ne pourrai lui en apprendre. La seule précaution à employer comme précaution sanitaire, c'est d'allumer de grands feux à l'entrée du caveau qu'on découvre et d'en purifier ainsi l'air avant d'y entrer. Comme ces caveaux sont souvent humides et malsains, il convient de ne pas y prendre trop longue séance, soit pour y dessiner, soit pour diriger les travailleurs. Pour ces derniers, il convient aussi de les changer d'heure en heure et de mettre aux coffres ceux qui piochent et pellettent. Ils travaillent ainsi alternativement au fond du caveau et au grand air'.

They were also given valuable help by the consular agents Tardieu in Nicosia and Acamas in Limassol. The latter wrote to Duthoit on the 31May 1862 concerning the vase of Amathus:[21] 'Le maçon qui l'a déblayé me rapporte qu'il est de toute beauté, qu'il a quinze pieds de diamètre et neuf pieds de hauteur, portant sur chacune de ses anses des lions de la grandeur d'un chat, et par dessus des initiales, et que la base très large repose sur une forte bâtisse de pierres de taille'.

Joseph von Hammer, who thought that the bulls were horses was, therefore, not the only one to be confused.[22] The help of consular agents was not limited to the excavations but extended to the storing, packing and shipping of the objects. We should also note that the mission benefited equally from letters of recommendation for lodging, in particular in remote villages like Yialousa or Kyrenia.

The results of the mission are well known, especially the acquisitions by the Louvre.

However, it should be remembered that Melchior de Vogüé was a private collector. His collection of coins is now in the Cabinet des Médailles in Paris and consists of a total of 1664 pieces. Cyprus is represented by 41 antique coins of which three are of the Evagoras, king of Salamis, and 124 from the time of the Crusades.[23] He bequeathed his collection of Cypriot antiquities to his daughter, Marthe de MacMahon, and it is now housed in the musée Rolin in Autun.[24] The collection comprises approximately 30 pieces of Cypriot antiquities rather small in height, dating from the earliest times to the Hellenistic age. It is quite varied and consists mainly of limestone or terracotta heads or figurines. Some pieces are particularly interesting, for

Fig. 17.4.

Fig. 17.5.

Figs 17.4 & 17.5: Head of a young man (inv. V. 20, Collection de Vogüé, Musée Rolin, Autin).

instance the head of a man wearing a crown of leaves (Figs 17.4 and 17.5), whose thick curly hair is typical of the Hellenistic period. Many pieces represent women, for example Kourotrophoi, 'Dea Tyria Gravida' or kanephoroi, dating from Cypro-Archaic II and Cypro-Classical I and II. Some of the women have been identified as musicians, including a tympanon player (Fig. 17.6), and a lyre player (Fig. 17.7). One of the nicest heads, representing a young woman, dates from Cypro-Archaic II. The severe expression of the face, the thick zigzag curly hair and the

Fig. 17.6: Tympanon player (inv. V. 14, Collection de Vogüé, Musée Rolin, Autin).

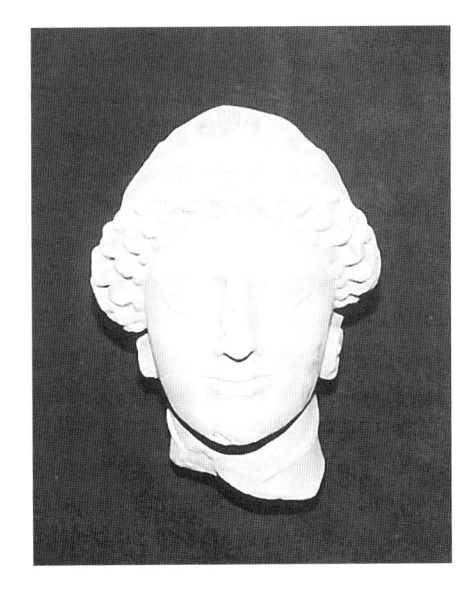

Fig. 17.8

Fig. 17.9

Figs 17.8 & 17.9: Head of a young woman (inv. V. 19, Collection de Vogüé, Musée Rolin, Autin).

Fig. 17.7: Lyre player (inv. V. 16, Collection de Vogüé, Musée Rolin, Autin).

kecryphale show strong Greek influence (Figs 17.8 and 17.9).

Unfortunately neither the Cabinet des Médailles nor the musée Rolin have any information about the origin of these objects. We can, however, assume that de Vogüé not only collected these from Dali or Athienou, but also undoubtedly bought, during his stay, some antiquities from consuls or consular agents, local scholars and collectors, or peasants. He equally acquired objects through the network of the French consulates while he was ambassador in Constantinople from 1871 to 1875 and later through antique dealer intermediaries like Paul Lambros or Aimé Péretié, in particular during the sales organised by the latter in Paris.[25] Even though Cyprus occupies a small part of Melchior de Vogüé's work, after the mission he published various important studies on coins of the kings of Jerusalem and Cyprus,[26] coins of the Phoenician Kings of Cyprus,[27] Phoenician inscriptions (five of Kition,[28] six of Idalion[29]) and eleven Cypriot inscriptions.[30]

Melchior de Vogüé did not only study epigraphy and Cypriot coins. What attracted him to the island in the first place was, as he said, the study of the 'monuments laissés par nos ancêtres sur le sol de l'Orient'.[31] In his archives is held a text about the monuments of the Middle Ages that is, as far as I know, unpublished. A passage about the abbey of Bellapais (Figs 17.10 and 17.11) reads:[32] 'Quand je visitais Lapaïs, au printemps de l'année 1862, l'île d'Aphrodite avait revêtu sa plus brillante parure et les flots tranquilles de la mer Egée frangeaient à peine d'un trait d'argent, le contour de ses côtes amollies. La vieille abbaye française semblait divaguer au milieu des caroubiers et des pistachiers en fleurs, au contact des palmiers dont les panaches rivalisaient d'élégance avec ses faisceaux de colonnettes et ses rosaces ajourées. Pour échapper au contraste, il fallait se réfugier à l'intérieur du monument abandonné, là, la France revivait sans mélange, avec le charme mystérieux du cloître, la puissante structure des salles voûtées, église, chambre capitulaire, long réfectoire à la fine chaire de pierre, vaste dortoir aux fenêtres donnant sur la mer'.

Finally, study of the correspondence of Melchior de Vogüé allows us to perceive the contacts that he maintained after the mission. Some names stand out from regular correspondence, notably the following: Dimitris Piéridès, who kept him informed on the inscriptions discovered in Cyprus, Sosthène Grasset who explained his method of deciphering Cypriot inscriptions and Aimé Péretié who offered him antiquities. On the French side, are held, for example, letters from Adrien de Longpérier, who asked for advice and support for the Cypriot antiquities of the Louvre and acted as an intermediary with antique dealers.

Many others can be cited, but their names only appear sporadically or even only once: Emmanuel Guillaume-Rey, Camille Enlart, Louis de Mas Latrie, Léon Heuzey, Robert Hamilton Lang, Michele Cirilli, Edouard du Tour, Georges Colonna Ceccaldi, etc.

What about Luigi Palma di Cesnola? It seems that he made contact with de Vogüé through George Henry Boker, Minister Resident in Turkey in 1874. He wrote from Larnaca on 22 April 1875:[33] 'Sur l'invitation de M. Boker, je me prends la liberté de vous adresser ces quelques lignes pour vous assurer que je serais bien heureux de vous faire part, de temps en temps, de mes nouvelles découvertes, si vous le désirez, et si vous me permettez de ne point faire attention à mon pauvre Français qui n'est pas certes, celui qu'on devrait user quand on écrit à un membre de l'Institut'. Having found no other letter from Cesnola, I think that this correspondence was not followed up. Nevertheless, an envelope, sent by Aimé Péretié in May 1870,[34] contains a great number of photographs of antiquities from Golgoï (Fig. 17.12) as well as a drawing of the temple by Cesnola himself (Fig. 17.13)[35] with the following annotation: 'en vert le terrain fouillé par le Milord français;[36] s'il n'avait pas suivi ses fouilles diagonalement, il aurait découvert le temple au lieu d'en détruire un coin sans le savoir; car on peut (sic) pas savoir si le temple avait deux ou quatre portes'.

Member of the Académie des Belles-Lettres in 1868, President of the Corpus des Inscriptions Sémitiques in 1892, and later member of the Institut, Melchior de Vogüé died in Paris on 10 November 1916 at the age of eighty-seven. A scholar, meticulous but modest, he had an exceptional personality that could only inspire respect and admiration.

Notes

1. Held at the Centre Historique des Archives Nationales (henceforth abbreviated CHAN).
2. See in particular. J. Charay, *Le marquis de Vogüé, Archéologue et Historien* (Aubenas 1968); J-B. Chabot, 'Le marquis de Vogüé, notice sur ses travaux d'épigraphie et d'archéologie orientale', *JA* XIe série, tome 9 (1916) 313–345; S. Reinach, 'Melchior de Vogüé', *RA* 3 (jan-juin 1916) 429–447; D. Sidersky, 'Le centenaire d'un grand français: de Vogüé', *Feuilleton du journal des débats du 19 octobre 1929, JA* (1929); L. Jalabert, 'Le Marquis de Vogüé, l'orientaliste et l'archéologue', *Etudes* 149 (20 décembre 1916) 709–740.
3. 'Fragment d'un voyage en Orient', *Bulletin de l'Athenaeum Français* (1854) 1089 and 1855, 138–140.
4. Draft of letter (CHAN 567AP229) published in L. Bonato, 'Chypre dans les archives de Melchior de Vogüé: à l'origine de la mission de 1862', *Centre d'Etudes Chypriotes. Cahier* 28 (1998) 105.
5. CHAN 567AP217, published in Bonato (n.4) 105–108.
6. Cf. Bonato (n.4) 105.
7. CHAN 567AP217, published in Bonato (n.4) 108–111.
8. Cf. O. Masson, A. Caubet, 'A propos d'antiquités chypriotes entrées au Musée du Louvre de 1863 à 1866', *RDAC* (1980) 140.
9. Under number AM 2754 or 979. Cf. A. Hermary, *Musée du Louvre. Les antiquités de Chypre, Sculptures* (Paris 1989).
10. See my discussion in Bonato (n.4) 109 n. 21.
11. CHAN 567AP217, published in L. Bonato, 'Chypre dans les archives de Melchior de Vogüé, II, correspondance de la "mission Vogüé" reçue au cours de l'année 1862', *Centre d'Etudes Chypriotes. Cahier* 29 (1999) 142–143.
12. Inscription found by Duthoit and Grasset and now held in the Louvre (inv. AM 1861).
13. Cf. J. Foucart-Borville, 'La correspondance chypriote

Fig. 17.10.

Fig. 17.11.

Figs 17.10 & 17.11: Bellapais Abbey (courtesy Rony van de Velde, Antwerp).

Fig. 17.12: Photographs of antiquities from Golgoï discovered by Luigi Palma di Cesnola (Ref. 567AP217, Melchior de Vogüé's archives, Centre Historique des Archives Nationales, Paris).

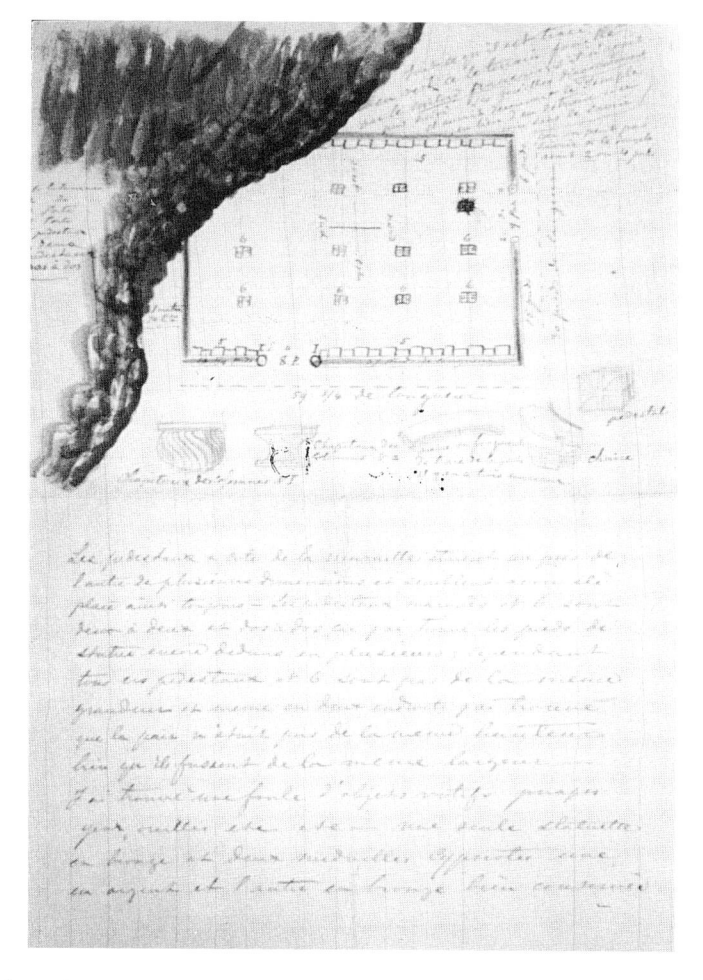

Fig. 17.13: The temple of Golgoï, drawing by Luigi Palma di Cesnola (Ref. 567AP217, Melchior de Vogüé's archives, Centre Historique des Archives Nationales, Paris).

d'Edmond Duthoit', *Centre d'Etudes Chypriotes. Cahier* 4 (1985) 16.
14. *RA* 1 (1862) 347.
15. Foucart-Borville (n.13) 17 and 23.
16. Letter from Dali, 6 April 1862 (CHAN 567AP217), published in Bonato (n.11) 152–154.
17. Masson and Caubet (n.8) 136–151.
18. N. Broc, *Dictionnaire illustré des explorateurs et grands voyageurs français au XIXe siècle, tome II, Asie* (Paris 1992) 203.
19. Letter from Ghazir, 11 January 1862 (CHAN 567AP217).
20. Letter from Saïda, 20 January 1862 (CHAN 567AP217), published in Bonato (n.11) 144–145.
21. Letter from Limassol, 31 May 1862 (CHAN 567AP217).
22. Cf. M-C. Hellmann, 'Les voyageurs' in P. Aupert, M-C. Hellmann, *Amathonte I, Testimonia I* (Paris 1984) 82.
23. Information kindly supplied by M. Michel Dhenin (Département des Monnaies, Médailles et Antiques, Bibliothèque Nationale de France (Paris).
24. Cf. A.J. Decaudun, *Les antiquités chypriotes dans les collections publiques françaises* (Nicosie 1987) 5–17, pl. III-VIII
25. Numerous letters in CHAN 567AP217, 229, etc.
26. Numerous articles in *La Revue Numismatique, Le Journal Asiatique, Le Journal des Savants* and *La Revue Archéologique.*
27. *RN* 12 (1867) 364–381.
28. *JA* 10 (1867) 85–176.
29. *JA* 5 (1875) 319–339.
30. One bilingual from Athienou, three from Koukla, one from Soli and two from Amathus: 'Inscriptions chypriotes inédites', *JA* 11 (1868) 491–502.
31. *RA* 2 (1862) 249.
32. CHAN 567AP224, published in L. Bonato, 'Chypre dans les archives de Melchior de Vogüé, III, impressions de Famagouste et de Bellapais', *Cahier d'Etudes Chypriotes. (forthcoming).*
33. CHAN 567AP197.
34. CHAN 567AP217.
35. Published in L. Palma di Cesnola, *Cyprus, its Cities, Tombs and Temples* (London 1877) 139.
36. In his letter already mentioned, Cesnola further specifies that the 'French Milord' is Melchior de Vogüé. He seems to have ignored that the excavations were directed by Edmond Duthoit.

18. The Ohnefalsch-Richter Collection in the Museum für Vor- und Frühgeschichte, Berlin

Melitta Brönner

As we know, M. Ohnefalsch-Richter (1850–1917, Fig. 18.1), besides his excavations in Cyprus, his scientific work and his lecturing tours around Europe and, in 1893, even in America, collected or purchased antiquities as a sideline, which he then sold again as opportunities arose, in order to secure his financial circumstances.[1] We cannot always establish precisely to what extent he was engaged in such dealings. According to different pieces of information in letters or references to sales in the years 1895 and 1896, they were, at least at that period, an important part of his enterprise.

After selling Cypriot objects in Vienna on 22 July 1895,[2] Ohnefalsch-Richter, already one month later, calls the attention of Wilhelm Fröhner of Paris (1834–1925) to more Cypriot finds in his possession, which he would like to sell at a good price, hoping for the addressee's support: 'Ich besitze eine große Sammlung cyprischer Alterthümer [...]. Aber vor einer Auction fürchte ich mich. Könnte ich die Sachen unter der Hand los werden, glaube ich[,] erziele ich mehr. Auch müßte ich bald Geld für d. Sachen haben, da ich meine ganze(n) Ersparniße in diese Ankäufe steckte'.[3] There is no evidence that Fröhner or Henri Hoffmann

Fig. 18.1: Max Ohnefalsch-Richter during his stay in Cyprus in 1910. After: The Illustrated London News *1911, 162, Fig. 7.*

Fig. 18.2: Rudolf Virchow (outstanding anthropologist, prehistorian, pathologist, physician and politician). Photo: Museum für Vor- und Frühgeschichte, Berlin.

Fig. 18.3: Copy of a letter of 13 February 1893 from the Erbprinz of Saxony-Meiningen, Bernhard II, to M. Ohnefalsch-Richter. The letter deals with the forthcoming reception by the Queen. Photo: Geheimes Staatsarchiv Berlin, Preußischer Kulturbesitz.

(1823–1897), who was related to him, accepted that offer in any way.[4]

Late in 1895 and in the first months of the following year, Ohnefalsch-Richter stayed in London, a fact he reports in letters to A. Furtwängler in Munich (1853–1907), and R. Virchow in Berlin (1821–1902, Fig. 18.2).[5] That extended visit to Britain may have been dictated primarily by concerns about his livelihood, as is hinted at in his letter to Furtwängler. The decisive motive certainly was the fact that excavations in Cyprus were not continuing, as Ohnefalsch-Richter briefly mentions in his letter to Furtwängler of 12 January 1896. After the excavations originally planned at Saxony's expense at Idalion and Vitsada until late April 1895,[6] he was going to set off for Polis tis Chrysochou, in order to find promising vases and jewellery.[7] Yet, as mentioned above, Ohnefalsch-Richter stayed in London in the winter of 1895/96 and did not leave for Germany until Easter 1896.[8]

We do not know for certain how Ohnefalsch-Richter earned his living in Britain. There are mentions of sales of antiquities, of a series of lectures, and of some extra earnings.[9] Apparently selling antiquities in London did not, however, yield large profits, as evidently not very many were actually sold. A lucrative offer from Liverpool seems to have been late, as the antiquities were already on their way to Germany.[10] We are, unfortunately, not in a position to establish whether these extra earnings resulted from a recommendation by Britain's Queen Victoria (1819–1901), to whom he had been introduced earlier through the good offices of Empress Friedrich (Princess Viktoria, 1840–1901) and of Erbprinz of Saxony-Meiningen, Bernhard II (1851–1929, Fig. 18.3).[11] Through them he also met ten high-ranking personalities, among them the Principal Librarian of the British Museum.[12] His letters, unfortunately, do not provide any details about these meetings.

Fig. 18.4: View of the Berlin Gewerbeausstellung, 1896, with the Spezial-Ausstellung Kairo in the background. Photo: Heimatmuseum, Berlin-Treptow.

Ohnefalsch-Richter had intended to make use of his London stay for continuing work on his *Tamassos und Idalion*, a book that was planned, but never published.[13] Here he met with some difficulties, as he was not, at the outset, sent important source materials from Germany.[14] We suppose that he was also occupied preparing a habilitation thesis on 'Der Ursprung der gesammten vorgeschichtlichen Cultur in Europa, Vorder-Asien und Nord-Africa', which would have given him the qualification to lecture in Prehistoric and Greco-Phoenician Culture at Berlin University. He failed, however, to realize that project for lack of time.[15]

When Ohnefalsch-Richter returned to Berlin in the spring of 1896 he wanted to fully concentrate on finishing *Tamassos und Idalion*.[16] But soon financial worries were to take hold of him again, so he had to focus all his energy on making money. He had no choice but to offer for sale in Germany what was left of his antiquities after his London sales. At that time, the last preparations for the Berlin Gewerbeausstellung, which was to take place in the grounds of today's Treptow Park, just outside the capital of the then German Reich, from 1 May until 15 October 1896 (Fig. 18.4), were in full swing.[17] Ohnefalsch-Richter, at short notice, had the chance of exhibiting his antiquities there at a pavilion he had to hire (store no. 30/30a) in a separate area, the 'Spezial-Ausstellung Kairo' (Fig. 18.5),[18] and of offering them for sale. In a letter to Virchow he reports on that opportunity: 'Meine Frau & ich haben unsere Ersparnisse in cyprische & kleinasiatische Alterthümer gesteckt. Einiges haben wir gut verkauft. Vieles besitzen wir noch, im Ganzen etwa im Werthe von 60 000 Mark. Man hat mir den Rath gegeben[,] die Alterthümer in d. Spezial-Ausstellung Kairo auszustellen & zu verkaufen.'[19] But as he did not possess sufficient financial means to provide the capital for, among other things, acquiring more antiquities to maintain his supply, he soon got into serious pecuniary difficulties. In that critical situation he placed all his confidence in Virchow's helpfulness, whose extensive and widespread relations he hoped would provide him with a financier's generous support. Such a person could not be found at once, so that on 1 July 1896 he was nearly on the brink of ruin.[20] From 11 June 1896, in several letters to Virchow, there occurs the name of Valentin Weisbach (1843–1899, Fig. 18.6), from whom Ohnefalsch-Richter hoped, among other things, for financial help.[21] Weisbach was certainly a possiblity inasmuch as that prosperous Berlin banker then enjoyed public esteem in Berlin through his different honorary functions, not only in the cultural-scientific, but also in the social field.[22] A personal relationship with Virchow, then Honorary Chairman of the Berlin Gesellschaft für Anthropologie, Ethnologie und Urgeschichte, resulted from Weisbach's mere membership

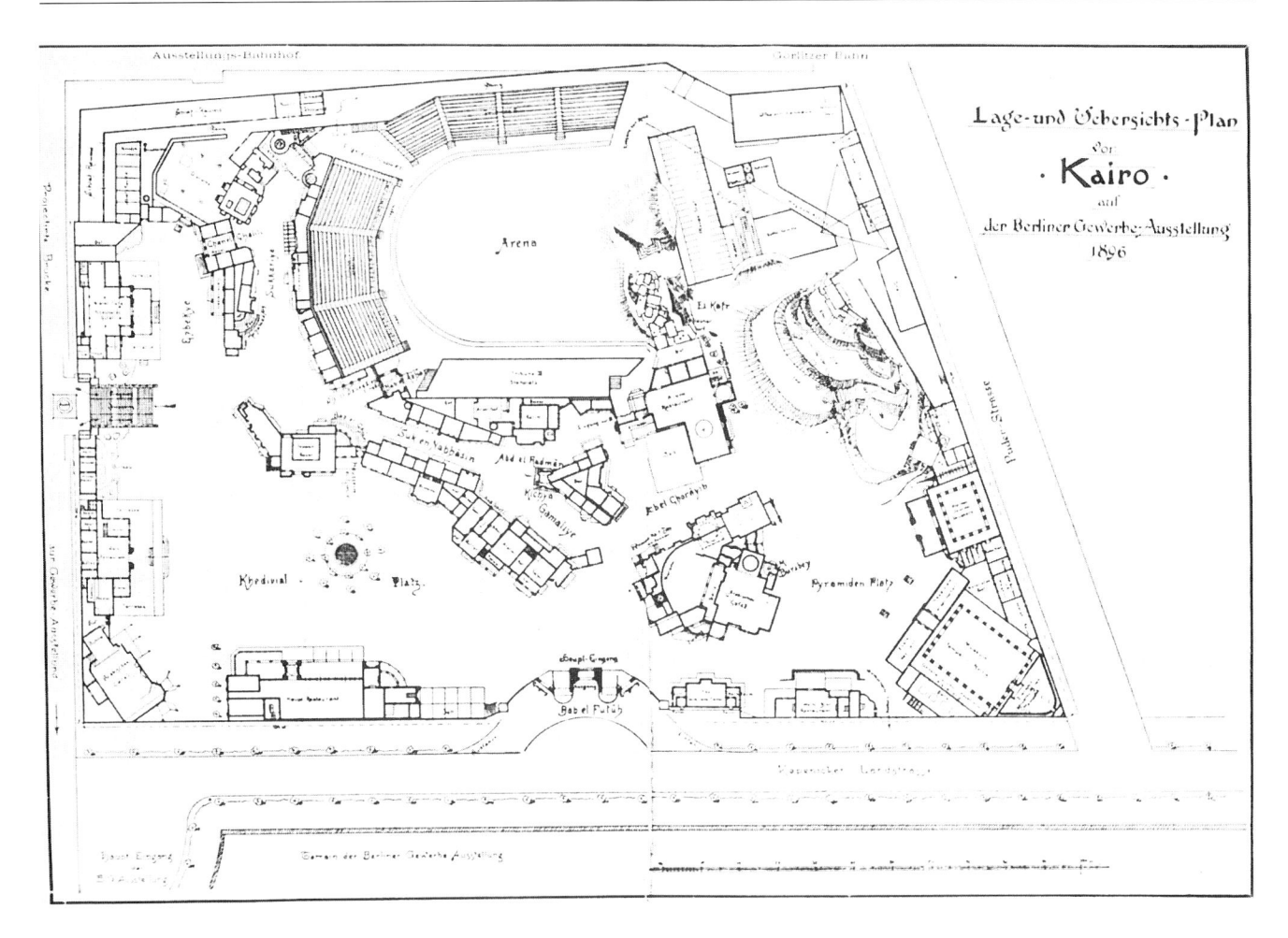

Fig. 18.5: Layout plan of the Spezial-Ausstellung Kairo. After: C. Krug, Offizieller Führer durch die Special-Abtheilung Kairo der Berliner Gewerbe-Ausstellung *(Berlin 1896).*

of that body, to which Ohnefalsch-Richter also belonged.[23] The latter had, at that time, presented a paper on his 'neueste Ausgrabungen auf Cypern' at a members' meeting.[24] We can certainly assume that Weisbach was among the audience.

It was in early July 1896 that Weisbach in fact relieved Ohnefalsch-Richter of his financial embarrassment, which was reported to Virchow by a letter of 6 July 1896.[25] Details concerning the event are not known, however. Weisbach possibly initially lent him a large amount of money, Ohnefalsch-Richter's antiquities perhaps acting as financial security. After the closing of the Berlin Gewerbeausstellung in mid-October of 1896, at the latest, the antiquities, not yet sold, probably passed into Weisbach's possession that same year.[26] The following year, Hermann Obst (1837–1906, Fig. 18.7), Director of the Museum für Völkerkunde at Leipzig, having exchanged letters with Ohnefalsch-Richter since 1890, received a note in that respect: 'Herr V. Weisbach hat sämmtliche Alterthümer, die ich besaß, übernommen & verschenkt sie an Museen'.[27] At the same time Ohnefalsch-Richter started mobilizing his efforts to interest Obst in the collection and influence Weisbach little by little to make him transfer it by donation to the Leipzig Museum. That actually happened in December 1898.[28]

There is a 44–page catalogue written by hand in the Leipzig collection of documents. In it, the pieces, arranged in 'collections', are listed with their selling prices.

According to that document, Weisbach may well have paid a total of 35,433.95 marks for them.[29] In addition, there are numerous old photographs mounted on cardboard, which relate either to single pieces, single groups or parts of whole collections. Some collections consist, according to the acquisition document, of pieces numbered successively without gaps, whereas other collections of finds show gaps that probably originate from sales conducted at the Berlin Gewerbeausstellung. The continuously numbered

Fig. 18.6: Valentin Weisbach (Berlin banker). Photo: Universitätsbibliothek, Basle.

Cypriot collections showing almost no gap, which were sold to V. Weisbach, are 'Elite Collection A' (Fig. 18.8) and 'Elite Collection B' (Fig. 18.9). More Cypriot collections, listed in the Leipzig acquisition document only by their numbers, are the 'Guten Collectionen A' and 'B' as well as the 'Typen Collectionen A' (Fig. 18.10), 'B', 'D' (Fig. 18.11), 'E', and 'F'. There is a handwritten note saying that the 'Gute Collection B', comprising 243 objects, was handed over to the Römisch-Germanisches Zentralmuseum at Mainz with Virchow acting as an intermediary.[30]

The question is when and why Ohnefalsch-Richter grouped his Cypriot antiquities in separate collections of just under 200 to 250 finds. It is quite possible that he arranged the finds already in Cyprus according to this principle. It cannot be ruled out either that he did not arrange such collections until the time of the Berlin Gewerbeausstellung or immediately afterwards. In any case, it certainly happened before 7 November 1897, when he mentioned his very rich Cypriot collections in a letter to H. Obst.[31] We can more easily answer the question as to why he assigned his finds to separate collections. The principle was probably not a general idea, but rather one of practicality to enable quick action whenever an opportunity for sale arose, since in the summer of 1896 Ohnefalsch-Richter had to be prepared not to dispose of his finds. He obviously had no reason for hoping that one of the big Berlin museums might purchase objects from him: 'Wenn ich Alles hier haben werde, was ich besitze, wird man mir vielleicht etwas abkaufen, vielleicht nicht'.[32] Apparently he saw more chances with minor museums. That is why he asked H. Obst in July 1896, long before the latter himself tried to get objects for his museum, for the addresses of smaller museums, so that he could offer to sell them his collections, which included antiquities from Egypt, Asia Minor and other places.[33] So far there is, however, no evidence that other museums besides the Römisch-Germanisches Zentralmuseum at Mainz received any special collections. Hence the collections purchased by V. Weisbach in 1896 went as a whole to Leipzig's Museum für Völkerkunde, for the time being.[34] Ohnefalsch-Richter congratulated its

Fig. 18.7: Hermann Obst (Director of Museum für Völkerkunde at Leipzig). Photo: Museum für Völkerkunde, Leipzig.

Fig. 18.8: 'Elite Collection A (Kupfer – Bronzezeit)'. Photo: M. Ohnefalsch-Richter. Museum für Vor- und Frühgeschichte, Berlin.

Fig. 18.9: 'Elite Collection B (Graecophoenikische Zeit)'. Photo: M. Ohnefalsch-Richter. Museum für Vor- und Frühgeschichte, Berlin.

Fig. 18.10: 'Typen Collection A (Bildwerke)'. Photo: M. Ohnefalsch-Richter. Museum für Vor- und Frühgeschichte, Berlin.

Fig. 18.11: 'Typen Collection D (Bildwerke)'. Photo: M. Ohnefalsch-Richter. Museum für Vor- und Frühgeschichte, Berlin.

Director, Hermann Obst, in a friendly manner: 'Ich gratuliere Ihnen zu einer solchen Sammlung. Sie sind der Mann mit dem weiten Blick & exceptioneller Intelligenz'.[35]

Notes

The letters of M. Ohnefalsch-Richter, to which most references are made, are now housed at the following institutions:

Letters to A. Furtwängler: Deutsches Archäologisches Institut, Berlin.
Letters to H. Obst: Museum für Völkerkunde, Leipzig.
Letters to R. Virchow: Berlin-Brandenburgische Akademie, Berlin, Nachlaß R. Virchow, no. 1587.

1. H.-G. Buchholz, 'Max Ohnefalsch-Richter als Archäologe auf Zypern', *Centre d'Etudes Chypriotes. Cahier* 11/12 (1989) 24 and 26; M. Krpata, ' Max Hermann Ohnefalsch-Richter. Bibliography and Biographical Remarks', *RDAC* (1992) 338.
2. Buchholz (n.1) 17.
3. Letter of 21 August 1895 of Ohnefalsch-Richter from Spangenberg Castle near Kassel to W. Fröhner, Paris: Stiftung Weimarer Klassik, Goethe- und Schiller-Archiv. Bestand W. Fröhner, no. 107/528. See also M.-Chr. Hellmann, 'W. Froehner et Chypre', *Centre d'Etudes Chypriotes. Cahier* 16 (1991) 17–28.
4. I would like to thank M.-Chr. Hellmann of the Bibliothèque Nationale, Paris for this information kindly provided on 16 May 1998
5. Letters of Ohnefalsch-Richter from London to A. Furtwängler of 28 December 1895, 2 January 1896, 5 January 1896, 12 January 1896, and of 29 January 1896; to R. Virchow of 2 February 1896, 11 February 1896, and 4 March 1896.
6. Ohnefalsch-Richter's circular letter of November 1894 to several Saxon institutions from Nisso countryseat, near Dali; Ohnefalsch-Richter's letters to H. Obst: Museum für Völkerkunde, Leipzig, nos 04490–04492.
7. Copy of a letter of 16 January 1895 of Ohnefalsch-Richter from Nisso countryseat, near Dali, to Th. Schreiber, Leipzig. Ohnefalsch-Richter's letters to H. Obst: Museum für Völkerkunde, Leipzig, nos 04833–04839.
8. Ohnefalsch-Richter's letter from Berlin of 15 April 1896 to R. Virchow.
9. Ohnefalsch-Richter's letters to R. Virchow of 4 March 1896 from London, and of 21 April 1896 from Berlin; to A. Furtwängler of 2 January 1896, of 12 January 1896 and of 29 January 1896 from London, and of May 1896 from Berlin.
10. Cf. Ohnefalsch-Richter's letters of 21 April 1896 from Berlin to H. Obst (no. 05219) and R. Virchow.
11. See copy of a letter of 13 February 1893 from Erbprinz Bernhard II to Ohnefalsch-Richter (Fig. 3), and National-Zeitung (Abend-Ausgabe) of 9 March 1893: Feuilleton. Geheimes Staatsarchiv, Preußischer Kulturbesitz, Berlin, Rep. 92, Althoff B, no. 140, vol. 1, 148 and 151.
12. Ohnefalsch-Richter's letters from London of 12 January 1896 and of 29 January 1896 to A. Furtwängler.
13. See Buchholz (n.1) 19, 21f.
14. Cf. Ohnefalsch-Richter's letters from London of 5 January 1896 and of 29 January 1896 to A Furtwängler.
15. See Ohnefalsch-Richter's letters from London of 2 February 1896, 11 February 1896, and 4 March 1896 to R. Virchow.
16. Ohnefalsch-Richter's letter from Berlin of 15 April 1896 to R. Virchow.
17. *Offizieller Haupt-Katalog der Berliner Gewerbe-Ausstellung* (Berlin not dated).
18. C. Krug, *Offizieller Führer durch die Spezial-Abtheilung Kairo der Berliner Gewerbe-Ausstellung 1896* (Berlin not dated) 118.
19. Ohnefalsch-Richter's letter from Berlin of 21 April 1896 to R. Virchow.
20. There are around 20 letters of Ohnefalsch-Richter from Berlin or from Treptow or from Adlershof (then near Berlin) to R. Virchow for the period from 21 April 1896 to 1 July 1896. In them, among other things, there is talk about financial problems connected with the intended sale at the Berlin Gewerbeausstellung, and Virchow is asked to recommend possible financiers or guarantors.
21. Ohnefalsch-Richter's letters from Treptow (then near Berlin) of 11 June 1896, 13 June 1896, 14 June 1896, 15 June 1896, 23 June 1896, and 26 June 1896 to R. Virchow.
22. For details see the memoirs of his son Werner Weisbach (1873–1953), an outstanding art historian: W. Weisbach, *Und alles ist zerstoben. Erinnerungen aus der Jahrhundertwende*, (Vienna, Leipzig, Zurich 1937) 95–107.
23. See the membership card index at the Berlin Gesellschaft für Anthropologie, Ethnologie und Urgeschichte.
24. At the "Außerordentliche Sitzung" of 13 June 1896. See ZEthn 28, 1896, Verhandlungen, 344.
25. Ohnefalsch-Richter's postcard from Treptow (then near Berlin) of 6 July 1896 to R. Virchow.
26. See V. Weisbach's Deed of Donation of 14 December 1898 to the Rat der Stadt Leipzig, in favour of the Museum für Völkerkunde, Leipzig: Stadtarchiv Leipzig. *Acta, das Deutsche Zentralmuseum für Völkerkunde betr.* Vol. 2, ch. 31, no. 12, 168.
27. Ohnefalsch-Richter's letter from Charlottenburg (Berlin) of 30 October 1897 to H. Obst (no. 05764).
28. For the later fate of the collection, which since 1992 has been in the Museum für Vor- und Frühgeschichte, Berlin, Charlottenburg Castle, see my article 'Zur Sammlung Ohnefalsch-Richter-Weisbach, einstmals in Leipzig – jetzt in Berlin', *Centre d'Etudes Chypriotes. Cahier* 28 (1998) 37–43. For details concerning Ohnefalsch-Richter's sale of antiquities at the Berlin Gewerbeausstellung and the later transfer to Leipzig of the objects not sold, see: M. Brönner, 'Ausstellung und Verkauf zyprischer Altertümer auf der Berliner Gewerbeausstellung 1896', *ActaPraehistA* 31 (1999) 107–123.
29. Museum für Völkerkunde, Leipzig, Erwerbsakte 1898/54 – Sammlung Valentin Weisbach (Ohnefalsch-Richter).
30. See F. Behn, *Vorhellenistische Altertümer der östlichen Mittelmeerländer* (Kataloge des Römisch-Germanischen Central-Museums No. 4, Mainz 1913) 67–97.

31. Ohnefalsch-Richter's letter of 7 November 1897 from Berlin to H. Obst (no. 05763).
32. Ohnefalsch-Richter's letter from Treptow (then near Berlin) of 25 June 1896 to R. Virchow.
33. Ohnefalsch-Richter's letter from Treptow (then near Berlin) of 28 July 1896 to H. Obst (no. 05218).
34. Weisbach may well, on his own, have given away finds to museums. See Ohnefalsch-Richter's letter from Charlottenburg (Berlin) of 30 October 1897 to H. Obst (no. 05764).
35. Ohnefalsch-Richter's letter from Berlin of 14 December 1898 to H. Obst (no. 06237).

19. Falkland Warren

H.-G. Buchholz

Das Leben der hier vorgestellten, 1834 geborenen Person, spielte sich – sieht man von Jugend- und Schulzeit ab – hauptsächlich in drei großen Abschnitten während der zweiten Hälfte des vorigen Jahrhunderts ab: Einer etwa dreizig Jahre dauernden militärischen Phase von 1852 an, als er achtzehn jährig in die königliche Artillerie eintrat, um Berufsoffizer zu werden. – Einer zweiten Phase seiner Verwendung in der Kolonialverwaltung von 1878 bis zum Ausscheiden aus dem aktiven Dienst und zwischenzeitlicher Beförderung zum Oberst (1881). – Schließlich in einem dritten Abschnitt, indem er mit der ganzen Familie nach Kanada auswanderte. Im Jahre 1890 verließ er Zypern, 1892 ebenso England und hielt sich bis 1908, seinem Todesjahr, in der Neuen Welt auf.

Wissenschaftsgeschichtlich ist allein die zweite Berufsphase von Colonel Warren interessant, beleuchtet sie doch einen Abschnitt kyprischer Archäologie, den man zu den Pionierleistungen derselben rechnen kann. Jedenfalls möchte man seine militärziet in Indien, die freilich das Selbstverständnis dieses Mannes weitgehend prägte, nicht einer besonderen biographischen Würdigung für Wert halten, entsprach sie doch vielen ähnlichen Lebensläufen englischer Kolonialoffiziere: 1857/58 war er an der Niederschlagung eines indischen Aufstandes beteiligt und wurde 1859 zum Hauptmann befördert. Im Jahre 1863 stand er an der indischen Nordwestgrenze im Kampf gegen kriegerische Bergstämme, 1864/65 nahm er am Bootan-Feldzug teil. 1872 erfolgte seine Beförderung zum Major, 1877 zum Oberstleutnant. Dem Studium englischer Kolonialgeschichte mag die Darstellung einer solchen Persönlichkeit dienlich sein, dem Studium der Entwicklung früher kyprischer Archäologie höchstens insofern die meisten archäologischen Aktivitäten der achtziger Jahre des vorigen Jahrhunderts von Militärpersonen durchgeführt, von ihnen geleitet oder durch sie beeinflußt wurden.

Abgesehen davon, daß zuvor L.P. di Cesnola im amerikanischen Bürgerkrieg ebenfalls Karriere bis zum General gemacht hatte und nicht eben als ausgebildeter Facharchäologe gelten konnte, erwarb sich der spätere Lord Kitchener unter den Militärs allein schon durch die Neuvermessung der Insel mit ihren antiken Denkmälern, Bergwerken und Schlackenhalden große Verdienste um die alten Kulturhinterlassenschaften. Jedenfalls ist seine Landkarte in mancher Hinsicht den Archäologen bis heute unentbehrlich.

Anläßlich der Neuordnung des Verhältnisses der europäischen Großmächte zueinander fiel Zypern 1878 auf dem Berliner Kongreß, auf dem sich Bismarck selber als 'ehrlichen Makler' bezeichnete, an das Britische Imperium, ohne völkerrechtlich die weitere Zugehörigkeit zum Osmanischen Reich zu verlieren. Deshalb behielten auch Gesetze wie das osmanische Denkmalsschutz- und Ausgrabungsrech, einschließlich der Fundteilung, ihre Gültigkeit. Es waren englische Kolonialtruppen aus Indien, welche sofort verfügbar waren. Gewiß erklärt sich somit aus den besonderen Umständen, daß Berufssofiziere das dominierende Element in der neuen Inselverwaltung bildeten. So begann Falkland Warren 1878 die neue Karriere als 'Assistant Commissioner' von Larnaka und wurde bereits Oktober desselben Jahres Commissioner von Limassol. Im August das folgenden Jahres wurde er zum 'Chief Secretary to the Government' in Nikosia erkannt. Dieses Amt bekleidete er zehn Jahre lang, bis er mit seinem 55sten Geburtstag, am 16. Juni 1889, in den Ruhestand trat. Doch die Insel verließ er erst, wie oben bereits erwähnt, am 13. Juli 1890.

Betrachten wir Falkland Warrens Ausgrabungstätigkeiten in dem angesprochenen Jahrzehnt, so sind die Quellen weder leicht zugänglich, noch eindeutig. Es ist wohl davon auszugehen, daß dieser Mann niemals auch nur annähernd etwas von dem lernte, was man praktische Feldarchäologie nennt. Allerdings verstand er es, erfahrene einheimische Arbeiter zu finden und sich ihrer zu bedienen. Sein Name ist in Sir Charles Newtons an die Trustees des British Museum gerichteten Bericht vom 8. Juli 1880 für das Jahr 1879/80 zusammen mit weiteren Namen genannt. Es werden dort Neuzugänge aus Larnaka, Aradippo, Limassol und Amathous aufgeführt. Der Bericht fährt fort: 'Mr. Newton would submit that the best thanks of the Trustees are due to Colonel Warren, R.A., now Chief Secretary at Cyprus, to Mr. Cobham, Commissioner at Larnaca, and to Lieutenant Kitchener, R.E., for their zeal and intelligence in collecting and preserving the antiquities now presented to the museum'.

Sir Charles Newton besuchte – so in dem genannten Bericht vermerkt – 1879 anläßlich seiner Zypernreise auch Amathous, '...and was shown the spot where General Cesnola discovered a remarkable archaic sarcophagus, now in New York ... Here a small tentative excavation has been subsequently made under the direction of Colonel Warren, while he was Commissioner at Limassol. This spot, and indeed the site of Amathus generally, would repay excavation'. Dr. Donald Bailey hat diesen Newton-Bericht schon vor vielen Jahren in den Archiven des British Museum ans Licht gezogen und in seinem schönen Aufsatz 'The Village Priest's Tomb ab Aradippou in Cyprus' abgedruckt und ausgewertet.

Weiterhin begegnet Colonel Warren als lizensierter Ausgräber während des Jahres 1883 in Kourion. Allerdings betätigte er sich in diesem Fall und häufiger nicht als Grabungsleiter vor Ort, sondern suchte sich gegen Bezahlung einen solchen. Er fand ihn in Gestalt des Deutschen Max Ohnefalsch-Richter. Da sich letzerer ständig in Geldnöten sah, war er zu unselbständigen Dienstleistungen solcher Art gezwungen. Im Jahre 1885 grub er für Colonel Warren, der wiederum Inhaber der betreffenden Grabungslizenz war, in der Nekropole Politiko-Alakati, einer Fundstätte bedeutender kypro-geometrischer und archaischer Vasen im antiken Stadtstaat Tamassos. Die wohl bekannteste ist ein „Bichrome IV-Krater' mit mythologischen und Jagdszenen im Besitz des British Museum, in den ersten Veröffentlichungen noch als aus Pera-Phrangissa stammend deklariert. Warren scheint einige Mühe gehabt zu haben, sich in den Besitz der Vase zu bringen, welche offenbar Ohenfalsch-Richter zurückzuhalten suchte. Denn in einem Brief des Jahres 1886 von Colonel Warren an Sir Charles Newton besagt ein Postscriptum: "Richter refused to give me the vase". Doch im Brief selber heißt es: 'The jar I have sent to Col. Thynne, Grenadier Guards, 62 Pont Street, and I have asked him to communicate with you ... I have had to go through three trials in a Court of Law, owing to that fellow Richter, while excavating for me at Tamassos, while paid by me and with workmen paid by me'. Welche Gerichtsverhandlungen gemeint sein werden, will ich weiter unten erörtern. Zugleich sei in diesem Zusammenhang auf den Beitrag von Michael Given verwiesen.

Bereits das bis hierher Vorgetragene zeigt, daß nicht allein von Falkland Warren, sondern seit Cesnolas Verkäufen kyprische Altertümer und ihre Gewinnung unter dem Aspekt des Gelderwerbs gesehen wurden. Auf der einen Seite war der Markt überflutet, wodurch die Preise nach unten gedrückt wurden, andererseits versprachen sich weiterhin Einheimische und Fremde von Ausgrabungen auf Zypern eine gute Dividende. Folgendes mag die Abnahmebereitschaft europäischer Museen und die generelle Einstellung sogenannter Wissenschaftler zum Geschäft beleuchten.

Aufschlußreich für die Einstellung der mitteleuropäischen Museumsverwaltungen in der letzten Dekade des vorigen Jahrhunderts bezüglich des Massen-Angebots kyprischer Altertümer ist die schriftliche Äußerung des erfahrenen E. Curtius, Inhaber des Berliner Lehrstuhls für Klassische Archäologie, seit 1872, nach dem frühen Tod von C. Friederichs, auch Leiter des Antiquariums in Berlin, vom 7. Januar 1895 an das preußische Kultusministerium: 'Es gehörte sich, daß Dr. Ohnefalsch-Richter Verzeichnisse und Photographien der Fundstücke einschicke und bei uns anfrage, ob wir sie haben wollen. Die Masse des vollkommen Gleichartigen ist übergroß'. Bei dem genannten Ausgräber übertrafen allerdings Geschäftsinteressen bei weitem die sachlichen Gesichtspunkte. So schrieb er am 7. November 1894 in einer Art Rundbrief, mit dem er bestimmte Dienststellen, Universitätseinrichtungen, Mäzene und Museen des Königsreichs Sachsen für seine Angebote erwärmen wollte: 'Ich glaube, daß Ausgrabungen, bei denen man für wenig Geld ein Drittel oder gar zwei Drittel aller Funde erhalten kann, platonischen, nur rein wissenschaftlich werthvollen Ausgrabungen vorzuziehen sind'.

Angebote in einem Brief Ohnefalsch-Richters an A. Furtwängler vom 18. April 1893, in New York verfaßt, lassen erkennen, daß man andererseits in der Neuen Welt einen Markt für antike Kunstwerke, nicht allein kyprische, vorfand und auf Interesse an einer möglichen Ausgrabungsbeteiligung in Zypern stieß. Erstens schreibt O.-R.: 'Für den Kopf von Brauron biete ich Ihnen 10000 Mark, d.h. etwas mehr: 2500 Dollar an, unter der Bedingung, daß ich davon $500 als Provision erhalte ... Sie erhalten etwa 4 Mark 15–18 pro Dollar'. Zweitens liebäugelt O.-R. damit, sämtliche Berliner Verbindungen bezüglich Zyperns preiszugeben, wenn es ihm gelänge, in Amerika an Mäzene zu gelangen: 'Ich ziehe sogar jetzt vor, den Zuschuß von 25000 Mark nicht mehr zu erhalten. Ich würde Ihnen sogar, falls ich Idalion für Amerika ausgraben könnte, sehr dankbar sein, wenn Sie trotzdem *Tamassos und Idalion* mit mir herausgeben würden, und könnte ich Ihnen dann 2000 Mark

Honorar mit Leichtigkeit verschaffen'. Und am 29. März hatte er, an Furtwängler von New York aus, vermerkt: 'Es geht ja nichts über Erfolge und diese heften sich, Gott sei Dank, förmlich an meine Fersen'.

In einem weiteren, ebenfalls an A. Furtwängler gerichteten Handschreiben, während seiner Amerikareise 1893 in Chikago verfaßt (aber nicht datiert, weil die ersten beiden Seiten fehlen), stellt O.-R. sein Verhältnis zum Antikenhandel völlig anders dar: 'Wie ich Ihnen wiederholt sagte, habe ich – bis jener unglückliche Prozeß Watkins-Warren stattfand – nie eine Commission von den Leuten erhalten, für die ich ausgrub und deren Sachen ich verkaufte. Ich bin stets in der uneigennützigsten und in ehrlicher Weise verfahren'. Doch dies bleibt schlicht die Unwahrheit, auch wenn man zu seinen Gunsten annimmt, daß er Einzelheiten früheren Antikenhandels verdrängte: In einem am 26. September 1884, mithin vor dem besagten Prozeß, in Marseille geschriebenen Brief an den Wiener Museumsdirektor Kenner fordert er 600 Goldfranken Provision für die Vermittlung der marmornen Artemis aus Larnaka, die seit dem Ankauf ein Glanzstück der Österreichischen Altertumsschätze bildet.

Soviel zum Verhältnis von Archäologie und Geld auf Zypern, hauptsächlich beleuchtet mit O.-R. Zitaten. Um korrekt zu sein, müßte man Fall für Fall durchgehen und unseren britischen Colonel nicht ausnehmen. Ihm wurde von Verwandten und Zeitgenossen, die ihn kannten, nachgesagt, daß er dazu neigte, auf großem Fuße zu leben, weshalb er sich ständig in finanziellen Nöten befand. Jedenfalls hatten auch die mehrfach erwähnte Ausgrabungs-Affäre des Jahres 1885, 'Pera-Phrangissa' betreffend, und der sich daraus ergebende Prozeß Watkins versus Warren nicht allein mit Prestige sondern zugleich mit Geld zu tun. Ich besprach ihn bereits im *Centre d' Études chypriotes. Cahier* 16 (1991) 3–15 unter dem Aspekt der gegenseitigen Übervorteilung der beteiligten Personen, und nunmehr betrachtet ihn M. Given in den 'Proceedings' unseres Kolloquiums von allen Seiten, hauptsächlich jedoch im Hinblick auf 'the control of excavations'. Die Öffentlichkeit Zyperns nahm lebhaften Anteil am Prozeßverlauf, wie ausführliche Berichte im *Cyprus Herald* anzeigen. Sie wurden von Given berücksichtigt. Auch O. Masson hatte bereits diesen Prozeß in die Vita unseres Obersten eingefügt: 'Le Colonel Falkland Warren à Chypre, 1878–1890', *Centre d'Études chypriotes.Cahier* 11/12 (1989) 29–34.

Immerhin war der Kläger C. Watkins, der sich durch Falkland Warren betrogen fühlte, kein Geringerer als der Direktor der Ottoman-Bank in Larnaka, jedenfalls ein nüchterner Geschäftsmann und nicht einmal ein leidenschaftlicher Liebhaber-Archäologe, sondern ein kühler Rechner, dem es beim Ausgraben um Gewinn ging. 1878 verfaßte er den 'Consular Report/Cyprus' Teil IV Seite 1364 für das Jahr 1877. Wir finden ihn seit Februar 1885 in und um Idalion aktiv. So sind die Nummern 31, 33, 36 und 37 in dem von Ohnefalsch-Richter in *Kypros, die Bibel und Homer* als Tafel 2 veröffentlichten Plan des Stadtgebietes von Idalion als Stätten des Lizenzinhabers Watkins angegeben, Nr. 20 als gemeinsames Projekt von C. Watkins und Dr. F. Dümmler. Im Jahre 1886 verfügte Watkins über die Lizenz für Ausgrabungen in Marion. Unter Ohnefalsch-Richters Karte der Gegend (Taf. 218) ist vermerkt: 'Marion wie 1885 von M. O.-R. auf eigene Kosten entdeckt. Seine Ausgrabungen für C. Watkins.....' 'Auf eigene Kosten' bedeutet in diesem wie in anderen Fällen: 'Dem O.-R. von Watkins abgekauft'!

Auf die Ausgrabungen des Jahres 1885 im Apollon-Heiligtum von Phrangissa will ich nicht ausführlich zurückkommen. Doch unter dem Plan desselber, ebenfalls in *Kypros, die Bibel und Homer* als Tafel 6 abgedruckt, steht links: 'Excav. Colonel Falk. Waren 1885', allerdings rechts: 'Antiqu. Cyprus & British Museum', ohne auszudrücken, welche Funktion oder Rechtssituation sich für die beiden Museen bezüglich des Planes oder der Ausgrabung aus ihrer Nennung ableiten soll. Der Aufmerksamkeit von Susan Sherratt und R. Merrillees verdanke ich die Kenntnis eines Briefes, den Ohnefalsch-Richter am 12. Februar 1886 in Nikosia an Mr. Evans in Oxford, den späteren Sir Arthur Evans, Ausgräber von Knossos, schrieb. Das Schriftstück setzt in Fachkreisen die Kenntnis der gerichtlichen Verwicklungen um die besagte Tamassos-Phrangissa-Grabung voraus und enthält folgende erstaunlichen Selbsterkenntnisse: 'I have written foolish letters ..., my honour has suffered by a partial judgment in the District court'. Immerhin wird deutlich, daß der sonst in diesem Prozeß stets nur als Zeuge auftretende Deutsche selber ebenfalls Angeklagter gewesen ist. So würden sich jene oben aus dem Brief Warren an Newton zitierten drei Gerichtsgänge in einem Fall als Klage um Herausgabe des 'Bichrome IV-Kraters', jetzt im British Museum, erklären und die Beschuldigung, welche Ohnefalsch-Richter schamhaft verschweigt, auf 'Herausgabe zu Unrecht zurückgehaltenen Ausgrabungsgutes' (also auf Diebstahl) lauten. Hier ist der noch unpublizierte Briefnützlich, in dem der Schreiber selber vermerkt, daß seine Englischkenntnisse schlecht seien. Im übrigen ergibt sich aus der Eingangsinformation, daß sich Falkland Warren 1886 in England aufgehalten haben muß:

Dear Mr Evans,   Nicosia 12/2 86
Prof. Furtwängler (Berlin Museum) will send you two of my reports 1.) f. S. Brown Esqu. 2.) f. Col. Warren, – both about excavations carried out in a prephoenician necropole near Nicosia. The big culture & art in prephoen. times at Cyprus was first demonstrated by me & accepted as true by Prof. Furtwängler & lately by Dr. Dümmler, send by the German Archaeol. Institut to Cyprus & continually present during these diggings.

I do not know where Professor A. H. Sayce is. The reports are written in English. I am anxious to have them published in England in any scientific paper. They are accompanied by drawings, plans & photographs. Could you help me with your friends to have published these reports or entirely or extracts of them, & having correct my bad English.

I am very glad to hear that you as the scholars & connoisseurs in generally are satisfied with the jar, I have procured you.

We had here now a trial of scandal *Watkins – Warren*. Unfortunately in consequence of my very nervous temper I have made mistakes myself in writing foolish letters to persuade both parties to earn an arrangement & being frightened by Warren. I am the principal witness in the trial of which trial I send you the first parts of the proceedings.

I have telegraphed & written to Germany & they will send me out a lawyer to defend myself or to prosecute. My honour has suffered by a partial judgement in the District Court. At the appeal (case also dismissed) nothing was said against my character.

All these for an extremely valuable discovering of a Temenos of Apollon, a colossal figure of pottery (Cypriote-Greek-Phoenician style) many most valuable statues, statuettes, heads – long bilingual inscriptions on marble Phoenician & Cypriote etc.

Yours very truly

Max Ohnefalsch-Richter

Die kyprischen Kolonialakten, in Nikosia archiviert, enthalten zwei Eingaben O.-R.s beim Hochkommissar Sir Henry Bulwer, datiert auf den 1. und 20. März 1887. Sie lassen sich als Beschwerden über Col. Warren verstehen: In der ersten behauptet O.-R., daß Warren gegen ihn arbeite und seine Absetzung als ehrenamtlichen Kurator des Cyprus Museum betreibe. In der zweiten ist auf den oben schon genannten 'Bichrome IV-Krater' im British Museum Bezug genommen. Wir erfahren als zusätzliche Information aus der Feder O.-R.s, daß Warren besagte Vase aus O.-R.s Haus geholt habe, 'obwohl sein Zimmer von der Polizei versiegelt gewesen sei' (hier übersetzt aus dem Englischen).

Bei der im Schreiben an Evans erwähnten 'Prephoenician Necropole near Nicosia' handelt es sich um Hagia Paraskevi, wiederum ein Unternehmen, wofür Falkland Warren Inhaber der Lizenz war, ebenfalls auf einen Antrag vom August 1885 zurückgehend. Auch diese Ausgrabung betrachtete er als seine persönliche. Ein gewisser W.H. Mallock beschreibt in einem Reisebericht *In an Enchanted Island, or a Winter's Retreat in Cyprus* (mir in der zweiten Auflage von 1889 zugänglich, die erste erschien unmittelbar nach den angesprochnenen Ausgrabungen des Herbstes/Winters 1885/86, also im Jahre 1886 in London) die Person unseres Obersten unter dem Pseudonym 'Colonel Falkland', seine Familie, die großzügige Haushaltung in einem alten, soliden städtischen Gebäude unmittelbar beim Paphostor und die sozial sehr gemischte Gesellschaft von Teegästen aus der englischen Kolonie in Nikosia. Dort heißt es: 'I learnt presently that I was not the only guest, but that a young professor from Cambridge, with his wife from Girton, were also staying in the house, being in Cyprus to superintend some excavations... Mr. Adam, as I will call the young professor, discussed, in a tone of placid academic refinement, which came to my ears like an echo of an Oxford common-room, the various spots where it might be desirable to excavate, and the various objects which had been unearthed already. Strange names of unknown places and people – men called Demetrius and Georgos, and places called Paraskévi and Morphou – buzzed in my ears like a sort of unintelligible spell. During déssert a basket was brought in full of prehistoric potery, with a bronze spear-head in addition – the fruits, as I gathered, of the afternoon's work...Colonal Falkland, who had lived much in the East, interwove with his talk about archaeology many interesting observations as to the unsuspected power, the politics, and the future of Islam. He explained to us problems of which in the Western world the very existence is hardly so much as dreamed...'

Soweit ein Zeitzeuge! Auf ein oder mehrere Rollsiegel aus jenen Hagia Paraskevi-Grabungen, jetzt in Baltimore, wird später zurückzukommen sein. Oberst Warrens Residenz ist übrigens dasselbe Haus mit schattigem Hof und kyprischer Bogenarchitektur, in welchem 1885 E.A. Carletti jene Sammelphotos der Phrangissa-Funde anfertigte, die mir ihre Wiederfindung ermöglichten. Ohenfalsch-Richters Passus 'die im Hause des Col. Warren mit ihm selbst aufgenommenen Photographien' bestätigt das Gesagte. Auf dreien dieser Bilder ist das Hausherr zu erkennen.

Daß es gute oder schlechte Verbindungen zwischen Warren und Ohnefalsch-Richter in dieser Zeit gab, war selbst bis zu Cesnola nach New York gedrungen. So fragte dieser in einem Brief vom 1.6.1886 bei Menardos, seinem Rechtsanwalt in Limassol an, welche Beziehungen, wenn überhaupt, zwischen dem französischen Konsul, Richter und Col. Warren bestünden (unpubliziert, Privatbesitz, Nikosia).

Bis Ende der achtziger Jahre hatte Warren ein buntes Gemisch gesammelter Gegenstände zusammengebracht, von denen kyprische Altertümer nur einen Teil ausmachten. So wie wir beiläufig erfuhren, daß sich seine berühmte Vase, der 'Bichrome IV-Krater' aus Tamassos, bereits 1886 in England befand, so ergibt sich nebenbei, daß ebenso die beiden Inschriftensteine aus Phrangissa mit ihren Bilinguen bereits 1886 Zypern verlassen hatten und dann in London auf der 'Colonial Exhibition' zu sehen waren. Warrens gelegentliche Abwesenheit von Zypern, oben aus einem Vermerk O.-R.s erschlossen, hatte unter anderem mit seiner Beteiligung an dieser Empire-Ausstellung zu tun. Nach *CCM* Seite VI fand die Ausstellung 1887 statt. 'Irreparable damage was done when part of the collection (des Cyprus Mus.) was sent, along with Col. Warren's exhibit, to the Colonial and Indian Exhibition of 1887'.

Der örtlichen Presse (*The Owl* Nr. 27, vom Sonnabend, dem 23. März 1889, Seite 3) ist zu entnehmen, daß während der Nacht vom 16. zum 17. März in Warrens Haus eingebrochen worden war und unter anderem folgende Gegenstände gestohlen wurden: 'A quantity of old coins, Ptolemy and Lusignan period (several of Amalric), seals and scarabai. A very peculiar shaped green stone engraved with a stag of rude style and a pair of large antique gold ear rings. A silver buckle with enamel plates set with stones appearing through old silk embroidery, a very peculiar shape, old Cypriote style'.

In *The Owl* Nr. 125 vom 19 September 1891, Seite 2 äußerte er sich selber zu seiner Sammeltätigkeit: 'I have during my twelve years' residence in Cyprus, collected, so far my means would allow, such coins as appeared to me to belong to the island... '. Wortgleich ist diese Bemerkung auch in seinen 'Notes on coins found in Cyprus' zu finden (*Numismatic Chronicle* 11 [1891] 140–151, Taf. 5). Als Empfänger der Warrenschen Münzsammlung habe ich allein das Museum der Johns Hopkins Universität in Baltimore und die National Art Gallery im kanadischen Ottawa ermitteln können. Es ist jedoch ohne weiteres möglich, daß auch andere amerikanische Museen Münzen, geschnittene Steine und Siegel aus Warrens Besitz angekauft haben. Aufs Ganze gesehen war er, der ehemalige Offizier, weder ein sehr systematischer Sammler noch ein sonderlich gerissener Händler vom Schlage Ohnefalsch-Richters. Im gedruckten Jahresbericht des kanadischen 'Department of Public Works' vom 22. April 1895, 217, Appendix Nr. 6 vom 23. März 1895, heißt es bezüglich der 'National Art Gallery': 'The collection of coins, pottery and antiquities from Cyprus, presented to the Gallery by Col. Warren, have for the most part been placed in suitable cases'.

Bezüglich der archäologischen Sammlungen der Johns-Hopkins-Universität besitzen wir für ihren Bestand Mitte der 80er Jahre unseres Jahrhunderts einen Bericht: E. Reeder-Williams, *The Archaeological Collection of the Johns Hopkins University* (1984). Auch wenn im einzelnen, wie es scheint, nicht immer die Herkunft der Objekte rekonstruierbar ist, erhielt das Museum 1900 einen wertvollen Zuwachs von hundertzweiundzwanzig kyprischen Sammlerstücken aus dem Privatbesitz unseres Falkland Warren. Dies ist nicht zur allgemeinen Kenntnis gedrungen, weil die Sammlung unter dem Namen 'Marburg Collection' registriert wurde. Und dies wiederum hängt damit zusammen, daß ein gewisser Theodore Marburg, ein Verwandter von Frau Warren, die Sammlung unserem Obersten abkaufte und sie sodann als seine Stiftung der genannten Universität vermachte. In einer Tageszeitung hieß es damals: 'It is impossible to place a money value on Marburg's gift'. In einigen Fällen steht fest, daß es sich um bronzezeitliche Funde aus Hagia Paraskevi, Kythraia und Larnaka handelt (im ganzen 13 Rollsiegel, davon sechs mit Keilschriftlegenden). Warren hatte zwar vermerkt, daß einiges aus seinen eigenen Ausgrabungen stamme, jedoch derartige Stücke nicht näher gekennzeichnet. Es handelt sich hauptsächlich um antiken Goldschmuck (49 Objekte, davon 42 Ohrringe und sieben Fingerringe), ferner um geschnittene Steine, Siegel und Gemmen (zusammen 20 Objekte, einmal mit einer kyprischen Sylabarinschrift), etwa 40 Skarabäen (wiederum einer mit einer Silbeninschrift) und weitere Kleinfunde, sowie einige Münzen. Als besonders wertvolle Kleinkunstwerke mit der Herkunft 'Zypern' sind ein Cameo mit den Köpfen Alexanders, des Zeus und des ägyptischen Gottes Ammon, sowie ein Intaglio mit der Göttin Athena im Titanenkampf bezeichnet worden (so Ch. Johnston, 'The Marburg Collection of Cypriote Antiquities' in *Journal of the American Oriental Society* 22 [1901] 18–19). Einen ausführlichen Bericht brachte bereits die *Baltimore Sun* vom 19. Dezember 1900, mit einem teilweisen Abdruck von Col. Warrens Katalog.

Weil der Name 'Warren' häufig ist, stammen längst nicht alle amerikanischen Antiken-Ankäufe, die unter diesem Namen geführt werden, aus dem Vorbesitz unseres Obersten. Außerdem befand sich ein gewisser C. Warren als Altertumsforscher ungefähr zur gleichen Zeit in der Levante wie Colonel Falkland Warren in Zypern. Der erstere gab 1884 mit C.R. Conder gemeinsam ein Buch unter dem Titel *The Survey of Western Palestine. A Complete Account of the Excavations and Researches in Jerusalem from 1866 to the Present Time* heraus.

Der weitaus bekanntere Antikenhändler jener Epoche in den USA war Edward Perry Warren, durch den zahlreiche bedeutende Objekte in den Besitz des Museums of Fine Arts in Boston gelangt waren. Allein im Bronzekatalog des Museums (1971) sind über hundert Objekte als von ihm stammend aufgeführt (dazu noch je ein Stück aus den Sammlungen eines gewissen S.D. Warren und einer Mrs. S.C. Warren). Über E.P. Warren haben O. Burdett und E.H. Goddard ein Buch geschrieben: *Edward Perry Warren, the Biography of a Connoisseur* (1941). Im Band 2 der gesammelten Schriften von Cornelius Vermeule *Art and Archaeology of Antiquity*, dessen Erscheinen man für August 1999 angesagt hat, wird sich ein Beitrag unter dem Titel *Collectors of Greek Art, Edward Perry Warren and his Successors* befinden. Ich verweise nicht ohne Grund auf diesen anderen Warren, weil es bereits Irrtümer gegeben hat. So liest man im Indexband des *Jahrbuches des Deutschen Archäologischen Instituts* für 1911: 'Warren, Colonel Falkland, cyprische Altertümer, Gegenstück des Ludovisischen Throns'. Richtig ist natürlich der Zusammenhang zwischen den kyprischen Altertümern und dem Colonel, falsch jedoch der Hinweis auf den 'Bostoner Thron', das Gegenstück zum Ludovisischen; denn das Denkmal in Boston gelangte dorthin über den anderen

Fig. 19.1: Falkland Warren (links) und drei weitere Personen hinter Köpfen von Figuren aus dem Apollon-Heiligtum von Phrangisa, aufgenommen 1885 in Nikosia. Sammelphoto 2 nach H.-G. Buchholz, centre d'Études Chypriotes, Cahier 16 (1991) 3ff. Taf. 3b.

Warren, und es kann keinen Zweifel geben, daß dieser es in Rom erwarb. Allerdings mochte die Verwechslung bei weniger Sachkundigen zu der Folgerung verleitet haben, daß das Monument aus Zypern stammt. Man vergleiche zu den Vorgängen E. Nash, 'Über die Auffindung und den Erwerb des Bostoner Throns' (*RM* 66, 1959, 104ff.). Zu berücksichtigen ist freilich auch, daß F. Studniczka im genannten Jahrbuch (Band 26, 1911, 50–192: 'Das Gegenstück der Ludovisischen Thronlehne') das verlorene Gesamtdenkmal, zu dem beide Teile (der Ludovisische und der Bostoner) ursprünglich gehörten, auf einen Aphrodite-Altar attisch-jonischen Stils des Gebietes in oder bei Amathous zurückgeführt hat.

Wie oben ausgeführt, verließ Warren 1890 mit seiner Familie die Insel. Darauf wies in Nikosia *The Owl* Nr. 65 vom Sonnabend, dem 12. Juli 1890, Seite 3 wie folgt hin: 'Colonel Falkland Warren, Chief Secretary to Government, leaves Cyprus on Sunday the 13th inst, on three months leave. At the expiration of this leave Colonel Warren will not return to Cyprus, so that we shall lose another of the few remaining officials who came here at the occupation...' In Nr. 52 derselben Zeitung, vom 22. März 1890, war eine Kurzmeldung vorausgegangen: 'We regret to hear that Col. Warren, one of the few remaining officials who came here at the British Occupation, is shortly leaving Cyprus for good'.

Die Mitgliederliste der Hellenic Society enthält ja eine Londoner Adresse von Col. Warren für die Jahre 1890 und 1897. Er hatte, wie es scheint, seine eigenen Fundstücke von der großen, oben erwähnten Kolonialausstellung nicht wieder zurück nach Zypern bringen lassen, vielmehr im British Museum deponiert. Seine Hoffnung eines günstigen Verkaufs gingen nicht in Erfüllung. Die beiden Bilinguen aus Phrangissa verblieben in der Vorderasiatischon Abteilung das Museums, anderes im Department of Greek and Roman Antiquities, davon eine stattliche Auswahl, Kallsteinskulpturen und Terrakotten, als Dauerleihgaben. Sie wechselten jedoch erst mit den 'Erwerbungen des British Museum im Jahre 1910' den Besitzer (A.H. Smith, *AA* 1911, 456 Nr. 5 und 462 Nr. 53: 'A series of limestone figures from Tamassos in Cyprus, collected by the late Colonel Falkland Warren...With the same collection were acquired some terracottas of similar type...a Cypriote Geometric vase, red ware painted with circles in black, from collection of Colonel Falkland Warren'). Veronica Tatton-Brown ist auf letzteren und diese Erwerbungen

Fig. 19.2: *Falkland Warren und Funde aus Phrangissa. Ober- und Unterteil des Kolossos gehören nicht zueinander. Nach Sammelphoto 5. Buchholz a.0. Taf. 5a.*

Fig. 19.3: *Falkland Warren (rechts) mit Köpfen und Figuren aus Phrangissa. Nach Sammelphoto 6, Buchholz a.0. Taf. 5b.*

mehrfach zurückgekommen, u.a. in *Ancient Cyprus* (1987) 4, 21–2, 31, 47, 50, 54, 68.

O.-R. hatte als Grabungsverantwortlicher in Phrangissa sehr wohl eine Vorstellung von der Menge der Funde, wußte überschlägig, was davon in Nikosia und in London existierte, begriff also, daß das Großteil dem wissenschaftlichen Zugriff völlig entzogen war. So schrieb er am 11. August 1893 von London aus vor seiner Fahrt nach Oxford an A. Furtwängler: 'Ich werde genaueres über die Frangissa-Sammlung erfahren. Aber daß sie nicht da ist, ist klar'. Noch eine Notiz O.-R.'s von 1909/10 in Berlin beweist, daß er über Jahrzehnte danach vergeblich fahndete: 'Col.Warren hat die Objekte mit nach Kanada genommien, und meine Nachforschungen nach ihrem Verbleib sind ergebnislos verlaufen'.

Der dritte und letzte Lebensabschnitt Falkland Warrens und seiner Familie spielte sich in der Neuen Welt, in Kanada, ab. Es ließen sich nur spärliche Details seiner Tätigkeiten vom Neubeginn bis zu seinen Tode (1908) finden. Eins davon betrifft den oben beschriebenen Antikenverkauf an Theodore Marburg, den Vetter seiner Frau. Demnach führte er wertvolle Objekte, unter anderem antiken Goldschuck, von der Einwanderung in Kanada bis zum Verkauf ungesichert mit sich, während er Monumentales, größere Kalksteinplastik, Terrakotten und Vasen gleich nach der Ankunft im Osten des amerikanischen Kontinents (in Ottawa) sicher deponierte. Im kanadischen Nationalarchiv existiert eins seiner Handschreiben an den Minister für öffentliche Arbeiten vom 6. Februar 1894. Es beginnt mit der Feststellung, daß seine 'Collection of Antiquities from an excavation of a Temple of Apollo made by me near Tamassus in Cyprus' in die Verantwortlichkeit des Angesprochenen gelangt sei. Warrens Hauptsorge bezieht sich auf die Möglichkeit, daß Nichtfachleute diese Funde manipulieren könntan. So besteht er darauf, daß sie so bleiben sollen, wie sie sind, es sei denn, es werde ein geschulter Restaurator ('a competent person') dafür gefunden und bezahlt. Der Kurator der National Art Gallery, J.W.W. Watts, gibt am 17. Februar 1894 dazu zu Protokoll, daß 'antiquities have been carefully unpacked and restauration has been done in the way of repairing damages ... and if any doubt arises the Curator will consult Col. Warren'.

Warrens Brief weist als Absendeort aus: 'The Grande Prairie via Ducks Station/British Columbia, Canadian Pacilif railway'. Im Dienste der im 'Wilden Westen' im Aufbau begriffenen Eisenbahn hat er dort in mehr als bescheidenen Verhältnissen gelebt. Ein Indianerdorf in British Columbia wurde zum Wohnsitz der Familie, die aus ihm, seiner Gattin, drei Söhnen und drei Töchtern bestand.

Im Jahre 1996, ziemlich genau hundert Jahre nach dem soeben vorgestellten Brief Warrens, meldete sich bei Neda Leipen im Royal Ontario Museum/Toronto ein gewisser Dr. med. Rupert Warren, der sich als Enkel unseres Falkland Warren vorstellte und sich gut an das Haus seines Großvaters in jenem Indianerdorf errinerte. Der Ort erhielt 1908, nach Warrens Tod, dessen Namen 'Falkland'. Allerdings wußte dieser Enkel nicht, daß sein Großvater jemals irgendwelche Altertümer besessen hätte. Andererseits waren ihm Rang und Ansehen der Familie während der Zeit in Zypern recht vertraut. In der Familienerinnerung war sein Großvater inzwischen zum 'Gouverneur von Zypern', aufgestiegen.

Aus den Beständen der 'Public Archives of Canada' wurde mir noch ein weiterer, in Vancouver geschriebener Brief Falkland Warrens vom 28. Dezember 1895 an den Minister of Public Works zugänglich (*L.G.* II/Volume 1074). Offensichtlich konnte einer der zuständigen Ministerialbeamten mit dem Absender 'Col. Warren' nichts anfangen und schrieb 'Geological Museum' an den Rand. Doch geriet das Schreiben danach ganz richtig an den bereits oben genannten Kurator der National Art Gallery, J.W.W. Watts, der es kommentierte. Warren erklärt seine Absicht, während des Sommers 1896 nach Ottawa zu reisen, sofern des Ministerium ihn mit einem 'Railway pass' versorgen könne. Er werde dann anhand von Photos und seinen Klassifikationen seine kyprischen Antiken näher bestimmen und bei deren Restauration beratend mitwirken können... 'He also refers to further collections which he would be willing to put on deposit in the National Art Gallery'.

Wer die Lebensgeschichte Warrens bis dahin rekonstruierte, mußte folgerichtig in Ottawa ansetzen, um die verschollenen Phrangissa-Funde wiederzufinden. Da es dort längst keinen Watts mehr gab, sondern eine aus China stammende Direktorin, kann man sich vorstellen, wie gering ihr Interesse an Kyprischem sein mochte. Obendrein hatte die National Art Gallery bereits im Jahre 1958 Warrens Phrangissa-Funde als Dauerleihgabe an das Royal Ontario Museum weitergegeben, allerdings ohne Begleitpapiere, welche deren Zusammenhang mit der Fundstätte 'Phrangissa' erklärten.

Als ich 1979 meine Suche auf Toronto ausdehnte und mich Neda Leipen in ein Magazin führte, in welchem sämtliche Objekte wohlverwahrt und unsichtbar hinter hölzernen Türen warteten, stand zufällig als einzelnes Gefäß oben auf einem der Schränke eine altertümliche kyprische, aber nicht antike 'Kornos-Kanne', die wegen ihrer Brüche an Hals und Mündung unverwechselbar mit einem ebensolchen Gefäß auf einer Sammelaufnahme übereinstimmte, die – wie oben ausgeführt – von E.A.Carletti, 1885 im damaligen Hause Warrens in Nikosia aufgenommen worden war. Auf dem Photo, in der Nähe dieser Kanne, liest man 'Excavations at Tamassus Cyprus by Colonel Warren R.A. in 1885'. Auf demselben Photo sind zur selben Zeit in Warrens Haus unter anderem ein

Zeus Ammon, zwei Sphingen als Thymiaterienträgerinnen und ein sorgfältig gearbeiteter ägyptisierender Jünglingstorso aufgenommen worden.

Sie alle – insgesamt über 350 Gegenstände – kamen 1979 in den Vitrinen und Schränken in Toronto zum Vorschein. Viele waren in der Tat weder gereinigt noch zusammengefügt. Sie stellen natürlich gegenüber den weniger als zwanzig Fundstücken, welche das Apollonheiligtum von Phrangissa im British Museum repräsentieren, eine ungleich reichere Dokumentation dar. Das Royal Ontario Museum, seinerzeit durch Neda Leipen vertreten, hat sie mir bereitwilligst zur Bearbeitung und Publikation überlassen. Die Vorbereitung ihrer Veröffentlichung im Rahmen meines Tamassos-Unternehmens ist nahezu abgeschlossen.

Danksagungen und Literatur:

Für Auskünfte, Übersendung von Photos, Urkunden-Ablichtungen und vielfache anderweitige Hilfe habe ich zu danken: Donald M. Bailey/British Museum. – Honor Frost/London. – John Hayes/Oxford, vormals Toronto. – Neda Leipen/Royal Ontario Museum, Toronto. – Dem verstorbenen Olivier Masson während eines jahrzehntelangen freundschaftlichen Erfahrungs- und Gedankenaustauschs, desgleichen: Robert Merrillees/Nicosia. – Alan Shapiro/Baltimore. – Susan Sherratt/Oxford. – Veronica Tatton-Brown/British Museum. – Außerdem Christa Sandner-Behringer/Gießen fürs Schreiben und Korrekturlesen.

CCM: J.L. Myres-M. Ohnefalsch-Richter, *A Catalogue of the Cyprus Museum* (Oxford 1899).
Léon Fivel: Pseudonym von O. Masson
KBH: M. Ohnefalsch-Richter, *Kypros, die Bibel und Homer* (Leipzig 1893). Die hier interessierenden Abschnitte stimmen wörtlich mit seiner Leipziger Dissertation 'Die antiken Cultusstätten auf Kypros' (Leipzig, 1891) überein, woher er sie übernommen hat.
Außer der nachfolgenden Literatur findet man weitere Titel unten im Beitrag von M. Given, 'The Fight for the Past, Watkins vs. Warren (1885–86) and the Control of Excavation'.

Brassey 1880: A. Brassey, *Sunshine and Storm in the East, or Cruises to Cyprus and Constantinople* (London 1880).

Buchholz 1985: H.-G. Buchholz, 'Die deutschen Ausgrabungen in Tamassos von 1970 bis heute', in *Praktika 2. Diethnous Kyprologikou Synhedriou, Nikosia 1982*, Band 1 (Nicosia 1885) 229–271, bes. 235–237.

Buchholz 1987: H.-G. Buchholz, 'Tamassos, 4. Bericht, 1977 bis 1986', *AA* 1987, 165–228, bes. 207–211 mit Abb. 36, 38a-d (Phrangissa, aus Warrens Besitz).

Buchholz 1989: H.-G. Buchholz, 'M. Ohnefalsch-Richter als Archäologe auf Zypern', *Centre d'Études Chypriotes. Cahier* 11/12 (1989) 3–27.

Buchholz 1991: H.-G. Buchholz, 'Tamassos-Phrangissa (1885)', *Centre d'Études Chypriotes. Cahier* 16 (1991) 3–15.

Buchholz & Untiedt 1996: H.-G. Buchholz und K. Untiedt, *Tamassos, ein antikes Königreich auf Zypern* (Jonsered 1996).

Fivel 1989: L. Fivel, 'Ohenfalsch-Richter (1850–1917), Essai de Bibliographie', *Centre d'Études Chypriotes. Cahier* 11/12 (1989) 35–40.

Fivel 1996: L. Fivel, 'Ohnefalsch-Richter, Vendeur d'Antiquités chypriotes (1895)', *Centre d'Études Chypriotes. Cahier* 25 (1996) 29–35.

Hermary 1997: A. Hermary, 'Nouveaux Documents sur le Sanctuaire d'Aphrodite à Idalion, Ohnefalsch-Richter 1885', *Centre des Études chypriotes. Cahier* 27 (1997) 97–108, bes. 98.

Hogarth 1889: D.G. Hogarth, *Devia Cypria, Notes of an archaeological journey in Cyprus 1888* (London 1889) 78.

Mallock 1889: W.H. Mallock, *In an enchanted Island, or a Winter's Retreat in Cyprus* (2nd. ed., London 1889) 48–62 (zu Falkland Warren)

Masson 1989: O. Masson, 'Le Colonel Falkland Warren à Chypre, 1878–1880', *Centre d'Études chypriotes. Cahier* 11/12 (1989) 29–34.

Masson 1995: O. Masson, 'Un album de photographiés chypriotes de Max et Magda Ohnefalsch-Richter (1895)', *Centre d'Études chypriotes. Cahier* 23 (1995) 37–39.

Vizetelly 1901: E. Vizetelly, *From Cyprus to Zanzibar* (London 1901) 44 und 46 (zu Falkland Warren).

Warren 1891: Falkland Warren, 'Notes on coins found in Cyprus', *Numismatic Chronicle* 11 (1891) 140–151.

20. Melchior de Vogüé *et alii* and Cyprus: Monsieur Péretié

Hélène Cassimatis

M. Péretié, the personality that we will be concerned with rather briefly, according to what we can learn about him, is an important figure of the nineteenth-century antiquarian world in Lebanon, Syria and Cyprus. The late Olivier Masson would have appreciated this new research about a figure of whom he said 'nous savons très peu de choses'. He belongs to that group of nineteenth-century people seen as part of a side-aspect of the history of archaeology, who nonetheless played a major role. The aim of this colloquium was indeed to bring forward the events and the people, notably the 'lesser' ones, who made history together with those, more famous, that history recalls with docility.

Péretié's name is mentioned in museum papers, archives or last century's publications either as a seller or as a donor. We come upon 'M. Péretié' in many reports and archives but, be it in private or official correspondence, he is always referred to without his full name, as at the time the Christian name was regularly omitted. This paved the way for later misinterpretations that bear heavily on our understanding of certain events.

My aim in bringing up Péretié is manifold. It concerns, mainly, the origin of some of the objects now in public collections of which many lack provenances. But even failing to fully succeed in this respect, a better knowledge of the period and the circumstances is rewarding enough for the historian of archaeology or the historian generally. This last instance conforms with the universal search for our roots as, faced with the ongoing destruction of memory at a pace never experienced before – even if, probably because of the urge, more and more time and money is spent to protect or retain it – it is necessary to try and gain a better understanding of why and how what is now considered the patrimony of the human race, in all its fields, has been collected. The success of museums, exhibitions, and the like, is not only due to the fact that more and more people gain access to knowledge. The prodigious rapidity of change causes unrest even in the young generations, who feel more and more the need to link their own present to a past, whether still near or clouded up centuries away. Next to prestige studies less ambitious ones are gaining interest, shedding light on the making of celebrities. What was considered side-history has become a new field of research, rich with potentialities. The famous collections, private and public, came to be not only because of the will of their initiators, but because of those on whom the former had to rely, the willingness of the latter to please, their wish to become a name in society, or just more trivially to make a living.

Monsieur Péretié was a provider for various collectors: the Duc de Luynes, Louis de Clercq, whose collection owes its greatest part to Péretié, but also Count Melchior de Vogüé whom he met in 1854, William Waddington and others, even Ernest Renan, all benefited from his activities and his experience. Had he not existed, many of the objects now in the Louvre and elsewhere, in the British Museum as well, would not have been there. Because of the availability of his correspondence with Melchior de Vogüé – thanks to the generosity of the family – new details have come to the fore, which otherwise would have remained unknown and the importance of the man forgotten.

Péretié wrote numerous letters to Count Melchior. Many have been saved; not all I am afraid, as there are gaps. Being on very friendly terms with him he wrote always freely, and often extensively, providing valuable information on various events of his day and place. Quite often he states where his finds came from: they were brought to him either by his own agents excavating on his behalf at Tartous or Saida, or by others selling what they had acquired or excavated themselves. It seems that he was a considerable figure in the small world of antiquarian activity.[1]

He was a worldly man too, well-acquainted with the important people of his time who, in turn, seem to have respected and thought highly of him, one of them being Hamilton Lang whose collection is housed in the British Museum (incidentally he provided Péretié, through Cesnola, with a full account of the conditions on which his collection was bought by the British Museum). Henrich Schliemann was another of the personalities acquainted with Péretié. He also knew Cesnola quite well and Cesnola tried to use him and his circle of friends to sell his collection to the Louvre; he provided him with photographs, now in the Vogüé archives, of some of the objects, some of which can be traced in the Metropolitan Museum in New York. Cesnola tried to convince Péretié to cross over to Cyprus to evaluate his finds, but the latter refused.

The private archives deposited at the Archives Nationales by the Vogüé family, together with the Louvre archives and those of the French Ministry of Foreign Affairs,[2] as well as the files kept at the Bibliothèque de l'Institut, help elucidate some points, the first being the identity of Péretié himself: we can now ascertain that his first name and the only one he uses is 'Aimé', and that he was never in charge of the French Consulate in Larnaca from 1889 to 1891, as is often stated, for he died in 1882. It was his son, Alfred, who ended his career in the country and town of his birth, Cyprus and Larnaca, and he was not an antiquarian. The antiquarian is AIME, the Consul is ALFRED, his son. Their biographies have been mixed up because both are mentioned simply as 'Péretié', both sign with an initial A and both were members of the French Consulate.[3] This confusion has given rise to false information.

That explains why Aimé Péretié is so badly known. This would have little to bear on the archaeological collections if the various sources had not shown that some precision can be gathered as to the provenance of various objects. What I am presenting is a short introduction to what is a complex affair and will eventually lead to a fuller publication. As this promises to be a long search, you will forgive my not being able to provide you as yet with full information.

The Péretié family migrated from Marseilles to Tartous or Tortosa in Lebanon in 1816. The father, a very prosperous merchant, seems to have suffered from adverse circumstances and lost his fortune. He had two sons, born in Marseilles: Antoine Gabriel born in 1804 and Aimé Antoine Napoléon born in 1808. Antoine Gabriel died in 1853 and need not delay us. The one we are concerned with is Aimé: after his father's death he had to earn his living. He first went to Larnaca as private secretary to M. Méchain, the French consul, probably in 1829. There he worked unofficially at the French Consulate as drogman and chancelier.[4] In 1831 Péretié married Marie Carpani, a

Fig. 20.1: The wedding certificate of Aimé Péretié in Larnaca: from the catholic parish of Larnaca, for which I thank Mme Pouradier-Duteil.

French girl living in Larnaca with her parents.[5] Their wedding certificate has been found, thanks to Mme Pouradier-Duteil. Their son Alfred was born in Larnaca in January 1832 and they all stayed in Cyprus until about 1834. These details strongly link the new Péretié family with Cyprus. Unfortunately that is about all we can recover from the Cypriote archives themselves as most seem to have been lost. However, I have not given up hope of finding more.

Aimé Péretié was surely a captivating personality. Important people, such as the poet Lamartine (a deputy at the time), who met Péretié in 1832 when he visited Cyprus, began harassing ministers to help the young man by providing him with a permanent job, which he finally obtained in 1834. He became first a 'Drogman auxiliaire' in Tripoli in Syria until 1839 – being a Drogman, in fact an interpreter, was a title that could be had only by following

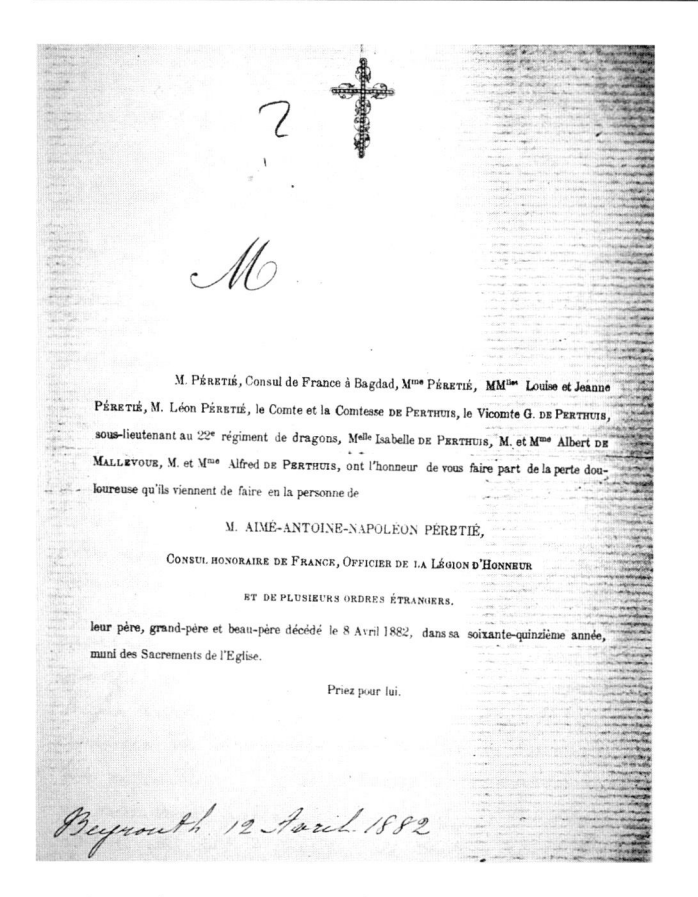

Fig. 20.2: The announcement of Pérétié's death in Beyrouth.

certain courses and obtaining a degree – then in 1843 'Drogman Chancelier' in Jerusalem for a short time, and finally in 1844 'Drogman Chancelier' in Beyrouth, where he remained until his death in April 1882. He died as '1er Drogman Chancelier du Consulat de France à Beyrouth, Officier de la Legion d'Honneur' and 'Consul honoraire' according to the French Foreign Affairs archives. His daughter Louise married Count Edmond de Perthuis in 1853.

Aimé Pérétié spent all of his career in Lebanon. I do not intend to deal much longer with his biography. What this first approach seeks to do is to firmly distinguish the father from the son and avoid any further misinterpretations. Alfred, the son, began as Drogman for a short time, then continued his career as consul in various places such as Mossoul, Baghdad and Smyrna, ending up in Larnaca as French Consul from 1889 to 1891. Alfred had little to do with archaeology, unlike his father Aimé, who was thoroughly engaged in antiquities, having excavations carried out for him, or even sometimes joining his team of excavators, in Beyrouth, Saida and Tortosa. From Aimé's letters to Vogüé we learn that he seemed to have been the person to whom were brought whatever objects were discovered, from Cyprus as well. He certainly went many times to Cyprus as his wife had her family there. How often? For the moment it is still a guess. What becomes clear is that, while some objects were bought by him personally in Cyprus when he happened to be there (as he states in a letter of May 1868), others were brought to him in Beyrouth. Such a case in point is a Greek inscription found in Larnaca. as Georges Colonna-Ceccaldi informs us, and brought to the French Consulate but now, he goes on to say, is in the hands of 'M. Pérétié'.[6] How and why? A clue may lie in a letter of his brother Tiburce Colonna-Ceccaldi of 14 February 1870 answering Froehner – the antiquarian in Paris – about an offer made by the antiquarian Hoffmann, in which he writes that he has first to consult with his associate M. Pérétié before accepting.[7] This implies that many transactions were carried out with Pérétié or with his knowledge. The correspondence with Vogüé informs us that all these men were well acquainted, being part of a small group sharing common interests. To discover more precise information it will be necessary to consult different archives.

Pérétié was a well-known collector as well. His interest in antiquities was twofold: first he bought and sold to make a better living, his salary being insufficient. At the time the officers of the various consulates had to find some means other than their meagre salary to make a decent living. Dealing in antiquities was recognised and accepted, and even encouraged by governments. In the French Foreign Affairs archives it is clearly stated that business was a necessity. Secondly he very quickly became really taken by the search for the past and the finds and by the historical knowledge he gained. He came to genuinely like it: he often expresses his happiness to be with his antiquities and his sadness to part with so many of them. He became an 'amateur éclairé' shrewd enough to recognise what he saw. He sent important lots to Paris that went to auction in 1851, 1854, 1855, 1856, and probably later. He donated many objects as well, and the Louvre benefited from his generosity. His last gift was an important fragment of a bronze statue: it is the whole right leg up to the hip of a male statue, of fine workmanship (inv. no. MNC 1190=Br69). It is still unpublished, but not unknown, as Langlotz had thought it could go with the Chatsworth head. This seems rather unlikely as the style of the head is so very different from that of the leg. The idea may have sprung from the fact that De Ridder, in his catalogue of the Louvre bronzes, attributes the fragment to Mattei as the donor and Cyprus as the place of origin. The Louvre archives tell another story: it is the last gift from Pérétié, handed over by his son and comes from Saida. Yet it is not that simple: in a letter to his mother dated 8 February 1862, Duthoit gives a vivid picture of various events and sights among which the existence of fragments of bronze statues found years

Fig. 20.3: The Pnytagoras stater in the Cabinet des Médailles, no. 4816. Courtesy M. Amandry, Bibliothèque Nationale Cabinet des Médailles.

ago by the Turks, one kept by Mattei and which he saw. He writes: 'dans une maison appartenant à M. Mattei Sancti on nous fit voir une cuisse de statue en bronze d'un fini exquis et d'une taille double ou triple nature. Il y a 27 ans environ des Turcs, en fouillant pour extraire des pierres, rencontrèrent cette figure complète et furent assez barbares pour la briser en mille pièces afin de s'en partager les morceaux...'[8] Could the Louvre leg belong to the same lot? It would be worth analyzing the bronze,[9] unless a letter of Péretié is found with some further information.

Among his numerous acquisitions are two gold staters of Pnytagoras, the Cypriote king of Salamis and contemporary of Alexander the Great. In a letter dated August 1863 to Melchior de Vogüé he proudly announces that he has just bought a stater of Pnytagoras and is informing Waddington; in due time it was forwarded to Waddington who published it. One at least is now in the Cabinet des Médailles of the Bibliothèque Nationale. The coins come from Saida and were found in three different very important and varied lots (as we learn from a letter to Waddington published by the latter). He also bought numerous coins of the Lusignans, some rare, which he enumerates in two other letters (dated April and May 1863) all coming from a large lot, found in Tortosa and published by Waddington as well.[10]

Of the many objects I will mention only a few.

One is the famous Phoenician sarcophagus of Eshmunazar found in 1855 now in the Louvre. Péretié states very clearly that it was found in the necropolis of Saida in the part belonging to him 'ce terrain m'appartient'. This is precise information and helps situate the other Phoenician sarcophagi: two in the Louvre and one in the British Museum. The Eshmunazar sarcophagus almost created a diplomatic incident between the French and British governments, as the British Consul there would not accept Péretié's claim. To end the quarrel, the Turkish government finally decided to send the monument to Constantinople (as the city was still named then in official correspondence), but through efficient diplomatic efforts it was handed as a gift to the French government. The Duc de Luynes paid Péretié his expenses and donated it to the Louvre, then published the inscriptions in 1856. In the Vogüé archives are three wash-paintings of Eshmunazar's tomb by Melchior de Vogüé. It would be very interesting to publish them in a future volume of the whole saga.

The other famous object is the bilingual tablet from Cyprus, now in the Cabinet des Médailles, which the Duc de Luynes bought from Péretié in 1850 and donated to the Bibliothèque Nationale.[11] For the moment there is no further information as to the exact location of its findspot, and I do not believe we will ever discover more as it was found and presented by peasants, who were always very reluctant to give precise details. All we can do is collect whatever information comes along and try to build up a picture of the findspots.[12]

It is also unclear where the embossed silver plate in the Louvre (AO 20134) was found. It was bought from Péretié, but has no provenance. According to Colonna-Ceccaldi it came from Idalion. In an article sent to the *Revue Archéologique*[13] his brother Count Tiburce writes: '...la colline à l'ouest [the site is Dali, Ambelliri] quand on fait face au village...Sur le sommet ont été trouvés il y a plus de 20 ans, 14 coupes en argent ciselé dont les paysans ont fait fondre 13 et la 14e fut rachetée par M. Péretié, puis cédée au Duc de Luynes..' (this brings us to the years 1849–50, and the Dali tablet was bought by de Luynes in 1850, which means that certain objects were part of a group and were discovered all in the same area and some of them together).

He writes that he bought in Beyrouth a series of Cypriote vases bearing painted inscriptions in Cypriote syllabary (that implies that he did not acquire them in Cyprus or through known excavations). Others came from Cesnola's collection according to De Ridder[14] and I quote, 'M. de Vogüé a étudié plusieurs des inscriptions et me communique: les deux vases proviennent de fouilles faites dans l'île de Chypre par M. de Cesnola, dans les années 1866, et suivantes. De la collection de M. de Cesnola ils passèrent dans celle de M. Péretié à Beyrouth où je les vis au mois de novembre 1868. M. Péretié les céda à M. de Clercq en 1872'. The vases were for de Clercq's collection as Péretié had an unwritten oral contract with him to provide antiquities. De Clercq[15] writes that from 1859 Péretié was his agent in Beyrouth and that all excavations he undertook were according to his (de Clercq's) instructions and with his funds.[16] This is going too far. Péretié got his funds from various sources: auctions or from what he sold directly himself, including to the French government, to others and de Clerq of course. He used his funds as he pleased. Had he been de Clercq's sole agent, he could not have sold his collections at official auctions in Paris. Furthermore Péretié had a better knowledge of the archaeology and topography of Syria and Lebanon than de Clercq. As to the Cypriote vases with painted inscriptions, they are yet to be found. They are not in the Louvre and were probably sold or donated elsewhere by de Clercq's descendants.

Among the objects donated by Péretié to the Louvre (apart from the bronze leg already mentioned MNC 1190= Br. 69), were three limestone heads from Cyprus brought over by de Saulcy, coming from Péretié according to the museum archives: two are rather small and not in very good condition, but the third is a colossal head of Phoenician style and excellent workmanship, according to Longpérier who saw them all and suggested that Péretié be thanked for his gift (letter of 1854). But these have not yet been located, as the Louvre inventories ignore them. What became of them? One possibility might be that they were sent to one of the provincial museums and could now be lying in a storeroom.

A thorough examination of all material available will shed more light on the origins and travels of many objects. This means going through many private and public archives of various sorts including those in the British Museum.[17] The Péretié archives themselves may still contain surprises, as the family still exists and holds some papers and probably photographs, which would give us a better image of their ancestor.

Notes

1. An extensive publication of the correspondence would provide much information in various fields.
2. Ministère des Affaires Etrangères: *Dossier Individuel Serie* 1 – Péretié no. 252.
3. S. Béraud, 'Liste des consuls français à Chypre de 1661 jusque'en 1959', *Kypriakai Spoudai* (1969) 149–154. In this list under the name 'Péretié Alfred consul' has been added 'archéologue amateur' perpetuating the confusion. Gustave Cirilli,'Choses et gens d'archéologie chypriote: le débarquement d'une "consulesse" américaine à Chypre', *Kypriaka Chronika* (June-July 1923) 175–177 lists a number of personalities who, from 1845, visited Cyprus. Among them is Péretié. Unfortunately Cirilli cites them at random and not chronologically, so we cannot know where Péretié fits in.
4. All the above information is to be found in a note written by Bottu, the next French consul in Larnaca (he died there in 1833), kept in the Péretié papers at the Ministère des Affaires Etrangères.
5. The Carpani family, originating in Cephallonia, migrated to Larnaca at the very beginning of the nineteenth century. Their name is mentioned among those asked to present themselves at the Consulate on 31 October 1801 in order to receive official residents' papers: A.L. Koudanari, 'Eptanesiake symbole eis ten koinonken synthesin tou kypriakou plethismou', *Kypriakai Spoudai* (1976) 87–103. They were 'French protégés' as from 1797 the Ionian islands were under the protectorate of France: cf. A.L. Koudonari, 'E katodos ton Eptanesion eis Kypron', *Acts of the 2nd congress of Cypriote Studies* (Nicosia 1987) 77–91. See also, A. Pouradier Duteil-Loizidou, 'La communauté française à Chypre á la fin du XVIIe et au début du XVIIIe siècle', in *Chypre et la Méditerranée orientale* (*Travaux de la Maison de l'Orient méditerranéen*, Lyon 1999) forthcoming. André Carpani (1783–1855) was to become Aimé Péretié's father-in-law: his daughter Marie (1810–1883) married Aimé in 1831 in Larnaca. Curiously her name is not mentioned in her husband's death announcement of 1882.
6. 'Nouvelles archéologiques et correspondance', *RA* n.s. 22 (1870–71) 56.
7. O. Masson, 'Correspondances chypriotes: lettres des frères Colonna-Ceccaldi et de L. Palma di Cesnola à Froehner', *Centre d'Études Chypriotes. Cahier* 14 (1990) 34 and n. 28.
8. J. Foucart-Borville, 'La correspondance chypriote d'Edmond Duthoit (1862 et 1865)', *Centre d'Etudes Chypriotes. Cahier* 4 (1985) 14. According to Foucart-Borville it belonged to the Tamassos Apollo.
9. This was suggested by Langlotz, but never carried out.
10. W.H. Waddington, *Mélanges de Numismatique* (*Académie des inscriptions et belles lettres, deuxième série,* Paris 1867) 33.
11. O. Masson, *Inscriptions syllabiques chypriotes* 2, (1983), no. 217 p. 235; Id. 'Les archeologues et voyageurs du XIXes', Kinyras. L'archeologie français à Chypre, Maison de l'Orient Mediterraneen (1993), p. 18 naming Peretie

"Antoine" and referring p. 19 to G. Perrot, 'L'île de Cypre. Son rôle dans l'histoire', *Revue des deux Mondes* (Janvier-Fevrier 1879) 572. "Achille", a name given to him in Musee de Cannes. Chypre dans l'antiquité, *Cahier du Centre d'Etudes Chypriotes* 19 (1993), he never possessed.
12. Georges Colonna Ceccaldi later wrote that some other objects found at Ambelliri came from the same find spot.
13. 'Lettres de Chypre', *RA* n.s.20 (1869) 208–213.
14. *Collection de Clercq. Antiquités chypriotes V* (Paris 1906) 329.
15. *Collection de Clercq II. Antiquités assyriennes* (Paris 1903) 213.
16. As n.15.
17. The editor notes that no mention of his name has yet been located in the archives already perused.

21. T. B. Sandwith and the beginnings of Cypriote archaeology

R. S. Merrillees

I would like to begin this paper with two quotations. Both are taken from the openings of archaeological works on Cyprus. The first is the following: 'Explanations for the rise of social complexity increasingly turn to politico-economic, social, or behavioural models that emphasize multivariate causality. Because the incipient stages in the development of social complexity on Cyprus have never been examined in an explicit, problem-oriented context, the material focus of this study is on the presentation and analysis of archaeological data from the Prehistoric Bronze Age ('Early-Middle Cypriot' periods). A broad range of evidence is discussed, and, in order to evaluate the inter-relationship amongst environment, production, exchange, and location in the development of power and prestige, the social implications of metallurgical and agricultural production are considered within a politico-economic framework' (Knapp 1990, 147). The second reads as follows: 'Recent excavations in Cyprus have brought to light a vast number of tombs of the primitive inhabitants of the Island, and a careful examination of the contents of these will help us to understand something of the manners, ideas, and artistic character of the different peoples whose remains are there deposited' (Sandwith 1880, 127). The first was written in the late 1980's by Dr A.B. Knapp, Reader in Archaeology at the University of Glasgow, and is a typical example of the prevailing academic jargon. The second was delivered in a communication to the Society of Antiquaries of London on 4 May 1871 by Her Britannic Majesty's Vice-Consul, Thomas B. Sandwith, Esquire, and still makes sense. The contrast between these two introductory paragraphs, which are separated by over a century's scholarly writing, reflects not just their fundamental difference in tone and expression, but extends to their divergent approaches to the discipline which has brought us together to-night.

Central to understanding the methodologies and mentalities of both generations of students is an appreciation of the audiences to which these quotations were directed. In the case of Thomas Backhouse Sandwith, there can be no doubt about the target of his presentation. His paper, entitled 'On the different styles of Pottery found in Ancient Tombs in the Island of Cyprus', was read to and subsequently published by the Fellows of the Society of Antiquaries of London, who represented at that time the pre-eminent body in England of those actively interested or engaged in archaeological research. Though Sandwith was not himself a Fellow, he and they evidently saw this association as the one most suitable for the purposes of receiving the outcome of his considered views on the cultural evolution of ancient Cyprus. He therefore appealed to the kinds of elite that people contemporary writings on Cypriote prehistory but exist only in the imaginings of those for whom the study of the island's past is more a matter of theories than facts. Through unflagging repetition, an approach along the lines of the first quotation has come to predominate in works on Cypriote antiquity, and nearly all the contributions made by the newer generation of researchers to this field have to a greater or lesser extent been influenced by the mindset and vocabulary therein represented. The audience, for which this statement was intended, was less the international archaeological community than a coterie of English speaking prehistorians who alone can understand it. Why Sandwith's ideas, unlike Knapp's, did not have the same early, tangible and widespread impact on the course of archaeological writing is worthy of consideration in its own right, and my paper is devoted to exploring and hopefully explaining the reasons for the initial failure and eventual success of this, the first academic attempt at synthesising the prehistory of Cyprus, in generating a new momentum in the study of the island's ancient remains.

Sandwith's sixteen-page article purports to reproduce the text of his lecture with a few footnotes and bibliographical references, and five plates of engravings, together with a number of illustrations in the text. As we shall see, the paper, though delivered in 1871, was subsequently revised and did not appear in print in *Archaeologia* until 1877, for reasons given in the endnote as follows: 'The delay in publishing this memoir has arisen from the small size of the sketches that accompanied it, which rendered them unsuitable for engraving. Advantage has, however, been taken of the author's having sent a portion of his collection to the Leeds Exhibition, 1875, to obtain larger drawings from selected examples. Where necessary these have been supplemented from the collections of Cyprian pottery in the British Museum' (Sandwith 1880, 142). In fact, though the volume of *Archaeologia* in which the article appears was issued in 1880, the text of the paper was separately printed in 1877, with its own title page and pagination, but containing plates published in 1876, with a reference in the top right hand corner to the pagination in the version that was included in *Archaeologia* Vol. XLV. From this we may infer that the text had been finalised for publication by 1877 at the latest. In my description of Sandwith's article I will use the pottery names and relative chronology canonised by the Swedish Cyprus Expedition in its series of volumes on the archaeology of Cyprus. This is no arbitrary or haphazard choice on my part, but one dictated by the need to use well-established and widely accepted empirical means to make typological comparisons and hence historical sense of the tangible evidence. It does not deny the value, still less the validity, of the results from the scientific analysis of the data, but presumes that these findings will be used not to replace, but to refine the nomenclature currently applied. Sandwith did not himself invent the terms by which we differentiate ceramic wares or periods of time, but for better or worse he laid the foundations for their development.

According to the Minute Book of the Ordinary Meeting of the Society of Antiquaries on 4 May 1871, Thomas B. Sandwith, British Consul at Crete, spoke on 'On the different styles of pottery found in the ancient tombs in the island of Cyprus'. In connection with this paper two exhibitions were laid before the Society. Colonel Lane Fox, who subsequently became General Pitt Rivers (Brown 1991; Masson 1996, 8), displayed Cypriote antiquities from the Cesnola collection, and Mr J.W. Flower displayed objects from the same source. 'Thanks were ordered to be returned for these Exhibitions and Collections'. The communication by Sandwith had been announced in the Executive Committee of the Society at its meeting on 19 April 1871, and the Committee resolved at its meeting on 3 May 1871 that the exhibitions of antiquities of Cyprus by Colonel Lane Fox and Mr Flower be noticed in the Proceedings. At its meeting on 10 May 1871 the Executive Committee of the Society recommended that Mr Sandwith's paper on Cypriote pottery be printed in *Archaeologia* with illustrations, but nothing further was done until the minutes of the Committee's meeting on 29 April 1875 record that a letter had been received from 'The Rev. H. Sandwith requesting that his brother's M.S. might be returned in order to be used for arranging some Cypriote pottery at the Leeds Exhibition. The Director undertook to return the M.S. as requested'. The next we hear of the plans for publication is the following entry in the Committee's minutes of its meeting on 16 March 1876 : 'The Director submitted to the Committee Mr Kell's Estimate (76.10.0) for 5 Plates of Cypriote Pottery and recommended to the Council that the same be approved subject to the opinion of the Treasurer'. The name of C.F. Kell appears at the bottom right hand corner of the plates. The draftsman, whose initials C.H.R. are printed in the bottom left hand corner, has not so far been identified.

Sandwith starts his paper with a straightforward description of the kinds of tombs from which the pottery came, and the cemeteries of which they formed part, the human remains and the funerary assemblages, noting that the bodies were not interred in coffins, but in a lying or sitting posture, accompanied by vessels for their sustenance in the after life (Sandwith 1880, 127–128). He then observes that 'the pottery excavated comprises an immense variety of styles, both in form and ornamentation, the styles, moreover, being so distinct as to make it easy to separate the cemeteries into different classes...'(Sandwith 1880, 128). 'Proceeding now to the classification of the pottery', as Sandwith states (1880, 129), he separates it into four groups, which turn out to be less ceramic subdivisions than chronological sequences based on the classes of cemetery which contain the same or similar kinds of pottery. This becomes evident, not only from the wording used to introduce each section, but in his observations about the geographical range of the cemeteries belonging to the same 'class'. Class I is characterised by 'a distinct and very remarkable style of pottery' made up of 'red vases, highly glazed, with lines incised in the clay when soft.... A plain bowl without a handle being a frequent form.... A few of the vases are black, and sometimes the black and red are blended, as if produced in baking' (Sandwith 1880, 129). Most of the pottery is Red Polished III of E.C. III to M.C. I, between 2100 and 1900 BC (Sandwith 1880, Pl. IX.4,5,6) with the occasional B.P. specimen (Sandwith 1880, Pl. IX.2), datable to M.C.I. He notes the existence of only three cemeteries, one near Dali in the centre of the island and the other two near Larnaca on the south-eastern coast, containing this 'species' of pottery, and records the presence in these tombs of bronze or copper spear heads.

In Class II, the most typical form of vase is the juglet of

Base-ring and Bucchero Wares (Sandwith 1880, Pl. IX.3,1) and the White Slip bowl (Sandwith 1880, Pl. X.1,2), which occur together with animal containers, most commonly the bull, presumably the Base-ring II bull vase, and the White Painted VI zoomorphic vase (Sandwith 1880, 130, Pl. III). Also represented is the Base-ring II female figurine, which he hesitated to identify as Venus (Sandwith 1880, 130, Pl. X. 4). Another vessel, described as having its pattern 'pricked into the clay while moist', is evidently not Pl. IX.5, to which reference is made in the text (Sandwith 1880, 130), and which was in any case previously cited (Sandwith 1880, 129), but Pl. IX.7, which is a unique Tell el Yahudiya acorn vase of a type not represented in Kaplan's corpus (Kaplan 1980, 36–7, 328–9, Figs 129.e,f; 130.a). While the one in the Sandwith collection had three bodies, the specimens listed by Kaplan have only one and all come from Palestine. It was obviously an import and can be dated to M.C. III or L.C. I between the seventeenth and the sixteenth centuries BC. All the other vases belong to the Late Bronze Age. Sandwith also illustrates some of the copper or bronze implements found in tombs of this class or phase (Sandwith 1880, 132, Ill.). They are typical of the Bronze Age before L.C. I. Sandwith states that the cemeteries in this group are more commonly met with than those of the preceding class, the existence of eight to ten being already recorded, and that the pottery recovered from these tombs had exact parallels in finds from the Delta site of Saïs in Lower Egypt (Sandwith 1880, 131). The specimens to which he refers were on display in the 'Boulak Museum' near Cairo, that is the 'Musée d'antiquités égyptiennes de S.A. le Khédive à Boulaq.' This museum, the first in Egypt to house relics of the Pharaonic civilisation of the Nile Valley, was founded by the pioneer French Egyptologist, Auguste Mariette-Bey (David 1994, 154 ff.), inaugurated in October 1863, and remained at Boulaq, a suburb of Cairo, until 1891, when it was transferred to the Palace of Giza before being relocated in its present building in 1900 (Drioton 1950; Dia ʿAbou-Ghazi 1988, 11).

The third class of cemeteries covered, according to Sandwith, a much wider area of the island than the first two (Sandwith 1880, 132) and produced pottery 'separated by a wide gulf from that previously described' (Sandwith 1880, 133). Characteristic forms are White Painted jugs (Sandwith 1880, Pl. X.5), bowls (Sandwith 1880, Pl. XI.3) and amphorae (Sandwith 1880, Pl. XIII) and Black Slip jugs (Sandwith 1880, Pl. XII.3), of the Cypro-Geometric period, and Bichrome jars (Sandwith 1880, Pls XI.1, XII.5), bowls (Sandwith 1880, Pl. XII.1) and jugs (Sandwith 1880, Pls X.7, XII.4), and Red-on-Black jugs (Sandwith 1880, Pl. XI.2), belonging to the Cypro-Archaic period. He refers to, but does not illustrate, a scene covering two thirds of a neck of a Bichrome amphora (the only fragment remaining), which shows 'a goat carried to sacrifice, tied to a pole borne on men's shoulders, followed by a man with uplifted arms, and wearing a high-crowned cap' (Sandwith 1880, 135). It was discovered by Robert (later Sir Robert) Hamilton Lang, of whom see further below, and is now in the Département des Antiquités Orientales of the Louvre (MNB322), where it is said have come from Pyla (Perrot and Chipiez 1885, 318 Fig. 255, and pp. 314, 317; Karageorghis and des Gagniers 1974, 48–9 no. VI. 2; Caubet et al. 1992, 86 no. 95; cf. Masson 1966; Caubet 1976, 168–9). In these deposits were also encountered figurines (Sandwith 1880, Pl. X.3) and lamps (Sandwith 1880, 136, Ill.). Class III clearly covers the Iron Age. In the fourth class of cemeteries, glass vessels are said to predominate, while the pottery is coarser and much less abundant (Sandwith 1880, 139). None was illustrated. Some tombs were built of masonry and contained sarcophagi as well as circular stone columns, which he calls stelae, and bore inscriptions (Sandwith 1880, 140–1). Jewellery was also encountered. This group can be assigned to the Cypro-Classical, but especially Roman times. Sandwith ends his paper with a detailed rebuttal of a claim by Luigi Palma di Cesnola, his American Consular colleague, that tombs belonging to Sandwith's third class were discovered by Cesnola 'lying many feet underneath the more modern ones containing glass' (Sandwith 1880, 141–2.).

As far as the critical apparatus is concerned, Sandwith's paper is singularly light. Such bibliography as there is, is nevertheless historiographically revealing. The earliest work he cites is an article by the Rev. Professor Rawlinson 'in the January number of the Sunday at Home for 1869' (Sandwith 1880, 133). He also quotes from the catalogue of an auction sale of Cypriote antiquities from the collection of Luigi Palma di Cesnola in Paris on 25 and 26 March 1870 (Sandwith 1880, 141; Masson 1990, 36ff.; 1992, 138–148), and draws attention to the fact that 'Dr. Birch, in his History of Pottery, states, that vases very similar in character to those now under consideration have been found at Athens, Santorin, and a few other places, and he thinks that they cannot belong to a later age than the seventh century B.C.' (Sandwith 1880, 138). No place or date of publication, or page reference is given, but the edition he consulted was not the first one published in 1857, but the second which came out in 1873, as the quotation occurs for the first time in the latter (Birch 1873, 180–4). For an analysis of 'Cyprian' metal objects, he refers the reader, in a footnote (a) on p. 132, to the *Compte Rendu du Congrès Préhistorique de Stockholm*, p. 346. What is being specified here is an article by A.W. Franks 'Sur la composition des instruments en métal trouvés dans l'île de Chypre, et sur d'autres trouvailles d'instruments en cuivre' in *Congrès international d'anthropologie et d'archéologie préhistoriques. Compte Rendu de la 7ᵉ Session, Stockholm 1874*, published in Stockholm in 1876 (pp. 346–351). Sandwith's knowledge of this work was evidently due to the author's association with Hamilton Lang (p. 348). The fact that these last two references must have been incorporated into the text of Sandwith's paper well after its delivery to the Society of Antiquaries in 1871 shows that it had been revised before being printed by 1877, and we have seen how the manuscript was withdrawn from the Society in 1875 (see above p. 223).

We now know, from a letter dated 18 March 1870 from Sir Charles Newton, then Keeper of the Department of Greek and Roman Antiquities in the British Museum, that it was at his instigation that Sandwith 'drew up and sent to the Museum an excellent report on the recently discovered Graeco-Phoenician tombs and remains in Cyprus'. It must have been originally completed before 1 June 1869, while Sandwith was still in Larnaca, for on that date Newton sent him a letter with the following P.S.: 'If you have no objection, I should like to have your Report printed in the Transactions of the Royal Society of Literature'. To which Sandwith replied, promptly and modestly, on 23 June 1869, in the following terms: 'If you think my paper on the Cyprian cemeteries worth printing, by all means let it be printed, and I cannot but feel flattered at the honour accorded it' (cf. Williams 1996, 102 n.2). What happened after that, and why it ended up being delivered to the Society of Antiquaries, is not recorded, but Newton was a Fellow of the Society and no doubt instrumental in arranging for its presentation under these auspices. We also know this was the first and only archaeological paper to have been written and published by Sandwith (cf. Goring 1988, 13–15). Indeed Sandwith was not an academic, but a Consular officer, who began his civil service career as Secretary to Mr Skene, Civil Commissioner to the Osmanli Irregular Cavalry, from 1855 to 1856 and was subsequently attached the next year to the British Consulate in Aleppo. He then served in other Consulates in the Levant from 1858 to 1864, before being appointed Vice-Consul at Larnaca in Cyprus on 12 October 1865. A promotion to the rank of Consul on 27 May 1870 took him from Cyprus, which he left on 13 September 1870, to Khania in Crete, whence he was transferred to Tunis on 20 March 1885 (Williams 1996, 100). His last consular posting was Odessa, from which he retired on 13 October 1891. All that we know of his educational background is that he went to Christ Church School in London, matriculated at London University in 1848, and graduated from St. Catherine's College, Cambridge, in 1856, with the degree of Bachelor of Arts.

An English Consulate is known to have existed in Cyprus as early as 1626 (Luke 1921, 87). Until 1825 all English Consular representatives were appointed and paid by the Levant Company (Luke 1921, 99), but because of the growing complexity of Turkey's relations with the Great Powers, it was decided to wind up the Company and transfer responsibility for the Consulates to the British Government (Luke 1921, 102). From that time on, the Consulates in the Levant were to report to the Consul General in Constantinople, for the information of the Minister at the Sublime Porte, 'all occurrences connected with their Consulate' (Luke 1921, 160). When Sandwith arrived on 1 May 1865 to take up his position as British Vice-Consul in Larnaca, the Consulate had been placed under the jurisdiction of the Consulate in Beirut in the Lebanon (Luke 1921, 215). There Sandwith joined the foreign Consular Corps, which had always had its residence in Larnaca. Under Turkish rule, Larnaca was the leading port in the island, the seat of the Commercial Court and the headquarters of the Sanitary, Quarantine and Customs Administration (Luke 1921, 9). According to Luke, it owed its commercial pre-eminence during this period to the fact that in it lived a small, but wealthy, community of Catholics, who virtually monopolised the foreign trade of the island. While of varied descent – French, Genoese, Ionian, Maltese, Syrian and Venetian – its members were under the protection of Britain, France or some other European power, and most of the European Consular representatives were chosen from amongst them. As has been previously pointed out, Sandwith was not locally engaged, but a Consul de la carrière.

All the Consuls in Larnaca, with the curious exception of the French, were, in the early nineteenth century at least, engaged in trade (Luke 1921, 146–7), but also performed many of the duties now assumed by diplomats, such as reporting on political, social and economic situations and developments, and making demarches to the local Turkish authorities as required. Sandwith's despatches to the Ambassador in Constantinople, for example, of 15 April 1867, on the treatment of Greek and other Christian subjects of the Sultan, and of 19 August 1867 and 19 June 1869, on taxation in the Ottoman provinces (Luke 1921, 216ff., 225ff., 238ff.), show him to have been very well informed, conscientious in fulfilling his professional duties, and balanced and judicious in his assessments. According to Gustave Laffon, a Levantine of French background who was employed in the French Consular office in Larnaca from 1865 or 1866 to 1874 (Milliex 1973, esp. 226), the European colony in Larnaca in 1867 was utterly decadent. It consisted of French and Italian merchants, who were all in desperate straits, and only the Greeks, whom he regarded as locals rather than Europeans, showed the commercial instinct which was their trademark. There was only one English representative, T.B. Sandwith, but he was the most important man in the island and had the backing of the Ottoman Bank, under Hamilton Lang (Hill 1952, 247–8). There was nothing, so far as we know, in Sandwith's training, background or previous experience to indicate a latent taste for antiquity, though he must have been exposed to the remains of the past during all his assignments in the Near East before coming to Cyprus.

According to Hamilton Lang, Sandwith first became interested in archaeological pursuits in the following way: 'In 1868, after a torrential rain, some peasants of Dali were passing along the base of a hillside to the north of their village on the summit of which is a well which gets the name of Laksha Nicoli. They found, evidently washed down from the hillside, a few pieces of ancient pottery in perfect preservation, and one of them representing a duck. The peasants at once thought that more might be found where these came from, and they set to work to turn over the ground on the hillside. To their surprise they got into tombs, and extracted pieces of pottery in great number, and some lances in bronze. News of the discovery soon spread, and as the villagers were in much distress, having lost most of their crops from the ravages of locusts, they repaired in great numbers to the pottery-diggings. The Sunday after, when walking with Mr. Pierides (who was my coadjutor in all connected with antiquities, and who was my instructor from his superior, nay, very exceptionally profound antiquarian and philological knowledge), I heard of these discoveries and without loss of time we arranged to send an intelligent *employé* to the seat of the find, with orders to acquire some objects and send them for inspection. This agent found Mr. Ceccaldi already on the spot. The objects were new and varied, and nearly all of them came to Mr. Ceccaldi or myself. This mine led to the discovery of many more, and the peasants of Dali came to spend all their time in searching for tombs and rifling them. The number of objects increased, and so did the purchasers. My friend Mr. Sandwith, the British vice-consul, began to acquire, and after him another friend came into the field, who although he began last, was destined to carry on his explorations longer than any of us, and with the most brilliant results, I mean, the American Consul-General de Cesnola. The novelty began to pass away, and yet new arrivals came to us daily. Our houses became like earthenware shops. The pieces found might be counted by tens of thousands, and the tombs opened by thousands' (Lang 1878, 331–2).

So far as we know, Sandwith did not conduct his own excavations, though, as Goring points out, there is a tantalising reference to his own fieldwork in the cemeteries around Dhali (Goring 1988, 13). The reason for this abstinence presumably lies in the fact that, in Hamilton Lang's words, 'of all the consular body at Larnaca the British Consul was the only one who was unable to obtain from Constantinople a firman for excavating. I applied officially to the British Embassy, and privately to Mr. Pisani, but the answer was that as the Porte itself had the intention of forming a museum no firman could be obtained. Of course the British Embassy, sacredly respecting Turkish rights, was bound to accept such an excuse. The American Ambassador laughed at it, and year after year his consul's firman was renewed. Fortunately my position in the island sufficed to secure that I should not be molested, and when the governor told me one day, during excavations at Dali, that he ought to stop me because I had no firman, I answered him jokingly that he needed a firman to stop me, which he had not' (Lang 1878, 338–9). Cesnola, who was most put out by Sandwith's criticism of his observations in the *Archaeologia* paper, asserted that Sandwith had never undertaken any extensive excavations at Dhali or for that matter elsewhere in Cyprus (Cesnola 1877, 83 n*). To judge by the Register of Correspondence of the Consulate in Larnaca from 1865 to 1872 (Public Record Office, Kew, FO 329 10), Sandwith's attempts to secure permission to dig were not exactly energetic, as the only references to his application for a *firman* occur in documents of 21 January 1867 and 10 February 1870. In fact the prime mover in the efforts to obtain the necessary authority from the Sublime Porte appears to have been Hamilton Lang himself.

Sandwith's inability to dig, at least on the same scale as his American colleague, Luigi Palma di Cesnola, his French colleague, Dominique-Albert-Edouard Colonna-Ceccaldi, Comte Tiburce, and Robert Hamilton Lang, Manager of the Imperial Ottoman Bank agency, in no way inhibited his acquisition of antiquities, undoubtedly through purchase. What is known of his collection shows that he favoured Bronze Age and Iron Age pottery and glass of the Classical period over stone sculpture, jewellery and inscriptions (cf. Goring 1988, 13–14), though he too was not averse to disposing of his objects by sale. Items from his collection are to be found in the Department of Greek and Roman Antiquities of the British Museum (Walters 1912; Williams 1996, 102 n.3), the National Museums of Scotland in Edinburgh (Goring 1988, 14), and the Ashmolean Museum, Oxford (Brown and Catling 1975, 25, Pl. X. b). This list is no doubt far from complete. In 1982 Dr J. S. Boys Smith, the grandson of T.B. Sandwith and the father of Mr Stephen Boys Smith, presented to the Fitzwilliam Museum in Cambridge a Cypriote Bichrome III krater of Cypro-Geometric III (GR. 96–1982 – kindly identified for me by Professor V. Karageorghis), which he had inherited from his grandfather (Fitzwilliam Museum 1982, 17). Part of Sandwith's original collection of both Cypriote and Cretan antiquities, numbering over 50 objects and including the Base-ring I juglet illustrated, without its base-ring, in the *Archaeologia* article (Sandwith 1880, Pl. IX. 3 – not 2 (Williams 1996, 102 n.20)), are still in private hands in England (cf. Williams 1996, 102 nn.1, 2). It is evident that after his departure from Larnaca in 1870, Sandwith kept his collection, at least up till the time the Yorkshire Exhibition opened on 13 May 1875, in the old Cloth Hall in Leeds, where he put part of it on display (Goring 1988, 13). The claim, in the visitors' guide to this exhibition, that Sandwith carried out excavations in Cyprus to alleviate a famine, by employing large numbers of starving people, is explained by Hamilton Lang's account, quoted above, of how Sandwith came to be interested in archaeology (Goring 1988, 14).

Sandwith clearly based the observations in his paper given to the Society of Antiquities in 1871 on the antiquities in his own collection. As we know, he supplemented the illustrations in *Archaeologia* Vol. XLV of pieces belonging to him, with drawings of others in the British Museum. He also drew on objects in the private possession of Hamilton Lang (see above), and acknowledged his 'great obligations to Mr. Lang for many valuable suggestions contained in this paper' (Sandwith 1880, 133). He also refers to Hamilton Lang as his friend, who was 'the first to establish, in an unpublished work on the ancient history of that island, that its primitive inhabitants were Aryan and not Semitic in race....' (Sandwith 1880, 133). Hamilton Lang (cf. Goring 1988, 7–10), who was also appointed acting British Vice-Consul in Sandwith's absence from 14 October 1865 to 23 April 1866, and from 15 April 1868 to 6 January 1869 (Lang 1878, v-vi), himself records writing details of the ancient and modern history of Cyprus during his assignment in Larnaca before 1869, and circulating them privately among friends (Lang 1878, vi-vii). Whether or not these notes dealt with the antiquities themselves, it is noteworthy that for an account of the ceramic finds, Lang selected a small number of Cypriote vases at the request of the eminent German Egyptologist, Professor Karl Richard Lepsius, and sent them to him in Berlin. Lepsius replied with his comments to Lang on 7 March 1872 (Lang 1878, 346–351), and Lang published this contribution with his own description of the rock cut tombs of Cyprus, which was written in the same year 'when all their peculiarities were fresh in my memory', and followed the same general outline as Sandwith's paper delivered in London in 1871 (Lang 1878, 340–345). A notable overlap in their coverage of the funerary customs was the claim by both authors that in some prehistoric interments the body had evidently been placed in a sitting 'posture' (Lang 1878, 342; Sandwith 1880, 128). This observation is sufficiently unusual, as well as being unverifiable, to suggest that one borrowed it from the other. It is evident that Sandwith and Lang maintained academically fruitful exchanges in the 1870's (see above and below, p.226), after they had both left Cyprus, and their friendly relations endured into the 1890's, as is attested by the diary kept of a visit to Egypt by Sandwith in 1893, when he was in regular touch with Lang, then on assignment in Cairo.

Sandwith's relations with Cesnola were evidently less close. In his paper he pays the American Consul the ambiguous compliment of describing him as the one who, 'more than any other person, has been instrumental in uncovering the archaeological treasures of the island' (Sandwith 1880, 141). As previously noted, he took Cesnola to task for misrepresenting the sequences of the finds he claimed to have made in the cemeteries around Dhali, and ended his critique, and the article, with the following sentence: 'In giving the above simple explanation of a phenomenon by no means extraordinary, I hope to have disposed of an untenable theory' (Sandwith 1880, 142). Cesnola, as we have seen, was not amused. At the same time, Sandwith gave proof of his own scientific approach, for he states that he went repeatedly over the ground to verify Cesnola's contentions and was even accompanied by the workmen who had excavated with Cesnola in these cemeteries (Sandwith 1880, 141–2.). The reserve, if not antipathy, shown by Sandwith towards Cesnola appears to have been cordially reciprocated, for Sandwith's name does not figure amongst those of his consular colleagues into whose 'pleasant society' he was introduced, though Cesnola got on well with the Colonna-Ceccaldi brothers as well as Hamilton Lang (Cesnola 1877, 44–5.). Indeed Lang went so far as to describe his relations with Cesnola as 'intimate' and marked by 'what in French is called *bonne camaraderie*' (Lang 1905, 636), and even Georges Colonna-Ceccaldi gratefully and graciously acknowledged the generous way in which Cesnola made his collection of antiquities accessible for study and publication (G. Colonna-Ceccaldi 1882, 288). It is, nevertheless, interesting to note that in June 1867 Sandwith sought and obtained approval to act for a time as Consul on behalf of his American colleague (Public Record Office, Kew, FO 329 10).

Cesnola's biographer, Elizabeth McFadden, who unfortunately calls Sandwith 'Sandwich' throughout her book, records that in 1868 Cesnola told Hamilton Fish, head of the New-York Historical Society, that the English Consul at Larnaca, described as 'his friend Sandwich', had informed the British Museum about their finds and that the Museum was to send an agent to Cyprus to buy them (McFadden 1971, 89). Indeed Sandwith's correspondence preserved in the Department of Greek and Roman Antiquities of the British Museum includes a letter of 17 March 1869 sent to Newton from Cyprus in which he has the following to say: 'Thinking it will interest you to form an idea of the antiquities recently found here, I enclose several photographs of pieces in Mr Cesnola's collection. You will see that one of the two jars surmounted by a female head has been purchased by Mr Piot who has been spending a month in the Island, and who is carrying away with him about 5000 francs worth of pieces from Mr Lang's and Mr Cesnola's collections.' The vase in question is most likely the Bichrome IV human headed jug of the Cypro-Archaic period which was illustrated in *The History of Art in Phoenicia and its Dependencies* by Perrot and Chipiez

(1885, 289–90, Pl. IV, 289–290; Piot 1890, 24 No. 94) and is now in the Ashmolean Museum, Oxford (Acc. No. 1974.437) (Brown and Catling 1980, 124, Fig. 73, No. 85 – I gratefully owe this reference to Ms Karin Nys). That there was certainly more than casual contact between Sandwith and Cesnola is demonstrated by a note dated 24 February 1875 to the Trustees of the British Museum from Newton who refers to 'an archaic vase discovered in the island of Cyprus by General Cesnola and purchased from him by Mr Consul Sandwith. The design painted on it represents a warrior standing in a chariot and drawing a bow, while his charioteer is urging his horse at full speed'. This is another Bichrome IV jug also in the Department of Greek and Roman Antiquities (B.M. 1875.3–10.1) (Smith and Pryce 1926, 9, Pl. 10 (Gr. Brit. 54) – with literature; Karageorghis and des Gagniers 1974, 25–6.).

Sandwith's relations with the Colonna-Ceccaldi brothers are potentially of much historiographical interest, but are the least well documented of any amongst the Consular and expatriate community in Larnaca. There is firstly no mention in Sandwith's *Archaeologia* article of Dominique-Albert-Edouard Colonna-Ceccaldi, comte Tiburce, usually referred to as Tiburce Colonna-Ceccaldi, who was French Consul in Larnaca from the end of January 1866 to the end of December 1869 (Masson 1992, 123), or of his younger brother, Georges Colonna-Ceccaldi, who served as French Consul in Beirut from September 1866 to October 1871, and made numerous visits to Cyprus (Masson 1992, 126). Both were active in archaeological pursuits, including excavations and collecting, as we have already seen, and both had papers published from 1868 onwards (G. Colonna-Ceccaldi 1882, 6–9, 293–308; Masson 1990, 1992). There is no hint of this bibliography in Sandwith's own study, and the Register of Correspondence of the Consulate in Larnaca from 1865 to 1872 contains almost no communications between Sandwith and Tiburce Colonna-Ceccaldi. Such exchanges as are noted concern exclusively matters of diplomatic politesse. This does not, of course, mean that there was no written or personal contact between them, as the Register deals only with official correspondence, and there was evidently no formal consular business between the British and French representatives during this period, as happened between Sandwith and Cesnola. Nor is there anything of archaeological interest mentioned, apart from the requests for a firman to excavate but, like all wise diplomats, Sandwith kept his academic pursuits as far as possible out of the sight and reach of his employers.

That Sandwith and the Colonna-Ceccaldi brothers did have some contact, even if only indirect, with each other is shown by the reference in Georges Colonna-Ceccaldi's paper on 'La céramique de Chypre' to a flat-based cup from Verghi belonging to the Sandwith collection (G. Colonna-Ceccaldi 1882, 276). From the description it is clear that the vase in question is the W.S.I. bowl illustrated in Sandwith's *Archaeologia* article (Sandwith 1880, Pl.X. 1), which was presented to the British Museum in 1876 by A.W. Franks and is now in the Department of Greek and Roman Antiquities (B.M. 1876.5 - 15.4; Walters 1912, 43). Georges certainly visited the collection belonging to Cesnola and housed in what he described as 'le musée du consulat américain à Larnaca' (G. Colonna-Ceccaldi 1882, 288), but there is no comparable indication that he ever went to Sandwith's residence. This makes a comparison between Sandwith's article and Georges Colonna-Ceccaldi's manuscript 'La céramique de Chypre' all the more intriguing. The latter was found amongst Georges Colonna-Ceccaldi's papers on his death in 1879 and consisted of an 'étude et fragments inédits', which were posthumously published in his collected works in 1882 (G. Colonna-Ceccaldi 1882, 269–280). No date can be given to the composition of this paper, but the main segment must have been completed after 1868 (G. Colonna-Ceccaldi 1882, 271, 272), and he was still writing up till the time of his death in 1879 (G. Colonna-Ceccaldi 1882, 285–8). Though the introductions to both studies differ in content and Colonna-Ceccaldi follows a succession of pottery styles based predominantly on fabric, instead of classes of cemetery, there are sufficient overlaps in format and substance to suggest that they drew not necessarily on each other, but on similar sources of information. Perhaps the most striking parallel in their accounts is the introduction into the comparative data of the pottery finds from excavations in 1867 at Sa el-Hagar, ancient Saïs, in the Delta of the Nile Valley (Helck and Otto 1984, cols 355–357). While Sandwith likens the material from Egypt to the ceramic remains of the Late Cypriote Bronze Age (see above p. 224), Colonna-Ceccaldi writes that 'Des poteries identiques [to Red Polished Ware of the Early and Middle Cypriote periods] ont été trouvées dans les fouilles de Saïs en 1867, ce qui indiquerait qu'un commerce de céramique existait autrefois entre Chypre et l'Égypte, à l'époque peut-être où l'île appartenait aux Ptolémées' (G. Colonna-Ceccaldi 1882, 271).

It is obvious that knowledge of the finds from Sa el-Hagar can have come only from a visit to the Museum at Boulaq, as they have never been published. The excavations in 1867 were presumably conducted by Auguste Mariette-Bey, to whom reference has previously been made (Mallet 1888, 77–8; cf. Mariette 1867, 102–3; cf. David 1994, 125, 277; see above, p. 224). There is, however, no mention of the pottery finds in the fourth edition in 1872 of his guide to the Boulaq Museum (Mariette 1872, 250), and the photographic album published by Délié and Béchard in Cairo in 1872, with an explanatory text by Mariette himself, who described the work as an illustrated catalogue of the Museum, shows no pottery said to have come from Saïs, and contains no reference to the site at all (Délié and Béchard 1872). W. J. Loftie, himself a Fellow of the Society of Antiquaries, devoted a whole chapter to 'The Boolak Museum' in his account of three visits to the Nile Valley which was published in 1879. There, he said, 'we find an arrangement, so far as anything can be arranged in the wretched building, which enables us to trace the history of Egypt and Egyptian art back step by step from the latest Roman bust to the earliest statue portrait' (Loftie 1879, 129). Saïs is not mentioned but he does state that 'at Boolak they know whence every piece came' (Loftie 1879, 126). In 1888 Henry Wallis was equally unflattering, for while acknowledging Mariette's achievements and the inadequacies of museums with Egyptian antiquities in Europe, he writes that 'the arrangement and classification of the contents of Boulaq leave much to be desired' (Wallis 1888, 110).

If there was any standoffishness or distance in the relations between Sandwith and the Colonna-Ceccaldi brothers, currently available data do not help pin point the actual cause(s). Circumstantially, however, there could be at least three explanations. The first, and most obvious, is the historical rivalry between Britain and France for influence beyond their shores. This was particularly acute in the nineteenth century AD when they found their expanding Empires running into each other world-wide. Symptomatic of the deep suspicions nurtured by each side towards the other was France's assumption, in the early 1860's, that Britain had designs on the huge stone vase from Amathus which the French were determined to gain for themselves, and which now graces the Louvre Museum (Foucart-Borville 1985, 7–8; Fivel 1990 – with bibliography). Of more immediate relevance to Sandwith's situation was the fact that his predecessor as Vice Consul in Larnaca, Horace White, enjoyed venomous relations with the predecessor of Tiburce Colonna-Ceccaldi, the comte de Maricourt, who died in July 1865 in Larnaca in the midst of a cholera epidemic. It seems that the comte de Maricourt was motivated in his hostility to White by the prospect that Prince Alfred, the second son of Queen Victoria, might become King of Greece, and therefore improve Britain's standing amongst all Greek-speaking peoples in the eastern Mediterranean, including Cyprus. White was no less antagonistic to his French counterpart for perceived impropriety and aggravation (Hill 1952, 231–5.; Béraud 1973, 39; Béraud 1990, 107). Be that as it may, there are no indications that the Colonna-Ceccaldi brothers harboured any anti-British sentiments, and indeed all the evidence points in the opposite direction. The very fact that Tiburce Colonna-Ceccaldi could have, in a letter dated 7 January 1868, offered the Trustees of the British Museum a collection of Cypriote antiquities, without mentioning Sandwith's name, not only illustrates his evident lack of chauvinism, but highlights the anomaly of his relations with the British Vice-Consul in Larnaca (Masson 1990, 35–6; Masson 1992, 137–8). No less reflective of the same abnormal situation is the fact that Mr Barron of the British Embassy in Constantinople submitted to the Foreign Office on 25 January 1870 a report from Tiburce Colonna-Ceccaldi on the question of land tenure in Cyprus. This account, which was published in French in the collection of papers presented to both Houses of Parliament in Westminster, was part of a larger document on the social and industrial condition of the island which Mr Barron had obtained 'from a friend, long resident in the Island of Cyprus as French Consul'. There is no hint that Sandwith was consulted or even informed about this commission, which in diplomatic practice must be regarded as highly unusual (Reports 1870, 272–3, 312 ff.). Furthermore I have encountered nothing which indicates what Sandwith felt about France if indeed he thought about it at all. In this his attitude was in striking contrast to that of Hamilton Lang, who prided himself on his French connections (e.g. Lang 1905, 629–30).

It is also possible that there was a degree of personal competitiveness between the two sides, since they were all actively involved in the search for and acquisition of antiquities, and this could have extended to the development of their respective academic interests in the subject of Cypriote archaeology. We know that there were informal exchanges of information and ideas between the expatriates in Larnaca sharing common antiquarian pursuits, and, as we have seen, they had no hesitation in drawing on these sources for composing their own historical essays. But who first drew the parallels between the pottery from Cyprus and the finds at Saïs in the Delta? This enigma is compounded by the discovery amongst the papers that descended from T. B. Sandwith to his great-grandson, Mr Stephen Boys Smith, of the off-print of an article from *Archäologische Zeitung* Neue Folge Bd. VI, printed in Berlin in 1874. This short paper is entitled 'Classification of Pottery from Cyprus' and was signed off by A. Lang in Alexandria in February 1873. It is not to be found in any of the standard bibliographies of Cyprus (Oberhummer 1893; Cobham 1908, 495–6; Jeffrey 1929, 32), and Sandwith's possession of it must have been due to the author himself. Internal evidence makes it clear that the writer of this completely forgotten article, which is reproduced in the Appendix to this article, was R.H. Lang and that the initial in the name at the end of the text was a misprint. It was far from being the only typographical error in the article, and was no doubt due to the unaccustomed appearance of a paper in English in this German periodical. Lang had by that time left Cyprus, from which he was re-assigned in March 1872 to head the Imperial Ottoman Bank in Alexandria, Egypt. He departed the island in May the same year (Lang 1878, vi, 338) and remained in Egypt until 1875.

Lang's paper is a remarkable study, not only because it shows that he applied himself to differentiating the pottery finds from the various sites around Dhali 'by sending an intelligent employée with the men to write the name of the cemetery upon the pieces, as they were found [by the peasants who brought him the objects]' (Lang 1873, 43), but because of the following observation: 'Some specimens of pottery exactly similar to that of Laksha Nicoli were found at Tyre, and Dr. Birch supposed them to be of Phoenician workmanship. I have also noticed a few specimens of this pottery in the Museum of Bonlac [sic], Cairo; but as the types are rare in Egypt, we may suppose them to be imported and not native workmanship' (Lang 1873, 43). Curiously enough, there are no acknowledgements in the article to any other person but Dr Birch, though by that time he had presumably received Lepsius' comments on the vases Lang had sent him in Berlin; the article was written and published after Lang had left Cyprus, in a German language periodical, but was not mentioned in his book on the island which came out in 1878; and that once again the ceramic material on display in the Museum at Boulaq is cited for comparative purposes, though without a reference to Saïs. Lang's essay was evidently written after Sandwith had delivered his paper to the Society of Antiquaries in London in 1871, but its chronological, never mind its substantive relationship to Georges Colonna-Ceccaldi's manuscript, cannot be readily established. For the record it should be noted that in a letter dated 14 June 1874 to Clermont-Ganneau, Georges mentions that he saw Lang in France during a visit to St Florentin, some 150 kilometres south-east of Paris (Institut de France M.S. 4108 Vol. I). In any case Lang is the only one to record that he actually saw the ceramic parallels in the Museum at Boulaq, though it is not clear from his narrative when this observation took place.

I could find no evidence that Sandwith had been to Egypt before the late 1870's until Mr Stephen Boys Smith showed me a photographic portrait of his great-grandfather taken by Schier and Schoefft, Court photographers in Alexandria, in 1868 when Sandwith was 37 years old (Williams 1996, Pl. 26.A – the date of 1878 in the caption is a misprint). The picture was presumably taken in Egypt, but leaves open the question of whether he ever visited the Museum at Boulaq himself in connection with his researches on Cyprus. On the other hand, Georges Colonna-Ceccaldi was no stranger to the Nile Valley. He had lived in Alexandria for two years from 1860 to 1862 and first became interested in archaeology at that time (G. Colonna-Ceccaldi 1882, 5). He revisited Egypt in 1866 on his way to Beirut (letter of 28 October 1866 to Charles Clermont-Ganneau in the Institut de France M.S. 4108 Vol. I), before, however, he began his trips to Cyprus, and mentioned in a letter of 3 March 1869 to the same correspondant that 'Je viens de recevoir le catalogue du Musée de Boulaq (Caire). Il est tout entier rédigé par Mariette'. He also wrote three articles on classical antiquities from Egypt, one of which appeared in 1869 (G. Colonna-Ceccaldi 1882, 6–7). While all this demonstrates his ongoing connections with Egypt, it does not prove that he personally saw the pottery from Saïs in Cairo, though none of the expatriates in Larnaca would have been as well placed as he to know about these finds in the Delta. It is worthy of note that, while Georges Colonna-Ceccaldi compared the finds from Saïs with the Early and Middle Bronze Age pottery from Cyprus, Sandwith equated them with the Late Cypriote ceramic material, and Lang with vases of the Iron Age! Lang was undoubtedly closer to the mark than the other two writers.

More titillating, perhaps, is a hint that Georges Colonna-Ceccaldi's interest in visiting Cyprus went well beyond the search for antiquities. He confesses in a letter of 6 August 1867 from Larnaca to Charles Clermont-Ganneau that: 'Larnaca est un petit sahara bien autrement chaud, sec, aride, désolé, brûlant que toute la Syrie, mais j'ai là mon frère et une charmante petite Anglaise....' (Masson 1992, 127). With the characteristic French respect for the private lives of others, Masson terminated the quotation at this point, but in the interests of scientific enquiry, and notwithstanding Kenneth Starr, I have consulted the relevant file in the Institut de France (M.S. 4108 Vol. I) and can now complete the reference, which continues: 'à qui je fais une cour respectueuse et dont je suis amoureux fou. Ajoutez qu'elle est rousse et fort jolie'. No name is given, but we must assume, in the way that small expatriate communities know each other's business, that Sandwith was well aware of the person concerned. If nothing else, this letter demonstrates that Georges Colonna-Ceccaldi, like his brother, had nothing against the English. In any case we know that Georges sent his scholarly works to the British Prime Minister, Mr Gladstone, the erudite statesman, who was in his own way courted by European scholars (cf. Fivel 1989, 38; Masson 1994, 8, 10, 13; Masson 1996 26) and whose office graciously replied to the author, acknowledging receipt of the publications (letter in 1872 to Charles Clermont-Ganneau).

Some nine months after Sandwith had left Cyprus, Georges Colonna-Ceccaldi wrote Clermont-Ganneau a letter dated 17 May 1871 and sent from Antoura near Beirut in which he said that: 'Vénus m'est apparue l'autre jour et elle m'a ordonné de hâter mon envoi à Chypre pour les fouilles [de] Paphos qui vont incessamment commencer. J'ai déposé...' (Masson 1992, 131). Masson has chosen to interpret this passage in a non-amorous manner, assuming that 'envoi' refers to something other than Georges himself, though he could not imagine what this was. Venus, it must be said, was Georges' favourite goddess and frequently invoked for all kinds of purposes in his correspondence with Clermont-Ganneau. What makes this passage mysterious is not only the difficulty of reconstructing why Georges should have been in any way involved with Cesnola's plans for digging at Kouklia, the site, of course, of the famed temple of Aphrodite (cf. Maier 1997, 128–9), but the fact that, as Masson has noted, the rest of this page of the letter has been cut off, as if to remove from the record certain indiscretions or intimacies. Judging by what was written and left on file in the correspondence from Georges Colonna-Ceccaldi to Clermont Ganneau in the Institut de France, the missing remarks must have been more than exceptionally delicate. Was there some way in which Georges, by his personal behaviour in Cyprus, had gravely offended mid-Victorian social and/or moral conventions amongst the British expatriate community, including Vice-Consul Sandwith? This should not, of course, have implicated Tiburce, except by association. In this respect it is interesting to note the differing links postulated by Sandwith and Georges Colonna-Ceccaldi respectively between Venus and the artefacts from ancient Cyprus. While, as previously noted, Sandwith was duly circumspect in identifying a Late Cypriote figurine from his own collection with Venus (Sandwith 1880, 130–1, Pl. X.4), Colonna-Ceccaldi attributed the W.P. containers of Middle Cypriote date in the shapes of birds, rams, cattle, fish and other beasts to the cult of Venus in Cyprus (G. Colonna-Ceccaldi 1882, 273).

At an early stage in my research, it had become clear that more details were required to fill in the gaps and resolve the uncertainties posed by the published sources of information. By chance, during a diplomatic visit to the island of Crete in 1996, I came across, in the Historical Museum and Archive in Khania, a collection of Cretan embroideries which had once belonged to T.B. Sandwith. They had been donated to the Museum in 1974 by Priscilla Boys Smith, the granddaughter of T.B. Sandwith. whose own daughter, Charlotte Cecilia, was born in Crete on 11 January 1871 and married the Rev. E.P. Boys Smith, Vicar of Hardle, Lymington, Hampshire, on 19 April 1898. The circumstances of this gift are not known, but the choice of the Historical Museum and Archive in Khania (not Herakleion – Williams 1996, 102 n.4) as the recipient was no accident as T.B. Sandwith had served as British Consul there for fifteen years, befriended the Cretans and stood up for them in their struggle against the Ottoman Turks (Hood 1987). Furthermore Charlotte Cecilia, Priscilla's mother, was almost certainly born in the town. Unfortunately neither the British Council nor the British Embassy in Athens could find any records about this transaction in which both of them were involved, but according to the Director of the Museum, Mrs Zacharenia Simandiraki, to whom I am grateful for her co-operation, the actual presentation took place on 24 May 1975. Thanks to Sir Brooks Richards, at one time British Ambassador to Greece, I learnt that another lot of Sandwith's Cretan embroideries had found their way to the Victorian and Albert Museum in London. In response to my enquiry Ms Jennifer Wearden, Assistant Curator, Textiles and Dress, willingly gave me as much information as she could, and Mr Roderick Taylor, who has just published a book on *Embroidery of the Greek Islands and Epirus* (London 1998), was equally forthcoming with his offers of assistance. I am very grateful to them both.

I then established in quick succession, thanks to the much appreciated intervention of Mr Nigel Williams, that T.B. Sandwith's personal file in the Foreign Office had long since been destroyed, and that the only Colonna-Ceccaldi file which the Association des Amis des Archives Diplomatiques du quai d'Orsay was able to locate in the French Ministry of Foreign Affairs contained three letters of no direct relevance to my enquiry. I have subsequently learnt that the personnel records of both Tiburce and Georges Colonna-Ceccaldi in the Quai d'Orsay may contain additional information on their careers, but have not so far been able to consult them. Through the co-operation of the British Embassy in Athens, which kindly supplied me with the addresses, I then wrote to every Sandwith listed in the United Kingdom telephone directory, seeking their assistance, and to the owners of the house at Hall Lands, Nutfield, Surrey, where T.B. Sandwith lived in retirement before his accidental death. This produced some valuable reactions, especially from Mr James D. Sandwith, whose contribution I gratefully acknowledge. He in his turn put me in touch with the great grandson of T.B. Sandwith, Mr Stephen W. Boys Smith, who had inherited some of his ancestor's papers and gathered anecdotal and other oral information about the latter's life and career. He has been the source of a number of valuable details and I am much endebted to him for his willingness to share them with me. I am no less beholden to Ms Rebecca Drought of the Surrey and South London Newspapers for the interest she took in my project and for letting me have a copy of T.B. Sandwith's obituary in *The Surrey Mirror* of 27 April 1900. Alas, none of this material shed much light on the relations between Sandwith and the Colonna-Ceccaldi brothers, nor have my efforts to track down the descendants and inheritors of Tiburce and Georges Colonna-Ceccaldi so far yielded any substantive results.

It is also fitting that at this point I should record my gratitude for all the generous help and hospitality I have received in connection with this study from Mme Annie Caubet, Dr Dominique Collon, Professor Nicolas Coldstream, Dr Nicola Coldstream, Mr Sinclair Hood, Mrs Miranda Pemberton-Pigott, Mrs Linda Boys Smith, Dr Veronica Tatton-Brown and Dr Dyfri Williams. My wife, Helen, cast a critical eye over the text and recommended that I make it more intelligible to the non-specialist. If you have followed me so far, it is due more to her than to me. Words are not enough to express my thanks.

Though Sandwith's paper had no sequel or immediate consequences, it should not be thought that it eventually went unnoticed or unappreciated. The first scholar to have used it appears to have been Dr J. Naue, who in an article on 'The Copper bronze and Iron Weapons of Cyprus' published in 1888 noted that 'Consul Sandwith had already in 1871 distinguished two chief divisions of the copper-bronze age' (Naue 1888, 21). In 1891 another German archaeologist, Dr Max Ohnefalsch-Richter, who was not known for his sensitive handling of colleagues and associates, paid Sandwith's work a glowing tribute, which is all the more remarkable for being so perceptive: 'If the facts observed by Lang at Idalion in a temple must be regarded as of fundamental importance for a proper comprehension of Cyprian religious usages, in the provinces of ceramic and metallic art, and indeed in the more general one of culture-history, the merits of Thomas Sandwith (a name little known in literature) are no less indisputably great. The paper read by him before the Society of Antiquaries on May 4th, 1871, and published with copious illustrations in the organ of the Society, 'Archaeologia' (Nicols & Sons) as late as 1877, must be styled a scientific performance of the first rank. I only came across it by a lucky chance in 1887, when my own excavations executed for Sir Charles Newton at Phoenidshais in 1883 had already led me to an independent delimitation of the Copper and Iron Periods. Had I in 1883 been acquainted with the work bearing the modest title "On the different styles of Pottery found in Ancient Tombs in the Island of Cyprus. By Thomas B. Sandwith Esq., H.B.M. Vice-Consul," I should have saved myself much labour, and would to-day have been further forward. It is, however, always a pleasure to be able to say that we have both independently arrived at the same main conclusions. To Sandwith belongs the merit of the first publication, the palm of first discovery. He points out correctly in what strata of tombs the metals are only represented by copper and bronze, iron being absent: he indicates correctly the chief types of the early weapons: he shows what kinds of vases belong, and what kinds are unknown, to the Copper-Bronze Period: he is perfectly aware what idol-types, and terracottas are characteristic of the different periods' (Ohnefalsch-Richter 1891, iii; cf. Oberhummer 1893, 76).

It is therefore curious to find that the novelty of Sandwith's work was not acknowledged in Myres' and Ohnefalsch-Richter's *A Catalogue of the Cyprus Museum*, published in Oxford in 1899. Instead the objects he illustrated in his *Archaeologia* article were used for comparative purposes only (Myres and Ohnefalsch-Richter 1899, 205, 222), though the sequence of Wares, described in the introduction to the Bronze Age, follows nearly the same order as Sandwith's, beginning with Red Polished, then Black Slip, though Sandwith here has Black Polished, followed by Base-ring; White Ware with Base-ring; Black Punctured Ware, now known as Tell el-Yahudiya Ware; Straw-plait Ware; Cypriote Bucchero Ware; Wheel-made Ware; White Ware, which is White Painted and exemplified in Sandwith's paper by a W.P.V Fine Line Style juglet (Sandwith 1880, Pl. IX.8 - this vase is not mentioned in the text but presumably belongs to Class I or II like the rest of the pottery in Pl. IX); Polished White Ware, which is evidently W.P. II; Black Glaze Ware, which is Red-on-Black and not mentioned by Sandwith; and White Slip Ware (Myres and Ohnefalsch-Richter 1899, 39–46). Since Ohnefalsch-Richter was already acquainted with Sandwith's work, and Myres in 1914 described Sandwith's paper as 'of fundamental importance on the ancient styles of pottery' (Myres 1914, xiii), their failure to refer to Sandwith's ceramic classification appears to be disingenuous, if not worse. The acrimonious correspondence between Ohnefalsch-Richter and Myres over the composition of this book, which is preserved in the Ashmolean Museum, sheds a little further light on the issue, for in a letter of 31 December 1895 Myres told Furtwängler that Ohnefalsch-Richter 'wishes to make the classification of the Cypriote pottery in the catalogue as nearly as possible the same as that in "Tamassos und Idalion" for convenience of reference'. I am much endebted to Dr Susan Sherratt for making this archive accessible. This does not in any way detract from the lasting value of this, the first catalogue raisonné produced by two practising archaeologists on the antiquities of Cyprus, but does raise questions about the sources of their inspiration.

In 1905, H.B. Walters, drawing on the work of Samuel Birch, was no less fulsome than Ohnefalsch-Richter in his praise of Sandwith's achievement: 'Another English consul, Mr. Sandwith, also made a collection of Cypriote pottery, and, with an acuteness in advance of his time, made a successful attempt to classify it according to periods and styles....The first attempt to classify the pottery of Cyprus, and to distinguish between the Bronze-Age wares and what are now known as the Graeco-Phoenician fabrics, was made by the late Mr. T.B. Sandwith in 1876. Considering the comparative poverty of material at his command, and the state of archaeological knowledge at the time, his brief but illuminating monograph is a wonderfully accurate and scientific contribution, and, so far as it goes, his classification can still be accepted in the main' (Walters 1905, 65, 240; cf. Walters 1912, xi). This assessment was implicitly sustained by Gjerstad in his influential thesis published in Uppsala in 1926 on *Studies on Prehistoric Cyprus*. In the section on 'Relative Chronology' he paid a double-edged compliment to Sandwith by opening the chapter with the following statement: 'Sandwith (1871) was the first to distinguish between the Bronze Age and the Iron Age in Cyprus by observation of the different styles of pottery found in the ancient tombs excavated – or rather robbed – at that time' (p. 262).

With that, Sandwith's study largely fades from the archaeological literature and has received, since the Second World War, only scant attention. Sir George Hill, in his monumental history of Cyprus, noted that Sandwith was the first to make a serious attempt at classifying the ancient pottery of Cyprus (Hill 1952, 238 n.4, 608 n.1); Frankel expressly recognised that 'the first real contribution toward a prehistory of Cyprus was the work of Sandwith...' (Frankel 1974, 1) and impartially analysed his synthesis; and Dr Dyfri Williams recently credited Sandwith with writing ' the first standard essay on Cypriot pottery' (Williams 1996, 100). On the other hand, Sandwith's paper was included in the bibliography of the 'Introduction' to *Cypriot Ceramics: Reading the Prehistoric Record,* which was edited by Barlow and others and published in Philadelphia in 1991, but it was mentioned only *en passant* in the text (Barlow *et al.*1991, 1–8). The question that must now be asked is why has Sandwith's paper been so perfunctorily treated this century ? The first and the most obvious explanation is that almost no one, including myself, has gone back to Sandwith's essay and studied it properly. From the historiographical analysis to which it has now been submitted, it clearly emerges as a work of singular originality, seeking to place different categories of cemeteries and ceramics in descending chronological order so as to illustrate the nature of each cultural episode and determine its historical implications. The fact that it proceeded from the data and not preconceptions gives it an enduring quality which, while not fully or widely recognised at the time, or responsible for immediately starting a new direction in interpreting Cypriote archaeological remains, provided the basis on which every subsequent attempt at classifying relics from the island's past has been built, and that includes the *Swedish Cyprus Expedition.* Only recently has its validity been challenged. Neglect of this seminal work can therefore only be due either to a lack of understanding of the way in which the analytical frameworks in current academic use have come into existence and/or to a rejection of this methodology on the grounds that anything written before the advent of the pseudo-scientific New Age archaeology must by definition be out-of-date, irrelevant and without value. No better example of this phenomenon could be found than the recent memoir by Coleman, Barlow, and others on the archaeological investigations by Cornell University in the Middle Bronze Age settlement at Alambra *Mouttes-Spileos* in central Cyprus (Coleman *et al.*1996).

Though technically this volume meets the highest standards of contemporary excavation and publication, the authors have deliberately foresworn using the classificatory system of the Swedish Cyprus Expedition on the questionable grounds that 'there has never been a clearly stated rationale for the conventional typologies' (Coleman *et al.* 1996, 237). The fact is that no less than three studies, by Sandwith, Hamilton Lang and Georges Colonna-Ceccaldi, all conceived in Larnaca in the late 1860's and all following the same basic outline, set down the principles for the system of pottery classification still currently in use, and I have attempted on two separate occasions, once in 1978 (Merrillees 1978, 14–28) and again in 1991, in *Cypriot Ceramics: Reading the Prehistoric Record,* to articulate the essential criteria (pp. 237–240). To dismiss this methodology as 'conservative', as Barlow has done (Barlow *et al.* 1991, 4), does not of course diminish its validity, but does suggest that Coleman and his co-authors have decided for their own reasons to ignore the relevant literature. The very fact that they have still been prepared to refer to the broad, and conventional headings of Red Polished, White Painted, etc, even if without the numerical subdivisions, indicates that they are merely following the longstanding practice of using taxonomies which are based on critical observation, not chemical analysis. This was no more or less than Sandwith did nearly 130 years ago, when he drew up a scheme of ceramic classification which depended on visible differences in colour, decoration and shape. This power of perception has been most tellingly delineated by McFadden in her biography of Luigi Palma de Cesnola, when she contrasts the exploits of her subject with the approach of his British colleague in Larnaca, in the following terms: 'In the dim first years of archaeology, the Englishmen had trained themselves by minute comparisons of form and style to be scholars rather than mere collectors' (McFadden 1971, 144). In this respect Sandwith stands out as the first to use his collection of antiquities, intellectual curiosity and historical instinct to compose and disseminate an analytical survey of the progression of material culture in ancient Cyprus, with no other purpose than to enlighten. In that endeavour he was materially helped not by another Englishman, but by a Scot, Robert Hamilton Lang, to whom McFadden's observation equally applies. That there was also some constructive interchange, direct or indirect, with the Colonna-Ceccaldi brothers is also apparent, but the extent of their contribution to Sandwith's study has yet to be fully clarified.

Sandwith's role in making Cypriote archaeology an academic discipline was disinterested, objective and scientific. He did not depend on the reception of his paper for his livelihood, advancement or standing. He did not follow it up with more studies in a similar vein, gave no further lectures on the subject or undertook any academic responsibilities even in retirement, and did not lobby to have his thesis accepted. It is not as if he lacked opportunities to do so, especially as he spent 15 years on consular posting in Crete and engaged in comparable antiquarian pursuits (Hood 1987). Indeed it was while he was resident in Khania that he finalised his paper for the Society of Antiquaries and saw it finally into print. His obituaries in *The Times* of London and *The Surrey Mirror* make no mention of his extracurricular interests and activities. The latter nevertheless describes him in the following terms: 'Mr Sandwith was a brilliant scholar, and spoke many languages, though no one, meeting him casually, would have taken him for a man of great gifts and erudition, so extremely modest and unassuming was he in his bearing. Probity was his great characteristic, and an enthusiastic friend believes that he never even thought a lie. He gave the best part of his life to his country in the consular service. His record was blameless, and the Government showed appreciation of his ability and uprightness by placing in him its full trust and confidence' (27 April 1900). If Sandwith had one particular intellectual strength, it was his belief in and commitment to the study of history for history's sake. Therein lies the remarkable achievement of his paper on Cypriote archaeology, delivered well over a century ago in the same city where we honoured the memory of Olivier Masson, epigraphist and historiographer *par excellence*.

Bibliography

Barlow *et al.* 1991: J.A.Barlow, D.L. Bolger and B.Kling (eds), *Cypriot Pottery:Reading the Prehistoric Record* (Philadelphia).
Béraud 1973: S. Béraud, 'Données historiques sur la colonie européenne de Larnaca au XIXème siècle', in *Acts of the First International Cypriological Congress (Nicosia, 14–19 April 1969)*, Vol. 3 (Nicosia), 37–43.
Béraud 1990: S. Béraud, *La culture française dans l'espace chypriote de 1192 à 1971* (Nicosia).
Birch 1873: S. Birch, *History of Ancient Pottery, Egyptian, Assyrian, Greek, Etruscan, and Roman* (new and rev. ed. London).
Brown 1991: A. Brown, 'Appendix. A Note on the two collections founded by General Pitt Rivers', *Centre d'Études Chypriotes. Cahier* 15, 29–30.
Brown and Catling 1975: A.C. Brown and H.W. Catling, *Ancient Cyprus* (Oxford).
Brown and Catling 1980: A.C. Brown and H.W. Catling, 'Additions to the Cypriot Collection in the Ashmolean Museum, Oxford, 1963–77', *Opuscula Atheniensia* 13, 91–137.
Caubet 1976: A. Caubet, 'La collection R. Hamilton Lang au Musée du Louvre: antiquités de Pyla', *Report of the Department of Antiquities Cyprus*, 168–177.
Caubet *et al.* 1992: A. Caubet, A. Hermary and V. Karageorghis, *Art antique de Chypre au Musée du Louvre du chalcolithique à l'époque romaine* (Paris).

Cesnola 1877: L.P. di Cesnola, *Cyprus: Its Ancient Cities, Tombs, and Temples* (London).
Cobham 1908: C.D. Cobham, *Excerpta Cypria. Materials for a History of Cyprus* (Cambridge).
Coleman *et al.* 1996: J.E. Coleman, J.A. Barlow, M.K. Mogelonsky and K.W. Schaar, *Alambra. A Middle Bronze Age Settlement in Cyprus* (Jonsered).
G. Colonna-Ceccaldi 1882: G. Colonna-Ceccaldi, *Monuments antiques de Chypre, de Syrie et d'Égypte* (Paris).
David 1994: E. David, *Mariette Pacha 1821 - 1881* (Paris).
Délié and Béchard 1872: Délié and Béchard, *Album du Musée de Boulaq comprenant quarante planches* (Cairo).
Dia' Abou-Ghazi 1988: Dia' Abou-Ghazi, *Introduction to Egyptian Archaeology with Special Reference to the Egyptian Museum, Cairo* (enlarged ed. Cairo).
Drioton 1950: E. Drioton, ' Le Musée de Boulac', in *Cahiers d'histoire égyptienne* Série III, Fasc. 1, 1–12.
Fitzwilliam Museum 1982: *Fitzwilliam Museum Cambridge. The Annual Reports of the Syndicate and of the Friends of the Fitzwilliam for the year ending 31 December 1982* (Cambridge).
Fivel 1989: L. Fivel, 'Ohnefalsch-Richter (1850–1917), essai de bibliographie', *Centre d'Etudes Chypriotes. Cahier* 11–12, 35–4 0.
Fivel 1990: L. Fivel, 'Le second vase d'Amathonte', *Centre d'Etudes Chypriotes. Cahier* 13, 11–13.
Foucart-Borville 1985: J. Foucart-Borville, ' La correspondance chypriote d'Edmond Duthoit (1862 et 1865)', *Centre d'Etudes Chypriotes. Cahier* 4, 3–60.
Frankel 1974: D. Frankel, *Middle Cypriot White Painted Pottery. An Analytical Study of the Decoration* (Göteborg).
Goring 1988: E. Goring, *A Mischievous Pastime. Digging in Cyprus in the Nineteenth Century* (Edinburgh).
Helck and Otto 1984: W. Helck and E. Otto, *Lexicon der Ägyptologie*. Band V (Wiesbaden).
Hill 1952: G. Hill, *A History of Cyprus*. Vol. IV (Cambridge).
Hood 1987: S. Hood, 'An Early British Interest in Knossos', *Annual of the British School at Athens* 82, 85–94.
Jeffrey 1929: G. Jeffrey (ed.), *An Attempt at a Bibliography of Cyprus* (new ed. Nicosia).
Kaplan 1980: M.F. Kaplan, *The Origin and Distribution of Tell el Yahudiyeh Ware* (Göteborg).
Karageorghis and des Gagniers 1974: V. Karageorghis and J. des Gagniers, *La céramique chypriote de style figuré. Âge de fer (1050–500 Av. J.-C.)* (Rome).
Knapp 1990: A.B. Knapp, 'Production, location and integration in Bronze Age Cyprus', *Current Anthropology* 31, 147–176.
Lang 1878: R.H. Lang, *Cyprus: its History, its Present Resources, and Future Prospects* (London).
Lang 1905: R.H. Lang, 'Reminiscences – Archaeological Researches in Cyprus', *Blackwood's Edinburgh Magazine* Vol. 177, no. 75, 622–639.
Loftie 1879: W.J. Loftie, *A Ride in Egypt* (London).
Luke 1921: H. Luke, *Cyprus under the Turks 1571–1878* (London).
McFadden 1971: E. McFadden, *The Glitter and the Gold* (New York).
Maier 1997: F.G. Maier, 'A Hundred Years after Hogarth:

Digging at Aphrodite's Sanctuary at Palaipaphos', *Centre d'Etudes Chypriotes. Cahier* 27, 127–136.

Mallet 1888: D. Mallet, *Le culte de Neit à Saïs* (Paris).

Mariette 1867: A. Mariette-Bey, *Exposition universelle de 1867. Aperçu de l'histoire ancienne d'Égypte* (Paris).

Mariette 1872: A. Mariette-Bey, *Notice des principaux monuments exposés dans les galeries provisoires du Musée d'antiquités égyptiennes de S.A. le Khédive à Boulaq* (4th ed. Paris).

Masson 1966: O. Masson, 'Kypriaka II. Recherches sur les antiquités de la région de Pyla', *Bulletin de correspondance hellénique* 90, 1–31.

Masson 1990: O. Masson, 'Correspondances chypriotes: lettres des frères Colonna-Ceccaldi et de L. Palma di Cesnola à W. Froehner', *Centre d'Etudes Chypriotes. Cahier* 14, 29–44.

Masson 1992: O. Masson, 'Diplomates et amateurs d'antiquités à Chypre vers 1866–1878', *Journal des savants*, 123–154.

Masson 1994: O. Masson, ' L. Palma di Cesnola, H. Schliemann et l'éditeur John Murray', *Centre d'Etudes Chypriotes. Cahier* 21, 7–14.

Masson 1996: O. Masson, 'La dispersion des antiquités chypriotes: les deux collections Cesnola', *Centre d'Etudes Chypriotes. Cahier* 25, 3–27.

Merrillees 1978: R.S. Merrillees, *Introduction to the Bronze Age Archaeology of Cyprus* (Gothenburg).

Milliex 1973: R. Milliex, 'Esquisse d'une biographe de Gustave Laffon (1835–1906)', in *Acts of the First International Cypriological Congress* (Nicosia, 14–19 April 1969) Vol. 3 (Nicosia) 221–236.

Myres 1914: J.L. Myres, *Handbook of the Cesnola Collection of Antiquities from Cyprus* (New York).

Myres and Ohnefalsch-Richter 1899: J.L. Myres and M. Ohnefalsch-Richter, *A Catalogue of the Cyprus Museum* (Oxford).

Naue 1888: J. Naue, 'The Copper Bronze and Iron Weapons of Cyprus', *The Owl Science Literature and Art* No. 3, 29th September, 17–23.

Oberhummer 1893: E. Oberhummer, 'Bericht über Geographie von Griechenland. III. Kypros', *Jahresbericht über die Fortschritte der classischen Altertumswissenschaft* Vol. 77, 29–96.

Ohnefalsch-Richter 1891: M. Ohnefalsch-Richter, *Ancient Places of Worship in Cyprus* (Berlin).

Perrot and Chipiez 1885: G. Perrot and G. Chipiez, *History of Art in Phoenicia and its Dependencies.* Vol. II (London).

Piot 1890: *Collection Eugène Piot. Antiquités dont la vente aux enchères aura lieu à l'Hôtel des commissaires-priseurs, 9 rue Drouot....Les Mardi 27, Mercredi 28, Jeudi 29 et Vendredi 30 Mai 1890Y..*(Paris).

Reports 1870: *Reports from Her Majesty's Representatives Respecting the Tenure of Land in the Several Countries of Europe: 1869–70* in *Accounts and Papers* 27. Vol. LXVII, Part II.

Sandwith 1880: T.B. Sandwith, 'On the Different Styles of Pottery Found in Ancient Tombs in the Island of Cyprus', *Archaeologia* Vol. 45, 127–142.

Smith and Pryce 1926: A.H. Smith and F.N. Pryce, *Corpus Vasorum Antiquorum. Great Britain British Museum (Department of Greek and Roman Antiquities). Fasc. II* (London).

Wallis 1888: H. Wallis, 'The Boulaq Museum', *The Art Journal* New Series 103–110.

Walters 1905: H.B. Walters, *History of Ancient Pottery, Greek, Etruscan, and Roman* (London).

Walters 1912: H.B. Walters, *Catalogue of the Greek and Etruscan Vases in the British Museum.* Vol. I. Part II (London).

Williams 1996: D. Williams, 'T.B. Sandwith's Cretan Collection', in D. Evely, I.S. Lemos and S. Sherratt (eds), *Minotaur and Centaur. Studies in the archaeology of Crete and Euboea presented to Mervyn Popham* (Oxford) 100–104.

Appendix

ARCHÄOLOGISCHE ZEITUNG.

Herausgeben

von

Ernst Curtius und Richard Schöne.

NEUE FOLGE

SECHSTER BAND

DER GANZEN FOLGE
EINUNDDREISSIGSTER
JAHRGANG.

BERLIN

DRUCK UND VERLAG VON
GEORG REIMER.

1874

CLASSIFICATION OF POTTERY FROM CYPRUS

In reference to my classification of pottery from ancient tombs in Cyprus I think it well to explain, how it was arrived at, and to give the reasons, which appear to me to justify its assumptions.

I had received for fully two years large quantities of that pottery and assisted at the opening of many tombs, when it occurred to me to keep separate the objects found in the different cemeteries. This was not as easily done as might appear at first sight; seeing that the peasants, who brought me the objects, wrought in large companies and mixed up all their discoveries. However, by sending an intelligent employée with the men to write the name of the cemetery upon the pieces, as they were found, I attained my object and the results were interesting beyond my expectations.

The first feature which struck me was, that I had distinct styles of pottery, which did not intermingle. To explain my meaning let me give three cases in point.

1. About 12 miles to the north of the village of Dali the cemetery, which first attracted the attention of the Dali men, was found. To distinguish it, I called it the cemetery of *Laksha Nicoli*.
2. At a village about 3 miles to the S.W. of Dali called *Alambra*, another cemetery was found.
3. Close to the village of *Dali* itself were also found extensive cemeteries.

Now my researches made apparent the singular facts, that the pottery of Laksha Nicoli was quite different in its characteristics from that of Alambra, and that the pottery found in the cemeteries close to Dali differed from both the other two. - in short, that each class of pottery presented such peculiarities that I could out of a large and mixed collection pick out the pieces, which had been found together, always excepting the large common jars, which were much the same in all. But I ought to add, that the distinctive features were more marked in the early epoch; in the later, when the artists had attained the proficiency of representing scenes and figures upon the ware, my distinctions frequently failed me.

Upon closer examination I was led to consider the pottery from tombs close to Dali more modern, but of the same family as those of Alambra, and I was confirmed in this opinion, when I found that the concentric circles - chief ornament of the pottery of Dali – were frequently found incised upon the ware of Alambra. I conclude therefore that the pottery of the Dali cemeteries is the sequence of the pottery of Alambra, and our classification is thus reduced to two types, namely that of Laksha Nicoli and that of Alambra. – In the two last mentioned tombs were found lances and instruments of bronze, but none were found in those of Dali; I presume therefore that the tombs of Laksha Nicoli and Alambra were nearly contemporaneous and I need not lose time in proving, that they are both of an early epoch. What that epoch was, can only be matter of opinion: it was, before vessels were ornamented by even figures of animals, and from the archaic nature of some small terracottas and a number of little objects, which attracted my attention, I feel inclined to put the epoch before the eighth century – it may be much earlier.

Of cemeteries yielding pottery like that of Laksha Nicoli the number and extent is limited, as compared with those of the other class. – Two of the number were near to Citium, and it will be remembered, that the city and Idalium were the chief Phoenician settlements in the Island.

Some specimens of pottery exactly similar to that of Laksha Nicoli were found at Tyre, and Dr. Birch supposed them to be of Phoenician workmanship. I have also noticed a few specimens of this pottery in the Museum of Bonlac, Cairo; but as the types are rare in Egypt, we may suppose them to be imported and not native workmanship.

To resume, the two distinct types of pottery appear to me to represent two distinct races, living amongst each other, but having separate cemeteries. The one pottery is found all over the Island, the other in limited districts. The two races thus represented I suppose to be: 1. a native race, which I call Cyprian and 2. a foreign, which I presume to be Phoenician. They are the same two races, which are addressed by Melekyatan, king of Citium and Idalion, on my Dali bilingual inscription in their respective languages, Phoenician and Cyprian. From the indications above given I am disposed to give the pottery of Laksha Nicoli to the Phoenicians.

Upon the pottery of Alambra we do not find any ornamentation in colours, but we do find it upon that of Laksha Nicoli. Might we not therefore suppose, that the Cypriotes acquired the art of colouring from the Phoenicians? Again the Cypriotes never seem to have acquired the manner of burning or preparation which produced the thin, brittle, dark-grained pottery, which is found in the Phoenician class, nor the manner of covering a dark ground with a creamy-white coating, just as copper-vessels are whitened for cooking – (see the vessels of this shape sent to the Museum of Berlin). Many other peculiarities in form and composition will strike the careful examiner of the specimens sent to the Museum. I never knew any glass found in tombs yielding pottery of Alambra-type and only one well-authenticated specimen from tombs of the Laksha-Nicoli type. This last specimen is in my possession, it represents in glass a little vase with three loops of a form, of which many specimens in pottery were found by me. The composition of the glass is quite peculiar, and I prize the piece highly, feeling confident that I can ascribe to it an antiquity of 2500 years.

In the Greek and Greco-Roman era glass vessels were buried in the tombs of Cyprus in lieu of earthen ware, and a few coincidences struck me:

1. The lamps in tombs, which contained small vessels in earthen-ware, were all of the common open kind, which we meet with in the earliest tombs and which you may still see burning in the khans of our day. The lamps in tombs, which contained glass-vessels, are mostly the covered greek lamps with some ornamentation on the top; sometimes even an inscription such as FAVSTI or such like.

2. In tombs containing glass-vessels jewellery is generally found; in those of Alambra jewellery never to my knowledge was found, but in those of Laksha Nicoli it was found in a few instances. The weight of ear-rings extracted from one tomb represented 25 p. St.

Alexandria, February 1873.   A. Lang

22. Lady Brassey, 1870–1886: traveller, writer, collector, educator, woman of means and the fate of her Cypriot artefacts

Lou Taylor

Annie, Lady Brassey (Fig. 22.1) funded an excavation at Kourion, probably in 1883–84, as a consequence of which about 800 antiquarian artefacts from Cyprus were sent privately to her in Britain.[2] The collection was dispersed between 1888 and 1920 and today the whereabouts of only some of these pieces are known. Of these, only those at Wolverhampton Museum, a few from a large collection at Hastings Museum and Art Gallery and those at Bexhill Museum, have yet been formally and adequately catalogued. This paper assesses the history of the Brassey Cypriot collection, its extent, *raison d'être* and its fate.

What is highly unusual in this story is that from the late 1860s, Annie Brassey became a woman collector, an enthusiastic female amasser of exotic 'things' on a vast scale. Thus, when she visited Cyprus in the Autumn of 1878 just four months after the British occupation troops had landed at Larnaca, it was not surprising that she quickly became enthused by the mystery and romance generated by excavations at Idalion and Kourion.

As well as highlighting the fate of these specific objects, the historiography of Annie Brassey's involvement with Cypriote artefacts exposes a specific layer of class tension and ambition at play in the earliest days of the British occupation of Cyprus in 1878 – a tension that lay between the Brasseys' expansionist world of new-monied British commerce and that of the firmly established British ruling and colonial social elite. This historiography of the Brassey-Cypriot collection also exposes the way in which precious ancient Cypriot artefacts became a tool of play within these tensions and ambitions.

Annie Brassey was the remarkable wife of the Liberal MP for Hastings, Thomas Brassey M.P. She became one of only a few British women in the last quarter of the nineteenth century able to personally undertake the large scale, private collecting of exotic artefacts. She was in other

Fig. 22.1: Photograph of Lady Brassey, about 1885, possibly wearing second mourning. Courtesy of Hastings Museum and Art Gallery.

Fig. 22.2: Photograph of Normanshurst, Catfield, near Battle, Lady Brassey's country home in Sussex, about 1870–80. Courtesy of Hastings Museum and Art Gallery.

respects a conventional member of wealthy, non-aristocratic, British society. She managed Normanshurst (Fig. 22.2), her large, new, neo-Gothic-styled country house near Battle, in Sussex. Faded photographs in the Brassey archives at Hastings Museum and Art Gallery show heavily decorated rooms, with complex, decorative plaster ceilings and cluttered furnishings and ornaments in a vaguely 'François Premier' style. Julian Porter's research and Brassey's own diaries indicate her love of fancy dress parties, of entertaining wealthy, foreign personages and, particularly her passion for hunting across the Sussex fields. Unlike her aristocratic neighbours in Sussex, once Thomas Brassey became the Liberal MP for Hastings in 1868, Annie and her husband became active Liberals. Annie Brassey had five children. Their second daughter Constance, nicknamed 'Sunbeam', died in 1873, aged five. As was her proper wifely duty, Annie Brassey's life centred around her family, her husband's business and political interests and managing her homes in London and Sussex.

Travel on the Sunbeam

Annie Brassey put together a 'natural science' collection of geological samples, plant specimens, stuffed animals and examples of ceramics, embroidery, wood carvings and metalwork from all over the world. She was able to do this because her husband, having inherited millions from his father, Thomas Brassey, Senior, the great railway builder, chose to spend large amounts of this fortune navigating himself around the world in luxury yachts with large holds. Brassey, Junior, was a skilled navigator and won his Master Mariner's ticket in 1873. 1874 saw the construction of his luxury steam yacht, 'the Sunbeam', named in memory of Constance. His expertise helped him eventually to become a civil Lord of the Admiralty and to gain a knighthood in 1881, and the Secretary of State to the Navy, under Gladstone. In 1895, having been granted a peerage, he became the Governor of Victoria, Australia in 1895. He was driven by a fusion of business, political and sea-faring interests and was, for example, Director of the British North Borneo Company.[3]

What is absolutely exceptional about Annie Brassey is that, rather than be left behind, she joined her husband on his sailing expeditions with their 4 young children. Between 1869 and 1887 they cruised the world, from 1876 in the *Sunbeam*, undertaking the world's first steam navigation of the world in 1876–78. Her accounts of her journeys indicate that, as well as innumerable pets, including a baby owl, a pet pig and various exotic creatures, the *Sunbeam* had a crew of at least twenty and a dozen staff on each voyage, including a doctor, an artist, Mr. Bingham, the 'tutor', a cook, a nurse, the children's maid, the Chief Steward, and the Mess Room boy.[4]

The Brassey family, like other internationally wealthy

Fig. 22.3: Illustration of the State room of the Sunbeam. Annie Brassey, Sunshine and Storm the East (London 1880). Courtesy of Josephine Keshishian.

yacht owners of the period, lived on board in great style taking their plutocratic life style with them (Fig. 22.3). They were able, for example, off the coast of Tahiti in December 1878, to eat 'some Devonshire butter ... which is as good now after ten thousand miles in the Tropics, as it was when first put on board'. Wherever they dropped anchor between 1869 and 1887 Annie Brassey, as well as inviting local dignitaries and/or colonial rulers to dinner in her splendid sea-going dining room, also assiduously collected local samples and specimens, some live and some ancient, such as her Cypriot artefacts.

Whilst in Cairo, for example, in April 1877, not only did she buy 'some quaint silver jewellery from Soudan and Abyssinia', but she also 'called on the Consul, the Vice Consul and our old friend Consul Burton, Haj Abdullah. He had just returned from a journey through the ancient land of Midian undertaken at the special request of the Viceroy'.[5] She amassed other antiquities, for example, from South America and China and ethnographical artefacts from Tahiti, Melanesia and the Solomon Islands. She took care to inform herself, either in advance or *in situ*, of local 'collectibles' and then scooped them up into the hold of the *Sunbeam*, with the intention of setting up her own private museum in her London for the education of working men. She amassed 6000 items from all over the world before her death, at the age of 47, probably, according to Julian Porter, Curator of Bexhill Museum, from malarial fever, contracted in Syria. David Devenish was more inclined to the belief that she picked up a fatal virus in the famous bat caves at Silam, in Borneo which she visited with her husband in 1886.[6] Whatever the cause, on 14 September 1887, after a long illness, she was buried at sea by her family and the crew of the *Sunbeam*, off the Australian coast, aged forty-seven.

Annie Brassey became famous in her own right after the popular success of her travel diaries which were translated into seventeen languages. *Sunshine and Storm in the East* or *Cruises to Cyprus and Constantinople* was published by Longmans Green in 1880. The original drawings were by the childrens' tutor, the Hon. A.Y. Bingham, (described by Sir Garnet Wolseley, as the 'son or brother of Lord Lucan, who, I presume is a sort of paid secretary').[7] *A Voyage in the Sunbeam*, was published with the same success by Longmans Green in 1881, having appeared in 1878 under the title *Around the World the World in the Yacht Sunbeam*. Cheap broadsheet versions were widely available. Lady Brassey became so well-known that Alberto Speranzo published a popular waltz called *the Sunbeam* dedicated 'by permission to Lady Brassey'.[8]

Despite her unconventional sea-faring life, Brassey's own highly conventional class attitudes surround her collection. Like others of her day, she sought the strange, the bizarre and the 'savage'. Off the coast of South America in December 1876, for example, she was disappointed that her sailors were unable to catch an albatross. She wanted to skin one 'to make tobacco pouches of its feet and pipe stems of the wing bones for presents'.[9] Items of inherent monetary value, or those with royal connections made them of supreme desirability. Julian Porter, Curator of Bexhill Museum, where Brassey's geological collection is housed, confirms that she fully 'realised the educational potential' of her collection whilst at the same time 'seeking out high status objects in lieu of family heirlooms'.[10] The royal feather cloak made for Queen Pomaré of Tahiti, probably in Hawaii, is just such an example. Porter notes that is an exceptionally significant piece and was 'extremely rare when Brassey collected her example'.[11] He also confirms that Brassey bought items from dealers, including Bryce Wright, who catalogued her collection in 1885.

It seems from the now bleached-out photographs of the interiors of Normanshurst, that her collection was not, as a norm, displayed in her home, but shown there during specific, ticket-only charity openings.

Thomas and Annie Brassey, returning from a world cruise, spent some twenty days, in November-December 1878, touring Cyprus with their entourage. Annie Brassey was, therefore, one of the first British women to inspect the island after the imposition of direct British military/Colonial rule during the summer of 1878. Indeed she arrived about six weeks before the wife of the first High Commissioner, Lt. General Sir Garnet (later to become Field Marshal Viscount) Wolseley. His wife, Loo, was still making preparations to leave London, via France, whilst the Brasseys were already making their tour of inspection of the island. Loo was charged with bringing her Britishness with her in the form of a vast range of items for the new Government House. These included, at Sir Garnet's very specific request, 'a set of lawn tennis things, really the best rackets and five dozen of the best covered balls'.[12] From the Wolseley's country estate Loo was instructed to send over dozens of plants for the gardens, including specific tree roots, grass seeds, 'mignonette, some sweet pea...some wall flowers, some heartsease seed and few dozen of crocus root'. Loo also had to order all the furniture and fittings for the new house, which Sir Garnet was desperately trying to complete before her arrival. Loo was more anxious about servant support in the new colonial Nicosia. She wrote from Paris on 12 November 'is it a housemaid we shall want? What sort of cook have you? I shall expect some titbits when I arrive'.[13]

However, when the Brasseys arrived in that first desperately hot November, none of this was in place. The Brasseys' nights in Nicosia were, therefore, spent in three hurriedly arranged wooden army huts at Wolseley's base with the 71st regiment. Travel for Annie Brassey was extremely hard, riding side-saddle on horseback in her riding habit, across 'sunburnt plains and between stony hills'. 'Truly' she wrote 'the sun of Cyprus is as raging as a lion'.[14]

The Brasseys' Cyprus visit was not simple tourism. Thomas Brassey, like other Colonial visitors of the same period, had a commercial eye on the island and was searching for viable export products. Despite the already recognised presence of a range of minerals, little, however, seemed on offer, though the *Illustrated London News* in 1878 suggested that 'the land is all for sale, and at most moderate rates'. Thomas Brassey, however, was (as indicated in a letter to the Times as soon as he returned from Cyprus on 26 December 1878) convinced that, if a settlement on the customs problem with Turkey could be reached, 'Cyprus would become the principal commercial depot for Syria and Southern Asia Minor'.[15]

Lady Brassey made her own investigations, but was not at all impressed.[16] Despite the fact that Sir Garnet has sent a crinkled Cyprus silk chemise to Queen Victoria, 'who has sent for two more', Annie Brassey found the typical silk of the island 'very ugly'. She also found the wine 'extremely nasty, being very strong and sweet with a marked flavour of tar'. She was further disappointed at the lack of game shooting possibilities in Cyprus ('the best bag I have heard of was six brace of partridges to two guns after a hard day's work') and she found that 'Venus certainly has not left behind her much of her beauty as a legacy'. She did ship home 'several large, pure white Turkeys' purchased from a fertile Armenian estate near Kythraea but finally declared that Cyprus 'is not likely to become anything more than a coaling station, unless the climate greatly changes'.[17]

But if Cyprus was poor in exportable raw materials, the island was immensely rich in collectible antiquities. It was these that caught Annie Brassey's attention. She may have been drawn to them, not only for their great romance, but also because involvement in the world of Cypriot archaeology meshed her, as an equal, within the status-giving world of the highest levels of Colonial administrators. They too were also enthralled by the mystery of the artefacts being unearthed from the soil of Cyprus. Thus the Brasseys were amongst the very first visitors who trekked to 'the village where General Cesnola has made his digs'. Immediately afterwards in Larnaca, Colonel White showed them 'the artefacts confiscated from Cesnola's excavations'.[18] When the *Sunbeam* then sailed around the coast to Limasol 'in these days before a law of 1905 ... restricted the export of antiquities'.[19] She bartered with the British Commissioner in Limassol, Colonel Falkland Warren (whom she may already have known in India), swopping new up-to-date English newspapers for 'old pots and earthenware vases, some of beautiful shapes from the tombs'.[20] Brassey's imagination was so fired by all these sights that she made arrangements with Falkland Warren to financially sponsor excavations at Kourion. These are now believed to have been carried out by Ohnefalsch-Richter in 1883–84. He had also arrived in 1878 and a year later he 'was entrusted with carrying out official excavations ...on behalf of the British government'.[21]

At the beginning of December 1878, the *Sunbeam* left the shores of Cyprus. By 1885 a flood of Brassey-Cypriot artefacts began to arrive in England – nearly eight hundred in all, 'mainly pottery vessels from the Bronze Age to the Roman period and Roman glass vessels'. 766 of these are described, albeit extremely briefly, in the original catalogue listing, which is still in use today in Hastings Museum and Art Gallery.[22]

Lady Brassey had begun exhibiting elements of her collection from 1881, firstly in the Brassey Institute's Hastings School of Art premises, then, in 1884, in Newlyn,

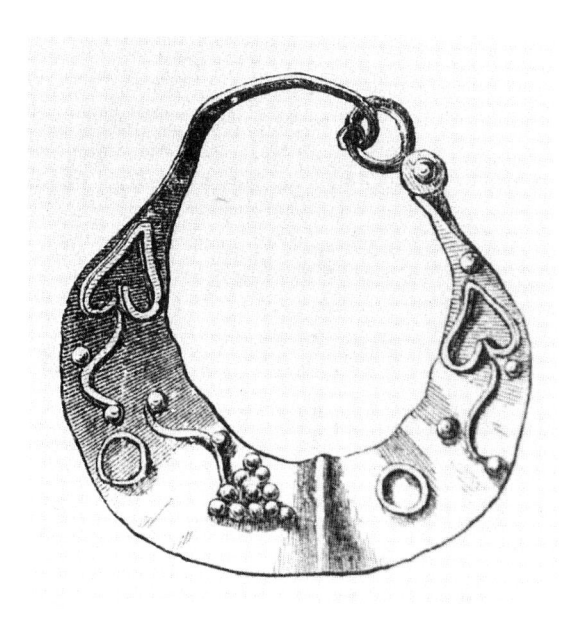

Fig. 22.4: Earring from Curium: drawing from Alfred Maskell, Antiquities in Cyprus, a short description of the collection of antiquities from excavations made for Lady Brassey at Cyprus, in Bryce Wright, Catalogue Raisonné of the Natural History, Ethnological Specimens and Curiosities collected by Lady Brassey during the voyages of the 'Sunbeam' 1876–1883 (London 1885).

Fig. 22.5: One of two very large hydria...sent to Lady Brassey by Colonel Warren. Photograph by the author from current display at Hastings Museum and Art Gallery. Courtesy of Hastings Museum and Art Gallery.

Cornwall (to help raise money for a new harbour), and once again in 1885 at the School of Fine Art, Hastings. It was for this last exhibition that the dealer, Bryce Wright, was commissioned by Annie Brassey to produce the *Catalogue Raisonné of the Natural History, Ethnological Specimens and Curiosities collected by Lady Brassey during the voyages of the 'Sunbeam' 1876–1883*, published by William Clowes, London in 1885. The Cypriot collection, though not yet complete, was already so extensive that a separate listing was commissioned from Alfred Maskell: *Antiquities in Cyprus, a short description of the collection of antiquities from excavations made for Lady Brassey at Cyprus.* 'The objects received up to the present time comprise about three hundred and twenty pieces of pottery, including vases of various kinds, lamps, and figures or fragments of figures; over a hundred examples of glass vessels......several ear-rings (Fig. 22.4), pendants, fragments of funeral wreaths and small objects in gold; one or two engraved gems and an Assyrian cylinder; seven pieces of silver work, or of lead; about fifty bronze fragments and three iron'. Maskell noted that the 'two very large hydria, or water jars, which were sent to Lady Brassey by Colonel Warren, are probably the largest specimens known of Cyprian pottery (Fig. 22.5)'.

What is already evident in this listing is that the confusion over the origin of these pieces was already in place by 1885. Maskell made it clear then that he was 'not in possession of sufficient details concerning the actual spots where the pieces have been found'. However, David Symons, now Curator of Antiquities in Birmingham Museums and Art Gallery, progressed the identification and the origins of the 59 Brassey Cypriot artefacts which found their way into the collection in Wolverhampton Museum through his 1984 research. He quotes Myres' and Ohnefalsch-Richter's 1899 account of excavations at Kourion 'by O-R for Col. Warren, S. Brown and others: determining the Graeco-Phoenician necropolis. Rich Hellenic tombs were found in the level ground east of the acropolis, near church of Ag. Hermogenis. A further investigation of the Ayios Ermoyenis necropolis was conducted by an expedition from the University Museum of Pennsylvania in 1940–41'. Symons believes that the Brassey artefacts in Wolverhampton 'also came from this Ayios Ermoyenis necropolis. This cannot be stated as a certainty as it is clear that Lady Brassey also acquired material from other sources in Cyprus'.[24]

After Lady Brassey's death in 1887, Thomas Brassey completed the plans for the Lady Brassey Museum in her memory, in a wing at the back of the family home at 24 Park Lane, London. The display was designed by Alfred Maskell, who had written the 1885 listing of the Brassey-Cypriot artefacts. The ground floor housed a lounge and smoking room, whilst the upper galleries contained the exhibits, including a case of oriental embroidery, and a library,[25] created in fulfilment of Annie Brassey's determined intent to afford 'information and recreation to the members of the Working Men's Clubs'.[26] Sofas (made for Sultan Abdul Aziz and covered in Turkish embroidery), which Annie Brassey had purchased in Cairo,[27] provided seating. The artefacts were divided into 14 sections which were built into the famous carved teak Durbar Hall, bought from the South Kensington Colonial and India exhibition of 1886. Thomas Brassey had been a Commissioner. Case 1 began with 'Personal Souvenirs of the late Annie Brassey' and Section 13 contained 'Savage Ornaments', whilst the Cyprus artefacts were included in Sections 10 and 11. The original museum description notes that these sections contained 'objects found in tombs excavated for Lady Brassey at Curium, of peoples extending from Phoenicia, through the Greek and Roman times, shown with South American gold ornaments and objects from the Pyramids, including the foot of a mummy picked up by Lady Brassey'.[28]

By 1888, one year after the death of his wife, Thomas Brassey began to disperse some of the Cypriot artefacts, perhaps simply because too many had arrived in London. As the original Brassey catalogue shows, the collection was finally split at least five ways. In 1888 donations were made to Wolverhampton Museum, 'Downing' and the Nicholson Institute, Leek. 59 pieces were 'presented to Wolverhampton Museum on April 18th, 1888, by Thomas, 1st Earl Brassey'. David Symons, whose research on this collection was published in 1984, commented on the very cursory descriptions 'of the Brassey artefacts in the original Maskell listing'. Symons noted that 'labels and tags went astray over the passing years. Only 29 pieces can be identified with certainty, while 27 probable and 3 possible attributions can be made'.[29] These specific artefacts have been professionally researched, cared for and catalogued. The same cannot be said for the Leek items, which seem to have gone missing at some point after the Nicholson Institute was reorganised in the 1960s. Enquiries by Symons, Porter and this author at the Potteries Museum and Art Gallery, Stoke-on Trent and Shugborough Hall, where the collection of Staffordshire Arts and Museum Service is housed, have as yet drawn a complete blank.

After Thomas Brassey's death in 1918, the entire eclectic Brassey collection seems to have weighed heavily and unwanted on the shoulders of his second wife, Sybil de Vere Capel, who he had married in 1890, and the children of his first marriage. In 1919, before his untimely death in a road accident in London, Annie Brassey's only son 'Tab' handed most of the collection over to Hastings Corporation and in 1920 his sister, Mabelle Egerton, gave the geology section to Bexhill Museum. After the death of 'Tab', Normanshurst was leased to a girls' school, finally burning down in 1951. Julian Porter is convinced that during this period not a few Brassey objects, probably abandoned in the house and out-houses, found their way into public auctions.[30]

However, in 1932, the new Brassey annexe at Hastings Museum and Art Gallery was finally created where, even now, items reflecting the whole breadth and historiography of the collection are displayed, (including one case of Cypriot artefacts) and stored in the original Durbar Hall. Thus in 1919 it would seem that Hastings Corporation certainly received most of the Brassey-Cypriot artefacts and that by 1932 they were being cared for by Prof. Stanley Adshead. In 1957, R.A. Higgins of the Department of Greek and Roman Antiquities at the British Museum, was asked by J. Mainwaring Baines, the Keeper of Hastings Museum and Art Gallery, to examine a small group of objects. Higgins identified a Bull Figure, as 'Cypriot, 1450 BC - the cult may be local to Cyprus'. Of two heads he wrote that 'the larger is Cypriot, 4th century BC, the smaller is Sicilian, late 5th century: I find it hard to believe that this piece comes from Cyprus'. Other items identified as Cypriot include three figures dancing, said to be from Vounous, north Cyprus, 2000–1800BC and a plank figure said to be from Kourion. A horse figurine is dated to 250–475 BC.

Porter discovered that in 1920 some Brassey items of Roman glass were donated to his museum along with the geology collection. These are catalogued and displayed. The remaining hundreds of Cypriot items are stored at Hastings Museum and Art Gallery in various boxes and cupboards and seem not to have been catalogued by a specialist in Cypriot archaeology to this day. Neither has any attempt been made to put back together a complete *catalogue raisonné* of the Brassey-Cypriot artefacts which survive in these various British institutions.

The unstable fate of the Brassey-Cypriot artefacts seems to reflect Lady Brassey's own unstable position in British society. Because of her death at the age of 47, before her husband climbed to a position of political power in

Gladstone's governments, she never did 'arrive' socially, despite her wealth, her title and her museum with its collection of Cypriot antiquities. Her very fame as an 'exotic' woman author-voyager may indeed have counted against her in this respect. If we can trust Wolseley's opinion, it would seem that Annie Brassey also failed to fit into British colonial circles, certainly in Cyprus.

Privately, Wolseley was quite unable to overcome his deep-rooted personal prejudices against her, though he liked Thomas Brassey: 'there is a good national ring about him'. Wolseley seemed to see in Annie Brassey the epitome of what he saw as the vulgar, nouveau riche woman of his day, who, as his diary makes abundantly clear, he profoundly despised. After the Brassey visit to his Nicosia camp on 10 November 1878, which Annie Brassey had found so exciting, Wolseley wrote in his diary that he had found her 'very pretentious and by no means clever. A very ordinary woman to whom riches gives some importance. How very plain she is'. Annie Brassey, having carefully arranged for a formal dress to be mailed over the appalling tracks from Larnaca to Nicosia in order that she could dress correctly for dinner with the High Commissioner, would have been enraged by the journal note written by Wolseley after supper that night. 'Mrs Brassey dressed magnificently in a grand brocaded silk for dinner. How thoroughly she looked like the maid in her mistress's clothes'.

The two parties met again in the Troodös mountains on 15 November 1878. Wolseley noted: 'we stopped and had a long parley'. Again, unable to resist comment on the Brassey entourage, he described the tutor, Mr Bingham, as 'the faithful loafer. ... If report be true and appearances would lead one to think, (he) makes love to her... I can only account for this by assuming him to be a cur of the lowest type'. Wolseley added finally: 'Mrs Brassey, as is her wont, had a brandy and soda (Fig. 22.6)'.

Wolseley's prejudices went on beyond condemnation of Annie Brassey's personal appearance and behaviour into the whole issue of the coded class and taste cultures of his day – and Annie Brassey's taste was found deeply wanting here too. Wolseley visited the *Sunbeam* whilst it was moored off Larnaca, and was happy enough to enjoy 'the first really delicious meal I have had since I left England, ... an exquisite luncheon which we washed down with dry champagne'. Nevertheless, he wrote later in his journal that he found the ship 'filled up like a flash sitting room owned by a lady of loose morals in St. John's Wood. Such taste!! Oh, how melancholy to see such riches at the disposal of a woman without, really, any taste at all'.[32]

There is sharp, cruel, period class snobbism at play here – a clear social and cultural taste clash. Letters sent by Wolseley's wife Loo to Cyprus in the same November of 1878, explain these taste differences. Whereas Annie Brassey's Sussex house and yacht were filled with new, elaborate historical-revival styled ornaments and furniture, Loo's tastes for her new Cyprus home were for far more modern, simple and intellectually progressive arts and crafts design. She ordered, for example, the interior furnishings for the new Government House in Nicosia from William Morris' shop in London. She wrote to her husband on 20 November 1878, that she had been to the 'shop where the designs of the famous draughtsman Morris were procurable'. Today I spend 5 hours at Morris's choosing papers and cretonnes. I bought with regard to economy you will be glad to hear'. She purchased enough fabric 'for 20 pairs of curtains ... I have papered all the bedrooms .. and I have more for the sitting room papers. I chose [*Bolton Sheetings*?] for curtains'. She had been advised by Colonel Walker on the problem of pests on the island eating unvarnished, unpainted wooden furniture. She wrote accordingly that 'all my furniture effects are founded on white ... so I am telegraphing to say it is to be painted white, the wood only'.[34]

Into this contemporary setting of Morris fabrics and plain white simple furniture, Loo also chose to place some of her favourite paintings and ornaments from those she had inherited from her father. These included a Lancret, four blue porcelain brackets and two white porcelain cockerels. 'I hope you will approve'.[35] Lady Brassey had no such eighteenth-century family heirlooms. Neither did her husband. Further, they made no attempt to hide the recent source of their family wealth.

The Wolseleys' letters and journal notes make it clear that, even in that first very difficult autumn, the British colonial rulers of Cyprus were determined to maintain the expected rules of British imperial behaviour and etiquette. Sir Garnet understood only too well the sophisticated and nuanced society codes signalled through dress and interior decoration, and found Annie Brassey badly wanting in every respect. Annie Brassey had taken her own specific brand of 'Britishness' with her to Cyprus, as indeed did the Wolseleys. Julian Porter insists that she was not 'ashamed of her family's industrial and mercantile background'.[36] A marble bust of Thomas Brassey Senior, by M. Wagmüller, of 1868 was, for example, always shown publicly and prominently within the Brassey collection, as it still is today. Thus, despite the fact that Wolseley liked Thomas Brassey, the class lines between the two social circles were clearly drawn.

For Lady Brassey, the attraction of funding excavations, and then owning Cypriot antiquities, seems not to have been related to the inherent history and characteristics of the objects themselves. She was probably not even particularly interested in them. They were, after all, only one of many groups of exotic collectibles she swept up on her world tours, just another passing acquisition. Her Cypriot antiquities were tools of her social ambition, like the

Fig. 22.6: 'Mrs Brassey, as is her wont, had a brandy and soda'. The Brasseys meeting the High Commissioner, Sir Garnet Wolseley in the Troodös mountains, November 1878. Drawing by A.Y. Bingham from Annie Brassey, Sunshine and storm in the East *(London 1880). Courtesy of Josephine Keshishian.*

acquisition of her royal feather cloak from Hawaii or 'the Royal robe of Japanese silk presented by the Mikado of Japan'.[37] What is very evident is that as the hundreds of Cypriot objects arrived, through the auspices of Falkland Warren, around and after 1885, many of them were not really wanted, and became the unwanted flotsam and jetsam of Imperial rule.

Out of a possible eight hundred pieces, nearly 60 at Wolverhampton Museum, and a further handful at Hastings Museum and Art Gallery and Bexill Museum have been formally identified. The rest remain to this day the neglected, and even lost, detritus of colonialism, sent to England because Annie Brassey, on her twenty-day tour of Cyprus in 1878, became caught up in the general fever of Imperial excavation of the island.

Neither her sponsorship of Kourion excavations, nor her eventual ownership of a large collection of Cypriot artefacts did, in fact win her a route into the elite social circles she may have desired. She would have been comforted to know that, through an advantageous marriage, her daughter, Marie, became the Marquess of Willington and Vicereine of India by 1936. Now, the only remaining traces of Annie Brassey's existence in her Sussex home in Catsfield are some splendid trees on the abandoned estate grounds, and a plaque in her memory placed in the local church by her grieving husband and family.

Annie Brassey, after her courageous travelling, did not leave her heart behind in the hot countryside of Cyprus. It lay firmly in the green fields of Sussex. On her return from the island, in time to celebrate Christmas of 1878, she wrote: 'there is no place like home, after all ... the soft warm air and bright blue skies of the sunny South – very pleasant it was to go hunting the next day after our arrival, and to gallop once more across the well known fields, and through the big woods of dear old Sussex'.[38]

Notes

1. I thank Josephine Keshishian for allowing me access to her collection of books on the post-1878 history of Cyprus. I also thank Julian Porter, Curator of Bexhill Museum, Sussex, for generous help over this research. His 1995, MA thesis, *Lady Brassey – a Victorian collector* is available through the Dept. of Museum Studies, University of Leicester. See also his *Lady Brassey– 1839–1887, Victorian Traveller, Collector and Writer* (Bexhill Museum, Bexhill, September 1996). I thank too Cathy Walling of Hastings Museum and Art Gallery, David Symons, Curator of Antiquities in Birmingham Museums and Art Gallery, Zoe

Lubowiecka, Archivist of the Wolseley Archives at Hove Reference Library and Graham Dawson, University of Brighton.
2. Information from Cathy Walling, Assistant Museum Curator, Hastings Museum and Art Gallery, September 1999. 766 Cypriote items are listed in a blue and gold leather-covered register.
3. D.C. Devenish, 'The Brassey Collection', *Curator* (4 April 1988) 269.
4. A. Brassey, *A Voyage in the Sunbeam* (London 1881) Appendix.
5. Brassey (n.4) 35 and 63. Some of this jewellery is displayed in Hastings Museums and Art Gallery.
6. Devenish (n.3) 272 and 270
7. A. Cavendish (ed.), *Cyprus 1878. The Journal of Sir Garnet Wolseley* (Nicosia 1991) 128.
8. Song sheet, published by Marriott and Williams, 295 Oxford Street, London, featuring an illustration of the *Sunbeam* on the front cover. Hastings Museum Art Gallery, Brassey Archives, no.988.56
9. Brassey (n.4) 22.
10. J. Porter, *Lady Brassey* (MA thesis, University of Leicester 1995) 37–39.
11. Porter (n.9) 26. The feather cloak is displayed at Hastings Museum and Art Gallery
12. WD 7/24i Wolseley Archives, Hove Reference Library.
13. L/WP/4ii/iv Wolseley Archives, Hove Reference Library. Unfortunately the Wolseleys moved on elsewhere before Loo's plans for Government House were completed.
14. A. Brassey, *Sunshine and Storm in the East and Cruises to Cyprus and Constantinople* (London 1880) 266, 262 and 274.
15. G. Hill, *A History of Cyprus Vol IV: The Ottoman Province, the British colony 1571–1948* (Cambridge 1952) 280–82.
16. Lady Brassey put together over seventy photographic albums. Some few are now in the East Sussex Records Office, Lewes but most were purchased by the Huntingdon Library, California. Notes in the Brassey Archives, Hastings, provided by Brita F. Mack, Curator of the Huntingdon Photography Archives, indicate that vol.36 covers Greece, Corfu and Cyprus and contains photos sold to Brassey on her travels.
17. Brassey (n.14) 276, 279, 297, 275.
18. Brassey (n.14) 279 and 281.
19. H.D. Purcell, *Cyprus* (London 1969) 217.
20. Brassey (n.14) 262, 279 and 259.
21. E. Goring, *A Mischievous Pastime. Digging in Cyprus in the Nineteenth Century* (Exhibition Catalogue, Edinburgh 1988) 18.
22. Information from Cathy Walling, Hastings Museum and Art Gallery, September 1998.
23. B. Wright, *Catalogue Raisonné of the Natural History, Ethnological Specimens and Curiosities collected by Lady Brassey during the voyages of the 'Sunbeam' 1876–1883* (London 1885) 100–108; A. Maskell, *Antiquities in Cyprus, a short description of the collection of antiquities from excavations made for Lady Brassey at Cyprus.*
24. D. Symons, *Cypriote Antiquities in Wolverhampton Art Gallery and Museums* (*Corpus of Cypriote Antiquities: Studies in Mediterranean Archaeology* vol. XX. 10, Gothenburg 1984) 2–3, quoting J.L Myres and M. Ohnefalsch-Richter, *A Catalogue of the Cyprus Museum* (Oxford 1899).
25. A. Bett and W. Ruskin Butterfield, *Guide to the Durbar Hall* (Hastings Museum 1932) 1. Brassey Archives, Hastings Museum and Art Gallery.
26. A. Brassey, *The Last Voyage* (London, published posthumously in 1889) from the introduction by Sir Thomas Brassey, p. 3; with thanks to Julian Porter.
27. These remain in place today in the Brassey display at Hastings Museum and Art Gallery
28. Anon, *Some Notes on a Few of the Principal Objects, Lady Brassey Museum, 24 Park Lane* (n.d.) 3 (in the archives, Hastings Museum and Art Gallery). The collection of ancient gold Columbian ornaments was sold off by Hastings Museum by auction to Birmingham Museum and Art Gallery in 1957.
29. Symons (n. 24).
30. Porter (n.10) Appendix 1, and personal interview September 1998.
31. Letter from Higgins to Mainwaring Baines, 21 January 1956, Brassey Archives, Hastings Museum and Art Gallery. In 1957, Mainwaring Baines added an iron age painted jug to the Hastings collection, which he purchased with official permission from a private collection in Cyprus.
32. Cavendish (n. 7) 129 and 145.
33. Linda Parry, Deputy Curator, Department of Textiles and Dress, Victoria and Albert Museum, suggests that this may be a plain coloured serge 'used both plain with braid and trimmings'. Letter to the author, 25 June 1999.
34. Letters from Lady Wolseley to her husband: Wolseley Archives, Hove Reference Library, LWP /94vi/- vi and LWP/49/I
35. Letters from Lady Wolseley to her husband: Wolseley Archives, Hove Reference Library, LW/p4/10.1.i and ii
36. J. Porter, *Lady Brassey: 1839–1887* (Bexhill 1996) 35.
37. Brassey (n. 4) 46.
38. Brassey (n. 4) 406.

23. Max Ohnefalsch-Richter and the Έσπερος[1]

Ioannis Violaris

In the *Catalogue of the Cyprus Museum* by John L. Myres and Max Ohnefalsch-Richter (1899), at page seven, in the section entitled 'Chronicle of Excavations undertaken in Cyprus since the British Occupation', it is briefly mentioned that 'O-R [wrote] four papers in *Έσπερος, Leipzig*'. The 184 issues of *Έσπερος* contain in fact five articles by Ohnefalsch-Richter and there is also a brief correspondence in one of the early issues, all written in Greek. The aim, therefore, of this paper is to present critically these articles, which remained so far unrecorded by the bibliography, and to try to place some of the information they bear in the wider context of his work concerning Cyprus. Moreover, some aspects of his personality and his conduct will be revealed.

Έσπερος was an illustrated Greek periodical, issued fortnightly, which dealt with a great variety of matters. It was issued, as mentioned above, in Leipzig by Ioannis Pervanoglou (1831–1911)[2] and its sixteen-page issues form eight annual volumes, the first seven of which were printed in Leipzig, and the last, after a short interruption, in Athens. Among the contributors to *Έσπερος* were a considerable number of well-known Greek intellectuals, writers and poets of the late nineteenth and early twentieth century, such as Alexandros Ragavis, Professor of archaeology in the University of Athens, a poet and Greek ambassador in Berlin for a certain period of time, Yeorghios Drosinis, writer and poet, Yeorghios Vizyinos, poet and intellectual and last, but not least, Constantinos Kavafis, who published some of his early poems in this periodical.

Έσπερος circulated not only in mainland Greece, but also in flourishing Greek communities all over Europe and of course Cyprus. Its wide range of content covering literature, politics, travellers' impressions, biographies, book reviews, etc., combined with its typographical elegance (Fig. 23.1), place it among the most remarkable and popular Greek family magazines of the nineteenth century.

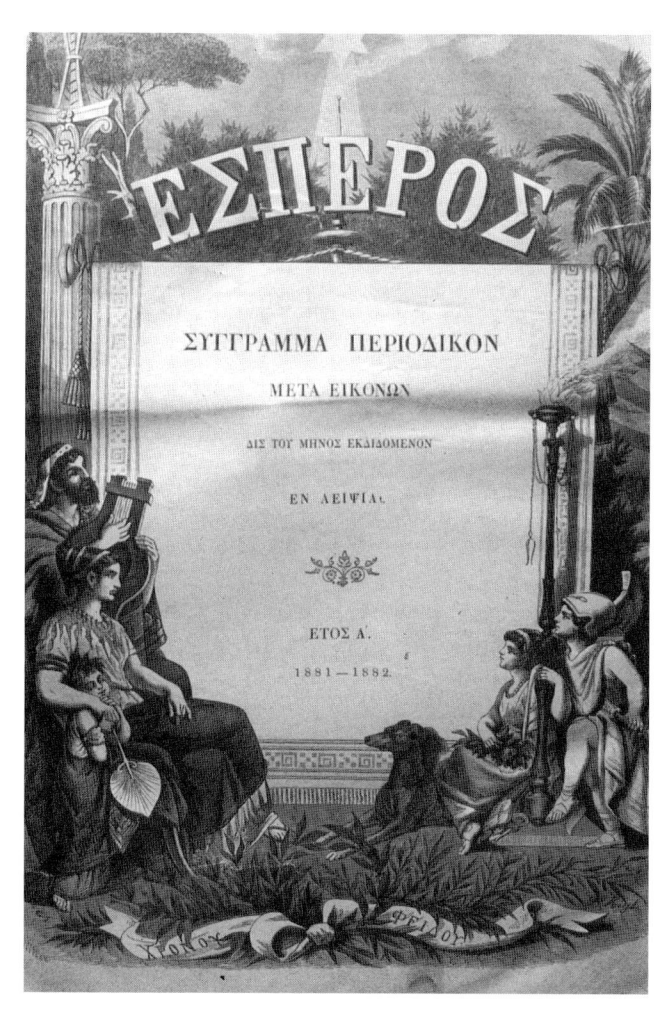

Fig. 23.1: The front page of the first annual volume of Έσπερος.

Fig. 23.2a: Artemis of Kition, Έσπερος 70 (1884).

Fig. 23.2b: Artemis of Kition, Kunsthistorisches Museum, from Magda Ohnefalsch-Richter, 8.

It is in this context that we have to read these articles, assessing them from the point of view of an average nineteenth-century intellectual, to whom they were addressed. As the writer states 'more comprehensive and more extensive specialized studies belong rather to the columns of specialized archaeological journals'.[3]

The first appearance of Max Ohnefalsch-Richter in the Έσπερος is in issue number seven of 1/13 August 1881. It takes the form of brief correspondence in which the discovery of a marble statue from Larnaka is announced.[4] Ohnefalsch-Richter attributes the statue to Styppax, a Cypriot sculptor mentioned by Pliny[5] and dates it during the first half of the fifth century. He claims that it represents Aphrodite Urania, and the statuette the Phoenician Astarte-Aphrodite. Three years later, however, in Έσπερος number 70 of 15/27 March 1884, he changed his mind, and decided that the statue represented Arthemis,[6] claiming that the arms were cut on purpose to serve certain practices of worship. In the *Catalogue of the Cyprus Museum* he also claims that the statue is an Artemis, but he dates it in the Hellenistic period,[7] while in *Kypros, The Bible and Homer* he attributes it to the fourth century.[8] Magda Ohnefalsch-Richter dates Artemis in the third century,[9] while later publications adopt a time-span between the end of fourth and the second century.[10]

Artemis was discovered accidentally by quarry-men during April 1880, while Ohnefalsch-Richter was digging for the British Museum and, when he found out, he kept it secret, until the buyer managed to export it illegally to France. Here it remained unsold until 1884 when Richter travelled to Paris and mediated for its sale to the Imperial and Royal Coin and Antiquity Collection (today the Kunsthistorisches Museum) at the Museums of the Emperor of Austria, receiving 600 francs.[11] It is interesting to compare the illustration of the statue which is given in the Έσπερος to the photograph in Magda's book, which was obviously taken after the statue was exhibited in Vienna. The illustration shows the statue as it was before the attachment of its right arm, and of the left one of the statuette (Fig. 23.2a,b).

The rest of Ohnefalsch-Richter's appearance in the Εσπερος is in the form of articles and they were all published in the year 1884, from March to June. They were delivered for publication before he started travelling in Europe in order to find sponsors for his excavations and sell antiquities. We might therefore deduce that one of the purposes of these articles was to prepare the ground for his forthcoming meetings with potential sponsors of excavations and purchasers of antiquities.[12]

In his first article in issue number 69 of 1/12 March 1884, Ohnefalsch-Richter states at the very beginning that he will prove that, since the British occupation, work has been done to benefit the science and the history of Cyprus, and considers the foundation of the Cyprus Museum as one of the first achievements under the British flag. He then goes on to mention that he had the honour to direct excavations for the British Museum and to express his gratitude to various people for their academic and financial help, and to others for their contribution to the foundation of the Museum. He concludes the acknowledgments by stating that 'unfortunately due to its limited funds the Museum cannot conduct excavations to a great extent and therefore, at least for the time being, individuals are allowed to excavate under certain conditions, according to which they have to deliver part of the finds to the Cyprus Museum'.[13] He notes also that scientific publications by the Museum had already started, thanks to the initiative of Falkland Warren, Chief Secretary to the Government, who arranged for these publications to be printed by the governmental printing office. Ohnefalsch-Richter does not omit to accuse the Cesnola brothers by saying, among other things, that their collections are 'commercial businesses'[14] and that their influence was more harmful than benefitial. He calls upon the reader not to be surprised if he arrives at totally different conclusions on matters concerning Cypriot culture from others, whose interpretations were based on a mixture of material, obviously implying Luigi Palma di Cesnola.

In the next paragraph he states that it is his belief that his article will be welcomed by the Greek readers, since he is going to talk mostly about the Greek element of ancient Cyprus, justly claiming that other researchers 'gave hellenism a minor role in Cyprus'.[15] We might therefore argue that we stand in front of a 'diplomat' who, on the one hand, praises the British colonists and on the other hand satisfies the nationalist feelings of the Greek readers of Έσπερος.[16] Of course, he refrains himself from exaggeration by noting that Greek art in Cyprus has never reached the perfection of the art of mainland Greece and the Ionic colonies. He also talks about the character of the ancient Cypriot as being given up 'to the enjoyment of the senses and to the worship of Astarte and Aphrodite and almost always in discord'[17] and therefore, according to the author, even in the extemely

Fig. 23.3: Terracottas, Έσπερος 69 (1884).

Fig. 23.4: Terracottas, Έσπερος 70 (1884).

rare case when a great Cypriot man would appear, he would emigrate, as in the case of the sculptor Styppax.

The rest of the article concentrates on ancient religion in Cyprus and especially on the worship of Artemis, by examining various terracottas (Fig. 23.3) which he identifies as the goddess.[18] The second article appears in the next issue of Έσπερος, number 70 of 15/27 March 1884. It is a continuation of the previous one and dated by the author 'Nicosia, February 1884'. It seems that Ohnefalsch - Richter sent both these articles as a single text which was published in two successive issues.

Fig. 23.5: Statues and temple boys, Ἕσπερος 73 (1884).

Fig. 23.6: Statues and other antiquities, Ἕσπερος 74 (1884).

In this second article he gives a description of the terracottas illustrated in both articles (Fig. 23.4) and tries to explain the evolution in the typology based on his own perception of change in worship practices and of course on the increasing Greek influence as we move from the Archaic to the Classical period. He also tries to show a connection between Artemis and Ekate by demonstrating an anthropomorphic incense-burner. He ends the article by claiming that it was Nicocles of Salamis, the successor of Evagoras, who put an end to the worship of Artemis by destroying her temples; this would give way to the erotic worship of Aphodite which, according to the author, was more suitable to his character.

The three last articles in the Ἕσπερος appear in three successive issues, numbers 73, 74 and 75 from May to June 1884 and they also form a single text dated by the author 'Nicosia, 1884'. Here he deals with Adonis, Apollo, Heracles, Zeus, Niki, and Athena. After observing that a lot of 'idols' which he excavated in various sanctuaries of Aphrodite have Phoenician influence, he once again assures his readers that he will remain 'loyal' to his subject and talk only about the Greek elements of ancient Cypriot religion.[19] He describes and interprets the seated statuettes as representing Adonis (Fig. 23.5).[20] Then he once more accuses Cesnola for his 'pseudotemple' of Aphrodite at Golgoi and for causing confusion to the 'wise men' of science.

The next god he deals with is Apollo and after stating that he was widely worshipped in Cyprus, he interprets the headless statue of Fig. 23.6 as representing Apollo and attributes the head in the same fig. to this statue. Then he talks about the connection between the worship of Apollo and Heracles in Cyprus and tries to support it by various finds. After a short discussion about Zeus and Niki,

Fig. 23.7: Bronze mirror from the baths of Salamis, Ἕσπερος 74 (1884).

Ohnefalsch-Richter talks about Athena by offering us a most sentimental and enthusiastic description of a bronze relief representing the goddes (Fig. 23.7). It is the back side of a mirror which he excavated in the baths of Salamis. Then he describes an engraved gem with a representation of Athena and he informs us that it was found by him in a tomb at Kourion and that it then belonged to Samuel Brown, Chief Engineer of Cyprus. Today it is in the British Museum.

The articles, presented above in a telegraphic manner, at most, apart from being an addition to the bibliography, certainly oppose the statement that the 'British Occupation of Cyprus in 1878 marks the close of what may be called the mythical age of Cypriote Archaeology'.[21] As far as Max Ohnefalsch-Richter is concerned, if he is either a 'famous ... plunderer of our ancestral relics'[22] or someone who contributed 'perhaps more than anybody else to the revealing of hitherto unknown facts about the island's past';[23] the discussion remains open.

Notes

1. This paper is dedicated in memory of Olivier Masson. My appreciation goes to Costis Kokkinoftas of the Kykkos Research Centre and to Mr Thanos Zintilis for making my participation to the Colloquium possible. I wish to thank Professor Vassos Karageorghis for his encouragement, Professor Demetrios Michaelides for his time, Marina Ieronymidou, Elena Prokopiou, Stella Demesticha and Dr. Rita Severis for their valuable help and last, but not least, Charalambos Bakirtzis for setting the necessary academic bases. Finally I am grateful to Angela Hadjigeorghiou for typing the text and Tony Paraskeva for some remarks.
2. Greek writer and philologist who studied in Munich and taught literature in the University of Athens. Around 1880 he settled in Leipzig until 1889, when he returned back to Athens. Information from Μεγάλη Ελληνική Εγκυκλοπαίδεια, vol.19 (2nd ed.)
3. M. Ohnefalsch-Richter, 'Αρχαιολογικαί Έρευναι εν Κύπρω', Έσπερος 69 (1884) 323.
4. It is not clear whether Ohnefalsch-Richter actually sent a text or the editor obtained the information from elsewhere. In *Kypros, The Bible and Homer* (London 1893) 309 Ohnefalsh-Richter informs us that he 'published in illustrated magazines an account of the work' and the footnote on the same page names several of them, but not Έσπερος. It seems therefore most likely that the correspondence follows earlier publications, which appeared a year earlier.
5. Plin. N.H. 34.81
6. Ohnefalsch-Richter (n.4) 309 n.2: 'To Friedlander belongs the credit of having first recognized in the group a representation of Artemis'.
7. J.L. Myres and M. Ohnefalsch-Richter, *A Catalogue of the Cyprus Museum* (Oxford 1899) 5.
8. Ohnefalsch-Richter (n.4) 311.
9. M. Ohnefalsch-Richter, *Griechische Sitten and Gebrauche auf Cypern* (Berlin 1913) 8.
10. M. Ohnefalsch-Richter, 'Cyprus, its Ancient Civilization', *Pall Mall Magazine* (1914) 749; E. Gjerstad, *The Swedish Cyprus Expedition* IV. 3, 236; V. Karageorghis, *Greek Gods and Heroes in Ancient Cyprus* (Athens 1998) 185
11. H-G. Buchholz, 'Max Ohnefalsch-Richter als Archaologe auf Zypern', *Centre d'Études Chypriotes. Cahier* 11–12 (1989) 9.
12. M. Krpata, 'Max Hermann Ohnefalsch-Richter. Bibliography and Biographical Remarks', *RDAC* (1992) 338.
13. Ohnefalsch-Richter (n.3) 323. This statement may well be considered to be an invitation to potential excavators.
14. Ohnefalsch-Richter (n.3) 323.
15. Ohnefalsch Richter (n.3) 323.
16. Ohnefalsch-Richter (n.10) 739: 'It is true that four-fifths of the Cypriotes are Greeks but as Greece has already doubled her territories since the Balkan wars, and as she will obtain most of the Aegean Islands, an annexation of far-off Cyprus would only be a great burden to her at the present time'. This statement is in the same mode as those in Έσπερος.
17. Ohnefalsch-Richter (n.3) 323
18. The top right illustration is a Bronze Age plank-shaped figurine.
19. M. Ohnefalsch-Richter, 'Κυπριακαί Αρχαιότητες', Έσπερος 73 (1884) 2.
20. At the bottom left of Fig. 5 we recognize a temple boy from the Cyprus Museum: C. Beer, *Temple Boys. A Study of Cypriot Votive Sculpture. Part 1. Catalogue* (Jonsered 1994) pl. 59.
21. Myres and Ohnefalsch-Richter (n.7) VIII.
22. Ι.Κ. Περιστάνη, *Γενική Ιστορία της Νήσου Κύπρου* (Λευκωσία 1995) 565.
23. Ohnefalsch-Richter (n.10) 741.

The Law

24. The fight for the past: Watkins vs. Warren (1885–6) and the control of excavation

Michael Given

The Permit

In early August, 1885, Lieutenant-Colonel Falkland George Edgeworth Warren, R.A. (retired), applied for permission to excavate at Paraskevi, Pera and Acanthou. His application was received by the Chief Clerk in the government offices, W.H. Bennett, and forwarded to the Chief Secretary, who happened to be Colonel Falkland Warren himself. Warren looked over the application and, in line with correct procedure, instructed Bennett, his Chief Clerk, to send it for comments to the Honorary Secretary of the Cyprus Museum Committee, one W.H. Bennett. The Honorary Secretary gave his approval and sent it back to the Chief Clerk (himself), who in turn passed it on to his superior, the Chief Secretary Colonel Falkland Warren. The Chief Secretary gave his permission, the application was countersigned in red ink by a busy High Commissioner, and in due course Colonel Falkland Warren heard the good news that he had indeed been granted an excavation permit (SA1/3380/1885).

This paper investigates the relationship between archaeology and colonial rule in late nineteenth-century Cyprus. Excavation of the island's many rewarding archaeological sites was a popular pastime for government officials and private individuals alike, and even as late as the 1910s a High Commissioner used to take his wife and Private Secretary out for a good day's 'tombing' (Luke 1953, 212). However genuine the interest and enthusiasm of such individuals, there was a strong ideological component to this activity. Imperial rule was certainly enforced by might, but it was also justified by rhetoric; and archaeology was a fruitful source of such legitimizing arguments.

The result of Colonel Warren's dubiously acquired excavation permit turned out to be rather different to what he had expected. For all the importance and value of his finds at Pera Frangissa, his excavations landed him in court within four months. He was publicly and ignominiously cross-examined, his evasive replies were published in the newspapers, and there were open calls for him to resign. Underlying the story of Warren's excavation and trial there lurks a fierce battle over the control of excavation, and it was only with the publication of the courtroom transcript in the *Cyprus Herald* that this battle came to public knowledge. With the help of what were then confidential documents in the Chief Secretary's Office and are now public records in the Cyprus State Archives, we can examine this unsavoury episode as an illuminating example of the close relationship between archaeology and colonial rule in the late nineteenth century.

Archaeology and Colonial Society

British imperial rule, when it came to the crunch, was based ultimately on might, and occasionally it suited them to declare this. When Britain took over the administration of Cyprus after the Congress of Berlin in 1878, the illustrated papers showed the British fleet filling the Bay of Larnaca, and the infantry landing at the beachhead and setting up camp in strategic areas. Outside such moments of crisis, it was more effective to sustain imperial rule by ideology, persuasion, and loudly stated conviction. Today we would call it the 'moral high ground'; then it was the White Man's Burden, the noble self-sacrifice made by imperial officials to bring organisation and order into the lives of their native subjects. Colonial rule was portrayed as paternalistic and strict, to be sure, but above all disinterested and just.

Precedent and parallel provide strong legalistic arguments, and so history and archaeology became important sources for this ideological justification. Past imperial situations demonstrated the long need for paternalistic control of eastern or southern peoples, while ancient artefacts and artistic styles could provide evidence for their character. An Oriental ancient Cyprus presupposed an Oriental modern Cyprus, and it was conventional wisdom that Orientals could not rule themselves. By argument that was careful, if inconsistent, any European or classical remains that did survive could be made to demonstrate the need for European guardianship which local people could not give.

Because of the ideological force of archaeology and history, it was important to control sources of information about the past, and to direct any interpretation that was made of them. One aspect of this was the careful selection and discussion of ancient textual references to Cyprus. To those positing an Oriental character for the island, for example, biblical references to Kittim were more pertinent than Isokrates' panegyrics on the quintessentially Hellenic Evagoras. As for archaeology, there was always a risk that new finds might prove embarrassing, as Ronald Storrs found in the 1920s (Given 1998, 15). Because of this, and because of a stated concern that excavation should be done properly, it was important to control who did the excavation.

In terms of government control, there had been considerable progress since the days of Sandwith, Lang and Cesnola. The new regime was all too happy to criticise the amateurs. Alessandro di Cesnola's finds were actually confiscated by the colonial government in 1878, and kept in the house of Claude Cobham, the Commissioner of Larnaca, for safe keeping (Brassey 1880, 281). Cobham may not have been too inconvenienced by this duty, as they remained there for some eleven years (SA1/702/1889). Excavation was now carried out by members of the government who were deemed responsible, if not necessarily expert: Hugh Sinclair, District Engineer of Larnaca and then Sir Robert Biddulph's Private Secretary; Herbert Kitchener, director of the Cyprus Survey; Claude Cobham; Falkland Warren; and, usually, the High Commissioner himself. The Cyprus Museum was set up in 1882 (*CH* 21 June 1882), with a committee dominated by members of the government and chaired ex-officio by the High Commissioner.

As for interpretation of the past, that too was done almost entirely by members of the government. Claude Cobham became the authority on the documentary history of the island. Tankerville Chamberlayne, the Commissioner of Kyrenia, catalogued and published medieval gravestones. Roland Michell, Commissioner of Limassol, investigated topics of local ethnographic interest such as the *linovamvaki*. By the end of the century academics from European universities and museums were excavating in Cyprus, but in close collaboration with the government; and even in the 1920s and 1930s the tradition of the 'scholar-official' continued with George Jeffery, Harry Luke, Rupert Gunnis, and Ronald Storrs.

There were outsiders, particularly British businessmen in Larnaca and Limassol, who also caught the excavation bug: John Williamson, a Limassol engineer and publisher; the brothers Charles, Percy and Frank Christian, who shared interests in mining, public works, and archaeology; and Charles Watkins, the respected director of the Imperial Ottoman Bank in Larnaca and member of the Legislative Council. As a correspondent to the *Cyprus Herald* wrote in December 1883, archaeology was the thing of the moment:

'Dear Sir,
So excavating's all the fashion!
And you yourself have not escaped the passion!
I, too, have digged, and it has been my fate
To find a Work of Art that wants a date:-
An interesting object, but whose history
And time of birth for me are wrap't in mystery. [...]
R.S.V.P. Believe me, Mr. Herald,
Your's truly, Papadópoulos Fitzgerald'.
(*CH* 10 December 1883)

But these non-government individuals found it hard to get excavation permits from the government, particularly when competing with their official compatriots such as Falkland Warren. Their only weapon was the independent press, and the pages of the *Cyprus Herald* from Limassol are full of angry denunciations against the government for reserving excavation for its own cronies (*CH* 31 December 1883; 7 January 1884; 12 December 1885). This rivalry between members of the government and private individuals divided the already small British community: the commercial operations and international contacts of businessmen in Larnaca and Limassol were a different world to the incestuous office politics and at-homes of inland Nicosia and its summer hill station on Mount Troodos.

There was one anomaly in Cypriot archaeology in the first twenty years of colonial rule: a photographer, forester, and self-taught archaeologist who was shunned for being German and pompous (or so British society declared): Max Ohnefalsch-Richter. The editor of the *Cyprus Herald's* reply to 'Papadopoullos Fitzgerald' about the unidentified vase is typical:

'[...] It looks such an excellent thing to make porridge in
I should rather have deemed it of Scotch than Greek origin.
While my friend Dr. Obersalz Dichter declares
With that look of deep wisdom he frequently wears,
While pronouncing it antique without hesitation,
"Off the motern it is a most kross imidashun"'.
(*CH* 17 December 1883)

The attack is all the more insulting for being so thinly veiled under a pseudonym which could fool nobody. In spite of this xenophobia, however, Ohnefalsch-Richter made himself indispensable to the regime, and after seven years of sheer persistence and obstinacy he obtained the largely unpaid position of 'Consulting Archaeologist and Superintendent of Excavations'.

The Excavation

When Colonel Falkland Warren applied for his permit to excavate at Paraskevi, Pera and Acanthou ('possibly ancient Carthage'), he had not of course found the sites himself. That had been done by Ohnefalsch-Richter. When work started on the site of ancient Tamassos near Pera at the end of September 1885, it was Ohnefalsch-Richter who directed the excavation, while Warren just visited on Sundays: the outcome he wanted consisted of finds of monetary and honorific value, rather than any actual personal experience. At Pera he was disappointed: a glass workshop with 'great quantities of glass droppings from the blow pipes' would be exciting to us today, but caused little enthusiasm then and remains unpublished (*CH* 2 November 1885, 1). A painted vase with a hunting scene was the only artefact of note from a series of tombs of 'poor class' (*CH* 2 November 1885, 1; 2 January 1886, 1b; for the vase see Ohnefalsch-Richter 1893, 7, 36–7, 327, 445, pl. 137:6).

While this was going on, dissatisfied with the results, Ohnefalsch-Richter went exploring on his days off, following up earlier leads from local people, and on 4 October he discovered what a judge later called 'a mine of antiquarian wealth' some three kilometres southeast of Pera, at the locality Frangissa (*CH* 9 January 1886, 3). So thick were the statuette fragments on the ground, he said later, they were 'like herrings in a barrel' (*CH* 2 January 1886, 3a). Instead of reporting the find to Warren, however, as might be expected, he wrote to another of his occasional employers, Charles Watkins, enthusing about the site and describing it as 'a most excellent money success beyond any doubt' (*CH* 9 January 1886, 3) – a telling comment on one of the main purposes of amateur excavation in the 1880s. Watkins was delighted; he sent Ohnefalsch-Richter £10 to hire the land, while he himself applied for a permit from the Government.

Ohnefalsch-Richter followed his instructions, without informing Warren, and on 5 October drew up the following contract with the landowner:

'Mr Richter will "hire a piece of land from Yoannui H. Loizi Argyre, which he will excavate for antiquities. He has hired it for 182 c. p. and there are 4 months duration for digging the whole field from 1 October to the 1 February 1886. And boundaries are: Hill, Channel Pandeli, H. Phillipou and Yoanni's H. Loizi. Wherefore for proof and assurance of the truth I give into his hands this my present writing in the presence of the below written witnesses, and they are to fill up the holes again"'
(*CH* 9 January 1886, 3).

Unfortunately for Watkins, he had to go to Beirut on business, leaving the Chief Secretary's office to deal with his permit application. Colonel Warren visited his excavations at Pera, as usual, on 15 October, with his official and antiquarian sidekick W.H. Bennett. Ohnefalsch-Richter made the tactical but understandable error of letting slip a reference to the glories of Frangissa. Warren, according to the judge's summing up at the trial, 'appears to have considered that the spot was within the limit of his own permit, and after a somewhat stormy interview ordered Richter to dig for him on the new site' (*CH* 9 January 1886, 3). Warren's bullying of the vulnerable and dependent Ohnefalsch-Richter comes over very clearly from Ohnefalsch-Richter's testimony in the trial (2 January 1886, 3a), in spite of Warren's ingenuous protestations (9 January 1886, 1a) and Bennett's clear evasion under oath (9 January 1886, 2b).

Ohnefalsch-Richter, browbeaten by the Chief Secretary to the Government, duly started work for Warren at Frangissa two days later. The results fully rewarded the expectations of the superintendent of excavations and his master. On a narrow river terrace above a dry stream bed Ohnefalsch-Richter excavated a walled enclosure fourteen metres long, crowded with statue bases, and packed with fragments of limestone and terracotta statuettes ranging from the terracotta colossus in the Cyprus Museum to 10cm high snowman figurines. Outside the entrance was an altar with 'hundreds' of chariot groups. Most famously, a slab built into the wall and another statue base from the enclosure carried bilingual inscriptions, written in Phoenician and Cypriot Syllabic Greek. (Ohnefalsch-Richter 1893, 7–10, pl. 6; Myres and Ohnefalsch-Richter 1899, 167–171; Masson 1964, 232–236; Masson 1983, nos. 215–216; Buchholz 1978, 209–210; Buchholz 1987, 207–211; Buchholz 1991; Buchholz 1996, 47–51).

Three days after work began at Frangissa, Charles Watkins returned from Beirut, to discover Ohnefalsch-Richter surprisingly silent about his promised site, and no word yet from the Chief Secretary's Office about his permit. The minute paper with the correspondence about this application (SA1/4262/1885) shows an astonishing series of prevarications and postponements. W.H. Bennett is clearly having difficulties separating his various roles as Chief Clerk, Honorary Secretary of the Cyprus Museum Committee, and Colonel Warren's lapdog. Five days after the receipt of Watkins' letter, he declares that Warren already has permission; a week later he pinpoints the exact spot; two days later he comes to the conclusion it is the same place as the one where Warren is digging.

By now, 7 November 1885, Ohnefalsch-Richter has actually completed the excavations at Frangissa, the finds have been installed in his house in Nicosia, and the winter rains have set in. But the bureaucratic stalling continues.

The Chief Secretary and the Chief Clerk decide Watkins cannot be granted a permit; but the High Commissioner, for once, intervenes, and declares that Watkins must be allowed to dig there if he wants, unless the site is reserved for the Cyprus Museum. The Chief Secretary inquires of the Honorary Secretary of the Museum Committee (via the Chief Clerk) as to whether the Museum wishes to excavate there. It turns out that the Museum does indeed wish to excavate, and on 17 November, over two weeks after the end of his excavations at Frangissa, Colonel Falkland Warren as Chief Secretary informs Watkins that his application to excavate has been rejected.

For Colonel Warren there only remained one problem, which became more and more alarming as Watkins' anger grew. Ohnefalsch-Richter had signed a contract with the owner of the land, and subsequently passed on his rights to Charles Watkins. On 25 November Warren visited Ohnefalsch-Richter's house in Nicosia, accompanied by George Smith, who was Assistant to the Chief Secretary and so Warren's immediate junior. Accounts of what happened on this occasion, unsurprisingly, do not entirely agree, but it is clear not just from Ohnefalsch-Richter's testimony (*CH* 2 January 1886, 3a, 3b) but even from Warren's (*CH* 9 January 1886, 1b) that Ohnefalsch-Richter was somehow persuaded into writing a declaration that Warren had a prior right to Watkins, and that Ohnefalsch-Richter then gave this document to Warren. When cross-examined by Watkins' advocate in court about the illegality of accepting such a fraudulent document (never mind obtaining it by force), Warren could only bleat pathetically 'I don't know what you mean', repeating it five times until his guilt was obvious, if unconfessed (*CH* 9 January 1886, 2a).

That still left the question of the contract to the land given by the landowner, which Warren clearly did not possess. On 2 December Mrs Falkland Warren mysteriously arrived at Ohnefalsch-Richter's house, and 'advised' him to go the village of Pera and make a contract for Frangissa in Warren's name in the presence of the landowner and the village judge, ante-dating it to 4 October, the day before the real contract had been drawn up by Ohnefalsch-Richter. Clearly intimidated, Ohnefalsch-Richter rode out to Pera the next day, drew up the false contract with the village judge, and delivered it to Colonel Falkland Warren in person. Warren denied all knowledge of his wife's involvement or any attempt to intimidate Ohnefalsch-Richter – but he made sure to accept the contract, and made Ohnefalsch-Richter sign a declaration he had 'brought this paper voluntarily without having been asked' (*CH* 2 January 1886, 3c).

At about this time Ohnefalsch-Richter drew up another false contract for Colonel Warren. This was for the land near Pera where he had discovered the painted vase, which at that point was considered to be worth over £500. The contract was ante-dated to 14 October, the day on which the vase had been found, and the owner received 10 shillings in return for waiving his rights for all material found on his land, including the £500 vase he had not been told about (*CH* 2 January 1886, 3c). The colonial establishment may well have preached the merits of the 'White Man's Burden', and flaunted its acts of self-sacrifice in supporting the poor natives who could not rule themselves. In their actual practice, however, it was clearly a very different story, even when the individual concerned was the second highest British official in the colony.

The Trial

Colonel Warren had good reason for being worried. Charles Watkins, although an independent businessman, had always been loyal to the regime, inviting its officials to his house (e.g. *CH* 22 January 1883, 3), speaking well of the government's road-building activities (Smith 1887, 149), and even serving for a year as President of the Municipal Council of Larnaca, in effect the mayor (*CH* 24 April 1884, 3). His unjust exclusion from a site he had legally acquired, however, along with Warren's blatant abuse of his position, angered him beyond endurance. In December 1885 he took the unprecedented step of taking the Chief Secretary of the island's government to court. He demanded one third of the antiquities, deriving from his rights to the land, and another third for damages, because of Warren's trespass. This trial, wrote the *Cyprus Herald* with considerable understatement, caused 'greater interest among the English Community in Cyprus than any other event since the Occupation' (*CH* 19 December 1885), and its notoriety even reached western Europe (Reinach 1891, 267, 294).

The forces that lined themselves up on each side of this battle for the past demonstrated very clearly the rift between the official and the private British communities. Watkins hired a well-known independent advocate and government-baiter, Ulick Burke, who had supported the Bishop of Kition against Falkland Warren in an earlier *cause célèbre*. Warren's defence lawyer was William Collyer, the Queen's Advocate and therefore the leading government lawyer and in effect a subordinate of Warren. Even more significantly, the judge was Charles Walpole, President of the District Court of Larnaca: although something of an expert in the Turkish Criminal Code, he was emphatically junior to both Warren and Collyer, and very much part of the official establishment.

This cronyism among the members of the government comes out most clearly in the discussion of the original contract made between Ohnefalsch-Richter, on Watkins' behalf, and the landowner. In the witness box was Christophi Christodoulos, the villager who had originally shown Ohnefalsch-Richter the site and arranged his meeting with the landowner. He described the signing of the contract and his own witnessing of it. This was clearly the major point supporting Watkins' case: he had a legally signed and witnessed contract giving him full rights to excavate Frangissa. The document itself had been handed in to the court, and all that was needed was for the witness to identify it. As recorded in the transcript, Ulick Burke, Watkins' advocate, duly asked for it to be produced:

'(Mr. Burke asked the court to hand over the contract to the witness but the contract could not be found. The Judge and the Barristers searched all over the place for it. The contract disappeared.) (Christophi continues). "I saw a contract written and myself and Abramo gave it to Richter". (Mr. Collyer said that the Govt. Engineer should provide the courts with boxes for the papers. Judge Walpole said that it was very difficult to get anything out of the Govt. Engineer. Mr. Collyer then remarked that if the two opposite windows are left open all the papers will be blown in the *potamos* (river). Justice Walpole said that they might at least be provided with stones from the *potamos* to use them as paper weights. Mr Collyer: otherwise we will be obliged to put the papers in our pockets)'.
(*CH* 2 January 1886, 4a).

What is clear from this farcical episode is not just the highly suspicious disappearance of the contract exactly when it would have proved Watkins' case, but also the cronyism between judge and defence lawyer, and the little in-jokes about the Government Engineer, who was often the butt of Government Office humour. Such is their position of institutional strength that they can even make jokes about their 'accidental' loss of the most critical item of evidence.

In the face of this opposition, the lawyers' actual arguments are almost irrelevant. Ulick Burke, speaking on behalf of Watkins, cited not just the elusive contract but also Article 17 of the 1874 Ottoman Antiquities Law, which remained in force, stating that government officials could not conduct excavations as private persons, for fear of them abusing the privileged position their official post placed them in. The relevance of this law was abundantly obvious. Defending Colonel Warren, his lawyer and official subordinate William Collyer gave the patently absurd riposte that 'Colonel Warren's jurisdiction is limited to his own office'. 'Here he may dig for permits', was Ulick Burke's *sotto voce* comment. The rest of Collyer's brief argument is limited to bold assertions, with no recorded evidence or argument to support his statements: 'As for Col. Warren abusing his position as chief secretary he has not done so' (*CH* 9 January 1886, 2).

It comes as no surprise that Colonel Warren won the case, and Watkins had to pay costs. The establishment had won the day, and Warren disregarded the calls for him to resign (*CH* 16 January 1886, 1–2). Even so, such a public split between compatriots was an embarrassment for the colonial government, which needed to preserve the façade of unity to keep its authority over the Cypriot people. So a scapegoat was found, someone who was easily mocked, already disliked, and who was above all not British: Max Ohnefalsch-Richter. 'Richter has been playing fast and loose with both Plaintiff and Defendant' pontificated Charles Walpole in his judgment. 'He began with the intention of deceiving the defendant and he has ended by cheating the plaintiff' (*CH* 9 January 1886, 3). Such rounded periods and neat symmetry unite the two Englishmen and make them the passive objects of the foreigner's active malice and dishonesty.

Conclusion

A year after the notorious trial, a short discussion of the two bilingual inscriptions appeared in the *Proceedings of the Society of Biblical Archaeology*. The ownership of these artefacts is not left open to any doubt

'Among the objects from Cyprus exhibited during the past summer at the Colonial Exhibition were two bilingual inscriptions, Phoenician and Cypriote, the property of Colonel F. Warren, R.A., who discovered them during his excavations at Frangissa, near the ancient town of Tamassos'.
(Wright 1886–87, 47).

Needless to say, there is no mention of Charles Watkins. Nor is any credit given to the man who did the work, Max Ohnefalsch-Richter, nor to the landowner Yianni Hadjiloizou (cf. Buchholz 1991, 4). This applies not just to one obscure scholarly publication, but to the Colonial and Indian Exhibition in London in 1886, where the inscriptions were displayed and labelled. The Cyprus Pavilion at this exhibition was attended by much of London society and by Queen Victoria herself (*CH* 17 July 1886, 2). As for Menahem and Abdasom, the authors of the two inscriptions, they had just become pawns in the power game of Colonel Warren and his contemporaries.

The same sense of victorious possession of the past is evident in the photographs taken of the artefacts from Frangissa by Edward Carletti, a clerk in the Land Registry Office, while they were still in Warren's house. In one photograph Warren joins a group of heads and statues which are smaller than life size (Buchholz 1991, pl. 5b); but in the photograph of the terracotta colossus he gets his servant to pose instead of him, in case he should appear dwarfed (pl. 4a). In another photograph Warren is shown in profile behind the artefacts, arms akimbo, as if posing with one foot on a record tiger he had just shot (pl. 5a).

Archaeology in the early days of colonial rule in Cyprus was clearly motivated by greed, power and self-display as much as by scholarly interest or academic enthusiasm. Any rival who was not a government official, or not British, was suppressed by the massive weight and power of the colonial establishment. The same applied to the artefacts and their users and creators. The past was not just fought over but was itself oppressed, so that ownership and interpretation became a prerogative of British colonial officials, and ancient people were compelled to support a modern regime.

Acknowledgements

The research for this paper was done with the aid of a Study Abroad Studentship from the Leverhulme Trust, to whom I am very grateful. I would also like to thank the Director and staff of the Cyprus State Archives, Nicosia, and the staff of the Cyprus Museum Library, Nicosia. The copyright of all documents from the Cyprus State Archives, Nicosia, remains with the Government of Cyprus. I am grateful to Hans-Günter Buchholz, Nicholas Stanley-Price, and Peter van Dommelen for their comments on an earlier version of this paper.

Bibliography

Brassey 1880: Annie Brassey, *Sunshine and Storm in the East, or Cruises to Cyprus and Constantinople*. (London).

Buchholz 1978: Hans-Günter Buchholz, 'Tamassos, Zypern, 1974–1976. 3. Bericht', *Archäologischer Anzeiger*, 155–230.

Buchholz 1987: Hans-Günter Buchholz, 'Tamassos, Zypern, 1977–1986. 4. Bericht', *Archäologischer Anzeiger*, 165–228.

Buchholz 1991: Hans-Günter Buchholz, 'Tamassos - Frangissa (1885)', *Centre d'Etudes Chypriotes. Cahier* 16, 3–15.

Buchholz 1996: Hans-Günter Buchholz, *Tamassos: Ein Antikes Königreich auf Zypern* (Jonsered).

CH: *Cyprus Herald* (weekly English-language newspaper published in Limassol from October 1881 to January 1887)

Given 1998: Michael Given, 'Inventing the Eteocypriots: Imperialist Archaeology and the Manipulation of Ethnic Identity', *Journal of Mediterranean Archaeology* 11, 3–29.

Luke 1953: Harry Charles Luke, *Cities and Men: An Autobiography. Volume 1: The First Thirty Years, 1884–1914* (London).

Masson 1964: Olivier Masson 'Kypriaka 1: Recherches sur les Antiquités de Tamassos', *BCH* 88, 199–238.

Masson 1983: Olivier Masson, 'Addenda Nova,' in *Études Chypriotes* 1 (Paris), 407–424.

Myres and Ohnefalsch-Richter 1899: John L. Myres and Max H. Ohnefalsch-Richter, *A Catalogue of the Cyprus Museum* (Oxford).

Ohnefalsch-Richter 1893: Max H. Ohnefalsch-Richter, *Kypros, the Bible and Homer (Oriental Civilization, Art and Religion in Ancient Times*, London).

Reinach 1891: Salomon Reinach, *Chronique d'Orient: Documents sur les Fouilles et Découvertes dans l'Orient Héllenique de 1883 à 1890* (Paris).

SA1: Unpublished government correspondence in the Cyprus State Archives, Nicosia.

Smith 1887: Agnes Smith, *Through Cyprus* (London).

Wright 1886–87: Professor Wright, Untitled [Bilingual Inscriptions from Tamassos], *Proceedings of the Society of Biblical Archaeology* 9, 47–49.

25. Archaeology and Islamic Law in Ottoman Cyprus

G. R. H. Wright

In the middle of the nineteenth century, when Cyprus had been part of the Ottoman Empire from time out of mind, the British consul in Larnaka was a young Scotsman named Hamilton Lang. According to reminiscences published much later he reckoned this the happiest period of his life, because of the opportunities afforded him to seek and collect antiquities. In this connection somewhere else he records that once, when supervising digging for antiquities (at Dhali, the ancient Idalion), he was hailed by his friend the Turkish Governor of the Island, who happened to be passing. The governor said to him mildly 'I suppose I should stop you. You need a firman *[Imperial decree]*. Have you got one?' Lang states that he replied 'No. You need a firman to stop me. Have you got one?'

On the face of it, this could pass as an example of the 'masterful manner' which Europeans of the day commonly assumed in their dealings with Ottoman officials. In fact, it is rather unlikely that it should be taken in this fashion. Hamilton Lang was a very able and intelligent man who had made a success of a varied career in the Middle East. He became a senior director of the newly founded Ottoman Bank and was very properly knighted. Far from being ill-conditioned verbiage, it is more likely that these remarks (implying utter confusion in the operation of law) represent a studied appraisal of the legal situation.

This episode introduces (in *medias res*) an interesting question – one of wide application extending to almost every province of the Ottoman Empire. It is manifested in Cyprus in its essential aspects; although, of course, there are local considerations. Nonetheless a brief outline of the question in Cyprus indicates, in principle, the position obtaining elsewhere, wherever remains, subsisting of an ancient past, became of topical interest to Western Europe (e.g. in Irak, Syria, Libya, etc).

Latterly the propriety of archaeological activities has become a matter of everyday interest, particularly concerning activities during the nineteenth century in the Eastern Mediterranean and the Middle East (where discussion is largely motivated by contemporary prejudices about imperialism). Here be it noted, virtually all areas of archaeological concern were then under Ottoman rule. In this way much has been, and now is, said to take seriously to task severally European archaeologists or Otttoman officials. In this debate it is not made explicit that the plane of discussion is a social one, or an ethical one, or an administrative one. Very rarely indeed are the matters discussed questions of law or questions which were referred to the law. No one wishes to say that legality is the be-all and end-all of every (or any) matter. However, it is manifestly unsatisfactory to discuss social matters entirely without reference to the law governing them, i.e. whether or not the proceedings under discussion were legal. Accordingly, in this preliminary notice, some attempt will be made to suggest what legal provisions might have been applicable to archaeological activities carried out in Cyprus during the nineteenth century, when it was part of Ottoman domains. It must be noted that the administrative status of Cyprus under Ottoman rule was changed continually back and forth. From being at first an independent province *(vilayet)*, it passed and repassed variously into a private *(khass)* domain (fief, we might say) first of the Lord High Admiral *(Kapudan Pasha)* and then of the Chief Minister *(vizier)*. In 1849 Cyprus was made a subsidiary division *(sanjak)* of the Aegean Islands *(Jeza'ir-i-bahir-i sefid)* governorate but there were further changes, so that at times its true status was not clear. However these administrative vicissitudes did not, in principle, affect the law applicable in the Island.

Cyprus was a late acquisition to the Islamic world, being conquered by the Ottomans in AD 1571 (=979 AH). However it was immediately thoroughly Islamicised, which meant in law and religion, since the latter two aspects of social life are closely connected – Islam being in considerable measure theocratic. This process conditioned completely attitudes towards the ancient past of the region. Islam did not comprehend a concern for pre-Islamic society as expressed in the material remains of its art and architecture. Absolutely to the contrary. Such a contrary attitude is implicit in other religions (e.g. a similar tendency was manifest in Early Christianity and has regularly resurfaced in fundamentalist revivals), however in Islam it is stated explicitly and emphatically.

Muhammad (like many visionaries) was a shrewd, practical man. He realised that his revealed faith (standing as it did on a marginal, provincial origin) was liable to censure on grounds of cultural limitation. It was thus very wise of him to characterise as essentially ignorant (hence boorish, barbaric) all cultures and civilisations (with a certain narrow exception) prior to his religious relation. This particular revelation has the force of all Koranic scripture, and thus in any discriminating judgement it is always possible to characterise the history of pre-Islamic times as of no consequence because it is essentially ignorant /foolish (except, that is, for the history of the 'people of the book' (*ahl al kitab*), i.e. biblical history).

The concept evolved by Muhammad is the *Jāhiliya*, the verbal root of which, *jahila*, means to be ignorant (not to know something), thus to be irrational, foolish, to behave foolishly. The noun *jahl* is ignorance; and the adjective *jāhil* is ignorant, uneducated, illiterate, foolish (which used as a substantive = a fool). From this root Muhammed evolved *Jāhili* as indicating all things pre-Islamic and *Jāhiliya* to signify the institutional state of ignorance – i.e. pre-Islamic religion and equally pre-Islamic society and its age and day. The concept resembles the Early Christian pejorative, heathen (rustics, dwellers in the heath) or pagan (peasants, workers of the fields); and note *Acts* 17.30

This incisive concept had to be continually tempered (or dismissed) in practical dealings, however it is dogma and its basic influence on Islamic attitude has been great – although not often specifically acknowledged. In the first instance Islam did not receive Graeco-Roman history and remains into what we now call its 'cultural heritage'. On the contrary it regarded the material remains as spoils and was struck with wonder at their fantastic wealth; originally to be seen above ground and forever afterwards to be found below the ground. This was so different from the sands of the Arabian desert. This sense of the imminence of treasure out of the *Jāhiliya* remains a striking feature of Islamic literature (cf in the *Thousand and One Nights*). The consequence of this is that Islamic governments never concerned themselves in practice with pre-Islamic antiquities. Even more significant and directly relevant to present concerns is the fact that, as Islamic Law came to be formulated out of religious principles, in principle, it did not address itself to questions concerning what we call antiquities. And the latter question must now be considered in more detail.

An outline of the origin, principles and working of Islamic Law evokes some incredulity in the first instance. To a modern European 'The Conflict of Laws' is something real enough, but it refers to the legal systems of different nations when (and as to when) they may be applicable in a given instance. It is in fact an alternative name for what is known as Private International Law. It is somewhat untoward to realise that this situation is endemic in Islamic Law within the one jurisdiction. Half a dozen sources (*uṣul*) of law may well be available in any one jurisdiction comprising customary law, secular (state) law, religious law (in four parallel recensions) – only the legal fiction is maintained that there is no conflict (or that apparent conflicts are always reconcilable).

Essentially the legal system obtaining in any Islamic land is based on the religious precepts of Islam – or such is the traditional position. However this has been qualified during the last century or so by the adoption, in many jurisdictions, of European legal provisions in a codified form, going back to the Code Napoleon. Nonetheless the traditional position is still revered in principle, and was operative in Cyprus during the period under discussion. The effect of this religious basis is that Islamic law often does not define impersonal categories and concepts as a western trained jurist would expect, but expresses itself rather in provisions regulating the conduct of persons so that they remain in a state of grace with God.

This religious Islamic Law (S*hari'a, Sheri'*) was developed during the second and third centuries of the Hegra (c. AD 780 – AD 850) at the flourishing period of Islamic scholarship, and thereafter, like much other Islamic thought, has tended to remain static. Several religious scholars during the period in question concerned themselves with studies (*fiqh* = intelligence, knowledge, specifically jurisprudence) to provide a legal system for the community. Eventually four such systems became accepted as orthodox religious law. The several systems have acquired preference or pre-eminence in various different geographical regions of the Islamic world – but in theory all are mutually acceptable and binding, on the legal fiction that they are all reconcilable by *ijtihad* = exertion (to form an opinion on a case). In practice what happened was that, while the Judge (*qādi*) would listen to any rule, he gave his decision in terms of the system to which he adhered. These systems (*madhhab*) are called rites (because of their religious origins) but perhaps schools seems a more appropriate term. The essential difference between them is the sources of law (*uṣul* = roots) they admitted, or the emphasis placed on these various sources. These sources were first and obviously the Koran (Quran) itself the direct word of God; next the words of Muhammad accepted by tradition (*Hadith/ Sunna*); then the statements of the companions (*ijmā* = agreement of those qualified i.e. contemporaries of the prophet), later extended to cover men of the succeeding two generations; and finally, applied human reason (*ra'y* = intelligence) i.e. legal interpretation *(qiyās* = analogy*)*.

While all schools of course accepted the Koranic material, the most rigid school (the *Hanbali* or *Hanabila*, that of Ahmad ibn Hanbal) sought to avoid virtually everything else. The school which was received by the Ottoman rulers and became the official doctrine of the Ottoman Empire (the *Hanafi* school or the *Hunafiya*, that of Abu Hanifa and his followers) was prepared to make use of rational, legal interpretation (*qiyās*) and accorded it more weight than some other schools. Fortunately Cyprus had no previous tradition of Islamic law when it was brought under Ottoman rule, therefore the *Hanafi* system did not encounter in Cyprus a previously established rival school of law (as, for example, in Syria and Egypt).

So much for what has always been held to be the essential body of Islamic law. However such law could not totally exclude, and thus was supplemented by, two other types of law: customary law (*'urf, 'āda*) and secular, state law (*qānūn*). Custom has a very strong force and Islamic law had to take cognisance of this willy-nilly. Thus early Islamic jurists were much concerned with the question of whether customary law survived islamisation or was rendered invalid and needed to be confirmed by Islamic law. Equally, on occasion, secular rulers had to be empowered to issue regulations and decrees. Often there was a connection. Such a law or ordinance might embody a custom or confirm a custom. In principle at first this process was reserved for circumstances where the *Shari'a* was little relevant, e.g. fiscal administration and criminal law. The Ottoman regime considerably developed Qānūn law, especially in a particular instance. This was the *firman/farman:* a decree issued in the name of the Sultan bearing his official cypher (*tughra*), sometimes endorsed or annotated by the sultan himself in his own hand to render it more august (compare *Khatt-i-Humayan, Khatt-i-Sherif*). It was thus a *Qānūn* but its characteristic was that it concerned itself with an individual affair rather than a public issue. In terms it was directed to specified officials or bodies ordering them *sub poena* to facilitate a certain specific activity or operation. In all this again the theory was that conflicts did not arise since customary and *Qānūn* law dealt with matters outside the *Shari'a* law. However, as the needs of the Ottoman administration became more complex, there was an increasing recourse to state law, and conflicts inevitably ensued with religious law.

It now remains to attempt some rationalisation of the legal position of acts concerned with antiquities in nineteenth-century Cyprus under Ottoman rule (i.e. AD 1800 – AD 1878). And initially it must be re-emphasized that the concern is to assess the position at law (i.e. *de jure*) and not what might have ensued in practice on the ground (i.e. *de facto*).

To begin with a simple issue. If the activities were carried out under the provisions of the Sultan's *firman* then, *de jure*, no complications arise. The *firman* was in effect a *qānūn* and was thus part of the organic law of the land. And from the moment of its issue it superseded (repealed, suspended, amended = *raskh*) all law relating to this particular instance. *Firmans* were as a rule very well draughted, and they enjoined all those concerned to see that the holder was able to carry out the activities desired without let or hindrance. So far as antiquities were concerned this, in general, meant not only to acquire them by excavation or other means, but also to take them out of the country – i.e. it granted exemption from whatever customs regulations may have been in force concerning such object. Very frequently antiquities operations in Ottoman lands were carried out under the terms of a *firman*, for example Lord Elgin's removal of the Parthenon sculptures at the beginning of the century. However, for one reason or another, some of the antiquities work in Cyprus during the middle of the nineteenth century was done without a *firman*. What was the position here according to the law of the land? That is the question.

In view of what has been said about the complex nature of Islamic law, it might be thought impossible to offer a brief resumé of this issue in an elementary approach. However, for the present purposes certain assumptions can be made fairly reasonably. First of all, it is possible to limit somewhat the body of law applicable. There is nothing to indicate the existence in Cyprus of any custom referring to antiquities. Equally nothing is known of any Ottoman *qānūn* specifically regulating antiquities. If such existed, logically, it might be mentioned in *firmans* issued to cover antiquities work, and so far as is evident, it never was. In particular there is no evidence for any *qānūn* specifying that it was forbidden *(yasak)* to carry out activities connected with antiquities in Ottoman lands unless in possession of the Sultan's *firman* authorising such activities. This in itself would have constituted an Antiquities Law *sui generis*, of which there is no record. Therefore it is *Shari'a* law which comes into question.

Cypriote antiquity has always remained of interest because of the Aphrodite connection in mythology. And in this way western Europeans who visited the Island in Turkish times were interested in its ancient remains. They looked out for them and copied inscriptions etc. However, it was only after the middle of the ninteenth century that western Europeans began to seek for antiquities in Cyprus by way of excavation. This work was in great measure carried out as a side line by consular representatives, notably the aforementioned Hamilton Lang and Cesnola, the American consul. In fact this phase was of short duration – continuing only for a decade or so about 1865–1875, before it was ruled out by the British occupation of the island in 1878. Nonetheless, during this period intensive work was undertaken at many sites in the Island and great quantities of antiquities were recovered. It has now become general to deprecate this work and represent it as spoliation and destruction, in which event odium also attaches to the Turkish authorities. Here the archaeological merit or propriety of this work is not in question, there is only the question as to whether it was legal according to Ottoman *Shari'a* law.

There are analytical digests published in European languages (French, English and Italian) of Ottoman *Shari'a* law – and this law was also partly codified by the Ottoman authorities themselves. The code (*Mejelle/Mecelle*) has been translated several times into both French and English. From these various instruments it is possible to gain some initial idea of the contents and concerns of *Shari'a* law. As suggested initially when considering the concept of *Jāhiliya*, no concern is evident in the *Shari'a* for antiquities as such. Therefore any judicial consideration of acts concerning them could only have proceeded by way of analogy (*qiyās*). In the present instance this could only arise out of land law, the law of real property (*aqar*); its ownership (*milk, mulk*), possession (*yad*) and its usufruct (*manfa'a*). In turn, the various legal incidents attached to real property varied according to the legal category of the land – and this in Cyprus was clearly defined and differentiated.

A question precedent is the capacity / incapacity of non-moslems to own and dispose of land. It appears that the post-conquest settlement of Cyprus did involve some concession to the Christian populace on this score. There was a capitulation in their favour enabling them to continue in the ownership, possession and enjoyment of their land and to deal freely with it by way of alienation etc. On occasions, in practice, infringements to this occurred, but these were incidental. Allied with this is the question of land ownership by foreigners (i.e. European residents). This in Ottoman lands at large was a contentious matter, with the underlying understanding that foreign nationals (i.e. Europeans) were debarred from enjoying such a privilege and the general right was specifically accorded only in the *Tanzimat* legislation, and not promulgated until 1867. However, in Cyprus, at least for members of the consular corps, it appears there was little of concern here. Both Cesnola and Lang possessed real property in Cyprus which they owned or leased. Lang, indeed, made a success of agriculture on a fairly large scale, being the proprietor of a chiftlik in the hinterland of Larnaka. It may therefore be taken that, during the period under consideration, European residents in Cyprus stood on the same footing as others with respect to the enjoyment of landed property.

It is now necessary to indicate the several legal categories of land obtaining in Cyprus, since these materially conditioned the rights of the user. For practical purposes, in the period under discussion, these were (together with their Turkish designations):

1. Private Land (*Arazi Memluké*)
2. Crown Land (*Arazi Mirié*)
3. Common Land (*Arazi Metrouké*)
4. Waste Land (*Arazi Mevat*)
5. 'Chantry' Land (*Arazi Mevkufi* = land in mortmain)

In principle, significant antiquities might be found on any of the above categories of land. Indeed, in some regions, for example Syria and Iraq, it is very possible that important ancient remains 'stand in the desert', i.e. occured in the remote wilderness far from human habitation and thus were on *Arazi Mevat* (Dead Land). However, the local circumstances in Cyprus are such that the great bulk of ancient remains brought to light were on privately owned land *(Milk/Mulki* land) with a residue on Crown Land (*Miri* land). Cyprus comprises, in the main, closely settled agricultural terrain; or at least the areas inhabited in antiquity were of this order. And in general, during the period under discussion, the activities of European investigators were not concerned with visible standing remains, but with remains buried under the earth, located during cultivation, well-digging etc. on private property (generally in fields). Thus either by purchase of these parcels, or by leasing them, or simply by operating under the license of the owner, the European excavator was legally entitled to exercise the property rights of ownership (*mulk*) or possession (*yad*) of the land. What then were these rights according to Shari'a law?

In the absence of any specific recognition of antiquities, the relevant provisions of Sharia law are probably to this effect. In principle the land owner owns what lies beneath his property (i.e. *cujus est solum* etc.), thus he is entitled to dig up the ground for whatever purpose, for example to sink wells. Therefore there is nothing forbidden (*yasak*) in excavating for antiquities on private land. However, all rights are subject to the legitimate interest of others and control by the state. Were there conditions or limitations to the excavator's enjoyment (*tasarruf*) of any antiquities he finds when digging up his land? Here since the *Shari'a* does not know antiquities, analogy *(qiyās)* must be applied. The closest analogy to excavated antiquities considered by *Shari'a* law are:

1. Mines *(ma'din)*
2. Treasure *(rikaz)*

With respect to mines, according to the Hunafiya, the owner of the ground owns the mine and enjoys its produce, but he must remit one fifth of this to the public treasure (*bait al mal*). If the ground has no owner, the mine belongs to the finder, under similar conditions. But other schools differ. The second instance, that of treasure, is obviously very close to that of antiquities, indeed well nigh congruent. The treasure belongs to the finder but (*de jure*) this ownership is heavily charged with conditions.

A treasure comprises precious materials (precious metals, precious stones, etc) hidden away under the earth. Here *Shari'a* law makes a sharp distinction according to the origin of the treasure, viz Islamic or non-Islamic. If the treasure belongs or belonged to Moslems, then an *animus revertendi* is presumed, and the rights of the original owner are given priority. The finder has only possession and he must 'cry' the treasure for a reasonable time. He then may use it, but is always liable to the original owner for its value, when ownership can be proved (all very unrealistic if, for example, the treasure consists of Abbasid coins!). On the other hand, if the treasure is non-Islamic in origin (i.e. from the *Jāhiliya*, which was the case with antiquities unearthed in Cyprus at the time) then the finder acquires ownership of the treasure. If the treasure was found on public land, then the finder must remit one fifth of the value to the state. However, if found on private land, he takes all and the state has no claim – but the authorities differ on details. In any event, if excavated antiquities in Cyprus were assimilated in law to treasure trove, then clearly the excavator was in a good position.

The gist of this rapid survey is to indicate that the archaeological activites, carried out by the likes of Lang and Cesnola on *mulki* land in the possession of the excavator, were not illegal according to Ottoman law in force at the time. There remained the question as to the liability of the excavator to render up to the public treasury a share of his finds. This would depend on the legal interpretations of his activities; but in any event, this burden was not an onerous one. As a matter of law, Lang was probably quite correct when he told his friend, the governor, that the latter would need a *firman* to stop him (legally) from continuing his excavation.

This, however, is certainly not the end of the story (from the excavator's point of view, that is). Both Lang and Cesnola make it clear that a significant motivation for their work was the benefit, accruing to both art and history, from transferring their finds to centres of western European civilisation, so that they could be properly studied and appreciated. They did not disdain financial reward to cover their expenses incurred in excavations, but they maintained that their basic aim and contribution was to keep the material intact and together, properly provenanced and made readily available for enlightened research by scholars. All this stood in contradiction to what would otherwise be the case: looting and chance finds smashed and abandoned with the items of commercial value dispersed into private hands without record of provenance. The merits of Cesnola in this connection are only now being made properly manifest after a lapse of more than a century, as the material is being exhaustively restudied in the research galleries of the Metropolitan Museum.

Now to achieve this aim it was necessary to export the material from Cyprus, and for this it had to be cleared through customs. In this question the preceeding analysis is entirely irrelevant. The customs everywhere are, and always have been, a law unto themselves. Thus, saving possession of the Sultan's *firman* specifically authorising export, excavators of antiquities were in bad case subject to the regulations (and whims) of the Cypriote customs. This situation they circumvented by various (illegal) devices. For smaller items they could manage fairly readily, but large items (i.e. valuable statuary) taxed their ingenuity. And they report, with a measure of professional pride, their success in these undertakings. Outwitting customs (in a good cause) always appears to have been reckoned fair game.

It is now advisable to close this account of a decade's activity in Cyprus, and to put it in perspective by referring to its immediate sequel. Precisely at the period (1865–1875) the European inspired reformist movement (the *Tanzimat*, the *Destur*) was struggling to gain expression in Ottoman governmental policy. Enlightened legislation on the broadest scale was expertly prepared. However, there was frequently a considerable lapse of time before it was actually promulgated. So it was with legislation concerning antiquities covering both excavations and museums. The Ottoman Antiquities Law *(Asar i-Atika)* was promulgated in 1874 when Lang had ceased his connection with antiquities, and Cesnola was about to leave the island to return to America and install both his collection and himself in the Metropolitan Museum.

The Turkish Antiquities law with its subsequent amendments and revisions incorporated all the provisions which have subsequently become canonical in regulating antiquities: vesting of all antiquities in the state; establishment of a responsible Department; no excavation without a permit issued by the Department and under the supervision of an appointed commissar (departmental representative); proper recording and handling of finds; no export of antiquities except with special permission of government etc, etc. Under the terms of this act, the work of Lang and Cesnola during the preceeding decade would have been illegal. Subsequently, excavators in other parts of the Ottoman Empire, for example Iraq, publicly complained that it was vexatious, and sighed for the good old days (of the Sultan's *firman*).

Was this act duly administered without delay by the Ottoman authorities in Cyprus? There are some items of evidence on this score. When Cesnola was arranging for the dispatch of his second collection to America in 1876, he records that he made a donation of a representative selection of this to the Imperial Museum in Istanbul. This material certainly made its way to Istanbul, where some of it is still on exhibition. However was it a gift or was it a squaring off under the terms of the new Antiquities Law? Recently it has been reported by Turkish publicists as a 'confiscation'. On the other hand, when Cesnola left Cyprus in 1876 his younger brother Alexander took on his mantle and continued with the same style of operations in and about Salamis. There is nothing to suggest that this work was carried under the terms of the new law. Accordingly in 1878, when the British occupied the island and administered it for the Sultan (according to Ottoman law), they immediately stopped Alexander di Cesnola's work on the grounds of its contravention of the 1874 act. Legal proceedings were taken against him and a part of his finds was confiscated. Since then antiquities work in Cyprus has always been subject to proper legislation – originally to the Ottoman Act and then subsequently to new Cypriote legislation.

Now, after more than a century has passed, the activities of 1865–75 are difficult to assess, in an utterly changed world, without technical knowledge and experience coupled with an extensive understanding of (local) history. Whatever view may be held of them now depends on personal historical bias. Concerning what is perhaps, a minor issue, the present study indicates that these activities were not illegal according to the law then prevailing.

A rather curious episode is mentioned in the present connection. When work on the Suez Canal and the associated development of Port Said got under way (1860–69), it gave rise to a continuing demand for first quality building material – good stone blocks. Some enterprising contractors catered for this by dismantling parts of the fine (Gothic) churches in Famagusta and shipping these to the builders in Port Said (at the rate of 5 blocks a penny!) for the construction of quays and hotels. It seems other coastal sites were likewise exploited, e.g. Soloi and Amathus. Now this activity was arguably in breach of the new Ottoman Penal Code of 1859 (Section 133: damage to public monuments). Nevertheless the dilapidation continued and the British Administration passed the Famagusta Stones Law (No. 14 of 1891) to remedy the practice. Nonetheless it seems the trade was still continuing at the end of 1899. This item obviously opens up a far-reaching subject, which has been studiously avoided here, *viz* legal provisions are one thing and their administration another.

Bibliography

1. Ottoman Cyprus and its antiquities in the nineteenth century

Cesnola 1877: L. Palma di Cesnola, *Cyprus: its ancient cities, tombs and temples* (London 1877).

Luke 1921: H. Luke, *Cyprus under the Turks* (Oxford 1921).

Hill 1952: Sir George Hill, *A History of Cyprus. The Ottoman Province, The British Colony*, Vol. IV (Cambridge 1952).

Lang 1878: R. Hamilton Lang, *Cyprus: its history, its present resources, and future prospects* (London 1878).

Lang 1903: R. Hamilton Lang, 'Archaeological researches in Cyprus', *Blackwood Edinburgh Magazine* Vol. 177, No.1075 (May 1903) 622–639.

Masson 1961: O. Masson, *Les Inscriptions Chypriotes Syllabiques* (Paris 1961) 17–24 (list of early activities).

Orr 1918: E.W.J. Orr, *Cyprus under British Rule* (London 1918) (brief account of the legal system as operating at the time of the British occupation and maintained by them).

Storrs: Ronald Storrs, *The Antiquities of Cyprus. The Near East and India Jan. 31st 1935* (brief account of the Ottoman Antiquities Law as applied in Cyprus from the beginning of the British occupation).

2. Islamic Law. General Introduction

Coulson 1964: N.J. Coulson, *A History of Islamic Law* (Edinburgh 1964).

Milliot 1953: L. Milliot, *Introduction à l'étude du Droit Musulman* (Paris 1953).

Schacht 1950: J. Schacht, *The origins of Islamic jurisprudence* (Oxford 1950).

Schacht 1964: J. Schacht, *An Introduction to Islamic Law* (Oxford 1964).

Tyan 1943: E. Tyan, *Organisation Judiciaire en Pays d'Islam* (Beirut 1943).

Custom, Customary Law (*'urf, 'āda*): *Encyclopaedia of Islam* I, 170–71.

Secular, Statute Law (*qānūn*): *Encyclopaedia of Islam* IV, 557–61.

Chap. X, 'Administration of Law. Ottoman Law and Law Reforms in the 19th Century', in Gibb and Bowen (eds), *Islamic Society and the West* II (Oxford 1957).

3. Ottoman Law and Law Reforms in the nineteenth century

d'Ohsson 1820: M. d'Ohsson, *Tableau General de L'Empire Othoman* (Paris 1820).

Gerber 1981: H. Gerber, *Shari'a, Kanun and Custom in the Ottoman Law*, *International Journal of Turkish Studies* 2, 131–147.

Imber 1996: C. Imber, *Studies in Ottoman History and Law* (Istanbul 1996).

Imber 1997: C. Imber, *Ebu s - su ud. The Islamic Legal Tradition* (Edinburgh 1997).

Tyser et al 1901: C.R. Tyser, D.C. Demetriades and Ismail Haqqi, *The Mejelle (Mecelle). The Ottoman Civil Code* (tr. Nicosia 1901).

Young 1905–6: G. Young, *Corps de Droit Ottoman. Receuil de Codes, Lois, Reglements, Ordonnances et Actes les plus importants du Droit Interieur, et d'Etudes sur le Droit Coutumier de l'Empire Ottoman* (Oxford 1905–6).

Farman/Firman: *Encyclopedia of Islam* II, 804–5.

26. The Ottoman Law on Antiquities (1874) and the founding of the Cyprus Museum[1]

Nicholas Stanley-Price

For more than twenty years after they took over the administration of Cyprus, the British authorities maintained in force the then current Ottoman antiquities legislation. This was based on a Regulation that had been issued by the Ottoman authorities in Constantinople in 1874. In many respects, the terms of this law were strictly applied by the British administration for defining the conditions on which excavations in the island could be officially authorized. The law also provided for the Government to receive a substantial portion of the excavated finds. Despite this provision, it was many years before the Cyprus Museum, following its founding in 1882, was able to acquire, inventory and put on public display a collection of Cypriote antiquities.

The Ottoman Antiquities Laws

When Great Britain took over the administration of Cyprus in 1878 under the Convention of Defensive Alliance with the Ottoman Empire, the island remained formally part of the Empire. Ottoman law remained in force. The Ottoman Civil Code, or Medjellé, had only recently been promulgated, in the years 1869–1876. No translation of it from Turkish to French had been made and apparently the Foreign Office had no copy of it.[2] Most of the Ottoman criminal law, however, was contained in the Ottoman Penal Code of 1857. Three volumes of the *Destour*, or authorized collection of Ottoman legislation, had been published in Greek and French translations in 1874, and two further volumes soon followed.[3] These were, therefore, available to the British administration. In 1882, the Cyprus Courts of Justice Order confirmed that the Ottoman Law that was in force on 13 July 1878 was to be administered in any action in which the defendant was an Ottoman subject (as were most of the population of Cyprus).

Nevertheless, the British Crown, in taking over the administration of a province of the Ottoman Empire, found it necessary to introduce new legislation in many spheres of government. Amongst the many ordinances and laws[4] that were passed by the British administration in its first twenty years were a number devoted to what would now be called conservation or preservation. To mention some examples: laws were passed for the protection of birds, the protection of moufflon, the protection of silkworm egg production, and the regulation of woods and forest activities and of sponge fisheries.[5]

Conspicuous by its absence, given the thriving market for them in Cyprus, is any law concerning antiquities. The only relevant Law that was passed in the period before 1900 is the Famagusta Stones Law of 1891.[6] This Law had the quite specific purpose of prohibiting the removal of stones from the ruined buildings of the old town of Famagusta. Its aim was consistent with a section of the Ottoman Penal Code that forbade the destruction of or damage to public buildings and monuments.[7] The 1891 Law is significant as the first one introduced under the British administration to legislate for improved antiquities protection. There were other moves afoot during the 1890's to introduce general legislation for antiquities.[8] But by the end of the century, the general law governing antiquities in Cyprus was still the Ottoman law that was in force on 13 July 1878, when the Occupation began.

The Law in question was the *Règlement sur les antiquités* issued in March 1874.[9] It was not, in fact, the first regulation concerning antiquities that was issued by the Ottoman authorities. In 1869 there had been issued a *Règlement sur les objets antiques*, consisting of only seven articles.[10] The 1869 regulation required that all requests to carry out excavations were to be addressed to the Minister of Public Instruction. The acceptance of any request concerning antiquities made by a foreign power must be the object of a special Imperial decree (Iradé). Furthermore, it was expressly forbidden to export any finds (with the exception of coins) that were made in authorized excavations. They could, however, be sold within the Empire either to individuals or to the State if it required them.

The 1869 regulation formalized policies for authorizing the search for antiquities that had previously been regulated through the granting of Imperial firmans to individuals. Thus, to take only one example from Cyprus, in 1862 Edmond Duthoit used his Imperial firman to obtain an inscription that was built into the wall of a peasant's house, and to overrule the objections of the local Madi to his excavating and removing stones from the site of Soloi.[11]

The same year of 1869 also saw the founding of a museum at Constantinople. In 1855 Ahmed Fethi Pasha, the grand master of artillery, started to form a public collection of antiquities in Constantinople, which he installed in the former church of Ayia Irini. This was formally established in 1869 as the Imperial Museum. Goold was made Director of the Museum and published a Catalogue of the collection in 1871. Under Mahmoud Nedim the post of Director was suppressed for reasons of economy, but Ahmed Vefik Pasha re-established it and appointed Philipp Déthier as Director. The latter, in March 1875, obtained Imperial permission authorising installation of the collection in the Tchinli Mosque. In 1880, on the death of Déthier, Osman Hamdi Bey was named Director of the Imperial Museum and charged Salomon Reinach with classifying and cataloguing the collection.[12]

The *Règlement sur les objets antiques* (1869) is important, not only because it appears to be the first such Ottoman regulation, but also because it seems to have conditioned the terms of the permits given to Luigi Palma di Cesnola for his later activities in Cyprus.

In January 1871, Cesnola reported to the Royal Academy of Sciences in Turin that the Turkish authorities had begun to raise objections to his excavations.[13] In the same year, the Turkish Governor-general informed Cesnola that the license that he had been given allowed him to excavate but not to export the finds.[14] The ban on export of finds outside the Empire reflected the terms of the 1869 legislation (quoted above). Cesnola also notes that, after four years of freedom to dig and to export his finds, he was now being told that his firman required him to send half of his collection of antiquities to the Museum in Constantinople.[15] The figure of four years given by Cesnola can therefore be explained as the period between his arrival in Cyprus in 1865 and the formal founding of the Imperial Museum and the passing of the regulation in 1869.

Another coincidence between the terms of the 1869 Regulation and Cesnola's own account of his activities concerns its Article 3. This states that every ancient object found on private property belonged to the owner of the land. This would explain Cesnola's action in hastening to Athienou to buy the land on which diggers working under his direction had found antiquities.[16] As the owner of the land, he could not be required to send half of his finds to Constantinople.

The brief Regulation on antique objects of 1869 was replaced only five years later by the much longer Regulation of 1874, consisting of 36 articles (see Appendix A). Not only was the new regulation much more detailed in its terms; it was at the same time stricter in defining State ownership of antiquities in the ground while also being more liberal concerning their export.

Article 3 states unequivocally that every antiquity discovered under the ground belongs to the Government. It then defines what was to happen to any antiquities that were found by those carrying out authorized excavations. As under the 1869 Regulation, permits to excavate could be given only on application to the Sublime Porte, for the approval of the Minister of Public Instruction (Article 8). One third of the antiquities that were found were to go to the Government, one third to the finder, and one third to the landowner. If the landowner was also the finder, he was assigned two-thirds and the Government one third.

A division of finds, in kind or by value, was to be carried out on the basis of an inventory of all discoveries. The inventory had to be kept in duplicate in a register which was also submitted to the Minister (Article 14). As to export of finds, the 1874 Law was more liberal than its predecessor. It allowed the export of antiquities from any part of the Empire with the permission of the same Minister. If the Government wished to acquire certain objects for the Imperial Museum, it would pay the price agreed with the owner. The rest would be allowed to be exported.

It is significant that it was the 1874 Law, with its liberal terms regarding the export of excavated antiquities, that continued to be applied by the British following their occupation of Cyprus. This law, according to Reinach,[17] had been drawn up by Déthier, the then Director of the Imperial Museum in Constantinople. But under his successor, Osman Hamdi Bey, the liberal terms of export were repealed in a new Law of 1884 which strictly forbade all export of antiquities.[18]

Consequently, in the late 1880s and 1890s, the ability of authorized foreign excavators in Cyprus to export the majority of the finds they made was anomalous in countries of the Ottoman Empire, of which Cyprus was still formally a part. This anomaly led to a later exchange of correspondence between Sir Austen Layard, the British Ambassador in Constantinople, and Sir Walter Sendall, the High Commissioner of Cyprus. The Minister of Foreign Affairs of the Ottoman Empire asked that all export of antiquities from Cyprus be stopped, citing the 1884 Law. Sendall replied that since the Turkish Law of 1884 was passed subsequent to the British occupation, it did not apply to Cyprus.[19] Cyprus therefore provides an interesting test-case of the application of the 1874 law, because of the British occupation of the island only four years later and the adoption of the then current Ottoman legislation.

The application of the 1874 Ottoman Law in Cyprus

The first case that illustrated the application of the 1874 Law in Cyprus under British rule came up only three months after their arrival. Alessandro Palma di Cesnola had returned to the island in 1876, to build up a collection to rival his brother's. His operational methods, and the reactions they caused, were similar to those of his mentor brother. On his own admission, he stopped digging at Curium in 1877 because of opposition by the local villagers and his activities were the subject of an official complaint from the Ottoman to the Italian Government.[20]

Whereas the Ottoman administration had used this diplomatic approach, the British in occupying Cyprus in July 1878, took more direct action against Alessandro di Cesnola. He was then commissioning excavations near Engomi (Enkomi). He claims that he had applied to Constantinople for a firman but, never having received a positive answer, he continued without it.[21]

The trial and sentencing of Alessandro di Cesnola at Larnaca in October 1878 strictly followed the terms of the 1874 Antiquities Law. Article 7 of the Law states that the antiquities found by illegal diggers would be seized in their totality; and that the transgressor would be fined from one to five Turkish pounds or would be imprisoned from three days to one week. In the younger Cesnola's case, the antiquities in his possession were confiscated, and he was fined £4, though the fine was then remitted.[22]

The High Commissioner Wolseley mentions in his diary that Cesnola had been told distinctly not to excavate.[23] In fact, Wolseley not only strictly applied the Ottoman Law requiring all excavations to be officially authorized but, within a few months of the Occupation, he issued a proclamation banning all excavations. Wolseley does not mention it in his diary, but it is referred to in contemporary sources. Perrot[24] states clearly that, as a result of a formal order from England, Wolseley introduced a ban on all excavations in August 1878. The ban was applicable to everyone, Europeans, foreigners and the island's inhabitants. The same ban is also mentioned by Mrs Scott-Stevenson[25] and Samuel Baker.[26] It is significant too that, according to Reinach,[27] Ohnefalsch-Richter (who arrived in the island in 1878) many times requested a permit to dig from Wolseley, but had to wait two years before being successful.

The complete ban on excavation, introduced in August 1878, appears to have lapsed with the departure of Sir Garnet Wolseley in May 1879. Policy for antiquities then continued to follow the 1874 Antiquities Law, with permission to excavate being restricted to learned institutions such as the British Museum and the South Kensington (now the Victoria and Albert) Museum. Beginning in September 1880, many of the excavations were undertaken by Ohnefalsch-Richter. He excavated officially for the Cyprus Government and for the British Museum, and later, following its founding, for the Cyprus Museum. He also excavated for private individuals who had secured a permit from the High Commissioner. As he himself recognized,[28] this sometimes led to a conflict of interest.

One of the justifications for authorising private excavations was that the Government share of finds from them helped to add to the collections of the Cyprus Museum. By 1887, however, a change in policy was announced by the High Commissioner, Sir Henry Bulwer, who had taken up this post in March 1886. As the President ex-officio of the Museum Committee, he had had a full year in which to observe the state of the Museum, and the nature of excavations being carried out. In a Minute to the Cyprus Museum Committee dated 16 June 1887, he announced that he had decided that private excavations were not good for the cause of historical or antiquarian knowledge, but only for speculative and commercial purposes. The Government had given the Cyprus Museum the rights of excavation which were held in trust for the public for education and science; therefore the Government must see those rights properly used. Henceforth, Bulwer decided, excavation permits would only be granted to foreign museums and recognised antiquarian institutions. These would be allowed to obtain, subject to some conditions, a share of the antiquities to be found in the island.[29]

It was under this new policy that first the Cyprus Exploration Fund and then the British Museum Turner Trust expedition worked in Cyprus in the late 1880s and 1890s. Both of them were subject to the regulations of the 1874 Law on Antiquities, as had been earlier excavations. In many respects, the Law was applied quite strictly.

For instance, the Law (Article 24) requires that landowners be compensated for any damage done to their lands as a result of excavations carried out by the Government. There are several references to the measures taken by excavators to backfill their excavations, for instance by Ohnefalsch-Richter at Tamassos,[30] by Munro and Tubbs at Salamis,[31] and by Ohnefalsch-Richter and Sinclair at Voni.[32]

Another article of the same Law [Article 19] states that no one person may carry out excavations at two different points at the same time. The Cyprus Exploration Fund was reminded of this when it asked to start excavations at Limnitis before it had completed its work at Polis.[33] The French were also caught out by the law in 1896. Fossey had been sent by the French School at Athens to excavate at Larnaca. When he fell ill, Perdrizet, who arrived to replace him, was not allowed to start work because the permit was in Fossey's name and could not be transferred.[34] This was a strict interpretation of Article 18 which states that the holder of a permit cannot concede or sell it to a third person.

As pointed out earlier, the question of the disposal of finds from excavations set Cyprus apart from its neighbours of the time. The three-way division of finds stipulated in the

1874 Law proved very generous for the excavator. As Hogarth explained,[35] the right to excavate on a certain site was obtained by making an agreement with the landowner. The landowner received a cash payment and a promise of compensation if the excavator damaged any crops or walls. In return, he leased the land and renounced all claims to any finds that might be made on it. So under this system, the excavator received two-thirds of the finds, giving only one third to the Government. Even this arrangement could be made more favourable to the excavator. In 1885 Ohnefalsch-Richter, as the self-styled Superintendent of Excavations for the Cyprus Museum, persuaded Watkins to pay him to dig at Idalion. He successfully persuaded Watkins to buy up, not only the rights of the proprietor of the land, but also the rights of the Government. As a result only a few duplicates had to be given to the Cyprus Museum.[36]

The Founding of the Cyprus Museum

The year 1883 is the usual date given for the founding of the Cyprus Museum.[37] In fact it was formally established on 15 June 1882, as the result of a meeting with the High Commissioner, Sir Robert Biddulph.[38] A Museum Committee was created that day and held a second meeting the following December.

There are two versions as to who should be given credit for founding the Museum. In one of them, Ohnefalsch-Richter in 1893 claimed credit for himself, in having formed a Committee for the foundation of a Cyprus Museum after securing the intervention of Gladstone in England to put pressure on the then High Commissioner to create a Museum.[39] There may be some truth in this claim, but I have not seen any contemporary documents that support it. Nor does Ohnefalsch-Richter's name appear anywhere in the founding membership of the Museum Committee. Not until December 1883 is his name mentioned when he is appointed an Honorary member of the Committee.[40] His claim therefore seems improbable.

In contrast, there is substantial evidence in favour of the other version, that Lieutenant Kitchener should be given credit. Kitchener was then in Cyprus carrying out his topographical survey of the island. He had already had extensive experience of surveying archaeological remains while working with C.R. Conder on the Survey of Western Palestine. While back in Britain in 1878 before being posted to Cyprus, he had given a paper at a meeting of the British Association for the Advancement of Science. He spoke about his survey in Galilee, and made a plea for the preservation of the synagogue that he had discovered at Capernaum.[41] This archaeological experience qualified him to be considered for undertaking archaeological work in Cyprus by the British Museum and by the South Kensington (now the Victoria and Albert) Museum, for which he duly directed excavations starting in January 1882.

Given these credentials of Kitchener as an archaeologist, it is reasonable to see him as the author of the letter to the Editor of the *Cyprus Herald* of 10 May 1882.[42] As was then the custom for letters to the Editor, the letter was signed anonymously, in this case by 'An Archaeologist'. It advocated the founding of a 'Museum of ancient and modern Arts and Industries in the capital of the Island'. Following letters of support in the next issue, the same 'Archaeologist' spelled out in a follow-up letter of 24 May his proposals for establishing a Cyprus Museum.[43] The wording of the terms in which the role of the Museum is described at its founding in the following month of June[44] reflects very closely the proposals of the 'Archaeologist' in this letter.

This was not the first time that the idea of a museum had been raised. Correspondence and editorials published in the Cyprus Herald in 1882 refer to the *revival* of the idea regarding the formation of a Museum of Cyprian Antiquities; and also to previous suggestions of forming local museums in Larnaca and Limassol.[45] But it was the practical suggestions put forward by 'An Archaeologist' that showed how a Cyprus Museum in Nicosia might be successfully established.

On 15 June 1882, only three weeks later, a deputation went to see the High Commissioner with a petition to found an Island Museum of Ancient Art. The petition was signed by the Cadi of Cyprus, the Archbishop of Cyprus, and the Mufti of Cyprus. The reasons given in favour of founding a museum were the positive influence that it would have on the mind and the cultivation of taste; as an island rich in antiquities, it would help promote the study of history, and would attract savants and foreigners to study antiquities. The museum thus established under the supervision of the Government of Cyprus would be considered a permanent National Institution. The High Commissioner approved the creation of a Museum; a Council was named; and Kitchener was appointed its Curator and Honorary Secretary.[46]

The key role of Kitchener in setting up the Museum was recognised by both the Greek and Turkish communities when he left the island in March 1883. In a farewell letter published in the press, the Greek community wrote: 'The formation of the Cyprus Museum for the preservation of the antiquities of the island is greatly due to your efforts. We beg therefore to send you this token of our esteem'. The letter was signed by the Archbishop, the Bishop of Kyrenia, the Abbot of Kykko, Mr. Peristiany, Mr Pascal Constantinides, Mr Efstathios Constantinides, and ten others. A similar address was sent to Captain Kitchener from the Turkish community signed by the Cadi, the Mufti, Fouad Effendi, Aouloussi effendi muhassabegi of Evkaf, and many others.[47]

Finally, the key role of Kitchener is confirmed by H.M.Sinclair, who succeeded Kitchener as Curator of the Museum. Writing in his autobiography forty years later, Sinclair states clearly that 'Kitchener started the idea of a Cyprus Museum to collect such objects of value as turned up'.[48] He also writes that Kitchener had received promises of subscriptions, but that had hardly made any progress by the time he left the island.

As with so many initiatives under the British Occupation, the Museum proposal received Biddulph's approval on condition that it should involve the least possible expenditure. It was to be sustained entirely by subscriptions and donations. The most that the Government would provide was the temporary loan of a room at the Government offices. In December 1882, the Museum Committee approved a budget that included the fitting-up of the room.[49] It is not clear that the room had already been allocated. Only in 1883 is it confirmed that two rooms of the new Government Offices were being used for the deposit of objects assigned to the Museum.[50] These two rooms are those that Myres, when he came to catalogue the collection in 1894, was to call the 'outhouses of the Commissioner's Office in Nicosia', otherwise known then as the Secretariat.[51]

The Government collections were not organized, so were liable to damage from those using the offices, and were not open to the public. Nevertheless, it seems that there were occasional visitors. The Cambridge scholar Guillemard, during his tour of Cyprus, wrote in his diary for 22 June 1887: 'Then to the "Museum", where I bought four glass things. A very poor place, nothing in it'.[52]

In the same month, exactly five years after the Museum had been founded, the High Commissioner Bulwer intervened. As its President, he reminded the Museum Committee of the aims with which the Museum had been founded. He pointed out that these aims had not been realized and demanded that the situation be improved.[53] Even so, it was two years before the Committee acted. In June 1889, the Committee took a lease on a house at number 7, Victoria Road, within the walled town, in what was then an Armenian quarter. It was to be rented for one year at £21. There was good security, since a caretaker with his wife were to be appointed at £12 p.a.[54] The collections were installed on the two floors of the house whose plan is published in Myres and Ohnefalsch-Richter's Catalogue of the collections prepared in 1894.[55]

In his preface to the Catalogue of 1894, Myres is unsparing in his criticism of the Government for failing to spend any funds on maintaining and properly storing the collection. Storage and cataloguing were quite inadequate. When loans were made from the collection, for instance to the Colonial and Indian Exhibition of 1887 in London, a number of items went missing and never returned.[56] Myres refers to objects that he found still in the Government Offices in 1894, long after the collections had been moved to Victoria Road.

The founding document of the Museum had proposed various ways in which its collections should be formed:[57] that the Government should hand over all antiquities rightly belonging to it, i.e. the Government's share of antiquities under the 1874 Law; that the museum should carry out excavations; that donations of antiquities from individuals should be sought; and that the government antiquities confiscated from Mr Cesnola should be deposited as a nucleus around which to work. These were, of course, those that were seized from Alessandro di Cesnola in October 1878 following his arrest.

The other issue, on which the High Commissioner had insisted in his instructions to the Museum Committee in 1887, was the opening of the Museum to the public. By 1891 apparently the Museum was better organized and was in a fit state to be visited. So it was decided to open it on the first Saturday of each month and on such public holidays as might be convenient. On 16 May 1891, the Cyprus Museum was opened to the public for the first time on this very limited basis.[58]

In summary, the two topics of this paper – the 1874 Antiquities Law and the founding of the Cyprus Museum – are linked in that the terms of the Law should have resulted in a substantial collection of antiquities being acquired by the Government for the central museum. In fact, the promise with which the museum was launched in 1882 took a long time to be realized. Only with the re-launching of the Cyprus Museum in 1908 in the purpose-built building in which it is now located did it begin to fulfil the hopes of its founding committee of twenty-five years earlier.

Notes

1. This paper is dedicated to the memory of Professor Olivier Masson, pioneer of research into antiquities in nineteenth-century Cyprus. Much of the research was conducted in 1997–98 while I was the holder of a National Endowment for the Humanities (NEH) Fellowship awarded through the Cyprus American Archaeological Research Institute (CAARI) in Nicosia. For making this research possible, I am grateful to the staff of CAARI and its library, and to the staff of the Cyprus State Archive, the Cyprus Museum Library, the Leventis Municipal Museum in Nicosia, and the Royal Military Academy at Woolwich. I am especially grateful to Dr Pavlos Flourentzos, Curator of the Cyprus Museum, for permission to refer to the Minutes of the Cyprus Museum Committee.
2. *Administration of Justice. Memorandum by Mr Reilly*, 26 August 1880. Biddulph Archive, NRA 25822, 1120, Box 4, Item 8.
3. C.R. Tyser and Mehmed Izzet, Preface in *Index to the contents of the Destour or Authorised collection of the Ottoman Laws* (Government Printing Office, Cyprus 1902). The French translation of the Destour was published as: Aristarchi Bey, Grégoire, *Législation Ottomane. Recueil des lois, règlements, ordonnances, traités, capitulations et autre documents officiels de l'Empire Ottoman*. Troisième partie. Droit Administratif (Demétrius Nicolaïdes, Constantinople 1874).
4. Laws enacted by the Local Legislature were called 'Ordinances' until May 1883; thereafter they were called 'Laws'.
5. *Index to the Statute Law of Cyprus. 1878 to 1902 Inclusive* (Waterlow & Sons, London 1903).

6. *Cyprus Gazette* 10 July 1891, Supplement, 1813–1814. Law XIV (1891), 'To provide for the preservation of ancient buildings in the town of Famagusta'.
7. Ottoman Penal Code, Art. 133 in G. Young, *Corps de Droit Ottoman. Recueil des codes, lois, règlements, ordinances et actes les plus importants du droit interieur, et d'etudes sur le droit coutoumier de l'Empire Ottoman* Vol. VII (Clarendon Press, Oxford 1906).
8. For example, the draft law 'To amend the existing Law with regard to the discovery of antiquities', published in the *Cyprus Gazette* 5 May 1897, 3342–3346.
9. 'Règlement sur les antiquités (le 20 Sefer 1291–24 mars 1874)' in *Législation Ottomane* (n.3) 162. The text is reproduced here in Appendix B.
10. 'Règlement sur les objets antiques (mars 1869)' in *Législation Ottomane* (n.3) 161. The text is reproduced here in Appendix A.
11. J. Foucart-Borville, 'La correspondance chypriote d'Edmond Duthoit (1862 et 1865)', *Centre d'Etudes Chypriotes. Cahier* 4 (1985) 3–60.
12. 'Titre XXXIX. Musée' in G. Young (n.7) Volume II, 388
13. E. McFadden, *The glitter and the gold. A spirited account of the Metropolitan Museum of Art's first director, the audacious and high-handed Luigi Palma di Cesnola* (New York 1971) 115–116.
14. McFadden (n.13) 116–117. In fact, Cesnola managed to evade this new imposition through his personal friendship with the Governor.
15. McFadden (n.13) 117.
16. L.P. di Cesnola, *Cyprus. Its ancient cities, tombs and temples* (London 1887) 125.
17. S. Reinach, *Chroniques d'Orient. Documents sur les fouilles et découvertes dans l'Orient Hellénique de 1883 à 1890* (Paris 1891) 171.
18. 'Antiquités règlement, texte XXXIX, 21 févr. 1884' in G. Young (n.6) Volume II, 389–394.
19. Colonial Office records, C.O. 67/76, 14 Oct. 1892; 77, 30 Nov.1892. Correspondence between Francis Clare Ford at Constantinople and Walter Sendall in Cyprus.
20. A.P. di Cesnola, *Salaminia (Cyprus): the history, treasures and antiquities of Salamis in the island of Cyprus* (2nd. ed., London 1884) xvii–xviii.
21. A.P. di Cesnola (n.20) xviii.
22. I hope to prepare for separate publication a study of the trial of Alessandro di Cesnola.
23. Sir G. Wolseley, *The journal of Sir Garnet Wolseley* (A. Cavendish (ed), Nicosia 1990 [1878]) 99, 116.
24. G. Perrot, 'L'Ile de Chypre. Son rôle dans l'histoire', *Entre deux mondes* (1879) 604. I have not been able to locate a text of this Proclamation.
25. Mrs. Scott-Stevenson, *Our home in Cyprus* (3rd. ed., London 1880) 208.
26. Sir S. Baker, *Cyprus as I saw it in 1879* (London 1879) 53–54.
27. Reinach (n.17) 170.
28. M. Ohnefalsch-Richter, *Kypros, The Bible and Homer* (London 1893) 7.
29. Cyprus Museum Committee, *Minutes of Meeting, 6 August 1887.* Copy of Minute from Bulwer, 16 June 1887.
30. Ohnefalsch-Richter (n. 28) 8.
31. J.A.R. Munro and H.A. Tubbs, 'Excavations in Cyprus, 1890' *JHS* 12 (1891) 99.
32. S. Reinach (n.17) 186.
33. J.A.R. Munro and H.A. Tubbs, 'Excavations in Cyprus, 1889', *JHS* 11 (1890) 18.
34. O. Masson, 'Kypriaka, X-XII. X. Archéologues français à Chypre en 1896', *BCH* 101 (1977) 313–4.
35. D.G. Hogarth, 'I. The first season's work: preliminary narrative' in E.A. Gardner et al., 'Excavations in Cyprus, 1887–8', *JHS* 9, no. 2 (1888) 161 n.1.
36. Ohnefalsch-Richter (n.28) 6.
37. J.L. Myres and M. Ohnefalsch-Richter, *A catalogue of the Cyprus Museum, with a chronicle of excavations undertaken since the British occupation and introductory notes on Cypriote archaeology* (Oxford 1899) vi.
38. 'Formation of a Museum in Cyprus', newsclipping dated 15 June 1882, in Cyprus Museum Committee Minute Book, Cyprus Museum, Nicosia. The correct date is noted too by A. Marangou in Magda Ohnefalsch-Richter, *Ellinika ithi kai ethima stin Kypro.* (ed. A. Marangou, Nicosia 1994) n.36.
39. 'Introduction' in Magda and Max Ohnefalsch-Richter, *Studies in Cyprus* (supervised by A. Marangou and A. Malecos, Nicosia n.d.).
40. Cyprus Museum Committee, *Minutes of Meeting, 3 December 1883.*
41. A. Hodges, *Lord Kitchener* (London 1936) 40; and P. Magnus, *Kitchener. Portrait of an imperialist* (London 1958).
42. *Cyprus Herald* 10 May 1882, 2.
43. *Cyprus Herald* 24 May 1882, 1882.
44. See n.38 above.
45. *Cyprus Herald* 14 June 1882; 5 August 1882.
46. See n.38 above.
47. *Cyprus Herald* 16 April 1883.
48. H.M. Sinclair, *Camp and society* (London 1926) 145.
49. Cyprus Museum Committee, *Minutes of Meeting, 6 December 1882.*
50. D. Pierides, *The Cyprus Museum. A short account of operations* (Larnaca, November 1883).
51. Myres and Ohnefalsch-Richter (n.36) vi. This is the building of the Government Offices which still stands today in Michalakis Karaolis Street.
52. F.H.H. Guillemard, *Cyprus: 1887, 1888* (unpublished ms. at CAARI, Nicosia) 51: entry for June 22, 1887. I am grateful to Dr Nancy Serwint, Director of CAARI, for permission to quote from the Diary. In the following year, Guillemard was one of the moving spirits behind the creation of the Cyprus Exploration Fund.
53. Cyprus Museum Committee, *Minutes of Meeting, 6 August 1887.* Copy of Minute from Bulwer, dated 16 June 1887; S. Reinach (n. 16) 441.
54. Cyprus Museum Committee, *Minutes of Meeting, June 20, 1889.*
55. J.L. Myres and M. Ohnefalsch-Richter (n. 36) x.
56. Cyprus Museum Committee, *Minutes of Meeting, June 6, 1890.*
57. See n.38 above.
58. Cyprus Museum Committee, *Minutes of Meeting, May 4, 1891.*

APPENDICES

THE OTTOMAN LAWS ON ANTIQUITIES OF 1869 AND 1874

Appendix A. Règlement sur les objets antiques (mars 1869).

ART. 1. Toute demande d'autorisation pour faire des fouilles dans les Etats de S.M.I. le Sultan, devra être désormais adressée au ministère de l'instruction publique, et nulle part il ne pourra être fait des fouilles de cette nature sans une autorisation officielle.

ART. 2. Il est expressément interdit aux personnes qui auront entrepris des fouilles dans l'Empire, avec l'autorisation du gouvernement, dans des endroits exempts d'inconvénients, d'exporter à l'étranger les objets antiques qu'elles pourront y découvrir. Faculté leur est laissée, cependant, de vendre ces objets dans l'Empire soit à des particuliers, soit à l'Etat, s'il le demande.

ART. 3. Tout object antique découvert dans les propriétés particulières, appartient au propriétaire du sol.

ART. 4. Les monnaies antiques de toute espèce sont exceptées de l'interdiction d'exportation prescrite par l'Art. 2.

ART. 5. Toute autorisation de faire des fouilles s'applique exclusivement aux objects gisant sous sol. Il ne sera permis à qui que ce soit de toucher ou d'endommager les monuments antiques de toute sorte, comme leurs accessoires, sis à la surface de la terre. Les personnes qui contreviendront à cette règle seront punies d'après la loi.

ART. 6. L'acceptation de toute demande faite officiellement par une puissance étrangère concernant les antiquités, dépendra d'un Iradé Impérial spécialement émané à cet égard.

ART. 7. Les personnes qui, possédant des connaissances spéciales pour la recherche et la découverte des antiquités, seront en état de le prouver au département de l'Instruction Publique, seront chargées de faire des fouilles aux frais de l'Etat et obtiendront dans le même but les missions spéciales du gouvernement impérial. Les personnes de cette catégorie sont, par conséquent, invitées à s'adresser au ministère de l'Instruction Publique.

Appendix B. Règlement sur les antiquités (le 20 Séfer 1291 – 24 Mars 1874).

ART. 1. Toute sorte d'objets d'art datant des temps anciens est une antiquité.

ART. 2. Il y a deux espèces d'antiquités: la première comprend les monnaies, et la seconde tout autre objet transportable ou non.

CHAPITRE I.
Du droit de possession d'antiquités et de tout ce qui y a rapport.

ART. 3. Toute antiquité non découverte (gisant sous sol), dans quelque endroit qu'elle se trouve, appartient au Gouvernement.

Quant aux antiquités trouvées par ceux qui effectueraient des fouilles par autorisation, un tiers appartiendra au Gouvernement, un autre tiers au trouveur et le reste au propriétaire du terrain où les antiquités ont été trouvés. Si le trouveur a trouvé les antiquités dans sa propriété, les deux tiers seront à lui et le reste au Gouvernement.

ART. 4. Pour toute recherche d'antiquités ou des trésors, on doit s'adresser directement ou par l'entremise de l'autorité local au Ministère de l'instruction publique.

ART. 5. La répartition des antiquités se fera, selon la demande du gouvernement, en nature ou en valeur.

ART. 6. Pour la conservation de monuments tels que temples et autres édifices complets qui se trouveraient dans les endroits appartenant à des particuliers, le Gouvernement désignera, selon le cas, des agents sur les lieux.

CHAPITRE II
Des conditions de la recherche et de l'excavation d'antiquités

ART. 7. Est interdite l'exécution de toute fouille entreprise speecialement pour la recherche d'antiquités et de trésors, sans autorisation officielle et sans le consentement du propriétaire du terrain. Les antiquitees trouvées par ceux qui contreviendraient à cette interdiction seront saisies totalement, et ils seront eux mêmes condamnés à une amende d'une livre turque à cinq, ou à un emprisonnement de trois jours à une semaine. En cas que les fouilles se seraient effectuées sur la propriété d'un tiers sans le consentement du propriétaire, celui-ci sera dédommagé, à sa requête, des pertes qui lui en auront été occasionées.

ART. 8. L'autorisation nécessaire à la recherche d'antiquités ou de trésors sera exclusivement accordée, *ad referendum*, à la S. Porte par le Ministère de l'instruction publique qui délivrera en même temps un livre imprimé et à souche, conforme au modèle à adopter pour l'enregistrement des antiquités qui auront été découvertes.

ART. 9. Le Ministère de la Police et l'autorité locale veilleront l'un à Constantinople, l'autre dans les vilayets, au point de savoir si les porteurs d'autorisation se conforment ou non aux conditions règlementaires dans l'exécution des fouilles et de tout ce qui s'y rapporte.

ART. 10. L'autorisation ne sera accordée que lorsqu'il aura été constaté que l'exécution des fouilles n'offre pas d'inconvénient sur les lieux, et que le requérant a produit un certificat légalisé par l'autorité locale, constatant le consentement du propriétaire du terrain. Dans le cas, le requérant sera tenu de déposer telle somme d'argent qu'elle aura été fixée par le Conseil de l'instruction publique ou de fournir une caution valable, et il sera perçu à cet effet un droit de 3 livres Ottomanes.

ART. 11. L'autorisation accordée pour la recherche d'antiquités ou de trésors, aura, au maximum, un terme de deux ans, qui ne sera jamais dépassé.

ART. 12. Le terme de l'autorisation pourra être prolongé, si, à l'expiration, l'on demande à continuer les fouilles.

ART. 13. L'autorisation donnée pour la recherche d'antiquités ou de trésors ne franchira guère les limites d'un village ou d'un bourg; le solliciteur d'autorisation sera tenu d'ailleurs de désigner l'emplacement et les limites du terrain recherche d'antiquités ou de trésors, à excaver et d'en présenter le plan, en cas de besoin.

ART. 14. L'exécution des fouilles dans les temples, tekkés, séminaires et dans les lieux tels que cimetières, aqueducs et voies publiques, dont l'excavation entraînerait des dommages publics, ne sera pas permise.

ART. 15. Si, postérieurement à l'obtention du permis et à l'entreprise des travaux d'excavation, l'on constate quelque inconvénient, les fouilles seront suspendues, après entente avec le Ministre de l'instruction publique, sans qu'on puisse formuler une demande en remboursement de frais par suite de cette suspension.

ART. 16. Si, pendant l'exécution des fouilles archéologiques, il en résulte quelque dommage, ou si, après l'achèvement des travaux, l'enquête effectuée par les soins de l'autorité locale sur les lieux excavés, constate que les fouilles ont porté préjudice au public, la part d'antiquités existantes due au chercheur sera retenue jusqu' à ce que le mal soit réparé à ses frais.

ART. 17. A aucun fonctionnaire du Gouvernement Impérial ou des Gouvernements étrangers ne sera accordée l'autorisation d'effectuer en son nom des fouilles archéologiques dans la cercle de sa jurisdiction, à moins qu'il ne soit le propriétaire du terrain.

ART. 18. Il n'est pas permis au porteur d'une autorisation de la céder ou de la vendre à un tiers.

ART. 19. Il ne sera permis à une même personne d'exécuter simultanément des fouilles sur deux points différents.

ART. 20. L'autorisation est considerée comme nulle et non avenue si l'on ne procède pas aux fouilles dans l'espace de 3 mois à partir de la date d'émission, ou si, après avoir été commencés, les travaux sont suspendus sans motif pendant 2 mois.

ART. 21. Si l'emplacement à fouiller se trouve séparé des localités peuplées par une distance qui rendrait toute surveillance continuelle de l'autorité difficile, un employé sera adjoint au possesseur d'autorisation aux frais de ce dernier.

ART. 22. Toute sorte de dépenses occasionées par les fouilles sera à la charge de celui qui possède l'autorisation.

ART. 23. Dans le cas où le Gouvernement voudrait exécuter lui même des fouilles sur des points qui ne sont pas mulk, ni dépendants de localités habitées et où la découverte d'antiquités serait probable, ces endroits ne seront cédés à personne.

ART. 24. Si les terres où le Gouvernement aura fait faire des fouilles sont en possession de particuliers, il dédommagera les propriétaires des pertes qui pourraient leur être occasionées.

CHAPITRE III
Des avertissements et des formalités concernant les antiquités et leur partage.

ART. 25. Ceux qui decouvriraient des antiquités, soit par hasard soit au moyen de recherches autorisées, seront tenus, s'ils ne sont pas accompagnés d'un employé aux termes de l'art. 21, d'en prévenir l'autorité local dans le délai de 10 jours au plus tard, sous peine de se voir condamnés au payement d'une amende équivalente au quart du prix des antiquités découvertes, non compris la part afférente au Gouvernement.

ART. 26. La nature et la quantité des antiquités annoncées conformément à l'art. précédent seront indiquées dans le livre imprimé à souche délivrée par le ministre de l'Instruction publique en même temps que l'autorisation. Ce livre sera signé ou scellé tant par l'autorité que par le trouveur et dûment légalisé; un exemplaire en sera remis à ce dernier et un autre sera envoyé au ministre de l'instruction publique, après avoir été enregistré dans la commission de l'instruction publique de la localité ou bien dans le conseil administratif.

ART. 27. Le partage des antiquités en nature ou en valeur se fera sur la base du livre dressé conformément à l'article

précédent; le mode de partage sera indiqué au bas du livre.
ART. 28. Dans le cas où l'autorité local hésiterait à procéder au partage en nature ou en valeur, elle doit s'en référer par télégraphe au ministre de l'instruction publique.
ART. 29. L'autorité et le trouveur désigneront chacun un expert pour estimer la contrevaleur des antiquités indivisibles. En cas de divergence d'avis entre ces deux experts, l'autorité désignera come arbitre un troisième expert dont la décision sera définitive.
ART. 30. Si, à l'expiration du terme ou avant, le concessionnaire annonce l'achèvement des fouilles et s'il est constaté qu'il a fidèlement rempli les conditions réglementaires, son dépôt lui sera restitué contre reçu.

CHAPITRE IV
Des dispositions concernant l'importation, l'exportation, l'achat, la vente, et la tenue en cachette d'antiquités.
ART. 31. Les antiquités importées de l'étranger dans l'Empire ou des autres parties de l'Empire à Constantinople, qu'elles consistent en monnaies ou dans d'autres objets, seront exemptes du droit de douane.
ART. 32. Une liste de monnaies ou d'autres objets antiques destinés à être exportés à l'étranger de quelque partie de l'Empire que ce soit, doit être transmise au Ministère de Instruction publique, sans l'autorisation duquel ces antiquités ne pourront être exportés. Si le Gouvernement veut faire l'acquisition de ces objets dont le Musée Impériale aura besoin, il en payera le prix fixé d'accord avec le propriétaire. Quant au reste, il lui sera permis de l'exporter.
ART. 33. Le Gouvernement autorisera la sortie des antiquités à exporter de l'Empire à l'étranger après l'accomplissement des formalités prescrites par l'art. 32 contre payement des droits de douane. Quant aux antiquités importées de l'étranger dans l'Empire, elles seront enregistrées séparement dans un livre spécial à la douane, et, à leur réexportation elles seront confrontées avec les registres, après quoi le permis (teskéré) d'usage sera délivré sans aucun prélèvement de droit.
ART. 34. Les antiquités saisies en flagrant délit de contrebande seront totalement confisquées.
ART. 35. Ceux qui auront démoli ou endommagé des antiquités élevées dans les lieux publics ou privés, tels qu'édifices et autres, seront condamnés, conformément à l'art. 131 du Code Pénal, à des dommages-intérêts et à l'amende, ainsi qu' à un emprisonnement d'un mois à une année.
ART. 36. Le produit du droit de courtage de 5% à percevoir sur les antiquités vendues aux enchères publiques, l'argent provenant du partage en valeur des antiquités, l'amende du droit de permis (Rouhsatié) ainsi que les recettes provenant des confiscations appartiendront à la caisse du Musée Impérial.

Cyprus in the 19th century AD: Fact, Fancy and Fiction
A Summing Up

R. S. Merrillees

The publication of the 27th issue of the *Cahier du Centre d'Etudes Chypriotes* is a melancholy reminder of all that we have lost through the untimely death of Olivier Masson. As you will see from the volume which is devoted to his memory, he was one of the major participants in the Centre and the *Cahier*, both of which he helped found. Scarcely an issue of the *Cahier* went by that did not have in it one or more of his articles, and his innate sense of modesty led him to disguise the full extent of his scholarly oeuvre by writing as well under the pseudonym of Léon Fivel. No colleague was more disinterested in his work than Olivier Masson. He was the quintessential scholar, devoted to assembling as much data as possible, published and unpublished, analysing it thoroughly and impartially, and drawing only such conclusions as the presentation of evidence allowed. Having nearly exhausted his primary field of philological research in Cyprus, he became increasingly intrigued by the historiography of Cypriote archaeological studies and made a singular and substantial contribution to elucidating the ways generations of Cypriote and foreign scholars have studied the island's past over the last 200 years. Eloquent tributes have been paid to his exceptional achievements by Professor Maurice Sznycer and Madame Emilia Masson, and I cannot but concur that Olivier would have liked nothing better, had he been alive, than to attend this colloquium. Indeed one of the last trips abroad he had planned was to visit the Pitt Rivers Museum in Oxford. That he wanted it to be known that he was working assiduously up to the end should serve as an inspiration to us all.

The meaning of history has been debated for centuries and continues to defy simple definition. Certainly everyone agrees that since history is either made by or interpreted by the human race, not by the natural sciences, it is not possible for us to reproduce exactly what happened in antiquity. Besides which, it is difficult for anyone to so divorce himself or herself from one's own era and society to be able to view with complete objectivity the past through the eyes of the people who created it for us. But on what basis should we review the achievements of our ancestors? Should we attempt to deal as dispassionately as possible with the discoveries of the past and those who made them, as though we were addressing inanimate objects or natural phenomena, or should we sit in judgement on what our predecessors did, or didn't do, in revealing ancient remains? Nearly all the papers presented have sought to place the archaeological exploration of Cyprus in the nineteenth century AD in the context of the convictions, mores and knowledge of the time, and to reflect on the strengths and weaknesses of that pioneering era in the recovery, exploitation and preservation of the relics of the island's long and turbulent history. By common consent it has been acknowledged that understanding the significance of the large number of antiquities which were brought to light and put into circulation in Cyprus, the Levant, Europe, North America and elsewhere, cannot be advanced without impartially establishing the circumstances of their recovery. At the same time those who were active in exploring the archaeological remains of Cyprus last century were as much involved in learning about the island's history as we are today, and to fail to heed the lessons from our own scholarly past would be a dereliction of academic duty. Indeed it was by observing, reviewing and improving on the techniques and findings of the nineteenth-century researchers that subsequent generations of students have perfected their approach to the subject. The answer to the two questions I previously posed is therefore in the affirmative, for it is both possible and proper to examine antiquities and excavators dispassionately as well as critically.

The mentality of our archaeological predecessors was

conditioned by several major considerations. In the first place they were motivated by the nineteenth-century passion for enquiry, exploration and collecting. The opportunity for wide-ranging travel, combined with a Classical and Christian education, prompted academics and others to begin investigations above and below the ground of countries and places long enshrined in Greek, Latin and Biblical literature. For the antiquaries of the last century, Cyprus was a land with strong Classical and Biblical associations, epitomised by Aphrodite and St Paul, and reflected in the assumption that the island's civilisation was shared between the Aryans and Semites, later translated into the Greeks and Phoenicians respectively. Cyprus in their minds already occupied the crossroads between east and west, and this perception was strengthened by the fact that most of the explorers of the island treated it as a stepping-stone on the way from the Occident to the Orient and back. Schliemann's sensational discoveries at Troy and Mycenae in the late nineteenth century were the culmination of the growing scholarly interest in the Levant, especially Cyprus, and transformed the outlooks and expectations of all those engaged in fieldwork and research in the eastern Mediterranean. Everyone had to find a treasure, locate an acropolis and establish a connection with Bronze Age Greece, and the Cesnola brothers, together with Max Ohnefalsch-Richter, amongst others, were only too willing to oblige.

These perceptions were also coloured by the rivalry for power and influence outside their own territories by the leading countries of Europe, especially Britain, France and Germany. This not only brought them into competition with each other, but engendered a contempt for the laws of the states where their interests converged. Foreigners visiting or living in Cyprus saw no reason to allow Ottoman and even British regulations on the excavation, ownership and export of antiquities to stand in the way of their archaeological ambitions. The diplomatic and consular representatives of the foreign nations *en poste* in Larnaca also considered that they had a right to dig, acquire and dispose of Cypriote relics with or without official approval, and did not hesitate to use their political influence, as well as their navies, to facilitate their acquisitions. Only the advent of the British administration in 1878, and the enforcement, ironically, of the existing Ottoman laws, put an end to the uncontrolled despoliation of the island's ancient remains. It was, however, some time before any order was put into the conduct of archaeological activities in Cyprus and the collection of the Government's share of antiquities, and the slow and hesitant progress towards an effective antiquities service, was due to the British administration's own lack of funds and unwillingness to accord any priority to the preservation of the island's cultural heritage.

British, and indeed Western ignorance of Cyprus in the nineteenth century AD was profound. However, when European and American visitors and residents who had been steeped in their own way of perceiving the island, actually came face to face with reality, certain practical adjustments became necessary. The abundance of ancient remains was treated not as an inalienable part of the island's history, but as an economic and artistic resource to be exploited for the benefit of those who had the means and the will to secure them for the purposes of decoration and trade. Tomb robbing and sanctuary gutting provided a plentiful harvest of saleable antiquities, but the habit of discarding fragmentary sculpture, plain pottery and sherds, and broken glass considered to be of no value, persisted well beyond the looting phase of exploring Cyprus' past, into the period of more controlled and scientific excavation. Archaeological sites also supplied convenient material for improving the island's primitive infrastructure, and no better illustration could be cited than the British army's use of the Bamboula at Kition to fill in the malaria infested marshes at Larnaca. And finally, through the tastes fostered by the Grand Tour, which did not, however, take in Cyprus, the removal of relics to adorn homes, offices and galleries abroad was considered a legitimate means of showing refinement, and much emphasis was placed on the acquisition of *objets d'art*. When what became the Victoria and Albert Museum in London reluctantly agreed to sponsor excavations at Salamis, the authorities specified that the fieldwork should produce aesthetic, not archaeological objects. For certain museums to-day this is still a guiding if unstated principle.

The nineteenth century AD saw the exploration of Cypriote antiquity evolve from a treasure hunt into an academic discipline, and paradoxically it was not the recognised scholars who expedited this process, but talented amateurs. While several experts such as Ross, the Marquis de Vogüé, Waddington, Duthoit, Perrot, Dörpfeld, Dümmler and the unfortunate Sigismond, all visited the island and published serious papers on its ancient remains, they did not set in train the academic movement that would lead to a reconstruction of Cypriote history through a scientific study of the archaeological record. This was left to the locals either living or stationed in Larnaca. Amongst them Demetrios Pierides, Luigi Palma di Cesnola and his brother Alessandro, Thomas B. Sandwith, Tiburce Colonna-Ceccaldi and his brother Georges, Robert Hamilton Lang and Max Ohnefalsch-Richter made the most significant contributions, directly and indirectly, towards the development of the techniques and understandings necessary to make historical sense of the multitude of artefacts and architectural remains they uncovered. This long period of gestation, when excavations were conducted by drunken sailors, absentee consuls and needy peasants, was completed when the Cyprus Exploration Fund sent its expedition to Cyprus in the 1880's and initiated the scientific era in archaeological exploration. And lest it be thought that all the consuls, bankers and educated people in Larnaca were engaged in antiquarian pursuits, there were evidently many who had no interest in the island's past whatsoever, including the Ottoman administrators.

The transition from looting to learning was a gradual and fitful process whose impetus was provided by self-educated individuals working, not in isolation from each other, but in enlightened collaboration. Indeed archaeological investigations in Cyprus last century were dominated less by pots, though, heaven knows, there were enough of them, than by personalities, many of them larger than life. Those responsible included artists, architects, consuls, bankers, officials, merchants, travellers, military officers, journalists, writers, and others, who shared little in common except a passion for archaeology engendered by their discovery on the spot of the wealth of Cyprus' past underground. They were typical of their epoch, often multilingual, always energetic, and not infrequently impecunious. Most of them paid for their antiquities, either through employing workmen to dig for them, or by purchasing them from peasants or dealers, and disposed of them by resale or donation. Much of the frenzied activity, by such pioneers as the Cesnola brothers and Ohnefalsch-Richter, was driven by their need to finance their acquisitions and even their lives. It was not therefore surprising that controversies and disputes often broke out, and much effort was expended in defending rights, interests and reputations. Again Luigi Palma di Cesnola and Ohnefalsch-Richter were at the forefront of these disagreements, and ironically they even criticised each other. Both were hypersensitive to attacks on their probity, and became embroiled in public contention over their archaeological activities. The most noteworthy of these fracas in the island was the court case of Warren *versus* Watkins, which directly implicated Ohnefalsch-Richter and cannot be said to have done much credit to the Superintendent of Excavations for the Cyprus Museum.

The nineteenth century AD saw the birth of our archaeological discipline and, for better or worse, laid the foundations on which all subsequent work has been built. Studying the finds of that era has shed much new light on objects and sites which have long since been lost from view or taken for granted, and this colloquium has heard highly informative accounts of the re-examination of the investigations last century at Kouklia Palaepaphos, Idalion, Salamis, Kourion, Nicosia, Ormidhia and other sites, and of collections of antiquities, particularly the Cesnola collection in the Metropolitan Museum of Art. Particularly interesting are the inscriptions and graffiti recently identified by Professor Hermary and Professor Karageorghis on one of the sculptures and silver bowls in New York. These descriptions have allowed us to observe, more comprehensively and factually than ever before, the precise nature of the fieldwork conducted under the often distant supervision of the expatriates who sponsored the diggings, and the academic backgrounds against which these discoveries were evaluated. It would be anachronistic to describe these activities as ahead of or behind their times, for they were of their time and valid in the terms in which they were carried out. In this respect it is important to give due recognition to the steps made by the nineteenth-century antiquarians to record the *in situ* disposition of their finds and to place them in their appropriate topographical, religious and ethnographical contexts. Each in his own way helped expand incrementally the way in which archaeological remains came to be recovered and interpreted for the benefit of future historians.

On behalf of you all, I would like to express our sincere gratitude to Dr Dyfri Williams and Dr Veronica Tatton-Brown for convening this unusual conference and forcing us to say something new. We are indebted as always to Mr and Mrs Leventis for their munificent hospitality and much more besides. The Hellenic Centre has greatly impressed us with its efficient organisation and warm welcome, and we could not have wished for better premises in which to hold this meeting. Keo has generously helped us slake our thirst after all this talking and listening, and many others have materially but anonymously contributed to the successful outcome of this colloquium. Let me thank them all most warmly for their valuable efforts. It remains only for me to say how personally delighted I have been to see here so many friends and colleagues, all united their desire to commemorate the historiographical legacy left to us by Olivier Masson, and to extend to you all a cordial welcome to the Cyprus American Archaeological Research Institute in Nicosia.